Migrants and Rights

The International Library of Essays on Rights
Series Editor: Tom Campbell

Titles in the Series:

Sexual Orientation and Rights
Nicholas Bamforth

Rights: Concepts and Contexts
Brian Bix and Horacio Spector

Disability Rights
Peter Blanck

The Right to a Fair Trial
Thom Brooks

Global Minority Rights
Joshua Castellino

Cultural Heritage Rights
Anthony J. Connolly

Indigenous Rights
Anthony J. Connolly

Migrants and Rights
Mary Crock

Refugees and Rights
Mary Crock

Civil Rights and Security
David Dyzenhaus

Democratic Rights
Ran Hirschl

Group Rights
Peter Jones

Human Rights and Corporations
David Kinley

Prisoners' Rights
John Kleinig

Genocide and Human Rights
Mark Lattimer

Language Rights
Stephen May

Animal Rights
Clare Palmer

Gender and Rights
Deborah L. Rhode and Carol Sanger

Economic, Social and Cultural Rights
Manisuli Ssenyonjo

Health Rights
Michael J. Selgelid and Thomas Pogge

Citizenship Rights
Jo Shaw and Igor Štiks

Theories of Rights
C.L. Ten

Bills of Rights
Mark Tushnet

Environmental Rights
Steve Vanderheiden

The Right to Bodily Integrity
A.M. Viens

Labour Rights
Marley S. Weiss

Religious Rights
Lorenzo Zucca

Migrants and Rights

Edited by

Mary Crock

University of Sydney, Australia

ASHGATE

Wherever possible, these reprints are made from a copy of the original printing, but these can themselves be of very variable quality. Whilst the publisher has made every effort to ensure the quality of the reprint, some variability may inevitably remain.

Published by
Ashgate Publishing Limited
Wey Court East
Union Road
Farnham
Surrey GU9 7PT
England

Ashgate Publishing Company
Suite 3-1
110 Cherry Street
Burlington
VT 05401-3818
USA

www.ashgate.com

British Library Cataloguing in Publication Data
A catalogue record for this book is available from the British Library.

Library of Congress Control Number: 2015932189

ISBN 9781472435972

MIX
Paper from responsible sources
FSC® C013985
FSC
www.fsc.org

Printed in the United Kingdom by Henry Ling Limited, at the Dorset Press, Dorchester, DT1 1HD

Contents

Acknowledgements

A number of Mary Crock's esteemed colleagues, researchers and friends provided advice and assistance in the selection of material for this volume. She wishes to thank Kate Bones, Lenni Benson, Laurie Berg, Stephen Castles, Vincent Chetail, Michelle Foster, Justin Gest, Stephen Legomsky, Jane McAdam, Hannah Martin, Gerald Neuman, Kim Rubenstein, Ben Saul and Laura Smith-Khan. Finally, special thanks are due to Mary's best critic and wisest friend, Ron McCallum AO. She accepts full responsibility for the choice of pieces included in this collection.

Ashgate would also like to thank the researchers and the contributing authors who provided copies, along with the following for their permission to reprint copyright material.

Ashgate Publishing Limited for the essays: Catherine Dauvergne (2004), 'Making People Illegal', in Peter Fitzpatrick and Patricia Tuitt (eds), *Critical Beings: Law, Nation and the Global Subject*, Aldershot: Ashgate, pp. 83–99. Copyright © 2004 Peter Fitzpatrick, Patricia Tuitt and the contributors; Bernard Ryan (2013), 'In Defence of the Migrant Workers Convention: Standard Setting for Contemporary Migration', in Satvinder S. Juss, *The Ashgate Research Companion to Migration Law, Theory and Policy*, Farnham: Ashgate, pp. 491–515. Copyright © 2013 Satvinder S. Juss and the contributors.

Australian Human Rights Centre and LexisNexis Australia for the essay: Ben Saul (2010), 'Migrating to Australia with Disabilities: Non-discrimination and the Convention on the Rights of Persons with Disabilities', *Australian Journal of Human Rights*, **16**, pp. 63–104.

Copyright Clearance Center for the essay: Ratna Kapur (2005), 'Travel Plans: Border Crossings and the Rights of Transnational Migrants', *Harvard Human Rights Journal*, **18**, pp. 107–38. Copyright © 2005 Harvard Law School.

Vincent Chetail (2013), 'The Human Rights of Migrants in General International Law: From Minimum Standards to Fundamental Rights', *Georgetown Immigration Law Journal*, **28**, pp. 225–55. Copyright © 2013 Vincent Chetail.

De Gruyter for the essay: Linda Bosniak (2007), 'Being Here: Ethical Territoriality and the Rights of Immigrants', *Theoretical Inquiries in Law*, **8**, pp. 389–410. Copyright © 2007 Walter de Gruyter GmbH.

Georgetown Immigration Law Journal for the essay: 'International Migrants Bill of Rights, with Commentary' (2013), *Georgetown Immigration Law Journal*, **28**, pp. 23–103.

Indiana University Press for the essay: Cathryn Costello (2012), 'Human Rights and the Elusive Universal Subject: Immigration Detention under International Human Rights and EU

Law', *Indiana Journal of Global Legal Studies*, **19**, pp. 257–303. Copyright © 2012 Indiana University Maurer School of Law.

International Law Association (Australian Branch) for the essay: Mary E. Crock (2013), 'Of Relative Rights and Putative Children: Rethinking the Critical Framework for the Protection of Refugee Children and Youth', *Australian International Law Journal*, **20**, pp. 33–53.

Intersentia Ltd for the essay: Sylvie Da Lomba (2010), 'Immigration Status and Basic Social Human Rights: A Comparative Study of Irregular Migrants' Right to Health Care in France, the UK and Canada', *Netherlands Quarterly of Human Rights*, **28**, pp. 6–40. Copyright © 2010 Netherlands Institute of Human Rights.

Johns Hopkins University Press for the essay: Jacqueline Bhabha (2009), 'Arendt's Children: Do Today's Migrant Children Have a Right to Have Rights?', *Human Rights Quarterly*, **31**, pp. 410–51. Copyright © 2009 Johns Hopkins University Press.

Melbourne Journal of International Law for the essay: Laurie Berg (2007), 'At the Border and Between the Cracks: The Precarious Position of Irregular Migrant Workers under International Human Rights Law', *Melbourne Journal of International Law*, **8**, pp. 1–34. Copyright © 2007 Melbourne Journal of International Law.

Oxford University Press for the essay: Siobhán Mullally (2014), 'Migration, Gender, and the Limits of Rights', in Ruth Rubio-Marín (ed.), *Human Rights and Immigration*, Oxford: Oxford University Press, pp. 145–76.

Thomson Reuters (Professional) UK Limited for the essay: John Finnis (2011), 'Nationality and Alienage', in *Human Rights and Common Good, Collected Essays: Volume III*, New York: Oxford University Press, pp. 133–49. Originally published *Law Quarterly Review*, **123** (2007), pp. 417–45.

University of North Carolina for the essay: Lenni B. Benson (2002), 'The Invisible Worker', *North Carolina Journal of International Law and Commercial Regulation*, **27**, pp. 483–96.

Vanderbilt Law Review for the essay: Scott Titshaw (2013), 'Revisiting the Meaning of Marriage: Immigration for Same-Sex Spouses in a Post-*Windsor* World', *Vanderbilt Law Review En Banc*, **66**, pp. 167–77. Copyright © 2013 Vanderbilt Law Review.

John Wiley & Sons for the essay: Martin Ruhs and Philip Martin (2008), 'Numbers vs. Rights: Trade-offs and Guest Worker Programs', *International Migration Review*, **42**, pp. 249–65. Copyright © 2008 Center for Migration Studies of New York.

Publisher's Note

The material in this volume has been reproduced using the facsimile method. This means we can retain the original pagination to facilitate easy and correct citation of the original essays. It also explains the variety of typefaces, page layouts and numbering.

Series Preface

Much of contemporary moral, political and legal discourse is conducted in terms of rights and increasingly in terms of human rights. Yet there is considerable disagreement about the nature of rights, their foundations and their practical implications and more concrete controversies as to the content, scope and force of particular rights. Consequently the discourse of rights calls for extensive analysis in its general meaning and significance, particularly in relation to the nature, location and content of the duties and responsibilities that correlate with rights. Equally important is the determination of the forms of argument that are appropriate to establish whether or not someone or some group has or has not a particular right, and what that might entail in practice.

This series brings together essays that exhibit careful analysis of the concept of rights and detailed knowledge of specific rights and the variety of systems of rights articulation, interpretation, protection and enforcement. Volumes deal with general philosophical and practical issues about different sorts of rights, taking account of international human rights, regional rights conventions and regimes, and domestic bills of rights, as well as the moral and political literature concerning the articulation and implementation of rights.

The volumes are intended to assist those engaged in scholarly research by making available the most important and enduring essays on particular topics. Essays are reproduced in full with the original pagination for ease of reference and citation.

The editors are selected for their eminence in the study of law, politics and philosophy. Each volume represents the editor's selection of the most seminal recent essays in English on an aspect of rights or on rights in a particular field. An introduction presents an overview of the issues in that particular area of rights together with comments on the background and significance of the selected essays.

TOM CAMPBELL
Series Editor
Professorial Fellow, The Centre for Applied Philosophy and Public Ethics (CAPPE),
Charles Sturt University, Canberra

Introduction

ACKNOWLEDGING THE 'OTHER': THE INTERSECTION OF HUMAN RIGHTS AND MIGRATION LAW

The concept of the migrant as rights-bearer at law is surprisingly recent and underdeveloped.[1] Within states, migrants have been seen traditionally as the obverse of citizens: aliens, outsiders, persons who are *in* society but not yet *of* a society. Migrants are at best invitees, 'guests' for whom presence in a country is a privilege. For those who enter or remain without the leave of official documentation, migrants are both non-citizen and out-law. The experience of countless irregular migrants around the globe attests the vulnerability of rightlessness. In the international domain, migrants have struggled to assert their personhood for the simple reason that states themselves are the traditional subjects of international law. Having said this, the very absence of legal status in the migrant has been a significant driver in the development and universalization of human rights law. Stripped of the protection of nationality, migrants remain undeniably human. In the iconic words of Max Frisch: 'We asked for workers, but people came' (1990, p. 219).[2]

This is the first volume of a two-volume collection of writings that trace the evolution in thinking about migrants as legal subjects and rights-holders. The intersection between migration law and human rights is now the subject of a vast literature – in many languages. The essays in this collection are taken from works in English published predominantly in academic journals or edited collections. Shorter essays have been favoured for reasons of space, even though the discursive nature of the subject matter has supported whole books on the topic.

In the introduction to his 2014 *Research Handbook on International Law and Migration*, Vincent Chetail organizes his discussion of international migration law around three 'pillars': Departure, Admission and Sojourn (Chetail and Bauloz, 2014, p. 71) . He attaches various rights to each. The right to leave is obviously associated with 'Departure'. Under 'Admission', he lists the right to return to one's own country, *non-refoulement*, family reunion of children, prohibition of arbitrary detention, access to consular protection, and prohibition of collective expulsion. Under 'Sojourn' Chetail includes non-discrimination, prohibition of forced labour and child labour, right to a fair trial, and freedom of conscience and association. While this does provide a useful scaffold for consideration of a notoriously polycentric area of law and public policy, in this collection I have drawn a broader distinction between essays on general migration (Volume I) and those addressing the special situation of refugees and forced

1 Lillich describes the international legal framework governing migration as a 'giant unassembled juridical jigsaw puzzle' with an uncertain number of pieces and only an emergent 'grand design' (1984, p. 122).

2 For an extended reflection on the humanizing effect of migrants on the law, see Motomura (2006).

migrants (Volume II). It is in the latter context that the right to leave, the right to return and *non-refoulement* are considered.

In virtually every country, the presence and treatment of non-citizens are matters of political sensitivity. With greater numbers of people on the move than in any time in human history (see Rubio-Marín, 2014, p. 1), immigration in many countries has polarized – and even paralysed – communities.[3] The difference in thinking about migrants is reflected in the academy. In this volume the two main approaches to migrants' rights that have emerged in liberal democracies are considered. The first proposes an ethic based on nationality (see, most famously, Arendt, 1951; see also Gibney, 1988; Miller, 1988; Kesby, 2012), while the second reaches beyond nationality to propose a more universalist schema based on physical presence and length of residence or depth of connection in or with a state (see Pogge, 1992; Held, 1995; Linklater, 1998; Satz, 1999).

While interrogating the breadth of issues and sub-issues surrounding migrants and the law, I have attempted to construct a balanced representation of the discourse. The collection includes contributions from both staunch defenders of state sovereignty and those who advocate openly for migrants' rights. Having said this, the brief given to me in adding these volumes to a series on human rights does contain an inherent bias. Among those minded to commit to writing serious academic pieces on migrants and rights, it is a minority who now argue against the proposition that migrants have rights of some kind that are worthy of protection.

The essays in this volume are divided into six categories. These range from issues around state sovereignty and migrants as subjects of international law in Part I, the articulation of rights (Part II), through different categories of migrants (Parts III and IV) and issues around health and disability (Part V). The volume closes with an extended essay on the proposal for an International Migrants' Bill of Rights (IMBR) made by an international consortium of academics and students (Part VI). In fact this volume begins and ends with pieces written for a special issue of the *Georgetown Immigration Law Journal* that was devoted to this initiative.

In this introduction I provide a brief overview of the essays and explain briefly how each fits into the overarching narrative on migrants and human rights. With such a rich body of work from which to choose, there may be inevitable idiosyncrasies in the selections made. In the main I have favoured essays that will resonate across countries and across time. At one level, migration law is naturally 'international'. The movement of persons across borders necessarily implicates at least two states (the sending and receiving countries) and often more. Yet, ironically, much writing about immigration law and policy is strongly domestic and issue-based in its focus.

Two Broad Approaches to Migrants' Rights in Liberal Democratic Theory

This volume begins with a series of essays that offer diverse perspectives on migrants as rights-bearers. Like others charged with constructing a collection of works on migrants

3 In 2014 the impact of the Syrian crisis on the bordering countries of Jordan, Lebanon and Turkey was an obvious example in point. See, more generally, Global Commission on International Migration (2005, p. 32); United Nations (2006).

and the law,[4] I have chosen Vincent Chetail as the opening contributor. A scholar with an encyclopedic knowledge of the literature who writes in both English and French, in Chapter 1 he tells the story of how international law has evolved to recognize and protect the human rights of migrants. As Chetail explains, the first recognition of rights in migrants occurred in the (relatively rare) cases where one state was prepared to confront another over the treatment of expatriate nationals. He provides an historical account of the international law on state responsibility for injuries to aliens. He then demonstrates how international human rights law absorbed the minimum standards articulated in the state responsibility cases, arguing that this became the foundation for the universalization of human rights norms. He posits that migrants' rights are universal and must be respected, because they are at base *human rights*.

The three essays that follow touch very lightly on the debate that has raged around the nature and extent of a state's responsibility towards migrants. To foreground these, it is worth expanding briefly on the two ethics outlined earlier, which are known variously as the 'nationalist' versus 'cosmopolitan' or 'postnationalist' approaches to migrants' rights (see Whelan, 1988; Pogge, 1992, p. 49; Bohman, 1998, p. 203; Barry, 1999).

The 'Nationalist' Approach

Writing from her direct experience of the totalitarianism of Nazi Germany, Hannah Arendt (1951) identified the absence of *citizenship* (*de factor* or *de jure*) as the single most important facto leading refugees, stateless persons and minority groups to be bereft of enforceable rights. She argued that human rights are little more than high theory unless an individual is accepted as a participating member of a polity that is prepared to respect and protect the person. Arendt describes citizenship as the enabling status that gives a person the 'right to have rights' (1951, pp. 296–97). Without a state being prepared to offer respect and protection, the minorities of Nazi Germany were not only denied access to justice and physical freedoms but also denied participation in the political process inherent in the functioning of a community (Arendt, 1951, p. 296).

Interestingly, Arendt's work has been used both by proponents of a very restrictive, even punitive view of migrants' rights and by those advocating human rights as universal entitlements.[5] Her observations find resonance with a number of scholars who defend the right of states to articulate physical and metaphysical boundaries that operate to exclude as well as to include. Michael Walzer considers membership in a bounded community to be the necessary pre-condition for many if not 'all the other' social goods (1983, pp. 29, 31 and 63; see also Miller, 1995, pp. 73–80, 90–98). For nationalists, borders facilitate 'popular sovereignty' over less democratic forms of social organization such as religion, race or sectarian interests.[6] The scholars see Arendt's theories as normative, accepting the rights of states to protect the interests of citizens over any rights that might vest in the foreigner.

---

4 See, for example, Rubio-Marín (2014) and the special issue on the IMBR in *Georgetown Immigration Law Journal* **28** (2014).

5 In this volume compare the essays by John Finnis (Chapter 2) and Jacqueline Bhabha (Chapter 9).

6 See Walzer's concern for a world comprised of a 'thousand petty fortresses' (1983, p. 39). See also Motomura (2014) and Bauböck (2011, pp. 358–64).

In Chapter 2, John Finnis demonstrates the way in which a nationalist approach to rights can operate to exclude and deny rights in the migrant. Finnis articulates as a constitutional principle inherent in statehood the right to expel the non-citizen who fails to comply with domestic laws. He argues that a state must accept risks to the public good posed by a *citizen*, but the same is not true for the non-citizen. In the case of the latter (but not the former), it is acceptable to obviate risk by expelling the (migrant) offender. Finnis argues that this is compatible with the principle of equality before the law. He invokes support for his position in parts of Raz's and other political theorists' discussion of multiculturalism and the conditions for a welfare and rule-of-law state.[7]

The Cosmopolitan or Post-national Approach

The problem with linking rights to membership of a community is that the interconnectedness of modern societies and the forces of globalization are redefining notions of community. Allegiances and identities are no longer simple and mono-dimensional, if they ever were (see, for example, Bohman, 1998). So it is that others have used Arendt's observations about rights and societal membership to speak against the acceptance of simple status dichotomies. These scholars read her scholarship in less normative terms to support a broader approach to citizenship and belonging. In Chapter 3, Linda Bosniak introduces the concept of ethical territoriality to challenge the notion that a person's status as citizen or non-citizen should be the sole determinant of the person's rights. She argues that rights and recognition should extend to all persons who are present on the territory of a state simply because of that presence. In this essay she explains and interrogates her argument that territorialism is preferable, on liberal democratic grounds, to status-based approaches to immigrants' rights. It is an essay in which Bosniak starts to look at both the nature of an individual's connection to territory and the circumstances in which individuals should be said to acquire rights by virtue of presence.[8]

Part II extends the discussions of territory and rights to explore the roles that law and language play in constructing identity, status and entitlement. In Chapter 4, Catherine Dauvergne examines the ways in which law and language strip migrants of their humanity and rights. She also considers the changes that have occurred in the way people relate to the notion of nation and state. In an essay that captures a thesis explored at greater length in her book of similar title (Dauvergne, 2008), she looks at how globalization has created a new category of person – the 'illegal' migrant. She concludes with an analysis of what labelling people 'illegal' does to their standing as rights-bearers. This and many of the essays that follow belong to what might be termed a critical rights discourse. For many strong believers in universal human rights, the treatment of migrants has prompted literature that laments the denial of rights in these people. Some seek explanations as to why migrants continue to be abject in the face of apparent improvements in human rights law and theory.

The theme of language, law and disentitlement is reprised in Chapter 5. In an essay published in 2005, Ratna Kapur traces the dissonances between the lived experience and complex identities of the migrant on the one hand and the 'regulatory apparatus' that governs who is permitted to move across borders. She argues that laws and policies often align badly

7 This argument is pursued at greater length in Finnis (2007).

8 For a fuller exposition of her ideas, see Bosniak (2006).

with the global factors that push people to cross borders – and produce the demand for migrants within states. She uses case studies to demonstrate how the 'complexities and layering of migrant existence are rolled and flattened' by law and policy (p. 96). She uses these to identify three ways in which transnational migrants are reduced to 'categories' that ultimately work to deny the identity and rights of these people. First are stereotypes of gender and race – traits that are immutable and unalterable, attracting 'subordinating and paternalistic' regulations (p. 96). The second response goes to the creation of 'the Other' through stereotyping described by Kapur as a 'cultural strip' that 'forces conformity to cultural and social norms' (p. 96). The third response is manifest in the characterization of migrants as threats to security or public health – 'contaminating force(s) to be excluded ... through incarceration or elimination' (p. 96). Kapur's ultimate message is that the use of rigid binaries – of 'us' and 'them', of domination and subordination – undermines the human rights of migrants and ultimately 'fail[s] to address the complex, fragmented, and blurred realities of our transnational world' (p. 97).

The third in a trilogy of pieces on rights and the characterization of migrants is Cathryn Costello's essay on the detention of transnational migrants (Chapter 6). She begins by noting the irony in the widespread use of immigration detention in the face of the universal acceptance in human rights instruments of the right to liberty and security of the person. She notes that it is the most vulnerable of migrants – asylum seekers – who are most susceptible to being detained. Costello examines the diverse jurisprudence on detention emanating from the UN Human Rights Committee, the European Court of Human Rights and the Court of Justice of the European Union. Noting the tendency to defer to the state's sovereign right to control immigration, she argues that greater interaction between these adjudicative bodies could deliver protection dividends for migrants in the form of rights-protective standards.

Fundamental Rights and Fundamental Failures: Family, Gender and the Rights of Children

In Part III, three essays examine the marginalization of women and children in the discourse on both human rights and migrant's rights. These are representative of an extensive literature on rights that traverses law and various aspects of social science.[9] Topics equally deserving of attention that are not included for reasons of space are the many splinter issues associated with the right to family: family unity (see, for example, Aceves, 2006; Elias, 2008; Foster, 2009), family violence and security (see, for example, Abuya, 2003; Weiss, 2009), gender and relationships, and issues around citizenship, identity and birthright (see, for example, Friedler, 1995; Shachar, 2009; Titshaw, 2010). In Chapter 7, Siobhán Mullally examines the significance of gender in three areas of law involving migration: human trafficking, migrant domestic workers and asylum claims involving gender. In theory, human rights law should underpin measures to redress the exploitation, abuse and disadvantage experienced by women in each of these contexts. Mullally argues that migrant women's rights claims in practice have

[9] See, for example, the other essays in the edited collection by Rubio-Marín (2014); Freeman (1996); Piper and Satterthwaite (2007). Note that the issue of human rights and sexual orientation is considered in the second volume in this collection, as is the treatment of women in the asylum process.

been used by states to justify increasing restrictions on legal pathways for safe and secure migration. On the one hand, migrant women are stereotyped as vulnerable and in need of protection. Conversely, women exercising autonomy and agency are characterized as a threat or potentially destabilizing.

Chapter 8 presents an exception to most of the essays in this collection, having a distinctly domestic (US) focus. Scott Titshaw's short essay on the treatment of same-sex relationships in the United States nevertheless opens a window on an issue that is faced by liberal democracies around the globe.

The two essays that follow provide a more detailed case study of a subgroup of migrants who are typically overlooked in practice and who have only recently attracted the attention they deserve in the academy. These are the children who, even more than women, have been invisible migrants. Within families, they pass unnoticed as dependents of responsible adults. Unaccompanied and separated children have been recognized as exquisitely at risk, and yet states have found many of ways to deny their rights – and a myriad of reasons to justify their actions. In Chapter 9, Jacqueline Bhabha embraces Arendt's critical theories to call for a new way of thinking about migrant children who she describes as 'functionally stateless' (p. 221). The focus of this essay is the many migrant children who enter countries and then slip into the shadows as irregular migrants. Bhabha shows that governments all around the world have been blind to the particular harms inflicted on children by laws and policies excluding irregular migrants.[10]

In Chapter 10, I make a closer study of the rationales used by states to deny rights to (and actually inflict harm on) migrant children – including those presenting as asylum seekers and refugees. I argue that the discourses developed to deny rights to these children turn on three 'disabling' ideas. First, I explore the hierarchies that have developed in thinking about human rights. However counter-intuitive to the notion of universal rights, in practice children's rights are seen most often as inferior to or dependent on the rights and interests of adults. Second, children suffer because of the primacy given to the state's right to control migration. Finally, I examine the harms caused to children by measures adopted to deter irregular migration. Of particular interest is the claim that regulatory measures offensive to basic human rights are justified because they will protect children against the greater dangers inherent in clandestine travel. In these instances the rights of the 'imputed' child are used to trump those of the embodied child.

Migrant Workers

The intersection between immigration and the human rights of workers is a topic that has also been slow to attract the academic interest it deserves (Freedland and Costello, 2014). Here the rich literature on human rights at work has often reflected a natural preference for the 'nationalist' ethic and a strongly domestic focus, with some notable exceptions (see, for example, Davies and Freedland, 1983). The reluctance to acknowledge the human rights of migrant workers is apparent in the time taken to negotiate a human rights treaty for these

[10] The themes in this essay have been explored at greater length in Bhabha (2011, 2014).

people – and the poor accession rate when such a convention was finally concluded.[11] In this volume I have chosen four essays to illustrate both the evolution in the literature and the divergence in thinking about the rights of migrant workers. Writing in 2007, Laurie Berg (Chapter 11) provides a thoughtful account of how international human rights law has been trumped consistently by state sovereignty in every attempt to protect foreign workers. She argues that regional judicial forums may prove more fruitful in the search for international legal doctrine to protect the human rights of the most vulnerable migrant workers – those who enter or remain in a country without authority.[12]

The second essay in this section is a contribution by social scientists Martin Ruhs and Philip Martin who have analysed the rights accorded to migrant workers in different countries. In Chapter 12, they present research suggesting that countries admitting large numbers of low-skilled migrant workers typically offer them far less rights than do countries which admit fewer and more select migrants. Ruhs argues that the discourse on universal human rights fails to recognize the competition in practice between migrants' rights and resource constraints. In an essay that is articulated more fully in his book (Ruhs, 2014), Ruhs calls for an explicit discussion of the number versus rights trade-off that occurs when states set their migration programmes. Somewhat controversially, Ruhs suggests that the idea of universalism should be abandoned in recognition that the rights of migrants must be relative to the numbers admitted by states (and to a state's resources).

In Chapter 13, Lenni Benson makes the simple point that the rights of migrant workers are predicated on the migrants being visible – and having access to the services devised to support and protect workers. In other words, rights will be rights theory only unless mechanisms are put in place to allow for the realization of the rights. Echoing Dauvergne and Kapur, Benson argues that the label of undocumented worker and the exclusionary force of the law create a whole class of invisible workers. She explains how even the most direct of protective measures – she gives the example of mobile teams charged with conducting health tests – fail to assist irregular migrant workers who have no identity papers and no formal identity within the state.

This section concludes in Chapter 14 with a reflective essay by Bernard Ryan, writing in defence of the Migrant Workers Convention. After describing its 'difficult' history, Ryan examines the effect of the Convention on the relatively small but growing number of states that have signed and ratified the instrument. He examines the migration experience of these states together with the work of the treaty body established in January 2004.[13] In a nice counterpoint to Ruhs, Ryan argues that the Convention has real potential as an effective and authoritative source of standards on the treatment of migrants.

---

11 International Convention on the Protection of the Rights of All Migrant Workers and Members of Their Families (entered into force 1 July 2003: 2220 UNTS 3; Doc A/RES/45/158). See Cholewinski, de Guchteneire and Pécoud (2009). See further Bernard Ryan, Chapter 14 in this volume.

12 For a more extensive treatment of this topic, see Berg (2015).

13 See Committee on Migrant Workers, details available at: http://www.ohchr.org/EN/HRBodies/CMW/Pages/CMWIndex.aspx (accessed 1 July 2015).

Health and Disability

Part V of this volume addresses issues of health and disability as they affect migrants in two contexts. In Chapter 15, Sylvie Da Lomba continues the discussion of the economic and social rights of irregular migrants, examining the right to health care. She reports on a comparative study of policy and practice in three developed countries: France, the United Kingdom and Canada. She argues that all three countries have been reluctant to extend the basic right to health care to these migrants, seeing the gesture as antithetical to the sovereign right to control immigration. This response is yet another illustration of how states subordinate human rights to immigration control.

The second essay in this section examines threshold criteria devised by states that operate as barriers to the admission of persons with disabilities. These are the rules applied to all migrants that go to issues such as a person's criminal record or the risk that an individual might pose to the public health of a country. In Chapter 16, Ben Saul examines the 'health test' devised by Australia and its application to persons with disabilities. He argues that the failure to distinguish between illness and disability and other features of the rules constitute unjustifiable discrimination against migrants with disabilities. The essay is one of the first to look at a system of migration rules against the new standards established by the UN Convention on the Rights of Persons with Disabilities (CRPD).[14] Saul notes that there is nothing inherently wrong with states imposing health requirements on migrants, for example to ensure that the scarce resources available are targeted on nationals rather than foreigners. However, he argues that Australia's laws go beyond measures designed to protect state interests to indirectly discriminate against persons with disabilities wishing to migrate. He asserts that the health rules routinely exclude migrants with disabilities who may pose no burden on the country. Making no distinction between disability and disease, the rules evince a 'medical' approach to disability that is directly at odds with the precepts of the CRPD.

Towards an International Migrants' Bill of Rights

This volume concludes with a long essay that presents an ambitious project of at least five years' standing aimed at creating an International Migrants Bill of Rights (IMBR).[15] In 2010, Harvard Professor Gerald Neuman opened his review of the exposure draft of the IMBR with

---

14 Convention on the Rights of Persons with Disabilities (CRPD), opened for signature 30 March 2007, 2515 UNTS 3 (entered into force 3 May 2008); Optional Protocol to the Convention on the Rights of Persons with Disabilities, opened for signature 30 March 2007 (2007) 46 ILM 443 (entered into force 3 May 2008). The texts of both instruments are available online at: www.un.org/disabilities/default.asp?navid=12&pid=150 (accessed 1 July 2015).

15 The IMBR project is a collaborative project of the Georgetown University Law Centre, The Minerva Center for Human Rights at the Hebrew University of Jerusalem and the Migration Studies Unit at London School of Economics.

the following reflections on the task before the IMBR consortium of scholars and students.[16] He wrote:

> In evaluating a human rights instrument, it may be important to bear in mind three possible aspects of a positive human rights norm.[17] First, a norm that acquires positive status through the agreement of states possesses a consensual aspect resulting from their participation in the adoption of the text and/or their ratification of the instrument as binding upon them. Second, the norm possesses a supra-positive aspect, to the extent that it gives effect in positive law, directly or indirectly, to extra-legal normative conceptions regarding the rights of human beings. Third, the norm may possess an institutional aspect, as a positive legal rule imposing duties on government actors, possibly subject to review by the courts or other bodies. Enforceable rules may need to be designed in a manner that facilitates compliance by the duty-holders and effective oversight. Aspirational instruments that neglect institutional concerns may need to be supplemented considerably if they are to be converted into effective legal rules. (Neuman, 2010, pp. 686–87)

Without the involvement of states or of international organizations to lend a consensual element to the IMBR initiative, the final document draws heavily on the language, principles and jurisprudence of the extant human rights treaties for its authority. The challenge for the project is that this body of hard and soft international law is not easily shaped into a monolithic whole that will sit comfortably with every iteration of 'migrant'.

The definition of migrant in Article 1(1) is described as 'purposefully broad and inclusive'. It covers all non-citizens within a state – permanent or temporary migrants, legal or illegal, official or otherwise. As Neuman (2010, p. 687) notes, tourists, diplomats, members of foreign armed forces may all be human beings with human rights, but their situations are dramatically different. The greatest challenge facing the drafters of the IMBR is that their instrument will quickly lose credibility and legitimacy if assertions of right or entitlement are made in respect of persons who are not obviously worthy of holding the rights in question. With the exception of rights not to be tortured or *refouled*, not all rights are owed by states to all migrants (thus so broadly defined).

It must be said that some aspects of the IMBR do give the document a strongly aspirational feel. An example in point is the inclusion of Article 14 of the Universal Declaration of Human Rights asserting that every migrant has the right to seek and enjoy asylum (Article 12). At the same time, this document does seem to have considered closely Neuman's critiques of the earlier draft. Less prominence is given to economic and social rights which will clearly vary according to the identity and status of different migrants.

The diversity of the migrant experience – and the legitimacy of states' interests in protecting their citizens – means that articulating a rights regime will always be complex. The significance of the IMBR is that the Georgetown consortium has opened a conversation that

---

16 Professor Neuman is the J. Sinclair Armstrong Professor of International, Foreign and Comparative Law, Harvard Law School. Between 2010 and 2014 he was a member of the United Nations Human Rights Committee, the elected body of experts that oversees states' compliance with the International Covenant on Civil and Political Rights.

17 See Neuman (2003, pp. 1866–72) for a discussion of these aspects with regard to individual rights provisions of constitutions and human rights treaties.

will only become more important as the forces of globalization grow and develop. The final aspiration of both this volume and of the IMBR is that scholars, policy-makers and thinkers everywhere embrace the challenge of engaging with the rights discourse so as to include the migrant, acknowledging the Other in our midst.

References

Abuya, Edwin Odhiambo (2003), 'The Pain of Love: Spousal Immigration and Domestic Violence in Australia – A Regime in Chaos?', *Pacific Rim Law and Policy Journal*, **12**, pp. 673–707.

Aceves, William J. (2006), 'Protecting the Right to Family Life in U.S. Immigration Proceedings: A Fundamental Right with a Limited Remedy', in Anne Bayefsky (ed.), *Human Rights and Refugees, Internally Displaced Persons and Migrant Workers: Essays in Memory of Joan Fitzpatrick and Arthur Helton*, The Hague: Martinus Nijhoff, pp. 349–83.

Arendt, Hannah (1951), *The Origins of Totalitarianism*, London: Harcourt Brace.

Barry, Brian (1999), 'Statism and Nationalism: A Cosmopolitan Critique', in Ian Shapiro and Lea Brilmayer (eds), *Nomos XLI: Global Justice*, New York: New York University Press, pp. 12–66.

Bauböck, Rainer (2011), 'Citizenship and Free Movement', in Rogers M. Smith (ed.), *Citizenship, Borders and Human Needs*, Philadelphia: University of Pennsylvania Press, pp. 343–76.

Berg, Laurie (2015), *Whose Rights at Work? Addressing Precariousness in Temporary and Unauthorised Migrant Labour in Australia*, Abingdon: Routledge.

Bhabha, Jacqueline (ed.) (2011), *Children without a State: A Global Human Rights Challenge*, Cambridge, MA: MIT Press.

Bhabha, Jacqueline (2014), *Child Migration and Human Rights in a Global Age*, Princeton: Princeton University Press.

Bohman, James (1998), 'The Globalization of the Public Sphere: Cosmopolitan Publicity and the Problem of Cultural Pluralism', *Philosophy and Social Criticism*, **24**, 2/3, pp. 199–216.

Bosniak, Linda (2006), *The Citizen and the Alien: Dilemmas of Contemporary Membership*, Princeton and Oxford: Princeton University Press.

Chetail, Vincent and Bauloz, Céline (eds) (2014), *Research Handbook on International Law and Migration*, Cheltenham: Edward Elgar.

Cholewinski, Ryszard, de Guchteneire, Paul and Pécoud, Antoine (eds) (2009), *Migration and Human Rights: The United Nations Convention on Migrant Workers' Rights*, Cambridge: Cambridge University Press.

Dauvergne, Catherine (2008), *Making People Illegal: What Globalisation Means for Migration and Law*, Cambridge: Cambridge University Press.

Davies, Paul L. and Freedland, Mark (eds) (1983), *Kahn-Freund's Labour and the Law* (3rd edn), London: Stevens & Sons.

Elias, Shaina N. (2008), 'From Bereavement to Banishment: The Deportation of Surviving Alien Spouses under the "Widow Penalty"', *George Washington Law Review*, **77**, pp. 172–215.

Global Commission on International Migration (2005), *Migration in an Interconnected World: New Directions for Action* (October), available at: http://www.gcim.org (accessed 18 May 2007).

Finnis, John (2007), 'Nationality, Alienage and Constitutional Principle', *Law Quarterly Review*, **123**, pp. 417–45.

Foster, Michelle (2009), 'An Alien by the Barest of Threads: The Legality of the Deportation of Long-term Residents from Australia', *Melbourne University Law Review*, **33**, pp. 483–541.

Freedland, Mark and Costello, Cathryn (2014), 'Migrants at Work and the Division of Labour Law', in Cathryn Costello and Mark Freedland (eds), *Migrants at Work: Immigration and Vulnerability in Labour Law*, Oxford: Oxford University Press, pp. 1–26.

Freeman, Michael (1996), *Children's Rights*, Aldershot: Ashgate Dartmouth.

Friedler, Edith Z. (1995), 'From Extreme Hardship to Extreme Deference: United States Deportation of its Own Children', *Hastings Constitutional Law Quarterly*, **22**, pp. 491–556.

Frisch, Max (1990), 'Überfremdung 1', in *Schweiz als Heimat? Versuche* über *50 Jahre*, ed. Walter Obschlager, Frankfurt am Main: Suhrkamp Verlag, pp. 219–21.

Gibney, Mark (1988), 'Introduction', in Mark Gibney (ed.), *Open Borders? Closed Societies? The Ethical and Political Issues*, London: Greenwood Press, pp. xiii–iv.

Held, David (1995), *Democracy and the Global Order: From the Modern State to Cosmopolitan Governance*, Cambridge: Polity Press.

Kesby, Alison (2012), *The Right to Have Rights: Citizenship, Humanity, and International Law*, Oxford: Oxford University Press.

Lillich, Richard B. (1984), *The Human Rights of Aliens in Contemporary International Law*, Manchester: Manchester University Press.

Linklater, Andrew (1998), 'Cosmopolitan Citizenship', *Citizenship Studies* **2**, 1, pp. 23–41.

Miller, David (1988), 'The Ethical Significance of Nationality', *Ethics*, **98**, pp. 647–62.

Miller, David (1995), *On Nationality*, Oxford: Clarendon Press.

Motomura, Hiroshi (2006), 'We Asked for Workers, but Families Came: Time, Law, and the Family in Immigration and Citizenship', *Virginia Journal of Social Policy and Law*, **14**, pp. 103–18.

Motomura, Hiroshi (2014), *Immigration Outside the Law*, Oxford: Oxford University Press.

Neuman, Gerald L. (2003), 'Human Rights and Constitutional Rights: Harmony and Dissonance', *Stanford Law Review*, **55**, pp. 1863–900.

Neuman, Gerald L. (2010), 'A Migrants' Bill of Rights – Between Restatement and Manifesto', *Georgetown Immigration Law Journal*, **24**, pp. 685–94.

Piper, Nicola and Satterthwaite, Margaret (2007), 'Migrant Women', in Ryszard Cholewinski, Richard Perruchoud and Ewan MacDonald (eds), *International Migration Law: Developing Paradigms and Key Challenges*, The Hague: TMC Asser Press, pp. 237–54.

Pogge, Thomas (1992), 'Cosmopolitanism and Sovereignty', *Ethics*, **103**, 1, pp. 48–75.

Rubio-Marín, Ruth (ed.) (2014), *Human Rights and Migration*, Oxford: Oxford University Press.

Ruhs, Martin (2014), *The Price of Rights: Regulating International Labor Migration*, Princeton: Princeton University Press.

Satz, Deborah (1999), 'Equality of What Among Whom? Thoughts on Cosmopolitan, Statism and Nationalism', in Ian Shapiro and Lea Brilmayer (eds), *Nomos XLI: Global Justice*, New York: New York University Press, pp. 67–85.

Shachar, Ayelet (2009), *The Birthright Lottery: Citizenship and Global Inequality*, Cambridge, MA: Harvard University Press.

Titshaw, Scott (2010), 'Sorry Ma'am, Your Baby is an Alien: Outdated Immigration Rules and Assistive Reproduction Technologies', *Florida Coastal Law Review*, **12**, pp. 47–134.

United Nations (2006), 'Summary of the High-Level Dialogue on International Migration and Development, Note by the President of the General Assembly', UN GAOR, 61st session, Agenda Item 55(b), UN Doc A/61/515 (13 October).

Walzer, Michael (1983), *Spheres of Justice*, New York: Basic Books.

Weiss, Adam (2009), 'Transnational Families in Crisis: An Analysis of the Domestic Violence Rule in EU Free Movement Law', *Michigan Journal of International Law*, **30**, pp. 841–79.

Whelan, Frederick G. (1988), 'Citizenship and Freedom of Movement: An Open Admission Policy?', in Mark Gibney (ed.), *Open Borders? Closed Societies? The Ethical and Political Issues*, London: Greenwood Press, pp. 3–39.

Select Bibliography

Migration and Human Rights

Aleinikoff, T.A. and Chetail, V. (eds) (2003), *Migration and International Legal Norms*, The Hague: TMC Asser Press.

Anderson, B. and Shutes, I. (eds) (2014), *Migration and Care Labour: Theory, Policy and Politics*, London: Palgrave.

Arendt, H. (1951), *The Origins of Totalitarianism*, London: Harcourt Brace.

Basok, T., Inclan, S. and Noonan, J. (2006), 'Citizenship, Human Rights and Social Justice', *Citizenship Studies*, **10**, pp. 267–73.

Benhabib, S. (2004), *The Rights of Others: Aliens, Residents and Citizens*, Cambridge: Cambridge University Press.

Betts, A. (2010), 'Towards a "Soft Law" Framework for the Protection of Vulnerable Irregular Migrants', *International Journal of Refugee Law*, **22**, 2 pp. 209–36.

Bogusz, B., Cholewinski, R., Cygan, A. and Szyszczak, E. (eds) (2004), *Irregular Migration and Human Rights: Theoretical, European and International Perspectives*, Dordrecht: Martinus Nijhoff.

Bosniak, L. (1991), 'Human Rights, State Sovereignty and the Protection of Undocumented Migrants under the International Migrant Workers Convention', *International Migration Review*, **25**, pp. 737–70.

Carens, J. (2008), 'The Rights of Irregular Migrants', *Ethics and International Affairs*, **22**, pp. 163–86.

Crock, M. (2008), 'Defining Strangers: Human Rights, Immigrants and the Foundations of a Just Society', *Melbourne University Law Review*, **31**, pp. 1053–71.

Dauvergne, C. (2008), *Making People Illegal: What Globalization Means for Migration and Law*, Cambridge: Cambridge University Press.

Dembour, M.-B. (ed.) (2011), *Are Human Rights for Migrants? Critical Reflections on the Status of Irregular Migrants in Europe and the United States*, Abingdon: Routledge.

Dummett, A. and Nicol, A. (1990), *Subjects, Citizens, Aliens and Others*, London: Weidenfeld and Nicolson.

Juss, S.S. (ed.) (2013), *The Ashgate Research Companion to Migration Law, Theory and Policy*, Farnham: Ashgate.

Legomsky, S. (2010), 'Citizens' Rights and Human Rights', *Israel Law Review*, **43**, pp. 67–98.

Neuman, G.L. (2010), 'A Migrants' Bill of Rights – Between Restatement and Manifesto', *Georgetown Immigration Law Journal*, **24**, pp. 685–94.

Opeskin, B., Perruchoud, R. and Redpath-Cross, J. (eds) (2012), *Foundations of International Migration Law*, Cambridge, Cambridge University Press.

Rubenstein, K. and Field, J. (2013), 'Conceptualising Australian Citizenship for Children: A Human Rights Perspective', *Australian International Law Journal*, **20**, pp. 77–93.

Rubio-Marín, R. (ed.) (2013), *Migration and Human Rights*, Oxford: Oxford University Press.

Tiburcio, C. (2001), *The Human Rights of Aliens under International and Comparative Law*, Dordrecht: Martinus Nijhoff.

Weissbrodt, D.S. (2008), *The Human Rights of Non-Citizens*, Oxford and New York: Oxford University Press.

State Responsibility for Injury to Aliens

Amerasinghe, C.F. (1967), *State Responsibility for Injuries to Aliens*, Oxford: Clarendon Press.

Freeman, A.V. (1938), *The International Responsibility of States for Denial of Justice*, London, New York and Toronto: Longmans.

Garcia-Amador, F., Sohn, L. and Baxter, R. (1974), *Recent Codification of the Law of State Responsibility for Injuries of Aliens*, Dobbs Ferry, NY and Leiden: Oceana and Sijthoff.

Lillich, R.B. (ed.) (1983), *International Law of State Responsibility for Injuries to Aliens*, Charlottesville: University Press of Virginia.

Roth, A.H. (1949), *The Minimum Standard of International Law Applied to Aliens*, Leiden: A.W. Sijthoff's Uitgeversmaatschappij N.V.

Migrants' Rights and Detention

Acer, E. and Goodman, J. (2010), 'Reaffirming Rights: Human Rights Protections of Migrants, Asylum Seekers, and Refugees in Immigration Detention', *Georgetown Immigration Law Journal*, **24**, pp. 507–31.

Cornelisse, G. (2010), *Immigration Detention and Human Rights: Rethinking Territorial Sovereignty*, Leiden: Martinus Nijhoff.

Costello, C. (2012), 'Human Rights and the Elusive Universal Subject: Immigration Detention under International Human Rights and EU Law', *Indiana Journal of Global Legal Studies*, **19**, 1, pp. 257–303.

Crock, M. (2002), 'You Have to Be Stronger Than Razor Wire: Legal Issues relating to the Detention of Asylum Seekers and Refugees', *Australian Journal of Administrative Law*, **10**, pp. 33–63.

Edwards, A. (2011), *Back to Basics: The Right to Liberty and Security of Person and 'Alternatives to Detention' of Refugees, Asylum-Seekers, Stateless Persons and Other Migrants*, UNHCR Legal and Protection Policy Research Series, Division of International Protection, PPLA/2011/01.Rev.1, Apr.

Vohra, S. (2007), 'Detention of Irregular Migrants and Asylum Seekers', in Ryszard Cholewinski, Richard Perruchoud and Ewan MacDonald (eds), *International Migration Law: Developing Paradigms and Key Challenges*, The Hague: TMC Asser Press, pp. 49–70.

Migration, Gender and Human Rights

Benhabib, S., Coopan, V. and Resnick, J. (eds) (2009), *Citizenship, Borders and Gender: Mobility and Immobility*, New Haven, CT: Yale University Press.

Bhabba, J. (2007), 'Border Rights and Rites: Generalisations, Stereotypes, and Gendered Migration', in S. Walsum and T. Spijkerboer (eds), *Women and Immigration Law: New Variations on Classical Feminist Themes*, Abingdon: Routledge Cavendish.

Chetail, V. and Bauloz, C. (eds) (2014), *Research Handbook on International Law and Migration*, Cheltenham: Edward Elgar.

Cronin, K. (1996), 'A Primary Consideration – Children in Australian Immigration Law', *Australian Journal of Human Rights*, **2**, 2; reprinted in Melinda Jones and Lee Ann Basser Marks (eds) (2001), *Children on the Agenda*, Sydney: Prospect Media, pp. 147–62.

Macklin, A. (2004), 'At the Border of Rights: Migration, Sex-Work and Trafficking', in N. Gordon (ed.), *On the Margins of Globalization: Critical Perspectives on Human Rights*, Lanham, MD: Lexington Books, pp. 161–91.

Macklin, A. (2008), 'Legal Aspects of Conflict Induced Migration by Women', *Reproductive Health Matters*, **16**, pp. 22–32; revised and republished in Susan Martin and John Tirman (eds) (2009), *Women, Migration and Conflict: Breaking a Deadly Circle*, New York: Springer, pp. 23–45.

Piper, N. and Satterthwaite, M. (2007), 'Migrant Women', in Ryszard Cholewinski, Richard Perruchoud and Ewan MacDonald (eds), *International Migration Law: Developing Paradigms and Key Challenges*, The Hague: TMC Asser Press, pp. 237–54.

Migration, Labour and Human Rights

Bosniak, L. (2009), 'Citizenship, Noncitizenship, and the Transnationalization of Domestic Work', in S. Benhabib and J. Resnik (eds), *Migration and Mobilities: Citizenship, Borders, and Gender*, New York: New York University Press, pp. 127–56.

Cholewinski, R. (1997), *Migrant Workers in International Human Rights Law: Their Protection in Countries of Employment*, Oxford: Oxford University Press.

Cholewinski, R. (2008), 'The Human Rights and Labor Rights of Migrants: Visions of Equality', *Georgetown Immigration Law Journal*, **22**, pp. 177–219.

Cholewinski, R. (2010), 'Labour Migration Management and the Rights of Migrant Workers', in A. Edwards and C. Ferstman (eds), *Human Security and Non-Citizens: Law, Policy and International Affairs*, Cambridge: Cambridge University Press, pp. 273–313.

Cholewinski, R., de Guchteneire, P. and Pécoud, A. (eds) (2009), *Migration and Human Rights: The United Nations Convention on Migrant Workers' Rights*, Cambridge: Cambridge University Press.

Cleveland, S. (2005), 'Legal Status and Rights of Undocumented Workers', *American Journal of International Law*, **99**, pp. 460–65.

Costello, C. and Freedland, M. (eds) (2014), *Migrants at Work: Immigration and Vulnerability in Labour Law*, Oxford: Oxford University Press.

Crock, M. and Lyon, K. (eds) (2002), *Nation Skilling: Immigration, Labour and the Law in Australia, Canada, New Zealand and the United States*, Sydney: Desert Pea Press and Australia Pacific Migration Research Network.

Dewhurst, E. (2011), 'The Right of Irregular Immigrants to Outstanding Remuneration under the EU Sanctions Directive: Rethinking Domestic Labour Policy in a Globalised World', *European Journal of Migration and Law*, **13**, pp. 389–410.

Fudge, J. (2012), 'Precarious Migrant Status and Precarious Employment: The Paradox of International Rights for Migrant Workers', *Comparative Labor Law & Policy Journal*, **34**, 1, pp. 95–131.

Gordon, J. (2005), *Suburban Sweatshops: The Fight for Immigrant Rights*, Cambridge, MA: Belknap/Harvard University Press.

Leary, V. (2003), 'The Paradox of Workers' Rights as Human Rights', in L. Compa and S. Diamond (eds), *Human Rights, Labor Rights and International Trade*, Philadelphia: University of Pennsylvania Press.

Lenard, P. and Straehle, C. (eds) (2012), *Legislated Inequality: Temporary Labour Migration in Canada*, Kingston: McGill-Queens University Press.

Ryan, B. (ed.) (2005), *Labour Migration and Employment Rights*, Melbourne: Institute of Employment Rights.

Ruhs, M. (2013), *The Price of Rights: Regulating International Labor Migration*, Princeton: Princeton University Press.

Wickramasekara, P. (2008), 'Globalisation, International Labor Migration and the Rights of Migrant Workers', *Third World Quarterly*, **29**, pp. 1247–64.

Migration and the Right to Family

Abram, E.F. (1995), 'The Child's Right to Family Unity in International Immigration Law', *Law & Policy*, **17**, 4, pp. 397–439.

Anderfuhren-Wayne, C.S. (1996), 'Family Unity in Immigration and Refugee Matters: United States and European Approaches', *International Journal of Refugee Law*, **8**, 3, pp. 347–82.
Bhabha, J. (2011), *Children without a State: A Global Human Rights Challenge*, Cambridge, MA: MIT Press.
Bhabha, J. (2014), *Child Migration and Human Rights in a Global Age*, Princeton: Princeton University Press.
Lahav, G. (1997), 'International versus National Constraints in Family-reunification Migration Policy', *Global Governance*, **3**, pp. 349–72.
Merin, Y. (2005), 'The Right to Family Life and Civil Marriage under International Law and its Implementation in the State of Israel', *Boston College International and Comparative Law Review*, **28**, pp. 79–147.
Starr, S. and Brilmayer, L. (2003), 'Family Separation as a Violation of International Law', *Berkeley Journal of International Law*, **21**, pp. 213–87.

Migration and Socioeconomic Rights

Chetail, V. and. Giacca, G. (2009), 'Who Cares? The Right to Health of Migrants', in A. Clapham and M. Robinson (eds), *Realizing the Right to Health*, Swiss Human Rights Book 3, Zurich: Rüffer & Rub, pp. 224–34.
Foster, M. (2009), *International Refugee Law and Socio-economic Rights: Refuge from Deprivation*, Cambridge: Cambridge University Press.
Grant, S. (2011), 'The Recognition of Migrants' Rights within the UN Human Rights System: The First 60 Years', in M.-B. Dembour (ed.), *Are Human Rights for Migrants? Critical Reflections on the Status of Irregular Migrants in Europe and the United States*, Abingdon: Routledge.
Guiraudon, V. (2000), 'The Marshallian Tryptich Reordered: The Role of Courts and Bureaucracies in Furthering Migrants' Social Rights', in M. Bommes and A. Geddes (eds), *Immigration and Welfare: Challenging the Borders of the Welfare State*, London: Routledge.
Trachtman, J.P. (2009), *The International Law of Economic Migration: Toward the Fourth Freedom*, Kalamazoo, MI: W.E. Upjohn Institute for Employment Research.

Part I
Challenging State Sovereignty: Migrants as Subjects of International Law

[1]

THE HUMAN RIGHTS OF MIGRANTS IN GENERAL INTERNATIONAL LAW: FROM MINIMUM STANDARDS TO FUNDAMENTAL RIGHTS

VINCENT CHETAIL*

I. INTRODUCTION

The story of migrants is frequently portrayed as a story of abuse, violence, and racism. This narrative of tragedy has become commonplace for triggering attention of mass media and highlighting—consciously or not—the perils of being a migrant. This article proposes another story: Migration is a permanent feature of history, and it is framed by public international law. There is nothing surprising in this; the movement of persons across borders is international by nature since it presupposes a triangular relationship between a migrant, a state of emigration, and a state of immigration.

Though it was not free from controversies, the legal protection of migrants has a long lineage in the history of international law. One can even argue that, from its inception, international law has had a symbiotic relationship with migration. The very term "*jus gentium*" designated the set of customary rules governing the legal status of aliens under the law of ancient Rome.[1] As far back as the 16th century, this Latin expression was specifically used to refer to the law of nations, before Jeremy Bentham coined the term "international law" in 1789.[2] In the meantime, the movement of persons across borders was a typical subject of discussions among the founding fathers of international

---

* Professor of International Law, Graduate Institute of International and Development Studies (Geneva); Director, Global Migration Centre; Editor-in-Chief, Refugee Survey Quarterly (Oxford University Press).

1. DAVID J. BEDERMAN, INTERNATIONAL LAW IN ANTIQUITY 85 (2004).

2. JEREMY BENTHAM, INTRODUCTION TO THE PRINCIPLES OF MORALS AND LEGISLATION ¶ XXV, at 236 (Batoche Books 1999) (1789).

law, such as Franciscus de Victoria,[3] Hugo Grotius,[4] and Emer de Vattel.[5]

Since then, migration has remained a topical issue of international concern, which mirrors the broader development of international law. A particularly telling case can be found in the human rights of migrants. The present article traces back their historical origins and analyses their primary features under contemporary international law. Though this issue has raised a considerable literature among contemporary scholars, human rights of migrants have been rarely approached from a general international law perspective.[6] Such an approach proves to be particularly valuable for many reasons. Most notably, it provides the global frame of migrants' rights and contributes to a better understanding of their legal environment and core content.

The systemic perspective proposed in the present article recalls that migrants' rights are anchored in international law and reflect its evolution. This underlines in turn that most migrants' rights are grounded in customary international law and are binding on every state. The legal protection of migrants has evolved from the notion of a minimum standard based on state responsibility to fundamental rights consecrated in human rights law, and, as such, available to every individual. As a result of this longstanding process, migrants' rights are universal and must be respected, because migrants' rights are human rights.

Against such a frame, part II of this article provides a historical account about the law of state responsibility for injuries committed to aliens. This was a classic question of international law which was crystallized through the notion of international minimum standards at the end of the 19th century and

3. FRANCISCUS DE VICTORIA, *The First Reflectio: On the Indians Lately Discovered*, *in* DE INDIS ET DE IVRE BELLI RELECTIONES, ¶ 386, at 151 (Ernest Nys ed., John Pawley Bate trans., Carnegie Institute of Washington 1917) (1532).

4. HUGO GROTIUS, DE JURE BELLI AC PACIS LIBRI TRES ¶ XXIV, at 253 (James Brown Scott ed., Francis W. Kelsey trans., Clarendon Press, 1925) (1625).

5. EMER DE VATTEL, THE LAW OF NATIONS, OR, PRINCIPLES OF THE LAW OF NATURE, APPLIED TO THE CONDUCT AND AFFAIRS OF NATIONS AND SOVEREIGNS, WITH THREE EARLY ESSAYS ON THE ORIGIN AND NATURE OF NATURAL LAW AND ON LUXURY ¶ 225, at 224 (Béla Kapossy & Richard Whatmore eds., Liberty Fund 2008) (1758).

6. The academic literature devoted to the human rights of migrants is prolific. *See generally* RYSZARD CHOLEWINSKI, MIGRANT WORKERS IN INTERNATIONAL HUMAN RIGHTS LAW: THEIR PROTECTION IN COUNTRIES OF EMPLOYMENT (1997); Joan Fitzpatrick, *The Human Rights of Migrants*, *in* MIGRATION AND INTERNATIONAL LEGAL NORMS 169 (T. Alexander Aleinikoff & Vincent Chetail eds., 2003); Guy S. Goodwin-Gill, *Migration: International Law and Human Rights*, *in* MANAGING MIGRATION: TIME FOR A NEW INTERNATIONAL REGIME? 160 (Bimal Ghosh ed., 2000); IRREGULAR MIGRATION AND HUMAN RIGHTS: THEORETICAL, EUROPEAN AND INTERNATIONAL PERSPECTIVES (Barbara Bogusz et al. eds., 2004); RICHARD B. LILLICH, THE HUMAN RIGHTS OF ALIENS IN CONTEMPORARY INTERNATIONAL LAW (1984); MIGRATION AND HUMAN RIGHTS: THE UNITED NATIONS CONVENTION ON MIGRANT WORKERS' RIGHTS (Paul de Guchteneire et al. eds., 2009) [hereinafter MIGRATION AND HUMAN RIGHTS]; 2 MONDIALISATION, MIGRATION ET DROITS DE L'HOMME: LE DROIT INTERNATIONAL EN QUESTION/GLOBALIZATION, MIGRATION AND HUMAN RIGHTS: INTERNATIONAL LAW UNDER REVIEW (Vincent Chetail ed., 2007) [hereinafter MONDIALISATION]; SYLVIE SAROLÉA, DROITS DE L'HOMME ET MIGRATIONS: DE LA PROTECTION DU MIGRANT AUX DROITS DE LA PERSONNE MIGRANTE (2006); CARMEN TIBURCIO, THE HUMAN RIGHTS OF ALIENS UNDER INTERNATIONAL AND COMPARATIVE LAW (2001); DAVID WEISSBRODT, THE HUMAN RIGHTS OF NON-CITIZENS (2008); Ryszard Cholewinski, *The Human and Labor Rights of Migrants: Visions of Equality*, 22 GEO. IMMIGR. L.J. 177 (2008).

the first half of the 20th century. Part III demonstrates how international human rights law has progressively encapsulated the notion of international minimum standards before constituting nowadays the primary source of protection. Part IV then focuses on the principle of non-discrimination as the ultimate benchmark of migrants' rights.

II. THE ORIGINS OF THE INTERNATIONAL MINIMUM STANDARD AND THE LAW OF STATE RESPONSIBILITY

Traditionally, the responsibility of states for injuries to aliens was a branch of international law on its own and, in fact, one of its most important branches.[7] In the century after 1840, some sixty mixed-claims commissions were set up to deal with disputes arising from this specific field.[8] Philip Jessup observed in 1948 that "[t]he international law governing the responsibility of states for injuries to aliens is one of the most highly developed branches of that law."[9] Its primary rationale was based on Vattel's well-known fiction: "Whoever uses a citizen ill, indirectly offends the state, which is bound to protect this citizen."[10]

According to this traditional stance, aliens are worthy of protection as nationals because they personify their own state. The legal status of aliens under classical international law is the result of a purely inter-state relationship: Both in practice and principle, aliens are under the dual dependency of the territorial state (where they sojourn) and of the personal state (of which they have nationality). This traditional position is well synthesized by the arbitral award delivered in 1928 in the famous *Island of Palmas* case: "Territorial sovereignty . . . involves the exclusive right to display the activities of a State. This right has as corollary a duty: the obligation to protect within the territory the rights . . . each State may claim for its nationals in foreign territory."[11]

This overlapping between the territorial and personal jurisdictions is

7. Among a rich literature, see C. F. AMERASINGHE, STATE RESPONSIBILITY FOR INJURIES TO ALIENS (1967); Dionisio Anzilotti, *La Responsabilité Internationale Des États À Raison Des Dommages Soufferts Par Les Étrangers*, *in* 13 REVUE GENERALE DE DROIT INTERNATIONAL PUBLIC 5, 5-29, 110-30 (photo. reprint 1987); EDWIN M. BORCHARD, THE DIPLOMATIC PROTECTION OF CITIZENS ABROAD OR THE LAW OF INTERNATIONAL CLAIMS (1925); A. DECENCIÈRE-FERRANDIÈRE, LA RESPONSABILITÉ INTERNATIONALE DES ÉTATS À RAISON DES DOMMAGES SUBIS PAR DES ÉTRANGERS (Rousseau & Co. ed., 1925); FREDERICK SHERWOOD DUNN, THE PROTECTION OF NATIONALS: A STUDY IN THE APPLICATION OF INTERNATIONAL LAW (1932); Jacques Dumas, *La Responsabilité Des Etats à Raison Des Crimes Et Délits Commis Sur Leur Territoire Au Préjudice D'Etrangers*, *in* 36 RECUEIL DES COURS 183 (1931); F. V. GARCÍA AMADOR ET AL., RECENT CODIFICATION OF THE LAW OF STATE RESPONSIBILITY FOR INJURIES TO ALIENS (1974); F. V. García Amador, *State Responsibility: Some New Problems*, *in* 94 RECUEIL DES COURS 365 (1958); INTERNATIONAL LAW OF STATE RESPONSIBILITY FOR INJURIES TO ALIENS (Richard B. Lillich ed., 1983).

8. IAN BROWNLIE, PRINCIPLES OF PUBLIC INTERNATIONAL LAW 500 (6th ed. 2003); MANLEY O. HUDSON, INTERNATIONAL TRIBUNALS: PAST AND FUTURE 196 (1944).

9. PHILIP C. JESSUP, A MODERN LAW OF NATIONS: AN INTRODUCTION 94 (1948).

10. VATTEL, *supra* note 5, at 298, § 71.

11. Island of Palmas (U.S. v. Neth.), Hague Ct. Rep. 2d (Scott) 83, 93 (Perm. Ct. Arb. 1928).

inherent to alienage. It further explains the longstanding interest of international law towards aliens. By contrast, classical international law has long been indifferent to the treatment of nationals within their own country who were left at the discretion of their sovereign state. As Hersch Lauterpacht observed, "the individual in his capacity as an alien enjoys a larger measure of protection by international law than in his character as the citizen of his own State."[12]

This paradox corresponds to a specific stage in the evolution of international law when the individual was literally considered an object of international law and not a subject in his own right.[13] The treatment reserved to aliens was not an exception but, on the contrary, a confirmation of this purely inter-state legal system. Individuals could be protected only because they embodied their state of nationality. This was epitomized by the *Mavrommatis* Judgment delivered in 1924 by the Permanent Court of International Justice:

> It is an elementary principle of international law that a State is entitled to protect its subjects, when injured by acts contrary to international law committed by another State, from whom they have been unable to obtain satisfaction through the ordinary channels. By taking up the case of one of its subjects and by resorting to diplomatic action or international judicial proceedings on his behalf, a State is in reality asserting its own rights-its right to ensure, in the person of its subjects, respect for the rules of international law.[14]

This inter-state monologue is further exacerbated by the discretionary nature of diplomatic protection. As restated by the ICJ, "[t]he State must be viewed as the sole judge to decide whether its protection will be granted, to what extent it is granted, and when it will cease."[15]

Thus, one should not be surprised that diplomatic protection has been a persistent source of tension among states—especially between western states and newly independent ones (notably in Latin America). Aliens in question were generally entrepreneurs from industrialized countries in search of new markets; furthermore, diplomatic protection was used as a common pretext for intervention in disregard of the principles of sovereign equality and non-interference in the domestic affairs of states, in this case developing

---

12. H. LAUTERPACHT, INTERNATIONAL LAW AND HUMAN RIGHTS 121 (photo. reprinted 1968) (1950).

13. *See* Walter George Frank Philimore, *Droits Et Devoirs Fondamentaux Des Etats*, *in* 1 RECUEIL DES COURS 62, 63 (1923). *See also* Vincent Chetail, *Le Droit D'avoir Des Droits En Droit International Public: Réflexions Sur La Subjectivité Internationale De L'Individu*, *in* LIRE HANNAH ARENDT AUJOURD'HUI: POUVOIR, GUERRE, PENSÉE, JUGEMENT POLITIQUE 217 (M. C. Caloz-Tschopp ed., 2008).

14. Mavrommatis Palestine Concessions (Greece v. U.K.), 1924 P.C.I.J. (ser. B) No. 3, ¶ 21 (Aug. 30). *See also* Panevezys-Saldutiskis Railway (Est. v. Lith.), 1939 P.C.I.J. (ser. A/B) No. 76, at 16 (Feb. 28).

15. Barcelona Traction (Belg. v. Spain), 1970 I.C.J. 3, ¶ 79 (Feb. 5).

states. As a result, "[t]he history of the development of the international law on the responsibility of states for injuries to aliens is thus an aspect of the history of 'imperialism,' or 'dollar diplomacy.'"[16]

The conflicting interests at stake have been reflected by two opposite conceptions of the standard of treatment granted to aliens. First, developing states have advanced the doctrine of national treatment: Aliens must be treated on an equal footing with nationals (with the obvious exception of political rights).[17] As a result, aliens cannot claim more rights than those granted to nationals and only a difference of treatment can trigger the responsibility of the host state. The doctrine of national treatment was endorsed at the First International Conference of American States held in Washington in 1889-1890.[18] It has been reinforced at the regional level in several treaties, including the 1902 Convention relative to the Rights of Aliens,[19] the 1928 Convention on the Status of Aliens,[20] as well as the famous Montevideo Convention on the Rights and Duties of States adopted in 1933.[21]

Nonetheless, international initiatives carried out by Latin American states have been primarily confined within their own region. At the universal level, the first Conference for the Codification of International Law, held in 1930 under the auspices of the League of Nations, demonstrated the absence of a broader consensus. The conference was unable to adopt the draft "Convention on Responsibility of States for Damage done in their Territory to the Person or Property of Foreigners" mainly because of the two different conceptions on the applicable standard: Seventeen states supported the doctrine of national treatment, whereas thirty-one others were opposed to it.[22]

In contrast to the national treatment, Western states have promoted the

16. JESSUP, *supra* note 9, at 96. *See also Barcelona Traction*, 1970 I.C.J. at 246 (separate opinion of Judge Padilla-Nervo). Among other well-known instances, the Boer War from 1899 to 1902 was officially justified by the UK in order to protect the British mine owners of Witwatersrand. *South African War*, ENCYCLOPAEDIA BRITANNICA, http://www.britannica.com/EBchecked/topic/555806/South-African-War (last updated Dec. 14, 2013).

17. 6 M. CHARLES CALVO, LE DROIT INTERNATIONAL: THEORIE ET PRATIQUE 230, § 256 (Paris, Arthur Rousseau, 5th ed. 1896). For further discussions, see also Alberto Guani, *La Solidarité Internationale Dans L'Amérique Latine*, *in* 8 RECUEIL DES COURS 209, 287 (1925); 1 J. DE LOUTER, LE DROIT INTERNATIONAL PUBLIC POSITIF 296-98 (1920); 2 ERNEST NYS, LE DROIT INTERNATIONAL: LES PRINCIPES, LES THEORIES, LES FAITS 266 (1912); J. M. Yepes, *Les Problèmes Fondamentaux Du Droit Des Gens En Amérique*, *in* 47 RECUEIL DES COURS 1, 106 (1934); Hormodio Arias, *The Non-Liability of States for Damages Suffered by Foreigners in the Course of a Riot, an Insurrection, or a Civil War*, 7 AM. J. INT'L L. 724 (1913).

18. THE INTERNATIONAL CONFERENCES OF AMERICAN STATES 1889-1928, at 45 (James Brown Scott ed., 1931).

19. *Id.* at 415-16.

20. *Id.*

21. Convention on Rights and Duties of States, Dec. 26, 1933, 49 Stat. 3097, 165 L.N.T.S. 19. As to the previous convention, the US made a reservation to Art. 9. *Id.*

22. *Conference for the Codification of International Law*, League of Nations Doc. C.351M.145 1930 V, at 188 (1930).

notion of minimum international standards, traditionally defined in the following terms:

> Each country is bound to give to the nationals of another country in its territory the benefit of the same laws, the same administration, the same protection, and the same redress for injury which it gives to its own citizens, and neither more nor less: provided the protection which the country gives to its own citizens conforms to the established standard of civilization.
>
> There is a standard of justice, very simple, very fundamental, and of such general acceptance by all civilized countries as to form a part of the international law of the world . . . . If any country's system of law and administration does not conform to that standard, although the people of the country may be content or compelled to live under it, no other country can be compelled to accept it as furnishing a satisfactory measure of treatment to its citizens.[23]

Thus, according to such a notion, aliens shall not be treated below a minimum standard which is required by general international law regardless of how a state treats its own nationals. This doctrine has been endorsed in a substantial amount of treaties and jurisprudence.[24] The content of the international minimum standard is, however, particularly vague. It has raised many controversies among states, some of them considering the ambiguity of the notion as the perfect excuse for justifying arbitrary interferences in host states. Nevertheless, as a result of these inter-state disputes, a considerable body of arbitral awards has progressively identified and refined the international minimum standard on a case-by-case basis. This incremental process has been crystallised in a core set of fundamental guarantees, including the right to life and respect for physical integrity, the right to recognition as a person before the law, freedom of conscience, prohibition of arbitrary detention, the right to a fair trial in civil and criminal matters, and the right to property (save public expropriation with fair compensation).[25]

---

23. Elihu Root, *The Basis of Protection to Citizens Residing Abroad*, 4 AM. SOC'Y INT'L PROC. 16, 20-21 (1910).

24. Among numerous arbitral awards, see most notably Hopkins v. United Mexican States (U.S. v. Mex.), 4 R.I.A.A. 41, 47 (Perm. Ct. Arb. 1926); Neer v. United Mexican States (U.S. Mex.), 4 R.I.A.A. 60, 64, 65 (Perm. Ct. Arb. 1926); Roberts v. United Mexican States (U.S. v. Mex.), 4 R.I.A.A. 77, 79-80 (Perm. Ct. Arb. 1926); British Claims in Spanish Zone of Morocco (U.K. v. Spain), 2 R.I.A.A. 615, 635, 644 (Perm Ct. Arb. 1925). *See also* Treaty of Friendship and Establishment, Egypt-Persia, arts. IV-VI, Nov. 28, 1928, 93 L.N.T.S. 381; Convention Respecting Conditions of Residence and Business and Jurisdiction arts. 1, 2, 13, 14, 17, July 24, 1923, 31 L.N.T.S. 11.

25. *See* S. Basdevant, *Théorie Générale De La Condition De L'étranger*, *in* 8 REPERTOIRE DE DROIT INTERNATIONAL 31-61 (A. De Lapradelle & J. P. Niboyet eds., 1930); ALWYN V. FREEMAN, THE INTERNATIONAL RESPONSIBILITY OF STATES FOR DENIAL OF JUSTICE 507-30 (1st ed. 1938); ANDREAS H. ROTH, THE MINIMUM STANDARD OF INTERNATIONAL LAW APPLIED TO ALIENS 185-86 (1949); Alfred Verdross, *Les Règles Internationales Concernant Le Traitement Des Étrangers*, *in* 37 RECUEIL DES COURS 323, 353-406 (1931).

As is apparent from this enumeration, the minimum standard of treatment has been the forerunner of human rights law at the international level. It has been critical for infusing the rule of law in the field of migration. Nowadays, while it still retains some residual value, the international minimum standard is to a large extent absorbed by human rights treaties and customary law.

III. THE EMERGENCE OF INTERNATIONAL HUMAN RIGHTS LAW AS THE PRIMARY SOURCE OF PROTECTION

The law of aliens inherited from the traditional notion of state responsibility has been progressively marginalized and arguably replaced by human rights law.[26] This reflects a more general and systemic evolution whereby human rights law is profoundly reshaping general international law.[27] Even the ICJ acknowledged in the *Diallo* Judgment of 2007 that:

> Owing to the substantive development of international law over recent decades in respect of the rights it accords to individuals, the scope *ratione materiae* of diplomatic protection, originally limited to alleged violations of the minimum standard of treatment of aliens, has subsequently widened to include, *inter alia*, internationally guaranteed human rights.[28]

Upon closer review, human rights law constitutes a normative synthesis between the two traditional conceptions of the treatment granted to aliens by international law. On the one hand, this branch of law ensures that a core content of basic rights is guaranteed by international law in line with the very notion of a minimum standard. On the other hand, human rights law asserts equality of treatment between citizens and non-citizens in accordance with

---

26. For further discussions about the impact of international human rights law on the law of state responsibility see Thomas E. Carbonneau, *The Convergence of the Law of State Responsibility for Injury to Aliens and International Human Rights Norms in the Revised Restatement*, 25 VA. J. INT'L L. 99, 100-02, 117, 136, 140 (1985); Alexandre-Charles Kiss, *La Condition Des Étrangers En Droit International Et Les Droits De L'Homme*, *in* MISCELLANEA: W.J. GANSHOF VAN DER MEERSCH 499, 509 (1972); Myres S. McDougal, Harold D. Lasswell & Lung-chu Chen, *Protection of Aliens from Discrimination and World Public Order: Responsibility of States Conjoined with Human Rights*, 70 AM. J. INT'L L. 432, 443, 452, 454, 461 (1976).

27. On this evolution, see generally Pierre-Marie Dupuy, *L'Individu et let Droit International: Théorie des Droits de L'Homme et Fondements du Droit International*, *in* 32 ARCHIVES DE PHILOSOPHIE DU DROIT: LE DROIT INTERNATIONAL 119 (Paris, Sirey 1987); THE IMPACT OF HUMAN RIGHTS LAW ON GENERAL INTERNATIONAL LAW (Menno T. Kamminga & Martin Scheinin eds., 2009); Theodor Meron, *International Law in the Age of Human Rights*, *in* A GENERAL COURSE ON PUBLIC INTERNATIONAL LAW, 301 RECUEIL DE COURSE 301 (2003); ANTONIO AUGUSTO CANÇADO TRINDADE, INTERNATIONAL LAW FOR HUMANKIND: TOWARDS A NEW *JUS GENTIUM* (The Hague Acad. of Int'l Law Monographs Ser. No. 8, 2013); Michel Virally, *Droits De L'Homme Et Théorie Générale Du Droit International*, *in* 4 RENE CASSIN AMICORUM DISIPULORUMQUE LIBER 323, 329 (1972); W. Michael Reisman, *Sovereignty and Human Rights in Contemporary International Law*, 84 AM. J. INT'L L. 866, 869, 876 (1990); Louis B. Sohn, *The New International Law: Protection of the Rights of Individuals Rather Than States*, 32 AM. U. L. REV. 1, 6 (1982).

28. Ahmadou Sadio Diallo (Guinea v. Dem. Rep. Congo), Preliminary Objections, 2007 I.C.J. 582, 599, ¶ 39 (May 24).

the national standard. Myres McDougal, Harold Lasswell, and Lung-chu Chen acknowledge in this sense:

> In sum, the principal thrust of the contemporary human rights movement is to accord nationals the same protection formerly accorded only to aliens, while at the same time raising the standard of protection for all human beings, nationals as well as aliens, far beyond the minimum international standard developed under the earlier customary law. . . . The consequence is thus . . . that continuing debate about the doctrines of the minimum international standard and equality of treatment has now become highly artificial; an international standard is now authoritatively prescribed for all human beings.[29]

Nevertheless, merging the old law of aliens and the new law of human rights has been progressive and it is still an ongoing process. One of the first systematic attempts was carried out by the International Law Commission (ILC). In 1953 the UN General Assembly requested that the ILC "undertake the codification of the principles of international law governing State responsibility."[30] García Amador was appointed as Special Rapporteur in 1955 and, from 1956 to 1961, he submitted six reports focusing on the responsibility of States for injuries caused to aliens within their territory.[31] His great ambition was "to change and adapt traditional law so that it will reflect the profound transformation which has occurred in international law. In other words, it will be necessary to bring the 'principles governing State responsibility' into line with international law at its present stage of development."[32]

According to Amador, traditional conceptions have shown their own limits for establishing clear-cut rules in this field.[33] They must be reassessed in

29. McDougal et al., *supra* note 26, at 464. Among many other similar accounts, see Charles G. Fenwick, *The Progress of International Law During the Past Forty Years*, *in* 79 RECUEIL DES COURS 44 (1951); Alwyn V. Freeman, *Human Rights and the Rights of Aliens*, 45 AM. SOC'Y INT'L L. PROC. 120, 122-23, 129 (1951); R.Y. Jennings, *The Responsibility of States*, *in* 121 RECUEIL DES COURSE 473, 480, 486-88 (1967); Kiss, *supra* note 26, at 509; HERMANN MOSLER, THE INTERNATIONAL SOCIETY AS A LEGAL COMMUNITY 72 (1980).

30. G.A. Res. 799 (VIII), U.N. GAOR, 8th Sess., Supp. No. 17, U.N. Doc. A/2630, at 52 (Dec. 7, 1953).

31. *Special Rapporteurs of the International Law Commission (1949–2013)*, INT'L L. COMM'N, http://legal.un.org/ilc/guide/annex3.htm (last updated Aug. 21, 2013).

32. *Special Rapporteur F. V. García Amador's International Responsibility*, [1956] 2 Y.B. Int'l L. Comm'n 173, at 176, U.N. Doc. A/CN.4/SER.A/1956/Add.1.

33. *Id.* at 175:

> [T]he subject of responsibility has always been one of the most vast and complex of international law; it would be difficult to find a topic beset with greater confusion and uncertainty. The cause lies not so much in the dominant part played by political factors in the shaping and development of this branch of international law, as in the glaring inconsistencies of traditional doctrine and practice. Perhaps because of the existence and influence of extraneous factors which are not always compatible with the law, artificial legal concepts and principles have been evolved which often appear markedly incongruent.

Id.

accordance with the dramatic transformations of contemporary international law deriving from the UN Charter and the international recognition of human rights:

> International law is not now concerned solely with regulating relations between States, for one of the objects of its rules is to protect interests and rights which are not truly vested in the State. Hence it is no longer true, as it was for centuries in the past, that international law exists only for, or finds its sole *raison d'être* in, the protection of the interests and rights of the State; rather, its function is now also to protect the rights and interests of its other subjects who may properly claim its protection . . . . International law today recognizes that individuals and other subjects are directly entitled to international rights, just as it places upon them certain international obligations.
>
> . . . .
>
> The basis of this new principle would be the "universal respect for, and observance of, human rights and fundamental freedoms" referred to in the Charter of the United Nations and in other general, regional and bilateral instruments. The object of the "internationalization" (to coin a term) of these rights and freedoms is to ensure the protection of the legitimate interests of the human person, irrespective of his nationality. Whether the person concerned is a citizen or an alien is then immaterial: human beings, as such, are under the direct protection of international law.[34]

Against such a "new" normative frame, the Special Rapporteur proposed in 1957 a draft Convention on international responsibility of the State for injuries caused in its territory to the person or property of aliens.[35] In its final version published in his last Report of 1961, article 1, paragraph 1 of the draft postulates that "aliens enjoy the same rights and the same legal guarantees as nationals," while specifying that as a minimum "these rights and guarantees shall in no case be less than the 'human rights and fundamental freedoms' recognized and defined in contemporary international instruments."[36] Its second paragraph then offers a non-exhaustive list of such fundamental human rights.[37]

---

34. *Id.* at 184, 192, 203.

35. *Special Rapporteur F. V. García Amador's International Responsibility: Second Report*, [1957] 2 Y.B. Int'l L. Comm'n 104, at 127-28, U.N. Doc. A/CN.4/SER.A/1957/Add.1.

36. *Special Rapporteur F. V. García Amador's International Responsibility: Sixth Report*, [1961] 2 Y.B. Int'l L. Comm'n 1, 46, U.N. Doc A/CN.4/SER.A/1961/Add.1.

37. *Id.* at 46-47:

> The 'human rights and fundamental freedoms' referred to in the foregoing paragraph are those enumerated below: (*a*) The right to life, liberty and security of person; (*b*) The right to own property; (*c*) The right to apply to the courts of justice or to the competent organs of the State,

At the time, however, this pioneer work was a "somewhat revolutionary approach," as Amador himself acknowledged.[38] In fact his draft received scant attention from the ILC and several members criticised his approach on the grounds that the individual was not a subject of international law and that the identification of human rights pertained to a different topic of codification than that of state responsibility.[39] A new Special Rapporteur, Roberto Ago, was designated with the aim to focus exclusively on the secondary rules of state responsibility.[40] That is to say, to define the general conditions under international law for the state to be considered responsible for wrongful actions or omissions, and the legal consequences to flow therefrom.[41] As a result of this new approach, primary rules—and in particular the substantive and more sensitive obligations regulating the protection of aliens—were excluded from the work of the ILC.[42]

This failed attempt at reconciling the old law of aliens with the new law of human rights was largely due to the political and legal context of the time. During the 1950s and 1960s, Latin American states were not yet ready to abandon their own doctrine of national treatment for another one so similar to the notion of minimum standard. In Africa and Asia, newly independent states were also unwilling to codify the rights of aliens which were associated with imperialism and the diplomacy of their former colonial powers. Further-

---

by means of remedies and proceedings which offer adequate and effective redress for violations of the aforesaid rights and freedoms; (*d*) The right to a public hearing, with proper safeguards, by the competent organs of the State, in the substantiation of any criminal charge or in the determination of rights and obligations under civil law; (*e*) In criminal matters, the right of the accused to be presumed innocent until proved guilty; the right to be informed of the charge made against him in a language which he understands; the right to present his defence personally or to be defended by a counsel of his choice; the right not to be convicted of any punishable offence on account of any act or omission which did not constitute an offence, under national or international law, at the time when it was committed; the right to be tried without delay or to be released." Article 1, paragraph 3 of the final draft further specifies that: "[t]he enjoyment and exercise of the rights and freedoms specified in paragraph 2 (*a*) and (*b*) are subject to such limitations or restrictions as the law expressly prescribes for reasons of internal security, the economic well-being of the nation, public order, health and morality, or to secure respect for the rights and freedoms of others.

38. Int'l Law Comm'n, Summ. Recs. of the 416th mtg. 169, at ¶ 18, U.N. Doc. A/CN.4/SR.416 (June 13, 1957).

39. *Special Rapporteur F. V. García Amador's International Responsibility: Third Report*, [1958] 2 Y.B. Int'l L. Comm'n 47, at 48-50, U.N. Doc A/CN.4/SER.A/1958/Add.1.

40. Georg Nolte, *From Dionisio Anzilotti to Roberto Ago: The Classical International Law of State Responsibility and the Traditional Primacy of a Bilateral Conception of Inter-State Relations*, 13 EUR. J. INT'L L. 1083, 1097 (2002).

41. *Special Rapporteur Roberto Ago's First Report on State Responsibility*, [1969] 2 Y.B. Int'l L. Comm'n 125, at 127, U.N. Doc A/CN.4/SER.A/1969/Add.1; *Special Rapporteur Roberto Ago's Second Report on State Responsibility*, [1970] 2 Y.B. Int'l L. Comm'n 177, U.N. Doc A/CN.4/SER.A/1970/Add.1 (Part 2).

42. Three succeeding Rapporteurs followed, finally leading to the adoption in 2001 of the Draft Articles on Responsibility of States for Internationally Wrongful Acts. *See* G.A. Res. 56/83, ¶ 1, U.N. Doc. A/RES/56/83 (Jan. 28, 2002); *Report of the Commission to the General Assembly on the Work of Its 53d Session*, [2001] 2 Y.B. Int'l L. Comm'n ¶¶ 69-71, at 26, U.N. Doc. A/CN.4/SER.A/2001/Add.1 (Part 2).

more, communist states still viewed human rights as a product of capitalism and thus resisted their international recognition. As a result of the cold war and the decolonisation process, it was not the moment to codify the legal status of aliens, and even less to relate it to human rights.

These political impediments were reinforced by purely legal ones. In 1961 when Amador submitted his final report,[43] the only universal instrument addressing human rights in a comprehensive way was the non-binding Universal Declaration of Human Rights.[44] At the regional level, only one treaty had been adopted, the European Convention for the Protection of Human Rights and Fundamental Freedoms.[45] Against such a background, merging the old and controversial law of aliens with the new and emerging field of human rights was bound to fail. It was simply too early.

The history of migrants' rights under international law steadily exemplifies that, in this area as well as in many others, the avant-garde of today frequently becomes the reality of tomorrow. However, quite ironically, while the notion of minimum standard was the forerunner of human rights on the international scene, the latter has been emancipated from the former to such an extent that the law of aliens now stands in the shadow of human rights law. Still, today the rights of non-citizens remain the poor cousins of human rights.

From a general international law perspective, the rights of non-citizens have been (re)discovered quite recently as a side effect of the normative expansion of international human rights law.[46] After a decade of lengthy discussions, the General Assembly adopted in December 1985 the Declaration on the Human Rights of Individuals Who Are Not Nationals of the Country in Which They Live.[47] The added value of this Declaration is more symbolic than substantial. While restating the plain applicability of human rights to non-nationals, it signals that the international protection of migrants is working in tandem with the development of human rights law.

Since then, due respect for the human rights of migrants has been restated on multiple occasions. Among the more well-known examples are the 1993 Vienna Conference on Human Rights;[48] the International Conference on

---

43. *Special Rapporteur F. V. García Amador's International Responsibility: Sixth Report*, [1961] 2 Y.B. Int'l L. Comm'n 1, U.N. Doc A/CN.4/SER.A/1961/Add.1.

44. Universal Declaration of Human Rights, G.A. Res. 217A (III), U.N. Doc. A/810, at 71 (Dec. 10, 1948) [hereinafter UDHR].

45. Council of Europe, Convention for the Protection of Human Rights and Fundamental Freedoms, *opened for signature* Apr. 11, 1950, C.E.T.S. No. 005 (entered into force Mar. 9, 1953).

46. For a similar process regarding the rights of refugees under international law, see Vincent Chetail, *Are Refugee Rights Human Rights?: An Unorthodox Questioning of the Relations Between Refugee Law and Human Rights Law*, *in* HUMAN RIGHTS AND IMMIGRATION 19 (Ruth Rubio-Marin ed., 2014).

47. G.A. Res. 40/144, U.N. Doc. A/RES/40/144 (Dec. 13, 1985).

48. World Conference on Human Rights, June 14-25, 1993, *Vienna Declaration and Programme of Action*, ¶¶ 33-35, U.N. Doc. A/CONF.157/23 (July 12, 1993).

Population and Development held the following year in Cairo;[49] the Summit for Social Development in Copenhagen in March 1995;[50] the fourth World Conference on Women organized in Beijing in September 1995;[51] and the 2001 World Conference against Racism, Racial Discrimination, Xenophobia and related Intolerance held in Durban.[52] Alongside similar restatements of regional organizations,[53] the UN General Assembly has further reaffirmed "the need for all States to protect fully the universally recognized human rights of migrants, especially women and children, regardless of their legal status."[54] From a systemic perspective, the very term "human rights of migrants" testifies to the appropriation of alienage by human rights law. However, such evolution is progressive and still incomplete in practice.

Despite the ancient lineage of migrants' rights in international law, it was not until 1990 that the UN adopted a specific convention on migrant workers: the International Convention on the Protection of the Rights of All Migrant

---

49. International Conference on Population and Development, Cairo, Egypt, Sept. 5-13, 1994, *Report of the International Conference on Population and Development*, at 135, U.N. Doc. A/CONF.171/13 (Oct. 18, 1994).

50. World Summit for Social Development, Copenhagen, Den., Mar. 6-12, 1995, *Report of the World Summit for Social Development*, at 99, U.N. Doc. A/CONF.166/9 (Apr. 19, 1995).

51. Fourth World Conference on Women, Beijing, China, Sept. 4-15, 1995, *Report of the Fourth World Conference on Women*, IV(D), U.N. Doc. A/CONF.177/20 (Oct. 17, 1995).

52. *See* World Conference against Racism, Racial Discrimination, Xenophobia and Related Intolerance, Aug. 31-Sept. 8, 2001, Durban, S. Afr., *Durban Declaration and Programme of Action*, ¶ 48, U.N. Doc. A/CONF.189/12 (Sept. 8, 2001).

53. *See* African Common Position on Migration and Development, Exec. Council of the Afr. Union, 9th Sess., June 25-29, 2006, ¶¶ 3.7-3.9, Doc. EX.CL/277 (IX), (June 29, 2006); ASEAN Declaration on the Protection and Promotion of the Rights of Migrant Workers, 12th ASEAN Summit, Cebu, Phil., ¶¶ 1-4 (Jan. 13, 2007); Inter-American Program for the Promotion and Protection of the Human Rights of Migrants, Including Migrant Workers and Their Families, I(A)(1), Doc. AG/RES. 2141 (XXXV-O/05) (June 7, 2005); European Council, The Stockholm Programme: An Open and Secure Europe Serving and Protecting Citizens, 2010 O.J. (C 115) 1, §§ 6.1.4-4.1.6.

54. G.A. Res. 58/190, ¶ 9, U.N. Doc. A/RES/58/190 (Dec. 22, 2003); G.A. Res. 57/218, ¶ 7, U.N. Doc. A/RES/57/218 (Dec. 18, 2002); Protection of Migrants, G.A. Res. 56/170, ¶ 5, U.N. Doc. A/RES/56/170 (Dec. 19, 2001); G.A. Res. 55/92, ¶ 5, U.N. Doc. A/RES/55/92 (Dec. 4, 2000); G.A. Res. 54/166, ¶ 4, U.N. Doc. A/RES/54/166 (Dec. 17, 1999). With slight changes in the wording, see Declaration of the High-Level Dialogue on International Migration and Development, G.A. Draft Res. 68/L.5, ¶ 5, U.N. Doc. A/68/L.5 (Oct. 3-4, 2013); G.A. Res. 67/172, ¶ 1, U.N. Doc. A/RES/67/172 (Dec. 20, 2012); G.A. Res. 66/172, ¶ 1, U.N. Doc. A/RES/66/172 (Dec. 19, 2011); G.A. Res. 65/212, ¶ 1, U.N. Doc. A/RES/65/212 (Dec. 21, 2010); G.A. Res. 64/166, ¶ 1, U.N. Doc. A/RES/64/166 (Dec. 18, 2009); G.A. Res. 63/184, ¶ 1, U.N. Doc. A/RES/63/184 (Dec. 18, 2008); G.A. Res. 62/156, ¶ 1, U.N. Doc. A/RES/62/156 (Dec. 18, 2007); G.A. Res. 61/165, ¶ 1, U.N. Doc. A/RES/61/165 (Dec. 19, 2006); G.A. Res. 60/169, ¶ 5, U.N. Doc. A/RES/60/169 (Dec. 16, 2005); G.A. Res. 59/194, ¶ 7, U.N. Doc. A/RES/59/194 (Dec. 20, 2004). The Millennium Declaration also endorses such a position. *See* United Nations Millennium Declaration, G.A. Res. 55/2, ¶¶ 24-25, U.N. Doc. A/RES/55/2 (Sept. 8, 2000). For the same idea in earlier resolutions inviting states to take all necessary and appropriate measures to ensure that the fundamental human rights, irrespective of their immigration status, are fully respected under their national legislation, see also Measures to Improve the Situation and Ensure the Human Rights and Dignity of All Migrant Workers, G.A. Res. 32/120, ¶ 2(c), U.N. Doc. A/RES/32/120 (Dec. 16, 1977); Measures to Improve the Situation and Ensure the Human Rights and Dignity of All Migrant Workers, G.A. Res. 31/127, ¶ 2(c), U.N. GAOR, 31st Sess., U.N. Doc A/RES/31/127, at 107 (Dec. 16, 1976). For a similar account among U.N. agencies, see International Labour Organization, Tripartite Meeting of Experts, *ILO Multilateral Framework on Labour Migration, Non-Binding Principles and Guidelines for a Rights-Based Approach to Labour Migration*, § 8, ILO Doc. TMMFLM/2005/1 (Rev.) (Oct. 31-Nov. 2, 2005).

Workers and Members of Their Families (ICRMW).[55] Though it mainly restates and sometimes specifies the applicability of rights already enshrined in more general instruments,[56] this Convention conspicuously confronted a slow ratification process, leading to both a late entry into force and a small number of parties. It experienced the longest period for its entry into force of any of the core binding UN human rights instruments. Adopted in December 1990, the ICRMW entered into force almost thirteen years later in July 2003.[57] Even today, it remains poorly ratified compared to the other core human rights treaties. The Convention counts only forty-seven parties,[58] with ratification by major western immigrant-receiving countries still lacking.[59]

A similarly poor number of ratifications can be observed with regard to the two conventions adopted by the International Labor Organization (ILO) for dealing with the specific situation of migrant workers. The 1949 Convention Concerning Migration for Employment (Revised) (No. 97)[60] is currently ratified by forty-nine states,[61] whereas the 1975 Convention Concerning Migrations in Abusive Conditions and the Promotion of Equality of Opportunity and Treatment of Migrant Workers (No. 143)[62] counts only twenty-three parties.[63]

However, this limited number of ratifications does not reflect the norma-

---

55. International Convention on the Protection of the Rights of All Migrant Workers and Members of Their Families, *adopted* Dec. 18, 1990, 2220 U.N.T.S. 3 [hereinafter ICRMW].

56. For a similar account, see United Nations, Human Rights Office of the High Comm'r, Europe Reg'l Office, Rights of Migrant Workers in Europe, at 11 (2011) (Marie D'Auchamp); ANNE T. GALLAGHER, THE INTERNATIONAL LAW OF HUMAN TRAFFICKING 169 (2010); Virginia A. Leary, *Labour Migration*, *in* MIGRATION AND INTERNATIONAL LEGAL NORMS 227, 235 (T. Alexander Aleinikoff & Vincent Chetail eds., 2003); David Weissbrodt & Stephen Meili, *Human Rights and Protection of Non-Citizens: Whither Universality and Indivisibility of Rights?*, 28 REFUGEE SURV. Q. 34, 43-44 (2010).

57. Ratification Status, *International Convention on the Protection of the Rights of All Migrant Workers and Members of their Families*, UNITED NATIONS TREATY COLLECTION (Mar. 17, 2014, 12 PM), https://treaties.un.org/Pages/ViewDetails.aspx?src=TREATY&mtdsg_no=IV-13&chapter=4&lang=en.

58. *Id.*

59. This number is still far from attaining the 193 States having ratified the Convention on the Rights of the Child, which was adopted only one year before the ICRMW. Obstacles to the ratification of the ICRMW have raised a substantial literature. Aside from the books on the ICRMW already quoted above in the introduction, see generally Shirley Hune & Jan Niessen, *Ratifying the UN Migrant Workers Convention: Current Difficulties and Prospects*, 12 NETH. Q. HUM. RTS. 393 (1994); Beth Lyon, *The Unsigned United Nations Migrant Worker Rights Convention: An Overlooked Opportunity to Change the 'Brown Collar' Migration Paradigm*, 42 N.Y.U. J. INT'L L. & POL. 389 (2010); Patrick Taran, *Status and Prospects for the UN Convention on Migrants' Rights*, 2 EUR. J. MIGRATION & L. 85 (2000); Dirk Vanheule, Marie Claire Foblets, Sander Loones & Steven Bouckaert, *The Significance of the UN Migrant Workers' Convention of 18 December 1990 in the Event of Ratification by Belgium*, 6 EUR. J. MIGRATION & L. 285 (2005).

60. Convention Concerning Migration for Employment, July 1, 1949, I.L.O. No. 97, 120 U.N.T.S. 70 (entered into force Jan. 22, 1952).

61. *Ratifications of C097*, INT'L LABOUR ORG. (Mar. 16, 2014, 8 PM), http://www.ilo.org/dyn/normlex/en/f?p=NORMLEXPUB:11300:0::NO:11300:P11300_INSTRUMENT_ID:312242:NO.

62. Convention Concerning Migrations in Abusive Conditions and the Promotion of Equality of Opportunity and Treatment of Migrant Workers, June 24, 1975, I.L.O. No. 143, 1120 U.N.T.S. 323.

63. *Ratifications of C143*, INT'L LABOUR ORG. (Mar. 16, 2014, 8 PM), http://www.ilo.org/dyn/normlex/en/f?p=NORMLEXPUB:11300:0::NO:11300:P11300_INSTRUMENT_ID:312288:NO.

tive density of the matter for two main reasons. First, a wide range of regional and bilateral treaties have been adopted for regulating various aspects of migration (including for labor purposes). To give only a few instances, more than 120 states are involved in regional economic integration schemes aimed at facilitating the movement of persons between states parties.[64] Furthermore, countries from the Organization for Economic Cooperation and Development (OECD) have alone entered into more than 176 bilateral labor recruitment agreements in 2004, a fivefold increase since 1990.[65]

Second, all human rights treaties—though drafted for a more general purpose—are still plainly relevant in the field of migration. Despite and because of the lack of worldwide ratification of treaties specifically devoted to migrant workers, general human rights instruments are bound to play a vital role. Indeed they are generally applicable to everyone irrespective of nationality and/or frequently include specific provisions applying to noncitizens. Besides the general principle of non-discrimination and equality before the law,[66] these instruments notably enshrine the right to leave any country and to return one's own country,[67] the right of children to acquire a nationality,[68] due process guarantees governing expulsion,[69] and protection against *refoulement*.[70] The added value of general human rights treaties is not only normative but also institutional: Their treaty bodies are crucial for advancing the protection of migrants within their respective mandates and

64. Patrick Taran, Rethinking Development and Migration: Some Elements for Discussion 4 (unpublished working paper) (on file with the author).

65. D. Bobeva & J.-P. Garson, *Overview of Bilateral Agreements and Other Forms of Labour Recruitment*, in OECD & Federal Office of Immigration, Integration and Emigration, MIGRATION FOR EMPLOYMENT. BILATERAL AGREEMENTS AT A CROSSROADS, OECD Publishing, 2004, 12.

66. *See* Convention on the Rights of Persons with Disabilities, arts. 1, 3(a), 4, 5, *opened for signature* Mar. 30, 2007, 2515 U.N.T.S. 3 [hereinafter CRPD]; Convention on the Rights of the Child, art. 2, *adopted* Nov. 20, 1989, 1577 U.N.T.S. 3 [hereinafter CRC]; Convention on the Elimination of All Forms of Discrimination against Women, arts. 1, 2, 15(1), *opened for signature* Mar. 1, 1980, 1249 U.N.T.S. 13 [hereinafter CEDAW]; International Covenant on Civil and Political Rights arts. 2(1), 26, *opened for signature* Dec. 16, 1966, 999 U.N.T.S. 171 (entered into force Mar. 23, 1976) [hereinafter ICCPR]); International Convention on the Elimination of All Forms of Racial Discrimination, arts. 1, 2, 5(a), *adopted* Dec. 21, 1965, 660 U.N.T.S. 195 [hereinafter ICERD].

67. *See* CRPD, *supra* note 66, art. 18(1)(d); CRC, *supra* note 66, art. 10(2); CEDAW, *supra* note 66, art. 15(4); ICCPR, *supra* note 66, arts. 12(2), 4; ICERD, *supra* note 66, art. 5(d)(ii).

68. *See* CRPD, *supra* note 66, art. 18(1)(a-b), (2); CRC, *supra* note 62, art. 7; CEDAW, *supra* note 66, art. 9; ICCPR, *supra* note 66, arts. 24(2), 3; ICERD, *supra* note 66, art. 5(d)(iii).

69. *See* ICCPR, *supra* note 66, art. 13. *See also* CRC, *supra* note 66, art. 10(1) (regarding family reunification).

70. *See* International Convention for the Protection of All Persons from Enforced Disappearances art. 16, *adopted* Dec. 20, 2006, 2715 U.N.T.S. Doc. A/61/448; Convention against Torture and Other Cruel, Inhuman, or Degrading Treatment or Punishment art. 3, *adopted* Dec. 10, 1984, 1465 U.N.T.S. 85. Furthermore, in line with other regional supervisory bodies, the Human Rights Committee and the Committee on the Rights of the Child have construed their respective instruments as encompassing an implicit duty of *non-refoulement*. *See* United Nations, Comm. on the Rights of the Child, General Comment No. 6: Treatment of Unaccompanied and Separated Children Outside Their Country of Origin, ¶ 27, U.N. Doc. CRC/GC/2005/6 (Sept. 1, 2005); United Nations, Human Rights Comm., General Comment No. 20: Article 7 (Prohibition of Torture and Cruel Treatment or Punishment), ¶ 9, U.N. Doc. HRI/GEN/1/Rev.9 (Vol. I) (Mar. 10, 1992).

instruments.[71] General comments adopted by UN treaty bodies not only restate the applicability of human rights to noncitizens, but they also usually devote particular attention to migrants.[72]

Furthermore, their concluding observations on State reports frequently address the rights of migrant workers as inferred from their relevant instruments. While the Human Rights Committee (HRC) is less systematic than the others,[73] the Committee on Economic, Social and Cultural Rights

71. For a similar account, see D. Weissbrodt & J. Rhodes, *UN Treaty Bodies and Migrant Workers*, in RESEARCH HANDBOOK ON INTERNATIONAL LAW AND MIGRATION 303-28 (Vincent Chetail & Céline Bauloz eds., 2014). *But see* Isabelle Slinckx, *Migrants' Rights in UN Human Rights Conventions*, *in* MIGRATION AND HUMAN RIGHTS 122, 143-148 (Paul de Guchteneire, Antoine Pécoud & Ryszard Cholewinski eds., 2009).

72. *See* United Nations, Comm. on Econ., Soc., & Cultural Rights, General Recommendation No. 27 on Older Women and Protection of Their Human Rights, ¶¶ 18, 50, U.N. Doc. CEDAW/C/GC/27 (Dec. 16, 2010); United Nations, Comm. on Econ., Soc., & Cultural Rights, General Recommendation No. 28 on the Core Obligations of States Parties Under Article 2 of the Convention on the Elimination of All Forms of Discrimination Against Women, ¶ 12, U.N. Doc. CEDAW/C/GC/28 (Dec. 16, 2010); United Nations, Comm. on Econ., Soc., & Cultural Rights, General Recommendation No. 26 on Women Migrant Workers, ¶ 27, U.N. Doc. CEDAW/C/2009/WP.1/R (Dec. 5, 2008); United Nations, Comm. on Econ., Soc., & Cultural Rights, General Comment No. 20: Non-Discrimination in Economic, Social and Cultural Rights, ¶ 30, U.N. Doc. E/C.12/GC/20 (July 2, 2009); United Nations, Comm. on Econ., Soc., & Cultural Rights, General Comment No. 19: The Right to Social Security, ¶¶ 36, 56, U.N. Doc. E/C.12/GC/19 (Feb. 4, 2008); United Nations, Comm. on Econ., Soc., & Cultural Rights, General Comment No. 18: The Right to Work, ¶¶ 18, 23, U.N. Doc. E/C.12/GC/18 (Feb. 6, 2006); United Nations, Comm. on Econ., Soc., & Cultural Rights, General Comment No. 15: The Right to Water, ¶ 16(f), U.N. Doc. E/C.12/2002/11 (Jan. 20, 2003); United Nations, Comm. on Econ., Soc., & Cultural Rights, General Comment No. 13: The Right to Education, ¶ 16, U.N. Doc. E/C.12/1999/10 (Dec. 8, 1999); United Nations, Int'l Human Rights Instruments, 1 Compilation of General Comments and General Recommendations Adopted by Human Rights Treaty Bodies, at 287, U.N. Doc. HRI/GEN/1/Rev.9 (Vol. II) (May 27, 2008) (Committee on the Elimination of Discrimination Against Women's General Recommendation No. 25 on Gender-Related Dimensions of Racial Discrimination); United Nations, Int'l Human Rights Instruments, 2 Compilation of General Comments and General Recommendations Adopted by Human Rights Treaty Bodies, at 303, 306, 34, U.N. Doc. HRI/GEN/1/Rev.9 (Vol. II) (May 27, 2008) (Comm. on the Elimination of Racial Discrimination's General Recommendation No. 30 on Discrimination Against Non-Citizens); United Nations, Int'l Human Rights Instruments, 1 Compilation of General Comments and General Recommendations Adopted by Human Rights Treaty Bodies, at 189, 34, U.N. Doc. HRI/GEN/1/Rev.9 (Vol. I) (May 27, 2008) (Human Rights Committee's General Comment No. 15 on the Position of Aliens Under the Covenant); United Nations, Human Rights Comm., General Comment No. 32: Right to Equality Before Courts and Tribunals and to a Fair Trial, ¶ 9, U.N. Doc. CCPR/C/GC/32 (Aug. 23, 2007); United Nations, Human Rights Comm., General Comment No. 31: The Nature of the General Legal Obligation Imposed on States Parties to the Covenant, ¶ 10, U.N. Doc. CCPR/C/21/Rev.1/Add.13 (May 26, 2004); United Nations, Human Rights Comm., General Comment No. 23, ¶ 5(2), U.N. Doc. CCPR/C/21/Rev.1/Add.5 (Apr. 26, 1994); United Nations, Comm. on the Rights of the Child, General Comment No. 11: Indigenous Children and Their Rights Under the Convention, ¶ 51, U.N. Doc. CRC/C/GC/11 (Feb. 12, 2009); United Nations, Comm. on the Rights of the Child, General Comment No. 6: Treatment of Unaccompanied and Separated Children Outside Their Country of Origin, ¶ 27, U.N. Doc. CRC/GC/2005/6 (Sept. 1, 2005).

73. See mainly the following concluding observations of the HRC, United Nations, Human Rights Comm., Consideration of Reports Submitted by States Parties Under Article 40 of the Covenant, ¶ 18, U.N. Doc. CCPR/C/KWT/CO/2 (Nov. 18, 2011) (regarding Kuwait); United Nations, Human Rights Comm., Consideration of Reports Submitted by States Parties Under Article 40 of the Covenant, ¶¶ 334-53, U.N. Doc. A/49/40 (Vol. 1) (Sept. 29, 1994) (regarding Slovenia); United Nations, Human Rights Comm., Consideration of Reports Submitted by States Parties Under Article 40 of the Covenant, ¶ 4, U.N. Doc. CCPR/C/79/Add.27 (Nov. 4, 1993) (regarding Norway).

(CESCR),[74] the Committee on the Elimination of Racial Discrimination (CERD),[75] the Committee on the Elimination of Discrimination Against

74. See the following concluding observations of the CESCR, United Nations, Comm. on Econ., Soc., & Cultural Rights, Consideration of Reports Submitted by States Parties Under Articles 16 and 17 of the Covenant, ¶¶ 20, 27, U.N. Doc. E/C.12/KAZ/CO/1 (July 1, 2010) (regarding Kazakhstan); United Nations, Comm. on Econ., Soc., & Cultural Rights, Consideration of Reports Submitted by States Parties Under Articles 16 and 17 of the Covenant, ¶ 22, U.N. Doc E/C.12/GBR/CO/5 (June 12, 2009) (regarding United Kingdom); United Nations, Comm. on Econ., Soc., & Cultural Rights, Consideration of Reports Submitted by States Parties Under Articles 16 and 17 of the Covenant, ¶¶ 14-15, 18, 21-22, U.N. Doc. E/C.12/CYP/CO/5 (June 12, 2009) (regarding Cyprus); United Nations, Comm. on Econ., Soc., & Cultural Rights, Consideration of Reports Submitted by States Parties Under Articles 16 and 17 of the Covenant, ¶¶ 22, 49, U.N. Doc. E/C.12/CAN/CO/4 (May 22, 2006) (regarding Canada); United Nations, Comm. on Econ., Soc., & Cultural Rights, Consideration of Reports Submitted by States Parties Under Articles 16 and 17 of the Covenant, ¶¶ 10-11, 27-29, U.N. Doc. E E/C.12/1/Add.109 (June 23, 2005) (regarding Norway); United Nations, Comm. on Econ., Soc., & Cultural Rights, Consideration of Reports Submitted by States Parties Under Articles 16 and 17 of the Covenant, ¶¶ 24, 53, 89, 114, 116, 124, 126, U.N. Doc. E/C.12/1/Add.107 (May 13, 2005) (regarding China); United Nations, Comm. on Econ., Soc., & Cultural Rights, Consideration of Reports Submitted by States Parties Under Articles 16 and 17 of the Covenant, ¶¶ 17, 36, U.N. Doc. E/C.12/1/Add.103 (Dec. 14, 2004) (regarding Italy); United Nations, Comm. on Econ., Soc., & Cultural Rights, Consideration of Reports Submitted by States Parties Under Articles 16 and 17 of the Covenant, ¶ 17, U.N. Doc. E/C.12/1/Add.94 (Dec. 12, 2003) (regarding Russian Federation); United Nations, Comm. on Econ., Soc., & Cultural Rights, Consideration of Reports Submitted by States Parties Under Articles 16 and 17 of the Covenant, ¶¶ 15, 37, U.N. Doc. E/C.12/1/Add.82 (Dec. 19, 2002) (regarding Poland); United Nations, Comm. on Econ., Soc., & Cultural Rights, Consideration of Reports Submitted by States Parties Under Articles 16 and 17 of the Covenant, ¶ 34, U.N. Doc. E/C.12/1/Add.16 (Dec. 12, 1997) (regarding Dominican Republic).

75. See in particular the following concluding observations of the CERD, United Nations, Comm. on the Elimination of Racial Discrimination, Consideration of Reports Submitted by States Parties Under Article 9 of the Convention, ¶ 11, U.N. Doc. CERD/C/MDV/CO/5-12 (Sept. 14, 2011) (regarding Maldives); United Nations, Comm. on the Elimination of Racial Discrimination, Consideration of Reports Submitted by States Parties Under Article 9 of the Convention, ¶ 20, U.N. Doc. CERD/C/CZE/CO/8-9 (Sept. 2, 2011) (regarding Czech Republic); United Nations, Comm. on the Elimination of Racial Discrimination, Consideration of Reports Submitted by States Parties Under Article 9 of the Convention, ¶ 18, U.N. Doc. CERD/C/ISL/CO/19-20 (Mar. 25, 2010) (regarding Iceland); United Nations, Comm. on the Elimination of Racial Discrimination, Consideration of Reports Submitted by States Parties Under Article 9 of the Convention, ¶ 16, 22, U.N. Doc. CERD/C/KAZ/CO/4-5 (Apr. 6, 2010) (regarding Kazakhstan); United Nations, Comm. on the Elimination of Racial Discrimination, Consideration of Reports Submitted by States Parties Under Article 9 of the Convention, ¶¶ 30, 33, U.N. Doc. CERD/C/CHN/CO/10-13 (Sept. 15, 2009) (regarding China); United Nations, Comm. on the Elimination of Racial Discrimination, Consideration of Reports Submitted by States Parties Under Article 9 of the Convention, ¶ 12, U.N. Doc. CERD/C/NGA/CO/18 (Mar. 27, 2007) (regarding Nigeria); United Nations, Comm. on the Elimination of Racial Discrimination, Consideration of Reports Submitted by States Parties Under Article 9 of the Convention, ¶¶ 15, 23, 25, U.N. Doc. CERD/C/IRL/CO/2 (Apr. 14, 2005) (regarding Ireland); United Nations, Comm. on the Elimination of Racial Discrimination, Consideration of Reports Submitted by States Parties Under Article 9 of the Convention, ¶ 15, U.N. Doc. CERD/C/BHR/CO/7 (Apr. 14, 2005) (regarding Bahrain); United Nations, Comm. on the Elimination of Racial Discrimination, Consideration of Reports Submitted by States Parties Under Article 9 of the Convention, ¶¶ 7, 10-11, U.N. Doc. CERD/C/64/CO/4 (May 10, 2004) (regarding Libya); United Nations, Comm. on the Elimination of Racial Discrimination, Consideration of Reports Submitted by States Parties Under Article 9 of the Convention, ¶ 11, U.N. Doc. CERD/C/64/CO/3 (Apr. 28 2004) (regarding Lebanon); United Nations, Comm. on the Elimination of Racial Discrimination, Consideration of Reports Submitted by States Parties Under Article 9 of the Convention, ¶¶ 4, 10, U.N. Doc. CERD/C/63/CO/9 (Dec. 10, 2003) (regarding Republic of Korea); United Nations, Comm. on the Elimination of Racial Discrimination, Consideration of Reports Submitted by States Parties Under Article 9 of the Convention, ¶¶ 16-20, U.N. Doc. CERD/C/62/CO/8 (Mar. 21, 2003) (regarding Saudi Arabia); United Nations, Comm. on the Elimination of Racial Discrimination, Consideration of Reports Submitted by States Parties Under Article 9 of the Convention, ¶¶ 12, 17, U.N. Doc. CERD/C/304/Add.81 (Apr. 12, 2001) (regarding Chile).

Women (CEDAW),[76] and the Committee on the Rights of the Child (CRC)[77] regularly insist on the need for protecting migrant workers under their respective instruments.

76. *See, e.g.*, United Nation, Comm. on the Elimination of Discrimination Against Women, Concluding Observations of the Committee on the Elimination of Discrimination Against Women: Albania, ¶¶ 19, 40-41, U.N. Doc. CEDAW/C/ALB/CO/3 (Sept. 16, 2010); United Nation, Comm. on the Elimination of Discrimination Against Women, Concluding Observations of the Committee on the Elimination of Discrimination Against Women: Australia, ¶¶ 44-45, U.N. Doc. CEDAW/C/AUS/CO/7 (Jul. 30, 2010); United Nation, Comm. on the Elimination of Discrimination Against Women, Concluding Observations of the Committee on the Elimination of Discrimination Against Women: Egypt, ¶¶ 35-36, U.N. Doc. CEDAW/C/EGY/CO/7 (Feb. 5, 2010); United Nation, Comm. on the Elimination of Discrimination Against Women, Concluding Observations of the Committee on the Elimination of Discrimination Against Women: United Arab Emirates, ¶¶ 10, 26-27, 36-37, U.N. Doc. CEDAW/C/ARE/CO/1 (Feb. 5, 2010); United Nation, Comm. on the Elimination of Discrimination Against Women, Concluding Observations of the Committee on the Elimination of Discrimination Against Women: Bahrain, U.N. Doc. CEDAW/C/BHR/CO/2 (Nov. 14, 2008); United Nation, Comm. on the Elimination of Discrimination Against Women, Concluding Observations of the Committee on the Elimination of Discrimination Against Women: Netherlands, ¶¶ 15-19, 21, 27-28, U.N. Doc. CEDAW/C/NLD/CO/4 (Feb. 2, 2007); United Nation, Comm. on the Elimination of Discrimination Against Women, Concluding Observations of the Committee on the Elimination of Discrimination against Women: Philippines, ¶¶ 21-22, U.N. Doc. CEDAW/C/PHI/CO/6 (Aug. 25, 2006); Rep. of the Comm. on the Elimination of Discrimination Against Women, 30th Sess., Jan. 12-30, 2004, ¶¶ 76-77, 79, U.N. Doc. A/59/38 (Part I) (Mar. 18, 2004) (regarding Kuwait); Rep. of the Comm. on the Elimination of Discrimination Against Women, U.N. GAOR, 58th Sess., Supp. No. 38, at 91, U.N. Doc. A/58/38 (Aug. 18, 2003) (regarding Costa Rica); Rep. of the Comm. on the Elimination of Discrimination Against Women, U.N. GAOR, 21st Sess., Supp. No. 38, at 33, U.N. Doc. A/54/38/Rev.1 (Feb. 5, 1999) (regarding Hong Kong Special Administrative Region).

77. See in particular the following concluding observations of the CRC, United Nation, Comm. on the Rights of the Child, Consideration of Reports Submitted by States Parties Under Article 44 of the Convention, ¶ 62, U.N. Doc. CRC/C/ITA/CO/3-4 (Oct. 31, 2011) (regarding Italy); United Nation, Comm. on the Rights of the Child, Consideration of Reports Submitted by States Parties Under Article 44 of the Convention, ¶¶ 36-37, U.N. Doc. CRC/C/ISL/CO/3-4 (Oct. 6, 2011) (regarding Iceland); United Nation, Comm. on the Rights of the Child, Consideration of Reports Submitted by States Parties Under Article 44 of the Convention, ¶¶ 36, 68-69, U.N. Doc. CRC/C/KOR/CO/3-4 (Oct. 6, 2011) (regarding Republic of Korea); United Nation, Comm. on the Rights of the Child, Consideration of Reports Submitted by States Parties Under Article 44 of the Convention, ¶¶ 10, 29-30, U.N. Doc. CRC/C/CRI/CO/4 (June 17, 2011) (regarding Costa Rica); United Nation, Comm. on the Rights of the Child, Consideration of Reports Submitted by States Parties Under Article 44 of the Convention, ¶¶ 37, 45, U.N. Doc. CRC/C/JPN/CO/3 (June 20, 2010) (regarding Japan); United Nation, Comm. on the Rights of the Child, Consideration of Reports Submitted by States Parties Under Article 44 of the Convention, ¶¶ 70-71, U.N. Doc. CRC/C/HND/CO/3 (May 3, 2007) (regarding Honduras); United Nation, Comm. on the Rights of the Child, Consideration of Reports Submitted by States Parties Under Article 44 of the Convention, ¶¶ 29, 63, U.N. Doc. CRC/C/CHL/CO/3 (Apr. 23, 2007) (regarding Chile); United Nation, Comm. on the Rights of the Child, Consideration of Reports Submitted by States Parties Under Article 44 of the Convention, ¶¶ 24-25, 59-60, U.N. Doc. CRC/C/OMN/CO/2 (Sept. 29, 2006) (regarding Oman); United Nation, Comm. on the Rights of the Child, Consideration of Reports Submitted by States Parties Under Article 44 of the Convention, ¶¶ 24-25, U.N. Doc. CRC/C/15/Add.233 (Jun. 30, 2004) (regarding Panama); United Nation, Comm. on the Rights of the Child, Consideration of Reports Submitted by States Parties Under Article 44 of the Convention, ¶¶ 24-25, U.N. Doc. CRC/C/15/Add.231 (Feb. 26, 2004) (regarding Japan); United Nation, Comm. on the Rights of the Child, Consideration of Reports Submitted by States Parties Under Article 44 of the Convention, ¶¶ 31-32, 58-59, U.N. Doc. CRC/C/15/Add.197 (Mar. 18, 2003) (regarding Republic of Korea); United Nation, Comm. on the Rights of the Child, Consideration of Reports Submitted by States Parties Under Article 44 of the Convention, ¶ 27, U.N. Doc. CRC/C/15/Add.185 (June 13, 2002) (regarding Spain); United Nation, Comm. on the Rights of the Child, Consideration of Reports Submitted by States Parties Under Article 44 of the Convention, ¶¶ 26-27, U.N. Doc. CRC/C/15/Add.151 (July 17, 2001) (regarding Denmark); United Nation, Comm. on the Rights of the Child, Consideration of Reports Submitted by States Parties Under Article 44 of the Convention, ¶ 32, U.N. Doc. CRC/C/15/Add.149 (Feb. 21, 2001) (regarding Palau).

Finally, migrants can also bring individual complaints to the seven existing UN supervisory bodies currently competent (namely the HRC, the CERD, the CAT, the CEDAW, the CESCR, the Committee on Enforced Disappearances, and the Committee on the Rights of Persons with Disabilities). The CAT is by far the most solicited UN treaty body. It has even become an anti-deportation committee, as between 80% and 90% of all individual complaints submitted to the CAT concern alleged violations of its Article 3 devoted to the principle of *non-refoulement*.[78] At the regional level, the European Court of Human Rights is another particularly active treaty-body, which has regularly sanctioned violations of human rights committed against migrants.[79] The European Court is not the only active regional body, as virtually all are concerned, such as the Inter-American and African Courts of human rights.[80]

In sum, as a result of a longstanding evolution, the traditional law of aliens grounded on diplomatic protection has been progressively superseded by human rights law, which has become in turn the primary source of migrants' protection. This process is not confined to the specific situation of migrants, but reflects the broader evolution of general international law during the last century. The consequences of this phenomenon are both normative and institutional. Already in 1984, Richard B. Lillich rightly observed in his seminal book, *The Human Rights of Aliens in Contemporary International Law*, that:

> What the international community is witnessing today is a major change—the significance of which cannot be overstated—in the way in which the rights of aliens are protected: from the classic system of diplomatic protection by the alien's State of nationality, invoking the traditional international law governing the treatment of aliens, to the direct protection of the individual alien's rights through his use of national and international procedures to enforce a set of reformulated international norms . . . .[81]

---

78. Vincent Chetail, *Le Comité des Nations Unies Contre la Torture et L'expulsion des Étrangers: Dix Ans de Jurisprudence*, *in* 26 REVUE SUISSE DE DROIT INTERNATIONAL ET EUROPÉEN 63, at 66 (2006); MANFRED NOWAK & ELIZABETH MCARTHUR, THE UNITED NATIONS CONVENTION AGAINST TORTURE: A COMMENTARY 159 (Philip Alston & Vaughan Lowe eds., 2008).

79. For recent condemnations see, for example, Othman (Abu Qatada) v. United Kingdom, 2012-I Eur. Ct. H.R. 159; Jamaa v. Italy, 2012-II Eur. Ct. H.R.; M.S.S. v. Belgium & Greece, 2011 Eur. Ct. H.R.

80. For recent condemnations pronounced by the Inter-American Court of Human Rights see, for example, Dorzema v. Dominican Republic, Merits, Reparations, and Costs, Judgement, Inter-Am. Ct. H.R. (ser. C) No. 12,688 (Oct. 24, 2012); Veles Loor v. Panama, Preliminary Objections, Merits, Reparations, and Costs, Judgement, Inter-Am. Ct. H.R. (ser. C) No. 12,581 (Nov. 23, 2010). Though the newly established African Court has not yet delivered a judgement in the field, the African Commission has already developed a substantial jurisprudence on the rights of migrants. *See* Good v. Bostwana, Afr. Comm'n H.R., Report No. 313/05 (2010); Modise v. Botswana, Afr. Comm'n H.R., Report No. 97/93 (2000).

81. RICHARD B. LILLICH, THE HUMAN RIGHTS OF ALIENS IN CONTEMPORARY INTERNATIONAL LAW 3 (Gillian M. White ed., 1984). This does not mean, however, that diplomatic protection has

IV. THE PRINCIPLE OF NON-DISCRIMINATION AS THE ULTIMATE BENCHMARK OF MIGRANT RIGHTS

The impact of international human rights law is not only procedural, but also substantial. It has substantially eroded the traditional *summa divisio* based on the distinction between citizens and non-citizens. This is all but surprising, for human rights are by definition inherent to human dignity without regard to nationality. The Universal Declaration of Human Rights and the two UN Covenants proclaim in the first recital of their preambles that human rights derive from the "recognition of the inherent dignity and of the equal and inalienable rights of all members of the human family."[82] Similarly, the preamble of the American Convention of Human Rights recalls in more explicit terms that, "the essential rights of man are not derived from one's being a national of a certain state, but are based upon attributes of the human personality."[83]

This philosophical and normative underpinning is reinforced by the principle of non-discrimination, which has been endorsed in all human rights treaties including Article 2(1) of the International Covenant on Civil and Political Rights (ICCPR):

> Each State Party to the present Covenant undertakes to respect and to ensure to all individuals within its territory and subject to its jurisdiction the rights recognized in the present Covenant, without distinction of any kind, such as race, [color], sex, language, religion, political or other opinion, national or social origin, property, birth or other status.[84]

disappeared; this traditional institution coexists with national and supranational procedures which are comparatively more reliable simply because, as methods of enforcement, the latter are not discretionary and more objective than the former.

82. ICCPR, *supra* note 66, pmbl.; UDHR, *supra* note 44, pmbl.

83. American Convention on Human Rights pmbl., ¶ 2, July 18, 1978, 1144 U.N.T.S. 123.

84. ICCPR, *supra* note 66, art. 2(1). Though nationality is not mentioned *expressis verbis* in this non-exhaustive list of prohibited grounds of discrimination, it is clearly covered by the one referring to "national origin." For further developments about the scope and content of the principle of non-discrimination *see* ODDNY MJYLL ARNARDOTTIR, EQUALITY AND DISCRIMINATION UNDER THE EUROPEAN CONVENTION ON HUMAN RIGHTS (2003); CURTIS F. J. DOEBBLER, THE PRINCIPLE OF NON-DISCRIMINATION IN INTERNATIONAL LAW (2007); WARWICK MCKEAN, EQUALITY AND NON-DISCRIMINATION UNDER INTERNATIONAL LAW (1983); DANIEL MOEKLI, HUMAN RIGHTS AND NON-DISCRIMINATION IN THE 'WAR ON TERROR' (2008); WOUTER VANDENHOLE, NON-DISCRIMINATION AND EQUALITY IN THE VIEW OF THE UN HUMAN RIGHTS TREATY BODIES (2005); E. W. VIERDAG, THE CONCEPT OF DISCRIMINATION IN INTERNATIONAL LAW (1973); LI WEIWEI, EQUALITY AND NON-DISCRIMINATION UNDER INTERNATIONAL HUMAN RIGHTS LAW (2004); Anne F. Bayefsky, *The Principle of Equality or Non-Discrimination in International Law*, 11 H.R.L.J. 1, 1-2 (1990); M. BOSSUYT, L'INTERDICTION DE LA DISCRIMINATION DANS LE DROIT INTERNATIONAL DES DROITS DE L'HOMME (1976); Mel Cousins, *The European Convention on Human Rights, Non-Discrimination and Social Security: Great Scope, Little Depth?*, 16 J. SOC. SEC. L. 3, 120-38 (2009); Aaron X. Fellmeth, *Non-discrimination as a Universal Human Right*, 34 YALE J. INT'L L. 558, 558-95 (2009).

The principle of non-discrimination is a well-recognized norm of general international law[85] and its impact on the legal position of non-citizens is quite straightforward. Interpreting Article 2(1) of the ICCPR, the HRC underlined:

> In general, the rights set forth in the Covenant apply to everyone, irrespective of reciprocity, and irrespective of his or her nationality or statelessness . . . . Thus, the general rule is that each one of the rights of the Covenant must be guaranteed without discrimination between citizens and aliens . . . . Exceptionally, some of the rights recognized in the Covenant are expressly applicable only to citizens (art. 25), while article 13 applies only to aliens.[86]

The HRC further delineated the basic rights of aliens deriving from the ICCPR. The list enumerated in its General Comment No. 15 on The Position of Aliens under the Covenant proves to be extensive:

> Aliens thus have an inherent right to life, protected by law, and may not be arbitrarily deprived of life. They must not be subjected to torture or to cruel, inhuman or degrading treatment or punishment; nor may they be held in slavery or servitude. Aliens have the full right to liberty and security of the person. If lawfully deprived of their liberty, they shall be treated with humanity and with respect for the inherent dignity of their person. Aliens may not be imprisoned for failure to fulfil a contractual obligation. They have the right to liberty of movement and free choice of residence; they shall be free to leave the country. Aliens shall be equal before the courts and tribunals, and shall be entitled to a fair and public hearing by a competent, independent and impartial tribunal established by law in the determination of any criminal charge or of rights and obligations in a suit at law. Aliens shall not be subjected to retrospective penal legislation, and are entitled to recognition before the law. They may not be subjected to arbitrary or unlawful interference with their privacy, family, home or correspondence. They have the right to freedom of thought, conscience and religion, and the right to hold opinions and to express them. Aliens receive the benefit of the right of peaceful assembly and of freedom of association. They may marry when at marriageable age. Their children are entitled to those measures of protection required by their status as minors. In those cases where aliens constitute a minority within the meaning of Article 27, they shall not be denied the right, in community with other members of their

85. According to the Inter-American Court of Human Rights, this is even a norm of *jus cogens*. Juridical Condition and Rights of the Undocumented Migrants, Advisory Opinion OC-18/03, Inter-Am. Ct. H.R. (ser. A) No. 18, ¶ 101 (Sept. 17, 2003).

86. United Nations, Int'l Human Rights Instruments, Compilation of General Comments and General Recommendations Adopted by Human Rights Treaty Bodies, at 18-19, ¶¶ 1-2, U.N. Doc. HRI/GEN/1/Rev.1 (July 29, 1994) (General Comment No. 15: The Position of Aliens Under the Covenant).

> group, to enjoy their own culture, to profess and [practice] their own religion and to use their own language. Aliens are entitled to equal protection by the law. There shall be no discrimination between aliens and citizens in the application of these rights. These rights of aliens may be qualified only by such limitations as may be lawfully imposed under the Covenant.[87]

The fundamental rights listed therein are not only applicable to non-citizens; most of them are generally considered part of customary international law.[88] Hence, the general applicability of human rights to non-citizens combined with the customary law nature of these fundamental rights have the consequence of anchoring migrants' rights within general international law.

However, the position of migrants under public international law is qualified by two main considerations. First, some of the rights listed above are conditioned by the legal status of their beneficiaries. It is true that such rights are not numerous; only two rights proclaimed in the ICCPR require a legal presence within the territory. Nevertheless, their impact is both significant and representative because the two rights in question specifically refer to the movement of persons: A regular presence is required for the right to liberty of movement and freedom to choose a residence within the territory,[89] as well as for due process guarantees governing expulsion from the territory.[90]

The combination of these two provisions graphically exhibits the specificities and the limits of the legal status of migrants under contemporary international law. A non-citizen must be lawfully within the territory of a state in order to benefit within that territory from the right to liberty of movement and freedom to choose his/her residence. But, even when lawfully within the territory, he or she may still be deported from that territory as long as some basic conditions and procedural guarantees are fulfilled.[91] This

87. *Id.* at 19, ¶ 7. Needless to say that all the rights consecrated in the ICCPR have been reaffirmed in many other human rights treaties notably at the regional level.

88. There is no room here for a detailed analysis of the customary law nature of the human rights referred therein. Among a plethora of literature, see, for example, LOUIS HENKIN, THE AGE OF RIGHTS 19 (1990); MYRES S. MCDOUGAL ET AL., HUMAN RIGHTS AND WORLD PUBLIC ORDER: THE BASIC POLICIES OF AN INTERNATIONAL LAW OF HUMAN DIGNITY 272 (1980); THEODOR MERON, HUMAN RIGHTS AND HUMANITARIAN NORMS AS CUSTOMARY LAW 79-135 (1989); OLIVIER DE SCHUTTER, INTERNATIONAL HUMAN RIGHTS LAW 50-56 (2010); Hurst Hannum, *The Status of the Universal Declaration of Human Rights in National and International Law*, 25 GA. J. INT'L & COMP. L. 287, 287-397 (1995); Richard B. Lillich, *The Growing Importance of Customary International Human Rights Law*, 25 GA. J. INT'L & COMP. L. 1 (1996); Louis B. Sohn, *The Human Rights Law of the Charter*, 12 TEX. INT'L L.J. 129, 133 (1977). *See also* RESTATEMENT (THIRD) OF THE FOREIGN RELATIONS LAW OF THE UNITED STATES (1987).

89. ICCPR, *supra* note 66, art. 12(1).

90. ICCPR, *supra* note 66, art. 13.

91. ICCPR, *supra* note 66, art. 13 ("An alien lawfully in the territory of a State Party to the present Covenant may be expelled therefrom only in pursuance of a decision reached in accordance with law and shall, except where compelling reasons of national security otherwise require, be

tension is a defining feature of alienage.

The rationale behind limiting rights based on an alien's legal status is clearly related to the traditional power of states to regulate entries and stays within their own territory.[92] As acknowledged by the HRC, "the question whether an alien is 'lawfully' within the territory of a State is a matter governed by domestic law, which may subject the entry of an alien to the territory of a State to restrictions, provided they are in compliance with the State's international obligations."[93] While states retain a substantial margin of appreciation, this does not mean that they have a purely discretionary power for deciding upon admission of non-citizens. Here again the legal position of migrants mirrors a broader transformation of the international legal order, which has evolved from a law of coexistence towards a law of interdependence. As a result of this structural evolution of public international law, territorial sovereignty is both a competence and a responsibility. Against such normative background, the competence to regulate admission in domestic legislation must be exercised in due accordance with the legal norms of international law.

The international legal norms governing migration control are more substantial and numerous than is frequently assumed by policy-makers. The most relevant ones are the principle of *non-refoulement*, the right to family unity, the prohibition of arbitrary detention, the prohibition of collective expulsion, and states' duties to admit their own nationals. Though their respective content and legal basis cannot be detailed here, each of these norms is not only acknowledged in numerous treaties but also arguably grounded in customary international law.[94]

---

allowed to submit the reasons against his expulsion and to have his case reviewed by, and be represented for the purpose before, the competent authority or a person or persons especially designated by the competent authority."). Similar conditions governing the deportation process can be found in other treaties. *See, e.g.*, Arab Charter on Human Rights art. 26(b), *adopted* May 23, 2004 *reprinted in* 12 INT'L HUM. RTS. REP. 893 (2005) (entered into force Mar. 15, 2008); Protocol No. 7 to the Convention for the Protection of Human Rights and Fundamental Freedoms, art. 1, Nov. 22, 1984, 1525 U.N.T.S. 195; African Charter on Human and Peoples' Rights art. 12(5), June 27, 1981, 1520 U.N.T.S. 217 (entered into force Oct. 21, 1986); American Convention on Human Rights, *supra* note 79, art. 22(6); Convention Relating to the Status of Refugees art. 32, July 28, 1951, 189 U.N.T.S. 137 (entered into force Apr. 22, 1954).

92. For further discussions see AM. SOC'Y OF INT'L LAW, THE MOVEMENT OF PERSONS ACROSS BORDERS 1-22 (Louis B. Sohn & Thomas Buergenthal eds., Studies in Transnational Legal Policy No. 23, 1992); Vincent Chetail, *Migration, Droits de L'Homme et Souveraineté: Le Droit International Dans Tous Ses Etats*, in MONDIALISATION, *supra* note 6, at 13-133; GUY S. GOODWIN-GILL, INTERNATIONAL LAW AND THE MOVEMENT OF PERSONS BETWEEN STATES (1978); David A. Martin, *The Authority and Responsibility of States*, *in* MIGRATION AND INTERNATIONAL LEGAL NORMS 31-45 (Thomas Alexander Aleinikoff & Vincent Chetail eds., 2003); RICHARD PLENDER, INTERNATIONAL MIGRATION LAW (2d ed. 1988); James A. R. Nafziger, *The General Admission of Aliens Under International Law*, 77 AM. J. INT'L L. 804, 804-47 (1983).

93. United Nations, Int'l Covenant on Civil & Political Rights, Human Rights Comm., General Comment No. 27: Freedom of Movement, ¶ 4, U.N. Doc. CCPR/C/21/Rev.1/Add.9 (Nov. 1, 1999).

94. For further discussions about their legal basis and content under customary international law see Vincent Chetail, *The Transnational Movement of Persons Under General International Law: Mapping the Customary Law Foundations of International Migration Law*, *in* RESEARCH HANDBOOK ON INTERNATIONAL LAW AND MIGRATION 1-74 (Vincent Chetail & Celine Bauloz eds., 2014).

Besides the limits deriving from the state's competence in the field of admission, the general principle of non-discrimination is subject to a second type of impediment closely related to the nature of the rights at stake. Indeed the position of migrants under general international law is more precarious when it comes to economic, social, and cultural rights.[95] From a purely legal perspective, this may be surprising for, in contrast to civil and political rights, none of the rights endorsed in the ICESCR[96] are conditioned by the nationality or legal status of their beneficiaries. However, most of these rights are progressively applicable depending on the resources available in each state.[97] The principle of non-discrimination is nonetheless well acknowledged as a basic guarantee which "is neither subject to progressive implementation nor dependent on available resources."[98]

This obligation of immediate implementation relies on the mandatory terms of Article 2(2) of ICESCR which requires each state party "to guarantee that the rights enunciated in the present Covenant will be exercised without discrimination of any kind as to race, colour, sex, language, religion, political or other opinion, national or social origin, property, birth or other status."[99] The CESCR rightly inferred from this fundamental and straightforward obligation that "[t]he Covenant rights apply to everyone including

95. For an overview, see, Vincent Chetail & Gilles Giacca, *Who Cares?: The Right to Health of Migrants*, *in* REALIZING THE RIGHT TO HEALTH 224–34 (Andrew Clapham & Mary Robinson eds., 2009); RYSZARD CHOLEWINSKI, STUDY ON OBSTACLES TO EFFECTIVE ACCESS OF IRREGULAR MIGRANTS TO MINIMUM SOCIAL RIGHTS (2005); Ryszard Cholewinski, *Economic and Social Rights of Refugees and Asylum Seekers in Europe*, 14 GEO. IMMIGR. L.J. 709, 709-55 (2000); Ockert Dupper, *Migrant Workers and the Right to Social Security: An International Perspective*, 18 STELLENBOSCH L. REV. 219–54 (2007); Sylvie Da Lomba, *Immigration Status and Basic Social Rights: A Comparative Study of Irregular Migrants' Right to Health Care in France, the UK and Canada*, 28 NETH. Q. HUM. RTS. 1, 6 (2010); Aliya Haider, *Out of the Shadows: Migrant Women's Reproductive Rights under International Human Rights Law*, 22 GEO. IMMIGR. L.J. 429 (2007-2008); Haina Lu, *The Personal Application of the Right to Work in the Age of Migration*, 26 NETH. Q. HUM. RTS. 1, 43-77 (2008); Ben Saul, *Waiting for Dignity in Australia: Migrant Rights to Social Security and Disability Support under International Human Rights Law*, 3 U.C. LONDON HUM. RTS. REV. 72 (2010).

96. International Covenant on Economic, Social and Cultural Rights, Dec. 16, 1966, 993 U.N.T.S. 3 (entered into force Jan. 3, 1976) [hereinafter ICESCR].

97. As underlined in Article 2(1) of the U.N. International Covenant on Economic, Social and Cultural Rights (ICESCR), "[e]ach States Parties to the present Covenant undertakes to take steps, individually and through international assistance and co-operation . . . to the maximum of its available resources, with a view to achieving progressively the full realization of the rights recognized in the present Covenant." ICESCR, *supra* note 95, art. 2(1).

98. United Nations, Comm. on Econ., Soc. & Cultural Rights, General Comment No. 18: The Right to Work, ¶ 33, U.N. Doc. E/C.12/GC/18 (Feb. 6, 2006). *See* United Nations, Comm. on Econ., Soc. & Cultural Rights, General Comment No. 20: Non-Discrimination in Economic, Social and Cultural Rights, ¶¶ 2, 7, U.N. Doc. E/C.12/GC/20 (July 2, 2009); United Nations, Comm. on Econ., Soc. & Cultural Rights, General Comment No. 9: The Domestic Application of the Covenant, ¶ 9, U.N. Doc. E/C.12/1998/24 (Dec. 3, 1998); United Nations, Comm. on Econ., Soc. & Cultural Rights, General Comment No. 3: The Nature of States Parties' Obligations, ¶ 287, at 83, U.N. Doc. E/1991/23, Annex III (Dec. 14, 1990). *See also* The Maastricht Guidelines on Violations of Economic, Social and Cultural Rights, ¶ 11, at 16, U.N. Doc. E/C.12/2000/13 (Oct. 2, 2000); United Nations, Comm'n on Human Rights, The Limburg Principles on the Implementation of the International Covenant on Economic, Social and Cultural Rights, ¶ 35, U.N. Doc. E/CN.4/1987/17, Annex I (Jan. 8, 1984) [hereinafter Limburg Principles].

99. ICESCR, *supra* note 96, art. 2(2).

non-nationals, such as refugees, asylum-seekers, stateless persons, migrant workers and victims of international trafficking, regardless of legal status and documentation."[100]

Nonetheless, contrary to its counterpart in the ICCPR, the principle of non-discrimination under the ICESCR is limited by a noteworthy—albeit circumstantiated—exception. According to Article 2(3), "developing countries, with due regard to human rights and their national economy, may determine to what extent they would guarantee the economic rights recognized in the present Covenant to non-nationals."[101] As any exception to a principle, this one should be restrictively interpreted (especially when the principle at stake is so fundamental and represents one of the funding backbones of the Covenant). Furthermore, the wording of this provision is circumscribed by three substantial cumulative conditions regarding the states concerned, the nature of the rights subjected to this exception, and the degree of permissible restrictions to them.

Regarding the first condition (the states concerned), Article 2(3) is a permissive, not a mandatory, provision which can be invoked only by "developing countries."[102] The notion of developing countries being a factual rather than a legal one, it is commonly understood as including "countries which have gained independence and which fall within the appropriate United Nations classifications of developing countries."[103] Although this kind of qualification referring to a particular type of State may be found in international trade law and other related areas, it remains quite unique in the field of human rights law. This specificity must be understood in the historical context which prevailed during the drafting of the ICESCR. Article 2(3) is a remnant of the traditional law of aliens and the longstanding debates between newly independent states and western states. The delegate of Indonesia who proposed this provision explained that its only purpose was to protect the rights of nationals of former colonies against the abuses deriving from "the dominant economic position enjoyed by [mostly western] foreigners as a result of the colonial system."[104] In summing up the debates between the delegations, the Third Committee of the General Assembly further insisted that:

100. United Nations, Comm. on Econ., Soc., & Cultural Rights, General Comment No. 20: Non-Discrimination in Economic, Social and Cultural Rights, ¶ 30, U.N. Doc. E/C.12/GC/20 (July 2, 2009). *See also* United Nations, Comm. on the Rights of the Child, General Comment No. 6: Treatment of Unaccompanied and Separated Children Outside Their Country of Origin, ¶¶ 12, 18, U.N. Doc. CRC/GC/2005/6 (Sept. 1, 2005).

101. ICESCR, *supra* note 96, art. 2, ¶ 3.

102. *Id.*

103. Limburg Principles, *supra* note 98, ¶ 44.

104. U.N. GAOR, 17th Sess., 1118th mtg. at 258, ¶ 37, U.N. Doc. A/C.3/SR.1185 (Nov. 16, 1962). Although the Committee on Economic, Social and Cultural Rights has not specified for the moment the meaning of this provision, the Limburg Principles reassert that "[t]he purpose of article 2(3) was to end the domination of certain economic groups of non-nationals during colonial times." Limburg Principles, *supra* note 98, ¶ 43.

> [T]he sole aim of the proposals in question was to rectify situations which frequently existed in the developing countries particularly those which recently won their independence. In such countries, the influence of non-nationals on the national economy—a heritage of the colonial era—was often such that nationals were prevented from enjoying the economic rights set forth in the draft Covenant.[105]

Article 2(3) was finally adopted by a small majority of states: forty-one votes to thirty-eight, with twelve abstentions.[106]

The second range of conditions governing Article 2(3)'s scope relates to the rights concerned by this exception to the principle of non-discrimination. Article 2(3) is exclusively limited to the "economic rights recognized in the present Covenant."[107] Although this notion is not explicitly defined in the Covenant, the ordinary meaning of the terms presupposes that the rights in question primarily consist of the right to work and other related rights,[108] such as the enjoyment of just and favourable conditions of work.[109] This excludes both social and cultural rights for which non-discrimination remains plainly operational.

Third, according to the cautious and restrictive wording of Article 2(3), developing countries are not allowed to suspend the rights of non-nationals, they can only "determine to what extent they would guarantee the[ir] economic rights."[110] They can thus merely envisage restrictions to the exercise of economic rights, which must be determined "with due regard to human rights and their national economy" as explicitly required by Article 2(3).[111] Possible restrictions on the economic rights of non-nationals are therefore deemed acceptable as long as they do not impair the enjoyment of other human rights. Following this stance, a general prohibition of the right to work imposed to non-citizens would not be justified if no welfare assistance is instead provided to them.[112]

In any event, Article 2(3) cannot justify any breach of economic rights and other related guarantees provided by other treaties. For example, it cannot be

---

105. U.N. GAOR, 17th Sess., 5365th plen. mtg. ¶ 68, U.N. Doc. A/5365 (Dec. 17, 1962).

106. U.N. GAOR, 17th Sess., 1206th mtg. ¶¶ 42-45, U.N. Doc. A/C.3/SR.1206 (Dec. 10, 1962).

107. ICESCR, *supra* note 96, art. 2, ¶ 3.

108. ICESCR, *supra* note 96, art. 6.

109. ICESCR, *supra* note 96, art. 7. *See also* CHOLEWINSKI, *supra* note 6, at 59; M. MAGDALENA SEPULVEDA, THE NATURE OF THE OBLIGATIONS UNDER THE INTERNATIONAL COVENANT ON ECONOMIC, SOCIAL AND CULTURAL RIGHTS 415 (Sch. of Human Rights Research Ser. Vol. 18, 2003); E. V. O. Dankwa, *Working Paper on Article 2(3) of the International Covenant on Economic, Social and Cultural Rights*, 9 HUM. RTS. Q. 230, 239-40 (1987).

110. ICESCR, *supra* note 96, art. 2, ¶ 3. During the drafting of Article 2(3), the delegate of Indonesia underlined that this provision "recognised the principle that non-nationals were entitled to enjoy the same economic rights as the nationals of a State; it was only the extent of such enjoyment that could be limited by the State." U.N. GAOR, 17th Sess., 1204th mtg. ¶ 2, U.N. Doc. A/C.3/SR.1204 (Dec. 6, 1962).

111. ICESCR, *supra* note 96, art. 2, ¶ 3.

112. *See also* Alice Edwards, *Human Rights, Refugees, and the Right 'to Enjoy' Asylum*, INT'L J. REFUGEE L. 293, 325-26 (2005).

used to avoid articles 17, 18, and 19 of the Refugee Convention governing access to employment.[113] Article 5(2) of the ICESCR ensures indeed that more favourable treatments granted by any other domestic legislation and treaties remain plainly applicable.[114] This safeguard clause has further far-reaching effects with regard to more favourable treatment enshrined in regional human rights treaties, for both the 1981 African Charter on Human and Peoples Rights[115] and the 1988 Additional Protocol to the American Convention on Human Rights in the Area of Economic, Social and Cultural Rights[116] guarantee the right to work without any discrimination. In such case, Article 2(3) is literally neutralised.

In addition to due respect for other human rights and more favourable treatment, restrictions on the economic rights of non-citizens are further conditioned by the state of their national economy. Although developing countries retain a substantial margin of appreciation, some commentators have argued that Article 2(3) can be triggered "only when the state of the economy of the nation as a whole so warrants."[117] In sum, despite the apparent vagueness of its wording, Article 2(3) represents a limited and balanced exception to the principle of non-discrimination. More fundamentally, it remains—for the moment at least—a rather virtual exception, for "no developing State has sought to invoke it."[118] Save for a possible future invocation of Article 2(3), the principle of non-discrimination constitutes thus an "immediate and cross-cutting obligation" binding all state parties.[119]

From the broader perspective of general international law, the prohibition of discrimination is acknowledged as a well-established principle. Nonetheless, its concrete implications are not always obvious as the principle of non-discrimination does not prohibit all differences of treatment. A differential treatment is still permissible provided that it has a legitimate aim and the criteria for such differentiation are "reasonable and objective."[120] The

113. Convention Relating to the Status of Refugees arts. 17-19, July 28, 1951, 189 U.N.T.S. 150 (entered into force Apr. 22, 1954).

114. ICESCR, *supra* note 96, art. 5, ¶ 2.

115. African Charter on Human and People's Rights art. 15, June 27, 1981, 1520 U.N.T.S. 217 (entered into force Oct. 21, 1986).

116. Organization of American States, Additional Protocol to the American Convention on Human Rights in the Area of Economic, Social and Cultural Rights art. 6, Nov. 17, 1988, O.A.S.T.S. No. 69 (entered into force Nov. 16, 1999) ("Protocol of San Salvador").

117. Dankwa, *supra* note 109, at 242.

118. SEPULVEDA, *supra* note 109, at 415. *See also* Matthew Craven, *The International Covenant on Economic, Social and Cultural Rights*, *in* AN INTRODUCTION TO THE INTERNATIONAL PROTECTION OF HUMAN RIGHTS: A TEXTBOOK 101, 111 (Raija Hanski & Markku Suksi eds., 2d rev. ed. 1999).

119. United Nations, Comm. on Econ., Soc., and Cultural Rights, General Comment No. 20: Non-Discrimination in Economic, Social and Cultural Rights, ¶ 7, U.N. Doc. E/C.12/GC/20 (July 2, 2009).

120. Gaygusuz v. Austria, 1996-IV Eur. Ct. H.R. 12, ¶ 42 (1996); United Nations, Comm. on Econ., Soc., and Cultural Rights, General Comment No. 20: Non-Discrimination in Economic, Social and Cultural Rights, ¶ 13, U.N. Doc. E/C.12/GC/20 (July 2, 2009); United Nations, Comm. on the Elimination of Racial Discrimination, General Recommendation No. 30: Discrimination Against Non-citizens, ¶ 4, U.N. Doc. CERD/C/64/Misc.11/Rev.3 (Oct. 1, 2004).

differentiation between citizens and non-citizens must thus be proportionate to the aims pursued by states.[121] This requires a subtle case-by-case assessment which confers on states a relatively broad margin of action.

Against such a frame, though equal access of non-citizens to economic and social rights remains controversial, there is a growing consensus for considering that this should be the case for a minimum core obligation. Equal access to the core content of economic and social rights has been notably endorsed by the CESCR. It has reaffirmed for instance that "[a]ll persons, irrespective of their nationality, residency or immigration status, are entitled to primary and emergency medical care."[122] In particular, "[r]efugees, stateless persons and asylum-seekers . . . should enjoy equal treatment in access to non-contributory social security schemes, including reasonable access to health care and family support, consistent with international standards."[123]

This general trend finds additional support in the general prohibition against degrading and inhuman treatment, a well-established norm of customary international law.[124] Indeed, violating a minimum of subsistence rights can cross the threshold of degrading treatment.[125] A similar evolution

---

121. *Gaygusuz v. Austria*, 1996-IV Eur. Ct. H.R. 12, ¶ 42; United Nations, Comm. on Econ., Soc., and Cultural Rights, General Comment No. 20: Non-Discrimination in Economic, Social and Cultural Rights, ¶ 13, U.N. Doc. E/C.12/GC/20 (July 2, 2009); United Nations, Comm. on the Elimination of Racial Discrimination, General Recommendation No. 30: Discrimination Against Non-citizens, ¶ 4, U.N. Doc. CERD/C/64/Misc.11/Rev.3 (Oct. 1, 2004).

122. United Nations, Comm. on Econ., Soc. & Cultural Rights, General Comment No. 19: The Right to Social Security, ¶ 37, U.N. Doc. E/C.12/GC/19 (Feb. 4, 2008). *See also* United Nations, Comm. on Econ., Soc. & Cultural Rights, General Comment No. 14: The Right to the Highest Attainable Standard of Health, ¶ 34, U.N Doc. E/C.12/200/4 (Aug. 11, 2000).

123. United Nations, Comm. on Econ., Soc. & Cultural Rights, General Comment No. 19: The Right to Social Security, ¶ 38, U.N. Doc. E/C.12/GC/19 (Feb. 4, 2008). As far the right to education, "the principle of non-discrimination extends to all persons of school age residing in the territory of a State party, including non-nationals, and irrespective of their legal status." United Nations, Comm. on Econ., Soc. & Cultural Rights, General Comment No. 13: The Right to Education, ¶ 34, U.N. Doc. E/C.12/1999/10 (Dec. 8, 1999). Article 3 of the Convention against Discrimination in Education also obliges States Parties to "give foreign nationals resident within their territory the same access to education as that given to their own nationals," without mentioning the nature of their migratory status. Convention against Discrimination in Education, Dec. 14, 1960, 429 U.N.T.S. 93 (entered into force May 22, 1962).

124. Its customary law nature has been notably acknowledged by the International Court of Justice. Ahmadou Sadio Diallo (Guinea v. Dem. Rep. Congo), Judgment, 1996 I.C.J. 639, ¶ 87 (Nov. 30).

125. This interpretation has been notably confirmed by the European Court in the *M.S.S.* case. M.S.S. v. Belgium & Greece, ¶¶ 365-67, 2011 Eur. Ct. H.R. Although it recalls, in line with its previous jurisprudence, that Article 3 does not "entail any general obligation to give refugees financial assistance to enable them to maintain a certain standard of living," the Court acknowledges the particular vulnerability of asylum-seekers: "[t]he Court attaches considerable importance to the applicant's status as an asylum seeker and, as such, a member of a particularly underprivileged and vulnerable population group in need of special protection. It notes the existence of a broad consensus at the international and European level concerning this need for special protection, as evidenced by the Geneva Convention, the remit and the activities of the UNHCR and the standards set out in the European Union Reception Directive." *Id.* ¶¶ 249, 251. While referring to the complementary obligation to provide decent material conditions under the EU Reception Directive, the Court concludes that "the situation in which he has found himself for several months, living in the street, with no resources or access to sanitary facilities, and without any means of providing for his essential

highlighting the interdependent and interrelated nature of human rights can be observed with regard to some of the core labour rights reaffirmed in several widely ratified ILO treaties.[126]

Besides the widespread and representative participation to these treaties, the customary nature of the basic norms enshrined therein can be inferred from the ILO Declaration on Fundamental Principles and Rights at Work:

> All Members, even if they have not ratified the Conventions in question, have an obligation arising from the very fact of membership in the Organization to respect, to promote and to realize, in good faith and in accordance with the Constitution, the principles concerning the fundamental rights which are the subject of those Conventions, namely:
>
> (a) freedom of association and the effective recognition of the right to collective bargaining;
> (b) the elimination of all forms of forced or compulsory labour;
> (c) the effective abolition of child labour; and
> (d) the elimination of discrimination in respect of employment and occupation.[127]

---

needs . . . . have attained the level of severity required to fall within the scope of Article 3 of the Convention." *Id.* ¶ 263.

126. *See* International Labour Organization, Convention Concerning Forced or Compulsory Labour, June 28, 1930, 39 U.N.T.S. 55 (entered into force May 1, 1932); International Labour Organization, Convention Concerning Freedom of Association and Protection of the Right to Organise, July 9, 1948, 68 U.N.T.S. 17 (entered into force July 4, 1950); International Labour Organization, Convention Concerning the Application of the Principles of the Right to Organise and to Bargain Collectively, July 1, 1949, 96 U.N.T.S. 257 (entered into force July 18, 1951); International Labour Organization, Convention Concerning Equal Remuneration for Men and Women Workers for Work of Equal Value, June 29, 1951, 165 U.N.T.S. 303 (entered into force May 23, 1953); International Labour Organization, Convention Concerning the Abolition of Forced Labour Convention, June 25, 1957, 320 U.N.T.S. 291 (entered into force Jan. 17, 1959); International Labour Organization, Convention Concerning Discrimination in Respect of Employment and Occupation, June 25, 1958, 362 U.N.T.S. 31 (entered into force June 15, 1960); International Labour Organization, Convention Concerning Minimum Age for Admission to Employment, June 26, 1973, 115 U.N.T.S. 298 (entered into force June 19, 1976); International Labour Organization, Convention the Prohibition and Immediate Action for the Elimination of the Worst Forms of Child Labour, June 17, 1999, 233 U.N.T.S. 161 (entered into force Nov. 19, 2000).

127. International Labour Conference, Geneva, Switz., June 18, 1998, *International Labour Organization Declaration on Fundamental Principles and Rights at Work and Its Follow-up*, at 1237-38, 37 I.L.M. 1237 (Annex rev. June 15, 2010). For further discussions about the customary law nature of the core rights reaffirmed in the ILO Declaration, see Yves Daudet, *Preface to* LAURENCE DUBIN, LA PROTECTION DES NORMES SOCIALES DANS LES ÉCHANGES INTERNATIONAUX, 3, 3-4 (Presses Universitaires d'Aix-Marseilles ed., 2003); Federico Lenzerini, *International Trade and Child Labour Standards*, *in* ENVIRONMENT, HUMAN RIGHTS AND INTERNATIONAL TRADE 287, 308 (Francesco Francioni ed., 2001); Edward E. Potter, *A Pragmatic Assessment from the Employers' Perspective*, *in* WORKERS' RIGHTS AS HUMAN RIGHTS 118, 123 (James A. Gross ed., 2003); Phillip Alston, *'Core Labour Standards' and the Transformation of International Labour Rights Regime*, 15 EUR. J. INT'L L. 457, 493 (2004); Janice R. Bellace, *The ILO Declaration of Fundamental Principles and Rights at Work*, 17 INT'L J. COMP. LAB. L. & INDUST. REL. 269, 272-73 (2001); Jason F. Hellwig, Note and Comment, *The Retreat of the State?: The Massachusetts Burma Law and Local Empowerment in the Context of Globalization(s)*, 18 WIS. INT'L L.J. 477, 504-05 (2000); Francis Maupain, *Revitalization Not Retreat: The Real Potential of the 1998 ILO Declaration for the Universal Protection of Workers' Rights*, 16 EUR. J. INT'L L. 439, 457-58 (2005); Jan Wouters & Bart De Meester, *The Role of International Law in Protecting Public Goods: Regional and Global Challenges* 21 (Leuven

The plain applicability of these basic rights to migrants has been further confirmed in 2004 at the 92nd International Labour Conference:

> The fundamental principles and rights at work are universal and applicable to all people in all States, regardless of the level of economic development. They thus apply to all migrant workers without distinction, whether they are temporary or permanent migrant workers, or whether they are regular migrants or migrants in an irregular situation.[128]

At the regional level, the Inter-American Court of Human Rights has come to a similar conclusion in its Advisory Opinion on *Juridical Condition and Rights of the Undocumented Migrants*.[129] The Court has deduced from the principle of non-discrimination and equality before the law some far-reaching assertions regarding labour rights of migrant workers:

> A person who enters a State and assumes an employment relationship, acquires his labor human rights in the State of employment, irrespective of his migratory status, because respect and guarantee of the enjoyment and exercise of those rights must be made without any discrimination. In this way, the migratory status of a person can never be a justification for depriving him of the enjoyment and exercise of his human rights, including those related to employment.[130]

V. CONCLUSION

Migration is framed by general international law. This has always been the case even if the trivialisation of immigration control has contributed to obscuring the role of international norms to such an extent that this field is

---

Interdisciplinary Research Grp. on Int'l Agreements & Dev., Working Paper No. 1, 2003). One should add that discrimination in employment is defined by Art. 1(1) of ILO Convention No. 111 as comprising "any distinction, exclusion or preference made on the basis of race, colour, sex, religion, political opinion, national extraction or social origin, which has the effect of nullifying or impairing equality of opportunity or treatment in employment or occupation." International Labour Organization, Convention Concerning Discrimination in Respect of Employment and Occupation art. 1, ¶ 1, June 25, 1958, 362 U.N.T.S. 31 (entered into force June 15, 1960). However, the prohibited ground of "national origin" that is traditionally retained in this kind of non-discrimination clause was substituted by the more ambiguous term "national extraction." *Id.*

128. International Labour Conference, June 1-17, 2004, *Towards a Fair Deal for Migrant Workers in the Global Economy*, ¶ 229.

129. Juridicial Condition and Rights of Undocumented Migrants, Advisory Opinion OC-18/03, Inter-Am. Ct. H.R. (ser. A) No. 18 (Sept. 17, 2003).

130. *Id.* ¶¶ 133-34. The rights in question notably include the prohibition of forced labour and child labour, freedom of association and to organize and join a trade union, fair wages and social security. *Id.* ¶ 157. For other regional restatements of non-discrimination in relation to economic and social rights of migrants, see Inst. for Human Rights & Dev. in Afr. (IHRDA) v. Republic of Angola, Comm. No. 292/2004, 2008 AHRLR 43, ¶ 80 (ACHPR 2008); International Federation of Human Rights Leagues (FIDH) v. France, Complaint No. 14/2003, ¶¶ 30-32 (Eur. Comm. of Social Rights May 4, 2005), *available at* http://www.coe.int/t/e/human_rights/esc/4_collective_complaints/list_of_collective_complaints/CC14Merits_en.pdf.

frequently confused with domestic jurisdiction. This article makes clear that the human rights of migrants are an integral part of public international law and mirror its broader evolution.

The main challenge remains in its implementation at the domestic level. This is arguably not so different from many other branches of international law which are at the crossroads of state sovereignty and individuals' rights (such as the law of armed conflicts). Nevertheless it has become a common place to observe the "gulf between proclaimed standards and their application to migrants," as regularly denounced by non-governmental organizations and the UN.[131] Migrants are structurally vulnerable to abuses as non-citizens, and their undocumented status can aggravate such vulnerability.[132] Other external factors—such as recurrent economic crises, the spectre of terrorist violence, political manipulations, and electioneering—have led to an environment fertile to violations of migrants' rights.

Nonetheless, the last decade has witnessed a growing awareness of their vulnerability and the corresponding need to ensure due respect for migrants' rights. A plethora of initiatives and instruments have been adopted by states and international organisations[133] with the result that "migrants' rights today are more clearly recognizable as human and labour rights."[134] From a more general perspective, this ongoing tension between rights and reality echoes the schizophrenic nature of an international legal system which is grounded on two contradictory driving forces. On the one hand, due respect of non-discrimination is primarily ensured by a decentralised scheme entrusted to nation states. On the other hand, the "universal respect for, and observance of, human rights and fundamental freedoms for all without distinction" is acknowledged as one of the founding principles of the international legal

---

131. Cholewinski, *supra* note 6, at 180.

132. Jorge A. Bustamante, *Extreme Vulnerability of Migrants: The Cases of the United States and Mexico*, 24 GEO. IMMIGR. L.J. 565, 565-66 (2010).

133. In addition to the already substantial number of resolutions and related soft law instruments mentioned above from footnotes 47 to 54, see U.N. High Comm'r for Refugees, Refugee Protection and Mixed Migration: A 10-Point Plan of Action (Jan. 2007); Council of Eur., Comm. of Ministers, *Twenty Guidelines on Forced Return*, 925th mtg., Doc. No. CM/Del/Dec(2005)924/10.1 (2005); Eur. Parl. Ass., *Resolution 1509: Human Rights of Irregular Migrants*, Doc. No. 10924 (2006); International Organization for Migration, *International Agenda for Migration Management: Common Understandings and Effective Practices for a Planned, Balanced, and Comprehensive Approach to the Management of Migration* 26-30 (Dec. 16-17, 2004). Though it cannot be confused with soft law instruments adopted by States and international organizations, similar academic initiatives can play a role for raising awareness of migrant's rights and promoting their effective respect. This is the noble purpose of the International Migrant Bill of Rights Initiative, which started in 2008 as a student-led project through Georgetown Law's Global Law Scholars Program. This twenty-three-article Bill of Rights mainly restates, sometimes elaborates and further develops well-established norms of international law though. INT'L MIGRANTS BILL OF RIGHTS (Int'l Migrants Bill of Rights Initiative 2014), *available at* http://www.law.georgetown.edu/academics/centers-institutes/isim/imbr/IMBR-Info.cfm, 28 GEO. IMMIGR. L.J. 9 (2014). As rightly observed by Gerald Neuman, it appears to be "a manifesto in the shape of a restatement." Gerald Neuman, *A Migrants' Bill of Rights—Between Restatement and Manifesto*, 24 GEO. IMMIGR. L.J. 685, 686 (2010).

134. Ryszard Cholewinski, *Human Rights of Migrants: The Dawn of A New Era?*, 24 GEO. IMMIGR. L.J. 585, 614 (2010).

order instituted by the UN Charter.[135] But much more remains to be done to draw all the normative and practical consequences for those who are not nationals of the country in which they live.

135. U.N. Charter, art. 55, para. c.

[2]

NATIONALITY AND ALIENAGE*

John Finnis

I. CONSTITUTIONAL PRINCIPLES: BASIC ASPECTS OF OUR COMMON GOOD

Our courts call some principles of our law 'constitutional'.[1] Some rights, too, were picked out as constitutional, well before the courts were charged with enforcing rights as 'human'.[2] Constitutional principles and rights prevail over ordinary norms of statutory interpretation; the presumption that statutes do not overturn these rights and principles qualifies the ordinary subordination of common law to parliamentary authority. They correspond to aspects of our common good which are of special concern to the judiciary. Many of them concern the responsibility of the courts themselves to be available to all, not least to protect everyone within their jurisdiction from legally unwarranted detention.

'The power to admit, exclude and expel aliens was among the earliest and most widely recognized powers of the sovereign state',[3] and the power

* 2007a ('Nationality, Alienage and Constitutional Principle'). Secs V and VI of the published original are here omitted for reasons of space. They argue that the widely acclaimed decision of the House of Lords in *A v Secretary of State for the Home Department* [2004] UKHL 56, [2005] 2 AC 68 was not only inattentive to the constitutional principle articulated in this essay but also radically erroneous because entirely neglectful of both (a) the court's duty under the Human Rights Act 1998, s. 3(1) to interpret legislation 'so far as it is possible to do so... in a way which is compatible with the [European] Convention [on Human Rights] rights' imported into English law by that Act and (b) the obvious possibility and good sense of reading the relevant statutory provision of the Anti-Terrorism, Crime and Security Act 2001 as authorizing detention of alien suspected international terrorists *just so long as good faith efforts* were demonstrably being made to deport them.

[1] e.g. *A v Secretary of State for the Home Department (No. 2)* [2005] UKHL 71, [2006] 2 AC 221 at paras 12, 51; *R (Gillan) v Commissioner of Police for the Metropolis* [2006] UKHL 12, [2006] 2 AC 307 at para. 1.

[2] *Bray v Ford* [1896] AC 44 at 49; *Scott v Scott* [1913] AC 417 at 477 (Lord Shaw of Dunfermline); Church of England Assembly (Powers) Act 1919, s. 3(3); *Wheeler v Leicester City Council* [1985] AC 1054 at 1065 (CA, Browne-Wilkinson LJ, dissenting).

[3] *R (European Roma Rights Centre) v Immigration Officer at Prague Airport* [2004] UKHL 55, [2005] 2 AC 1 at para. 11 (Lord Bingham of Cornhill).

remains 'undoubted'.[4] But unless it is understood to be a constitutional principle, or the instrument of constitutional principle, the power will crumble, eroded by newly enforceable constitutional principles of equality before the law, and by rights as ancient as liberty (immunity from coercion or imprisonment) or as newly fecund as 'respect for [one's] private life'. For *principle*, adequately conceived, is not merely a matter of general normative propositions; more fundamentally, it retains its connotative link to *principium*, a starting point and source. And the source of normativity, in legal or moral schemes of right, is value, purpose, point—in short, common good. So the power of exclusion needs to be understood with its underlying principle, which in turn needs to be understood as one of those elements of the common good which the law of our constitution articulates and promotes.

The fundamentally equal protection which our law has long accorded aliens (foreigners)[5] within the realm is grounded on a venerable constitutional maxim of reciprocity: presence within the realm entitles foreigners to the protection of subjects and with it the obligations of subjects. Taken with the abolition of banishment as an option for dealing with risks posed by our own nationals, and the contemporaneous re-articulation of the liability of foreigners to be expelled when their presence is responsibly determined to be adverse to our public good, it yields a principle of constitutional weight:

> Risks to the public good that must be accepted when posed by the potential conduct of a national (citizen) need not be accepted when posed by a foreigner, and may be obviated by the foreigner's exclusion or expulsion.

Though a foreigner's legally cognizable misconduct, actual or reasonably apprehended, does not automatically nullify the onerous obligations of protection which our law and government accept as arising from his presence, the consequent damage or risk to the common good entitles the public authorities to prevent or terminate that presence by lawful process. A foreigner's recalcitrant failure to assimilate his conduct, in matters of weight, to the particular conceptions of common and public good that are embodied in our constitution and law can lawfully and appropriately be met by refusing him entry, or requiring his departure. These applications of the deep principle of reciprocity cohere with, support, and are supported by the mutual trust, the give and take, and tolerance of shared risks that

[4] Counsel for seven of the nine appellant applicant detainees in *A v Secretary of State for the Home Department* [2004] UKHL 56, [2005] 2 AC 68 at 78.

[5] This essay uses these two words interchangeably and synonymously, to mean non-national/non-citizen.

are a precondition for democracy, social welfare, the defence of the realm, and the constitutional rule of law. The Lords in *A v Home Secretary* (2004)[6] were led away from these constitutional principles by argumentation which seems partly erroneous and partly *per incuriam*.[7]

II. ALIENS AS CONDITIONAL SUBJECTS

The maxim of reciprocity was articulated by Coke, with the Lord Chancellor and almost all England's judges, in *Calvin's Case* (1608): *protectio trahit subjectionem, et subjectio protectionem*: protection entails subjection, and the status of subject entails entitlement to protection by Crown, law, and courts.[8] So the presence within the realm of a friendly (non-enemy) alien, by drawing with it the protection of those institutions, entails the alien's duty of allegiance during his stay.[9] Commenting on Littleton, Coke would ground the legal status of foreigners present within the realm upon their right to sue in personal actions, a right he was the first to assert firmly.[10] Magna Carta, regularly treated by Coke as declaring common law rights, had distinguished enemy from non-enemy foreigners (s. 41). So the supposed incapacity of aliens to pursue personal actions at law was limited, he concluded, to enemy aliens: subjects of a state at war with the Crown.

Thus, in the seventeenth-century doctrinal and political settlement which shapes the constitutions of English-speaking countries around the world, foreigners within the realm (speaking always of non-enemy aliens)[11] enjoy the subject's common law right to freedom from every act of a government servant or agent which if done by a private person would be a tort. Because the Crown can neither do nor authorize wrong, any such act of an official against an alien must be tortious unless demonstrably warranted by common law or statute.[12] And this inference will underlie both the doubt of eighteenth-century lawyers about the existence of a prerogative of expelling aliens, and the Crown's long abstention from

[6] *A v Secretary of State for the Home Department* [2004] UKHL 56, [2005] 2 AC 68.

[7] In this the case resembles other notable cases where skilful advocacy led the House of Lords unanimously astray: e.g. *Haughton v Smith* [1975] AC 476, and again *Anderton v Ryan* [1985] AC 560. *A v Home Secretary* is not quite unanimous, but Lord Walker of Gestingthorpe's dissent scarcely challenges the six majority judgments at their questionable roots.

[8] *Calvin's Case* (1608) 7 Co Rep 1a, 5a; *Joyce v DPP* [1946] AC 347 at 366.

[9] *Calvin's Case* at 5b–6a.

[10] Coke, *Commentary on Littleton* (1628), 129b; Hale, *Historia Placitorum Coronae* (1678) I, 542 ratifies the doctrine; Holdsworth, *Hist.* ix, 95.

[11] But 'even alien enemies, if they were resident in this country with the express or even with the tacit permission of the Crown, must be treated as alien friends': Holdsworth, *Hist.* x, 396; ix, 101. Holdsworth's 'must' takes for granted that Parliament can dispose otherwise.

[12] Holdsworth, *Hist.* ix, 98.

purported exercise of it. If expulsion were by royal proclamation, defiance of it must go without penalty since the Crown cannot make criminal what hitherto was not criminal.[13] But if it were by arrest, detention, and forcible movement towards the boundaries of the realm, would it not be mere assault, trespass, and false imprisonment, axiomatically incapable of non-statutory authorization, and liable to the alien's personal action for damages against the officers and their agents? Dicey dramatized the constitutional position evocatively, in 1885: if 'foreign anarchists come to England and are thought by the police on strong grounds of suspicion to be engaged in a plot, say for blowing up the Houses of Parliament', but the responsible minister is not in a position to put them on trial, there are 'no means of arresting them, or of expelling them from the country'. No rule of common or statutory law authorized interference with their liberty, Dicey implied, and their application for habeas corpus must succeed.[14]

But when Dicey last passed this passage for the press in 1908, the law had begun to leave him behind. In authorizing detention pending deportation, the Aliens Act 1905 did not deal with Dicey's unconvicted foreign terrorists.[15] But soon after its enactment, the Judicial Committee of the Privy Council articulated constitutional foundations for doing so:

> One of the rights possessed by the supreme power in every State is the right to refuse to permit an alien to enter that State, to annex what conditions it pleases to the permission to enter it, and to expel or deport from the State, at pleasure, even a friendly alien, especially if it considers his presence in the State opposed to its peace, order, and good government, or to its social or material interests: *Vattel, Law of Nations* book 1 s. 231; book 2, s. 125.[16]

By carefully not specifying 'the supreme power of the State', the Privy Council skirted the unresolved question whether *our* executive has any inherent power of excluding foreigners, or is altogether dependent upon parliamentary authority for doing so.

Johnstone v Pedlar (1921) riveted into our constitution the fundamental and extensive equality, within the realm, of friendly aliens and British nationals. But each Law Lord pointed, without deciding, to a prerogative or inherent power of the Crown to 'revoke its licence expressed or implied to

[13] *Case of Proclamations* (1611) 12 Co Rep 74 at 75, 76.

[14] Dicey, *Introduction to the Study of the Law of the Constitution* (1st edn, 1885), 239–40; (7th edn, 1908), 226–7.

[15] On the occasion and limited purpose of the Aliens Act 1905, see Beatson, 'Aliens, Friendly Aliens and Friendly Enemy Aliens' at 80.

[16] *A-G for Canada v Cain* [1906] AC 542, 546, quoted in the single judgment in *R (Saadi) v Secretary of State for the Home Department* [2002] UKHL 41, [2002] 1 WLR 3131 at para. 31, and described there as 'this principle'; quoted by Lord Bingham in *R (European Roma Rights) v Prague Immigration Officer* [2004] UKHL 55, [2005] 2 AC 1 at para. 12.

an alien to reside'.[17] The Crown having made no such purported revocation, its officer's seizure of the alien Pedlar's money was simply tortious, and actionable at his suit, despite all the trappings of a Secretary of State's ratification and the treasonable savour of the alien's activities. The issues, decided and undecided, rest today where the Privy Council left them in 1906 and 1921: there is constitutional authority, whether by prerogative or not,[18] to exclude an alien in the interests of the community's well-being. Since 1919, at latest, Parliament as the state's supreme authority has vigorously asserted, and ever more carefully regulated, our state's (nation's, political community's) capacity lawfully and rightfully to exclude.[19]

III. THE DEVELOPED CONSTITUTIONAL DIFFERENTIATION AND ITS PRINCIPLE

The legislation made by or under parliamentary authority during the first twenty years of the twentieth century defines principal effects of the constitutional distinction between nationals and aliens. Aliens have no liberty to enter the realm without leave of an immigration officer, may be admitted subject to 'such conditions as the Secretary of State may think fit',[20] and may be deported either (i) if a court sentencing them for an offence punishable only with imprisonment so recommends and the Secretary of State concurs or (ii) 'if the Secretary of State deems it to be conducive to the public good'.[21] Where a deportation order has been made, or a certificate has been given by a court with a view to the Secretary of State making such an order, a foreigner may be detained pending removal.[22] This basic pattern of duties and (Hohfeldian) liabilities is confirmed in the next great settling of status, the Immigration Act 1971, which begins with 'General Principles':

1. All those who are in this Act expressed to have the right of abode in the United Kingdom shall be free to live in, and to come and go into and

[17] [1921] 2 AC 263 at 283, per Lord Atkinson; see also 273 (Viscount Finlay), 276 (Viscount Cave), 293–4 (Lord Sumner, concessively), 297 (Lord Phillimore). Holdsworth, *Hist.* x, 393–400, assembles the seventeenth-century practices and judicial dicta, and the eighteenth and nineteenth-century opinions of lawyers, firmly asserting a prerogative of both exclusion and expulsion.

[18] Prerogative powers are preserved, if not asserted, in successive statutory saving clauses, e.g. Immigration Act 1971, s. 33(5).

[19] See Aliens Restriction Act 1919, authorizing the Aliens Order 1920, S.R. & O. 1920/448 and 2262. The Order as amended remained in force until 1953, its provisions being eventually transformed into the Immigration Act 1971 and the associated Immigration Rules.

[20] Aliens Order 1920, art. 1(4).

[21] *Ibid.*, art. 12(6)(c).

[22] *Ibid.*, art. 12(4). Powers of detention pending actual removal from the realm were created by the Aliens Act 1905, e.g. s. 7(3) (detention in custody awaiting a ship's departure or pending the Secretary of State's determination after certification by a court of conviction for a deportable offence).

from, the United Kingdom without let or hindrance except such as may be required under and in accordance with this Act to enable their right to be established or as may be otherwise lawfully imposed on any person.

2. Those not having that right may live, work and settle in the United Kingdom by permission and subject to such regulation and control of their entry into, stay in and departure from the United Kingdom as is imposed by this Act....

The right of abode, under the Act, is defined in the next section as belonging to United Kingdom citizens (since 1981 called British citizens) and a now vestigial sub-class of Commonwealth citizens. The third section's 'general provisions for regulation and control' provide first for exclusion—grant or refusal of leave to enter, and the conditions which may be attached to such leave, all regulated by Rules made under parliamentary scrutiny—and then for expulsion by deportation of any who overstay their leave of entry or fail to observe any of its conditions, or who obtain leave to enter by deception, or are recommended by a court for deportation on their conviction for an imprisonable offence,[23] or whose deportation the Secretary of State 'deems to be *conducive to the public good*'. More drastically, the British Nationality Act 1981, s. 40,[24] empowers the Secretary of State to make an order depriving of that status a British citizen who, he is satisfied, has done 'anything seriously prejudicial to the vital interests of the United Kingdom or a British overseas territory', unless such deprivation would result in statelessness.

The constitutional scheme's main features embody two legal constitutional principles, each resting on a moral-constitutional principle. (1) Subject to the limitations on employment or occupation that may have been imposed as conditions of their entry, and to liabilities which, for all foreigners, are entailed by the Crown's authority to expel them, non-enemy aliens present within the realm have all the rights and obligations that nationals have.[25] This rests on the justificatory (moral-constitutional) principle that resident aliens, having the duties of subjects, should reciprocally enjoy the rights of subjects. (2) The citizen, on the other hand,

[23] For the principles on which the courts exercise this function, see *R v Nazari* [1980] 1 WLR 1366; [1980] 3 All ER 880, CA. A court's refusal to make such a recommendation creates no presumption that the Secretary of State should not order deportation, although the court's recommendation does create some presumption in favour of such an order: *M v Secretary of State for the Home Department* [2003] EWCA Civ 146, [2003] 1 WLR 1980.

[24] As substituted by Nationality, Immigration and Asylum Act 2002, s. 4. On the wider (in certain respects) effect of s. 40 as enacted in 1981, see *Secretary of State for the Home Department v Hicks* [2006] EWCA Civ 400, [2006] INLR 203.

[25] *R v Secretary of State for the Home Department, ex p. Khawaja* [1984] 1 AC 74 at 111–12, per Lord Scarman. The alien's rights are subject to another exception: those rights that, as Aristotle said, define the central case and focal sense of citizenship, viz., rights of participation in governing (electorally, legislatively, executively, or judicially): *Pol.* III.1, 2 and 7; *NLNR* 253–4, 259.

can never be excluded from the realm: this was the trajectory and principle[26] albeit not the letter[27] of our law long before the United Kingdom signed up to a strict articulation of that proposition in Art. 3 of Protocol No. 4 (1963) to the European Convention on Human Rights ('ECHR').[28]

What principle underlies the executive's authority—now highly regulated both legislatively and judicially[29]—to exclude foreigners? Connoted by 'not conducive to the public good' (which doubtless means 'in some way deleterious to, or putting at risk, the public good'), the principle is this: the political community, while it cannot shift to other communities the risks presented by one of its own nationals,[30] need not unconditionally accept the *risk presented by aliens*. That is, the presence in the community of an alien who, individually considered,[31] can fairly be said to present some genuine *risk*, even relatively slight, to the rights of others, or to national security, public safety, the prevention of crime, the protection of health or morals or maintenance of *l'ordre public*, or to anything else of 'public interest in a democratic society', *need not be accepted*. Instead such risk can properly be sought to be prevented by exclusion, or terminated by expulsion, on the grounds that such presence within the community, even if it has not been already forfeited by commission of an imprisonable offence, is nonetheless 'not conducive to the public good'.

This principle is fully compatible with our moral and legal obligations to accept refugees or other immigrants, and to accept some costs and burdens in doing so. Vattel said that 'the first general law to be found in the very end of the society of nations is that each nation should contribute as far as it can to the happiness and advancement of other nations,'[32] and that 'no nation may, without good reason, refuse even a perpetual residence to one who has

[26] See e.g. Co. Litt. 133a; Blackstone, *Commentaries* I, 133 [137]; Holdsworth, *Hist.* x, 393.

[27] Provisions enacted in 1829 for the banishment or transportation for life of e.g. Jesuits were not repealed until the Roman Catholic Relief Act 1926, but had long been in desuetude. On expatriation, banishment and related concepts, see *Trop v Dulles* 356 US 86 (1958) at 102.

[28] Lest it confer a right of abode on certain classes of people belonging to present or former dependent territories, the United Kingdom has not yet ratified the Fourth Protocol, which subject to the usual kinds of authorized restrictions provides that 'No one shall be expelled, by means either of an individual or of a collective measure, from the territory of the State of which he is a national' and 'No one shall be deprived of the right to enter the territory of the state of which he is a national'.

[29] Immigration Act 1971, s. 15(1), conferring rights of appeal against any deportation order except (by s. 15(3)) any order made purportedly 'in the interests of national security or of the relations between the United Kingdom and any other country or for other reasons of a political nature'; that exception was disapproved by the European Court of Human Rights ('ECtHR') in *Chahal v United Kingdom* (1996) 23 EHRR 413, resulting in the rights of appeal to a Special Immigration Appeals Commission ('SIAC') established by the Special Immigration Appeals Commission Act 1997. See *Secretary of State for the Home Department v Rehman* [2001] UKHL 47, [2003] 1 AC 153.

[30] Dual nationality would be accommodated by a more precise statement of the principle.

[31] ECHR Protocol No. 6, Art. 4: 'Collective expulsion of aliens is prohibited.' Exclusion (denial of permission to enter) of wide classes (collectivities) of foreigners on grounds of their numbers or their collective characteristics is a different matter.

[32] Vattel, *Le Droit des Gens* (1758), Introduction sec. 13.

been driven from his country',[33] or to a body of fugitives or exiles unless its own territory 'could scarcely supply the needs of its own citizens'.[34] We might accept all this and more—even an extensive immigration programme, adopted as a duty of justice[35]—and yet justly demand of the foreigners that, at peril of being expelled (even if only to make way for others), they abstain from conduct (act or omission) that damages or puts at risk the public good. Indeed, we might hold that the more extensive the nation's willingness to accept newcomers, the less willing it need be to accept dangers created by the presence, especially the actual or reasonably foreseeable conduct, of particular foreigners (or, indeed—while eschewing collective expulsion—particular kinds of foreigners).

IV. DETENTION PENDING (WITH A PURPOSE OF) REMOVAL

The principle that *risks to the public good which must be accepted when arising from the presence of a national need not be accepted from the presence of an alien and may be obviated by the alien's exclusion or expulsion* has long been recognized as having an immediate practical consequence. Foreigners who are to be lawfully removed from the country may be detained pending their removal. Indeed, where reasonable grounds appear for investigating and deciding whether to remove particular foreigners, they may be detained pending the decision and its execution. Provision for such detention was made in the Aliens Act 1905 and more fully in all later enactments governing expulsion. The ECHR provides in Art. 5(1)(f) that the right to liberty and security of person is not infringed by '(f) the lawful... detention of a person... against whom action is being taken with a view to deportation...'.

The key concept in Art. 5(1)(f) is of ongoing purposive activity: the detention must at all times be part of action being taken 'with a view to' the non-citizen's removal from the territory. Likewise, in the governing provision of the Immigration Act 1971, Sch. 3, para. 2(3):

> Where a deportation order is in force against any person, he may be detained under the authority of the Secretary of State pending his removal or departure from the United Kingdom...

[33] *Ibid.*, book I sec. 231. [34] *Ibid.*

[35] The original commonality of all the earth's resources, as available in justice for all and each of earth's human inhabitants, is abrogated neither by the instituting of private property (see n. 62 below) nor by the appropriation of territories to states; and just as property rights are subject to a kind of moral trust or 'social mortgage' (a requirement of justice not merely of charity) for the benefit of the poor in their necessity (see *Aquinas* 188–96; *NLNR* 169–73), so the right of states to exclude aliens from their territory is subject in principle to an analogous qualification or burden. See sec. V below, and essays 7 and 8.

Here an ongoing purpose of removal is connoted not only by the word 'pending' but by the provision on which Sch. 3 depends, s. 5(5).[36]

As judicially interpreted, these provisions for detention 'pending' and 'with a view to' deportation, like similar provisions in other countries, fall far short of providing that an alien against whom a deportation order has been made may be detained for as long as ministers wish and regardless of their purposes and methods. The *locus classicus* is a dictum, largely if not wholly obiter, of Woolf J in *ex parte Hardial Singh* (1984). The case concerned very dilatory arrangements for a deportation, but there was little or no suggestion that deportation might even temporarily be 'impossible', in the sense of prevented by obstacles immovable for the foreseeable future. However, Woolf J's statement concerns itself mainly with that hypothesis, although it does not neglect to give primacy to *purpose of removal*:

> Although the power which is given to the Secretary of State in paragraph 2 to detain individuals is not subject to any express limitation of time, I am quite satisfied that it is subject to limitations. First of all, it can only authorise detention if the individual is being detained...pending his removal. *It cannot be used for any other purpose.* Secondly, as the power is given in order to enable the machinery of deportation to be carried out, I regard the power of detention as being impliedly limited to a period which is *reasonably necessary for that purpose.* The period which is reasonable will depend upon the circumstances of the particular case. What is more, if there is a situation where it is apparent to the Secretary of State that he is not going to be able to operate the machinery provided in the Act for removing persons who are intended to be deported within a reasonable period, it seems to me that it would be wrong for the Secretary of State to seek to exercise his power of detention.[37]

Woolf J here assumes that inability to deport 'within a reasonable period' is somehow incompatible with maintaining and acting on a purpose of deporting, and/or with that being reasonable. As will become apparent, such an assumption is questionable and has been challenged both legislatively and judicially.

Woolf J's dicta were treated as a sound guide in interpreting Hong Kong's more elaborate statutory provisions in *Tan Te Lam v Superintendent of Tai A Chau Detention Centre* (1996).[38] The Judicial Committee of the Privy Council ruled that 'if it becomes clear that removal is not going to be possible within a reasonable time, further detention is not authorized'. But dicta and ruling alike were treated as implications of a governing

[36] Immigration Act 1971, s. 5(5): 'The provisions of Schedule 3...shall have effect with respect to...the detention...of persons *in connection with deportation*' (emphasis added).

[37] *R v Governor of Durham Prison, ex p. Hardial Singh* [1984] 1 WLR 704 at 706 (emphases added). The suggestion that detention might be improper *ab initio* goes wider than the treatment of Art. 5(1)(f) in *Chahal v United Kingdom*, 23 EHHR 413; see nn. 55–8 below.

[38] [1997] AC 97.

principle: 'in conferring such a power to interfere with individual liberty the legislature intended that such power could only be exercised reasonably'.[39] The Judicial Committee expressed agreement with the trial judge's findings that, although the period during which the applicant Vietnamese boat people had been in detention pending deportation (in one case over five years in all)[40] was 'truly shocking' and 'at first blush, an affront to the standards of...civilized society', it was *nonetheless reasonable* and lawful, given circumstances such as the policies and practices of the Vietnamese authorities, the refusal of some detainees to apply for repatriation, and in another case the detainee's apparent withdrawal of his application.[41]

Detention for removal was subjected to a 'reasonable length of time' limitation, by constitutionally motivated statutory interpretation, in the US Supreme Court's decision in *Zadvydas v Davis* ten weeks before 9/11 (the New York and Washington atrocities of 11 September 2001).[42] The statute provided for a ninety-day removal period, after which certain categories of foreigners (criminals, security risks, persons certified likely to abscond or a risk to the community, etc.)[43] 'may be detained beyond the removal period and, if released, shall be subject to... supervision'. By majority the Court held that this post-'removal period' detention could[44] continue only 'for such time as is reasonably necessary to secure the alien's removal', and presumptively only for a further ninety days, after which even criminal or risky aliens would be entitled to release if they 'provide good reason to believe that there is no significant likelihood of removal in the reasonably foreseeable future'.[45] Reasonableness is to be measured 'primarily in terms of the statute's basic purpose, namely assuring the alien's presence at the moment of removal'.[46] The consequent risks to the public could be obviated:

> the alien's release may and should be conditioned on any of the various forms of supervised release that are appropriate in the circumstances, and the alien may no doubt be returned to custody upon a violation of those conditions.[47]

[39] *Ibid.* at 111.

[40] By the time of the determination of the appeal, 40 months 'pending removal'.

[41] [1997] AC at 109, 114–15 (no need to decide, since applicants successful on another ground).

[42] 533 US 678, 150 L Ed 2d 653 (2001).

[43] But in the case of terrorist aliens ordered to be removed but whom 'no country is willing to receive', Congress had authorized the Attorney-General 'notwithstanding any law, [to] retain the alien in custody' on six-monthly administrative review, a provision noted without adverse comment by the Court (533 US at 697).

[44] The Court (at 696) seems to accept that, notwithstanding the resident alien's constitutionally significant liberty interest, Congress could have authorized (if sufficiently explicit about its intent) the indefinite detention of a deportee for whom there was no reasonable prospect of finding any receiving country within a reasonable period.

[45] 533 US at 701. [46] 533 US at 699. [47] 533 US at 700.

The Court seems to imply that such conditions of supervision, perhaps stringent, might equally be 'indefinite and potentially permanent', so long as the certified flight risk or danger to the community persists and is reaffirmed from time to time with procedural due process, and provided always that the government's purpose remains to deport this person as soon as possible.

Into the notably more severe[48] Australian statutory scheme—mandatory removal of all unlawful non-citizens 'as soon as reasonably practicable' and *mandatory* detention 'until . . . removed'—the High Court read restrictions pertaining to the purpose of the detention as ancillary to the purpose of removal. Although *Al Kateb v Godwin*[49] (6 August 2004) declines to read into the statute a temporal limitation of the *Hardial* or *Zadvydas* type (terminating detention when there is 'no real likelihood or prospect of removal in the reasonably foreseeable future'), it implicitly accepts[50] the Solicitor-General's submission that 'detention cannot continue indefinitely without bona fide efforts being made to remove the detainee, and the court has power to order that reasonable efforts be made' and to 'review . . . whether reasonable efforts are being made to effect removal'.[51] The majority Justices[52] vigorously reject the claim that extended or even indefinite delay is incompatible with maintaining the indispensable *purpose* of deporting the detainee. As Hayne J (Heydon J agreeing) puts it:

> the most that could ever be said in a particular case where it is not now, and has not been, reasonably practicable to effect removal, is that there is *now* no country which will receive a particular non-citizen whom Australia seeks to remove, and it cannot *now* be predicted when that will happen. . . . That is not to say that it will *never* happen.

[48] Note, however, that ECHR Art. 5(1)(f), on its face, authorizes detention without limit of time 'to prevent [a person's] effecting an unauthorized entry into the country'.

[49] [2004] HCA 37, (2004) 219 CLR 562, decided simultaneously with *Minister for Immigration & Multicultural & Indigenous Affairs v Al Khafaji* [2004] HCA 38, (2004) 219 CLR 664, with the same majority (McHugh, Hayne, Callinan, and Heydon JJ) and minority.

[50] See [224–5] (Hayne J, Heydon J agreeing), [294] (Callinan J, who at [290–1], however, goes further and holds that the purpose of removing the detainee is to be presumed unless 'formally and unequivocally abandoned'—perhaps too narrow a version of the implied limitation by purpose).

[51] 219 CLR at 567 per Bennett S-G., who prefaced this with: 'Removal will never be impossible because it is always possible that there will be a change of regime or a change of mind in the subject country or that some other country will take an altruistic view.'

[52] Gleeson CJ, dissenting, also accepted that 'it cannot be said that it will never be reasonably practicable to remove [the detainee]'. But he considered that where removal is not 'currently practicable, and is not likely to become practicable in the foreseeable future', the detention's primary purpose of removal is 'in suspense' (para. 18), and that in respect of such cases the statute should be presumed not to have intended to authorize indefinite detention regardless of 'the circumstances of individual cases, including, in particular, danger to the community and likelihood of absconding' (para. 22).

Even a finding of '"no real likelihood or prospect of removal in the reasonably foreseeable future"... does not mean that continued detention is not for the purpose of subsequent removal' or that the purpose of detention for removal is spent.[53] What matters is that the executive keep trying to carry out their duty to remove, by taking what reasonable steps they can to accomplish what may at present seem not reasonably practicable.

Had *Al Kateb* been cited in *A v Home Secretary* (argued in October 2004), neither counsel nor Law Lords could have been as carefree as they were in treating the appellant detainees as persons who *'cannot'* be deported, a simplification which reaches its extreme in Baroness Hale of Richmond's summary: 'These foreigners are only being detained because they cannot be deported. They are just like a British national who cannot be deported'![54] The Australian majority judges, like the dissenters in *Zadvydas*, demonstrate that what is 'temporarily impossible', or 'not possible for the indefinite future', may tomorrow become possible because of some change of regime abroad, or a breakthrough in negotiations with some other state; and that therefore it would be quite wrong to treat either of these phrases (or other similar phrases) as equivalent to '[simply] impossible [in practice]'. Removal in such a situation (assuming always that the executive had not begun to treat removal as impossible, and ceased trying to work around the obstacles) would better be said to be 'prevented (temporarily or indefinitely)'. And that was the language of the statutory provision condemned, with no attention to the spectrum of situations it signified, in *A v Home Secretary*.

That condemnation took the form of a declaration of incompatibility with ECHR Arts 5 and 14, made effective in the United Kingdom by the Human Rights Act 1998 ('HRA'). So the requirements stated in *Hardial* are now reinforced by Art. 5(1)(f), permitting detention while 'action is being taken with a view to deportation'. In *Chahal v United Kingdom* (1996), the ECtHR had held that, if action is being taken with due diligence[55] with a view to deportation, Art. 5(1)(f) does *not* require that the detention be considered necessary, 'for example to prevent his committing an offence or

[53] 219 CLR at paras 229, 231. To the same effect is Callinan J at paras 290, 291 and in *Al Khafaji*, 219 CLR at para. 45:

> The reference of [the trial judge] to reasonable practicability and reasonable foreseeability was directed to the situation 'at present'. The Migration Act imposes no such temporal qualification. It is to purpose [that] attention must be paid, and the purpose of deportation has not been abandoned. As I have observed in *Al-Kateb*, in the nature of human and international affairs, long periods may be involved just as circumstances may change very quickly.

[54] *A v Home Secretary* [2004] UKHL 54, [2005] 2 AC 68, para. 235; see also paras 222 and 228; the simplification is explicit in paras 9 and 13 (Bingham), 84 (Nicholls), 126 (Hope), 162 and 188 (Rodger), and 210 (Walker).

[55] 23 EHHR 413 at para. 113.

fleeing'.[56] It held, moreover, that the proceedings for Chahal's deportation had been conducted with such diligence that four (indeed, over six) years' detention of the alien deportee was compatible with Art. 5(1)(f). And this despite the fact that, so the Court also held, the purpose of deporting him to his national territory, India, was at all relevant times incompatible with the requirements of Art. 3, prohibiting torture and ill-treatment. It was not unreasonable for the Secretary of State to have taken over thirteen months to deliberate about the alien's claim that his deportation to India would contravene Art. 3. Thus the question whether an alien 'cannot be deported' (because there is a 'real risk' of torture or ill-treatment) is not open and shut, but 'involves considerations of an extremely serious and weighty nature' and decisions that should not 'be taken hastily, without due regard to all the relevant issues and evidence'.[57]

Since 1998, of course, deportation 'contrary to' Art. 3 as read or misread by *Chahal*[58] is now 'impossible', if not strictly as a matter of law (though

[56] At para. 112.

[57] At para. 117. Lord Bingham's statement in *A v Secretary of State for Home Department* at para. 9 of what *Chahal* decided about Art. 5(1)(f) is mistaken or at best elliptical:

> [the ECtHR] reasserted (para 113) that 'any deprivation of liberty under article 5(1)(f) will be justified only for as long as deportation proceedings are in progress'. In a case like Mr Chahal's, where deportation proceedings are precluded by article 3, article 5(1)(f) would not sanction detention because the non-nationals would not be 'a person against whom action is being taken with a view to deportation'.

In fact, however, the court held that, although Chahal's deportation was precluded by Art. 3, his detention for four or six years *was sanctioned* by Art. 5(1)(f) while the authorities took action to ascertain whether or not his deportation could be carried out compatibly with the United Kingdom's obligations. No doubt those authorities did not have the clear view of Art. 3 imposed in that case by the court. But even if they had had such a view, they might reasonably have taken steps, with all deliberate speed (on the part of the United Kingdom authorities) but perhaps lengthy in duration (not least if lengthened by the dilatoriness of foreign governments), to ascertain the risks and seek ways of obviating them by agreement with India or some other state.

[58] If *Chahal*'s rulings on Art. 5 are unhelpfully terse, its pronouncements on Art. 3, both in the majority and the principal dissenting judgments, are notably ill-reasoned. The absoluteness of a state's obligation not to engage in torture and other practices contrary to Art. 3 in no way entails that the person with such an absolute right has thereby the right not to be subjected to any form of treatment (e.g. deportation) that might have the foreseeable but unintended and unwelcome side effect of his being tortured or ill-treated by some other persons. All who seriously reflect upon normative absolutes recognize that they would entail intolerable paradoxes and deliberative incoherence unless their exceptionless prohibitions define the excluded conduct by reference to the *proximate intentions* (or *object*) of the person(s) they bind: see *MA* 68–74, 81–3. It is one thing for a state to deliver persons to another state *so as* to enable the latter to torture them, and quite another matter to remove/deliver them to another state with all practically possible precaution against their being tortured thereafter and with the sole object of removing the real threat their presence poses to the lives of people in the removing state. *Chahal*'s Art. 3 ruling treats the intentions of the removing state as completely irrelevant and declares that the deportee's activities, '*however undesirable or dangerous*, cannot be a material consideration' ([80], emphasis added). Taking into account Art. 3's extension beyond torture to 'degrading treatment', and the breadth of that concept in recent ECtHR jurisprudence, *Chahal*'s ruling on Art. 3 is juridically unsound by over-breadth, and shocking to conscience by its indifference to the human rights threatened *by* the would-be deportee. [The same is regrettably true of the ECtHR Grand Chamber's unanimous ratification of this central ruling in *Chahal* in *Saadi v Italy* [2008] ECHR 179, 49 EHRR 30; on all the main

that is how the courts unhesitatingly treat it), at least as a matter of treaty obligation. But even as it articulated this rule, *Chahal* made it clear that the rule's application to particular cases may involve contingencies which preclude, as unacceptably simplistic, any notion that deportation is from the outset impossible. Rather, the existence of a 'real risk' that the deportee would be tortured or ill-treated will in various cases not be so indisputable as to render deportation (and thus detention with a view to removal) impossible from the outset or at any definable moment thereafter. So this is yet another way in which the 'possibility' or 'impossibility' of removal, and of having a purpose of removing, is often relative, provisional, qualified and arguable.

V. THE CONSTITUTIONAL PRINCIPLE'S RATIONALE

What, then, is the rationale or, in the more rigid language of ECHR jurisprudence, 'legitimating aim', of the principle of nationality-differentiated risk-acceptability? What basic aspect of the common good does it represent, promote or protect?

The principle informs two undoubted rules, not merely one: foreigners can be deported; nationals cannot. Associated with the latter is the rule that nationals cannot be deprived of their citizenship if doing so would leave them without a nationality. The rules signal a fundamental understanding and disposition: the human community is politically and juridically organized into states, groups that are national political communities ('nations'). Whoever and wherever one may be, one is both entitled and bound to regard oneself as belonging to one of them: statelessness is an anomaly, a disability, and presumptively an injustice, to be systematically minimized.[59]

What constitutes such a political community? Aristotle famously tried out the hypothesis that a *polis* (state) is a set of people given identity-establishing *form* by a constitution (*politeia*), with the entailment that the identity of the *polis* (state) changes when its constitution changes, say from

points the submissions of the United Kingdom, intervening, were sound but rejected by the Court with the mantra that Art. 3 is absolute (sc. in all its extensions and applications however extended or indirect).]

[59] Measures for rectifying the anomaly are instituted by the Convention relating to the Status of Stateless Persons 1954 (ratified by the United Kingdom in 1959 and in force since 1960), which provides for the state of their lawful residence to treat them so far as possible as other aliens, and looks (Art. 32) towards eventual 'assimilation and naturalization', subject (Art. 2) to the stateless person's duties 'to the country in which he finds himself', in particular to 'conform to its laws and regulations as well as to measures taken for the maintenance of public order'.

a tyranny to a democracy. But this will not do, as Aristotle tacitly concedes by concluding his discussion with the question whether agreements entered into and debts incurred by the state under the previous constitution can rightly be repudiated (or regarded as nullities) by the new state—a question which he promises but fails to try to answer.[60] Working out the implications of Kelsen's and Hart's accounts of legal systems, Joseph Raz and I, quite independently, concluded that a legal system's subsisting unity through time cannot be explained without foundational reference to the group whose legal system it is.[61]

To be sure, groups with a complex and far-reaching membership and purpose such as a worldwide and ecclesial religion may reasonably organize and count themselves as having a legal system, parallel to and in principle compatible with the legal systems of the states in which their adherents are citizens. And those states are appropriately many and particular, not universal. For just as experience shows compellingly that the resources on which human life and well-being depend are best husbanded, developed, and made available by a system of appropriation of particular resources to particular owners,[62] so experience compellingly shows—and the *international* order by its structures and regulating principles confirms—that human persons need to live in polities or states, political communities which hold as their own a defined territory subject to a national legal system defining, inter alia, a national constitution.

About this need we can and should be still more specific. Addressing an ethnically and culturally diverse audience in Germany, Raz showed why political societies need a common bond. They authoritatively require individuals to make sacrifices for the benefit of other members: witness redistributive taxation and all the other institutions of the welfare state. But 'the willingness to share is not purchased easily. Without it political society soon disintegrates, or has to rely on extensive force and coercion.' And this willingness to share itself cannot be maintained without a common culture, grounding the needed 'ability of people to feel for others', which 'depends on their ability to understand and empathise with other people's experiences, aspirations and anxieties'. Thus the political unity presupposed by any welfare state

> depends on people's free and willing identification with the political society they belong to: on the fact that they feel German, that their sense of their own identity

[60] *Pol.* III.3: 1276a7–b15; *Aquinas* 28, 53.

[61] *CLS* 101–5, 188, 210; and essay IV.21 (1971a).

[62] See *NLNR* 170–1 (and see n. 35 above on the defeasibility of all such appropriations).

as German is totally instinctive and unproblematic. And it depends on the fact that they are proud to be German.[63]

States, occupying valuable territory as they do, can be confronted, moreover, with challenges more urgent and far-reaching, more existential, than maintaining the welfare state. These challenges too will call upon their members' sense of identification with their fellow members—upon the 'solidarity among citizens that', as David Miller argues, 'democratic politics requires'.[64] Much recent political theory shows how equal laws, public probity, impartial government, social justice, and democratic deliberation towards the undertaking of collective commitments and obligations and international action all depend upon—and in turn foster—a generalized trust sufficient to outweigh *competing* bonds of kin, caste, religion, or ethnicity, a level of trust and common sympathies attainable only within bounded political communities, nation-states.[65] The distinction between nationals and aliens is an indispensable framework for articulating, expressing, ratifying, and demanding such willingness to share, such awareness of being part owner of a shared inheritance and future,[66] such integration in and assimilation to *this* nation-state rather than some other.

But that willingness, as joint and common inheritors, to share a common fate, promote a common life, and accept and contribute towards common burdens and benefits, should not be conceived as suppressing the liberties of individuals, families, and other associations to occupy their own space and enjoy, as of right, their own freedom of initiative, self-direction, and self-determination. Such freedoms entail, as a side effect, the unintended but real creating of risks to others and to the common life. (This reciprocity underpins the reciprocity of protection and subjection that *Calvin's Case* articulated in the language of allegiance, language which should not obscure either the duties of governors or the truth that everyone's root political and legal-moral obligations are not so fundamentally to our rulers or institutions of governance as to our fellow subjects.[67]) The

[63] Raz, 'Multiculturalism' at 202–3. Since policies of assimilation or integration may be intended precisely to preserve the benefits, for all, of national solidarity which are so cogently described by Raz, his further thesis that such policies insult the members of immigrant cultures is mistaken.

[64] Miller, *Citizenship & National Identity*, 62.

[65] See Canovan, *Nationhood & Political Theory*, 44 and passim. To witness an unabashedly national pride—patriotism—being rooted in history and used as a ground of judicial reasoning and decision, see e.g. *A v Secretary of State for the Home Department (No. 2)* [2005] UKHL 71, [2006] 2 AC 221, at [82], [99], [152], [171]; or again *A v Secretary of State for the Home Department* [2004] UKHL 56, [2005] 2 AC 68 at [86], [96] (Lord Hoffmann).

[66] See Canovan, 54–75; also Raz, *Ethics in the Public Domain*, 172–3, on a common culture as needed for the civic solidarity which in turn is 'essential to the existence of a well-ordered political society' (172). [On this, and the issues in nn. 63–65, see essay II.7.]

[67] *NLNR* 359.

benefits of those politically (legally) respected and defended freedoms, and the burdens of the attendant risks, are part of what we share as members of this political community. And this is the rationale of the principle that we should be willing to accept from fellow members a level of adverse risk that we need not accept from non-members.

Here our constitutional law intervenes to remind us that while they are among us, non-members are to be treated as members so far as is compatible with maintaining the core of the distinction between members and non-members—between members by right and members by revocable permission. So our justifiable lesser willingness to accept risks from non-members warrants, not a set of special duties, liabilities, or disabilities of foreigners within the realm, but only their individual liability to be removed from the nation's territory and, with a view to and pending that removal, to be kept apart from the community by humane detention or control.[68]

The problem of the indefinitely 'irremovable' foreigner, as in *Zadvydas v Davis*, in *Al Kateb v Godwin*, and in *A v Home Secretary*, is a boundary problem of the intersection of these two building blocks of our constitutional scheme. The argumentation in the American and Australian judgments, majority and minority alike, reveals the problem's contours perceptively;[69] *A v Home Secretary* does not.

Beyond that boundary problem there lies, of course, the deeper challenge to constitutional order and theory posed by *nationals* who regard their nationality as a form of alienage because, doubtless like some if not all the detainees in *A v Home Secretary*, they believe their true Nation lies altogether beyond—but is ordained to have dominion over—the bounds and territories, and the constitutional principles and rights,[70] that frame and structure our nation's common good.

[68] The liability of *enemy aliens*—a category not considered in this essay, and hitherto conceived of as nationals of a state at war with ours—to statutorily authorized detention in time of war might be understood as a form which that liability to removal reasonably takes when circumstances prevent (or make unreasonable) actual removal.

[69] So too does the Canadian Supreme Court's decision in *Charkaoui v Canada* [2007] SC 9, which accepts that there need be no breach of human or constitutional rights in open-ended detention for the purposes of deportation provided that regular review keeps all factors in view, not least the burden on the detainee compared with any remaining danger he presents to national security or the safety of any person: see paras 110, 126–7.

[70] See the Cairo Declaration on Human Rights in Islam, unanimously approved by 45 states at the Nineteenth Islamic Conference of Foreign Ministers, 5 August 1990, English trans. UN Doc. A/CONF.157/PC/62/Add.18 (UN GAOR, World Conference on Human Rights., 4th Sess., Agenda Item 5) (1993), especially preamble and Arts 10, 19, 22–5; and see generally essay II.7; essay V.1 (2009c) sec. VII; essay V.4 sec. VII (2006a at 122–7); and essay 2009e, sec. 4.

[3]

Being Here: Ethical Territoriality and the Rights of Immigrants

Linda Bosniak[*]

In this Article, I examine a normative idea of territoriality which I call ethical territoriality. By ethical territoriality, I mean the conviction that rights and recognition should extend to all persons who are territorially present within the geographical space of a national state simply by virtue of that presence. I start by briefly reprising a claim I have developed elsewhere — that territorialism is preferable, on liberal democratic grounds, to status-based approaches to immigrants' rights. Here, though, I set out to interrogate the logic of ethical territoriality itself. I ask why the mere fact of a person's territorial presence should serve as the basis for rights and recognition. Further, even conceding that it should, I ask how this commitment is to be operationalized. What is the scope of the territory in which presence figures so significantly in normative terms, and who, precisely, gets access to presence in that territory? My purpose in this Article is to get beyond the status vs. territorial presence-as-basis-for-membership dispute in the immigration debates and to begin a (self-) critical discussion of the ethical territorial commitment itself.

I.

This Article is about a normative idea of territoriality which I will call ethical territoriality. By ethical territoriality, I mean the conviction that rights and

---

* Professor of Law, Rutgers Law School-Camden. Thanks to participants in the Why Citizenship? workshop at the University of Toronto in May 2006, to workshop organizers Audrey Macklin and Guy Mundlak for facilitating an excellent intellectual exchange, and to Rainer Bauböck and Guy Mundlak for perceptive readings of an earlier draft.

recognition should extend to all persons who are territorially present within the geographical space of a national state by virtue of that presence. What I wish to do is demonstrate the significance of this commitment in liberal legal thought about immigration, and then raise some questions about it. I will ask why the mere fact of a person's territorial presence should serve as the basis for rights and recognition, and then consider some implications of thinking about things in this way.

As a general matter, a person's territorial presence or lack thereof in a particular state has a host of legal consequences for that person's treatment under the state's law. From criminal due process rights to taxation requirements to attribution of citizenship, territoriality matters.[1] My own focus here is territoriality in relation to the status of noncitizen immigrants. Although my observations will be relevant to many liberal democratic states, my discussion is informed especially by legal and theoretical debates in the United States.

To set the stage, I must first make clear why territoriality is a defining question in the debate over immigrants' rights. To be very simple and reductive about things, the rights and recognition enjoyed by immigrants are usually understood to derive from either their formal status under law or their territorial presence. According to the status-based conception, a person's rights are determined by the specific legal category she occupies in the country's immigration and nationality regime. The status of citizenship is understood to represent membership's culmination — the moment the individual is entitled to enjoy full rights and entitlements and duties — whereas alienage status of various kinds entails lesser rights.

Two aspects of the status-based approach are significant for my purposes here. The first is differentiation. Legal status is not distributed uniformly among residents. The operation of a state's immigration admissions and citizenship allocation systems produces an array of statuses among members of the society's population, so that at any given time, some people are citizens and some are aliens, and among aliens, there are various status locations assigned by the state. The result is that different people in the society enjoy different sets of rights and recognition by virtue of their legal status assignment.

The second aspect of the status-based approach that interests me is what I will call graduation. Rights are conceived in a graduated, or scalar, fashion;

1 For an excellent recent analysis of the legal significance in the United States of geographical presence and lack thereof, see Kal Raustiala, *The Geography of Justice*, 73 FORDHAM L. REV. 2501 (2005).

they are understood to increase in extent and significance the closer to the status of citizenship the individual progresses. Whether this graduated scale is conceived in linear terms — with formal citizenship the end-point on a continuous axis — or in concentrically-circular terms — with citizenship the prize at the core of a series of membership circles[2] — the status account of rights is, normatively, a story of incremental progress from less to more. In this account, progress along the membership continuum both presupposes and requires state consent.

In contrast to the status-based approach, the territorial conception of rights for immigrants treats a person's geographical presence itself as a sufficient basis for core aspects of membership. Instead of focusing on assigned legal categories, the territorial conception stresses the normative significance of the physical fact of presence in the national space.[3] This presence is not necessarily tied to, or preceded by, political consent, although it may be. The territorial conception repudiates the notion of differential levels of inclusion, regarding the maintenance of partial membership statuses as illegitimate under liberal and democratic principles. It thus treats the conception of belonging as more of a binary than a continuum. It says: once someone is in the geographical territory of the state, that person must, for most purposes, be treated as fully *in*. The fact of a person's "hereness" itself triggers the extension of extensive rights and recognition.

I have elsewhere described the divergence between status-based and presence-based conceptions of immigrant inclusion as a defining divide in the debates over the treatment of noncitizens in liberal societies.[4] This is not to suggest that they are always directly opposed in practice; what I have described are merely ideal types. In fact, many exponents of the status-based membership model recognize territorial presence as a consequential event sometimes deserving of acknowledgement in the assignment of status. At the same time, most territorialists presume the existence of formal status

---

2 On this account, a person's rights increase the closer to the center that the she or he progresses. *See* T. ALEXANDER ALEINIKOFF ET AL., IMMIGRATION AND CITIZENSHIP: PROCESS AND POLICY 2 (5th ed. 2003).

3 To say territoriality is a physical fact is not quite accurate, as I will explain below. *See infra* text accompanying notes 31-34.

4 Linda Bosniak, *Membership, Equality, and the Difference That Alienage Makes*, 69 N.Y.U. L. REV. 1047 (1994); *see also* LINDA BOSNIAK, THE CITIZEN AND THE ALIEN: DILEMMAS OF CONTEMPORARY MEMBERSHIP ch. 3 (2006) [hereinafter BOSNIAK, THE CITIZEN AND THE ALIEN]. In *The Citizen and the Alien*, my concern is the tensions between these commitments, whereas in this Article, I consider what they share in common.

differences among the territorially present and recognize or concede that these differences may have consequences for their treatment, at least in some domains.

Nevertheless, these two approaches to immigrants' rights find themselves directly at odds in some settings. The distinction between them is clearest when we focus on the situation of unauthorized immigrants — people who are territorially present within a national society but who have, as a formal matter, failed to play by the formal rules of graduated membership. Although geographically here, these are people who are out of line, both literally and figuratively. For status exponents, the illegality of their presence places them outside the community of membership for most purposes, or else in its outermost circle. For territorialists, the fact of their presence often trumps the irregularity of their status for purposes of allocating rights and recognition.

In the incessant tug-of-war between status-based and territorially-based conceptions of membership, I am generally sympathetic to the territorial approach. It seems to me that ethical territoriality appropriately insists on treating membership as a matter of social fact rather than as a legal formality. And by opposing the imposition of less-than-complete-membership on classes of residents, ethical territoriality honors the egalitarian and anti-caste commitments to which liberal constitutionalism purports to aspire.[5]

Despite its virtues, however, the territorial model begs its own questions, and it is these that I am interested in exploring here. Why, first of all, should the fact of territorial presence matter so significantly in the allocation of rights and recognition? And even conceding that it should, how is this commitment to be operationalized? What is the scope of the territory in which presence figures so significantly in normative terms, and who, precisely, gets access to presence in that territory? My purpose in this Article is to get beyond the status vs. territorial presence-as-basis-for-membership dispute in the immigration debates and to begin a (self-) critical discussion of the ethical territorial commitment itself.

II.

The ethical territorial view was explicitly articulated by political theorist Michael Walzer in his book *Spheres of Justice*. In the chapter on "Membership," Walzer defends a principle of "political inclusiveness" for

---

5 I elaborate these arguments at length in BOSNIAK, THE CITIZEN AND THE ALIEN, *supra* note 4.

immigrants residing within the territory of a democratic political community. To the extent that individuals who inhabit a national community are not recognized as members, he writes, they are subject to nothing short of political and social "tyranny."[6] As a paradigmatic example of such tyranny, Walzer cites the case of the metics of ancient Athens who lived and worked in the city but enjoyed neither political rights nor "welfare rights," nor any prospect of acquiring citizenship in the future. They were, Walzer says, "the subjects of a band of citizen tyrants, governed without consent."[7] What makes the status of metics wrong, from a democratic point of view, is the fact that they share territory with the citizens but nevertheless subsist as a class of political and social outsiders. Democratic justice requires that membership's rights and rule "be open, and equally open, to all those men and women who live within [a political community's] territory . . . and are subject to local law."[8] For "the state owes something to its inhabitants simply, without reference to their collective or national identity," but merely by virtue of that inhabitance.[9]

The territorial conception of rights and recognition that Walzer endorses is embraced, in some form, by many political liberals and progressives. These commentators argue that people who are here, by virtue of *being here*, are entitled to rights and recognition within the national society. This embrace is apparent in much of the liberal scholarly literature on the rights of noncitizens, but the commitment is not merely academic. A commitment to the territorial conception of rights is, in fact, expressed in the fundamental law of many liberal democratic systems. In many countries, every person who is territorially present — citizen or not, legally present or not — is entitled to fundamental forms of due process, to contract and property rights, to access to the courts, and to core rights in the educational and employment spheres.[10] The territorial imperative was powerfully articulated by the United States Supreme Court in late nineteenth century (this, notably, in a case involving noncitizens of Chinese descent at the height of the Chinese exclusion period):

> [Fundamental rights] are not confined to the protection of citizens. . . .

---

6 MICHAEL WALZER, SPHERES OF JUSTICE: A DEFENSE OF PLURALISM AND EQUALITY 59 (1983).

7 *Id.*

8 *Id.* at 60-61. The European guestworker programs of the 1970s were similarly defective: ostensibly democratic communities imported foreigners to function as "live-in servants" to do the society's "dirty work," but these workers had no prospect of ever moving beyond that status.

9 *Id.* at 43.

10 BOSNIAK, THE CITIZEN AND THE ALIEN, *supra* note 4, ch. 3.

> These provisions are universal in their application to all persons within the territorial jurisdiction, without regard to any differences of race, of color, or of nationality.[11]

The territorialist claim is not, however, an unequivocal claim that citizenship status is irrelevant in the treatment of the nation's inhabitants. American courts have never held that all of the rights liberal societies hold as fundamental must be extended to all territorially present persons.[12] Nor are those liberal scholars who advocate the territorial conception entirely strict about it; they do not maintain that there cannot be *any* differences in treatment between citizens and territorially-present noncitizens. Most territorialists, for example, accept that the franchise does not necessarily extend to all persons who are territorially present. Even Walzer bends in his discussion of contemporary immigrant policy; he allows that noncitizens need not be afforded the vote. They must have swift and easy access to citizenship status through naturalization, he insists, which will itself put them in a position to vote. But accession to citizenship first is essential. Yet this exception does not swallow the rule for Walzer, for voting is the only exception to the principle of territorial inclusion that he (directly) accepts.[13] He claims that, otherwise, it is illegitimate for a democratic society to maintain a caste of residents who subsist in a lesser status than that of full members.[14]

I identify a great deal, as I have said, with the universalist, anti-caste commitment that animates the territorialist position. In the territorialist view, rights and recognition are owed not merely to formal status citizens but to

---

11 Yick Wo v. Hopkins, 118 U.S. 356, 369 (1886). This is a powerful strand of constitutional doctrine that has fundamentally structured the treatment of noncitizens in the United States. It is the strand that has competed with the so-called "plenary power doctrine" in immigration law, according to which the national state is largely unconstrained in exercising its sovereign right to regulate borders. In fact, noncitizens are subject to both regimes, which are often in conflict. *See* BOSNIAK, THE CITIZEN AND THE ALIEN, *supra* note 4, ch. 3.

12 For discussion of the difference that alienage makes in U.S. law, see BOSNIAK, THE CITIZEN AND THE ALIEN, *supra* note 4, chs. 3, 4.

13 I say "directly" because Walzer does not appear to oppose all indirect forms of constraint on the rights of noncitizens. Given Walzer's commitment to a national community's right to maintain an admissions policy, he presumably would endorse the community's authority to deport noncitizens in some circumstances. However, the deployment of the deportation threat as a means of social control is subject to explicit critique by Walzer. *See infra* note 26.

14 Again, in Walzer's formulation, "to the extent that immigrants who live and work within a national community are not recognized as members, they are subject to nothing short of 'tyranny.'" WALZER, *supra* note 6, at 59.

all persons present in the national society. On this commitment, it is both anti-democratic and morally wrong in liberal terms to allow for treatment of a class of persons who are living among us as social and political outsiders. Territorialism embodies an ethic of inclusiveness and equality: it is the ground (both literally and figuratively) of national community belonging.

And yet: a shift in gaze and a little reflection make clear that the territorialist view is hardly all about inclusion. When we step back from a purely intranational focus and survey the landscape more broadly, we can see that ethical territorialism also has a constitutive exclusionary element. Almost every version of inclusion-within-the-territory is coupled with a vision of a bounded territorial community *within which* inclusion is to take place. Ethical territorialists, that is to say, invariably presuppose the existence of borders around the territory in question. In some cases, they affirmatively embrace those borders.

Walzer himself expressly embraces borders and the exclusionary work they do. His views on the legitimacy of a country's immigration control policy are well-known. Political communities must have the right to distribute membership according to their own values and commitments — to fashion their own "admissions policies," in his memorable formulation.[15] According to Walzer, a country is a membership community, a "world of common meanings" and "shared ways of life," which its members are entitled to preserve. Since the unimpeded entry of strangers would render such preservation impossible, members of a national community must have the right to "control and sometimes restrain the flow of immigrants."[16] Walzer insists, in short, not only on the imperatives of inclusion within the territory but also on the legitimacy of exclusion at territory's edges.

One might, perhaps, wonder how it is possible for Walzer to maintain his robust national inclusionism while simultaneously defending the imperatives of national closure. Walzer, however, does not regard these dual commitments as standing in conflict at all. For him, in fact, they are entirely and necessarily complementary.[17] This is because, in his view, border and interior are distinct regulatory and social domains whose governing logics are entirely separate. His approach relies on a conception of border and interior as divided jurisdictions, with different normative practices applying to each.

---

15 *Id.* at 39.

16 *Id.* The last two sentences in the text appear in almost identical form in my discussion of Walzer in BOSNIAK, THE CITIZEN AND THE ALIEN, *supra* note 4, at 40.

17 As Walzer says, "the theory of distributive justice must vindicate at one and the same time the . . . right of closure and the political inclusiveness of existing communities." WALZER, *supra* note 6, at 63.

Boundedness governs at the community's edges, while inclusiveness prevails within.[18] This conception of membership based on jurisdictional splitting between border and interior — whereby anti-caste values apply *within* the community, while the community possesses the right to limit the ingress of outsiders *into* the community[19] — is widespread among liberals and progressives in and out of the immigration debate. The inclusive universalism of territorialism is commonly understood to be framed, and enabled, by a hard or hard-ish shell around the territorial perimeter. Membership is, in this normative conception, "hard-on-the-outside and soft-on-the-inside."

A recent lead essay in the *Boston Review* on immigrants' rights was structured precisely around this spatially divided conception of membership. The author, constitutional scholar Owen Fiss, takes as given the current restrictions on immigrant admissions.[20] "My point," he writes, "is not to subvert the admission process or otherwise open the borders," but rather, to focus on the treatment of those immigrants who are already here. In his essay, Fiss "insist[s] that laws regarding admission cannot be enforced or implemented in ways that would transform immigrants into pariahs."[21] Whatever restrictions are enforced at the border, Fiss argues, we must maintain egalitarian values within, in relation to those who are territorially present.

I understand the appeal of this "hard-outside/soft-inside" model of membership. Liberal democratic thought is notoriously plagued by tensions between universalist and particularist conceptions of responsibility and belonging,[22] and a division of normative labor between inside and edges

18 I have called this construct a "hard-on-the-outside and soft-on-the-inside" conception of citizenship. BOSNIAK, THE CITIZEN AND THE ALIEN, *supra* note 4, chs. 1, 5, 6.

19 Sphere separation is a central concern of Walzer's throughout *Spheres of Justice*. See the discussion in BOSNIAK, THE CITIZEN AND THE ALIEN, *supra* note 4, ch. 3. In his work, separation is not merely a descriptive reality but also a normative imperative.

20 "I am not surreptitiously questioning the validity of laws regulating the admission of immigrants to this country. For present purposes, I am prepared to assert that these laws are just." Owen Fiss, *The Immigrant as Pariah*, BOSTON REV., Oct.-Nov. 1998, at 4, *reprinted in* A COMMUNITY OF EQUALS: THE CONSTITUTIONAL PROTECTION OF NEW AMERICANS 3, 16 (Joshua Cohen & Joel Rogers eds., 1999) [hereinafter Fiss, *The Immigrant as Pariah*]. See response by Mark Tushnet, *Open Borders*, *in* A COMMUNITY OF EQUALS: THE CONSTITUTIONAL PROTECTION OF NEW AMERICANS, *supra*, at 69, 69 ("Owen Fiss's proposal doesn't go far enough. He assumes that an immigration policy founded on creating legal barriers to people's entry into this country is just.").

21 Fiss, *The Immigrant as Pariah*, *supra* note 20, at 16.

22 See especially SAMUEL SCHEFFLER, BOUNDARIES AND ALLEGIANCES: PROBLEMS OF JUSTICE AND RESPONSIBILITY IN LIBERAL THOUGHT (2002).

would seem to hold out the promise that we can have it all: we can have our universalist cake on the inside, and eat our particularist cake, too, at the border. Jurisdictional division seems to resolve the dilemma, for at least some purposes.

Attractive as this splitting strategy might seem, however,[23] it is actually not terribly functional in practical terms. The problem is that it is based on empirical premises about the possibility of maintaining separation between the community's inside and its edges that simply do not hold. Fiss's account itself makes this clear. He writes:

> Admission laws can be enforced by fences at the borders, deportation proceedings, or criminal sanctions, not, I maintain, by imposing social disabilities.[24]

The operation of border norms via exclusionary "fences" at the threshold is not, as Fiss himself recognizes, the only mode of administering admissions laws. Exclusion functions also inside the territory — most significantly through the power and practice of deportation. The nation-state's power of exclusion, in other words, does not disappear the moment an individual physically enters the state's territory. Through a complex regime of immigration regulation — one that includes government authorization to detain and deport noncitizens under some circumstances — the "border" — conceived as regulatory sphere — follows the immigrant into the national geographic space and shapes her experience there.

The result is that squarely *within* the space of the national society liberal egalitarian norms work alongside exclusionary border norms. Both occupy the same, geographically internal, terrain. And given their joint applicability, what happens, in practical terms, is that they often compete for primacy.[25] Whether an issue pertaining to the treatment of the undocumented — say, their access to driver's licenses or workers' compensation insurance

---

23 There are certainly debates to be had about its normative attractiveness in the first instance. The commitment to exclusion at the borders has been criticized by a number of analysts. *See* discussion *infra* text accompanying note 27.

24 Fiss, *The Immigrant as Pariah*, *supra* note 20, at 16.

25 In fact, a lot of the fights over the rights of immigrants in the U.S. are disputes over the question of how far the border legitimately extends within the national society. So, for example, in the debates over whether undocumented immigrants should be entitled to driver's licenses, we are arguing about whether this is legitimately a border control question or whether it is a question about the rights of territorially present persons. For further discussion, see LINDA BOSNIAK, THE UNDOCUMENTED IMMIGRANT: CONTENDING POLICY APPROACHES IN DEBATING IMMIGRATION (Carol Swain ed., forthcoming 2007).

or disaster relief — is properly viewed as an "immigration question" or an "equality question" perennially plagues legal actors and policy-makers in the field. Indeed, the competition between immigration control prerogatives and equality norms constitutes the structural substratum of all of our legal and policy debates about the status of immigrants in liberal democratic states. One significant practical consequence of this competition, notably, is that the rights that many noncitizens do enjoy by virtue of their territorial presence are often drastically curtailed by the internal operation of the border. As is well-known, unauthorized immigrants are often reluctant to avail themselves of the rights that are formally extended to them out of fear of attracting the attention of the immigration authorities. As a result, they are subject to various abuses of public and private power even where formal law would seem to otherwise protect them.[26]

The point, in short, is that the normative divide between the community's inside and its edges that the territorialists presume possible — that, indeed, is foundational to them — is chimerical. For even when noncitizens are geographically here, and are therefore theoretically embraced within the territorialist ethic of inclusion, they remain subject to the jurisdiction of the internally-implemented border as well. And as such, the rights and recognition they are meant to enjoy by virtue of being here are often (though not always) undercut, both directly and indirectly.

III.

Ethical territorialism's first problem, therefore, is that it is self-undermining in practical terms. The territorial boundaries that are understood to be universalism's enabling frame are not, in fact, confined to the territory's physical threshold but penetrate the territorial interior as well, and there function to thwart ethical territorialism's own internal universalist project. Yet even if it were possible to confine the border to the territory's physical edges — even if, once inside, a person would truly be insulated from the action of the border — ethical territorialism would raise other concerns, both analytical and normative. In this part of the discussion, I want to briefly raise two of these.

26 This is an effect Walzer recognizes, though not specifically in relation to the undocumented: a democratic community is undermined when some of its residents are subject to what he calls the "everpresent threat of deportation." WALZER, *supra* note 6, at 58.

There is, first of all, the question of access to territory. The question is: "territoriality for whom?" In a normative regime in which territoriality is so unsurpassingly important, we will need to establish who it is who gets to be territorially present in the first place. How, exactly, is physical territoriality going to be distributed?

As I have said, the ethical territorialist view usually presumes that access to territory will continue to be restricted. It insists on rights and recognition for everyone who is here, but *being here* continues to be a limited commodity. States are usually understood to have a right to restrict territorial access (here is the hard-on-the-outside conception again) through regulation of both immigration and citizenship acquisition and transmission. Consequently, not everyone who would wish to be here can or will achieve it. This is not to say that the norm of border control is necessarily entailed by the territoriality position. One could certainly take a stance on behalf of rights and recognition for the territorially-present while also espousing an open borders policy, as some have done. But most advocates of territorial inclusion tend either to affirmatively embrace an ethic of border restriction or at least to concede it.

However, limitations on access to territory via restrictive immigration and citizenship rules raise their own problems of justification. To state the case briefly, why should the fortuities of birthplace and parentage — which today establish the background rules for distribution of territoriality through domicile or residence — be permitted to dictate people's life chances so unalterably? Why should national states be able to stand in the way of those individuals lacking in privileged pre-given birthplace or parentage ties who wish to improve their life chances through cross-border movement to other territories?[27] In much the same way that limitations on opportunities for formal immigration raise profound questions of normative justice for liberal thought, limitations on access to physical territoriality do as well.

There is, moreover, the practical point that even the most stringent border restrictions will not halt the territorial ingress of national outsiders. Many do, and will continue to, arrive notwithstanding. What happens then? A strict territorialist position would seem to say: the exercise of border control

27 These points have been powerfully made by a handful of theorists in legal and political theory, including Joseph Carens and, more recently, Ayelet Shachar. *See* Joseph Carens, *Aliens and Citizens: The Case for Open Borders*, 49 REV. POL. 251 (1987); Ayelet Shachar, *Children of a Lesser State: Sustaining Global Inequality Through Citizenship Laws*, *in* NOMOS XLIV: CHILD, FAMILY AND THE STATE 13 (Stephen Macedo & Iris Marion Young eds., 2002). But these arguments tend to be regarded as utopian in nature and fail to have much influence on the mainstream debates, not merely in the policy arena but in the academy as well.

must be confined to the nation's geographic perimeter. Once a person has touched national soil, he or she is to be considered part of the universal "we." In means *in*.

In practice, of course, this would result in something like a rolling legalization program whereby everyone who manages to set foot in the national space is automatically recognized as a national member. Defending such a position is not unthinkable. Indeed, some countries, including the United States, have had approximations of it embodied in policy at various times.[28] Yet I am certain that many advocates of ethical territorialism today would find themselves wishing to disavow such a scenario, not merely because it would be politically unpopular (though unquestionably it would) but also because it presents inherent difficulties for them. On the one hand, a "touch the territory and you're in" policy could surely threaten the very commitment to territorial boundedness that most ethical territorialists presuppose, since the existence of such a rule would arguably serve as a powerful incentive to irregular entry.[29] This might not be a bad thing if you want to critique the existence of borders to entry in the first place, but assuming you want to stick with them, this would be self-defeating. On the other hand, any effort to avoid this difficulty by allowing for, or insisting upon, a drawing of distinctions among categories of the territorially present (by, for instance, privileging legal or long-term immigrants over irregular entrants or just-over-the-line entrants or opportunistic entrants, however this latter would be defined)[30]

---

28 According to Mae Ngai,

> Before 1891 there were no provisions in our immigration laws to deport an immigrant who entered without permission. (Indeed, hardly any requirements for admission existed.) Thereafter, Congress enacted statutes of limitations of one to five years for deportable offenses. This policy recognized an important reality about illegal immigrants: They settle, raise families and acquire property — in other words, they become part of the nation's economic and social fabric. In the first decades of the 20th century, it was considered unconscionable to expel such people. Judge Learned Hand of New York said that deportation, especially when it tore people from their homes and families, was "barbarous and cruel."

Mae M. Ngai, *We Need a Deportation Deadline: Statute of Limitations on Unlawful Entry Would Humanely Address Illegal Immigration*, WASH. POST, June 14, 2005, at A21.

29 This is the same concern that opponents of various amnesty or legalization programs express.

30 It is the same charge of territorial opportunism that is directed against so-called birth tourists. The iconic image is that of the impoverished Mexican woman who manages to drag herself across the Rio Grande just before giving birth in order to convey U.S. birthright citizenship on her newborn. But there are more affluent versions as well. *See* Barbara Demick, *Women Take Trips to Give Birth in U.S.: For South Koreans, American Citizenship*

would mean adopting a graduated conception of rights and recognition among the territorially-here and, to that extent, abandoning a strict commitment to the equal membership imperative underlying ethical territoriality in the first place.

A second question to ask about ethical territoriality relates to the precise scope of the territory within which presence counts as so normatively consequential. What is the geographic space that constitutes any state's territory anyway? Conceding for the moment that being within national territory should serve as the basis for rights and recognition, how do we decide what the scope of that territory is? Where does this territory begin and end? Answering these questions is not simply a matter of looking at a map of the world. What counts as "our territory" is itself subject to all kinds of contestation. Territory is gained through conquest and lost through secession. Disputes among states about the proper locations of territorial borders are legion. Indeed, determining what constitutes the legitimate scope of a particular state's territory is what many wars are all about.

Most often, these conflicts concern the legitimacy of a state's exercise of power, or sovereignty, in a particular geographic space. But disputes over the scope-of-territory question are not confined to disputes over government rule. Sometimes they concern the scope of government responsibility as well. As we have seen, liberal democratic states commonly regard themselves as owing fundamental obligations — if not total equality of treatment — to persons who are present within their territory. Sometimes, however, states opportunistically define the contours of their territory in restrictive terms to limit, or disavow, the obligations they would otherwise maintain to those persons. The most vivid recent example of this for any country is the case of Guantanamo, which the United States government sought to describe as "outside" the territory of the U.S. precisely in order to avoid the territorially-based requirement that it extend constitutional protections to prisoners it was holding on its military bases there.[31] Another example of longer standing in the U.S. context is the case of Puerto Rico, which

---

is Best Present for Baby, MILWAUKEE J. SENTINEL, June 2, 2002, *available at* http://www.findarticles.com/p/articles/mi_qn4196/is_20020602/ai_n10796512.

31 The government sought to take advantage of the rule in U.S. law that noncitizens located outside U.S. territory are entirely unprotected by the Constitution. *See* Johnson v. Eistentrager, 339 U.S. 763 (1950). This is, of course, a territoriality rule that is both the inverse, and corollary, of the one I am concerned with in this Article. In this context, *lack* of territorial presence — at least for noncitizens — means lack of rights and recognition.

In *Rasul v. Bush*, 542 U.S. 466 (2004), the U.S. Supreme Court repudiated the government's claim that Guantanamo is outside the U.S., holding that the individuals

the United States claims as its territory for most purposes yet describes as "foreign" when defining the constitutional rights of its inhabitants.[32] Notably, in neither Guantanamo nor Puerto Rico has the U.S. relinquished any claim to exercise sovereign control. What it has done, instead, through manipulation of the idea of territoriality, is decouple rule and obligation.

States employ other legal fictions to avoid the obligations of territoriality. Among them is the fiction that certain individuals who are in fact physically within the territorial space are "not here" as a legal matter. Under U.S. immigration law, for example, people detained at the border by the immigration authorities are deemed not to be "within the United States" and therefore not entitled to the rights that come with territorial presence.[33] The distinction drawn between physical and legal presence, among other things, has been read to allow the government to hold individuals in indefinite detention without falling afoul of the Constitution's due process requirements.

The manipulability of territorial scope is seen, finally, in the power states exercise to remove noncitizens from their territorial jurisdiction. Usually, we regard a state's physical removal of foreigners from its territory as an instance of that state's immigration regulatory authority; in this context, deportation is just one of the mechanisms the state employs to maintain control of the composition of its national political community. Sometimes, however, the practice of physical removal of foreigners represents something else: it is a strategy that allows the state to avoid the obligations that a person's continued territorial presence would otherwise impose upon it. Thus, for example, the recent practice of prisoner "rendition" from the U.S. to Egypt, Syria, and other countries would appear to be motivated less by a desire to rid the country of the presence of these individuals than by the wish to

---

seeking redress have "for more than two years . . . been imprisoned in territory over which the United States exercises exclusive jurisdiction and control." *Id.* at 467.

32 According to the Supreme Court, Puerto Rico is "foreign in a domestic sense." Downes v. Bidwell, 182 U.S. 244 (1901). For an important volume addressing the meaning and import of this phrase, see CHRISTINA DUFFY BURNETT & BURKE MARSHALL, FOREIGN IN A DOMESTIC SENSE: PUERTO RICO, AMERICAN EXPANSION AND THE CONSTITUTION (2001).

33 The entry fiction "holds that excludable aliens are to be treated as if detained at the border despite their physical presence in the United States." Lynch v. Cannatella, 810 F.2d 1363, 1373 (5th Cir. 1987). See especially Shaughnessy v. United States *ex rel* Mezei, 345 U.S. 206 (1953), which held that a returning lawful permanent resident being held on Ellis Island was not within the United States and therefore not entitled to invoke the Constitution on his behalf to challenge his indefinite detention. This case has never been overruled and is still invoked by the Court as governing law. *See* Zadvydas v. Davis, 121 S. Ct. 2491 (2001).

avoid the legal constraints on the individuals' treatment that their territorial presence would otherwise impose.[34]

We can see, therefore, that the scope of what constitutes a state's territory is far more contestable and manipulable than ethical territorialism tends to presume. A political community's territory is neither naturally given nor fixed in its contours; boundaries are endlessly drawn and redrawn and fought over. This malleability in itself casts some doubt on the workability, if not the defensibility, of an ethical commitment that makes rights and recognition contingent on being territorially inside.

IV.

Beyond questions about territorial access and territorial scope, the most fundamental question we need to ask about ethical territoriality is the "why" question: Why privilege territorial presence at all? Why should being on *this* side of the territorial line rather than the other side be so normatively significant?[35] As Kal Raustiala has asked in another context, what accounts for the "magic" worked by geographical presence?[36]

Of course, the magic involved here is not of a kind that comes down from the heavens. This magic is a function of political and social practices. People who live inside territorial communities often choose to ascribe certain recognition and rights upon those with whom they occupy the same territory. Some would want to ascribe more. These are rights and recognition generally *not* extended to nonterritorial others. Understanding the magic of territoriality, therefore, requires understanding what it is about the fact of sharing territorial space that gives rise to this sense of heightened

34 "Rendition is the CIA's antiseptic term for its practice of sending captured terrorist suspects to other countries for interrogation." David Ignatius, *Rendition Realities*, WASH. POST, Mar. 9, 2005, at A21. *See generally* Jane Mayer, *Outsourcing Torture*, NEW YORKER, Feb. 14, 2005, at 106.

35 It is interesting to note that this is a question that anti-immigrant advocates pose all the time. They query why the fact that a person has managed, by hook or by crook, to get herself "in" should, by itself, confer advantage. Implicit in such a critique is not merely unhappiness about possible irregular entry but also the conviction that merely being here should not be enough to trigger obligations and recognition; there has to be something more. The "something more" that many anti-immigrant advocates believe must exist is formal legal status, acquired through rule-following and state consent. But even if we reject such formalism, we are still faced with the question of why territoriality alone should be enough.

36 Raustiala, *supra* note 1, at 2546.

obligation.[37] Why should the fact of territorial presence have particular ethical significance? How do we make sense of this commitment? It seems to me that there are three different kinds of answers to these questions that exponents of ethical territorialism might submit as an account of their position. When not explicitly articulated, they are at least implicit in the territorialist discourse. Each of these accounts is meritorious in important respects, but each raises difficulties as well.

One kind of answer is the "affiliations" answer.[38] On this account, the physical sharing of national territory serves to tie people together through proximity and linkage to place.[39] Extending rights and recognition to co-territorial inhabitants acknowledges the common bonds that develop among those who share physical context.[40] On this account, it is not so much the connection with the land per se that is salient;[41] rather, the impulse seems to be

---

37 There are, of course, other uses of the term "territoriality." With the rise of the Westphalian State system, territoriality became the rule associated with the scope of sovereign state power: In the classic model, a sovereign state enjoyed plenary power within the territory and was constrained from acting outside it. But territoriality as a rule about scope of power — about jurisdiction — and territoriality as a rule about the basis for rights and recognition of individuals are not the same thing; indeed, they could be in tension. Classically, a sovereign was entitled to treat persons within its territory as it desired, without constraint. The commitment to ethical territoriality, in contrast, specifically acts as a limit on state discretion; it is a requirement of a particular kind of state action toward individuals within that state's territory.

38 In using the language of "affiliations," I am borrowing from HIROSHI MOTOMURA, AMERICANS IN WAITING: THE LOST STORY OF IMMIGRATION AND CITIZENSHIP IN THE UNITED STATES (2006). Motomura describes "immigration as affiliation" as a way of viewing the rights and incorporation of immigrants that "depend[s] on the ties that they have formed in this country." *Id.* at 11. My use of affiliation is also meant to reference the "ties formed" by immigrants. But my account differs from Motomura's in this respect: Motomura regards "immigration as affiliation" as an approach to immigrants' rights that "evolved" out of an earlier commitment to "territorial personhood," pursuant to which "simply being present in the United States bestows certain . . . rights." *Id.* at 10. In contrast, I am using the idea of affiliation to explain why ethical territorialism has emotional and political resonance. I view an affiliations conception of membership, in other words, as a way of making sense of territorialism's purchase — although in my analysis I also show how territorialism and affiliationism are in some ways distinct.

39 Yishai Blank, *Spheres of Citizenship*, 8 THEORETICAL INQUIRIES L. 411 (2007).

40 Doreen Massey, *Geographies of Responsibility*, 86B GEOGRAFISKA ANNALER 5 (2004).

41 Some characterize the relationship that exists between particular people and their territory in quasi-essentialist terms. For instance, David Miller writes,

> Through custom and practice as well as by explicit political decision [members

to acknowledge attachments and social ties that often develop among persons who are leading a common life within a single territorial space.

But while the affiliations account is intuitively appealing in many respects, analytically it presents various difficulties. For one thing, to the extent that the affiliations response depends on people's "leading a common life" to trigger the obligation, it would appear to contain a requirement that goes beyond the sheer fact of a person's physical location within the territorial space. It would seem to require that the person to whom we owe our co-territorial obligation actually reside or dwell (lead a life) within the territory. The mere fact of a person's physically *being here* — just passing through, for example, or just visiting for the weekend — would not seem to meet the standard.[42] On the other hand, what *would* be enough to meet it? How long would we require that a person be here in order to regard her as someone with whom we "lead a common life"? Is it two weeks, or two months, or two years? And can length of stay, alone, be the defining variable in any event? Is the operative principle indeed "the longer the stay, the stronger the claim," in Joseph Caren's phrase?[43] What about the terms, or circumstances, of that stay? For instance, what about a person who was arrested abroad months ago and forcibly brought to the United States to stand trial?[44] How about the immigrant who has been residing here for months or years but is present in an unauthorized status?[45] And what, finally, about the fact of work? Doesn't

> of a political community] create laws, establish individual or collective property rights, engage in public works, shape the physical appearance of the territory. Over time this takes on symbolic significance as they bury their dead in certain places, establish shrines or secular monuments and so forth. All of these activities give them an attachment to the land that cannot be matched by any rival claimants.

DAVID MILLER, *Secession and the Principle of Nationality*, *in* CITIZENSHIP AND NATIONAL IDENTITY 110, 116 (2000). An "attachment to the land" concept does not seem to support the ethical territorial position, because it presupposes an already-existing membership community that maintains an ongoing relationship with the land in question. The ethical territorial view is far more open, holding that the fact of presence within the state's borders, even if of recent vintage, is itself the basis for community membership.

42 The word "inhabit" interestingly highlights this ambiguity regarding the ethical significance of territorial presence versus residence. The American Heritage Dictionary contains two definitions for the term: "1. To live or reside in. 2. To be present in; fill." AMERICAN HERITAGE DICTIONARY 901 (4th ed. 2000).

43 Joseph Carens, *On Belonging: What We Owe People Who Stay*, BOSTON REV., Summer 2005, at 16.

44 *See generally* United States v. Verdugo-Urquidez, 494 U.S. 259 (1990).

45 *See* Carens, *supra* note 43, at 19 ("The general principle with which I began — the longer the stay, the stronger the claim — applies even in the case of those who have settled without authorization, and for the same reasons. When people settle in a

the social contribution of the working immigrant, ipso facto, qualify her as someone with whom we share a common life irrespective of her length of stay?[46] Inevitably, the line drawing here is going to be controversial.

Notice, however, that to the extent we draw any line that requires more than sheer physical presence in the territory, we are implicitly smuggling additional requirements into the equation. The ethical principle now depends not on territoriality alone but on territoriality-plus (with the precise content of the "plus" itself uncertain). But if this is true, then arguably a person who is geographically here but just passing through is not differently situated than a person who is located on the other side of the border. Territorial presence per se has lost its purchase.

My point so far is that ethical territorialists who are animated by an affiliations justification actually wish to privilege territorial co-residents rather than co-occupants — although again we must acknowledge the real difficulties involved in drawing the line between these two categories. There is, however, a further problem with the affiliations account of the ethical territorialist commitment. This is the fact that co-residence within a territory is a highly imperfect proxy for the existence of attachments and affiliations in any event. No doubt, certain kinds of connections do often develop among people who share a physical context. But it is also true that many people reside within a common territory who are distinctly unattached to their co-inhabitants. And correspondingly, plenty of territorial residents maintain very close affiliations and attachments with people located outside the territory — attachments both physical (through travel) and virtual (through distance-shrinking technologies) — which may be far more engaged and central to them than those they maintain with their co-territorial residents.[47] Add to this that a nation-state territory is far larger than the kind of shared physical space (say, a town or even a city) in which the possibilities for face-to-face or other physically proximate contact are possible or likely in any event.[48] To the extent that the logic of the ethical territoriality rule rests on a

---

country they form connections and attachments that over time make them members of the society. After a while, the conditions of admission become irrelevant.").

46 Walzer emphasizes the normative significance of the social contribution through labor made by immigrant workers in his examination of alien status. WALZER, *supra* note 6, at 52-61.

47 *See* Linda Bosniak, *Citizenship Denationalized*, 7 IND. J. GLOBAL LEGAL STUD. 447, 470-88 (2000).

48 If the world is too big for the development of community affiliations, so, too, is a nation. *See* Bruce Robbins, *Introduction: Part I*, *in* COSMOPOLITICS: THINKING AND FEELING BEYOND THE NATION 6 (Pheng Chea & Bruce Robbins eds., 1998).

desire to acknowledge the importance and salience of physically proximate human attachments, it therefore seems both too broad and too narrow.

A second answer to the "why territoriality" question — and one which quite expressly animates many ethical territorialists — is what I will call the "anti-caste" answer. To maintain its democratic character, the argument goes, a national community cannot abide the existence of caste. Yet to the extent we allow for a class of persons to subsist among us in a less-than-fully-incorporated status, we will have entrenched and institutionalized caste-based distinctions. This is a consequentialist argument, pitched in the negative: if we do not extend rights and recognition to co-inhabitants, if we allow for the maintenance of what Walzer calls "a class of live-in servants" who are perpetually disadvantaged under law, we will, to that extent, poison the democratic community at its heart.

I identify with the anti-caste commitment in ethical terms, and I agree as a descriptive matter that democracy suffers when differential caste-like status is permitted. But rendering this commitment as a rule about territoriality is problematic for several reasons. First, as I argued above, so long as the territory in question is bordered by policed boundaries and so long as those boundaries operate not merely at the geographic edges but inside the territorial interior by way of the deportation power, differences in status among those within can never be eliminated completely. Even those noncitizens who are formally extended substantial rights and recognition are, by virtue of being noncitizens, subject to the exercise of the immigration regulatory regime and inevitably find themselves, to that extent, less than full social members.

Second, and more fundamentally, it is not clear why the commitment to egalitarianism that underlies the anti-caste vision should be confined to the world within the national territory. I recognize that this is the conventional understanding: equal justice is a national project. People are by nature particularistically motivated, and the idea that we could be compelled to extend solidarities of justice to the world at large is politically utopian and sociologically naive. There is, however, an important case to be made — and it is one that some scholars and activists have been making — first, that responsibilities of justice extend beyond the bounds of the territorial nation-state and, second, that as a matter of fact, people are increasingly experiencing themselves as ethically and politically connected to others across national borders.[49] Paying attention to the global — to global justice and to the movement for increased democracy at the global level — makes it

49 For further discussion, see Bosniak, *supra* note 47, at 489-509.

harder to take as a given that a person's being territorially "in here" rather than "out there" should be the dispositive factor in allocating rights and recognition.

In addition to the affiliations answer and the anti-caste answer to the "why territoriality" question, there is, finally, a third answer — one concerned with state power and its constraints. This "jurisdictional" answer begins from the proposition that a state is a body that possesses legitimate authority to rule over a particular territory. To the extent that a state exercises power in a territorial space, the argument goes, every person present within that space, and "subject to the jurisdiction" of that power, should be armed with individual protections against its exercise. Walzer's account of the rights of immigrants relies, in part, on this conception. He writes, "Men and women are either subject to the state's authority, or they are not; and if they are subject, they must be given a say, and ultimately an equal say, in what that authority does."[50]

The jurisdictional argument, grounded in a conception of "mutuality of obligation," embodies a crucially important principle on behalf of individual rights.[51] It is this principle that underlies the extension of fundamental constitutional rights to territorially-present noncitizens in most liberal democratic states. In the U.S. context, as explained above, all territorially present persons are entitled to rights against government power and to affirmative protections in a variety of crucial settings, whether or not they possess citizenship status.

Yet important as it is, the mutuality of protection afforded to territorially present noncitizens is incomplete. For one thing, noncitizen immigrants remain subject to various forms of government discrimination, notwithstanding the extension to them of certain core rights. And once again, noncitizens are always vulnerable to ejection from the jurisdiction altogether. Mutuality, in short, only goes so far.

Additionally, we might ask why the mutuality of obligation involved should be territorially circumscribed at all. If the core principle here is availability of protections against power where power is exercised, then it is unclear why those noncitizens located abroad who are subject to the exercise of a sovereign's power are not entitled to protection against that sovereign as well. Many states wield power in ways that affect people

---

50 WALZER, *supra* note 6, at 61. Gerald Neuman has described such a concept in American constitutional law as the "mutuality of obligation" approach. GERALD L. NEUMAN, STRANGERS TO THE CONSTITUTION: IMMIGRANTS, BORDERS AND FUNDAMENTAL LAW (1996) (especially ch. 6). *See also* Raustiala, *supra* note 1.

51 See NEUMAN, *supra* note 50, on "mutuality of obligation."

outside the territorial boundaries of their states and yet deny obligations to them.[52] Arguably, those so affected should enjoy protections from its exercise irrespective of their geographical location and as well as their citizenship status.[53]

V.

Ethical territoriality has a great deal to recommend it. In the debates over the status of noncitizen immigrants, it is, I believe, far preferable to the formalist, status-centered framework embraced by so many dominant voices. Ethical territoriality is especially valuable in its effort to acknowledge and honor the real attachments people develop in their daily lives, in its commitment against the perpetuation of caste in democratic political communities, and in its insistence on ensuring individual protections against the exercise of state power.

But ethical territoriality has its own hang-ups. First, it promises more than it delivers. The rights and recognition it actually demands for territorially-present noncitizens are limited. The trouble is that ethical territorialists fail to come to terms with the defining condition of alienage itself. So long as persons are present in a territorial community *as* aliens, they remain outsiders to some degree, for alienage entails a conditionality of presence that often trumps whatever formal rights and recognition are extended. Furthermore, when read through the lenses of globalization, we see that territoriality is beginning to fray at the edges. Territoriality as an ethical concept is becoming less authoritative, largely because territory itself no longer organizes social and political life in the determinative way it once did.

This is not to say that territory no longer matters; on the contrary, it continues to structure many of our most significant relationships and associated obligations. Nevertheless, in a world in which affiliations and

---

52 In U.S. constitutional law, citizens abroad may claim protections against the exercise of American power, but aliens abroad may not. *Compare* Reid v. Covert, 354 U.S. 1 (1957), *with* Johnson v. Eistentrager, 339 U.S. 763 (1950). *See generally* NEUMAN, *supra* note 50, at 99-100 (arguing on behalf of a "modern form of the mutuality [of obligation] approach . . . [which] extends constitutional rights to aliens abroad . . . in those situations in which the United States claims an individual's obedience to its commands on the basis of its legitimate authority").

53 Kal Raustiala's outline of a "despatialized understanding of legal rules and protections" is a good starting point. *See* Raustiala, *supra* note 1.

memberships and political engagements do often press beyond the confines of territory, our ethical commitments must be understood to do so as well. A normative political and legal theory that attends to these transnational connections is still in its infancy, but the issues are increasingly on the agenda in scholarly and political debate. I suspect Iris Young's later work will be regarded as important in placing it there. In 2006, Young wrote that

> obligations of justice arise between persons by virtue of the social processes that connect them . . . . Claims that obligations of justice extend globally for some issues, then, are grounded in the fact that some structural social processes connect people across the world without regard to political boundaries.[54]

We are sure to see development of this line of theory in the coming years.

In the meanwhile, those of us working on behalf of immigrants find ourselves facing a lag-time between our social reality and our prevailing political concepts. In most policy debates over immigration, the normative significance of territoriality is unquestioned, and issues of global ethics barely register. Our debates are structured, instead, by competing visions of inward-looking, nation-centered ethics, with ethical territoriality but one version. In such a setting, and given the alternatives, ethical territoriality still represents the best argument for immigrants' rights that we have.

---

54 Iris Marion Young, *Responsibility and Global Justice: A Social Connection Model*, 23 SOC. PHIL. & POL'Y 102, 102 (2006); *see also* Iris Young, *From Guilt to Solidarity: Sweatshops and Political Responsibility*, DISSENT, Spring 2003, at 39. Many other theorists across the disciplines have certainly paved the way. *See, e.g.*, CHARLES BEITZ, POLITICAL THEORY AND INTERNATIONAL RELATIONS (1979); Thomas Pogge, *Cosmopolitanism and Sovereignty*, 103 ETHICS 48 (1992); Martha Nussbaum, *Patriotism and Cosmopolitanism*, BOSTON REV., Oct.-Nov. 1994, at 19; Robbins, *supra* note 48; Massey, *supra* note 41.

Part II
Defining Rights across Borders

[4]
Making People Illegal

Catherine Dauvergne

In August 2001 a ship called the *Tampa* captured the Australian public imagination. It incited the most divisive public discourse of more than a decade and dominated a late 2001 national election campaign which returned the centre-right Liberal-National coalition government to power for a third term.[1] The *Tampa* was a Norwegian freighter that rescued a group of people in an unseaworthy craft attempting to cross from Indonesia to Australia to make asylum claims. Following the rescue, Australia refused to allow the *Tampa* to deliver the 'rescuees' to its shores. The following few weeks featured the deployment of SAS troops, international pressure from Indonesia, Norway and the United Nations High Commission for Refugees, a habeas corpus claim brought to the Federal Court[2] and, ultimately, a challenge to international refugee law that the government labeled its 'Pacific Solution'.[3] The presence of the *Tampa* in the Australian collective imagination will endure long past the return or resettlement of the people on board the boat, and beyond the duration of the government it helped to elect. In spite of this, however, the 438 people on board the *Tampa* represent a small fraction of the estimated 60,103 people who were in Australia without legal authorization at the time, and an almost infinitesimally small fraction of the people on the move without legal authorization around the globe.

The *Tampa* incident is, however, emblematic of the character of migration and migration laws at the opening of the twenty-first century. It demonstrates in miniature the new twists that have appeared in the old coupling of nation and migration in the era of globalization. Perhaps the most significant of these is the coalescing of 'illegal' as an identity.

The rhetorical battle that raged in the press over the *Tampa* crisis was marked by hesitancy over how to refer to the people at the centre of the drama. They were referred to as asylum-seekers, queue jumpers, refugees, boatpeople[4] and, most ubiquitously, illegals. Of all of these, illegal was the easiest, as the needs of accuracy and of generalization coincided. To refer to these people as illegal entrants was legally correct given Australia's universal visa requirement. Illegal was also a label that obscured difference and individuality, labelling all in one swathe. Some attempts were made in the press to refer to those on the boat by national identity labels. Early on they were reported to be Afghanis and, later, Afghanis as well as Iraqis and Pakistanis. It seemed that certainty about national identities was difficult to come by, making the label 'illegal' a better catch-all on this count as well. Thus, illegal was treated as a neutral term. 'Afghani' or 'Pakistani' tended to influence opinions based on one's views of whether the regime in power was cause enough to leave. 'Asylum-seekers', 'queue jumpers' or 'refugees' each display a political and legal perspective. The problem with 'illegal' as a rhetorical solution is, of course, that 'illegal' is not neutral.

The nominalization of illegal in this sense and its function as a false liberal legal neutral category are my central concerns in this chapter. I argue that the dynamics of globalization are shifting the boundaries of the insider–outsider dichotomy. Formerly, this boundary fitted neatly around the border of the nation, with discrete categories of 'us' and 'them' corresponding to legal categories of citizen and alien. The new label names the other not only as an outsider to a particular nation, but as an outsider to any nation. As such, the other is outside the law itself, in a word, illegal. I explore this argument in three stages. First, I briefly outline the relationship between migration law and nation that is shifting in the era of globalization. Second, I consider what aspects of the globalizing phenomenon are most important in turning illegal into an identity category. Finally, I conclude by analysing illegal people as a 'globalized' consequence of liberalism's exclusions.

Migration Laws and the Nation

The modern political world is divided into nations. Subject only to exceptions such as the high seas and Antarctica, the geography of the entire globe is 'nationalized'. There is no empty, non-nation space where people can exist beyond the reach of nation. In the contemporary post-colonial era, nations have been formally equalized by transforming colonial space into 'new' national space. The importance of 'state' in disciplines such as international relations, the precise definition it is afforded in law through the Montevideo Convention on the Rights and Duties of States 1933 and the ambiguity of the nation state couplet have not succeeded in diminishing the prevalence of nation.

Despite this prevalence, however, nation is elusive. Attempts to pin 'nation' down with academic precision have resorted to central terms which themselves suggest instability. Smith's attempt to define 'nation' by reference to ethnicity nonetheless conceded that this could not be the case with new nations such as the USA, Australia or Canada (Smith, 1991, p. 40), and presumably a large number of colonially constructed nations as well. Given the importance of his exceptions, he instead asserted that these nations existed by providing a sense of belonging to individuals which were similar in a mythic sense to ethnic nations. The importance of mythic fabrication is a good part of what sustains this account in the world beyond Europe. Gellner's conception of nation puts myth in a central role (Gellner, 1983). Anderson's seminal work isolates collective imagining as vital in forming the 'imagined communities' of his title (Anderson, 1991).[5] Hobsbawn asserts the importance of invented traditions and of the 'assumptions, hopes, needs, longings and interests of ordinary people' (Hobsbawn, 1983, pp. 13–14).

These trends in scholarship point up two things which are significant for the relationship between migration law and nation. First is that nation is inseparable from people – its people – ultimately its citizens. Accordingly, in each of these analyses nation and national identity – a perception of myth, symbol, imagination – are linked. Second, in contrasting the difficulty of defining nation and the instability woven into all attempts to do so with the predominance of nation in the political world, we are confronted with a concept which must have, against these odds, a stable appearance. This stability is necessary for any particular nation to be defined, and is at the crux of nation's relationship with law and especially migration law.

The importance of people, therefore, is one aspect of the interweaving of migration law and nation. Of all the subcategories and subdivisions of law, migration law is that which controls the membership of the nation. Legal frameworks for controlling entry – systems of passports, visas, entry permits, refusals, deportations – are inscribed in the texts of migration laws. More than any other type of law, migration laws make borders meaningful for the movement of people.[6] Migration laws are also responsible for prescribing degrees of membership. Their provisions establish rights for citizens, permanent residents, visaed students, guest workers, refugees and visitors, and through these categories of rights conjure these identities into being. For the 'new' nations of migration like the USA, Australia, Canada or New Zealand, migration laws are crucially bound up with populating the nation and the exercise of nation-building. In only slightly earlier times, they provided a framework for 'settlement' and regulated the composition of the 'founding' population. The importance of migration to the mythic foundations of these 'nations of immigration' plays an important role both in silencing and in marking the absence of the voices of indigenous populations. In nations which have well-developed contemporary immigration programmes, migration law provides the effective controls on the full membership which is inscribed in citizenship law. The particular, bodily, unequal hurdles to permanent residency which are written in migration law texts provide an effective population screen, leaving to citizenship law symbolic matters such as allegiance and equality (Dauvergne, 2000a). In these ways, migration law is essential to creating the population which can become the nation.

This gatekeeping function of migration laws is the first layer of the nation and migration law intertwinement. Migration law, in addition, provides a key support for the mirage of stability essential for an identity as nation. The texts of migration laws are written as frameworks to accommodate changing conceptions of national values and priorities. Rather than engraving a fixed set of values, migration law provides both an assertion that there is such a set, and a practical method for fluidity. In the long-standing Canadian Immigration Act (RSC, 1985, c.I-2) this was accomplished by listing a set of objectives in the act which ranged from border protection to upholding humanitarian traditions, some of which were contradictory.[7] In the crucial test for administrative decision-makers, no act of discretion within the framework of the act could fail to conform to at least some of these objectives. In the Australian Migration Act (1958 (Cth)), the hodge-podge of objectives is avoided by referring simply to controlling borders for the national interest.[8] As the national interest is ever changing and impossible to define, the scope of the Act is limitless. Administrative conformity requires only that a claim can be made in the name of national interest. In matters of migration which are ever present on the public agenda, claims of national interest are often mustered to each side of any argument.

The malleability of these migration statutes does not stop with these types of introductory statements which become the subject of parliamentary debate when the law comes round for renewal. The nitty-gritty regulatory teeth of these frameworks are also structured to accommodate shifts, and this capacity is insidious because of its invisibility. In both Canada and Australia, two aspects of the law are central to determining who will be admitted: the 'point system' and the number of visas given out. The mechanics are not identical in the two nations, but the central ideas are. In both places, the number of visas to be provided in a year in various categories and subcategories is not written into the law but is decided by the executive and reported to parliament. This allows control over admission to be finely tuned and reduces both democratic and public scrutiny as the final numbers are reported, not debated.

The point system is the way of 'scoring' applicants for admission over a range of criteria such as education, (labour) market value and English language ability. It was introduced in both places in the 1970s when racially based exclusions were dismantled. The point system was preferred for the neutrality it provided, presumably because it produced a number. The point system is set out in each Act's regulations, but the actual points awarded for factors such as a particular type of education and the total points required to cross the threshold are subject to frequent bureaucratic adjustment. Changes are so frequent that they rarely attract any public attention.

Thus at both the lofty level of aspirational statement and the lowly level of bureaucratic number-crunching, migration laws are written to accommodate an ever-changing view of national value, priority and identity. And despite this malleability, they retain the reassuring solidity of the law. The regulatory minutiae of migration law provide a banal illustration of the mutual reliance of law and nation, within which the relationship of migration law and nation is an easily observable instance.

Peter Fitzpatrick has described the relation between law and nation as one of complementarity, where they 'mutually compensate for their intrinsic inadequacies'. In his analysis, 'the irresolution of nation's identity is "overcome" by law and the irresolution of law's identity is "overcome" by nation' (Fitzpatrick, 2001, p. 129). As migration law is concerned with the limit of the nation, the border itself and the mythology of national identity, it constitutes a site where complementarity is easily observed. The 'overcoming' essential to Fitzpatrick's argument is illustrated in the incessant adjustment of migration law to meet national need and the use of national need as a device to justify migration statutes. Migration law is an easy case. The commonality of nation and law which is the crux of Fitzpatrick's thesis is their need for a boundary. The importance of the boundary for the concept of nation is demonstrated in theories of nation discussed above, especially Anderson, whose imaginary communities are necessarily limited (Anderson, 1991, p. 7). The importance of boundary for a theorization of law has meant that a limit to the community is an essential Rawlsian assumption (Rawls, 1985, p. 233),[9] and a precondition for Dworkin's community of principle (Dworkin, 1986, p. 209). Migration law is concerned directly with the boundary. As law writ large, it offers the boundary the veneer of stability which allows it to function as such.

The veneer of stability is reinforced from time to time by SAS troops boarding ships like the *Tampa*.[10] The malleability of migration law to national need was highlighted during the *Tampa* 'incident' by the government's hasty changes to the law to fit it to its actions, and by the fact that putting the public spotlight on Australia's 'vulnerability' in this way secured the opposition party's support for a series of migration law adjustments it had long resisted.[11] The migration law–national identity coupling is not new. It is characteristic of the era of migration control which coincides relatively neatly with the twentieth century (Dummett and Nicol, 1990; Torpey, 2000). What is emerging at the outset of the twenty-first century in response to the growing forces of globalization is a new twist on this relationship, the nub of which is encapsulated by the idea of people 'being illegal'.

Globalization and Extra-legal Migration

While the *Tampa* was anchored in international waters near the Australian territory of Christmas Island, one of the tactics that was used in the raging public debate was to assert that Australia's international reputation was being damaged by the affair. This allegation was supported in various ways, including, for example, conducting person-in-the-street interviews with Norwegians in the hometown of the *Tampa*'s captain and broadcasting these on Australian television, or reporting in Australian newspapers stories about the stories which had been run in newspapers in Britain or the USA. A sub-debate even developed about whether or not Australia's international reputation was indeed harmed.

The technological conduct of this argument marks the story as belonging to the era of globalization. Globalizing technologies of communication make it possible, or even conceivable, for Norwegian opinion to be collected and broadcast in this way. Similar technologies facilitate Australian newspapers reporting on American newspapers reporting on Australia contemporaneously, or given the international dateline, even sooner. Moreover, our routine acceptance of these technologies which shrink the globe makes the views of people in Oslo or Baltimore or Nottingham relevant to a kitchen-table debate in Wagga Wagga or Perth.

Definitions of globalization are now as diffuse as the phenomenon they attempt to pin down. They routinely make reference to economic factors such as exchange rates, securities markets and Starbucks, and to communication technologies such as the new wireless era, SMS messaging and the routinization of innovations like email and the Internet. Globalization is about these things and, importantly also about the conceptual shifts which accompany them. That is, the globalizing forces which have economic or communication effects also affect the way we envision the world and our place in it. Our capacity to imagine the world, including our perceptions of international borders and of nations as entities, and the way that imagination seeps into our retelling of the world, are also part of globalization.

A vast theoretical literature has flourished alongside other globalizing phenomena. The significant debates within this theory[12] include whether globalization is a new phenomenon, whether it is inevitable, whether it is liberal and whether it heralds the end of the nation state era. Perhaps overarching all of these is an attempt to normatively evaluate it. My examination of illegal migration in this chapter offers some insight into both how the nation-state is responding to globalization and to unearthing the liberal nature of at least some of globalization's aspects. Situating my work normatively is harder, for, although my analysis focuses on exclusion and marginalization in the matrix of globalization I am also resolutely optimistic about some of the potential of broader prosperity which globalizing forces could offer and completely free of nostalgia for the cold war and other earlier versions of global alignment.

The debate about the nation-state in globalization theory covers the spectrum from those who assert that the nation-state has already been eclipsed (Ohmae, 1995), to those claiming it 'is anything but irrelevant' (Ruggie, 1993, p. 142), to others who claim it is gaining in importance (Weiss, 1998). That people are less mobile than money or ideas is often a factor in assessments of the resilience of the nation-state. For Hirst and Thompson the fact the people remain 'nationalized' is the crucial element ensuring the continued importance of the nation state (Hirst and Thompson 1996, ch. 8). Their analysis focuses on the elements of migration law – passports, visas, employment authorizations – and highlights the role of the nation-state as the legitimator of law. Regardless of one's assessment of the resilience of the nation-state, there is a consensus that the nation-state is under threats of some sort and that the globalizing era has ushered in challenges for governance, especially economic ones. It is my argument, detailed below, that the present pervasive 'crackdown' on illegal migration responds to these perceived or real threats.

The question of whether globalization is a liberal force runs alongside discussions of free trade (trade 'liberalization'), 'democratization' and the spread of human rights doctrines. As such, it sometimes appears as a kind of post-cold war triumphalism. In a markedly different context, Tom Young (1995) points out that liberalism has always had a globalizing agenda. This observation is vital both to an assessment of globalization theory and to fitting together globalization, law and nation. Liberalism is marked by a tension between the universal and the particular.[13] This tension maps onto the tension between the universal and the particular which Fitzpatrick finds in the essence of law and of nation (Fitzpatrick, 1992; 2001, ch. 4). The three level correspondence which results calls attention to the challenge of reading liberal law and liberal nation in the global era. For extra-legal migrants, globalization transforms old liberal exclusions into new via a transformation in the migration law and nation correspondence.

It is difficult to assess the place of population movements within the story of globalization. In an extensively researched analysis forming part of their systematic evaluation of globalization David Held and his co-authors examine human migration patterns throughout history on the basis of their extensity, intensity, velocity, and impact on host and home states and societies (Held et al., 1999, ch. 6). Their conclusion is tentative, stating that if present trends continue the contemporary pattern of migration 'may supersede its predecessors in terms of intensity as well as extensity' (ibid., p. 312). It is inaccurate to suggest that more people are on the move than ever before. The increasingly free movement of goods, capital and ideas which marks globalization has not been accompanied by an opening of borders to people. Even the much publicized open borders within the European Union are only open to nationals; only concern a relatively small geographic area and only provide mobility between states with broadly similar living and legal standards (cf. Paliwala, 1995). The fact that the removal of border controls has not resulted in significant population migrations[14] suggests that those who were motivated to move within Europe were qualified to do so under the previous migration law regimes and that open borders alone do not generate population shifts.

Despite the lack of coincidence between globalization and migration generally, tales of illegal migration are increasingly prevalent. It is not an exaggeration to suggest that the global media report stories of illegal migration at least every week. The past year has brought memorable stories of stowaways dying in a lorry at Dover, of asylum-seekers attempting to run through the Channel Tunnel, of people making 'suicide run' attempts to cross the border between Mexico and the USA, of boats reaching Canada's Atlantic shore, of Albanians dying aboard a ship reaching France and of a string of vessels attempting to reach Australia waters. While it is impossible – by its nature – to know if extra-legal migration really is increasing in raw numbers, the press alone suggests that it is not premature to diagnose a 'moral panic'.[15] The dimensions of this panic owe much to globalizing forces, as does the antidote typically applied – more stringent laws.

One thing that each of these stories has in common is 'class' dimension: nationals of 'poor' nations moving towards the borders of 'prosperous' nations. Despite borders being transgressed around the world, sometimes by the same people in transit to their ultimately headline capturing destinations, only certain borders are defended in the international press. The 'us' and 'them' line, so familiarly drawn to constitute the nation is shifted in this discourse to embrace a new 'us'. It is the 'Fortress Europe' mentality expanding to a new 'Fortress OECD' or 'Fortress Rich'.

The seemingly simultaneous arrival of illegal migrants at borders around the world is an effect of the technologies of globalization. We can see three of these stories side by side in the same newspaper, or one after another on the same programme, because of the same communication technologies that spread them and gave the *Tampa* story international play. This fuels the moral panic, 'we' the rich are under siege – it is happening everywhere, all the time. Technologies of globalization are also involved in the mechanics of the people-smuggling trade which supports at least some of this migration. The highly organized snakehead gangs of China's Fujian province make use of the same technologies of communication, finance and transport to organize 'delivery' of paying customers to Britain, Canada, Australia or the USA.

But just as globalization's technologies multiply and re-broadcast to the 'us' group images of the threat at 'our' doorstep on the other side of the earth, the same technologies present to potential migrants images of alternate lives. Prosperous countries are no longer unimaginably distant, impossible to visualize. Flight is easier to imagine, and choices are more tangible.[16] Those who make perilous illegal journeys, however, encounter the sharp contradiction of globalization mythology: the geographies compressed are metaphorical – when travelling in an airtight lorry container each kilometre counts.

The moral panic of illegal migration which is made possible by globalizing technologies is perceived as one of the many ways that globalization threatens the capacity of nation-states. As such, a series of legal measures in prosperous nations which represent a 'crackdown' on illegal migration must be read as one way of nations asserting their resilience to globalization. Over the past few years, many of the prosperous destination nations have tightened legal controls aimed at regulating entry. The USA passed the Illegal Immigration Reform and Immigrant Responsibility Act in 1996 (Pub.L. 104-208, Div. C, 110 Stat. 3009–546) aimed at limiting the welfare state access and labour market participation of extra-legal migrants, and has devoted additional funds to 'enforcing' its southern border with Mexico (Kitfield, 1997; Palafox, 1996). Canada's new immigration legislation penalizes those who do not co-operate in efforts to obtain identity documents from their home state and also names a 'new' crime of people smuggling as the most serious transgression of the Act (S.C. 2001 c. 27). Australia has created a new category of refugee visa, with fewer rights attached, to single out refugees who arrive by boat (visa class 785). And in Europe, discussions are afoot about how to better secure the 'Fortress' against asylum-seekers (Nacheman, 2001).[17]

These actions mark the nation as strong. In this era when the capacity of a nation to control its borders and make them meaningful is being questioned in many fora, moving to reinforce them against 'outsiders' is an assertion to the contrary. Through this spate of new legislation, nations reassert their sovereignty. Not a new sovereignty transformed by globalizing forces (Jayasuriya, 1999) nor a sovereignty ebbing away to the benefit of all concerned (MacCormick, 1993), but simple traditional territorial sovereignty controlling people in place. By moving to reinforce the borderline between us and them, nations seek to bolster their self-identity, their way of being nations. When the Australian Prime Minister took his 'tough stance' against the 400-plus tired, hungry and unarmed men, women and children rescued by the *Tampa*, he did it in the name of 'defending Australia'. This sentiment resonated in public discourse showing that while the notion of a physical threat to the nation was patently ridiculous, the threat to the idea/ideal of the nation was palpable.

In addition to asserting sovereignty as traditionally understood, this newest round of regulation against illegal migrants is also part of a new facet of the migration law – nation relation. This development occurs in two ways. First, as both the moral panic over illegal migration and the legal responses to it are not limited to one nation. Globalization gives both factors the appearance of happening all over the world, all at once. This is not true, of course, but that matters little to the mythologizing of globalization. It is equally not true that McDonald's exists the world over or that everyone can access the Internet – globalization is marked by uneven penetration (Twining, 2002, fn. 32 and surrounding text). The impression that the 'problem' of illegal migration is a global one, and the fact that those who seek to migrate outside the law have access to a geographically broader range of options than in earlier eras, contribute to the construction of an identity category of people named by the new noun 'illegal'. We create in this way the impression that the people who seek entry to Australia via Indonesia by boat are *the same as* those who attempt to walk the length of the Channel Tunnel or swim the Rio Grande. This allows talk of 'illegals', in international and intranational discourses as though the term had some fixed meaning besides being an adjectival description of legal transgression.

The second emerging facet of the migration law – nation relation which is demonstrated by the crackdown on illegal migration – is an enhanced power of exclusion. Capturing the moral panic about extra-legal migrants and enshrining it in law allows governments control which their borders lack. When a part of the population is labelled 'illegal' it is excluded from within. Despite their (sometimes long-term) presence and their contribution to the economy, debate about appropriate participation in the political and social community is all but silenced by the label illegal. This is markedly different from the tenor of debate which surrounds the entitlements of long-term guest workers, for example (Brubaker, 1989). The difference is underlined by the arguments that Legomsky musters to urge that restricting the sizeable illegal population of the USA is counterproductive: as illegals they provide labour which Americans will not, receive no state benefits and abide by the law to avoid deportation (Legomsky, 1998). When the nation is unable to assert its traditional sovereignty by closing its borders, it retains its power to separate us from them through this labelling, although the exclusion is now diffuse and no longer lines up neatly with the clear bright lines of a map. Those excluded are outside the law, regardless of which nation they enter or attempt to enter.

On Being Illegal

The label 'illegal' is empty of content. It says even less than other identity slots in the migration hierarchy: resident, visitor, guest worker or refugee. It circumscribes identity solely in terms of a relationship with law: those who are illegal have broken (our) law. Discourse about illegals gathers together a shred of common meaning, some pejorative connotation and a fixed idea of the law. The lowest common denominator approach which made the word look 'neutral' in the *Tampa* debate is false: illegals are transgressors – and nothing else – by definition.

The minimal content of the term 'illegal' operates in two ways, obscuring the identities of those to whom it is affixed and extending the identity of nation into the global era. Migration laws set out myriad requirements for legal presence within a state. Only citizens are immunized from the regulatory structures these laws erect.[18] In a technical legal sense anyone who breaches one of these regulations would be 'an illegal'. In reality, however, the label connotes those who are poor and brown and destitute. The backpacking tourist who overstays his or her visa and the business person who fails to renew papers on time are not who comes to mind when we label illegals. In Australia in 2001 the largest group of 'illegals' were visitors who had outstayed their legal welcome and among these the largest nationality group was British[19] – hardly those who people our imaginary sweatshops and brothels.

We imagine illegals as desperate and needy and other. The label obscures differences among the individuals it is applied to, even those differences that matter to the law which could, for example, carry an entitlement to remain as a refugee. Homogenizing individual identities under this label which has so little content of its own clears mental space for inscribing the other with any attributes we desire. This fits well within the migration law – nation relationship as the changing needs of a national identity require an other whose attributes are equally variant. The desperation of the illegal other appears in contrast with our prosperity as a nation. We 'have' and they 'have not'; entitlement to membership is ours to bestow. One of the shifts which is occurring at present is that as 'illegal' emerges as a globally meaningful identity label, the characteristics of all of those nations against which this other is imagined also tend to merge. The line between having and not having can no longer be easily conceived as fitting around the border of *a* nation and must instead fit around the border of *all* prosperous nations, creating a global understanding of 'insiders' and 'outsiders'. This conception also resonates with the pedigree of the emotive term 'nation': prosperous Western nation-states are closer to the ideal of nation than others. Their desirability as destinations for extra-legal migrants functions as a measure of their status and standing as nations. While globalization may bring some characteristics of the nation-state under threat, it also allows the exclusion which is essential to the existence of nations to expand. National actions designed to assert traditional sovereignty also contribute to a globalizing of sovereignty in this new way.

'Illegal' emerges in reference to the law. The othering process facilitates a fixed idea of nation and does so relying on a fixed idea of the law. The two are necessarily intertwined. As we have seen, the content of migration law – especially the most important parts for determining who will be admitted and who will not – is easily and frequently altered. As the label 'illegal' has no content aside from being against the law, it accommodates similarly frequent changes. The law and the nation name the other in this way as not-us and not-legal.

In the present state of international law, the importance of making people illegal in this way is most problematic for refugees. The legal category and legal identity of refugees is subsumed by that of illegals. Those who are refugees can make claim to a narrow and tenuous 'right to remain' in many prosperous states;[20] they cannot however make a claim to entry of any state where they are not nationals. For this reason, many refugees have transgressed migration laws as a prerequisite to making a refugee claim. The connotations of the label 'illegal' are thus attached to them. Whether their claim is ultimately successful, part of this homogenizing, vilifying, othering label remains with them.

Making people illegal reflects an increasingly globally coherent view that there are proper and improper reasons to migrate. The force of sanctions against extra-legal migration are often aimed at 'mere economic migrants'. Being destitute, or even being poor or 'average' and wanting a better life in return for abandoning all that is familiar and starting one's life over again, are insufficient reasons to migrate today. Those who are 'merely' seeking a better life are the prime targets of the constricting global migration net. This is a key marker of migration regimes in the twenty-first century. The massive population movements of the nineteenth and twentieth centuries were made up in significant part of people seeking to better their life circumstances. Being poor and willing to start one's life again was formerly a primary reason to migrate, not a reason to be excluded from doing so. While Held and his co-authors can track intense population movements in the present era, those who are on the move are the privileged. People with an abundance of education, training, labour and entrepreneurial experience are welcome and encouraged to migrate. Globalization has in this sense reframed traditional 'class' lines. While the basic contours of privilege are still similar shifts are visible along the edges. Workers in the emerging information technology industry servicing globalization's technology increasingly enjoy worldwide mobility despite comparatively low levels of education and no connections to traditional wealth. Knowledge workers such as academics are included in the global elite despite often being paid little enough that they will never own property. It is common in both groups to develop career patterns that span the globe.

The concept of citizenship was forged alongside the idea of nation. Citizens emerged along with nations in Europe's Enlightenment, and extended its moniker of belonging to the nations of Europe's colonial expansion. Citizenship retains its inclusive and equalizing power despite a strong tradition of scholarship admonishing its exclusions. The new global elite are sometimes referred to as 'global citizens'. They belong to the world in its entirety, not to any one nation. As such they are 'insiders' despite mixed and overlapping allegiances in a traditional sense. Over the past 50 years, the legal strictures of citizenship have become more flexible. Dual citizenship is more frequently accepted, denationalization is rarer. Nations which have had rigid barriers to citizenship are relaxing them (Rubenstein, 1998; Rubenstein and Adler, 2000). It is easier to be or become a citizen of an increasing number of nations.

This pattern in citizenship law coincides with the tightening of restrictions on extra-legal migration, and reveals the essence of liberalism and nation within globalization. When we calibrate our instruments to measure inclusion we find it to be on the increase. But similarly, exclusions are multiplying. As the entitlements of citizenship are increasingly standardized and accessible, so the exclusions of illegal status are increasingly homogenized and universalized. The liberal project of universalization includes within it a potential to universalize exclusion. This is concomitantly the logic of the nation. In order for inclusion within the nation to increase, the exclusion of the other against which the nation is imagined must also increase. The illegal creates a blank slate against which the other can be inscribed as required. The threat which globalization brings to some aspects of the nation-state does not threaten the logic which underpins the nation. What emerges may at some point in the globalized future have a different name than nation, but its reliance on an 'us' and 'them' line seems secure. Just as the citizen was a universal subject for the nation, the illegal is constituted as a universal subject for the global era.

The story of the *Tampa* is not finished as I write. Since the 'rescue' an intriguing combination of migration law amendments and naval deployment have ensured that no asylum-seekers have reached Australian shores. An unknown number of people are waiting in Naura and in Papua New Guinea, for the culmination of the Pacific Solution.[21] The co-operation of those nations has been purchased at considerable price by the Australian government.[22] The illegals are awaiting their fate in the company of those too poor to enforce their sovereignty in the same traditional way Australia has. The Norwegians in the street and American editorialists have forgotten the Pacific Solution, understandably in the face of the first war of the twenty-first century. But the contours of new understandings of 'us' and 'them', new ways of reading nation and exclusion, are inscribed in both events.

Notes

1 The Liberal National Coalition won a third successive majority government on 11 November 2001, in an election where some commentators suggested that the *Tampa*'s rescue action and the government's response were a crucial turning point. The opposition Labour Party, which had polled well leading into the election, aligned itself with most of the government's policies related to the *Tampa* incident, despite the divisive nature of the public and legal debate.

2 *Victorian Council for Civil Liberties Inc* v. *Minister for Immigration and Multicultural Affairs* [2001] FCA 1297 (11 September 2001); overturned by *Ruddock* v. *Vadarlis* (includes corrigendum dated 20 September 2001) [2001] FCA 1329 (18 September 2001); leave to appeal to the High Court of Australia denied.

3 So named because it involves removing those attempting to reach Australia to nearby Pacific nations to have their asylum claims assessed. In the government's rhetoric, this is a regional solution for a regional problem. As of early 2002, it is not yet clear how many who are determined to have valid claims will be allowed to resettle in Australia. To date, Papua New Guinea and Nauru have hosted people moved under this plan. This challenges international refugee law because it depends on an aggressive turning away of boats carrying people seeking asylum to nations which are further away.

4 The Australian press has made this one word since 1999 when the number of illegal boat arrivals jumped sharply to a total of approximately 4000 for the fiscal year 1999–2000.

5 Peter Fitzpatrick offers a compelling critique of these attempts to define nation in Fitzpatrick (2001, pp. 114–20).

6 A myriad of other legal frameworks make borders meaningful for goods or money or ideas, which are vitally important to the people whose border passage is regulated in migration texts.

7 The list in full includes supporting demographic goals, enriching Canada's cultural and social fabric, facilitating family reunion, encouraging adaptation to Canadian society, facilitating visitor entry, ensuring standards of non-discrimination for admission, fulfilling international legal obligations, supporting the humanitarian tradition, fostering economic development, maintaining the health, safety and good order of Canadian society, and promoting international order and justice.

8 The most important subsection reads: 'the object of this Act is to regulate, in the national interest, the coming into and presence in, Australia of non-citizens' (subs 4(1)).

9 Rawls assumes as a precursor to his theory of justice that one enters a community at birth and leaves at death. This assumption has been the subject of extensive criticism, to which Rawls (1999) responds in his *The Law of Peoples*.

10 As occurred several days after the rescue because the boat had entered Australian waters.

11 These included changes to how the refugee definition would be interpreted and the addition of a privative clause to the Migration Act.

12 I canvass this theory in more detail in 'Illegal Migration and Sovereignty' (Dauvergre, 2002).

13 Fishkin (1982) formulates this in the device of the threshold of heroism: liberalism is sufficiently focused on the individual that as a moral philosophy it does not require sacrifices which require more than minimal sacrifice.

14 See annual net migration rates reported at www.europa.eu.int/comm/eurostat/Public/datashop/print-product/EN?catalogue=Eurostat&product=3-po020in-EN&mode=download.

15 I borrow this phrase from Stuart Hall et al. of *Policing the Crisis: Mugging, the State and Law and Order* (1978).

16 It was reported at the time of the *Tampa* affair that Australia was the least expensive destination for people smuggled to offer to Afghanis living in refugee camps in Pakistan.
17 It is difficult if not impossible in the new regulatory net to separate the traffickers from the trafficked. While most legal regimes reserve their harshest penalties for traffickers, it is necessarily true that those who are most often punished are the migrants themselves. No nation has yet attempted to limit its crackdown exclusively to traffickers.
18 It is possible for some citizens to be deported, but usually a preliminary step is to strip them of their citizenship on the grounds that it was fraudulently obtained.
19 The UK is ranked first on the list of countries with the most overstayers at 30 June 2001 with 6273 overstayers, 10.5 per cent of the total. The US accounts for 8.6 per cent of the total. Third on the list is the People's Republic of China with 6.5 per cent (www.immi. gov.au/ facts/86overstayers_1.htm).
20 I have argued elsewhere that this right is elusive and that rights discourse is a poor tool for refugees because much of refugee law and political discourse is grounded in liberalism's humanitarian consensus. See Dauvergne (2000b).
21 Some of the original *Tampa* rescuees had their refugee status claims assessed in New Zealand as well. This was a much smaller number, processed more quickly.
22 The government has not publicized the actual amount spent, however, in addition to covering all related costs, significant financial incentives have been offered and some rumours suggest the cost may be in the order of several hundred thousand Australian dollars per claimant.

References

Anderson, B. (1991), *Imagined Communities: Reflections on the Origin and Spread of Nationalism*, revd edn, London and New York: Verso.

Brubaker, W.R. (1989), 'Introduction', in Brubaker, W.R. (ed.) *Imagination and the Politics of Citizenship in Europe and North America*, Lanham, MD: University Press of America.

Dauvergne, C. (2000a), 'Citizenship, migration laws and women: gendering permanent residency statistics', *Melbourne University Law Review*, 24, 280.

Dauvergne, C. (2000b), 'The dilemma of rights for refugees', *University of New South Wales Law Journal*, 23, 56.

Dauvergne, C. (2002), 'Illegal Migration and Sovereignty', in Dauvergne, C. (ed.), *Jurisprudence for an Interconnected Globe*, Aldershot: Ashgate.

Dummett, A. and Nicol, A. (1990), *Subjects, Citizens Aliens and Others: Nationality and Immigration Law*, London: Weidenfeld and Nicolson.

Dworkin, R. (1986), *Law's Empire*, Cambridge, MA: Belknap Press.

Fishkin, J. (1982), *The Limits of Obligation*, New Haven, CT: Yale University Press.

Fitzpatrick, P. (1992), *The Mythology of Modern Law*, London and New York: Routledge.

Fitzpatrick, P. (2001), *Modernism and the Grounds of Law*, Cambridge: Cambridge University Press.

Gellner, E. (1983), *Nations and Nationalism*, Ithaca, NY: Cornell University Press.

Hall, S., Critcher, C., Jefferson, T., Clarke, J. and Robert, B. (1978), *Policing the Crisis: Mugging the State and Law and Order*, London: Macmillan.

Held, D., McGrew, A., Goldblatt, D. and Perraton, J. (1999), *Global Transformations: Politics, Economics and Culture*, Cambridge: Polity Press.
Hirst, P. and Thompson, G. (1996), *Globalization in Question*, Cambridge: Polity Press.
Hobsbawn, E.J. (1983), 'Introduction', in Hobsbawn, E.J. and Ranger, T. (eds) *The Invention of Tradition*, Cambridge: Cambridge University Press.
Hobsbawn, E.J. (1992), *Nations and Nationalism since 1780: Programme, Myth, Reality*, (2nd edn) Cambridge: Cambridge University Press.
Jayasuriya, K. (1999), 'Globalisation, law and the transformation of sovereignty: the emergence of global regulatory governance', *Indiana Journal of Global Legal Studies*, 6, 425.
Legomsky, S. (1998), 'Employer sanctions: past and future', in Duignan, P. and Gann, L.H. (eds), *The Debate in the United States over Immigration*, Hoover Institution Press, Oxford: Clarendon Press.
MacCormick, N. (1993), 'Beyond the Sovereign State', *Modern Law Review*, 56, 1.
Ohmae, K. (1995), *End of the Nation State*, London: HarperCollins.
Paliwala, A. (1995), 'Law and the Constitution of the "Immigrant" in Europe: A UK Policy Perspective', in Fitzpatrick, P. (ed.) *Nationalism, Racism and the Rule of Law*, Aldershot: Dartmouth.
Rawls, J. (1971), *A Theory of Justice*, Oxford: Oxford University Press.
Rawls, J. (1985), 'Justice as fairness: political not metaphysical', *Philosophy and Public Affairs*, 14, 223.
Rawls, J. (1999), *The Law of Peoples*, Cambridge, MA: Harvard University Press.
Rubenstein, K. (1998), 'Citizenship in a Borderless World', in Anghie, A. and Sturgess, G. (eds), *Legal Visions of the 21st Century: Essays in Honour of Judge Christopher Weeramantry*, Kluwer Law International, The Hague: Boston.
Rubenstein, K. and Adler, D. (2000), 'International citizenship: the future of nationality in a globalized world', *Indiana Journal of Global Legal Studies*, 7, 519.
Ruggie, J.G. (1993), 'Territoriality and beyond: problematizing modernity in international relations', *International Organization*, 47, 139.
Smith, A.D. (1986), *The Ethnic Origins of Nations*, Oxford and New York: Blackwell.
Smith, A.D. (1991), *National Identity*, London and New York: Penguin.
Torpey, J. (2000), *The Invention of the Passport: Surveillance, Citizenship and the State*, Cambridge: Cambridge University Press.
Twining, W. (2002), 'The Province of Jurisprudence Re-examined', in Dauvergne, C. (ed.), *Jurisprudence for an Interconnected Globe*, Aldershot: Ashgate.
Weiss, L. (1998), *The Myth of the Powerless State: Governing the Economy in a Global Era*, Cambridge: Polity Press.
Young, T. (1995), '"A Project to be Realised": global liberalism and contemporary Africa', *Millenium*, 24, 527.

Selected Newspaper and Magazine Articles

'A victory crafted by John Howard', *The Age*, 12 November 2001, 22.
'Refugees and others', *Sydney Morning Herald*, 28 December 2001, 14.
'Tampa Crisis won't be a slur on Australia, claims Howard', *The West Australian*, 9 March 2001 (on line version).
Barton, M. (2002), 'Ruddock warns off UN', *The West Australian*, 9 January (on line version).
Clennel, A. (2002), 'New Zealand denies it's a new magnet for people smugglers', *Sydney Morning Herald*, 18 January, 4.
Henderson, G. (2001), 'Too late for PM to abandon refugees ship', *Sydney Morning Herald*, 13 November, 14.
Kitfield, J. (1997), 'Crossing the line', *Government Executive Magazine*, 1 July at www.govevec.com/features/0797s5.html
Mares, P. (2001), 'If not the Pacific Solution, then what?', *Australian Financial Review*, 21 December, 4.
Nacheman, A. (2001), 'EU moves to tighten immigration, asylum, human trafficking', *Agence France Press*, 11 February, accessed at Dow Jones Interactive.
Palafox, J. (1996), 'Militarizing the border', *Covert Action Quarterly*, 56, at www.caq.com/CAQ56border.html

[5]

Travel Plans: Border Crossings and the Rights of Transnational Migrants

Ratna Kapur*

> We are the people you never see.[1]
>
> [Y]ou begin to give up the very idea of belonging. Suddenly, this thing, this belonging, it seems like some long, dirty lie.[2]
>
> Come on, mohajir! Immigrant. . . . Pack-up double quick and be off to what gutter you choose.[3]

I. Introduction

Dirty Pretty Things, a compelling, cross-cultural thriller from the United Kingdom, tells the complex stories of illegals, semi-illegals, and the other side of London life. These lives are far from the story of the good old English chap, the ritz and glitz of Oxford Street, the grandeur and chimes of Big Ben, and the formal sterility of Buckingham palace. It is the story of foreigners forced to make a living in the shadows of the British capital—the busboys, taxi drivers, chambermaids, porters, hookers, and hospital orderlies who feed, clean, and sexually service the rich and powerful, keeping London looking pretty, or at least glisteningly sterile. The film foregrounds the stories of Okwe, a Nigerian doctor who has been run out of his homeland and is an undocumented worker, and Senay, a Muslim Turkish chambermaid, granted asylum, but without the right to work. Both have taken up employment in a West London hotel run by a Spaniard, Señor "Sneaky." It is the sort of place where mundane underground businesses like drug dealing, sex work, and more sinister ones—like organ trafficking—take place. Senay dreams of go-

---

* Fellow, Program for the Study of International Law at the Graduate Institute of International Studies in Geneva; Director, Centre for Feminist Legal Research in New Delhi; Visiting Global Faculty, NYU School of Law. Different versions of this Article have been presented at the New International Law Conference, Birkbeck College, University of London, June 2003; Gendered Borders Conference, Amsterdam University Faculty of Law, September 2004. My thanks to all those who gave feedback and comments on early drafts of this Article and on the presentations. I am particularly grateful to Susan Marks, Dianne Otto, Kamala Kempadoo, Lynn Savery, and Thuy Do for their comments and feedback. My thanks to Jayne Huckerby and Angelina Fisher for research assistance.

1. Dirty Pretty Things (BBC 2002).
2. Zadie Smith, White Teeth 337 (2000).
3. Salman Rushdie, Shame 89 (1983).

ing to New York, a city of fantasy and wonder, and is willing to sell her body and possibly even her kidneys to provide her with the means to pursue her dream. Okwe just wants to get back home to his wife and daughter.

The film represents the plight of a besieged community of illegal immigrants from a variety of countries, and delves into the complexities of the existence of the subaltern life and the life of the "Other" who has crossed borders, willing to take on the considerable risks that accompany such movements, especially movements that are illegal, stigmatized, and even criminalized. The film serves as a point of entry into the central issue addressed in this Article: how the transnational migrant subject is addressed through a spectrum of legal rules and criteria designed to question her legitimacy at the point of crossing borders. I expose how the complexities and layering of migrant existence are rolled and flattened through a regulatory apparatus that fails to engage with the broader transnational processes that produce the global demand for migrants. International and domestic laws are serving as sites where the emergence of the transnational migrant on the global stage is being resisted and her human rights compromised. These legal interventions are constructed along frameworks rooted in the boundaries of difference, the sovereignty of the nation-state, and the myth of the liberal subject, which all fail to address the challenges posed by the transnational migrant.

I discuss three responses to the transnational migrant that characterize some of the legal interventions. The first response is reinforcing difference through categories such as gender and race, which regard these traits as immutable and unalterable and subject them to subordinating and paternalistic legal regulations. The second response involves the assimilation of the Other, which forces conformity to cultural and social norms partly through the performance of a "cultural strip." Finally, there is the perception of the transnational migrant as a threat—a dangerous and contaminating force—to be excluded either through incarceration or elimination. These three approaches are reflected in the three situations that I set out in this Article.

First, I briefly examine how difference is reinforced in my discussion of the legal regulation of women who migrate for work, including sex work. Second, I examine the assimilationist move in the context of the legal responses to transnational migrants in countries that have adopted new emotional, cultural, and citizenship criteria to determine eligibility for citizenship and immigrant status. I discuss the recent initiatives in the U.K. and how these expose a neo-colonial anxiety about the Other and a desire to prevent the erosion of the social and cultural cohesion on which such societies are ostensibly built. In the third example, I examine how the global response to terrorism in and through the "War on Terror," which promotes fear of the Other, has impacted Australia's legal response to refugees and asylum-seekers fleeing persecution and conflict.

The diverse responses to the transnational migrant subject are not clear-cut and distinct measures: they frequently overlap. These subjects are at times represented as victims and at times as perpetrators capable of the most terrifying violence. The common element in the examples I discuss is the attempt to examine and respond to border crossings by transnational subjects along the rigid binaries of "us" and "them," and domination and subordination. These binaries undermine the human rights of the transnational migrant subject and fail to address the complex, fragmented, and blurred realities of our transnational world.

II. THE "OTHER" SIDE OF UNIVERSALITY

There is already considerable scholarship setting out how law's claim to truth resides in the ideal rather than the actual practice of law.[4] Although law continues to fall short of its ideal, it continues to situate itself as an authoritative discourse, its authority derived in part through scientific legal method and rigor, and its projection as a unified discipline with an internally coherent logic that is transcendent and divorced from the world.[5] In this section, I examine how the legal responses to the transnational migrant reflect a theoretical tension between assumptions about law as an objective, external, neutral truth, and the exclusionary potential of legal discourse. I illustrate how legal discourse actually constitutes the transnational migrant subject and justifies her exclusion from certain rights and benefits. In developing this argument, I borrow from the insights of postcolonial theory and the subaltern studies project.[6]

Throughout this Article I use the term transnational migrant subject, which refers quite specifically to the subject who crosses borders and occupies a subaltern position. The subaltern studies project regards hegemonic history as part of modernity's power/knowledge complex, which in the context of colonialism was deeply implicated in the "general epistemic violence of imperialism."[7] It reads the official archive against the grain and focuses on "listening to the small voice of history," including the voices of peasants, women, and even religious, sexual, and racial minorities.[8] In the context of the transnational migrant subject, the subaltern project challenges the traditional assumptions about universality, neutrality, and objectivity on which legal

4. CAROL SMART, FEMINISM AND THE POWER OF LAW 11 (1989). Legal realists as well as critical legal scholars of the 20th century have made critiques about the difference between the promise of law and its actual application.

5. *Id.* at 12–13.

6. For an elaboration of the postcolonial project and law, see Eve Darian-Smith & Peter Fitzpatrick, *Laws of the Postcolonial: An Insistent Introduction*, *in* LAWS OF THE POSTCOLONIAL 1, 1–2 (Eve Darian-Smith & Peter Fitzpatrick eds., 1999); Dianne Otto, *Postcolonialism, and Law?: Guest Editor's Introduction*, THIRD WORLD LEGAL STUD. vii (1998–99); RATNA KAPUR, EROTIC JUSTICE: LAW AND THE NEW POLITICS OF POSTCOLONIALISM (forthcoming 2005) (manuscript at ch. 2, on file with author).

7. Gayatri Chakravorty Spivak, *Three Women's Texts and a Critique of Imperialism*, 12 CRITICAL INQUIRY 242, 251 (1985); Dianne Otto, *Subalternity and International Law: The Problems of Global Community and the Incommensurability of Difference*, 5 SOC. & LEGAL STUD. 337–38 (1996).

8. *See generally* Ranajit Guha, *The Small Voice of History*, *in* SUBALTERN STUD. IX, at 1 (S. Amin & D. Chakrabarty eds., 1996).

concepts are based, exposing how law produces exclusions and contributes to the construction of the transnational migrant subject's subaltern location.

Subaltern studies and postcolonial scholarship have exposed how the identity of the West and the European has been constructed in opposition to an Other. In the context of the transnational migrant subject, this opposition exposes an incommensurable tension between the West's claims to universality and inclusion, which continue to inform traditional assumptions about law, and the politics of exclusion of the Other from the project of universality.[9] These exclusions, whether based on gender, sexual status, race, ethnicity, or religion, are constructed along what are perceived to be "real differences." The law produces the binaries of "us and them," "here and there," and "civilized and uncivilized" by representing the migrant subject as distinct and different. These distinctions become the lynchpin for determining who to include and who to exclude when it comes to formulating legal responses to those who cross borders.

Modernity posits a set of claims to universal truth about equality, citizenship, and representation in law. Yet these universal concepts have continuously been exposed as resting on exclusions, as in the context of slavery, apartheid, empire, and gender discrimination. For example, in the context of empire, colonialism has been coterminous with modernity.

While Europe was developing ideas of political freedom, particularly in France, Britain, and Holland, it simultaneously amassed vast empires where such freedoms were either absent or severely attenuated for the majority of native inhabitants.[10] There were two primary ways in which it was possible to legitimize this relationship and reconcile the freedoms associated with liberalism with the exclusionary impact of colonialism. First, reconciliation involved linking the capacity to reason with adherence to some notion of a universal natural law, applicable to all.[11] These norms were premised on European practices to which the colonial subjects had to conform if they were to avoid sanctions and achieve full membership.

The second way in which to reconcile domination with freedom and equality was through the discourse of difference, in which the eligibility and capacity for freedom and progress was biologically determined, and colonial subjugation legitimized as the natural subordination of lesser races to higher ones.[12]

9. Darian-Smith & Fitzpatrick, *supra* note 6, at 1–2.

10. UDAY SINGH MEHTA, LIBERALISM AND EMPIRE: A STUDY IN NINETEENTH CENTURY BRITISH LIBERAL THOUGHT 46–54 (1999). Mehta argues that imperialism stemmed from liberal assumptions about reason and historical progress. He unpacks the inclusionary potential of liberal theory and the exclusionary effects of liberal practices. *Id.* at 46. He illustrates this argument through an examination of the colonial encounter with India, and finds that British liberals justified the denial of rights and benefits to the colonial subject on the grounds that such unfamiliar cultures were infantile and backward.

11. Ratna Kapur & Tayyab Mahmud, *Hegemony, Coercion, and Their Teeth-Gritting Harmony: A Commentary on Power, Culture and Sexuality in Franco's Spain*, 33 U. MICH. J.L. REFORM 995, 1012–14 (2000); *see also* MEHTA, *supra* note 10, at 102.

12. *See* Tayyab Mahmud, *Colonialism and Modern Constructions of Race: A Preliminary Inquiry*, 53 U. MIAMI L. REV. 1219 (1999); *see also* MEHTA, *supra* note 10, at 64–71.

The purportedly universal rights of man could be denied to those not considered to be men or even human. Liberal discourses of rights, inclusion, and equality could be reconciled with the colonial policies of exclusion and discrimination only by presuming absolute differences between different types of individuals.[13]

A similar logic justified the continued subordination of women, where women were understood as different from men—specifically, as weaker, subordinate, and in need of protection.[14] Curiously, in the colonial relationship, gender difference was conflated with cultural backwardness, where the native treatment of women was used in part as a justification for colonial intervention and the civilizing mission.[15] The British Empire was quite consistently able to position itself as the defender of women's rights in the colonial context without fundamentally changing its own position on gender difference and the representation of women as the weak and subordinate sex. The British continued to take the existence of gender differences as natural and inevitable. And difference was partly constructed through the capacity to consent and the capacity to reason. The Other was deemed unfathomable, inscrutable, distant, and removed, demonstrating that this subject was civilizationally backward and savage or infantile.[16] Colonial subjugation became one way to rectify past deficiencies, and the civilizing mission of imperialism became justified in societies perceived as stagnant and mired in the stranglehold of custom. The Empire was the "engine that tows societies stalled in their past into contemporary time and history."[17] It was a necessary precondition to progress.

---

13. MEHTA, *supra* note 10, at 69–70.

14. *See generally* Joan Scott, *Deconstructing Equality Versus Difference: Or, the Uses of Poststructuralist Theory for Feminism*, 14 FEMINIST STUD. 33 (1988); *see also* MARTHA MINOW, MAKING ALL THE DIFFERENCE: INCLUSION, EXCLUSION AND AMERICAN LAW (1990); LYNNE FORD, WOMEN AND POLITICS: THE PURSUIT OF EQUALITY (2002).

15. KATHERINE MAYO, MOTHER INDIA: SELECTIONS FROM THE CONTROVERSIAL 1927 TEXT 3–4 (Mrinalini Sinha ed., 2000) (claiming that imperial intervention was justified on grounds that the native woman must be rescued from her plight and the harms of a backward and barbaric culture). *See generally* TANIKA SARKAR, HINDU WIFE, HINDU NATION: COMMUNITY, RELIGION, AND CULTURAL NATIONALISM (2001). Sarkar posits that Hindu ideas and traditions were in part products of the colonial encounter, which influenced the development of ideas and traditions that have shaped hegemonic and dominant conceptions of Indian womanhood, domesticity, wifeliness, mothering, and India as a Hindu nation. The Hindu nationalists embraced the very aspects of the tradition that the colonial power argued were symbols of India's backwardness and a justification for the continued colonial rule.

16. MEHTA, *supra* note 10, at 68–73; JOHANNES FABIAN, TIME AND ITS OTHER: HOW ANTHROPOLOGY MAKES ITS OBJECTS (1983) (discussing how the anthropologist engages with her subject as existing at a different time from herself, in some mythical, and hence primitive past); ROBERT YOUNG, WHITE MYTHOLOGIES: WRITING HISTORY AND THE WEST 21–27 (1990) (arguing that the notion of the Other as savage and primitive is partly contingent on the way in which history is recited. Young critiques various Marxist accounts of a single world history, which have represented the "Third World" as unassimilable, constituting a surplus to the narrative of the "West." Decolonizing history is a part of the project of deconstructing the "West" and understanding how the truth about the Other comes to be produced.).

17. MEHTA, *supra* note 10, at 82.

Law became one site at which to deal with difference and legitimize the pursuit of the civilizing mission.[18] The native was entitled to certain rights and benefits to the extent that he could reinvent himself as an Englishman and successfully perform the mime.[19] Otherwise, "backwardness" and lack of "civilizational maturity" were regarded as limitations. They were deficiencies to be tolerated, even if they could not be altered, or to be eliminated if they posed too great a threat.[20] Furthermore, this deficiency was in part emphasized through a focus on the natives' treatment of their own women, even as the colonial powers themselves accepted gender difference as intrinsic and immutable.

Thus, while there was an assumption that certain political ideals—liberty, equality, and fraternity—were universal, these ideals seemed to stumble and falter at the moment of their encounter with the unfamiliar, the Other. One response to a world where there were so many different ways of organizing social and political life was simple: colonialism. Today, assumptions that underscore these "universal" values meet with some of the same difficulties as they encounter difference and unfamiliarity in a postcolonial and increasingly transmigratory, transnational world.[21] Universality is always accompanied by what Denise da Silva evocatively describes as "the other side of universality."[22] This "moral and legal *no man's land*, where universality finds its *spatial* limit," is built upon the foundation of difference.[23]

These responses to the Other are still present in the contemporary moment in the context of the legal treatment of the transnational migrant subject. I examine these responses through a sampling of legal interventions and unpack the assumptions about the Other and difference on which they are based. The discussion exposes the failure to recognize the global movement of people as a part of the globalization process, and how legal interventions, which continue to operate along the dichotomies of "here and there" and "us and

18. *See* Wilhem Grewe, The Epochs of International Law 457 (Michael Byers trans., 2000):

> The principal, practical effect of the linkage of international law to the standards of civilization was the system of "capitulations" or, in other words, the "unequal" treaties by which the civilized nations reserved a special jurisdiction . . . over their own nationals, whom they did not wish to have subjected to the legal order and justice system of a half-civilized or uncivilized country.

19. See discussion of mimicry in Homi Bhabha, The Location of Culture (1994). Bhabha argues that while colonial mimicry represents the desire of the native to be reformed and recognizable, it also reveals a certain transgressive recalcitrance since the difference continues to pose an imminent threat to "both 'normalized' knowledge and disciplinary power." *Id.* at 85–86. Colonial mimicry is thus characterized by ambivalence.

20. Antony Anghie, *Finding the Peripheries: Sovereignty and Colonialism in Nineteenth-Century International Law*, 40 Harv. Int'l L.J. 3, 3–5 (1999); *see generally* Helen Fein, Imperial Crime and Punishment: The Massacre at Jallianwala Bagh and British Judgment, 1919–1920 (1977); Savita Narain, The Historiography of the Jallianwalla Bagh Massacre, 1919 (1998).

21. Tayyab Mahmud, *Migration, Identity and the Colonial Encounter*, 76 Or. L. Rev. 633, 634 (1997).

22. Denise Ferreira da Silva, *Toward a Critique of the Socio-Logos of Justice: The Analytics of Raciality and the Production of Universality*, 7 Soc. Identities 421, 421 (2001).

23. *Id.* at 422.

them," are actually contributing to the production of a clandestine migrant mobility regime.

A. *Re-entrenching the Native Subject*

Over the past several years, sex workers (male, female, and transgendered), their families, and their support communities have crossed international borders and converged on different cities in India to celebrate the International Sex Workers' Rights Day on March 3.[24] At the epicenter of their debates and protests has been a challenge to the anti-trafficking initiatives being promoted by Western and South Asian countries, feminists, and human rights groups.[25] These communities argue that such measures have resulted in targeting of migration from the south, promotion of a highly conservative moral agenda, and a denial to sex workers and other migrants of their right to work, family, and mobility.[26] I discuss how anti-trafficking initiatives assume that persons in situations of trafficking, especially women, are "victims" incapable of choosing to cross borders, and how they fail to address the push factors that compel such "unsafe" movements.[27] Instead, these responses focus on border

---

24. Roshni Basu, Report on the "Shanti Utsav," *at* http://www.kit.nl/gcg/assets/images/mela_report.doc (last visited Dec. 15, 2004). The Durbar Mahila Samanwaya Committee (DMSC), more widely known as the Sonagachi Project, is an organized sex workers' rights movement based in Calcutta and consisting of over 60,000 sex workers. By gathering and organizing information, it has been able to reduce the transmission of HIV as well as the trafficking of minors within sex work. The anti-trafficking initiatives rely on the participation of residents in red light areas in monitoring the entry of minors into the area and assisting in the return of any who try to enter. For DMSC's general principles, see *Sex-workers Manifesto* (theme paper of the First National Conference of Sex Workers in India, Nov. 14–16, 1997), *available at* http://www.walnet.org/csis/groups/nswp/conferences/manifesto.html. The Sex Workers' Forum in Kerala, a southern state in India, organized the third Sex Workers' Conference of January 17–19, 2003 under the theme "The Festival of Pleasure." The conference addressed the problems of sex workers and the violations of their rights. *Festival of Pleasure: Your Questions, Our Answers*, *at* http://www.heart-intl.net/HEpatitis,%20AIDS,%20Research%20Trust/International%20Studies/Complete/Festival%20of%20Pleasre-India.htm (last updated Apr. 24, 2003).

25. *See, e.g.*, Lisa Batiwalla, Infochange India News & Features, *Women's Groups, Feminists Often Ignore Sex Workers' Rights*, *at* http://www.infochangeindia.org/WomenItop.jsp?recordno=3437&section_idv=1#3386 (Sept. 6, 2004).

26. *See, e.g.*, Laxmi Murthy, *Our Rights are Human Rights*, 1:4 Vampnews (Apr. 2004), *available at* http://www.vampnews.org/vol01no04/world.html. Some of these concerns are expressed in Tales of the Night Fairies (Centre for Feminist Legal Research & Mamacash 2002), directed by Shohini Ghosh, which documents the Sonagachi Project. The film cuts between shots of the Sex Workers Millennium Carnival held in Calcutta in 2001, the stories the sex workers tell about their work and lives, the violation of their rights, and the double standards on issues of sexuality.

The empowered representations of the sex workers in Ghosh's film stand in sharp contrast to the images of victimization and violence represented in the more highly publicized documentaries of the sex workers in Calcutta by Andrew Levine, The Day My God Died (PBS 2003), and by Ross Kauffman and Zana Briski, Born Into Brothels (HBO/Cinemax Documentary Films 2003). Neither film addresses the fact that Calcutta is a city where the red-light district is a safe refuge for its sex workers and their trade. These sex workers and their activist comrades have set up—however rudimentary—financial institutions, health clinics, sex education schools, and blood banks for the surrounding community. Levine and Briski's films portray these women and their families as exploited subjects, who have been "saved" either by the benevolence of the Christian white man or the film makers themselves.

27. Ratna Kapur, *The Tragedy of Victimization Rhetoric: Resurrecting the "Native" Subject in International/Post-Colonial Feminist Legal Politics*, 15 Harv. Hum. Rts. J. 1 (2002).

controls and the prosecution of "traffickers," who range from transport agents to the "victims'" families who consent to the movement. They are designed to discourage women's mobility and to stigmatize her (Third World) family, conveying a simple message: Keep the "native" at home. The anti-trafficking initiatives reproduce assumptions about women as passive, incapable of decision-making, and in need of protection. They also fail to address the concerns of anti-trafficking advocates, as they are frequently used merely as a façade to deter the entry of certain categories of migrants or to clean up establishments within the sex industry.[28] The anti-trafficking framework has not succeeded in detaching itself from these hidden agendas, and consequently it has proven to do little good for the trafficked person and great harm to migrants and women in the sex industry.[29]

Statistics in the area of trafficking are unavailable primarily due to the imprecise nature of the term "trafficking," the lack of systematic research in this area, and the clandestine nature of the activity.[30] In addition, statistics

28. Some examples include the recent amendments to the Swedish prostitution laws, which criminalize the purchasing of sexual services in the name of combating trafficking. Act Prohibiting the Purchase of Sexual Services (1998:408) (Swed.); *see also* SAARC Convention on Preventing and Combating Trafficking in Women and Children for Prostitution, Jan. 5, 2002, *available at* www.saarc-sec.org/old/freepubs/conv-traffiking.pdf; REPORT OF THE INTERNATIONAL LAW ASSOCIATION: NEW DELHI CONFERENCE COMMITTEE ON FEMINISM AND INTERNATIONAL LAW (2002).

29. *See, e.g.*, EMPOWER CHIANG MAI, REPORT ON THE HUMAN RIGHTS VIOLATIONS WOMEN ARE SUBJECTED TO WHEN "RESCUED" BY ANTI-TRAFFICKING GROUPS WHO EMPLOY METHODS USING DECEPTION, FORCE AND COERCION (June 2003); Statement from the Network of Sex Work Projects, The Anti-Sex Work Anti-Trafficking Agenda: A Threat to Sex Workers' Health and Human Rights, at the XIV International Conference on AIDS, Barcelona, Spain (July 2004), *available at* http://www.nswp.org/nswp/conferences/xivaids/nswp-0207.html; Melissa Ditmore & Marjan Wijers, *The Negotiations on the U.N. Protocol on Trafficking in Persons*, 4 NEMESIS 79 (2003); Sunera Thobani, *Benevolent State, Law-Breaking Smugglers, and Deportable and Expendable Women: An Analysis of the Canadian State's Strategy to Address Trafficking in Women*, 19:4 Refuge 24 (2001); Jo Doezema, *Forced to Choose: Beyond the Voluntary vs. Forced Prostitution Dichotomy*, *in* GLOBAL SEX WORKERS: RIGHTS, RESISTANCE AND REDEFINITION 34, 44–46 (Kamala Kempadoo & Jo Doezema eds., 1998) [hereinafter GLOBAL SEX WORKERS].

30. The Global Alliance Against Traffic in Women undertook a study on behalf of the U.N. Special Rapporteur on Violence Against Women, in which it stated that it was extremely difficult to find reliable statistics on the extent of trafficking that was taking place. MARJAN WIJERS & LIN LAP-CHEW, TRAFFICKING IN WOMEN, FORCED LABOUR AND SLAVERY-LIKE PRACTICES IN MARRIAGE, DOMESTIC LABOR AND PROSTITUTION 15 (1997). A searchable database on different statistics of trafficking provided by various governments is available at the UNESCO Trafficking Statistics Project database, http://www.unescobkk.org/culture/trafficking/matrix/matrix.asp (last visited Jan. 3, 2005). Accurate statistics on migration flows more generally are not readily available. This lack is due in part to the absence of any universal methodology for collecting such statistics, a lack of commitment on the part of governments to collect these statistics, the absence of a common definition amongst countries of who constitutes an international migrant, and the difficulty in collecting data given the clandestine nature of some forms of migration. *See* U.N. DEP'T OF ECO. & SOC. AFFAIRS, STATISTICS DIV., RECOMMENDATIONS ON STATISTICS OF INTERNATIONAL MIGRATION, at 12–15, U.N. Doc. ST/ESA/STAT/SER.M/58/Rev.1, U.N. Sales No. E.98.XVII.14 (1998). However, some official U.N. estimates provide information about the numbers involved in cross-border movements. The U.N.'s International Migration Report 2002 estimated that there were 175 million migrants, defined as persons outside their country of birth or citizenship for twelve months or more. About 60% of migrants were in "developed countries," including 56 million in Europe, 50 million in Asia, and 41 million in North America. During the 1990s, the number of migrants in developed countries rose by 23 million, or 28%, and immigration accounted for almost two-thirds of the population growth in industrial countries. Between 1995 and 2000, the more developed countries received nearly 12 million migrants from lesser developed countries, about 2.3 million migrants a year, including 1.4

are sometimes cited without identifying any substantiating research. For example, the Coalition Against Trafficking in Women—Asia-Pacific sets out the numbers of women trafficked in several countries, often without citing any research or source for their statistics.[31] Similarly, the 1995 Human Rights Watch report on trafficking between Nepal and India states that "[a]t least hundreds of thousands, and probably more than a million women and children are employed in Indian brothels."[32] Human Rights Watch further states in its 1993 report on trafficking between Burma and Thailand that there are an "estimated 800,000 to two million prostitutes currently working in Thailand."[33] Neither report, however, provide any sources for its statistics.

Kamala Kempadoo has stated that there are often extreme variations in the estimates of the number of women in prostitution in Asia. She questions the veracity of these figures, arguing that such discrepancies are grounds for questioning the reliability of the research.[34] Despite such criticism, in the context of sex work, prostitution, and the conflation of these activities with trafficking, standards are compromised and such figures are cited without any question.

These questionable statistics reinforce confusion about trafficking, migration, and sex work. In contemporary discourse, human trafficking has come to be interlinked with migration (mainly illegal), clandestine border crossing, and smuggling of humans. On a parallel plane, trafficking in women and girls is conflated with their sale and forced consignment to brothels as sex workers. This conflation of trafficking in persons with various manifestations of migration and mobility on the one hand, and with prostitution and sex work on the other, lies at the very core of the confusion underpinning the contemporary discourse on the global, national, and regional trafficking of women and girls.

---

million a year in North America and 800,000 a year in Europe. *International Migration Report 2002*, Dept. of Econ. and Soc. Affairs, Population Div., U.N. Doc. ST/ESA/SER.A/220, U.N. Sales No. E.03.XIII.4 (2002). In 2001, the United Nations High Commissioner for Refugees estimated that of the 21.8 million people the Commission was responsible for, 12 million were refugees. *Global Refugee Trends: January–September, 2001, A Statistical Overview of Refugee Populations, New Arrivals, Durable Solutions and Refugee Status, Determination Procedures in Some 90 Countries*, Populations Data Unit, Population and Geographical Data Section, 2001 U.N.H.C.R. Statistical Y.B. 12. Several million people are missing from these estimates because they are illegal and do not appear in the official census. *Id.* at 12–15.

31. Coalition Against Trafficking in Women—Asia-Pacific, *at* http://www.catw-ap.org/ (last visited Oct. 23, 2004).

32. HUMAN RIGHTS WATCH, RAPE FOR PROFIT: TRAFFICKING OF NEPALI GIRLS AND WOMEN TO INDIA'S BROTHELS 1 (1995).

33. WOMEN'S RIGHTS PROJECT, HUMAN RIGHTS WATCH, A MODERN FORM OF SLAVERY: TRAFFICKING OF BURMESE WOMEN AND GIRLS INTO BROTHELS IN THAILAND 1 (1993).

34. Kamala Kempadoo, *Introduction: Globalizing Sex Workers' Rights*, *in* GLOBAL SEX WORKERS, *supra* note 29, at 1, 15 (elaborating on the inaccuracy in the statistics on the number of people who are trafficked, which often go unchallenged, as well as the uncritical acceptance of the view that the problem of trafficking has increased).

B. Conflating Migration With Trafficking

In 2000, the United Nations adopted an international definition of trafficking. The Protocol defines trafficking as follows:

> "Trafficking in persons" shall mean the recruitment, transportation, transfer, harbouring or receipt of persons, by means of the threat or use of force or other forms of coercion, of abduction, of fraud, of deception, of the abuse of power or of a position of vulnerability or of the giving or receiving of payments or benefits to achieve the consent of a person having control over another person, for the purpose of exploitation. Exploitation shall include, at a minimum, the exploitation of the prostitution of others or other forms of sexual exploitation, forced labour or services, slavery or practices similar to slavery, servitude or the removal of organs.[35]

The definition marks an important development insofar as it shifts toward a newer, relatively more widely acceptable and inclusive definition of trafficking. Since the definition is very recent, its impact will only be realized once it begins to be applied and tested. A striking feature of the definition is that it includes trafficking for purposes other than prostitution, such as for forced labor, forced marriage, and other slavery-like practices. There is also some acknowledgement that trafficking is a problem of human rights and not a law and order or public morality issue related to prostitution.

However, the new definition is not fully coherent and still conflates trafficking with migration and prostitution. Women move and are moved, with or without their consent, for a variety of reasons.[36] They frequently find their way into the job market as domestic helpers or sex industry workers, partly because these are the largest available enclaves in the job market of receiving countries.[37] The definition of trafficking in the Protocol fails to clearly distinguish between trafficking and voluntary consensual migration, often conflating women's migratory movement with trafficking.[38] A number of states

35. Protocol to Prevent, Suppress and Punish Trafficking in Persons, Especially Women and Children, Supplementing the United Nations Convention Against Transnational Organized Crime, Annex II, Dec. 12, 2000, G.A. Res. 55/25, U.N. Doc. A/55/383 (2000) [hereinafter Trafficking Protocol].

36. *See* Doreen Indra, *Not a "Room of One's Own": Engendering Forced Migration Theory and Practice, in* ENGENDERED FORCED MIGRATION: THEORY AND PRACTICE 1–23 (Doreen Indra ed., 1999); *cf.* Saskia Sassen, *Toward a Feminist Analytics of the Global Economy*, 4 IND. J. GLOBAL LEGAL STUD. 7 (1996).

37. *See generally* WIJERS & LAP-CHEW, *supra* note 30; Marjan Wijers, *European Union Policies on Trafficking in Women, in* GENDER POLICIES IN THE EUROPEAN UNION 209 (Mariagrazia Rossilli ed., 2000).

38. The issue of consent or lack of consent is important, but does not address the broader factors that contribute to the problem of trafficking. Women may choose to move due to the lack of economic opportunities in their own country as well as the fact that there is an increasing demand for cheap, exploitable labor within the context of globalization. *See* CENTRE FOR FEMINIST LEGAL RESEARCH, REPORT OF THE INTERNATIONAL SEMINAR ON CROSS BORDER MOVEMENTS AND HUMAN RIGHTS (2004). The issue of demand is not addressed by the Protocol nor is the fact that women move into domestic work and the sex industry because these are the largest enclaves available to women in the job market. There is evidence that due to the lack of safe passages for movement, women are resorting to traffickers and smugglers to facilitate their voluntary movement. Rutvica Andrijasevic, *The Difference Borders Make: (Il)legality, Migra-*

parties to the Protocol have also interpreted it, both consciously and inadvertently, as foregrounding prostitution as the main site of trafficking, relegating the issue of the consent of the "victim" to irrelevance.[39]

Additionally, the Protocol does not require states parties to provide any measures of redress, assistance, or service to individuals who have been trafficked, or to their families. In all these ways, the trafficking definition delegitimizes the woman's cross border movement.

The various tensions that characterize the anti-trafficking debates have become evident in the Protocol and its definition.[40] Equating trafficking with migration has led to simplistic and unrealistic solutions: in order to prevent trafficking, there has been a conscious or inadvertent move to prevent altogether the migration of those who are deemed vulnerable to exploitation.[41] Even when curbing migration is not a stated focus of a program, there is an inadvertent tendency to try to dissuade women and girls from moving in order to protect them from harm. Anti-trafficking measures are frequently made applicable to "women and girls," thereby failing to accord women a separate identity as adults and confer rights that flow from that status, including the right to choose to move and to control one's life and body. This language also emphasizes women's role primarily as caretakers for children and fails to consider that their roles have altered. A woman's identity as the sole supporter of dependent family members, and hence as an economic migrant in search of work, is completely overlooked by these legal initiatives. Conflating trafficking with migration reinforces the assumption that women and girls are incapable of decision making or consent, and are therefore in need of constant male or state protection. The logical consequence of such an assumption is the curtailment of a woman's right to movement or right to earn a living in the manner she chooses. Indeed, policies that appear to be

---

tion and Trafficking in Italy Among Eastern European Women in Prostitution, *in* UPROOTINGS/REGROUNDINGS: QUESTIONS OF HOME AND MIGRATION 251, 263–64 (Sara Ahmed et al. eds., 2003).

39. For example, the Council of Europe, in its Parliamentary Assembly Recommendation 1545 of 2002, stated that "[i]n European societies, trafficking is a very complex subject which is closely linked to prostitution and hidden forms of exploitation, such as domestic slavery, catalogue marriages and sex tourism. Some 78% of women victims of trafficking are, in one way or another, exploited sexually." No citations are provided for this statistic. The practice of foregrounding sexual exploitation in the discourse on trafficking stands in contrast to another field report regarding trafficking issues in southeastern Europe by Barbara Limanowska, *Victim Referral and Assistance System and Gaps Therein in Southeastern Europe* (Nov. 18–22, 2002) (paper for the Expert Group Meeting on "Trafficking in Women and Girls," Nov. 18–22, 2002), *available at* http://www.un.org/womenwatch/daw/egm/trafficking2002/reports/EP-Limanowska.PDF (last visited Oct. 26, 2004).

40. Kara Abramson, *Beyond Consent, Toward Safeguarding Human Rights: Implementing the United Nations Trafficking Protocol*, 44 HARV. INT'L L.J. 473, 474–76 (2003) (arguing for the need to move beyond the focus on consent and address the issues of illegal movement and illicit forms of labor).

41. A number of non-governmental organizations and women's groups have developed border interception strategies with law enforcement officials in order to prevent the migration of women who are moving under what seem like "suspicious" circumstances and place them in protective care. *See* CENTRE FOR FEMINIST LEGAL RESEARCH, *supra* note 38, at 21. Such interventions merely result in restricting women's rights or encouraging corruption. DALE HUNTINGTON, POPULATION COUNCIL, ANTI-TRAFFICKING PROGRAMS IN SOUTH ASIA: APPROPRIATE ACTIVITIES, INDICATORS AND EVALUATION METHODOLOGIES 21 (Mar. 2002), *available at* http://www.popcouncil.org/pdfs/rr/anti_trafficking_asia.pdf.

initiated for the *benefit* of women often contribute to further victimization and infantilization of female migrants.[42] The construction of women who move (or are moved) as victims of a web of criminal networks lies in tension with the counter-narrative that regards the movement of labor as part of the globalization process in which the emergence of human trafficking and smuggling networks are parallel responses to the migration phenomenon that nation-states, especially in the global North, refuse to address other than as an issue of immigration or criminality.

The approach that arises out of constructing women as victims delegitimizes women's movement, while the problem of trafficking—the ostensible purpose of these measures—never gets resolved. Curbing migration does not stop trafficking, it merely drives the activity further underground, making it more invisible. Borders cannot be made impermeable, and stricter immigration measures result in pushing the victims further into situations of violence and abuse. As a result, women who migrate are pushed into further dependence on an informal and illegal network of agents and rendered even more vulnerable to economic and physical abuse, exploitation, and harm.

International law has constructed a response to "trafficking" that fails to draw clear conceptual distinctions between migration and trafficking. As a result, migration becomes equated with trafficking, which also means that the number of victims of trafficking comes to include the number of those who have migrated voluntarily. This logic operates particularly in the case of adolescent and adult female migrants, rather than in the case of male migrants. As a result, surveys on trafficking in "risk-prone" and "affected" districts, such as various South Asian countries, are conducted using flawed methodology. If women or girls are absent from a village or town, they are assumed to be "missing persons" and, therefore, trafficked. It is a logic that has resulted in the viewing of all consensual migrant females as trafficked individuals.

Anti-trafficking advocates also conflate women's cross-border movements with sex work or prostitution, producing at least two contradictory responses.[43]

---

42. For example, in the early 1990s, Bangladesh, India, and Indonesia imposed minimum age limits for women workers going abroad for employment. In 1998, Bangladesh banned women from going abroad as domestic workers. In 2002, the government of Bangladesh announced that it was considering removing the ban; however, to date the ban appears to have remained in effect. In 2003, the Indonesian government similarly announced the imposition of a temporary ban on female migrant workers. *See* Irene Fernandez, *Ban on Female Workers by Indonesia is Not the Solution* (Mar. 5, 2003), *at* http://www.december18.net/web/papers/view.php?paperID=672&menuID=41&lang=EN. In the same vein, although not entirely prohibiting migration by women, section 12 of the Nepal Foreign Employment Act (1985), prohibits the issuance of employment licenses to work overseas to women without the consent of the woman's guardian. *Id.* at 2042. Similarly, the government of Burma, reacting to the publication of a report by Human Rights Watch about the trafficking of Burmese women and girls into Thailand's sex industry from the eastern Shan state, imposed rules prohibiting all women in that area between the ages of 16 and 25 from traveling without a legal guardian. *See* Brenda Belak, *Migration and Trafficking of Women and Girls, in* GATHERING STRENGTH: WOMEN FROM BURMA ON THEIR RIGHTS 194, 195 (2002). Even passports are difficult to acquire for women, especially those under 25. The government states that such restrictions are intended to protect women from being coerced into working in night clubs or as commercial sex workers. *Id.* at 198.

43. One recent stark example of this conflation is the SAARC Convention on Preventing and Combat-

Collapsing the process with the purpose equates the abuse and violence that a woman may experience in the course of transport with the ultimate purpose of her journey. Many anti-trafficking measures are invariably anti-prostitution or intended to curtail sex work. Prostitution as the mutually exclusive purpose of trafficking is an untenable assumption because not all victims of trafficking are prostitutes nor have all prostitutes been trafficked. At the same time, if women are deemed to have participated in the process of trafficking, they are immediately recast as immoral subjects or criminals undeserving of legal protection.

Restrictive migration and immigration policies of countries of transit and destination have decreased the possibilities for regular, legal, and safe migration throughout the world. This phenomenon has resulted in the growth of a clandestine migrant-mobility regime in which traffickers and smugglers facilitate the movement of migrants, often providing false travel documents and identification papers for them. It is a regime born from people's desire and need to migrate produced, in part, by the demand for cheap exploitative labor across borders. The anti-trafficking legal initiatives fail to recognize and respect the rights of transnational migrant subjects such that women's agency and the rights of their families in the course of their movement are all but forgotten. These initiatives continue to address women (especially from the global South) as victims, infantilizing them as incapable of rationally choosing to migrate in a clandestine fashion, although a bevy of factors—including market demands and the lack of safe migration options—can make clandestine migration methods a rational, viable option.

Anti-trafficking initiatives also tend to criminalize women and their families by regarding families as part of the trafficking chain, failing to recognize that women move in part to seek better economic opportunities to support their families.[44] Although the women migrating on the behalf of their family can still be subject to subtle and forceful coercion from their family members, the anti-trafficking initiatives assume criminality indiscriminately for all female migrants. Furthermore, by invariably associating trafficking with sexual exploitation, women who move are implicitly suspected of crossing borders for the purposes of sex, which stigmatizes their movement. As such, women and their movement are viewed through the lenses of criminality and stigma, and the woman herself is rendered both a victim as well as an immoral subject.

ing Trafficking in Women and Children for Prostitution, *supra* note 28. For a criticism of this conflation, see Report of the International Law Association: New Delhi Conference Committee on Feminism and International Law, *supra* note 28. See also Anne Gallagher's background paper cited in the annex of Advisory Council of Jurists, Consideration of the Issue of Trafficking: Final Report 89–92 (Dec. 2002), *available at* http://www.asiapacificforum.net/jurists/trafficking/Final_Report.doc (last visited Oct. 26, 2004).

44. The Trafficking Protocol has been adopted under the terms of the Convention Against Transnational Organized Crime, Nov. 15, 2000, 40 I.L.M. 335, 353 (entered into force Sept. 29, 2003).

C. Assimilation and the Cultural Strip

> Almost the same, but not quite . . . almost the same, but not white.[45]

> [M]ost migrants learn, and become disguises.[46]

The global flow of people across borders and within borders is generated by a plethora of reasons: the reconfiguration of the global economy, displacement and dispossession of marginalized populations, the desire to provide education to children, the awareness through consciousness-raising that there are better options elsewhere, armed conflict, and, of course, the basic human aspiration to explore the world.[47] The global patterns of economics and trade have increased the demand for low wage labor as well as the demand of poor countries for remittances from immigrants in the global North that will assist in social welfare that the state is neither able nor willing to provide.[48] The World Bank's report on Global Development Finance 2003 estimates that migrant remittances to developing countries reached almost $80 billion in 2002. Poorer countries thus have little interest in controlling outward movement, whether legal or clandestine.[49]

There are several human rights documents and provisions in international and human rights law that address some of the harms and abuses to which migrants may be exposed, such as slavery, forced labor, and debt bondage.[50] The recently ratified International Convention on the Protection of the Rights of All Migrant Workers and Members of Their Families ("CMW") is the first international convention to address the issue of irregular or illegal migration from a rights perspective. It affords some recognition and substantial rights to migrants and undocumented workers.[51] The primary purpose of

45. BHABHA, *supra* note 19, at 86.

46. SALMAN RUSHDIE, IMAGINARY HOMELANDS 49 (1988).

47. *See* MYRON WEINER, THE GLOBAL MIGRATION CRISIS: CHALLENGE TO STATES AND TO HUMAN RIGHTS 21–44 (1995) (providing an overview of the causes and consequences of international global migration, including the challenges that it brings to the meaning of sovereignty, security and social justice); *see also* James Hollifield, *Migration, Trade and the Nation-State: The Myth of Globalization*, 3 UCLA J. INT'L & FOREIGN AFF. 595 (1998) (arguing that migration and trade are inextricably linked).

48. *See generally* Kerry Rittich, *Transformed Pursuits: The Quest for Equality in Globalized Markets*, HARV. HUM. RTS. J. 231, 241–42 (2000).

49. *See* Claudia M. Buch et al., Kiel Inst. for World Econ., *Worker Remittances and Capital Flows* (2002), *at* http://www.uni-kiel.de/ifw/pub/kap/2002/kap1130.pdf. Buch argues that worker remittances constitute an important method for transferring resources from developed to developing countries. Worker remittances are ranked as the second largest source, next to foreign direct investment, of external funding for developing countries.

50. *See* Supplementary Convention on the Elaboration of Slavery, the Slave Trade and Institutions and Practices Similar to Slavery, Sept. 7, 1956, 226 U.N.T.S. 3; *see also* International Covenant on Civil and Political Rights, *opened for signature* Dec. 16, 1966, art. 8, 999 U.N.T.S. 171, 175 (entered into force Mar. 23, 1976); *see also* International Covenant on Economic Social and Cultural Rights, *opened for signature* Dec. 16, 1966, arts. 6, 11, 993 U.N.T.S. 3 (entered into force Jan. 3, 1976).

51. International Convention on the Protection of the Rights of All Migrant Workers and Members of Their Families, G.A. Res. 45/158, U.N. GAOR, 45th Sess., Supp. No. 49A, at 261, U.N. Doc. A/45/49 (1990) (entered into force July 1, 2003) [hereinafter CMW].

the Convention is to protect the human rights of legal and illegal migrants and their families, and to ensure there is no arbitrary interference with their rights to liberty and security.[52] The CMW imposes positive obligations on the state to provide housing and other benefits to migrants, both documented and undocumented.[53] Despite the rights provided under the CMW, it suffers from a number of shortcomings, such as a failure to address the obstacles posed by immigration laws and restrictions.[54] Additionally, as of this writing, the treaty has not been ratified by a single country in the global North.

At the same time, there is a resistance on the part of states to address the transnational migrant within the framework of international and human rights law. The primary response of states to the global movement of people has been to enact new citizenship and nationality laws to enable transnational migrants to be part of the universal project of rights and acquire legitimacy through the process of assimilation. However, these initiatives are also being promoted alongside tighter immigration laws and procedures that address immigrant-status migrants and increased border control mechanisms that target those who refuse to assimilate.

Transnational movements are challenging nation-states and their borders, and reconfiguring the map of national, political, and cultural identity. The need to secure the sovereign nation-state and the sovereign subject results in an unwillingness to countenance such a challenge. New laws enacted to defend and consolidate the cultural, social, and national cohesion of individual states—through a combination of assimilating criteria and exclusionary cultural boundaries—reveal continuing neo-colonial anxieties about the Other.

The U.K. Government's response to this neo-colonial anxiety, as well as to the racial tensions that gripped the country in the summer of 2001, is the government's new policy on immigration and citizenship set out in its White Paper entitled *Secure Borders, Safe Haven*.[55] Consistent with the policy of pursuing tighter immigration measures rather than addressing the anxieties and

---

52. *Id.* arts. 8–35.

53. *Id.* arts. 64–71.

54. A comprehensive critique of the CMW is beyond the scope of this Article. As it is a relatively new Convention that only recently came into force, it has not been subjected to extensive analysis and review. What is evident, however, is that sending countries have a greater incentive to ratify the document than receiving countries. The Convention represents a major positive shift towards acknowledging the trend of increasing migrations. However, there are still some substantial limitations and problems with the definitions as well as substantive provisions of the Convention. The major shortcoming is that the Convention fails to consider the issue of migration from the perspective of the migrant and restricts the rights of migrant workers, especially female migrants.

55. U.K. HOME OFFICE, SECURE BORDERS, SAFE HAVEN: INTEGRATION WITH DIVERSITY IN MODERN BRITAIN 10–11 (2002) [hereinafter SECURE BORDERS, SAFE HAVEN] ("The reports into last summer's disturbances in Bradford Oldham and Burnley painted a vivid picture of fractured and divided communities, lacking a sense of common values or shared civic identity to unite around. The reports signaled the need for us to foster and renew the social fabric of our communities, and rebuild a sense of common citizenship, which embraces the different and diverse experiences of today's Britain."); *see generally* TED CANTLE, U.K. HOME OFFICE, COMMUNITY COHESION: A REPORT OF THE INDEPENDENT REVIEW TEAM (2002); *see also* OLDHAM INDEPENDENT REVIEW, PANEL REPORT (2001) (providing a general discussion and analysis of race riots and community relations in Britain).

national security issues posed by the transnational migrant within the framework of international and human rights law, the U.K. government has not ratified the CMW and asserts—though not uncontestedly—that there is inevitably a tradeoff between migrant rights and immigration controls.[56] The national immigration measures target the transnational migrant subject through new cultural, emotional, and citizenship criteria. Most of these criteria have found their way into the British Nationality, Immigration, and Asylum Act of 2002.[57]

Secure Borders, Safe Haven is based on two primary objectives. The first is to build social cohesion and a sense of British identity in "an increasingly diverse world."[58] The government considers it critical to ensure that local residents feel secure in their own identity and community and that those who want to settle in the U.K. "develop a sense of belonging, an identity and shared mutual understanding, which can be passed from one generation to another."[59] The second is to address economic considerations by ensuring that people who want to work in the United Kingdom can do so without entering the country through illegal routes.[60] These two objectives are pursued under a policy of "managing migration."[61] Managing migration seeks to integrate migrants into the British economy and society in ways in which the existing population will welcome them. The migrants are to be "managed" in their literal crossing of borders as well as in their identity construction once in the U.K. Through new nationality, citizenship, and integration policies, the migrant is reshaped in the British mold. As Home Secretary David Blunkett has asserted, the migrants should be trained to "uphold common values and understand how they can play their part in our society while upholding our status as subjects of [Her Majesty] The Queen."[62] Blunkett therefore proposes that people who want to become U.K. citizens take a compulsory English language test and an exam on the ways of British life, British society, and British institutions.[63] Migrants would also be required to take a citizenship pledge.[64] This move toward assimilation requires a "cultural strip."

56. In a recent report by the International Development Committee of the House of Commons, the government was requested to explain why it had not ratified CMW and to provide the committee with evidence to support the assumption that there is a trade-off between migrants' rights and immigration control. *See* INTERNATIONAL DEVELOPMENT COMMITTEE, MIGRATION AND DEVELOPMENT: HOW TO MAKE MIGRATION WORK FOR POVERTY REDUCTION, SIXTH REPORT, 2004, Cm. HC 79-I, at 86.

57. Nationality, Immigration, and Asylum Act, 2002, c.41 (Eng.).

58. SECURE BORDERS, SAFE HAVEN, *supra* note 55, at 11.

59. *Id.* at 27.

60. *Id.*

61. *Id.* at 22.

62. *Id.* at 29.

63. *Id.* at 32–33.

64. *Id.* at 34–35, 111; *see* Nationality, Immigration and Asylum Act, *supra* note 57, §§ 1, 3 (pertaining to knowledge of language and society for naturalization and bringing into effect Schedule 1 of the Act, pertaining to the citizenship ceremony, oath and pledge).

As part of a "cultural strip," cultural practices that are perceived as being contrary to British tradition and values must be rooted out. For example, *Secure Borders, Safe Haven* targets "bogus marriages," defined as marriages entered into solely for the purpose of bringing friends and relatives into Britain through one of the easiest routes still permitted by U.K. immigration rules.[65] According to the definition, bogus marriages are entered into for "wrong" (not personal or romantic) reasons.[66] There is a normative bias in Blunkett's focus on "arranged" marriages that implies such arrangements are not real marriages. Moreover, while he recognizes the desire on the part of parents to choose partners of a similar cultural background for their children, he expresses the hope that eventually such parents will seek to choose such partners from within their own settled communities in Britain. He states that only certain marital norms will be acceptable in the U.K., and that polygamous or forced marriages will not be tolerated.[67] However, his proposals create a blurring of distinctions between forced marriages and arranged marriages, especially when such marriages are arranged between a U.K. citizen and a person living abroad.

Blunkett has proposed the introduction of a "probationary period" of two years for new marriages before allowing the couple to apply for settlement in the U.K.[68] During those two years the couple would have to support themselves without recourse to public funds, a hardship Blunkett claims will "not greatly inconvenience or penalize those in genuine relationships."[69] The subjection of the relationship to some form of economic hardship over the course of two years would, according to the Home Secretary's view, be unsustainable in the context of "sham marriages": "it would be harder to sustain a relationship for this longer period with a duped partner and it is more likely that, when questioned or interviewed, the lack of a genuine and subsisting relationship will become apparent."[70] These recommendations have yet to be explicitly enacted into law. They nevertheless serve as a telling illustration of some of the cultural and gendered assumptions that the government retains with respect to foreigners, assumptions that will no doubt influence the decisions of those who evaluate immigration applications.

The Blunkett proposal to introduce new regulations into the relationships of immigrant populations requires couples with a migrant spouse to demonstrate instrumental, emotional, and cultural components to prove the "au-

65. SECURE BORDERS, SAFE HAVEN, *supra* note 55, at 99–102.

66. Indeed, very recently one London newspaper columnist expressed anxiety over the ease with which even gay men assisted foreign women to get their residency in the U.K. by marrying them. Matthew Parris, *Bogus Marriages Should Be Our Target, Not Asylum-Seekers*, TIMES (London), Sept. 18, 2004, at 26. Parris further expressed a fear that the enactment of civil partnership laws in the U.K. would accentuate the problem by extending the facility of marriage for the purposes of bringing in foreign, gay men, especially from Cuba and Brazil.

67. SECURE BORDERS, SAFE HAVEN, *supra* note 55, at 99.

68. *Id.* at 100.

69. *Id.*

70. *Id.*

thenticity" of their marriages. The instrumental element measures the strength and genuineness of the marital arrangement as contingent upon the length of time a couple remains together: the longer the couple stays together, the more legitimate the arrangement. The emotional element quite specifically requires proof of love. In other words, the proposal targets marriages that may be consensual, but that are entered into for reasons other than romance or love. Yet not all such "non-genuine" arrangements are targeted. The proposal quite specifically hones in on arranged marriages, presuming that they are less genuine because they are not based on "sincere" emotions, and hence more likely to be based on impermissible motives such as immigration benefits.[71]

Finally, the cultural element is based on the idea that the practice of arranged marriages is a universal one among the people from the Indian subcontinent. Not only is this an inaccurate perception, it undermines the understanding of culture in the postcolonial context as heterogeneous, fluid, and malleable.[72] Conjugality was a contested site in the colonial encounter. Arranged marriages constituted part of the political and cultural authenticity move against the British colonial power during its period of rule over the Indian subcontinent. Hindu nationalists declared that arranged marriage was the site of pure Hindu culture beyond the reach of colonial legal intervention.[73] My argument is not intended as a defense of arranged marriages. It is to highlight how marriage has been, and continues to be, entered into for political, cultural, and material reasons, and not exclusively for emotional ones. However, in an effort to curtail illegal migration, the British White Paper has singled out a legal consensual arrangement and subjected it to an implicit standard that only normalizes marriages that are "love"-based. Arranged marriages, as a result, are draped in a cultural cloth and cast as alien, insincere, and deceptive.

---

71. The U.K. is not the only country to target arranged marriages in order to distinguish "genuine" marriages and those intended for the purpose of obtaining the right to settle. Denmark has introduced a host of new criteria based on strict age and connection requirements under its family reunification policy before permitting immigrant status migrants to secure a resident permit. *See generally* Lovbekg. Nr. 685 af 24.07.2003 Lovtidende, 4357. One critical precondition that has especially sparked a great deal of controversy requires that both parties should be over the age of twenty-three in order to reduce the number of coerced marriages. Malcolm Brabant, *Denmark Cracks Down on Migrant Marriage*, BBC NEWS, June 24, 2002, *at* http://news.bbc.co.uk/1/hi/world/europe/2057594.stm (last visited Sept. 29, 2004). For a more detailed source on Danish restrictions and immigration laws, see the Danish Immigration Service's online service, *Spouses and Cohabitating* Companions, *at* http://www.udlst.dk/english/Family+Reunification/Spouses/Default.htm (last visited Jan. 3, 2005).

72. *See, e.g.*, SEYLA BENHABIB, THE CLAIMS OF CULTURE: EQUALITY AND DIVERSITY IN THE GLOBAL ERA (2002). Benhabib argues that cultures are not static wholes, but riddled with contradiction and dissent, torn apart and disputed within their own boundaries. Benhabib's discussion comes in the context of how liberal democracy can co-exist with multiculturalism. For a fictionalized account of the nonessential and ever-shifting fluidity of culture, see SMITH, *supra* note 2.

73. In fact, the marriage arrangement was also cast as a more loving and spiritual union than those practiced in the West. SARKAR, *supra* note 15, at 40. Sarkar writes that the non-consensual, indissoluble, infant marriage was projected as a higher form of love that countered the "utilitarian, materialist and narrowly contractual Western arrangement."

The proposals in the White Paper disregard the fact that marriage provides institutional access to a wide array of state benefits, and the right to settle is only one of them. The proposals are based on a static and naturalized understanding of marriage, whereas individuals marry for a variety of reasons both in and outside of Britain. People "here" and "there" marry for love, economic status, title and privilege, procreative purposes, as well as for the fact that the marital arrangement is the only state-recognized arrangement that is accorded maximum legitimacy by the state and access to state benefits, rights, and privileges. People opting for arranged marriages are motivated by all or some of these considerations and cannot be assessed exclusively from the perspective of "love" and other limited normative standards.

The White Paper proposals operate along a cultural divide that reinforces cultural stereotypes about the Other as different and inferior. The Home Secretary expresses the need for future generations of immigrants to grow up "feeling British."[74] Yet this "feeling" is assumed and never examined. It signals a return to a "crude and flawed mythology of a mono-racial, culturally uniform British identity in which non-white people's presence is tolerated—and even then only conditionally."[75] The "British" identity is neither defined nor explained, but it does, according to the Home Secretary, involve a process of integration through adopting British "norms of acceptability," studying British history and culture, and embracing "our laws, our values, our institutions."[76] Part of being British includes more than simply not tolerating practices unacceptable in the United Kingdom, such as enforced marriages. It involves a more aggressive assimilation move, which seeks in part to press the Other into conforming with the prevailing sexual, marital, and cultural norms in Britain, and also to erase cultural difference. For the Home Secretary, being British involves assimilation into a society that is assumed to be advanced, civilized, and homogenous. To ensure that immigrant practices do not infiltrate or compromise "British values," the White Paper lays down the criteria for encouraging assimilation and excluding all those subaltern arrangements that do not conform to or resemble the norm—a norm that is both white and middle class. The White Paper proposals are located on a slippery slope, where the line between belongingness and non-belongingness is increasingly drawn in an insular, culturally intolerant direction.

The White Paper permits the possibility of the Other metamorphosing into someone who is familiar and recognizable: the assimilated immigrant. The goal of controlling who should and should not live in Britain is being partly secured through the proposal to regulate whom a section of society should and should not marry. The White Paper represents a return to a highly exclusivist form of cultural and national identity. It is reminiscent of a time

74. *Immigrants "Should Try to Feel British,"* BBC NEWS, Dec. 9, 2001, *at* http://news.bbc.co.uk/hi/English/uk_politics/newsid_1699000/1699847.stm.

75. Gary Younge, *Britain is Again White*, GUARDIAN (London), Feb. 18, 2002, at 13.

76. Warren Hoge, *Britain's Nonwhites Feel Un-British, Report Says*, N.Y. TIMES, Apr. 4, 2002, at A13.

when English identity felt it could command, "within [its] own discourses, the discourses of almost everybody else; not quite everybody, but almost everyone else at a certain moment in history."[77] The underlying message of the proposals is that in order to be treated the same as everyone else, to try to be like everyone else. The "everyone else" standard constitutes the unstated universal norm from which "being British" emerges.

D. Demonizing the Other

> [T]he evil, barbarity, and licentiousness of the colonized Other are what make possible the goodness, civility, and propriety of the European Self.[78]

The treatment of the transnational migrant has remained ambiguous and contested, based at times on simply a lack of knowledge or desire to know the Other, or at times on a fear that the migrant was arriving in hordes to disrupt the social cohesion of or take away jobs from the (white, Christian) global North. In the contemporary period, demographic deficits and labor demands for nannies, maids, and domestic workers—among other factors—have pressed nations into adopting policies that negotiate between national cultural purity and cohesion, and economic demands. The tensions generated by these different fears, concerns, and demands have not been addressed exclusively within the framework of administrative and ministerial decisions. There has been an explosion of actors involved in the debates on immigration, including non-governmental networks or organizations representing the rights of migrants, ethnic lobbies, and anti-immigration parties. The issue has been the centerpiece of elections and at the heart of cultural debates and struggles.

After the terrorist attacks of September 11, the new "War on Terror" commenced, and there has been a heightened anxiety about the Other, who is increasingly perceived as a threat to the security of the nation. The line of difference is being redrawn along very stark divides—friend versus enemy, the good versus the evil. After September 11, the Other has been increasingly transformed into a fanatic and a potential enemy. The failure to define either the purpose or limits of the "War on Terror" has resulted in a serious casualty: groups and communities simply not liked have become targets.[79] Additionally, the failings of the international legal definition of terrorism—flowing precisely from the disagreement over who is a terrorist and what

77. Stuart Hall, *The Local and the Global: Globalization and Ethnicity*, *in* CULTURE, GLOBALIZATION AND THE WORLD SYSTEM: CONTEMPORARY CONDITIONS FOR THE REPRESENTATION OF IDENTITY 19, 19–39 (Anthony D. King ed., 1997).

78. MICHAEL HARDT & ANTONIO NEGRI, EMPIRE 127 (2000).

79. *See* Madeline Bunting, *Intolerant Liberalism*, GUARDIAN (London), Oct. 8, 2001, *available at* http://www.guardian.co.uk/waronterror/story/0,1361,565215,00.html.

constitutes terrorism—have resulted in the unbounded, unrestrained use of the concept of the "War on Terror."[80]

The casting of the Other as a dangerous and negative force to be contained finds its most explicit expression in Australia. Asylum-seekers who have attempted to enter Australia through clandestine means have been cast as people who are attempting to blackmail the Australian government.[81] In response, the Australian government has adopted a policy that regards asylum-seekers with fear and loathing, and post–September 11, as a danger and threat to the nation.[82]

Australia is a party to the 1951 Convention Relating to the Status of Refugees.[83] Australian law defines refugees as people who are outside their country of nationality or usual country of residence and are unable or unwilling to return to or seek the protection of that country because of a well-founded fear of being persecuted for reasons of race, religion, nationality, membership to a particular social group, or for holding a particular political opinion.[84] Australia has declared its commitment to provide protection to refugees under the terms of the Convention and ensure that asylum-seekers within Australia are treated in accordance with internationally recognized human rights standards. These commitments include a commitment not to send people back to a country where they would be exposed to human rights violations. Under the Australian law, asylum-seekers are categorized into two

80. TERRORISM AND POLITICAL VIOLENCE: LIMITS & POSSIBILITIES OF LEGAL CONTROL (Henry H. Han ed., 1993) (providing a general understanding of the state of international law and terrorism); *see also* TERRORISM AND INTERNATIONAL LAW (Rosalyn Higgins & Maurice Flory eds., 1997).

81. William Maley, *Asylum-seekers in Australia's International Relations*, 57:1 AUSTRALIAN J. INT'L AFF. 187, 192 (2003) (analyzing the relationship between notions of sovereignty and border controls and how this plays out in the legal and policy responses to asylum-seekers in Australia, representing them as 'bogus' and 'flooding' into the country); *see also* Jane Perlez, *Deep Fears Behind Australia's Immigration Policy*, N.Y. TIMES, May 8, 2002, at A3.

82. *See* Don McMaster, *Asylum-seekers and the Insecurity of a Nation*, 56 AUSTRALIAN J. INT'L AFF. 279 (2002) (discussing how the assertion of national sovereignty and a history of a white or discriminatory immigration policy have been at the core of Australia's treatment of its "Others"); *see also* Don McMaster, *Refugees: Where to Now?: White Australia to Tampa: The Politics of Fear*, 21 ACADEMY SOC. SCI. IN AUSTRALIAN DIALOGUE 3 (2002).

83. Convention Relating to the Status of Refugees, *adopted* July 28, 1951, 19 U.S.T. 6223, 189 U.N.T.S. 137, 152.

84. The definition of "refugee" incorporated into the Migration Act 1958 (Cth) (Austl.) by s36(2), which deals with the granting of protection visas, and provides that a criterion for a protection visa is that the applicant is a non-citizen "to whom . . . Australia has protection obligations under the Refugees Convention as amended by the Refugees Protocol." In September 2001 the Australian Parliament passed the Migration Legislation Amendment Act (No.6) 2001 (Cth). The amendments to the Migration Act 1958 included definitions of key Convention definition terms: persecution, particular social group, non-political crime, and serious crime. The definitions are contained in part 2, division 3, sub-division AI of the Migration Act 1958 (Cth). Persecution is defined in section 91R(1) that: (a) the Convention grounds (or "reasons") must be the "essential and significant" reason/s for persecution; (b) the persecution must involve serious harm; (c) the persecution must involve "systematic and discriminatory conduct." Section 91R(2) lists some examples of "serious harm," e.g., threat to life or liberty or "significant economic hardship that threatens the person's capacity to subsist." The definition of membership of a particular social group is refined in section 91S by stating that when the particular social group is a family, then the administrative decision maker should disregard any persecution experienced by other members of the family.

groups: those who enter legally and those who enter unlawfully.[85] Australia's Humanitarian Program offers a legitimate means of entry, and sets a quota of permitted entries from different parts of the world.[86] Those admitted under the program are referred to as "refugees" and are entitled to permanent residency, health checks, and permission to remain in the community while their applications are processed.

Persons entering Australia illegally—without proper travel documents—are categorized as "unlawful non-citizens" and confined to a detention center until their cases are reviewed. Upon review, these migrants are either granted a visa to remain in Australia, ordered to leave the country voluntarily, or deported. The mandatory detention policy was adopted in 1994 when nine detention centers were established to deal with the increasing number of persons fleeing to Australia through smuggling routes via Indonesia. There are several reasons provided for the adoption of these stringent and at times harsh new policies toward asylum-seekers.[87] One justification is that these "boat people" are not genuine asylum-seekers, but economic migrants and "queue-jumpers" seeking to enter Australia illegally. Accordingly, it is believed that these migrants are seeking asylum specifically in Australia, rather than in safe haven third countries through which they pass on their way to Australia.[88] Asylum-seekers are thus divided into "good" and "bad" refugees.[89] The good ones are selected through Australia's diplomatic missions and the Commonwealth pays for their airfare. They are immediately entitled to permanent residency and given access to assistance programs. "Bad" asylum-seekers arrive without invitation, illegally, and of their own accord. These refugees are locked up until their cases are determined.[90] There is a sense that the latter group of people is violating Australia's egalitarian values by not awaiting its turn and playing by the rules.

However, under the Refugee Convention, there is no "queue" to jump. The Convention imposes an obligation on a state party in relation to persons within its territory regardless of whether they arrived with a visa. William Maley has argued that "[t]he notion of a 'queue' is unrelated to refugee protection: instead, it reflects the wish of governments to be able to 'pick and

85. Dep't of Immigration and Multicultural and Indigenous Affairs, Fact Sheet 61: Seeking Asylum Within Australia (2004), *available at* http://www.immi.gov.au/facts/61asylum.htm (last visited Feb. 7, 2005).

86. Dep't of Immigration and Multicultural and Indigenous Affairs, Fact Sheet 60: Australia's Refugee and Humanitarian Program (2004), *available at* http://www.immi.gov.au/facts/60refugee.htm.

87. *See* U.S. Committee For Refugees, Sea Change: Australia's New Approach to Asylum Seekers (2002) (providing an overview of the changes in Australia's response to asylum-seekers).

88. Peter Mares, Borderline: Australia's Treatment of Refugees and Asylum Seekers 24 (2001) (stating that the Australian government's primary argument is that the "boat people" who try to enter the country unlawfully are denying legitimate refugees—who apply for asylum offshore, waiting patiently for a decision—the right to be considered for resettlement in Australia); *see also* John Menadue, *The Myth Howard Calls a Queue*, Age (Melbourne), July 19, 2002.

89. Maley, *supra* note 81, at 196.

90. Mares, *supra* note 88, at 24.

choose' which refugees to help (the educated rather than the unskilled, the healthy rather than the disabled, the quiescent rather than the 'troublesome')."[91] Furthermore, the effectiveness of a policy of incarceration and deportation is undermined since it does not stop the flow of economic migrants who constitute a portion of the unregulated movement of people.[92] The issue of demand remains unaddressed through such initiatives, and the unregulated flow of people will continue until the issue of demand is addressed.

One of the effects of the mandatory detention policy has been the arbitrary incarceration of immigrants and their families who enter Australia through unregulated or clandestine means in detention centers, the conditions of which have been regarded as bordering on inhumane.[93] Under international standards, detention must be for exceptional reasons, temporary in nature, and not used as a form of punishment.[94] Some refugees, including children, are locked up in medium security prisons, often in remote and inhospitable locations, sometimes spending years behind razor wire fencing while their applications are processed.[95] In light of this situation, in July 2000, the Human Rights Committee stated that the Australian government should reassess its policies and legislation on mandatory detentions.[96] It specifically stated that the mandatory detention of "unlawful non-citizens," including asylum-seekers,

91. William Maley, *A Global Refugee Crisis?*, *in* KEYNOTES: REFUGEES AND THE MYTH OF THE BORDERLESS WORLD 1, 4 (Christian Reus-Smit & Mary-Louise Hickey eds., 2002).

92. *See* Guido Friebel & Sergei Guriev, Human Trafficking and Illegal Migration (Feb. 2002), *available at* http://www.nes.ru/english/about/10th-Anniversary/papers-pdf/guriev_isnie_paper.pdf (arguing that more lenient deportation policies and amnesties towards migrants decrease illegal migration flows).

93. *See* Amnesty International Australia, *A Continuing Shame: The Mandatory Detention of Asylum-Seekers*, AI Index AUS/POL/REF (June 1998) (stating that the detention policy has been criticized by a number of the human rights groups including Amnesty International and by the Human Rights Committee as violating article 7 of the International Covenant on Civil and Political Rights); *see also* HEATHER TYLER, ASYLUM: VOICES BEHIND THE RAZOR WIRE (2003) (documenting the conditions of the detention centers by reproducing the voices and stories of detained inmates and attempting to humanize the Other in the process of such documentation).

94. *See Conclusion No. 44—Detention of Refugees and Asylum-Seekers, in Addendum to the Report of the United Nations High Commissioner for Refugees*, Executive Comm. of U.N. High Comm'r for Refugees, at 31, ¶ b, U.N. GAOR, 41st Sess., U.N. Doc. A/41/12/ADD.1 (1986) (stating that "in view of the hardship which it involves, detention should normally be avoided," although the conclusion does recognize the right a state has to temporarily detain an asylum-seeker in exceptional cases where detention is necessary in order to:

> verify identity, determine the elements on which the claim to refugee status or asylum is based; to deal with cases where refugees or asylum-seekers have destroyed their travel and/or identity documents or have used fraudulent documents in order to mislead the authorities of the State in which they intend to claim asylum; or to protect national security or public order.)

95. *See generally* PHILIP FLOOD, REPORT OF INQUIRY INTO IMMIGRATION DETENTION PROCEDURES (2001); *see also* DEP'T OF IMMIGRATION AND MULTICULTURAL AND INDIGENOUS AFFAIRS, REPORT OF AN OWN MOTION INVESTIGATION INTO THE DEP'T OF IMMIGRATION AND MULTICULTURAL AFFAIRS' IMMIGRATION DETENTION CENTRES 3, 19 (2001) *available at* http://www.ombudsman.gov.au./publications_information/Special_Reports/IDCMarch1.pdf (stating that under the prevailing conditions at immigration detention centers, refugees had fewer rights than convicted criminals in Australia, and as of June 30, 2000, there were almost 800 women and children in detention); *see also* Amnesty International, *supra* note 93.

96. *Concluding Observations of the Human Rights Committee, Australia: 24/07/2000*, Office of the High Comm'r for Hum. Rts., ¶¶ 498–528, U.N. Doc. A/55/40 (2000).

under the Migration Act raises questions about compliance with article 9.1 of the International Covenant on Civil and Political Rights. This article provides that no person shall be subjected to arbitrary detention.

The situation of the transnational migrant has been aggravated by a paranoia that hoards of asylum-seekers are threatening to enter the country, and threatening the social and cultural cohesion of Australian society.[97] More recently, in the aftermath of the September 11, 2001 attacks, there has been an amplification of voices depicting the transnational migrant subjects as potential terrorists.[98] In the interest of national security, the Australian government has enacted several pieces of legislation prioritizing border control, and security has become a further justification for Australia's detention policy.[99] More recently, under further amendments to the migration regulations, asylum-seekers arriving in an unauthorized manner are refused family reunification rights for a minimum of thirty months after they receive refugee status and are not provided with travel documents.[100] As a result, women and children might be detained even though they may have a male family member in Australia who is on a temporary protection visa ("TPV"). The policy has had two inadvertent effects. Women and children are increasingly accompanying husbands and fathers on boats for fear of otherwise being permanently separated. Secondly, if it is not possible to raise enough funds for the entire family to travel, the refugees who are on a TPV are motivated to maintain contact with criminal networks as their only hope of being reunited with their family members.[101]

---

97. *See* Mungo MacCullum, *Girt by Sea: Australia, the Refugees and the Politics of Fear*, 5 Q. ESSAY 1 (2002) (outlining the politics of fear that have influenced the current policies in the context of Australian history and the process of delegitimizing asylum-seekers and treating them as criminals); *see also* McMaster, *supra* note 82.

98. Maley, *supra* note 91, at 5.

99. The initiatives permit certain Australian territories and "excised offshore places" to be removed from the migration zone for the purposes of limiting the ability of unlawful non-citizens to make a valid visa application. The Migration Amendment (Excision from Migration Zone) Act 2001 amends the definition of "excised offshore place" in section 5 of the Migration Act 1958. The note accompanying the definition is: "The effect of this definition is to excise the listed places and installations from the migration zone for the purposes of limiting the ability of offshore entry persons to make valid visa applications." The new provisions also prevent any legal proceeding from being initiated against the government in respect of the entry, status, detention, and transfer of any unlawful non-citizen entering Australia and an excised offshore place. The Migration Amendment (Excision from Migration Zone) (Consequential Provisions) Act 2001 introduces a new regime for people who arrive unlawfully at an offshore excised place. It includes powers to move the person to another country where claims for Australia's protection can be considered. This Act inserts sections 198(A) and 494(AA) into the Migration Act 1958. By removing any infrastructure or facilities to process claims, the intention is to discourage boats from landing at the nearest land destination or from undertaking the journey in the first place.

100. In October 1999, Australia amended the regulations to the Migration Act 1958. Migration Amendment Regulations 1999 to Migration Regulations 1994. Since October 1999, under the Migration Regulations 1994, asylum-seekers who arrive without authority are released from detention if their application is successful, but they are only entitled to receive a temporary protection visa ("TPV") for a period of three years. If they leave the country for any reason, they cannot re-enter. Every three years they must reapply for their visa and their cases are re-evaluated to determine whether or not they still face persecution. The TPV affords refugees limited access to health care, but relatively few other services.

101. Since August 2003, there have been further changes made to the migration regulations. Prior to

The policy toward "unlawful non-citizens" in Australia has treated the families of asylum-seekers as though they were criminal and dangerous, reprehensible for their condition.[102] And the detention policy is reinforced through the representation of these families as uncaring, even brutal and barbaric, as illustrated in the "Children Overboard Scandal." In October, the Australian navy fired at an Indonesian ship carrying over 300 asylum-seekers in an attempt to force the ship to leave Australian waters. The government announced that the refugees were throwing their children overboard to force the navy to rescue them and in an attempt to blackmail the government.[103] The government stated that they had photographs of this outrageous conduct proving that the actions of the refugees were premeditated.[104] This publicity incident fueled the image of the uncaring and uncivilized Other at a time when the issue of asylum-seekers was a hot election topic.[105] Howard stated that "[t]here is something to me incompatible between somebody who claims to be a refugee and somebody who would throw their own child into the sea. . . . It offends the natural instinct of protection and delivering security and safety to your children."[106] In February, well after the Howard government was safely ensconced back in power, the Prime Minister confessed that the photographs were not genuine and that he had knowledge of this fact just three days prior to the election, but chose not to divulge the information.[107]

During 2002, refugees in detention centers across the country began to protest the government's repressive policy and the appalling conditions of the centers. In February 2002, detainees at Woomera began a hunger strike, protesting the conditions in the centers, especially the situation of children and young adults.[108] Several of the detainees, including children, took up the horrifying protest method of drinking detergent and shampoo and sewing their lips together in a symbolic gesture of resistance against the oppression and imposed silence that they were experiencing in the detention centers.[109]

September 2001, those who had been granted a TPV were entitled to apply for a permanent protection visa after thirty months. This option has now been withdrawn after Migration Amendment Regulations 2003 amended the Migration Regulations 1994. TPV holders who did not apply for a permanent protection visa prior to September 21, 2001 are ineligible to do so after that date. All TPV holders, even those who entered Australia lawfully on genuine documents, are covered by the changes. A TPV holder can apply for another TPV if she or he can demonstrate that she or he is in continuing need of protection.

102. *See* HUMAN RIGHTS WATCH, BY INVITATION ONLY: AUSTRALIAN ASYLUM POLICY (2002).

103. S. Douez & M. Forbes, *Boat People "Threw Children Overboard,"* AGE (Melbourne), Oct. 8, 2001, at 1.

104. A. Cock & M. Ludlow, *Parents Throw Children Off Ship—Navy Intercepts Asylum Boat*, DAILY TELEGRAPH (Sydney), Oct. 8, 2001, at 11.

105. Patrick Barkham, *Australia Votes on How Tightly to Close the Door: Illegal Migration is at the Heart of Australia's Cliffhanger General Election Today*, GUARDIAN UNLIMITED (London), Nov. 10, 2001.

106. *PM Accuses Boatpeople of Moral Blackmail*, AAP NEWSFEED, Oct. 8, 2001.

107. Andrew Clennell, *Overboard Photos: I Knew They Were Doubtful, PM Admits*, SYDNEY MORNING HERALD, Feb. 20, 2002, at 1; Frank Walker, *Sailor Hero Betrayed as Truth Tossed Overboard*, SUN-HERALD (Sydney), Feb. 24, 2002, at 4.

108. *See* Russell Skelton, *Tales from Behind the Fence*, AGE (Melbourne), Mar. 18, 2002, at 9.

109. *See Fresh Hunt for Fleeing Refugees as Protesters Break Camp in Australia*, AGENCE FRANCE-PRESSE,

The government once again cast the refugees as uncivilized child abusers who stitched together the lips of their children.[110] One columnist supporting the government's tough policies toward illegal immigrants deplored the acts of lip stitching, stating that "[t]he test is simple: who wants as neighbors the people who have stitched shut the mouths of their children?"[111] The families' actions were characterized as a form of blackmail against the government, rather than as acts of desperation.[112]

Although this method of resistance was a particularly disturbing one, it could be interpreted, as characterized by the Australian Human Rights and Equal Opportunities Commission, as a response to the "atmosphere of despair in which [the refugee children] live."[113] The Commissioners observed that the provision of education for the children in the detention center was confined to those who were twelve years old or under, but that the quality of education was not comparable to the quality received by Australian twelve-year olds.[114] For children over twelve, little or no education was provided.[115] In April 2003, the Woomera detention center was shut down. However, the government remains steadfast in the pursuit of its refugee policy. In response to the protests over conditions at Woomera, it proposed that the children be placed in the care of foster parents while their parents remained in detention centers. The proposal is reminiscent of the notorious policy that placed Australia's aboriginal children in the care of Christian, white families who would teach them how to be real Australians.[116] The assimilationist civilizing strategy relegates the subaltern parents into the category of savage and criminal, unfit to care for their own children.

Australia's policy toward asylum-seekers has historically been problematic. A trickle of people, especially those who are non-white and non-Christian,

---

Apr. 1, 2002. There were several subsequent attempts by the detainees to break out of the detention complex at Woomera with the support of local demonstrators. This act strengthened the government's resolve to take a tough stand on the arrival of illegal immigrants. *See also* Farah Farouque, *Police Hunt for 14 Detainees*, AGE (London), Apr. 1, 2002, at 2. However, the publicity and the protests did ultimately result in the closing down of the Woomera detention center.

110. *See* Patrick Barkham, *PM Calls Asylum Protest Blackmail*, GUARDIAN UNLIMITED (London), Jan. 26, 2002, at 18 (quoting the Prime Minister as stating, "[c]hildren in proper positive care of their parents don't sew their lips together, do they?"); *see also* Hugh Mackay, *Australians All Let Us Be Judged*, AGE (Melbourne), Mar. 30, 2002, at 7 (arguing that Australians must be held accountable for the wrongs that are being committed against asylum-seekers and the maltreatment of their children).

111. Heather Tyler, *Australia Unmoved by Detainees*, MIDDLE EAST TIMES, *available at* http://64.233.179.104/search?q=cache:-srBUsXfPSgJ:www.metimes.com/2K2/issue2002-4/reg/australia_unmoved_by.htm+%22heather+tyler%22+%22australia+unmoved+by+detainees%22&hl=en (last visited Jan. 6, 2005).

112. M. Steketee & I. Henderson, *PM Labels Lip Sewing Blackmail*, AUSTRALIAN, Jan. 26, 2001.

113. Media Statement, President Professor Alice Tay AM & Dr Sev Ozdowski, Human Rights Commissioner OAM, *Woomera Immigrations Detention Centre Report of Visit by HREOC Officers* (Feb. 6, 2002), *at* http://www.hreoc.gov.au/media_releases/2002/05_02.html.

114. *Id.*

115. *Id.*

116. *See generally* HUM. RTS. AND EQUAL OPPORTUNITY COMM'N, BRINGING THEM HOME: REPORT OF THE NATIONAL INQUIRY INTO THE SEPARATION OF ABORIGINAL AND TORRES STRAIT ISLANDER CHILDREN FROM THEIR FAMILIES (1997).

triggers a fear of an imminent flood.[117] This fear in the contemporary moment has been most explicitly expressed against the "Muslim."[118] Disproportionate numbers of individuals from Islamic and third world countries are placed in detention.[119] These "boat people" have been subjected to a new form of hate speech and Islamaphobia, which expresses itself in terms of a fear of a "Muslim invasion." The fear of hoards of immigrants flooding into the country is not substantiated by statistics.[120]

This fear has been constructed in part through the rhetoric of the far right, especially the One Nation Party, which was a significant force in 1998.[121] The party's fortunes have declined since then, but its rhetoric has succeeded in influencing public discourse on asylum-seekers. Since September 11, the Howard government has also been able to capitalize on this fear through recourse to the "War on Terror," which casts the Other as evil and dangerous. Howard was able to fight a successful election campaign in 2001 by portraying the cross-border movements by immigrants, refugees, and asylum-seekers into Australia as a potential terrorist threat. In the buildup to the national elections in 2001, the two main national parties resorted to the powerful rhetoric of the threats of terrorism and evil. Howard declared: "[y]ou don't know who's coming, and you don't know whether they do have terrorist links or not."[122] Howard's hard line position—that these asylum-seekers were unwelcome, to be denied entry into Australia, or to be incarcerated upon entry—won the day.

In the Australian context, the transnational migrant is undermined through two delegitimizing moves. These subjects are cast as blackmailers, using their situations of hardship to extract sympathy and material benefits from the Australian government. They are also cast as primitive and barbaric, as demonstrated in the representation of these families in the media and gov-

117. William Maley, *Security, People-Smuggling and Australia's New Afghan Refugees*, 55:3 AUSTRALIAN J. INT'L AFF. 351 (2001).

118. *See* DEP'T OF IMMIGRATION AND MULTICULTURAL AND INDIGENOUS AFFAIRS, POPULATION FLOWS: IMMIGRATION ASPECTS 26–27 (2000), *available at* http://www.immi.gov.au/statistics/publications/popflows/popflows.htm (last visited Feb. 27, 2005). In Australia, European refugees received 45.6% of the offshore Humanitarian Visa Grants, compared to the 29.4% of grants that went to refugees from the Middle East and South Asia.

119. DEP'T OF IMMIGRATION AND MULTICULTURAL AND INDIGENOUS AFFAIRS, FACT SHEET 82: IMMIGRATION DETENTION IN AUSTRALIA, *available at* http://www.immi.gov.au/facts/82detention.htm (last visited Nov. 2, 2003).

120. In a recent report by the United Nations High Commissioner for Refugees, the total number of "boat people" arriving into Australia between 1999–2000 was only 4174, in sharp contrast to the number of asylum applications received in the United Kingdom, which was 97,900 in the year 2000. The number of applications received in other liberal democracies also far outnumber the ones received by Australia. In the year 2000, Germany received 78,800; the Netherlands, 43,900; Belgium, 42,690; and France, 38,590. U.N. HIGH COMM'R FOR REFUGEES, ASYLUM APPLICATIONS SUBMITTED IN EUROPE (2000).

121. Maley, *supra* note 81, at 192–93.

122. Seth Mydans, *Which Australian Candidate Has the Harder Heart*, N.Y. TIMES, Nov. 9, 2001, at A3; *see also* ANTHONY BURKE, IN FEAR OF SECURITY: AUSTRALIA'S INVASION ANXIETY (2001) (discussing the security discourse and how Australia's general security concern may have affected the country's refugee policies).

ernment statements regarding the "Children Overboard Scandal," as well as the Woomera protests. Both of these responses are based on a fear of the Other that has heavily influenced Australian policy in an increasingly borderless world, as well as on assumptions that the security of the nation-state is achieved through the denial of the transnational migrant's security. Fear and prejudice have been accentuated post–September 11, adding another layer of aversion to the Other, who is now also regarded as a threat to the security of the nation.[123]

The new "War on Terrorism" has created space for a more strident and alarming response to the global movements of people, reducing it at times to nothing more than an evil threat.[124] If terrorism is defined as a transnational crime, then by merely committing the crime of seeking illegal movement and illegal entry, many anti-immigration parties might seize upon a series of logically flawed deductions to conclude that migrants could be defined as terrorists. Such simple and faulty equations can lead to a disjuncture between the reality of the illegal migrant and the issue of terrorism. The conflation of the migrant with the terrorist is not new, but it has received greater attention since September 11. It has afforded more space for the representation of the Other as a fanatic, both dangerous and opposed to freedom.[125]

III. Conclusions: "Somewhere in Between"

The legal interventions in the lives of transnational migrants have been articulated primarily from the perspective of the host country. The perspec-

123. Even those subjects who propose to come to Australia through legitimate means, especially from the Middle East, are discouraged through a complete "othering" of their habits, lifestyles, and relationships as distinct and incompatible with "Western" (civilized) norms and values. A kit prepared for Philip Ruddock, Australia's former Immigration Minister, for a tour in the Middle East contained a document entitled, Dep't of Immigration and Multicultural and Indigenous Affairs, Questions and Answers provided by the Australian Minister for Immigration and Multicultural Affairs, Philip Ruddock (2001), which included a series of questions and answers for Middle Easterners who are considering relocating to Australia. In response to a hypothetical query, "[w]ouldn't my family have a better life," the document gives the response: "No. Even if you can bring your family to join you, your children will abandon your traditional way of life in favor of modern 'western' ways. You will lose control of your children, who will rebel and question your authority and your religious beliefs." The relationships of the Muslim or "Middle Easterner" are constructed as repressive and un-democratic, and Australia as a land only suitable to "Westerners" and a family structure that comprehends "western values" and autonomy; *see* Maley, *supra* note 117, at 364 (discussing the contents of the kit in greater detail).

124. *See* David Frum & Richard Perle, An End to Evil: How to Win the War on Terror (2003).

125. *See* Bruce W. Nelan, *The Dark Side of Islam*, Time, Oct. 4, 1993, at 62–64 ("The clash between Islamic religious and political authority is more widespread and in some places more threatening now than it was then. . . . [T]his is the dark side of Islam, which shows its face in violence and terrorism intended to overthrow modernizing, more secular regimes and harm the Western nations that support them. Its influence far outweighs its numbers. . . . [T]hese disparate cells of angry young men seem to boil up from the broad opposition growing in the largely undemocratic countries of the region, in a self-proclaimed war to force pure, undiluted Islamic law on the societies that have failed them."); *see also The Changing Face of Terrorism*, BBC News, Aug. 12, 1998, *at* http://news.bbc.co.uk/1/hi/world/africa/149090.stm (statement of John Bolton, former U.S. Secretary of State: "I think the U.S. is viewed as principal target of Islamic terrorists who are trying—at a minimum—to get the U.S. in effect to withdraw from the Middle East.").

tives of the migrant subject are omitted from these interventions. However, these are the perspectives that can assist in untangling the conflations and confusions that are taking place between trafficking, migration, and terrorism in the international and domestic legal arenas. The perspective and location of the transnational migrant subject must be foregrounded—not as a terrorist, nor as a victim, but as a complex subject affected by contemporary global processes.

In all three situations discussed in the Article, the focus of the regulatory effort has been on the borders. These efforts are based on the assumption that the movement of the transnational migrant subject is a consequence of organized criminal networks and "evildoers" and their manipulative and devious maneuvers. The consequence of this assumption is that the receiving country is not in any way implicated in these movements—it is simply the passive recipient. This assumption is not universal, but the legal interventions reviewed in this Article suggest that the larger part of the responsibility lies with those who move. As a result, the transnational migrant becomes the site of accountability as well as the site for enforcement. The three examples illustrate how legal interventions tend to individualize the nature of the movement, regard it as a deliberate transgression and a threat. However, the broader global canvas against which such transnational migrations occur is not addressed. The global push and pull factors that compel movement cannot be addressed through responses that locate such movement exclusively in the individualized transnational subject.

Cross-border movements are an integral aspect of globalization and thus have become a fundamental feature of the contemporary moment. Although a new legal order has emerged to deal with, and facilitate the cross-border movement, of capital, goods, and services, there has not been a simultaneous response to deal with the concomitant cross-border movement of people and labor.[126] Instead states have sought refuge in traditional notions of nation-state identity and sovereignty to resist cross-border movements.[127] This assertion of national identity is deployed through assimilationist and essentializing policies, as well as through the production of fear of the Other as a threat to the nation's security.

Prior to September 11, there was some recognition that the cross-border movements needed to be addressed in more transnational terms. After the

126. An example of a legal order established to facilitate the movement of capital and goods is the Schengen Treaty of 1985. At one level Schengen marks an attempt to abolish borders between member states and allow the free circulation of goods, capital, and services as well as citizens. However, this move could also be read as an assimilationist one, intended to create a culturally homogenous and economically protected area. It produces an expanded notion of the national subject as a European citizen, and a national sovereign extending to the external borders of the European Union. *See* Ginette Verstraete, *Technological Frontiers and the Politics of Mobility in the European Union*, *in* UPROOTINGS/REGROUNDINGS: QUESTIONS OF HOME AND MIGRATION 226 (Sara Ahmed et al. eds., 2003); *see also* Robert Goodin, *If People Were Money*, *in* FREE MOVEMENT: ETHICAL ISSUES IN THE TRANSITIONAL MIGRATION OF PEOPLE AND OF MONEY 6 (1992).

127. *See* HEATHER RAE, STATE IDENTITIES AND THE HOMOGENISATION OF PEOPLES (2002).

attacks on the World Trade Center, these conversations have become muted, and inversely, the targeting of the transnational migrant has become more acute.[128] After September 11, the urgency of the situation has been underscored by the "War on Terror" and the fear of imminent threats to national security.[129] Legal reforms are further alienating those who have been cast as the "new enemy."[130] The recourse to border controls and constructions of ethnic purity, cultural values, and nationalism arise out of the anxieties of dealing with difference, and serve to stigmatize, penalize, and criminalize the transnational migrant. Cross-border movements have been caught within the framework of a "war" fought along the simple binaries of good versus evil, and civilization versus barbarism. The issues of border crossing cannot be adequately addressed through such binaries. Indeed this myopic response will do little to discourage the illegal crossing of borders or the determination of those who want to move. These responses push us further away from addressing the complexity of cross-border movements and the equally complex legal and political responses required to address the issues raised by such movements.

In order to address the issue of cross-border movements, we cannot simply remain confined to the domestic arena, where regulatory enforcement is focused on the individual and the border. Nor can this process be addressed in the international legal arena purely in terms of criminality or trafficking. It is important to recognize that the erection of borders through immigration policy, anti-terrorist legislation, and anti-trafficking laws, or by a simple policy of incarceration, will not succeed in stopping cross border movements, meeting a nation's security needs, or protecting the sovereign subject. People will continue to move illegally if legal means are not available. Indeed, migrants are moving through irregular and clandestine channels precisely because of the system of political, social, cultural, and economic exclusions that are being produced, in part, through legal interventions.

The problems produced through trafficking, smuggling, and unlawful movement can only partly be alleviated by the expansion of immigration laws that acknowledge and accommodate the entry of people other than those who are part of the highly skilled information technology work force.[131]

128. Statement by Genevieve Gencianos of Migrants Rights International, Oral Intervention on Item 14(a): Migrant Workers, delivered to the U.N. Comm'n on Hum. Rts. (Apr. 17, 2003), *available at* http://www.migrantwatch.org/mri/whats_new/MRI_oral_intervention_on_agenda_item_14.htm (acknowledging that "[t]he war against terrorism and the war against Iraq are intimately linked to the war against the human rights of migrants").

129. *See* Human Rights Watch, World Report 2002, *available at* http://www.hrw.org/wr2k2/. Some of this fear or aversion is expressed in the enactments of anti-terrorist legislation around the globe which are vaguely drafted, over inclusive and are likely to be used to target legitimate protest which may be disapproved.

130. *Id.*

131. *See* Nandita Sharama, *Race, Class and Gender and the Making of Difference: The Social Organization of "Migrant Workers" in Canada*, 24:2 Atlantis: Women's Stud. J. 5 (2000). Restrictive immigration policies adopted by states have not stemmed the flow of people moving across borders. Rather, restrictive policies create a decline in the number of people coming as legal immigrants and documented migrants,

At the same time, the conferring of legal rights does not address some of the normative challenges produced by the transnational migrant. Her movement across borders exposes the porosity of national borders and breaks down the binaries, the "us and them," "here and there" distinctions that inform the legal regulation of transnational migrants and reveals her location somewhere in between these binaries. She exposes how legal discourse produces exclusions and reinforces differences by drawing bright lines delineating legitimacy of border crossings. Transnational migrants have continuously disrupted these lines and upset the neat boundaries between the domestic and the international, between the national and the transnational, and between the local and the global.

Transnational movements therefore require a transnational response and analysis—they cannot be stuck within older frameworks. A radical departure is required in the area of legal responses to migration. The story of the transnational migrant subject must be told in the context of globalization. This subject exposes the need to think about law and rights in ways that are not confined to the boxes of sovereignty, the nation-state, and the autonomous subject of liberal rights discourse. The liberal state and the liberal subject are based on the idea of fixed borders, with clearly identifiable interests and identities. They are imbued with the power to decide, choose, and act autonomously. Yet the challenge of globalization, which brings the challenge of migration and non-state actors to the legitimacy of the borders of the sovereign state and the autonomous subject, indicates otherwise. The complexity of new global formations and the dynamic character of the individual who crosses borders challenge any notion that the state and individual are hermetically sealed or capable of exercising control through self-contained power. The inability to distinguish those who constitute national subjects from those who are alien or foreign reflects the uneasy location of a distinct national entity with distinct borders and a distinct national subject with borders. The legitimizing tools of cohesion, unity, and sovereignty become blunt in the face of a more complex and integrated world and global economy.

The shift to a transnational framework is neither easily achieved nor persuasive. The right to determine who is entitled to enter into a country remains a prized prerogative of nation-states. However, this discussion reveals that current strategies are not stopping entry, but merely encouraging the production of a clandestine migrant mobility regime that facilitates clandestine movement. A transnational framework can challenge the complex global processes that instigate such movements and moves away from viewing the Other as the main producer of illegality and criminality. In the process, it can serve to break down the binaries, the "us and them," "here and there" distinctions, and exposes how these oppositions are partly produced in and through legal discourse and the focus on a state-centered framework. As long as

but increase the flow of migrants categorized as indentured, temporary, or undocumented migrants, all often clubbed under the rubric of "illegals."

nation-states neglect to view the issue of transnational migration through the complex lens of globalization and market demand, the (in)security of the nation-state and the rights of the transnational migrant will remain unaddressed, thereby contributing to the growing instability of both the host country and this itinerant population.

The transnational migrant is a subject who remains present and disruptive of any legal project that continues to compel assimilation, exclude, marginalize, or erase her presence. In *Dirty Pretty Things*, every move to unearth, capture, or remove this clandestine subject is subverted, and the migrant continues to pursue her dreams and direction undeterred although her situation remains fraught and vulnerable to exploitation. It is only through the centering of this new global actor that law can begin to address the real issues that emerge in the context of cross-border movements and engage with the new challenges that are being posed in the contemporary moment of globalization.

[6]

Human Rights and the Elusive Universal Subject: Immigration Detention Under International Human Rights and EU Law

CATHRYN COSTELLO*

ABSTRACT

The right to liberty is ubiquitous in human rights instruments, in essence protecting all individuals from arbitrary arrest and detention. Yet, in practice, immigration detention is increasingly routine, even automatic, across Europe. Asylum seekers in particular have been targeted for detention. While international human rights law limits detention, its protections against immigration detention are weaker than in other contexts, as the state's immigration control prerogatives are given sway. In spite of the overlapping authority of international and regional human rights bodies, the caselaw in this field is diverse. Focusing on the U.N. Human Rights Committee, the European Court of Human Rights, and the Court of Justice of the European Union, this Article explores how greater interaction between these bodies could produce more rights-protective standards.

INTRODUCTION

The right to liberty is ubiquitous in human rights instruments, in essence protecting all individuals from arbitrary arrest and detention. It should go without saying that deprivations of liberty

---

* Fellow and Tutor in EU and Public Law at Worcester College, Oxford. I thank participants at the 2011 Nordic Asylum Law Seminar on The State of International Refugee Law; the Indiana Journal of Global Legal Studies Spring Symposium on Globalization and Migration; the VU University Amsterdam Seminar on Migration Law and European Integration, Bergen aan Zee; and the Workshop on the Meaning and Practice of Immigration Detention, St. Antony's College, Oxford for helpful comments on earlier drafts, in particular Galina Cornelisse, Catherine Dauvergne, Jeff King, Gregor Noll, and Thomas Spijkerboer. I am particularly indebted to Aaron Rathmell for research assistance and to the Journal's reviewers and editorial staff for their helpful suggestions. Unless otherwise noted, all translations are my own. The usual disclaimer applies.

require the strongest possible justification. Yet, in practice, immigration detention[1] is increasingly routine, even automatic, across Europe.[2] Often detention is justified on the basis that categories of immigrants are "illegal," either in entering a state's territory without authorization or in staying after they have been told to leave. Asylum seekers in particular have been targeted for detention.[3] While international human rights law (IHRL)[4] limits detention, we see that the protections afforded to migrants are often weaker than in other contexts.[5] The state's migration control powers seem to be given greater sway than others, reflecting an uneasy

---

1. "Immigration detention" is understood as referring to the detention of migrants (in the broadest sense, to include all individuals entering the territory of a state other than their own, be it as refugees, asylum-seekers, stateless persons, irregular migrants, or regular migrants) either upon seeking entry to a territory or pending deportation, removal, or return from a territory.

2. *See generally* COUNCIL OF EUR., PARL. ASS., *Report of the Comm. on Migration, Refugees and Population on the Detention of Asylum Seekers and Irregular Migrants in Europe*, Doc. No. 12105 (2010); ANA CATARINA MENDONÇA, *Explanatory Memorandum* to THE DETENTION OF ASYLUM SEEKERS AND IRREGULAR MIGRANTS IN EUROPE (2010); MICHAEL FLYNN & CECILIA CANNON, GLOBAL DETENTION PROJECT, DETENTION AT THE BORDERS OF EUROPE: REPORT ON THE JOINT GLOBAL DETENTION PROJECT–INTERNATIONAL DETENTION COALITION WORKSHOP IN GENEVA, SWITZERLAND, 2-3 OCTOBER 2010 (2010).

3. *See generally* Michael Welsh & Liza Schuster, *Detention of Asylum Seekers in the US, UK, France, Germany and Italy: A Critical View of the Globalizing Culture of Control*, 5 CRIMINOLOGY & CRIM. JUST. 331 (2005).

4. "International human rights law" is used here to connote the broad body of international law that is rooted in the Universal Declaration of Human Rights (UDHR) and the two key covenants: the International Covenant on Civil and Political Rights (ICCPR) and the International Covenant on Economic Social and Cultural Rights (ICESCR). It also includes the regional human rights instruments, in the European context being those of the Council of Europe, principally the European Convention on Human Rights (ECHR) and the European Social Charters (ESC). For present purposes, I focus on the ICCPR and ECHR. Also pertinent is the Refugee Convention (RC) (Geneva Convention of 28 July 1951 and the Protocol of 31 January 1967 relating to the status of refugees). The RC may not, on one view, be part of IHRL, because its main function is palliative, in that it only applies when flight to another country triggers its legal protections. However, I include it within the notion of IHRL here as the key instrument that sets out the rights and obligations of states towards a vulnerable category of foreigners, namely asylum seekers and refugees. Space precludes considering detention of children, so for that reason alone the Convention on the Rights of the Child (CRC) is not examined.

5. *See generally* ALICE EDWARDS, BACK TO BASICS: THE RIGHT TO LIBERTY AND SECURITY OF PERSON AND 'ALTERNATIVES TO DETENTION' OF REFUGEES, ASYLUM-SEEKERS, STATELESS PERSONS AND OTHER MIGRANTS (2011); INT'L DETENTION COAL., LEGAL FRAMEWORK AND STANDARDS RELATING TO THE DETENTION OF REFUGEES, ASYLUM SEEKERS AND MIGRANTS: A GUIDE (2011); INT'L COMM'N OF JURISTS, MIGRATION AND INTERNATIONAL HUMAN RIGHTS LAW: PRACTITIONERS GUIDE NO. 6, at 147-90 (2011).

tension between the universal right to liberty and the state's border control prerogatives. My starting point is the acknowledgment of this tension. I set out to examine how it is resolved over time when migrants challenge their detention before human rights courts and bodies.[6]

Accordingly, this Article focuses in particular on the roles of the U.N. Human Rights Committee (HRC), the European Court of Human Rights (ECtHR or Strasbourg), and the Court of Justice of the European Union (CJEU or Luxembourg) in this context. The HRC is the monitoring body for the International Covenant for Civil and Political Rights (ICCPR), while the ECtHR is the court that enforces the European Convention on Human Rights (ECHR). The CJEU is the main court of EU law. Since 1997, the EU Member States have conferred competence on the European Union (EU) to adopt binding laws relating to immigration, asylum, and "combating illegal immigration" from outside the EU.[7] Now, there is a significant body of EU law governing immigration detention, in particular, the detention of asylum seekers under the Procedures Directive (PD)[8] and Reception Conditions Directive (RCD)[9] and of those facing deportation under the Returns Directive (RD).[10] Thus, as of late, the CJEU has become part

6. The principal focus is on the permissibility of detention per se, rather than procedural protections and detention conditions, although the latter also raise serious human rights concerns, usually scrutinized under guarantees against inhuman and degrading detention conditions. *See, e.g.*, European Convention on Human Rights art. 3, *opened for signature* Nov. 4, 1950, C.E.T.S. no. 194. Particular concerns are also raised in relation to the detention of children. *See, e.g.*, Mayeka & Mitunga v. Belgium, App. No. 13178/03 Eur. Ct. H.R. (2006) http://www.echr.coe.int/echr/en/hudoc (follow "HUDOC database" hyperlink; search "Application Number 13178/03"). As will be seen though, the two issues are intertwined, as detention conditions do bear on the permissibility of detention, in particular under the case law of the European Court of Human Rights, discussed below at *infra* Part II.C.

7. Consolidated Version of the Treaty on the Functioning of the European Union art. 79(1), May 9, 2008, 2008 O.J. (C 83) 47, 77 [hereinafter TFEU] (stating aims for the development of an EU common immigration policy).

8. *See* Council Directive 2005/85/EC, On Minimum Standards on Procedures in Member States for Granting and Withdrawing Refugee Status, 2005 O.J. (L326) 13 [hereinafter PD] (this directive is currently being revised, and the outcome of the reform process is not yet clear). *See also Amended Proposal for a Directive of the European Parliament and of the Council on Common Procedures for Granting and Withdrawing International Protection Status*, COM (2011) 319 final (June 1, 2011).

9. Council Directive 2003/9, Laying Down Minimum Standards for the Reception of Asylum Seekers, 2003 O.J. (L31) 18 [hereinafter RCD] (this directive is being revised at present). *See Amended Proposal for a Directive of the European Parliament and of the Council Laying Down Standards for the Reception of Asylum Seekers*, COM (2011) 320 final, (June 1, 2011).

10. *See* Directive 2008/18, of the European Parliament and of the Council of 18 December 2008 on Common Standards and Procedures in Member States for

of the apparatus of supranational human rights adjudication over the bulk of immigration detention by EU Member States.[11]

The main aim of this article is to analyze the jurisprudence of all three bodies on immigration detention. In comparing and contrasting their different jurisprudence, I illustrate how different human rights bodies speak with different voices on detention, a phenomenon that is at least in part explained by their different institutional contexts and decisional autonomy.[12] Given that the resultant human rights standards overlap significantly, I urge greater mutual engagement between regimes, so that a "constructive human rights pluralism" might emerge, drawing on a thesis developed at length elsewhere.[13] Constructive human rights pluralism describes the desirable mode of interaction between human rights regimes, whereby each cultivates a degree of openness to the others, while maintaining its own integrity.[14]

Returning Illegally Staying Third-Country Nationals, 2008 O.J. (L 348) 98 [hereinafter RD].

11. This article focuses on the easy case where Member States implement these directives in detaining third-country nationals (TCNs) and are therefore subject to EU norms. It is also arguable that in other situations Member State detention practices may fall within the scope of EU law, in particular if the detention practices derogate from other EU norms.

12. Of course, the degree of decisional autonomy or "zone of discretion" (to use Sweet's term) will only be a crude indicator. As he puts it,

> Mapping a zone of discretion cannot tell us what constitutional courts [a term he applies to the ECtHR, CJEU and WTO Appellate Body] will actually do with their powers. The best we can do is to predict that, given a steady case load, constitutional judges operating in a relatively larger zone will come to exercise more influence over the evolution of the polity than those operating in relatively smaller zones.

Alec Stone Sweet, *Constitutionalism, Legal Pluralism, and International Regimes* 16 IND. J. OF GLOBAL LEGAL STUD. 621, 640-41 (2009).

13. Cathryn Costello, Destination Europe: Human Rights & Admissions to the EU's Area of Freedom, Security and Justice (Jan. 14, 2010) (unpublished doctoral thesis in law, University of Oxford) (on file with author). *See* Miguel Poiares Maduro, *Interpreting European Law: Judicial Adjudication in a Context of Constitutional Pluralism*, 1 EUR. J. LEGAL STUD. 1 (2007). *See also* Miguel Poiares Maduro, *Courts and Pluralism: Essay on a Theory of Judicial Adjudication in the Context of Legal and Constitutional Pluralism*, *in* RULING THE WORLD? CONSTITUTIONALISM, INTERNATIONAL LAW, AND GLOBAL GOVERNANCE 356 (Jeffrey Dunoff & Joel Trachtman eds., 2009).

14. This piece focuses on the interactions across key international and regional regimes, rather than between the international and domestic. On the latter, see generally Gerald L. Neuman, *Human Rights and Constitutional Rights: Harmony and Dissonance*, 55 STAN. L. REV. 1863 (2003); Gráinne de Búrca & Oliver Gerstenberg, *The Denationalization of Constitutional Law*, 47 HARV. INT'L L. J. 243 (2006); Anne-Marie Slaughter & William Burke-White, *The Future of International Law is Domestic (or, The European Way of Law)*, 47 HARV. INT'L L. J. 327 (2006).

I. TOWARDS CONSTRUCTIVE HUMAN RIGHTS PLURALISM

A. *Human Rights Between Universalism and Statism*

Human rights tend to be conceived of as universal, in that they are rights all people have simply in virtue of being human. That premise sits uneasily with statist border control, which presupposes rights enjoyed within bounded states that have a sovereign right to control admissions. A distinctive conception of sovereignty dominates immigration discourse and law, tending to equate sovereignty and unfettered state discretion.[15] I refer throughout to the "statist entry control assumption" or, simply, the "statist assumption" to connote this notion that states have a sovereign right to exclude aliens without justification. Undoubtedly, this notion warrants challenge on ethical grounds[16] and cries out for historical corrective.[17] The statist assumption seems out of place in an age of human rights and increasing transnational economic and social interpenetration. Yet, in the migration context, it remains stubbornly ingrained.[18]

This statist assumption is reflected in the Universal Declaration of Human Rights (UDHR) and percolates through other instruments. The UDHR speaks of "the right to a nationality" but not in the country of one's residence or choosing. It affirms the right "to freedom of movement and residence," but only "within the borders of each State,"[19] and the "right to leave any country, including his own, and to return to his country,"[20] but not to enter another. Article 14(1) of the UDHR enshrines the right to seek, but not to be granted, asylum, stating "everyone has the right to seek and to enjoy . . . asylum from persecution." The formulation was controversial, reflecting states' unease at inclusion of a right to be granted

15. *See generally* GALINA CORNELISSE, IMMIGRATION DETENTION AND HUMAN RIGHTS: RETHINKING TERRITORIAL SOVEREIGNTY (2010) (arguing that it is a distinctively territorial account that distorts human rights in the immigration field).

16. *See generally* Veit Bader, *The Ethics of Immigration*, 12 CONSTELLATIONS 331 (2005).

17. For critiques of the presentation of the statist assumption in light of the historical development of public international law, see James A. R. Nafziger, *The General Admission of Aliens Under International Law*, 77 AM. J. INT'L L. 804 (1983); Satvinder S. Juss, *Free Movement and the World Order*, 16 INT'L J. REFUGEE L. 289 (2004).

18. *See, e.g.*, CATHERINE DAUVERGNE, MAKING PEOPLE ILLEGAL: WHAT GLOBALIZATION MEANS FOR MIGRATION AND LAW (2008); Catherine Dauvergne, *Sovereignty, Migration and the Rule of Law in Global Times*, 67 MOD. L. REV. 588 (2004).

19. Universal Declaration of Human Rights art. 13(1), G.A. Res. 217(III) A, U.N. Doc. A/RES/217(III) (Dec. 10, 1948) [hereinafter UDHR].

20. *Id.* art. 13(2).

asylum, lest it create a subjective right to enter their territory.[21] Broadly speaking, both the ICCPR[22] and the ECHR[23] follow this pattern. Even the Refugee Convention (RC) does not create a right of admission to the territory per se.[24] As Seyla Benhabib puts it, "a series of internal contradictions between universal human rights and territorial sovereignty are built into the logic of the most comprehensive international law documents in our world."[25]

Scholars examining the tensions between human rights and border control tend to fall within three broad categories. Yasemin Soysal exemplifies the universal. She argues that the development of IHRL marked a transition from nationality to humanity as the primary reference for the enjoyment of rights, diminishing the distinction between citizens and aliens.[26] On the other extreme, we find scholars who emphasize the persistent significance of migration control and alienage within IHRL.[27] Rather than open up space to resolve tensions between universal human rights and migration control, IHRL tends to reify this conflict, supporting the statist assumption. In this vein, it has been suggested that the international legal character of IHRL instruments tie

21. *See* GUY S. GOODWIN-GILL & JANE MCADAM, THE REFUGEE IN INTERNATIONAL LAW 358-61 (3d ed. 2007).

22. International Covenant on Civil and Political Rights, G.A. Res. 2200A (XXI), 21 U.N. Doc. A/6316 (Dec. 16, 1966), 999 U.N.T.S. 171, *entered into force* Mar. 23, 1976 [hereinafter ICCPR].

23. Protocol No. 4 to the Convention for the Protection of Human Rights and Fundamental Freedoms, Securing Certain Rights and Freedoms Other than Those Already Included in the Convention and in the First Protocol Thereto, art. 2, 3, Sept. 16, 1963, E.T.S. No. 46.

24. As Goodwin-Gill and McAdam put it, "[s]tates were not prepared to include in the [RC] any article on admission of refugees; *non-refoulement* in the sense of even a limited obligation to allow entry may well have been seen as coming too close to the unwished-for duty to grant asylum." GOODWIN-GILL & MCADAM, *supra* note 21, at 206-07. *See* Charter of Fundamental Rights of the European Union art. 18, Dec. 7, 2000, 2000 O.J. (C 364) 1, 12 (stating that, "The right to asylum shall be guaranteed with due respect for the rules of the [RC] and in accordance with the Treaty establishing the European Community") [hereinafter EUCFR]. *But see* Maria-Teresa Gil-Bazo, *The Charter of Fundamental Rights of the European Union and the Right to be Granted Asylum in the Union's Law*, 27 REFUGEE SURVEY Q. 33, 34 (2008) (arguing that EUCFR art. 18 indicates that, "the right to be granted asylum has become a subjective right of individuals under the Union's legal order").

25. SEYLA BENHABIB, THE RIGHTS OF OTHERS: ALIENS, RESIDENTS, AND CITIZENS 11 (2004).

26. *See generally* YASEMIN SOYSAL, LIMITS OF CITIZENSHIP MIGRANTS AND POSTNATIONAL MEMBERSHIP IN EUROPE (1994).

27. *See, e.g.*, Linda Bosniak, *Universal Citizenship and the Problem of Alienage*, 94 NW. U. L. REV. 963 (2000).

them to the state system.[28] Accordingly, norms that manifest state sovereignty "alter and shape human rights provisions."[29] This Article locates itself on the more ambivalent middle terrain, inspired by the work of Benhabib. She identifies the apparently "irresolvable contradiction" between universal human rights and democratic self-determination.[30] Yet, while she accepts that this apparent contradiction cannot be overcome, she argues that it can be mediated and mitigated through "democratic iterations" including "jurisgenerative politics."[31] These are the deliberative processes in which universalist rights claims are contested and contextualized.[32] Courts are exemplars of "strong public bodies"[33] engaged in these processes, as are other human rights adjudicatory bodies like the HRC. The ECtHR has unsettled statist border control assumptions, albeit in tentative fashion. Relocating matters of asylum and immigration into the EU realm is replete with further transformative potential.

B. A Plurality of Overlapping Instruments and Institutions

Overlapping, even competing, human rights jurisdiction is the institutional reality.[34] The authority of the HRC and the ECtHR overlap, as all Council of Europe members are also parties to the ICCPR.[35] Although the HRC may decline to hear complaints if the

---

28. *See generally* SALADIN MECKLED-GARCÍA & BAŞAK ÇALI, *Lost in Translation: The Human Rights Ideal and International Human Rights Law*, *in* THE LEGALIZATION OF HUMAN RIGHTS: MULTIDISCIPLINARY PERSPECTIVES ON HUMAN RIGHTS AND HUMAN RIGHTS LAW 11 (2006).

29. *Id.* at 16.

30. *Id.* at 19.

31. *Id.* at 176-81. *See generally* Robert M. Cover, *Foreword: Nomos and Narrative*, 97 HARV. L. REV. 4 (1983); Frank Michelman, *Law's Republic*, 97 YALE L.J. 1493 (1988).

32. *See* MECKLED-GARCÍA & ÇALI, *supra* note 28, at 179. *See also* Seyla Benhabib, *Claiming Rights Across Borders: International Human Rights and Democratic Sovereignty*, 103 AM. POL. SCI. REV. 691 (2009).

33. MECKLED-GARCÍA & ÇALI, *supra* note 28, at 179 (distinguishing between "strong" public bodies like the legislature, judiciary, and executive, and "weak" publics of civil society associations and the media). My account differs in that it focuses not so much on domestic public bodies so much as international and supranational ones.

34. *See generally* Liora Lazarus, Cathryn Costello, Nazila Ghanea, and Katja Zeigler, *Study for Parliament on the Evolution of Fundamental Rights Charters and Case Law: A Comparison of the United Nations, Council of Europe and European Union Systems of Human Rights Protection*, Directorate-General for Internal Policies (Feb. 2011), *available at* http://www.europarl.europa.eu/activities/committees/studies/download.do?language=en&file=34751.

35. For a list of parties to the ICCPR, see *Databases*, UNITED NATIONS TREATY COLLECTION, http://treaties.un.org/Pages/ViewDetails.aspx?src=TREATY&mtdsg_no=IV-4&chapter=4&lang=en (last visited Mar. 2, 2012).

matter is already before the ECtHR,[36] it inevitably pronounces on issues (if not individual complaints) that are also raised before the ECtHR given that both instruments deal with similar civil and political rights. All EU Member States are parties to the ECHR, and the EU itself is about to accede.[37] Pending accession, the EU institutions have internalized ECHR standards, and the CJEU uses them to scrutinize both the validity of EU acts[38] and of pertinent national ones.[39] The ECtHR, for its part, has deferred to the autonomy of the EU system, satisfied that the EU generally provides "equivalent protection" of human rights.[40] In order to rebut this presumption, applicants must demonstrate "manifestly deficient" protection within the EU system.[41] Most EU law is implemented by the EU Member States, and provided they exercise some discretion in so doing, they remain answerable before the ECtHR for their actions.[42] When EU Member States detain third-country national (TCN) migrants, they are increasingly within the scope of EU law, giving the CJEU jurisdiction as well.

Four vivid illustrations of the overlapping Luxembourg/Strasbourg jurisdictions are pertinent and current. First, the individual at the center of the CJEU's first ruling on predeportation detention (*Kadzoev*)[43] still has a case pending before the ECtHR concerning the

---

36. Catherine Phuong, *The Relationship Between the European Court of Human Rights and the Human Rights Committee: Has the 'Same Matter' Already Been 'Examined'?*, 7(2) HUM. RTS. L. REV. 385, 394 (2007).

37. *See* Consolidated Version of the Treaty on European Union art. 6(2), Dec. 13, 2007, 2008 O.J. (C 115) 13, 19 (stating that, "The Union shall accede to the [ECHR]. Such accession shall not affect the Union's competences as defined in the Treaties") [hereinafter TEU]. *See also* Council of Europe Informal Group on Accession of the European Union to the Convention, *Final Version of the Draft Legal Instruments on the Accession of the European Union to the European Convention on Human Rights* (July 19, 2011), *available at* http://www.coe.int/t/dghl/standardsetting/hrpolicy/cddh-ue/cddh-ue_documents_EN.asp; Tobias Lock, *EU Accession to the ECHR: Implications for Judicial Review in Strasbourg* 35 EUR. L. REV. 777 (2010).

38. *E.g.*, Case C-540/03, Parliament v. Council, 2006 E.C.R. I-5769.

39. *E.g.*, Case C-60/00, Carpenter v. Sec'y of State for the Home Dep't, 2002 E.C.R. I-6279.

40. Bosphorus Hava Yollari Turizm Ve Ticaret Anonim Sirketi v. Ireland, 42 Eur. Ct. H.R. 1, 46 (2005). *See generally* Cathryn Costello, *The* Bosphorus *Ruling of the European Court of Human Rights: Fundamental Rights and Blurred Boundaries in Europe*, 6 HUM. RTS. L. REV. 87 (2006); Tobias Lock, *Beyond* Bosphorus*: the European Court of Human Rights' Case Law on the Responsibility of Member States of International Organizations Under the European Convention on Human Rights*, 10 HUM. RTS. L. REV. 529 (2010) (providing an account of the jurisprudential developments since the *Bosphorus* decision).

41. *See Bosphorus*, 42 Eur. Ct. H.R. at 46.

42. *See* M.S.S. v. Belgium & Greece, App. No. 30696/09 Eur. Ct. H.R. (2011), http://www.echr.coe.int/echr/en/hudoc (follow "HUDOC database" hyperlink; search "Application Number 30696/09").

43. Case C-357/09 PPU, Kadzoev, 2009 E.C.R. I-11189.

lawfulness of his detention under the ECHR.[44] Second, the CJEU's other ruling on predeportation detention (*El-Dridi*)[45] raises some similar issues on the detention-deportation nexus, as were considered by the ECtHR only weeks before in *Mikolenko v. Estonia*.[46] Third, Strasbourg recently ruled on the duties of EU Member States when transferring asylum seekers under the EU's Dublin Regulation[47] in *M.S.S. v. Belgium & Greece*.[48] A case on similar issues has been argued before the CJEU.[49] Fourth, the most recent ECtHR case on detention of asylum seekers, *Lokpo & Touré v. Hungary*,[50] concerned detention under domestic legislation adopted to give effect to the EU PD.[51] The applicants in any of these cases could invoke the ICCPR, if not domestically, then by complaining to the HRC about their treatment.

IHRL has a common metaframework in the UDHR.[52] On this basis, some cross-fertilization, perhaps even leading to an international jus commune on human rights across various human rights instruments, may be envisaged. Certainly, convergence across different human rights instruments and bodies would seem to be desirable with a view to ensuring coherence and equality.[53] Such convergence raises fewer difficult institutional questions than the integration of human rights

44. Kadzoev v. Bulgaria, App. No. 56437/07 Eur. Ct. H.R. (introduced Dec. 20, 2007 and communicated Feb. 2, 2009).

45. *See* Case C-61/11 PPU, Hassen El-Dridi alias Karim Soufi, 2011 ECJ EUR-Lex CELEX LEXIS 1027 (Apr. 28, 2011).

46. Mikolenko v. Estonia, App. No. 10664/05, Eur. Ct. H.R. (2009), http://www.echr.coe.int/echr/en/hudoc (follow "HUDOC database" hyperlink; search "Application Number 10664/05").

47. *See* Council Regulation 343/2003, Establishing the Criteria and Mechanisms for Determining the Member State Responsible for Examining an Asylum Application Lodged in One of the Member States by a Third-Country National, 2003 O.J. (L 50) 1 (EC).

48. *See* M.S.S. v. Belgium & Greece, App. No. 30696/09 Eur. Ct. H.R. (2011), http://www.echr.coe.int/echr/en/hudoc (follow "HUDOC database" hyperlink; search "Application Number 30696/09").

49. Press Release, Opinions of the Advocate General in Joined Cases C-411/10 N.S. v. Secretary of State for the Home Dep't and C-493/10 M.E. and Others v. Refugee Applications Commissioner and Minister for Justice, Equality and Law Reform (Sept. 22, 2011) [hereinafter Opinions of AG Trstenjak in *NS/ME*].

50. Lokpo & Touré v. Hungary, App. No. 10816/10 Eur. Ct. H. R. 7, para. 16 (2011), http://www.echr.coe.int/echr/en/hudoc (follow "HUDOC database" hyperlink; search "Application Number 10816/10").

51. *Id.* para. 15.

52. *See*, OLIVIER DE SCHUTTER, INTERNATIONAL HUMAN RIGHTS LAW 31-32 (2010) ("Whether they are adopted at the universal or the regional levels, all human rights treaties are derived from the UDHR, from which they borrow, sometimes quite literally, much of their language. It is therefore quite natural for international courts or quasi-judicial bodies . . . to cite one another.").

53. This is not to suggest that convergence is in all cases desirable. Convergence at the lowest common denominator is clearly undesirable.

standards into other regimes, such as those dealing with international trade or investment, where that integration may be seen to expand the functional regime's scope.[54] Indeed, the sort of mutual engagement between overlapping human rights systems advocated here is much less contentious than the citation of foreign law sources across constitutional jurisdictions.[55] While all three of the bodies under discussion here, the HRC, the ECtHR, and the CJEU, are charged with enforcing a particular instrument or body of law, they also have the means, and indeed, the obligation, to take into account other instruments and jurisprudence. For instance, the ECHR contains a provision referring to obligations under other human rights instruments.[56] Similarly, the EU Charter of Fundamental Rights (EUCFR), a binding part of EU law since 2009, and the general principles of EU law, which contain binding fundamental rights norms predating the Charter, are both synthetic in character, drawing on outside human rights standards.[57]

For instruments with broader scope to influence the narrower regional ones seems entirely fitting. In particular, it is legally and institutionally problematic for the ECHR standards to fall below the

54. *See* Anne Van Aaken, *Defragmentation of Public International Law Through Interpretation: A Methodological Proposal*, 16 IND. J. GLOBAL LEGAL STUD. 483, 483 (2009).

55. *See, e.g.*, Christopher McCrudden, *Judicial Comparativism and Human Rights*, *in* COMPARATIVE LAW: A HANDBOOK 371 (Esin Örücü & David Nelken eds., 2007). As Waters notes, much of the U.S. debate conflates the citation of "foreign" domestic sources and international law. Melissa Waters, *Creeping Monism: The Judicial Trend Toward Interpretative Incorporation of Human Rights Treaties*, 107 COLUM. L. REV. 628 (2007).

56. The ECHR provides in Article 53 (ex Article 60), entitled "Safeguard for Existing Human Rights," that "nothing in this Convention shall be construed as limiting or derogating from any of the human rights and fundamental freedoms which may be ensured under the laws of any High Contracting Party or under any other agreement to which it is a Party." European Convention on Human Rights, *supra* note 6, art. 53.

57. Charter of Fundamental Rights of the European Union, art. 6(1), 2007 O.J. (C 303) 1. The TEU now provides that, "The Union recognizes the rights, freedoms and principles set out in the Charter of Fundamental Rights of the European Union of 7 December 2000, as adapted at Strasbourg, on 12 December 2007, which shall have the same legal value as the Treaties. . . ." The Charter contains Article 53, entitled "Level of Protection," which provides:

> Nothing in this Charter shall be interpreted as restricting or adversely affecting human rights and fundamental freedoms as recognized, in their respective fields of application, by Union law and international law and by international agreements to which the Union or all the Member States are party, including the European Convention for the Protection of Human Rights and Fundamental Freedoms, and by the Member States' constitutions.

Id. Furthermore, Article 52(3) provides the EUCFR rights which "correspond" to ECHR rights and shall have the same meaning and scope, although EU law may provide higher protection. On this provision, see Opinions of AG Trstenjak in *NS/ME*, *supra* note 49, ¶¶ 142-48.

ICCPR. The ICCPR embodies a global minimum; it is undesirable, not only legally, but also institutionally, for a regional system to fall below that standard. Individuals from regions with developed human rights systems should not have to look to protection at the U.N. level. When they do, it signals a double failure, at both the domestic and the regional level. In contrast, for the narrower regional system to prompt progressive developments in the broader one may raise objections from the states that are not party to the narrower regional system. Nonetheless, under certain conditions it may be appropriate. For instance, EU standards may provide evidence for an evolving consensus that the ECtHR should regard according to its own established interpretative methodology.[58] Also, there are means whereby the wider system may reinforce the narrower one. For instance, the Strasbourg Court sometimes takes into account Member States' obligations under EU law in assessing states' limitation of certain rights,[59] or even in determining whether states meet their positive duties under absolute guarantees such as Article 3 of the ECHR.[60]

This Article is also concerned with the particular legal position of asylum seekers and refugees, so the RC is pertinent. This instrument lacks a dedicated court or monitoring body.[61] Given that absence, asylum seekers and refugees in Europe often have recourse to the ECtHR, as the Strasbourg system offers comparative enforcement advantages over the RC.[62] Over the years, Strasbourg has developed an extensive jurisprudence on asylum seekers and refugees, taking into account, but not enforcing, the RC.[63] For instance, the ECtHR in *Amuur*

58. *See*, Camille Dautricourt, *A Strasbourg Perspective on the Autonomous Development of Fundamental Rights in EU Law: Trends and Implications* (Jean Monnet Working Paper No. 10/10, 2010), *available at* http://centers.law.nyu.edu/jeanmonnet/papers/10/101001.html, 30-35.

59. Mendizabal v. France, App. No. 51431/99 Eur. Ct. H. R. (2006), http://www.echr.coe.int/echr/en/hudoc (follow "HUDOC database" hyperlink; search "Application Number 51431/99"). See also the varying examples in Dautricourt, *supra* note 58, at 36-39.

60. Thus, controversially, in *M.S.S v. Belgium & Greece* the ECtHR had regard to Greece's obligations under the EU RCD to assess whether its treatment of asylum seekers was "inhumane and degrading" contrary to Article 3 ECHR. *See*, M.S.S. v. Belgium & Greece, App. No. 30696/09 Eur. Ct. H.R. (2011), http://www.echr.coe.int/echr/en/hudoc (follow "HUDOC database" hyperlink; search "Application Number 30696/09").

61. Convention Relating to the Status of Refugees, July 28, 1951, 189 U.N.T.S. 137 [hereinafter RC]. The RC states parties may, under Article 38, accord the ICJ jurisdiction over the instrument. However, this jurisdiction has never been invoked, leading to what is known as the "Article 38 deficit."

62. Hélène Lambert, *Protection Against Refoulement from Europe: Human Rights Law Comes to the Rescue*, 48 INT'L & COMP. L. Q. 543 (1999).

63. *See generally* NUALA MOLE & CATHERINE MEREDITH, ASYLUM AND THE EUROPEAN CONVENTION ON HUMAN RIGHTS (2010).

v. France noted, but did not explore, the import of the RC on detention.[64] Similarly, the ECtHR protects many asylum seekers and refugees from removal, bolstering and extending the RC's *non-refoulement* guarantee.[65] The EU, for its part, legislates on asylum and refugee matters. In so doing, it is required to adopt measures which are "in accordance with the [RC] and other relevant treaties."[66] In legislating on the scope of refugee protection in Europe, the EU codified not only the RC concept of persecution "within the meaning of article 1A of the [RC],"[67] but also a broader notion of serious harm encompassing some of the ECHR *non-refoulement* protection and some protection for those fleeing indiscriminate violence.[68]

Notwithstanding IHRL's common basis in a set of metaprinciples, and the appropriateness of cross-referencing between different systems, the specter of a fragmentation of IHRL looms. While the ECtHR has integrated various other human rights standards, it has done so in a somewhat piecemeal and inconsistent way.[69] The CJEU's use of sources other than the ECHR has been "parsimonious."[70] In particular, the CJEU has been strikingly dismissive of the jurisprudence of quasi-judicial bodies, including the HRC. It noted that the HRC is "not a

---

64. *Amuur v. France,* App. No. 19776/92 Eur. H.R. Rep. para 43 (1996).

> Such confinement, accompanied by suitable safeguards for the persons concerned, is acceptable only in order to enable States to prevent unlawful immigration while complying with their international obligations, particularly under the 1951 Geneva Convention Relating to the Status of Refugees and the European Convention on Human Rights. States' legitimate concern to foil the increasingly frequent attempts to circumvent immigration restrictions must not deprive asylum-seekers of the protection afforded by these conventions.

65. However, it has also been suggested that in demanding a high degree of individuation of risk in order to trigger protection from removal, "the coexistence of the two systems [RC and ECHR] appears to have aggravated the restrictive tendencies of both—in other words, competition between the two systems has resulted in constraining the protection opportunities of asylum seekers, instead of amplifying them, as it should." Jean François Durieux *Salah Sheekh is a Refugee: New Insights into Primary and Subsidiary Forms of Protection* (Refugee Studies Centre Working, Paper No. 49, 2008).

66. See TFEU, *supra* note 7—the pertinent provision is now Article 78 (1).

67. Council Directive 2004/83, art. 9(1), On Minimum Standards for the Qualification and Status of Third Country Nationals or Stateless Persons as Refugees or as Persons Who Otherwise Need International Protection and the Content of the Protection Granted, 2004 O.J. (L 304) 12 (QD).

68. *See id.*, art. 15. *See also Elgafaji v. Staatssecreteris van Justitie,* App. No. 465/07 Eur. Ct. H.R. (2009), http://www.echr.coe.int/echr/en/hudoc (follow "HUDOC database" hyperlink; search "Application Number 465/07").

69. *See generally* MAGDALENA FOROWICZ, THE RECEPTION OF INTERNATIONAL LAW IN THE EUROPEAN COURT OF HUMAN RIGHTS (2010).

70. Israel Jesús Butler & Olivier de Schutter, *Binding the EU to International Human Rights Law*, 27 Y.B. OF EUR. L. 277, 282 (2008).

judicial institution" and that its "findings [had] no binding force in law."[71] While it is appropriate for one body to take into account the others' institutional context when reading its output, the CJEU position is too dismissive. Its characterization of the HRC is certainly at odds with the HRC's self-perception.[72] As will be seen, immigration detention also is a domain where the appropriate constructive engagement is lacking.

C. Contrasting Institutional Contexts

Although both the ECtHR and CJEU are evidently courts, their institutional setup differs significantly. The ECtHR is accessible only once domestic remedies have been exhausted. Nonetheless, it disposes of a massive, growing caseload, acting as a supranational court for human rights across the forty-seven countries of the Council of Europe. The ECtHR is now inundated with cases, and reforms have been undertaken to allow it to deem more cases inadmissible and dispose of cases more efficiently.[73] Although the ECHR is under some accounts characterized as a constitutional instrument,[74] its domestic effect varies across contracting states.[75]

The CJEU, in contrast, has jurisdiction over a range of different actions against the EU institutions and the Member States, to ensure compliance with the vast body of EU law, including treaties, legislation, and general principles. Most of the CJEU's caseload comprises references from national judges, often concerned (albeit indirectly) with the compatibility of domestic laws and practices with EU norms. Unlike the HRC and the ECtHR, the CJEU is not exclusively or even predominantly a human rights court. Its human rights jurisdiction arises where there are some pre-existing questions of EU law. EU human rights norms then bind the EU institutions and the Member States when they act within the scope of EU law.[76]

71. Case C-249/96, Grant v. South-West Trains Ltd., 1998 E.C.R. I-621, para. 46.

72. *See generally infra* notes 87-89.

73. COUNCIL OF EUR., PROTOCOL 14 THE REFORM OF THE EUROPEAN COURT OF HUMAN RIGHTS FACT SHEET, *available at* www.echr.coe.int/NR/rdonlyres/57211BCC-C88A-43C6-B540-AF0642E81D2C/0/CPProtocole14EN.pdf.

74. *See, e.g.*, Alec Stone Sweet, *Sur la constitutionalisation de la Convention européenne des droits de l'homme conçue comme une Cour constitutionnelle*, 80 REVUE TRIMESTRIELLE DES DROITS DE L'HOMME 923 (2009).

75. For an overview, see generally, A EUROPE OF RIGHTS: THE IMPACT OF THE ECHR ON NATIONAL LEGAL SYSTEMS (Helen Keller & Alec Stone Sweet eds., 2008).

76. The phrase "within the scope of EU law" is contentious. The binding EU Charter of Fundamental Rights purports to bind the EU Member States only when they are "implementing" EU law (Article 51(1) EUCFR); although it may be interpreted to

In exercising their judicial review tasks, both courts must be mindful of securing compliance with their rulings. In this endeavor, Strasbourg is in a weaker position than Luxembourg, in that it lacks the direct line of communication with national judges inherent in the preliminary reference procedure, and it has a wider and more diverse pool of states to keep in check. For Karen Alter, "[the CJEU] is about the most powerful and influential international court that is realistically possible."[77] These institutional positions have led to different approaches to the domestic status of EU and ECHR law. The ECHR requires domestic incorporation,[78] while the CJEU obliges national judges to give EU law full effect, interpreting domestic law to comply with EU law,[79] and, if necessary, to set aside conflicting domestic norms.[80] Should the national court have any doubts as to the meaning or effect of any particular EU provision, it may refer questions to the CJEU.[81]

Contrasting domestic statuses both reflect and temper the courts' respective jurisprudence on national remedies. The ECtHR's starting point is that it is a subsidiary organ, and the primary guarantors of ECHR rights are the Member States. In contrast, the CJEU stipulates

---

encompass the same scenarios as the broader phrase "within the scope of EU law." *See generally* Dautricourt, *supra* note 58, at 49-51; Opinions of AG Trstenjak in *NS/ME*, *supra* note 49.

77. Karen Alter, *The European Court of Justice's Political Power Across Space and Time* 3 (Nw. Univ. Sch. of Law and Econ., Working Paper No. 09-03, 2009).

78. *See generally*, Rick Lawson, *The Monitoring of Fundamental Rights in the Union as a Contribution to the European Legal Space (III): The Role of the European Court of Human Rights* (Reflexive Governance in the Pub. Interest, Working Paper No. REFGOV-FR-7, 2006).

79. This doctrine of "indirect effect" has its origins in Case C-106/89, Marleasing SA v. La Comercial Internacional de Alimentacion SA, 1990 E.C.R. I-4135. For an application in the EU refugee law context, see C-465/07, Elgafaji v. Staatssecreteris van Justitie, 2009 E.C.R. I-921.

80. *See* Case 106/77, Amministrazione delle Finanze dello Stato v. Simmenthal S.p.A., 1978 E.C.R. 629. For an application in the context of immigration detention, see Case C-61/11 PPU, Hassen El-Dridi alias Karim Soufi, 2011 ECJ EUR-Lex CELEX LEXIS 1027 (Apr. 28, 2011).

81. Before the entry into force of the Treaty of Lisbon, under Article 68 EC only national courts and tribunals "against whose decisions there is no judicial remedy under national law" were empowered to refer questions concerning EU asylum and immigration law. *See generally* Steve Peers, *EC Immigration Law and EC Association Agreements: Fragmentation or Integration*? 34 EUR. L. REV. 628 (2009). However, the Treaty of Lisbon has removed this anomalous restriction so that all national courts and tribunals may make such references. For the most part, whether to refer is in the discretion of the national judge, although judges of final instance are obliged to refer questions of EU law, which are necessary to resolve the case before them, unless the matter is already settled and clear. Article 267 TFEU. Case 283/81, Srl CILFIT & Lanificio di Gavardo SpA v. Ministry of Health, 1982 E.C.R. 3415.

duties for national judges directly, reflecting their shared role as EU law judges. As a result, the ECtHR case law on remedies is more tentative than that of the CJEU. In particular, concerning migration status, the ECtHR tends to leave states control over formal migration status, even when it deems individuals to be nonremovable for human rights reasons.[82] However, the CJEU does not hesitate in deeming that EU law creates stable residence rights in other EU Member countries for those who come within its scope.[83] The overall result is captured in Virginie Guiraudon's stylized contrast between the CJEU and the ECtHR. She posits a "bold [CJEU] and a tamer [ECtHR]" and predicts "that the [CJEU] will have less fear of increasing its competence and [issuing] controversial rulings, while the [ECtHR] will adopt a self-limiting approach to slowly gain legitimacy and avoid provoking nation-states."[84] We can see some hints of that prediction coming to pass in the immigration detention case law.

The ICCPR's monitoring body, the HRC, has been empowered to examine individual complaints since 1985.[85] While its scrutiny of states' regular reports forms the bulk of its work, it is becoming increasingly court-like in its adjudication of individual grievances.[86] While initially it was assumed that its decisions (known as views) in response to these individual complaints were not legally binding as such, over time the HRC has asserted that states do have an obligation to allow both views and interim measures[87] to take legal effect within their national legal

82. *See, e.g.*, Bonger v. Netherlands, App. No. 10154/04, Eur. Ct. H.R. (2005), http://www.echr.coe.int/echr/en/hudoc (follow "HUDOC database" hyperlink; search "Application Number 10154/04").

83. *See, e.g.*, Case 48/75, Joel Noel Royer, 1976 E.C.R. 497; Case C-60/00, Carpenter v. Sec'y of State for the Home Dep't, 2002 E.C.R. I-6279; Case C-127/08, Metock v. Minister for Justice, Equal. & Law Reform 2008 E.C.R. I-6241. Admittedly, these cases concern EU Citizens and their TNC family members. However, where TCNs derive rights of residence from other EU measures, we see similar approaches emerging. *E.g.*, Case C-578/08, Chakroun v. Minister van Buitenlandse Zaken, 2010 E.C.R. I-1839.

84. Virginie Guiraudon, *European Courts and Foreigners' Rights: A Comparative Study of Norm Diffusion*, 34 INT'L MIGRATION REV. 1088, 1094 (2000).

85. *See* Liz Heffernan, *A Comparative View of the Individual Petition Procedures under the European Convention on Human Rights and the International Covenant on Civil and Political Rights*, 19 HUM. RTS. Q. 78 (1997); *see generally* Dominic McGoldrick, *The Human Rights Committee: Its Role in the Development of the International Covenant on Civil and Political Rights* (1991).

86. FOROWICZ, *supra* note 69, at 152-53.

87. *See* Weiss v. Austria, U.N. Human Rights Comm., 77th Sess., Comm. No. 1086/2002 at ¶ 11.1, U.N. Doc. CCPR/C/77/D/1086/2002 (May 24, 2002). The HRC decision was cited by the ECtHR when it established an analogous principle in Mamatkulov v. Turkey, App. Nos. 46827/99 & 46951/99 Eur. Ct. H.R. Feb. 4, 2005, http://www.echr.coe.int/echr/en/hudoc (follow "HUDOC database" hyperlink; search "Application Number 46827/99"). For

order.[88] The domestic effects of the ICCPR vary greatly in practice though.[89] The HRC may find violations and specify a particular remedy. Compliance is then monitored through a process of periodic review.[90] The institutional differences sketched in this part will illuminate the substantive discussion in the next part.

II. IMMIGRATION DETENTION & HUMAN RIGHTS

Immigration detention is garnering increasing attention in international human rights fora. Within the U.N. system, the Working Group on Arbitrary Detention (WGAD) has considered immigration detention since 1997.[91] The U.N. Special Rapporteur on the Human Rights of Migrants[92] and the U.N. High Commissioner for Human Rights have also engaged with this issue.[93] Within the Council of Europe, the Committee of Ministers adopted the *Twenty Guidelines on Forced Return* in 2005,[94] while its Parliamentary Assembly adopted an

discussion of this development as a manifestation of the emerging jus commune of human rights, see Butler & de Schutter, *supra* note 70, at 37-39.

88. André Nollkaemper & Rosanne Van Alebeek, *The Legal Status of Decisions by Human Rights Treaty Bodies in National Law* 2 (Amsterdam Center for International Law, Research Paper No. 2011-02, Apr. 11, 2011); Scott Davidson, *Intention and Effect: The Legal Status of the Final Views of the Human Rights Committee*, 2001 N.Z. L. REV. 125, 131-32 (2001).

89. *See* Christopher Harland, *The Status of the International Covenant on Civil and Political Rights (ICCPR) in the Domestic Law of State Parties: An Initial Global Survey Through UN Human Rights Committee Documents*, 22 HUM. RTS. Q. 187, 189 (2000).

90. For a defense of this dialogic process, see Michael O'Flaherty, *The Concluding Observations of United Nations Human Rights Treaty Bodies*, 6 HUM. RTS. L. REV. 27 (2006).

91. Human Rights Commission Res.1997/5 (15 Apr. 1997); UN Docs. E/CN.4/1999/63 (1998), E/CN.4/2004/3 (2003), E/CN.4/2006/7 (2005), A/HRC/10/21 (2008), and A/HRC/13/30 (2010). A specific recent report on Italy deals extensively with immigration detention. *See* Report of the WGAD on its Mission to Italy, UN Docs A/HRC/10/21/Add.5 (2009) [hereinafter Report of the WGAD].

92. Special Rapporteur on Migrant Workers, *Report of the Special Rapporteur, Ms. Gabriela Rodriguez Pizarro*, U.N. Comm'n on Human Rights, UN Doc. E/CN.4/2003/85 (Dec. 30, 2002) (by Gabriela Rodriguez Pizarro); Special Rapporteur on the Human Rights of Migrants, *Promotion and Protection of All Human Rights, Civil, Political, Economic, Social and Cultural Rights, Including the Right to Development*, Human Rights Council, UN Doc. A/HRC/11/7 (May 14, 2009) (by Jorge Bustamante).

93. *See Immigration Control Must Not Compromise Human Rights*, OFFICE OF THE UNITED NATIONS HIGH COMM'R (Sept. 22, 2009), http://www.ohchr.org/EN/NEWSEVENTS/Pages/MigrationPanel.aspx.

94. COUNCIL OF EUR., COMM. OF MINISTERS, *Twenty Guidelines on Forced Return*, 925th Meeting of the Ministers' Deputies (May 4, 2005) [hereinafter *Twenty Guidelines on Forced Return*]. The Parliamentary Assembly prompted the compilation of these

important resolution and recommendation in early 2010 specifically on immigration detention.[95] Significantly, an UNHCR-OHCHR Global Roundtable on Alternatives to Immigration Detention was held in May 2011 in Geneva.[96] Additionally, the EU's Fundamental Rights Agency (FRA) recently reported on preremoval detention.[97] These political initiatives, and the soft law principles espoused therein, form an important backdrop to this article.

A. *International Covenant on Civil and Political Rights (ICCPR)*

As discussed below, while one might expect the weak institutional framework of the ICCPR to produce tentative rulings on immigration detention, the HRC has developed a relatively robust line of jurisprudence.[98] Detention must be lawful and nonarbitrary in order to meet the Article 9 standards.[99] While the notion of lawfulness is similar to that employed by the ECtHR, as will be seen, the HRC notion of arbitrariness is thicker, connoting "elements of inappropriateness, injustice and lack of predictability" as well as reasonableness and necessity "in all the circumstances for a specific purpose."[100] In this context, the HRC also applies the principle of proportionality.[101]

Article 9 does not expressly limit the legitimate purposes of detention, unlike Article 5 of the ECHR. However, the HRC has clarified that detention must pursue a specific purpose. Crucially, for immigration detention purposes, illegal entry alone does not justify

guidelines. EUR. PARL. ASS., *Expulsion Procedures in Conformity with Human Rights and Enforced with Respect for Safety and Dignity*, 3d Sitting, Doc. No. 9196, (2002).

95. *See* EUR. PARL. ASS., *The Detention of Asylum Seekers and Irregular Migrants in Europe*, Doc. No. 12105 (Jan. 11, 2010).

96. *See* U.N. High Comm'r for Refugees & U.N. High Comm'r for Human Rights, Concept Note on the Global Roundtable on Alternatives to Detention of Asylum-Seekers, Refugees, Migrants and Stateless Persons (May 11-12, 2011), http://www.unhcr.org/4dde23ab9.pdf.

97. *See* Fundamental Rights Agency, *Detention of Third-Country Nationals in Return Procedures*, at 80-81 (2010), *available at* http://fra.europa.eu/fraWebsite/research/publications/publications_per_year/pub_detention_en.htm#.

98. For an extensive analysis, see generally CORNELISSE, *supra* note 15.

99. "Everyone has the right to liberty and security of person. No one shall be subjected to arbitrary arrest or detention. No one shall be deprived of his liberty except on such grounds and in accordance with such procedures as are established by law." ICCPR, *supra* note 22, at art. 9.1.

100. Human Rights Comm., van Alphen v. Netherlands, Commc'n No. 305/1988, ¶ 5.8, U.N. Doc. CCPR/C/39/D/305/1988 (1990).

101. Human Rights Comm., A. v. Australia, Commc'n. No. 560/1993, ¶ 9.2, U.N. Doc. CCPR/C/59/D/560/1993 (1997).

detention.[102] In this respect, the HRC has set a more demanding standard than the ECtHR in its case law on "detention to prevent unauthorised entry."[103] The HRC demands that there are other additional factors particular to the individual, "such as the likelihood of absconding and lack of cooperation, which may justify detention for a period."[104]

Not only must detention pursue a narrow specific aim, it must be necessary and proportionate in the individual circumstances.[105] The HRC repeatedly condemned Australia's detention practices for failure to provide individual justifications.[106] Detention may not be justified on the basis of the country's "general experience that asylum seekers abscond if not retained in custody,"[107] an assumption that does not appear grounded in empirical reality in any event.[108] In *C. v. Australia*,[109] the HRC condemned a detention where the state had failed to assess whether other means (such as the imposition of reporting obligations, sureties, or other conditions) would have met the aim of ensuring compliance with immigration law.[110] In contrast, in *Jalloh v. Netherlands*, the detention in question was found justified as the applicant had previously fled an open facility.[111]

---

102. *Id.* para. 9.4.

103. *See infra* Part II.C.3.

104. Human Rights Comm., A. v. Australia, Commc'n. No. 560/1993, ¶ 9.4, U.N. Doc. CCPR/C/59/D/560/1993 (1997).

105. *Id.* para. 9.2.

106. *See generally id.*; Human Rights Comm., Saed Shams v. Australia, Comm. No. 1225/2004, CCPR/C/90/D/1255 (2007); Human Rights Comm., D and E and Their Two Children v. Australia, Comm. No. 1050/2002, CCPR/C/87/D/1050/2002 (2006); Human Rights Comm., Shafiq v. Australia, Comm. No. 1324/2004, CCPR/C/88/D/1324/2004 (2006); Human Rights Comm., Baban v. Australia, Comm. No. 1014/2001, CCPR/C/78/D/1014/2001 (2003); Human Rights Comm., Bakhtiyari v. Australia, Comm. No. 1069/2002, CCPR/C/79/D/1069/2002 (2003); Human Rights Comm., C. v. Australia, Comm. No. 900/1999, U.N. Doc. CCPR/C/76/D/900/1999 (2002). In spite of these views, Australia continues its practice of automatic detention. *See* Australian Human Rights Comm., *Submission to the Joint Select Committee on Australia's Immigration Detention Network* 11-27 (Aug. 2011), http://www.hreoc.gov.au/legal/submissions/2011/201108_immigration.html.

107. Human Rights Comm., Shafiq v. Australia, Commc'n No. 1324/2004, ¶ 7.3, U.N. Doc. CCPR/C/88/D/1324/2004 (2006).

108. *See* Office of the United Nations High Comm'r, *Alternatives to Detention of Asylum Seekers and Refugees*, (Apr. 2006), www.unhcr.org/refworld/pdfid/4472e8b84.pdf (Ophelia Field & Alice Edwards).

109. Human Rights Comm., C. v. Australia, Commc'n No. 900/1999, ¶. 8.2, U.N. Doc. CCPR/C/76/D/900/1999 (2002).

110. *Id.*

111. Human Rights Comm., Jalloh v. Netherlands, Commc'n. No. 794/1998, ¶ 8.2, U.N. Doc. CCPR/C/74/D/794/1998 (2002).

B. Refugee Convention

The RC establishes a spectrum of rights allocated according to the degree of attachment between the refugee and the state in question.[112] Article 26 on freedom of movement applies to those "lawfully in" the territory.[113] While Article 26 clearly applies to recognized refugees, there is debate as to whether it applies to asylum seekers too. One view holds that Article 26 should apply to asylum seekers whose applications have been presented.[114] In this view, then, asylum seekers should generally enjoy a right to free movement once formally in the asylum process, although their movement may be restricted under the same conditions as are "applicable to aliens generally in the same circumstances."[115] Notably, several European governments still contest the applicability of Article 26 to asylum seekers.[116] Such contestation reflects a more general movement, whereby governments have distorted the scope of the RC, by seeking to limit the rights attaching to the category of "asylum seeker." In contrast, the RC is based on the premise that asylum seekers are presumptive refugees, and to be treated accordingly, particularly in light of the declaratory character of refugee status.[117]

Article 31, the nonpenalization clause, is concerned with those who are illegally present in a state, provided that they "present themselves without delay to the authorities and show good cause for their illegal entry or presence." They are to be immune from penalties and subject only to such restrictions on free movement as are necessary. As to the meaning of "penalties," while some take the view that only criminal sanctions are precluded,[118] several authoritative commentators take the

112. Hathaway describes this as the "structure of entitlement" under the RC. JAMES C. HATHAWAY, THE RIGHTS OF REFUGEES UNDER INTERNATIONAL LAW 154 (2005). *See* GOODWIN-GILL, *supra* note 21, at 524-28, who described it as "criteria of entitlement."

113. The full text of the article states that "[e]ach Contracting State shall accord to refugees lawfully in its territory the right to choose their place of residence to move freely within its territory, subject to any regulations applicable to aliens generally in the same circumstances." RC, *supra* note 61, art. 26.

114. See HATHAWAY, *supra* note 112, at 173, for extensive consideration of the meaning of "lawful stay."

115. RC, *supra* note 61, art. 26.

116. *See* Reinhard Marx, *Article 26 (Freedom of Movement/Liberté de Circulation), in* THE 1951 CONVENTION RELATING TO THE STATUS OF REFUGEES AND ITS 1967 PROTOCOL: A COMMENTARY 1147, 1161-64 (Andreas Zimmermann et al. eds., 2011).

117. *See* Office of the United Nations High Comm'r, *Handbook on Procedures and Criteria for Determining Refugee Status under the 1951 Convention and the 1967 Protocol Relating to the Status of Refugees*, ¶ 28, HCR/IP/4/Eng/REV.1 (1992) *quoted in* James Hathaway, *What's in a Label?*, 5 EUR. J. MIGRATION & L. 1, 9-10 (2003).

118. Cornelisse simply asserts that "[i]t is not plausible that this provision would be violated when a refugee is detained on account of his illegal entry, if the deprivation of

view that at least some forms of detention should be precluded as punitive.[119] Alternatively, even if detention is not always regarded as a "penalty," Article 31(2) provides that the asylum seeker may be subjected only to such restrictions as are necessary.[120]

The UNHCR's *Revised Guidelines on Detention of Asylum Seekers* confirm that "[a]s a general principle, asylum-seekers should not be detained," and that detention is only permissible in exceptional circumstances, when it is reasonable, proportional, and necessary in order to attain a limited range of objectives.[121] However the range of purposes is broad, allowing detention in order:

> To verify identity; to determine the elements on which the claim to refugee status or asylum is based; to deal with cases where refugees or asylum-seekers have destroyed their travel and/or identity documents or have used fraudulent documents in order to mislead the authorities of the State in which they intend to claim asylum; or to protect national security or public order.[122]

The breadth of the grounds seems liable to undermine the commitment to ensuring that detention is an exceptional practice.

Regrettably, as Goodwin-Gill notes:

---

liberty is an administrative measure and is not categorized as a criminal sanction as such." CORNELISSE, *supra* note 15, at 262. She assumes that only Article 31(2) limits detention, requiring it to be "proportional in view of the individual circumstances of each and every individual." *Id.*

119. Guy Goodwin-Gill, *Article 31 of the 1951 Convention Relating to the Status of Refugees: Non-penalization, Detention and Protection*, *in* REFUGEE PROTECTION IN INTERNATIONAL LAW: UNHCR'S GLOBAL CONSULTATIONS ON INTERNATIONAL PROTECTION 185, 195-96 (Erika Feller, Volker Türk & Frances Nicholson eds., 2003). *See also* EDWARDS, *supra* note 5, at 11 (citing Gregor Noll, *Article 31 (Refuges Unlawfully in the Country of Refuget/Réfugés en Situation Irrégulière dans le Pays d' Accueil)*, *in* THE 1951 CONVENTION RELATING TO THE STATUS OF REFUGEES AND ITS 1967 PROTOCOL: A COMMENTARY 1243, 1263-64 (Andreas Zimmermann et al. eds., 2011)).

120. Hathaway explains the "strictly provisional" nature of the detention power under Article 31(2), with Article 26 of the RC as the general provision applicable to most asylum seekers who have been admitted to the asylum procedure. HATHAWAY, *supra* note 112, at 414, 418-19. Hathaway also discusses "necessity." *Id.* at 423-39.

121. Office of the United Nations High Comm'r for Refugees, UNHCR's Guidelines on Applicable Criteria and Standards Relating to the Detention of Asylum-Seekers 3, (Feb. 1999), http://www.unhcr.org/refworld/docid/3c2b3f844.html.

122. Detention of Refugees and Asylum Seekers, Office of the United Nations High Comm'r for Refugees, 41st Sess., Jan. 13 1987, ¶ 128(b), U.N. Doc. 12A (A/41/12/Add.1) (1987).

> Comparatively few states have taken any formal steps to incorporate the exemption from penalties required by Article 31 . . . Even where legislative provisions exist, however, refugees and asylum seekers can still face loss of liberty. They are subject to the same law as is applied to non-nationals generally, and are thus exposed to prosecution, punishment, and/or detention, on account of illegal entry, entry without documents, or entry without falsified documents.[123]

His conclusion reflects the RC's relative lack of enforcement apparatus, as does the contestation over the scope of Article 26 of the RC.

C. *European Convention on Human Rights* (ECHR)

In contrast to the ICCPR, the ECHR enumerates a finite list of specific grounds of permitted detention, including two forms of immigration detention.[124] Article 5(1)(f) permits detention "to prevent . . . unauthorised entry into the country" and "of a person against whom action is being taken with a view to deportation or extradition."[125] Both

---

123. Goodwin-Gill, *supra* note 119, at 226.

124. Article 5(1) provides:

> No one shall be deprived of his liberty save in the following cases and in accordance with a procedure prescribed by law:
> (a) the lawful detention of a person after conviction by a competent court;
> (b) the lawful arrest or detention of a person for non-compliance with the lawful order of a court or in order to secure the fulfilment of any obligation prescribed by law;
> (c) the lawful arrest or detention of a person effected for the purpose of bringing him before the competent legal authority of reasonable suspicion of having committed and offence or when it is reasonably considered necessary to prevent his committing an offence or fleeing after having done so;
> (d) the detention of a minor by lawful order for the purpose of educational supervision or his lawful detention for the purpose of bringing him before the competent legal authority;
> (e) the lawful detention of persons for the prevention of the spreading of infectious diseases, of persons of unsound mind, alcoholics or drug addicts, or vagrants;
> (f) the lawful arrest or detention of a person to prevent his effecting an unauthorized entry into the country or of a person against whom action is being taken with a view to deportation or extradition.

European Convention on Human Rights, *supra* note 6, art. 5(1).

125. *Id.*

forms of detention must be "in accordance with a procedure prescribed by law."[126]

1. *The Requirement of Legality*

The requirement of legality, as is commonly the case under the ECHR, refers not only to conformity with enacted domestic law, but also entails rule of law criteria, particularly relating to the accessibility, precision, and foreseeability of the standards and procedures governing detention.[127] On occasion, the requirement of legality encompasses more general concerns relating to detention conditions, such as when detention of vulnerable individuals or children is at issue.[128] "In accordance with law" has a further, somewhat latent significance under the ECHR: where the state has additional obligations under EU law and potentially other international legal norms, these are liable to be incorporated into the notion of "in accordance with law."[129] Accordingly, there is much potential to read other legal standards into the ECtHR's rule of law conception.

The ECtHR frequently finds violations of Article 5(1) for lack of adherence to rule of law criteria.[130] Some cases concern egregious breaches of domestic law: in *Riad & Idiab v. Belgium*, the respondent state kept the applicants in detention despite two domestic court rulings to release them, rendering the detention unlawful under the

126. Articles 5(4) and (5) set out the right to have the lawfulness of detention tested "speedily by a court" and to compensation for unlawful detention, respectively. ECHR, *supra* note 4, art. 5(4)-(5). The procedural safeguard in Article 5(3) applies to those arrested or detained under Article 5(1)(c), but not to those detained under Article 5(1)(f). European Convention on Human Rights, *supra* note 6, art. 5(3).

127. Amuur v. France, App. No. 19776/92, 22 Eur. H.R. Rep. 533, 559 (1996).

128. *See* Muskhadzhiyeva v. Belgium, App. No. 41442/07 Eur. Ct. H.R. (2010), http://www.echr.coe.int/echr/en/hudoc (follow "HUDOC database" hyperlink; search "Application Number 41442/07"). Mayeka v. Belgium, App. No. 13178/03 Eur. Ct. H.R. (2006), http://www.echr.coe.int/echr/en/hudoc (follow "HUDOC database" hyperlink; search "Application Number 13178/03").

129. In *Mendizabal v. France*, the ECtHR treated the EU right of residence of a Spanish national in France as an aspect of its Article 8 ECHR legal patrimony. Mendizabal v. France, App. No. 51431/99, 50 Eur. H.R. Rep. 50 (2006).

130. *See* Al-Agha v. Romania, App. No. 40933/02 Eur. Ct. H.R. (2010), http://www.echr.coe.int/echr/en/hudoc (follow "HUDOC database" hyperlink; search "Application Number 40933/02"); Soldatenko v. Ukraine, App. No. 2440/07 Eur. Ct. H.R. (2008), http://www.echr.coe.int/echr/en/hudoc (follow "HUDOC database" hyperlink; search "Application Number 2440/07"); John v. Greece, App. No. 199/05 Eur. Ct. H.R. (2007), http://www.echr.coe.int/echr/en/hudoc (follow "HUDOC database" hyperlink; search "Application Number 199/05"); Shamsa v. Poland, App. No. 45355/99 Eur. Ct. H.R. (2003), http://www.echr.coe.int/echr/en/hudoc (follow "HUDOC database" hyperlink; search "Application Number 45355/99").

ECHR also.[131] The ECtHR has found repeated serious infractions of the requirement of legality by Turkey,[132] Malta,[133] and Russia.[134] The ECtHR also scrutinizes conformity with domestic law with increasing intensity, at times effectively finding that the domestic courts have

131. Riad v. Belgium, App. No. 29787/03 Eur. Ct. H.R. at 74-76 (2008), http://www.echr.coe.int/echr/en/hudoc (follow "HUDOC database" hyperlink; search "Application Number 29787/03").

132. *See* Dbouba v. Turkey, App. No. 15916/09 Eur. Ct. H.R. (2010), http://www.echr.coe.int/echr/en/hudoc (follow "HUDOC database" hyperlink; search "Application Number 15916/09"); Tehrani v. Turkey, App. No. 32940/08 Eur. Ct. H.R. (2010), http://www.echr.coe.int/echr/en/hudoc (follow "HUDOC database" hyperlink; search "Application Number 32940/08"); Z.N.S. v. Turkey, App. No. 21896/08 Eur. Ct. H.R. (2010), http://www.echr.coe.int/echr/en/hudoc (follow "HUDOC database" hyperlink; search "Application Number 21896/08"); Abdolkhani v. Turkey, App. No. 30471/08 Eur. Ct. H.R. (2009), http://www.echr.coe.int/echr/en/hudoc (follow "HUDOC database" hyperlink; search "Application Number 30471/08"). Researcher Michael Flynn reports that "Turkey has refused to acknowledge, despite successive legal rulings against it, that its systematic confinement of irregular migrants in so-called guesthouses amounts to deprivation of liberty." Michael Flynn, *Immigration Detention and Proportionality* 8 (Global Detention Project, Working Paper No. 4, 2001), *available at* http://www.globaldetentionproject.org/fileadmin/publications/GDP_detention_and_proportionality_workingpaper.pdf.

133. *See* Massoud v. Malta, App. No. 24340/08 Eur. Ct. H.R. (2010), http://www.echr.coe.int/echr/en/hudoc (follow "HUDOC database" hyperlink; search "Application Number 24340/08"); Kadem v. Malta, App. No. 55263/00 Eur. Ct. H.R. (2003), http://www.echr.coe.int/echr/en/hudoc (follow "HUDOC database" hyperlink; search "Application Number 55263/00"); Ali v. Malta, App. No. 35892/97 Eur. Ct. H.R. (2000), http://www.echr.coe.int/echr/en/hudoc (follow "HUDOC database" hyperlink; search "Application Number 35892/97"). Malta persists in automatically detaining asylum seekers, notwithstanding these rulings. *See Report by Thomas Hammarberg, Commissioner for Human Rights of the Council of Europe, Following His Visit to Malta from 23 to 25 March 2011*, CommDH(2011)17 (2011), https://wcd.coe.int/wcd/ViewDoc.jsp?id=1797917 (prepared by Thomas Hammarberg).

134. *See* Sultanov v. Russia, App. No. 15303/09 Eur. Ct. H.R. (2010), http://www.echr.coe.int/echr/en/hudoc (follow "HUDOC database" hyperlink; search "Application Number 15303/09"); Iskandarov v. Russia, App. No. 17185/05 Eur. Ct. H.R. (2010), http://www.echr.coe.int/echr/en/hudoc (follow "HUDOC database" hyperlink; search "Application Number 17185/05"); Yuldashev v. Russia, App. No. 1248/09 Eur. Ct. H.R. (2010), http://www.echr.coe.int/echr/en/hudoc (follow "HUDOC database" hyperlink; search "Application Number 1248/09"); Isakov v. Russia, App. No. 14049/08 Eur. Ct. H.R. (2010), http://www.echr.coe.int/echr/en/hudoc (follow "HUDOC database" hyperlink; search "Application Number 14049/08"); Nolan v. Russia, App. No. 2512/04 Eur. Ct. H.R. (2009), http://www.echr.coe.int/echr/en/hudoc (follow "HUDOC database" hyperlink; search "Application Number 2512/04"); Muminov v. Russia, App. No. 42502/06 Eur. Ct. H.R. (2008), http://www.echr.coe.int/echr/en/hudoc (follow "HUDOC database" hyperlink; search "Application Number 42502/06"); Nasrulloyev v. Russia, App. No. 656/06 Eur. Ct. H.R. (2007), http://www.echr.coe.int/echr/en/hudoc (follow "HUDOC database" hyperlink; search "Application Number 656/06"); Garabayev v. Russia, App. No. 38411/02 Eur. Ct. H.R. (2007), http://www.echr.coe.int/echr/en/hudoc (follow "HUDOC database" hyperlink; search "Application Number 38411/02").

erred in their application of domestic law. In *Rusu v. Austria*,[135] the Court ensured strict adherence with the necessity test in the applicable domestic law, although the Court does not incorporate this standard into its own requirements for Article 5(1)(f) detention.[136] Other cases push the notion of "lawfulness" even further. For instance, in a case in which the decision to detain was ostensibly based on national security concerns, the Court deemed the detention to be unlawful as no specific allegations or charges were brought against the applicants, nothwithstanding that the detention was authorized under published law.[137] In *Lokpo & Touré v. Hungary*,[138] the detention of asylum seekers was deemed unlawful due to the authority's failure to make a reasoned decision to continue detention: mere acquiescence ("non-action"[139] or "mere silence"[140]) in the continued detention was deemed insufficient to meet the requirement of legality.[141] Although the legislation in question was adopted to give effect to the EU PD, the ECtHR did not take the opportunity to condemn the detention as unlawful, even though it appeared to violate the EU measure's

135. Rusu v. Austria, App. No. 34082/02, ¶ 48 Eur. Ct. H.R (2008), http://www.echr.coe.int/echr/en/hudoc (follow "HUDOC database" hyperlink; search "Application Number 34082/02"). For a discussion, *see* MOLE & MEREDITH, *supra* note 63, at 158-61. For an intense review of the application of domestic law, *see* Jusic v. Switzerland, App. No. 4691/06 Eur. Ct. H.R. (2010), http://www.echr.coe.int/echr/en/hudoc (follow "HUDOC database" hyperlink; search "Application Number 4691/06").

136. *See infra* Part II.C.2.

137. *See* Al-Agha v. Romania, App. No. 40933/02 Eur. Ct. H. R. (2010), http://www.echr.coe.int/echr/en/hudoc (follow "HUDOC database" hyperlink; search "Application Number 40933/02"); Ahmed v. Romania, App. No. 34621/03 Eur. Ct. H.R. (2010), http://www.echr.coe.int/echr/en/hudoc (follow "HUDOC database" hyperlink; search "Application Number 34621/03"). In both rulings, the Court emphasized that national security grounds needed particular safeguards against abuse, in particular to ensure effective judicial protection, lest "*sous le couvert de défendre la démocratie, de telles mesures risquent de la saper, voire de la détruire.*" *Al-Agha*, ¶ 90 ("under the guise of defending democracy, these measures risk undermining it, even destroying it"); *see also Ahmed*, ¶ 33, (quoting Rotaru v. Romania, App. No. 28341/95 Eur. Ct. H.R. (2000), http://www.echr.coe.int/echr/en/hudoc (follow "HUDOC database" hyperlink; search "Application Number 28341/95")).

138. Lokpo v. Hungary, App. No. 10816/10, ¶ 16-24 Eur. Ct. H.R. (2011), http://www.echr.coe.int/echr/en/hudoc (follow "HUDOC database" hyperlink; search "Application Number 10816/10").

139. *Id.* para 23.

140. *Id.* para 24.

141. *But cf. id.* (Jočienė & Björgvinsson, J., dissenting) (arguing that the Court had strayed too far into the interpretation of national law, and that the continued detention should be assumed to be on the same grounds as the initial one—and if there was a deficit of judicial scrutiny, this might have been raised as an issue under Article 5(4) ECHR but had not been).

requirement that detention not be for the "sole reason"[142] that the applicants were asylum seekers.

2. Predeportation Detention—the Rejection of a Test of 'Reasonable Necessity'

The leading case on predeportation detention is *Chahal v. U.K.*[143] The Court stated in *Chahal*, and has reiterated since, that Article 5(1)(f) "does not demand that the detention of a person against whom action is being taken with a view to deportation be reasonably considered necessary, for example to prevent his committing an offence or fleeing."[144] The only requirement was that the individual face deportation. Whether the underlying decision to expel could be justified under national or ECHR law was also deemed immaterial for the purposes of Article 5(1)(f).[145] Having rejected the criterion of "reasonable necessity," the Court asserted that detention was only lawful as long as deportation proceedings were in progress and prosecuted with "due diligence."[146] Strikingly, the Court held that detention while the asylum claim was still being assessed fell under Article 5(1)(f).[147] By thirteen votes to six, it found no violation of Article 5(1), but unanimously found a violation of Article 5(4), as the domestic courts were unable to conduct a proper review due to the national security constraints on them.

The Court is increasingly insistent that states demonstrate that deportation must be a realistic prospect. If removal is not feasible due to the absence of travel documents, for example, detention will not be justified.[148] The most recent Grand Chamber ruling on this matter, *A. & Others v. U.K.*,[149] concerned the detention of foreign terrorist suspects. The Court accepted that they were nonremovable under the ECHR

142. PD, *supra* note 8, art. 18(1).

143. Chahal v. United Kingdom, App. No. 22414/93, 23 Eur. H.R. Rep. 413 (1997).

144. *Id.* para. 112.

145. *Id.*

146. *See id.* para. 113; *see also* Quinn v. France, App. No. 18580/91, 21 Eur. H.R. Rep. 529, para. 48 (1995); Singh v. Czech Republic, App. No. 60538/00, para. 61 Eur. Ct. H.R. (2005), (follow "HUDOC database" hyperlink; search "Application Number 60538/00") (offering more recent applications of "due diligence" criterion).

147. *See Chahal* paras. 115-16.

148. *See* Ali v. Switzerland, App. No. 24881/94, 28 Eur. H.R. Rep. 304, para. 12 (1998); *see also* Mikolenko v. Estonia, App. No. 10664/05, para. 10 Eur. Ct. H.R. (2009), http://www.echr.coe.int/echr/en/hudoc (follow "HUDOC database" hyperlink; search "Application Number 10664/05"); Raza v. Bulgaria, App. No. 31465/08, paras. 11, 16 Eur. Ct. H.R. (2010), http://www.echr.coe.int/echr/en/hudoc (follow "HUDOC database" hyperlink; search "Application Number 31465/08").

149. A. v. United Kingdom, App. No. 3455/05 Eur. Ct. H.R. (2009) http://www.echr.coe.int/echr/en/hudoc (follow "HUDOC database" hyperlink; search "Application Number 3455/05").

standards, due to human rights concerns in their countries of origin. Nonetheless, the United Kingdom sought to justify their detention under Article 5(1)(f) as it was keeping the possibility of removal "under active review."[150] The Court rejected the United Kingdom's argument, as this review was not "sufficiently certain or determinative to amount to 'action . . . being taken with a view to deportation.'"[151] The Grand Chamber distinguished *Chahal,* stating that the earlier case proceedings were being "actively and diligently pursued" in order to determine whether removal would violate Article 3 of the ECHR.[152] In contrast, in *A & Others*, the proceedings concerned the legality of detention, the prohibition of deportation having been conceded.[153]

The position of asylum seekers is precarious. It is arguable that in order to comply with the RC's and the ECtHR *non-refoulement* guarantees, they cannot be removed until their claims have been fully examined, and so should be regarded as temporarily lawfully present. Where domestic law reflects this position, the Court has held that asylum seekers are not lawfully in predeportation detention, as is seen in *S.D. v. Greece* and *R.U. v. Greece.*[154] These cases are in tension with *Chahal* because, in the earlier case, the period in detention as an asylum seeker was deemed to be lawful predeportation detention.[155] As yet, as discussed in the next section, the Court has shied away from insisting that, as a matter of ECHR law, asylum seekers are not in predeportation detention, as they are temporarily authorized entrants.

3. *Deportation to Prevent Unauthorized Entry: Statism Writ Large*

Article 5(1)(f) also permits detention to prevent unauthorized entry. The leading case is *Saadi v. U.K.*[156] The applicant was an Iraqi doctor

150. *Id.* para. 167.

151. *Id.*

152. *See id.* para. 169.

153. *See id.* paras. 169-70.

154. *See* S.D. v. Greece, App. No. 53541/07, para. 62 Eur. Ct. H.R. (2009), http://www.echr.coe.int/echr/en/hudoc (follow "HUDOC database" hyperlink; search "Application Number 53541/07") (referring specifically to the fact that *national law* precluded detention unless the deportation was executable); *see also* R.U. v. Greece, App. No. 2237/08, paras. 95-96 Eur. Ct. H.R. (2011), http://www.echr.coe.int/echr/en/hudoc (follow "HUDOC database" hyperlink; search "Application Number 2237/08") (noting that both national law and the RC prevented removal and that, accordingly, the detention was not lawful under domestic law).

155. *See also* Lokpo v. Hungary, App. No. 10816/10, para. 16 Eur. Ct. H.R. (2011), http://www.echr.coe.int/echr/en/hudoc (follow "HUDOC database" hyperlink; search "Application Number 10816/10") (noting that it was common ground between the parties that the applicants, although asylum seekers, were being detained with a view to deportation).

156. Saadi v. United Kingdom, App. No. 13229/03, 47 Eur. H.R. Rep. 17 (2008). *See*

who claimed asylum on arrival to the United Kingdom at Heathrow Airport. At that point, he was temporarily released and requested to return to the airport immigration authorities. He complied with the request, and four days later was detained and transferred to a detention center. The real reason for detention, in fact the entire institutional rationale for the particular detention center, was to facilitate fast-track processing of claims.[157]

The central premise of the majority in the Grand Chamber was that detention of those whose entry had not been authorized was a "necessary adjunct" to "undeniable sovereign right to control aliens entry into and residence in their territory."[158] This "necessary adjunct" imports the statist assumption into detention practices. The Court also imported *Chahal's* rejection of a necessity test. The next move in the reasoning places asylum seekers and other migrants in a legally naked position: until a state has formally authorized entry, "any entry [is] 'unauthorized.'"[159] Accordingly, the detention of anyone seeking entry who did not yet have the requisite authorization fell under Article 5(1)(f).[160] However, the Court was at pains to stress that the state did not dispose of an open-ended right to detain, and so it tailored four context-specific requirements to avoid arbitrariness. Detention must be (1) carried out in good faith; (2) closely connected to the purpose of preventing unauthorized entry of the person; (3) in an appropriate place and under appropriate conditions bearing in mind that detainee has not "committed criminal offences" but rather may have fled fearing for his life; and (4) the length of the detention should not exceed that reasonably required for the purpose pursued.[161] Applying these criteria to the facts, the majority held that seven days in a "specifically adapted" place of detention was not arbitrary, in light of the difficult administrative problems that confronted the United Kingdom during the period in question.[162]

---

generally Violeta Moreno Lax, *Beyond* SAADI v UK: *The "Necessity" Requirement for Administrative Detention of Asylum Seekers in the EU*, (Reflexive Governance in the Pub. Interest, Working Paper No. REFGOV-FR-31 2010), *available at* http://refgov.cpdr.ucl.ac.be/?go=publications&dc=561a56161f4c3720ba64e53b6bf6ea61d4ee4a84; Helen O'Nions, *No Right to Liberty: The Detention of Asylum Seekers for Administrative Convenience*, 10 EUR. J. MIGRATION & L. 149 (2008).

157. *See Saadi* paras. 23-25.

158. *See id.* para. 64 (citing Amuur v. France, 22 Eur. H.R. Rep. 533, 556-57, para. 43 (1996); Chahal v. United Kingdom, 23 Eur. H.R. Rep. 413, 454-55, para. 73 (1996); Abdulaziz v. United Kingdom, 7 Eur. H.R. Rep. 471, 497-98, paras. 67-68 (1985)).

159. *See id.* para. 65.

160. *See id.*

161. *Id.* para. 74.

162. *See id.* para. 80.

The partly dissenting opinion of Judges Rozakis, Tulkens, Kovler, Hajiyev, Spielmann, and Hirvelä set out powerful counterarguments, which urge greater fidelity to other IHRL standards. First, they noted that the majority failed to distinguish between different categories of migrants, subjecting them all to the "[s]tates' unlimited sovereignty."[163] The dissenters viewed the majority's treatment of detention as the adjunct of sovereign entry control as sitting "uncomfortably with the principle that asylum seekers who have presented a claim for international protection are *ipso facto* lawfully within the territory of a State . . . ."[164] It should be noted that the majority and the minority cite the HRC for authority of this proposition.[165] Dismissing the notion of a statist carte blanche to deem any entry unauthorized, they found that in the particular case it had "in no sense been established in the present case, as the applicant did not enter or attempt to enter the country unlawfully."[166] On this point, the dissenters are in a difficult position, because if they deem *all* asylum seekers to be lawful entrants in all circumstances, then the state has no power to detain them under Article 5(1)(f). In a deft move then, the suggestion is that asylum seekers be treated as having a purpose-specific temporary admission. Accordingly, while it is not permissible to detain "refugees on the sole ground that they have made a claim for asylum," where evidence exists that they may abscond before the claim is determined, then detention would be permissible. In contrast, the United Kingdom's detention of Saadi was explicitly for the purpose of making the asylum determination process more efficient. The dissenters deemed that rationale improper, in terms worth setting out in full:

> [N]ot just in the context of asylum but also in other situations involving deprivation of liberty, to maintain that detention is in the interests of the person concerned appears to us an exceedingly dangerous stance to adopt. Furthermore, to contend in the present case that detention is in the interests not merely of the asylum seekers themselves "but of those increasingly in the queue" is equally unacceptable. In no circumstances can

163. *See id.* at para. 32 (Rozakis, Tulkens, Kovler, Hajiyev, Spielmann & Hirvelä, J., dissenting).

164. *Id.* at para. 31.

165. *See id.* para. 32, 35 (citing U.N. Human Rights Comm., Celepli v. Sweden, Commc'n No. 456/1991, U.N. DOC. CCPR/C/51/D/456/1991 (1994).

166. *See id.* at para. 33 (Rozakis, Tulkens, Kovler, Hajiyev, Spielmann and Hirvelä, J., dissenting).

> the end justify the means; no person, no human being may be used as a means towards an end.[167]

Under the majority's approach, the asylum seeker "becomes an object rather than a subject of law."[168]

On the application of the test to the facts, they further questioned how to determine how long detention might last: If seven days was reasonable, "where and how do we draw the line for what is unacceptable?"[169] The dissenters also took issue with the failure to examine alternatives to detention as part of the nonarbitrariness assessment.[170]

Of central interest for present purposes is the approach of the minority to IHRL more generally. The minority also noted that the ECHR "[does] not apply in a vacuum,"[171] setting out the key HRC jurisprudence[172] and EU norms, noting that Article 18(1) of the PD, precluding detention for the "sole reason" of being a refugee, should be regarded as "the minimum guarantee."[173] On the majority's lack of fidelity to the other international standards, described as the "crux of the matter," the minority opinion ends with the following stinging rebuke:

> Ultimately, are we now also to accept that Article 5 [of the ECHR], which has played a major role in ensuring controls of arbitrary detention, should afford a lower level of protection as regards asylum and immigration which, in social and human terms, are the most crucial issues facing us in the years to come? Is it a crime to be a foreigner? We do not think so.

The Council of Europe's Parliamentary Assembly criticized the *Saadi* judgment. First, the interpretation of "unauthorized entry" meant that the state could detain "ad infinitum." [174] Secondly, it was in "blatant conflict" with the UNHCR guidelines on detention in allowing detention throughout the entire asylum process.[175] The Parliamentary Assembly's

167. *Id.*
168. *Id.* at para. 34.
169. *See id.*
170. *See id.*
171. *Id.*
172. *See id.* at paras. 34-35.
173. *See id.* at para. 35.
174. *See* MENDONÇA, *supra* note 2, at 19.
175. *Id.*

Rapporteur called on the Court to reexamine its case law "taking fully into account other international sources of law and views of the international community."[176]

Since *Saadi*, the Court has come back to the issue of detention to prevent unauthorized entry only once, in *Rusu v. Austria*.[177] As outlined above, in *Rusu* the detention was deemed arbitrary mainly due to the failure to adhere to the Austrian domestic legal standards, in particular its necessity test. However, the Court also emphasized that it was implausible on the facts to treat the applicant as attempting to effectuate an unauthorized entry, when she was in fact trying to leave Austria. This ruling may signal a more intense judicial review of both adherence to domestic standards and the factual matrix surrounding the claim of unauthorized entry.[178]

4. *Assessment of the Strasbourg Case Law*

Overall, the case law is predominantly concerned with legality criteria. Certainly, this preoccupation reflects in part the types of violations coming before the ECtHR, wherein states have internalized the statist assumption, and erroneously regarded their own prerogatives as not requiring legal authority in the normal sense. Yet, it also reflects a choice on the part of the ECtHR to emphasize the domestic protection of rights. However, without clear ECtHR review of the purposes and necessity of detention, domestic law and rule of law criteria may offer little protection in practice.

The two weak points in the Strasbourg case law are the approach to the determination of "unauthorized entry" and the loose nexus required between deportation and detention. On the former, the notion of the state's carte blanche to authorize entry is also ill fitting when legal authority is exercised at different levels. The RC, and the EU law giving effect to it, clearly envisages asylum seekers as temporarily authorized entrants, as are many other categories of individuals who enjoy rights of entry and residence under EU law. For a court of IHRL to ignore these obligations is to treat states as plenipotentiaries over a matter that they

176. *Id.* at 21.

177. *See* Rusu v. Austria, App. No. 34082/02, 49 Eur. H.R. Rep. 28 (2009).

178. *See* MOLE & MEREDITH, *supra* note 63, at 151 (pointing out that *Rusu* is a Chamber judgment delivered by seven judges, four of whom had been dissenters in *Saadi v. United Kingdom*, and two of whom had voted with the majority); *see also* CORNELISSE, *supra* note 15, at 312 (suggesting that this "one case" where the court closely analyzed the proportionality of the detention was striking in that it concerned "a person who was not at all 'out of place' in the global territorial ideal, but instead on her way back to the country where she 'belonged'").

have already ceded discretion. Strasbourg moved in the right directive in *R.U. v. Greece*[179] and *S.D. v. Greece,*[180] but regrettably did not engage with the question of EU standards in *Lokpo & Touré v. Hungary.*[181]

On the deportation-detention nexus, by rejecting the necessity test, the Court explicitly sets a lower standard of protection for immigration detention than for other forms.[182] The "necessary adjunct" construct in fact allowed states to transplant the degree of discretion they (putatively) disposed of over admission to the territory to another domain, detention. It would be appropriate for the ECtHR to take a prompt from the HRC jurisprudence and EU norms, and read requirements of necessity and proportionality into Article 5(1)(f). Normally under the ECHR, rights restrictions must be proportionate,[183] meaning that the restriction must be suitable to achieve the particular legitimate aim. Thus necessary and proportionate are used in the strict sense, which involves examining alternative less rights-intrusive means. Such is the "ubiquity of proportionality analysis"[184] that some defend as *the* central principle of human rights adjudication.[185] Without necessarily endorsing that view, for the ECtHR to be textually faithful to Article 5, the ECHR requires it to insist on finite permissible grounds for detention. But the failure to insist on the appropriate demonstrable link between the detention in question and the ground in question (be it to effectuate deportation *or* to prevent unauthorized entry) undermines the textual commitment to limit detention to specified grounds.

---

179. R.U. v. Greece, App. No. 2237/08 Eur. Ct. H.R. (2011), http://www.echr.coe.int/echr/en/hudoc (follow "HUDOC database" hyperlink; search "Application Number 2237/08").

180. S.D. v. Greece, App. No. 53541/07 Eur. Ct. H.R. (2011), http://www.echr.coe.int/echr/en/hudoc (follow "HUDOC database" hyperlink; search "Application Number 53541/07").

181. Lokpo v. Hungary, App. No. 10816/10 Eur. Ct. H.R. (2011), http://www.echr.coe.int/echr/en/hudoc (follow "HUDOC database" hyperlink; search "Application Number 10816/10").

182. *See* CORNELISSE, *supra* note 15, at 279, 305-08 (comparing case law under Article 5(1)(e), which concerns "the lawful detention of persons for the prevention of the spreading of infectious diseases, of persons of unsound mind, alcoholics or drug addicts, or vagrants," with that of Article 5(1)(f)); *see also* CLARE OVEY & ROBIN WHITE, JACOBS & WHITE: EUROPEAN CONVENTION ON HUMAN RIGHTS 133 (2002).

183. European Convention on Human Rights, *supra* note 6, art. 8-11. Admittedly, there is often a textual basis, as the restrictions in question must be "necessary in a democratic society" under the relevant Treaty Article. However, the principle is built into the structure of analysis beyond those provisions as well.

184. Mattias Kumm, *The Idea of Socratic Contestation and the Right to Justification: The Point of Rights-Based Proportionality Review*, 4 LAW & ETHICS HUM. RTS. 140, 142 (2010).

185. *See* DAVID BEATTY, THE ULTIMATE RULE OF LAW 187 (2004). *See generally* ROBERT ALEXY, A THEORY OF CONSTITUTIONAL RIGHTS (2002).

Constructive human rights pluralism is evident in the minority opinion in *Saadi*. The minority opinion shows that appropriate engagement with the external standards of the HRC and RC, would have led to a different result. Strasbourg's failure to engage with the ICCPR standards in all of its immigration detention cases is striking.[186]

D. EU Law

The EU legislation governing immigration detention takes the form of directives. These are binding norms that envisage further legislative implementation by the Member States.[187] However, once the implementation date prescribed has passed, individuals may invoke those provisions of the directive that are sufficiently clear and precise.[188] This doctrine of direct effect allows individuals to invoke the unimplemented Directive against the state but not vice versa.[189] Once an EU directive's implementation date has passed, individuals and their lawyers will have no hesitation to invoke those of its provisions that may be beneficial.[190] This helps explain how even an apparently repressive measure like the RD, discussed below, produces cases that are protective of migrants' rights, at least when Member States are dilatory in implementation. Given EU law's strong normative punch,

186. *See* Ian Bryan & Peter Langford, *The Lawful Detention of Unauthorised Aliens Under the European System for the Protection of Human* Rights, 80 NORDIC J. OF INT'L L. 193, 203-04 (2011).

187. *See* TFEU *supra* note 7, art. 228.

188. Case 41/74, Van Duyn v. Home Office, 1974 E.C.R. 1337 (describing the doctrine of "vertical direct effect").

189. The opinion of Advocate General Ruiz-Jarabo Colomer in Joined Cases C-152-154/07, Arcor v. Germany, 2008 E.C.R. I-5959, para. 98 accurately captures the legal position:

> The doctrine of direct effect operates on a vertical, one-way plane (from an individual to the State), in that traffic in the opposite direction (reverse vertical relationships) (citing Joined Cases C-74/95 and C-129/95 *X*, 1996 E.C.R. I-6609) and perpendicular routes which would enable a directive to be relied on between individuals (horizontal direct effect) are both prohibited. (citing Case 152/84, Marshall v. Southampton and South-West Hampshire Area Health Authority, 1986 E.C.R. 723).

See also, Case C-61/11 PPU, Hassen El-Dridi alias Karim Soufi, 2011 ECJ EUR-Lex CELEX LEXIS 1027, para. 28 (Apr. 28, 2011) (view of Advocate General Jàn Mazák).

190. *See, e.g.*, Serge Slama, *Le Noël Des Sans-Papiers : invoquez directement la directive "retour" et la charte des droits fondamentaux...*, COMBATS POUR LES DROITS DE L'HOMME (CPDH) BLOG (Dec. 26, 2010), http://combatsdroitshomme.blog.lemonde.fr/les-suites-du-noel-des-sans-papiers-invocabilite-de-la-directive-retour-du-16-decembre-2008-depuis-le-24-decembre-2010/. The title "Le Noël des sans-papiers" (The Christmas of Undocumented Migrants) refers to the RD's implementation date of December 24, 2010. After that time, migrants could invoke the RD against the State.

national governments that form part of the main EU legislative body are loath to commit to legislative norms that will constrain them excessively. Yet, the combination of terse laconic norms and strong judicial enforcement may have unanticipated consequences for national executives.

1. *Detention of Asylum Seekers*

Both the RCD[191] and PD[192] make references to detention. In addition, the EU is currently revising the Dublin Regulation to include detention rules.[193] At present, the Regulation does not contain any provisions on detention, but in practice it is seen to have contributed to the increase in detention of asylum seekers across Europe, as it increases the cohort of asylum seekers who are amenable to removal before the claims have been processed.[194]

The original proposal for the RCD contained a detailed provision on detention, largely modeled on Executive Committee Conclusion Number 44.[195] However, negotiating wrangles produced oblique, piecemeal provisions instead. Article 7 of the RCD provides that "[a]sylum seekers may move freely within the territory of the host Member States." However, Member States may decide on "the residence of the asylum seeker for reasons of public interest, public order, or, when necessary, for the swift processing and effective monitoring of his or her application."[196] This provision seems to fall far short of Article 26 of the RC.[197]

---

191. RCD, *supra* note 9.

192. PD, *supra* note 8. For analysis of both, see Dan Wilsher, *Immigration Detention and the Common European Asylum Policy*, *in* WHOSE FREEDOM, SECURITY AND JUSTICE?: EU IMMIGRATION AND ASYLUM LAW AND POLICY 395, 418-25 (Annelise Baldaccini et al. eds., 2007); Kay Hailbronner, *Detention of Asylum Seekers* 9 EUR. J. OF MIGRATION & L. 159, 169 (2007).

193. Council Regulation 343/2003, *supra* note 47. The recast proposal contains a new provision (Article 27) on detention. *See Proposal for a Regulation of the European Parliament and of the Council Establishing the Criteria and Mechanisms for Determining the Member State Responsible for Examining an Application for International Protection Lodged in One of the Member States by a Third-Country National or a Stateless Person (Recast)*, at 48, COM (2008) 820 final (Mar. 12, 2008).

194. For some qualitative evidence, see *Dublin II: A Summary of JRS Experiences in Europe*, JESUIT REFUGEE SERV. (Oct. 2008), www.jrseurope.org/AdvocacyPages/Dublin%20Regulation/DublinSummaryJRSResponsesFinal.pdf.

195. *See generally* U.N. High Comm'r for Refugees, Exec. Comm., *No. 44 Detention of Refugees and Asylum-Seekers* (1986), http://www.unhcr.org/cgi-bin/texis/vtx/home/opendocPDFViewer.html?docid=4aa764389&query=detention%20of%20refugees%20and%20asylum-seekers%20no.%2044; *see also*, Wilsher, *supra* note 192, at 422.

196. RCD, *supra* note 9, art. 7(2).

197. Marx, *supra* note 116, at 1163-64.

On detention stricto sensu, Article 18(1) of the PD states plainly that detention should not be for the sole reason that the individual is an applicant for asylum.[198] Article 7(3) of the RCD states that "[w]hen it proves necessary, for example for legal reasons or reasons of public order, Member States may confine an applicant to a particular place in accordance with their national law."[199] Here we find the necessity criterion that is absent in the Strasbourg case law.[200] However, the guarantee is undermined by the vague open-ended grounds expressed as, "for example for legal reasons or reasons of public order." The vagueness of these grounds sits uneasily with the approach of the HRC, in particular. The border procedures provision in Article 15(4) of the PD seems to envisage confinement of asylum seekers at the border for a prolonged period of up to four weeks, detention in all but name.

The provisions are replete with transformative potential. The PD recognizes the right of the asylum seeker to be on the territory of the Member States.[201] On this basis alone, it seems difficult for an EU Member State to treat asylum seekers' presence as unauthorized; at the very least the approach of the minority in *Saadi* would have to be applied. Similarly, asylum seekers could not be normally regarded as in predeportation detention, following the approach in *R.U. v. Greece* and *S.D. v. Greece*.[202] The remaining leeway to detain asylum seekers is

198. Article 18 provides:
"1. Member States shall not hold a person in detention for the sole reason that he/she is an applicant for asylum. 2. Where an applicant for asylum is held in detention, Member States shall ensure that there is a possibility of speedy judicial review." PD, *supra* note 8, at 23.

199. RCD, *supra* note 9, art. 7(3).

200. *See generally* Lax, *supra* note 156.

201. *See* PD, *supra* note 8, at 18 ("Applicants shall be allowed to remain in the Member State, for the sole purpose of the procedure, until the determining authority has made a decision in accordance with the procedures at first instance set out in Chapter III. This right to remain shall not constitute an entitlement to a residence permit.") *See also* Council Directive 2008/115, 2008 O.J. (L 348) 98 (EC). ("In accordance with [the PD] a [TCN] who has applied for asylum in a Member State should not be regarded as staying illegally on the territory of that Member State until a negative decision on the application, or a decision ending his or her right of stay as asylum seeker has entered into force"). The PD appears to leave it to Member States to decide whether there is a right to remain pending resolution of any appeals or reviews of first instance decisions. However, the case law of the ECtHR requires suspensive effect of appeals to vindicate Articles 3 (where such risks pertain) and 13 ECHR. *See* Gebremedhin v France, App. No. 25389/05, ¶ 34 Eur. Ct. H.R. (2007), http://www.echr.coe.int/echr/en/hudoc (follow "HUDOC database" hyperlink; search "Application Number 25389/05"). *See also* Thomas Spijkerboer, *Subsidiarity and 'Arguability': The European Court of Human Rights' Case Law on Judicial Review in Asylum Cases* 21 INT'L J. REFUGEE L. 48, 69-73 (2009).

202. *See* S.D. v. Greece, App. No. 53541/07 Eur. Ct. H.R. (2009), http://www.echr.coe.int/echr/en/hudoc (follow "HUDOC database" hyperlink; search "Application Number

accordingly diminished, and would require some infraction on the part of the individual asylum seeker in order to render her stay unauthorized. Even in that instance, the detention would need to be demonstrated as a necessary means to achieve the particular legitimate aim in view. Proportionality, encompassing the three elements of suitability, necessity, and least restrictive means, is a ubiquitous feature of EU law.[203] The building blocks for a new, more rigorous adjudicatory framework are contained in these terse rules. Whether that potential is exploited depends largely on suitably crafted references from national courts coming before the CJEU.

2. Predeportation Detention and the CJEU Kadzoev and El Dridi Rulings

The RD sets out rules governing the conditions and procedures for the return (i.e., deportation) of illegal TCNs.[204] Once a Member State deems someone "illegal" the RD sets out "a horizontal set of rules, applicable to *all* [TCNs] who do not or who no longer fulfill the conditions for entry, stay or residence in a Member State."[205] Like the asylum directives, it took prolonged negotiations to reach agreement on the RD, though involving the European Parliament as a colegislator.[206] Some of the standards in the RD are lamentably low, prompting a broad-based international campaign against its adoption, during which

53541/07"); *see also* R.U. v. Greece, App. No. 2237/08 Eur. Ct. H.R. (2011), http://www.echr.coe.int/echr/en/hudoc (follow "HUDOC database" hyperlink; search "Application Number 2237/08").

203. Proportionality is a general principle of EU law. In addition, the EUCFR contains a general limitation clause in Article 52(1). *See* Charter of Fundamental Rights of the European Union, *supra* note 57, art. 52(1) (stating, "Any limitation on the exercise of the rights and freedoms recognised by this Charter must be provided for by law and respect the essence of those rights and freedoms. Subject to the *principle of proportionality*, limitations may be made only if they are *necessary* and genuinely meet objectives of general interest recognised by the Union or the need to protect the rights and freedoms of others" (emphasis added)).

204. For detailed analysis, see Anneliese Baldaccini, *The Return and Removal of Irregular Migrants Under EU Law: An Analysis of the Returns Directive*, 11 EUR. J. MIGRATION & L. 1 (2009). *See also* Anneliese Baldaccini, *The EU Directive on Return: Principles and Protest*, 28 REFUGEE SURV. Q. 114 (2010); Martin Schieffer, *Chapter V. Termination of Residence*, *in* EU IMMIGRATION AND ASYLUM LAW: COMMENTARY ON EU REGULATIONS AND DIRECTIVES (Kai Hailbronner ed., 2010).

205. Council Directive 2008/115, *supra* note 201, at 98.

206. *See generally* Diego Acosta, *The Good, the Bad and the Ugly in EU Migration Law: Is the European Parliament Becoming Bad and Ugly?*, 11 EUR. J. MIGRATION & L. 19 (2009) (discussing the different steps in the adoption of the Directive); *see also* FABIAN LUTZ, THE NEGOTIATIONS ON THE RETURN DIRECTIVE: COMMENTS AND MATERIALS (2010).

it was condemned as a "shameful" and "outrageous" measure.[207] The eighteen-month outer time limit for detention has been the focus of the most criticism.[208] While Member States are not obliged to permit such long detention, in practice several have increased detention times in implementing the Directive.[209] Further, reentry bans reinforce the impression of a repressive measure.[210]

Yet, the RD integrates human rights principles,[211] in particular the principle of proportionality.[212] It aims to encourage voluntary return, so the coercive moves to detain and deport may only be engaged after a waiting period.[213] The preamble cites the Council of Europe's Twenty Guidelines on Forced Return.[214] Concerning detention, Recital 16 provides:

---

207. *See, e.g., No to the Outrageous Directive*, www.statewatch.org/news/2007/dec/eu-returns-ngo-compilation.pdf (document prepared by 14 European pro-migrant NGOs, subsequently supported by 400 European organizations and more than 8,000 citizens); *see also* Press Release, European Council on Refugees and Exiles (ECRE), Returns Directive: EU Fails to Uphold Human Rights (June 18, 2008), http://www.ecre.org/files/ECRE%20press%20release%20Returns%20Dir.pdf; U.N. High Comm'r. for Refugees, *UNHCR Position on the Proposal for a Directive on Common Standards and Procedures in Member States for Returning Illegally Staying Third-Country Nationals* (June 16, 2008), http://www.unhcr.org/refworld/pdfid/4856322c2.pdf; Press Release UN Experts Express Concern About Proposed EU Return Directive, UN Press Release (July 18, 2008).

208. *See, e.g.*, EUR. PARL. ASS. DEB. 7th Sess. para. 5 (Jan. 28, 2010) ("The European Union Return Directive, which provides for a maximum length of detention for irregular migrants of up to eighteen months, can be criticised for adopting the lowest common standard with regard to length of detention . . . and increasing the possibility for states to increase their minimum duration of detention."). *See generally* Report of the Working Group on Arbitrary Detention, U.N. Doc. A/HRC/13/30 (Jan. 18, 2010).

209. *See* Michael Flynn & Cecilia Cannon, *Detention at the Borders of Europe: Report on the Joint Global Detention Project*, GLOBAL DETENTION PROJECT, Oct. 2-3, 2010, at 5. (stating "Greece, Italy, and Spain have all increased detention times since adopting the Return Directive. A fourth country, Hungary, is set to double maximum detention terms when newly adopted legislation enters into force at the end of 2010"). For a detailed overview of detention time limits, see Fundamental Rights Agency, *supra* note 97, at 31-35. On implementation more generally, see THE RETURNS DIRECTIVE: CENTRAL THEMES, PROBLEM ISSUES, AND IMPLEMENTATION IN SELECTED MEMBER STATES (Karin Zwaan ed., 2011).

210. *See generally* Council Directive 2008/115, *supra* note 201, art. 11. (explaining the issuing of entry bans).

211. *See id.* at Recital 2 (referring to "full respect for . . . fundamental rights and dignity"); *see also id.* at Recital 24 (asserting that "[t]his Directive respects the fundamental rights and observes the principles recognised in particular by the Charter of Fundamental Rights of the European Union.").

212. *See id.* at Recitals 13, 16.

213. *See id.* at Recital 10, art. 7. The period envisaged is between seven and thirty days.

214. *Id.* at Recital 3. *Twenty Guidelines on Forced Return*, *supra* note 94. On many contentious issues in the negotiations, the Twenty Guidelines provided compromise solutions. *See* Schieffer, *supra* note 204, at 1506.

> The use of detention for the purpose of removal should be limited and subject to the principle of proportionality with regard to the means used and objectives pursued. Detention is justified only to prepare the return or carry out the removal process and if the application of less coercive measures would not be sufficient.

Article 15 requires that detention only be used as a last resort, for as short a period as possible, with the specific purpose of preparing and carrying out the return process and crucially for as long as it is "necessary to ensure successful removal."[215] Two specific purposes are given as examples of when detention would be necessary: when there is a risk of absconding, or when the individual concerned avoids or hampers the preparation of return or of the removal process. Reflective of the ECtHR case law, detention is only permissible "as long as removal arrangements are in progress and executed with due diligence."[216] In the absence of a "reasonable prospect of removal," detention must cease. Article 15's terms are clearly stricter than the ECtHR case law in incorporating a necessity requirement.

The CJEU has given two rulings on the legality of predeportation detention under the RD, *Kadzoev*,[217] and *El-Dridi*,[218] both under its new urgent preliminary reference procedure.[219]

a. *Kadzoev*[220]

Kadzoev's prolonged detention in Bulgaria shows the sharp end of EU detention practices.[221] At the time of the references, he had spent

215. Council Directive 2008/115, *supra* note 201, art. 15.

216. *Id.* art. 15(1).

217. Case C-357/09 PPU, Kadzoev, 2009 E.C.R. I-11189.

218. *See* Case C-61/11 PPU, Hassen El-Dridi alias Karim Soufi, 2011 ECJ EUR-Lex CELEX LEXIS 1027 (Apr. 28, 2011).

219. *See* TFEU, *supra* note 7, art. 267 (stating, "[i]f such a question is raised in a case pending before a court or tribunal of a Member State with regard to a person in custody, the Court of Justice of the European Union shall act with the minimum of delay"); *see also* Consolidated Version of the Rules of Procedure of the Court of Justice (CJEU), art. 104b, 2010 O.J. (C 177) 1, 28. For a general discussion, see Catherine Barnard, *The PPU: Is it Worth the Candle? An Early Assessment*, 34 EUR. L. REV. 281 (2009).

220. *See generally* Elitsa Mincheva, *Case Report on Kadzoev, 30 November 2009*, 12 EUR. J. MIGRATION & L. 361 (2010) (detailing the *Kadzoev* case).

221. Concerning Kadzoev's particular case, see *Fear of Forcible Return/Fear of Torture or Ill-Treatment*, AMNESTY INT'L (Apr. 18, 2008), http://amnesty.org/en/library/asset/EUR15/001/2008/en/90cd1485-0d65-11dd-a114-e974a1f25b3e/eur150012008eng.pdf. *See also Report of the Special Rapporteur on Torture and Other Cruel, Inhuman or Degrading Treatment or Punishment*, 42-43, U.N. Doc. A/HRC/10/44/Add4 (Feb. 17, 2009) (by Manfred Nowak).

thirty-four months in detention, despite bringing unsuccessful asylum claims and judicial reviews in order to secure his release. The reference arose when the domestic court was seized by a request from the Directorate for Migration at the Ministry of the Interior requesting it to rule ex officio on the legality of the duration of detention. The questions referred concerned the temporal and material scope of Article 15 of the RD in light of the particular facts of the case. The first two questions concerned the determination of which periods were covered by the prescribed maximum detention period. The first question concerned periods predating the Directive's entry into force, while the second question raised the crucial question of how the periods while asylum applications were pending should be regarded. The third question concerned periods when the execution of the removal was suspended pending appeal. The fourth question went to the meaning of removal being "reasonably possible," raising fact-specific concerns pertaining to the noncooperation of the Russian authorities. The fifth and final question asked what the Bulgarian authorities were to do if the maximum detention period had passed and "there [was still] a doubt as to [the applicant's] identity, he [was] aggressive in his conduct, he [had] no means of supporting himself and there [was] no third person who has undertaken to provide for his subsistence?"[222]

The specific answers may be summarized quickly: the period spent in detention prior to the entry into force of the RD did count toward the maximum period, when proceedings were ongoing after its entry into force.[223] Periods spent as an asylum seeker did not count toward the period, as a separate regime addressed this issue, and, crucially, asylum seekers were not "illegal," so they did not fall under the RD. If, however, no specific decision had been taken to detain Kadzoev under the asylum rules, the time under the RD would continue to run.[224] Similarly, periods in detention when deportation was suspended pending appeal did count toward the RD time limit.[225] The "reasonable prospect of removal" meant a realistic prospect, which would not pertain if the receiving country was unlikely to admit the individual within a "reasonable period" (according to the Advocate General (AG))[226] or the period set out in the RD (according to the Court).[227] Once the detention

Concerning detention practices in general in Bulgaria, see Valeria Ilareva, *Bulgaria's Treatment of Asylum Seekers*, 29 FORCED MIGRATION REV. 60 (2007), *available at* www.fmreview.org/FMRpdfs/FMR29/60-61.pdf.

222. Case C-357/09 PPU, Kadzoev, 2009 E.C.R. I-11189, para. 30.

223. *Id.* paras. 34-39.

224. *Id.* paras. 40-48.

225. *Id.* paras. 49-57.

226. *Id.* paras. 65-66.

227. *Id.*

period was up, there was no further basis to detain the individual under EU law, and immediate release was required,[228] notwithstanding the facts the Bulgarian government sought to rely on.[229] In a footnote, the AG acknowledged the possibility of residual Member State competence to detain "because of aggressive behaviour on the basis of national legislation intended to maintain public order or the criminal law, for example."[230] The Court was silent on this crucial question of the extent to which Member State action had been preempted by the RD.

b. El-Dridi

El-Dridi[231] delves even more deeply into the immigration detention practices of the Member State concerned, Italy, and raises precisely those preemption questions that were left unanswered in *Kadzoev*.

Italy has been at the forefront of the criminalization of irregular migration, a trend seen increasingly across Europe.[232] Detention for committing a crime is conceptually and legally distinct from immigration detention, as Article 5 of the ECHR reflects. However, immigrant populations increasingly fall foul of criminal laws specifically designed to criminalize their presence. In Italy, it is a criminal offense for a foreigner to remain in the country once a legal order to leave the territory has been issued.[233] Although the Italian Constitutional Court has tempered the strictness of the offense, the crime of illegal presence remains.[234] Notably, the Italian Constitutional Court has recently issued a number of rulings undermining some elements of the repressive anti-immigrant legislation, known as the "security package."[235] *El-Dridi* may be viewed as part of this process of judicial

228. *Id.* paras. 68-71.

229. *Id.* para. 71.

230. *Id.*, n.38 (view of Advocate General Jàn Mazák). *See also* Galina Cornelisse, *Casenote on C-357/09 PPU,* 48 COMMON MKT. L. REV. 925, 933 (2011).

231. *See* Case C-61/11 PPU, Hassen El-Dridi alias Karim Soufi, 2011 ECJ EUR-Lex LEXIS 1027 (Apr. 28, 2011).

232. *See generally* Council of Eur.: Comm'r for Human Rights, *Criminalisation of Migration in Europe: Human Rights Implications* (Feb. 4, 2010), *available at* http://www.unhcr.org/refworld/docid/4b6a9fef2.html.

233. See *El-Dridi,* 2011 ECJ EUR-Lex LEXIS 1027, para. 17 for the full text of the synopsized provisions.

234. See Report of the WGAD, *supra* note 91, ¶¶ 57-67 for an extensive discussion of both Italy's "extraordinary measures in the fight against crime by irregular migrants" and immigration detention stricto sensu. The Italian Constitutional Court has reviewed this law, and precluded its application in cases where noncompliance with the order to leave was justified. *See* Cass., sez. un., 17 dicembre 2010, n. 359, (It.) (Case No. 359/2010).

235. All, bar one (Case C-144/11, Abdallah, 2011 O.J. (C 152) 17), have been terminated in light of *El-Dridi* (*see* YASHA MACCANICO, STATEWATCH ANALYSIS: ITALY – SERIES OF

action to constrain the states' immigration decrees. Italian judges sent a raft of similar preliminary references on the topic.[236] The questions referred merit setting out in full:

> In the light of the principle of sincere cooperation, the purpose of which is to ensure the attainment of the objectives of the directive, and the principle that the penalty must be proportionate, appropriate and reasonable, do Articles 15 and 16 [RD] preclude:
>
> –the possibility that criminal penalties may be imposed in respect of a breach of an intermediate stage in the administrative return procedure, before that procedure is completed, by having recourse to the most severe administrative measure of constraint which remains available?
>
> –the possibility of a sentence of up to four years' imprisonment being imposed in respect of a simple failure to cooperate in the deportation procedure on the part of the person concerned, in particular where the first removal order issued by the administrative authorities has not been complied with?[237]

DEFEATS IN COURT FOR THE "SECURITY PACKAGE" (Statewatch, 2011), *available at* www.statewatch.org/analyses/no-137-italy-security-package.pdf). *See generally* Italian Constitutional Court, 25 July 2011, No. 245 (striking down a law restricting the right to marry of irregular migrants); Italian Constitutional Court, 8 July 2010, No. 249 (striking down a law imposing additional criminal penalties on irregular migrants); Italian Constitutional Court, 4 Apr. 2011, Case No. 115 (striking down a law conferring excessive powers on local government to combat irregular migration), *available at* http://www.cortecostituzionale.it/actionPronuncia.do.

236. *See* Case C-43/11, Assane Samb, 2011 O.J. (C 113) 7; Case C-50/11, Lucky Emegor, 2011 O.J. (C 113) 7, 2011 O.J. (C 252) 28 (withdrawn); Case C-61/11, Mrad, 2011 O.J. (C 113) 8, 2011 O.J. (C 252) 28 (withdrawn); Case C-63/11, John Austine, 2011 O.J. (C 120) 5, 2011 O.J. (C 252) 28 (withdrawn); Case C-94/11, Survival Godwin, 2011 O.J. (C 139) 14, 2011 (C 252) 29 (withdrawn); Case C-113/11, Cherni, 2011 (C 238) 4 (withdrawn); Case C-120/11, Yeboah Kwadwo, 2011 O.J. (C 145) 17 (removed from register); Case C-140/11, Demba Ngagne, 2011 O.J. (C 152) 16, 2011 O.J. (C 252) 29 (removed from register); Case C-156/11, Ibrahim Music, 2011 O.J. (C 269) 20 (removed from register); Case C-169/11, Conteh, 2011 O.J. (C 173) 8 (removed from register); Case Case C-187/11, Vermisheva, 2011 (C 211) 11 (removed from register).

237. Case C-61/11 PPU, Hassen El-Dridi alias Karim Soufi, 2011 ECJ EUR-Lex LEXIS 1027, para. 25 (Apr. 28, 2011).

The Italian government argued that its use of criminal law put the detention outside the scope of the RD, relying on Article 2(2)(b).[238] In one sentence, the Court rejected that plea.[239] The AG clarified that the exception only applied where the return obligation was applied as a result of a criminal conviction. In the instant case, the return obligation was the predicate act to the criminal offense, and so the exception was not applicable.[240]

The CJEU characterized the national legislation as providing for detention "on the sole ground" that the migrant was in breach of the order to leave.[241] In contrast, the Court described the RD as establishing a "fixed order" of "various, successive stages" of the removal process,[242] which must employ the "least coercive measures possible."[243] Detention, the "most serious constraining measure," was "strictly regulated" in order to ensure observance of fundamental rights.[244] Having confirmed the direct effect of Articles 15 and 16 of the RD,[245] the CJEU identified various ways in which "the removal procedure provided for by the Italian legislation at issue in the main proceedings [was] significantly different from that established by that directive."[246] These differences included the absence of a period for voluntary departure[247] and the recourse to criminal detention.[248]

The CJEU reassured the Member States that they may still take "[coercive] measures, including criminal law measures, aimed inter alia at dissuading those nationals from remaining illegally on those States' territory."[249] However, those measures, even in the criminal law field, must be adjusted to ensure compliance with EU law,[250] and ensure its effectiveness.[251] The principles of proportionality and effectiveness precluded any national rule that provided for a custodial sentence "on the sole ground" that the TCN continued to stay illegally after the order has been issued. Instead, Member States must "pursue their efforts to

238. *Id.* para. 49.

239. *Id.* paras. 48-49. At issue was the exclusion of those facing deportation for criminal reasons under Article 2(2)(b) of the Returns Directive. *See* RD, *supra* note 10, art. 2(2)(b).

240. *El-Dridi*, 2011 ECJ EUR-Lex LEXIS 1027, paras 22-28.

241. *Id.* para. 29.

242. *Id.* para. 34.

243. *Id.* para 39.

244. *Id.* para. 42.

245. *Id.* paras. 44-47.

246. *Id.* para. 50.

247. *Id.* para. 51.

248. *Id.* paras. 52-60.

249. *Id.* para. 52.

250. *Id.* para. 54.

251. *Id.* paras. 55-56.

enforce the return decision, which continues to produce its effects."[252] The CJEU noted that detention in this circumstance risked making removal more difficult.[253]

The result is startling: The RD precludes the Italian law. As EU law is supreme over national law, national courts are obliged not to apply those provisions of the Italian law which are incompatible with the RD, taking into account the general principle "of the retroactive application of the more lenient penalty."[254] This duty, incumbent on all national judges irrespective of their position in the national judicial hierarchy, has been a hallmark of EU law since its early years.[255]

3. *The Looming Question of Preemption*

EU law's capacity not only to penetrate the domestic legal order, but also to shift aside other domestic norms and make way for its own "full effectiveness" is truly distinctive. The question left unasked and unanswered in *Kadzoev* is of great constitutional significance for the relationship between the EU and its Member States. If Kadzoev can no longer be detained under the RD, what residual power does the Member State have detention-wise?[256] *El-Dridi* takes up this issue in regard to criminal detention. The AG and the CJEU are not ad idem on the extent of preemption. The AG notably took issue with the inherent nature of criminal law, described as a "repressive reaction."[257] For the AG, both criminalization per se and detention as the specific penalty were liable to impede the achievement of the RD's aim.[258] In contrast, the Court expressly leaves more leeway for national criminal measures in this field.[259] Indeed, in emphasizing that the offending

252. *Id.* para. 58.
253. *Id.* para. 59.
254. *Id.* para. 61.
255. *See* Case 106/77, Simmenthal, 1978 E.C.R. 629.
256. This form of preemption, where the EU rules preempt national ones because the latter impede the effectiveness of the former is "the most hazy and ill-defined" form of preemption in EU law. Amedeo Arena, *The Doctrine of Union Preemption in the EU Single Market: Between* Sein *and* Sollen 31 (The Jean Monnet Ctr. for Int'l and Reg'l Econ. Law & Justice, Working Paper 03/10, 2010). The other forms are field pre-emption (where EU rules in the field preclude national action in that field) and rule pre-emption (where an EU norm precludes a contradictory national one.) Arena's account focuses on pre-emption in the context of the EU's single market. He notes in his conclusion that investigating the "preemptive effects on EU legislation in the area of freedom, security and justice" is of "paramount importance." *Id.* at 90.
257. Case C-61/11 PPU, Hassen El-Dridi alias Karim Soufi, 2011 ECJ EUR-Lex CELEX LEXIS 1027, para. 40 (Apr. 28, 2011).
258. *Id.* para. 43.
259. *Id.* para. 52.

aspect of the Italian legislation was that detention was "on the sole ground" of staying in the face of the order to leave, the CJEU seems to implicitly allow for other criminal offenses based on illegal residence coupled with some other elements of wrong-doing, provided that this did not make deportation more difficult. The difference in approach between the AG and the Court will require resolution shortly.[260] While the approach in *El-Dridi* seems capable of taming some of the punitive excesses of the moves toward the criminalization of migration, it brings a sense of disquiet too. If criminalization was demonstrated to be effective in achieving deportation, then one would fall back on the principle of proportionality alone to restrain it under EU law, in which case the notion that the RD would preempt the national rules would be a much more audacious claim.

As for the notion of residual "public order" detention powers, there is certainly no general "public order" power to detain under Article 5 ECHR. The grounds for detention set out there are finite.[261] The Court has interpreted the potentially broadest ground, which permits detention "to secure the fulfillment of an obligation prescribed by law" narrowly, requiring a specific identifiable legal obligation in view.[262] Even in times of emergency, detention powers must be exercised in a nondiscriminatory fashion. Singling out foreigners for special forms of detention, other than under Article 5(1)(f), is not permissible. This is best illustrated by the rulings in the *Belmarsh* litigation saga, culminating in the ECtHR Grand Chamber ruling in *A. v. U.K.*[263] Nonetheless, many Member States do have anomalous detention grounds that cannot be subsumed under the ECHR purposes,[264] and so are of questionable legality under the ECHR. If such grounds impede the effectiveness of the removal, the RD may also preclude them.

260. Case C-329/11 Alexandre Achughbabian v Préfet du Val-de-Marne, lodged on 29 June 2011.

261. For a discussion, see Fundamental Rights Agency, *supra* note 97, at 19.

262. Engel v. Netherlands, 1 Eur. H.R. Rep. 647 (1976).

263. A. v. United Kingdom, App. No. 3455/05 Eur. Ct. H.R. (2009) http://www.echr.coe.int/echr/en/hudoc (follow "HUDOC database" hyperlink; search "Application Number 3455/05").

264. As the FRA has recently highlighted, in the Czech Republic, Finland, Greece, Germany, and Hungary, additional reasons (such as the threat posed to public order) are used to determine whether to place individuals in predeportation detention. The practices are difficult to square with the requirement that detention be strictly necessary for the purpose of effectuating removal. In other Member States (Latvia, Lithuania, and Malta), public order and other non-Article 5 grounds, seem per se to justify detention of foreigners. Fundamental Rights Agency, *supra* note 97, at 19-20.

4. CJEU—ECtHR Interactions

In *Kadzoev*, the reasoning of AG Mazák and of the Court are similar, but, as is typically the case, the AG's View is more elaborate, particularly in its engagement with the ECtHR authorities. In regard to the "reasonable prospect of removal" under Article 15(4) of the RD, the AG cited the Council of Europe material, in particular the CAHAR Guideline Number Seven on Forced Return.[265] The AG noted that EU law also incorporated the Article 5(1)(f) ECHR standards,[266] citing *Chahal*[267] and *Mikolenko*.[268] The AG emphasized the ECtHR requirement of due diligence, in order to ensure that periods in detention are as short as possible.[269] The AG's view was decided on November 10, 2009, less than a month after the ECtHR ruled in *Mikolenko* that detention was unlawful as there was no reasonable prospect of removal.[270] Given the proximity in time, it is unsurprising that the AG would cite this case, particularly since both cases concern impediments to removal due to insufficient cooperation from the receiving country. Unlike the Court, the AG gave a strong indication that the detention should be regarded as unlawful in the absence of a reasonable prospect of removal.

However, *Kadzoev* signals that the RD standards are *higher* than the ECHR in other crucial respects, namely in requiring that detention is necessary to effectuate removal,[271] and in imposing a strict time limit. In *El-Dridi*, the Court noted that the RD was intended to take account of both the Strasbourg case law "according to which the principle of proportionality requires that the detention of a person against whom a deportation or extradition procedure is under way should not continue for an unreasonable length of time, that is, its length should not exceed that required for the purpose pursued" and the guideline providing that detention is to be "for as short a period as possible."[272] In this way, the

265. Case C-357/09 PPU, Kadzoev, 2009 E.C.R. I-11189.

266. *Id.* para. 53 (citing Chahal v. United Kingdom, App. No. 22414/93, 23 Eur. H.R. Rep. 413 (1997); Mikolenko v. Estonia, App. No. 10664/05 Eur. Ct. H.R. (2009), http://www.echr.coe.int/echr/en/hudoc (follow "HUDOC database" hyperlink; search "Application Number 10664/05"); *Twenty Guidelines on Forced Return*, *supra* note 94 (Guideline No. 7)).

267. Chahal v. United Kingdom, App. No. 22414/93, 23 Eur. H.R. Rep. 413 (1997).

268. Mikolenko v. Estonia, App. No. 10664/05 Eur. Ct. H.R. (2009), http://www.echr.coe.int/echr/en/hudoc (follow "HUDOC database" hyperlink; search "Application Number 10664/05").

269. Case C-357/09 PPU, Kadzoev, 2009 E.C.R. I-11189, para. 4.

270. Mikolenko, App. No. 10664/05 Eur. Ct. H.R. (2009).

271. Case C-357/09 PPU, Kadzoev, 2009 E.C.R. I-11189, para. 64.

272. *See* Case C-61/11 PPU, Hassen El-Dridi alias Karim Soufi, 2011 ECJ EUR-Lex LEXIS 1027, para. 43 (Apr. 28, 2011) (citing to Saadi v. United Kingdom, App. No. 13229/03, 47 Eur. H.R. Rep. 17, para. 72, para. 74 (2008); *Twenty Guidelines on Forced Return*, *supra* note 94 (Guideline No. 8)).

CJEU reads in the Strasbourg requirements as to the duration of detention, making clear that the eighteen-month time limit is the outer limit, which will not be justified in all cases. However, as we have seen, the ECtHR rejects the requirements of necessity and proportionality in its case law, but reads the requirement of "reasonable time" into its conception of nonarbitrariness. It would be regrettable if the distinctive EU version of proportionality were to be sapped of vigor by converging on the weak ECHR non-arbitrariness standard.

The AG in *Kadzoev* also cited the Strasbourg case law to clarify that although asylum seekers could not be detained under the RD, "detention of an asylum applicant [was] not, as such, prohibited under the international and [EU] law of asylum."[273] While the judgment is crucially important in delimiting the detention of asylum seekers from those facing deportation, it should not be taken to endorse the view that the ECHR standards in *Saadi*[274] should be incorporated into EU law in toto. Rather, as demonstrated above, the EU legislative framework contains the building blocks for more rigorous scrutiny of detention of asylum seekers. Constructive human rights pluralism stands for critical engagement, not automatic integration. The EU legislative framework and its imminent commitment to rigorous proportionality review, warrant a different approach.

CONCLUSION

The proliferation of rights sources and adjudicative bodies with overlapping jurisdiction may give the appearance of a rights surfeit. Yet, the cases reveal a burgeoning practice of immigration detention. The HRC has used a vague, capacious notion of "arbitrariness" to condemn automatic detention of migrants, instead demanding individual justification. But, the permissible aims of detention remain open under its jurisprudence. Regrettably, neither the ECtHR nor the CJEU gives due weight to the HRC authorities. The ECtHR takes an eccentric course, particularly in refusing to apply its standard proportionality approach, and in allowing the state unlimited leeway to deem migrants unauthorized. The two leading rulings, *Chahal* and *Saadi*, sit poorly with the authority of the HRC and the RC, as well as

273. Case C-357/09 PPU, Kadzoev, 2009 E.C.R. I-11189, para. 85 (citing, e.g., Saadi v. United Kingdom, App. No. 13229/03, 47 Eur. H.R. Rep. 17 (2008); Riad v. Belgium, App. No. 29787/03 Eur. Ct. H.R. at 74-76 (2008), http://www.echr.coe.int/echr/en/hudoc (follow "HUDOC database" hyperlink; search "Application Number 29787/03 "); Human Rights Comm., A. v. Australia, Commc'n. No. 560/1993, para. 9.2, U.N. Doc. CCPR/C/59/D/560/1993 (1997).

274. *Saadi*, App. No. 13229/03, 47 Eur. H.R. Rep. 17 (2008).

with the standards now binding on the bulk of ECHR parties via EU law. A necessity test and authorized presence at least for asylum seekers once admitted to the procedure are acknowledged features of the EU regime.

Constructive human rights pluralism would have Strasbourg engage in a less perfunctory manner with the IHRL standards and align with them, when appropriate. The existence of the EU standards should exert pressure for that movement from within. EU law, despite the apparently unpromising legislative framework, has integrated the better aspects of the ECtHR jurisprudence, superimposing the necessity requirement that the ECtHR erroneously rejected. Guiraudon's prediction of the "bold" CJEU and the "tamer" ECtHR seems to be playing out.[275] It would be wrong for the EU to converge on the ECHR minimum when it is called upon to articulate its own interpretation of the right to liberty. Thus far, given the nature of the claims before it, textual fidelity to the RD has produced outcomes that are evidently more rights-protective than the ECHR. In future cases, it may be called upon to develop its own distinctive jurisprudence on the right to liberty and should be wary of the overblown statism that animates the Strasbourg case law.

Much depends on national judges. They trigger preliminary references, and their questions not only dictate the scope of the CJEU's jurisdiction but may nudge the Luxembourg judges in particular directions. While the referring court in *Kadzoev* seemed incredulous that release from detention was required as a matter of EU law, the questions referred in *El-Dridi* seem part of a concerted judicial effort to thwart the criminalization of irregular migration in Italy. The Italian government's argument in *El-Dridi*, that its use of criminal law prevented the application of the RD, has a naïve ring to it. The outcome, wherein the RD instead "precludes" the Italian law, shows that the state qua EU Member no longer controls the exception. At the other end of the enforcement spectrum, we might contrast the distortion of the scope of the RC by governments keen to treat "asylum seekers" as presumptively "bogus" rather than presumptive refugees. The article began with the statist assumption, and the migrant's vulnerability to naked state power. EU law takes a different view of the state, unsettling statist assumptions, and opening up space for greater normative contestation. The universal subject, the rights-bearer, appears a more vivid prospect under EU law than under IHRL.

And yet, I have not described a continent at ease. Immigration detention continues to increase, and Member States are raising

275. *See* Guiraudon, *supra* note 84.

detention time limits in response to the RD. EU law brings us "[d]etainees [who] have more rights, but they are detained for longer periods of time."[276] But at least, once the maximum period of detention expires, release is required. But then what? Once *Kadzoev* and *El-Dridi* are released from detention, their irregular status remains. Periodic mass regularizations of irregular migrants are routine in EU Member States,[277] and increasingly justified in human rights terms.[278] Mincheva suggests the implicit next step for *Kadzoev* should be regularization.[279] Yet, EU law offers no solution at present and may even be seen to exert an anti-regularization ethos over its Member States.[280] The ECHR protects some migrants from removal based on their long residence, but does not provide them with a formal status in the host state.[281] There is no clear supranational legal remedy at present. It appears the best we can hope for is that supranational courts and authority will prompt inclusive political and judicial moves at the domestic level.

276. FLYNN & CANNON, *supra* note 2, at 9 (reporting the statement of an EU workshop participant).

277. For an overview of regularization practices, see MARTIN BALDWIN-EDWARDS & ALBERT KRALER, INT'L CTR. FOR MIGRATION POLICY DEV., REGINE: REGULARIZATIONS IN EUROPE: STUDY ON PRACTICES IN THE AREA OF REGULARIZATION IN THE MEMBER STATES OF THE EU—FINAL REPORT (2009).

278. *See* Albert Kraler, *Fixing, Adjusting, Regulating, Protecting Human Rights—The Shifting Uses of Regularisations in the European Union,* 13 EUR. J. OF MIGRATION AND L. 297 (2011).

279. *See* Mincheva, *supra* note 220.

280. The problems posed by nonremovable irregular migrants have long been noted, but even a suggestion to study the various Member State practices concerning nonremovable migrants with a view to developing some common principles at the EU level was dropped. Kraler, *supra* note 278, at 301.

281. *See, e.g.,* Bonger v. The Netherlands, App. No. 10154/04 Eur. Ct. H.R. (2005) http://www.echr.coe.int/echr/en/hudoc (follow "HUDOC database" hyperlink; search "Application Number 10154/04"). In rare cases, Article 8 ECHR may provide a basis for a claim to regularize a migrant's stay. *See generally* Daniel Thym, *Respect for Private and Family Life Under Article 8 ECHR in Immigration Cases: A Human Right to Regularize Illegal Stay?,* 57 INT'L & COMP. L. Q. 87 (2008).

Part III
Family, Gender and the Rights of Children

[7]

Migration, Gender, and the Limits of Rights

Siobhán Mullally

The significance of gender in the context of migration has attracted increasing attention in recent years. The 'feminization of migration', noted in many policy documents and academic commentaries, points to the increasing numbers of women now migrating independently to seek work and the diverse geographical regions within which women are migrating.[1] Reflecting this phenomenon, significant developments have taken place in international human rights law specifically addressing migrant women.[2] As many commentators have noted, however, there are costs to inclusion in the register of human rights discourse.[3] This is particularly true for migrant women who do not fit easily into the inherited structures of human rights law. The terms of inclusion may reinforce gendered and racialized stereotypes of the 'abject' third-world woman or lead to alliances with conservative agendas that further limit migration possibilities. 'Border norms' do not stop at the border.[4] They follow migrants within the territorial borders of states and entrench distinctions not just between citizens and non-citizens, but also between categories of migrants. Gender plays a key role in determining the precariousness and vulnerability experienced by migrants, in shaping the migration routes that are taken, and in determining the terms of belonging imposed by states. Migrant women crossing borders pose significant challenges to the inherited structures and frameworks of international human rights law raising questions as to its transformative potential.

This chapter examines the significance of gender in three areas of law relating to migration: human trafficking, migrant domestic workers, and gender-related asylum law. It starts from the premise that human rights norms, properly interpreted, may challenge the exclusion, exploitation, and abuses experienced by many migrant women. It argues that human rights norms have the potential to address and respond to overlapping axes of discrimination and disadvantage, including 'race', ethnicity,

[1] N. Piper, 'Feminisation of Migration and the Social Dimensions of Development: the Asian case', 29 *Third World Quarterly* (2008) 1287.

[2] See, eg, UN Committee on the Elimination of All Forms of Discrimination Against Women, *General Recommendation no. 26 on Women Migrant Workers* (2009) UN Doc CEDAW/C/2009/WP.1/R.

[3] D. Otto, 'Exile of Inclusion: Reflections on Gender Issues in International Law over the Last Decade, The Feature: Reflections on a Decade of International Law' 10 *Melbourne Journal of International Law* (2009) 11.

[4] L. Bosniak, *The Citizen and the Alien: Dilemmas of Contemporary Membership* (2006).

migration status, and gender. It recognizes, however, that the permeability of human rights law is not without limits, particularly in the context of migration where sovereign prerogatives continue to resist human rights claims. It also matters who is promoting the gender equality agenda and to what end.[5] In the context of migration, migrant women's rights claims have been instrumentalized by states so as to legitimize the expansion of criminal laws (in the context of human trafficking and irregular migration) and to restrict pathways to safe and secure migration.[6] Migrant women are frequently positioned by law as vulnerable to abuse and in need of protection. This constructed vulnerability, in turn, is presumed to justify the coercive interventions of the state. As we shall see, the normative re-emergence of protective categories does little to enhance women's autonomy, agency, or equality, as the 'sexed subject' of human rights law continues to position migrant women at its limits. To the extent that women's autonomy is recognized, such autonomy is viewed as threatening, potentially destabilizing to the certainties required for neoliberal models of migration management, and further evidence that the protections afforded by law may be unnecessary (or undeserved).[7] This duality is reflected in the law's responses to migrant women. The resulting tensions, as we shall see, limit the transformative potential of human rights norms and projects of law reform, both domestically and internationally.

I. Human Trafficking: Rights, Vulnerabilities, and Reform

Attempts to add the harms endured by trafficked persons into the framework of international human rights law have met with many obstacles, revealing the reluctance of states to yield traditional sovereign prerogatives on immigration even in the face of egregious harms.[8] The protective stereotypes of migrant women persist, as trafficked women are positioned as victims but denied the resources and supports most needed to move to a secure and safe migration status. For women who are victims of human trafficking, access to legal protections, effective remedies, and to secure migration status, remains difficult. The trafficked person, although a victim of an egregious harm, is also an irregular migrant in the eyes of the state. An irregular migrant with a possible claim to international protection poses a significant challenge to a state's claim to control its borders and to manage migration. Her potential claim to 'be here' and to remain is one that has been resisted as states have proven reluctant to remedy the fundamental irregularity of her presence. As Gallagher has argued, the trafficked woman is de facto stateless, unlikely to receive effective protection from her country of origin and denied the very form of protection most likely to vindicate her human rights claims to secure residence and access to safe migration pathways.[9]

[5] See V. Munro, 'Of Rights and Rhetoric: Discourses of Degradation and Exploitation in the Context of Sex Trafficking', 25 *Journal of Law & Society* (2008) 240.

[6] V. Munro, 'Stopping Traffic: A Comparative Study of Responses to the Trafficking in Women for Prostitution', 46 *British Journal of Criminology* (2006) 318.

[7] Munro (n 6).

[8] A. Gallagher, *The International Law of Human Trafficking* (2010).

[9] Gallagher (n 8).

Recent years have witnessed the adoption of a growing body of anti-trafficking laws and policies at domestic and international levels. To borrow Agamben's evocative term, we have seen an explosion of laws[10] on human trafficking and in the context of trafficking for purposes of sexual exploitation, a continuing circulation of sexual panic. Many feminist commentators have responded with concern to this proliferation of laws and to the accompanying expansion of sovereign power to regulate migration.[11] The unintended consequences of anti-trafficking measures have included an expansion of state power to regulate border crossings and a further closing off of regular migration pathways for migrant women. This crisis response has negative consequences for migrant women and for longer-term analysis of the substantive impact of anti-trafficking law on gender equality. The preoccupation with criminalization of trafficking and related activities has narrowed the space for responses that foreground the human rights of trafficked persons. As a crisis governance response takes hold, reform proposals that recognize the intersecting axes of discrimination and power linked to gender, 'race', and migration status are marginalized.

This ideological capture is not complete, however. In the practice of human rights law, there is potential for law to move beyond the binary divides that have characterized the crisis governance response to human trafficking to date. In recent years, we have seen a growing resistance to the expansion of criminal law and greater recognition of the requirements of due process in anti-trafficking reforms. There is some, albeit limited, resistance increasingly visible in the incremental changes occurring in relation to residence claims, recovery periods, and restrictions on return of trafficked persons, as well as recognition of states' positive duties to prevent human trafficking and to provide effective remedies to victims. These incremental changes reflect the need to move beyond stereotypical portrayals of the 'victim subject' of human trafficking that have marginalized the agency of the trafficked person and limited the transformative potential of human rights.

A. Standard-setting: problems of definition and competing narratives

As noted in the introduction, who 'sponsors' feminist goals matters a great deal, as becomes very clear when one examines the genealogy and contemporary practice of anti-trafficking measures. The adoption of the Protocol to Prevent, Suppress and Punish Trafficking in Persons, especially Women and Children (Palermo Protocol) in 2000 marked a significant moment in the development of international legal standards on human trafficking.[12] The inclusion of an anti-trafficking instrument in the panoply of international legal instruments, through a Protocol to the Convention on Transnational Organized Crime was also significant, reflecting

[10] G. Agamben, *Means Without End: Notes on Politics* (2000).

[11] See Munro, n 6, and A. T. Gallagher, *Recommended Principles and Guidelines on Human Rights and Human Trafficking: Commentary* (2010); available at: <http://works.bepress.com/anne_gallagher/15>; accessed 20 March 2012.

[12] Protocol to Prevent, Suppress and Punish Trafficking in Persons Especially Women and Children, supplementing the United Nations Convention against Transnational Organized Crime (2000).

the international community's preoccupation with organized crime and irregular movements across borders. The failure to ensure stronger protections for trafficked persons in the Protocol reflects the reluctance of states to recognize the rights claims that arise in the context of irregular migration and the continuing dominance of security and sovereignty concerns.

A key issue in defining the crime of human trafficking is the question of whether consent may be raised as a defence. This issue is a particularly complex one in the context of allegations of trafficking for the purposes of sexual exploitation, where conflicting positions on the appropriate domestic legal responses to sex work muddy the process of reform. The difficult negotiating history of the Palermo Protocol, the delays in securing agreement on the legal definition of trafficking, and the ensuing divisions that arose between human rights activists during the drafting process reflect broader disagreements on the regulation of sex work. The question of how or whether to allow for possible defences of consent to be raised was the subject of protracted negotiation and often acrimonious debate.[13] Familiar disagreements came to the fore in these negotiations. For those pursuing an abolitionist position on prostitution, the possibility of a woman consenting to engage in the commercial sex industry as a sex worker could not be countenanced as a defensible legal position.[14] The move to disallow possible defences of consent being raised follows from this abolitionist position.

The possible consequences of such a position for diverse national systems of criminal law including those that do not criminalize the purchase of sexual services, and the potential for conflict with fair trial rights, led to a compromise in the final text of the Protocol. The possibility of a defence of consent being raised where the victim in question was a child is denied, in recognition of the child's inherent vulnerability.[15] Outside of the context of child trafficking, where any of the aggravating factors of exploitation were found to exist, including the use of force

[13] See Gallagher (n 8).

[14] See C. MacKinnon, 'Prostitution and Civil Rights', 1 *Michigan Journal of Gender and Law* (1993) 13.

[15] Art. 3 of the Protocol provides:

For the purposes of this Protocol:

(a) 'Trafficking in persons' shall mean the recruitment, transportation, transfer, harbouring or receipt of persons, by means of the threat or use of force or other forms of coercion, of abduction, of fraud, of deception, of the abuse of power, or of a position of vulnerability or of the giving or receiving of payments or benefits to achieve the consent of a person having control over another person, for the purpose of exploitation. Exploitation shall include, at a minimum, the exploitation of the prostitution of others or other forms of sexual exploitation, forced labour or services, slavery or practices similar to slavery, servitude, or the removal of organs;

(b) The consent of a victim of trafficking in persons to the intended exploitation set forth in subparagraph (a) of this article shall be irrelevant where any of the means set forth in subparagraph (a) have been used;

(c) The recruitment, transportation, transfer, harbouring, or receipt of a child for the purpose of exploitation shall be considered 'trafficking in persons' even if this does not involve any of the means set forth in subparagraph (a) of this article;

(d) 'Child' shall mean any person under eighteen years of age.

or coercion, consent was deemed to be irrelevant.[16] The compromise adopted leaves open the possibility that women may have chosen to engage in sex work and as such could not be presumed to be victims of violence per se. This position was subsequently followed in the later 2005 Council of Europe Convention on Action Against Trafficking in Human Beings[17] and is also reflected in the position taken by the drafters of the UN Convention on the Elimination of All Forms of Discrimination Against Women (CEDAW).[18]

The compromises adopted in the Palermo Protocol and other international legal instruments fall short of the more radical position taken by Barry et al., who argue that sex work (or the preferred term, prostitution) is inherently exploitative.[19] A 'wrongful use' view of sexual exploitation sees harm as essential to prostitution itself. In this view, regardless of whether a decision to engage in sex work was rational or preferential given the 'pre-transaction baseline' and terms of engagement, exploitation is presumed to occur.[20]

Divisions between regulatory and abolitionist positions on sex work continue to manifest themselves in the context of proposals to criminalize the purchase of sexual services, including the services of a trafficked person.[21] States' positive obligations to prevent human trafficking are increasingly linked to these debates. On the question of combating demand for the services of trafficked persons, the Palermo Protocol requires states to adopt legislative or other measures to discourage the demand that leads to trafficking.[22] While the regulation of prostitution is left to states, it is argued by some that there is a positive obligation on states to combat demand for exploitative commercial sexual services, which encourages human trafficking and ultimately engages states' obligations of deterrence and prevention.[23] The call to criminalize the purchase of sexual services seeks to tackle the apparently 'insatiable demand for cheap labour' that fuels the commercial sex industry and creates a buoyant market for traffickers.[24]

The UN CEDAW Committee has not pursued an abolitionist model, preferring to focus on the substantive impact of regulatory or abolitionist responses to sex work on women, including, in particular, women migrants. In its Concluding Observations on both the Dutch and Swedish reports, the Committee has questioned the impact of differing responses—regulatory and abolitionist—adopted at domestic level and sought concrete data and analysis on the impact of differing

16 See Art. 3(b). 17 Arts 4(a) and (b).

18 Convention on the Elimination of All Forms of Discrimination Against Women (1979), 1249 UNTS 13. See Art. 6.

19 K. Barry, *The Prostitution of Sexuality* (1996); MacKinnon (n 14); C. A. MacKinnon, *Are Women Human? And Other International Dialogues* (2006).

20 Munro (n 5) at 260–1.

21 See, eg, recent legal reforms in the UK, Policing and Crime Act 2009 (ss. 14–15). These proposals draw, in particular, on developments in Sweden following the adoption of the Act Prohibiting the Purchase of Sexual Services (1999).

22 See Art. 9.

23 Statement of Ms Sigma Huda, Special Rapporteur on Trafficking in Persons, at CSW- Beijing + 10 Review, 7 March 2005; available at: <http://www.un.org/webcast/csw2005/statements/050307traffickinginpersons-e.pdf>.

24 Munro (n 5) at 242.

regimes on the health, well-being, and rights of sex workers.[25] The 2005 Council of Europe Trafficking Convention adopts a similar compromise, leaving it open to states to consider the introduction of criminal sanctions, but requiring all states at a minimum to address the problem of demand in the context of a growing market for the services of trafficked persons.[26] The 2011 EU Directive on preventing and combating trafficking in human beings and protecting its victims[27] addresses the question of demand for the services of trafficked persons in general, but limits the imposition of positive obligations to prevent human trafficking to programmatic measures relating to education, training, and raising of awareness.[28] States are required only to 'consider' the introduction of offences to criminalize the purchase of the services of a trafficked person with the knowledge that the person is a victim.[29] An earlier European Commission proposal to require states to criminalize the use of such services was not adopted, reflecting disagreements on the regulation of sex work at member state level. The specific reference in the 2011 Directive to use of the services of trafficked persons with knowledge that the person is the victim of an offence, would seem to allow states to move beyond the binary divisions of abolition or regulation of sex work and instead to target specifically the phenomenon of human trafficking. For proponents of an abolitionist response, this position is not enough as the commercialization and sale of sex is, in itself, presumed to be exploitative and to fuel the human trafficking industry.[30]

In *Rantsev v. Cyprus and Russia*,[31] the European Court of Human Rights, while not directly addressing the links between demand for commercial sex services and human trafficking per se, did read Article 4 of the European Convention on Human Rights (ECHR) as imposing positive obligations on states to prevent trafficking for the purposes of sexual exploitation. Specifically, the Court noted that Article 4 requires member states to put in place adequate measures to regulate businesses frequently used as a cover for human trafficking and to ensure that domestic legislation provides 'practical and effective protection of the rights of victims and potential victims of trafficking'.[32] The links between a failure to regulate the sex industry and heightened risks of trafficking on this reading may engage the responsibility of the State. In *Rantsev*, the inconsistencies in the Cypriot government position became evident. The government had earlier introduced a range of anti-trafficking measures including a national action plan to combat trafficking, while at the same time maintaining a widely criticized '*cabaret artiste*'

[25] *Concluding comments of the Committee on the Elimination of Discrimination against Women: Netherlands*, UN Doc CEDAW/C/NLD/CO/4, 2 February 2007, paras 20–22; *Concluding observations of the Committee on the Elimination of Discrimination against Women: Sweden*, 8 April 2008, UN Doc CEDAW/C/SWE/CO/7, para. 33.

[26] Council of Europe Convention on Action against Trafficking in Human Beings, Warsaw, 16 May 2005, Art. 6: Measures to discourage the demand.

[27] Directive 2011/36/EU of the European Parliament and of the Council, OJ 2011 L 101/1, 5 April 2011, on preventing and combating trafficking in human beings and protecting its victims, and replacing Council Framework Decision 2002/629/JHA.

[28] See Art. 18. [29] Art. 18(4). [30] Barry (n 19).

[31] ECHR (2010) Appl. No. 25965/04, judgment of 7 January 2010.

[32] ECHR (2010), n 31, judgment of 7 January 2010, para. 284.

visa scheme.[33] The Court commented that it had 'no doubt' that the Cypriot authorities were aware that the visa scheme was being used by traffickers for the purposes of sexual exploitation.[34]

Ultimately, the Court concluded that the Cypriot government had failed to meet its positive obligations under the Convention by failing to regulate employment in the '*cabaret artiste*' industry, maintaining a visa regime for cabaret artists that did not provide effective protection against trafficking, and failing to carry out an effective investigation into the death of Oxana Rantsev.[35] Audrey Macklin has written elsewhere on similar inconsistencies in Canadian immigration policy, arising from the operation of the so-called 'exotic-dancer' visa scheme.[36] Destination states, she points out, may be complicit in human trafficking by continuing to operate immigration schemes that significantly increase the vulnerability of migrant women.[37] It was this complicity that was recognized in the *Rantsev* judgment. In a far-reaching statement, the Court found that Article 4 requires States to:

> put in place adequate measures regulating businesses often used as a cover for human trafficking. Furthermore, a State's immigration rules must address relevant concerns relating to encouragement, facilitation or tolerance of trafficking. (para. 284)

The next step of opening up safer migration routes is not one that is usually taken, however, reflecting a wider reluctance on the part of states to recognize the links between access to safe migration routes, application of human rights norms to immigration law and policy, and the potential to reduce migrant women's vulnerability to trafficking.

B. The rights of trafficked persons: recognizing the nexus

The Palermo Protocol makes only limited reference to states' obligations to provide support and services to trafficked persons. In contrast, significant attention is given to states' duties of law enforcement and prevention. While states are required to take various steps to criminalize trafficking and to ensure more effective investigation and prosecution of trafficking crimes, the provisions on victim support and services are more cautious. States parties are required only to 'consider'

[33] The position of the Cypriot government had been subject to detailed criticism by the Council of Europe Commissioner for Human Rights. See Report by Thomas Hammarberg, Commissioner for Human Rights of the Council of Europe, following his visit to the Republic of Cyprus on 7–10 July 2008, Strasbourg, 12 December 2008, CommDH(2008) 36, paras 32–53.

[34] ECHR (2010) (n 31) para. 294.

[35] Concerning Cyprus, the Court found it had violated its procedural obligations under Art. 2 ECHR, 'because of the failure to conduct an effective investigation into Ms Rantseva's death' (paras 241–242). The Court, in a novel interpretation of the Convention, found that the corollary of the duty to secure evidence from other relevant countries during an investigation had as a corollary that such countries should, within their means and competence, render such assistance if requested. The procedural obligations under Art. 2 included therefore a duty of transnational cooperation and investigation.

[36] A. Macklin, 'Dancing across Borders: "Exotic Dancers," Trafficking, and Canadian Immigration Policy', 37 *International Migration Review* (2003) 464.

[37] Macklin (n 36) 495.

implementing measures to provide for the physical, psychological, and social recovery of victims, in 'appropriate cases'.[38] On the status of trafficked persons, states are again required only to 'consider' adopting measures in 'appropriate cases' to allow for the issuing of temporary or permanent residence permissions.[39]

The question of status for trafficked persons is one that goes to the heart of states' wider reluctance to recognize rights to be within their borders, particularly in the context of irregular migration. If we are to take trafficking seriously as a human rights violation and if we admit the contributory role played by receiving countries, the provision of secure immigration status would be viewed as a human rights remedy and not merely as 'munificence' on the part of the host country or as 'a contingent benefit conditional upon cooperation with legal authorities'.[40] As yet, a positive obligation to provide secure residence and safe migration pathways as human rights remedies has not been accepted by states. Cautious steps have been taken towards challenging this refusal in an attempt to highlight the complicity of states that limit access to safe migration routes or fail to exercise due diligence in preventing human trafficking. The Council of Europe Convention Against Trafficking goes further than the Palermo Protocol in recognizing the rights claims of trafficked persons. States parties are required to provide for recovery and reflection periods of at least thirty days[41] and for renewable residence permits where such permits are considered necessary either because of the personal situation of the victim or to facilitate cooperation in criminal proceedings.[42] These provisions are in contrast to the conditionality attached to the issuing of residence permits in EU law for trafficked persons.

The 2004 EU Directive on short-term residence permits for victims of trafficking specifically conditions the issuing of residence permits on the trafficked person's cooperation in criminal proceedings.[43] Despite widespread criticism, the Directive remains in force.[44] The 2011 Directive was adopted specifically to enhance support for victims. The motivation behind this reform was not entirely or even primarily a humanitarian one. It was recognized that enhanced victim protections, in particular concerning residence and recovery periods, could strengthen the likelihood of effective trafficking investigations and prosecutions. Following the adoption of the 2011 Directive, member states are now required to ensure that support provided to trafficked persons is not made conditional on cooperation with criminal investigations, prosecution, or trial proceedings. This requirement, however, is 'without prejudice' to the provisions of the 2004 Directive or 'similar national rules',[45] with the result that the issuing of short-term residence permits

[38] See Art. 6. [39] Art. 7. [40] See Macklin, n 36, at 495.

[41] Council of Europe Convention on Action against Trafficking in Human Beings (n 26) Art. 13.

[42] Council of Europe Convention on Action against Trafficking in Human Beings (n 26) Art. 14.

[43] Council Directive 2004/81/EC, OJ 2004 L 261, 29 April 2004 on the residence permit issued to third-country nationals who are victims of trafficking in human beings or who have been the subject of an action to facilitate illegal immigration, who cooperate with the competent authorities.

[44] S. Egan, 'Protecting the Victims of Trafficking: Problems and Prospects', 1 *European Human Rights Law Review* (2008) 106.

[45] Directive 2011/36/EU of the European Parliament and of the Council (n 27) Art. 11(3).

to trafficked persons may continue to be conditional on cooperation with a criminal process. The possibility of continuing conditionality, given the importance of secure residence for trafficked persons and associated risks of re-trafficking, reflects the continuing tensions between member states' interests in migration control and recognition of the rights claims of trafficked persons.

These tensions are evident also in the jurisprudence of the European Court of Human Rights. In *Siliadin v. France*, the Court recognized for the first time that Article 4 ECHR could give rise to positive obligations for states.[46] It failed, however, to recognize that such obligations could extend to regularization of a victim's migration status and positive obligations of rehabilitation.[47] The Court's focus on the need for more effective criminal justice responses to problems of servitude fits within the predominantly prosecutorial model that has shaped international legal developments on human trafficking. It falls short, however, of a response that would support recognition of the complex rights claims of trafficked persons, particularly of children. In *Rantsev*, as already discussed, the Court acknowledged the links between safe migration routes, effective monitoring of immigration regimes, and vulnerability to human trafficking. However, it did not take the additional step of recommending that states expand access to safe migration routes.

In the recent case of *Osman v. Denmark*,[48] the Court was required to distinguish between caring work provided by a minor in a family context and the boundaries of human trafficking. The case concerned a young Somali national who had lived from the age of seven in Denmark. When she was fifteen, her father brought her to Kenya (with her mother's permission), for what was presumed to be a short family visit. She was subsequently left by her father at the Hagadera refugee camp to provide ongoing 24-hour care to her ailing paternal grandmother. After two years, she left the camp and sought to return to Denmark to join her mother and siblings. The Danish authorities refused to reinstate her residence status, however. The Court found that this refusal constituted an interference with her rights to both private and family life and that it was not proportionate to the aim pursued.[49] The AIRE Centre, representing the applicant, had sought to argue that Osman had been subject to intra-familial human trafficking and that the state had failed in its obligation to investigate and prosecute the offence of trafficking.[50] The Danish

[46] ECHR 2005, Appl. No. 73316/01, judgment of 26 July 2005. Further cases on Art. 4 are now pending before the Court, and also involve alleged violations of Art. 4 in the context of domestic service. See *Kawogo v. United Kingdom*, Appl. No. 56921/09; *Milanova and Others v. Italy and Bulgaria*, Appl. No. 40020/03; *C. N. v. United Kingdom*, Appl. No. 4239/08; *O.G.O. v. United Kingdom*, Appl. No. 13950/12, lodged 8 March 2012.

[47] For a detailed analysis of the case, including the Court's finding that the state had breached its positive obligation to provide specific and effective protection against violations of the European Convention on Human Rights, see H. Cullen 'Siliadin v. France: Positive Obligations Under Article 4 of the European Convention on Human Rights', 6 *Human Rights Law Review* (2006) 585.

[48] *Osman v. Denmark*, ECHR (2011) Appl. No. 38058/09, judgment of 14 June 2011.

[49] *Osman v. Denmark*, (n 48), in particular at paras 51–77.

[50] *Osman v. Denmark*, (n 48) at paras 46 and 62.

authorities had a duty, they argued, to look beyond the exercise of parental authority in order to protect the child's best interest.[51] The Court rejected this argument, noting that the applicant had not at any time complained of trafficking to the Danish authorities. The Court also, however, sought to distinguish the work done as part of everyday family life, from the exploitation that constitutes an element of human trafficking offences. Specifically, it noted that 'the exercise of parental rights constitutes a fundamental element of family life, and that the care and upbringing of children normally and necessarily require that the parents... impose, or authorise others to impose, various restrictions on the child's liberty'.[52] Interestingly, in finding against Denmark for refusing to reinstate the applicant's residence permit, the Court noted that 'in respecting parental rights, the authorities cannot ignore the child's interest including its own right to respect for private and family life'.[53] The assertion of the child's interests in the context of the alleged intra-familial trafficking did not trump the Court's deference to parental authority, however.

The case is a difficult one, taking place as it does against a background of increasing scrutiny by many European states of the normativity of migrant family life. This scrutiny has been accompanied by an expansion of the human trafficking framework, with all the attendant problems of potential over-reach of the criminal law. The response to the Court's judgment has been mixed, with some welcoming the decision not to pursue the question of human trafficking, while others have pointed to the need to address the problem of intra-familial trafficking particularly for the purposes of forced domestic labour. Given the wider policy context of increasing criminalization of migration, the space for reasoned dialogue on exploitative practices in the context of migration is limited.

The link between safe migration procedures and fulfilment of states' human rights obligations is explicitly recognized in CEDAW's *General Recommendation No. 26 on women migrant workers* (2009).[54] The CEDAW Committee notes that states are entitled to control their borders and regulate migration but must do so in compliance with their obligations to 'respect, protect and fulfil the human rights of women throughout the migration cycle'.[55] The rights claims arising when determining claims to remain within a host state are not yet fully recognized by this emerging international law of migration. Recommendation No. 26 does not address the issue of human trafficking directly. However, it does note its relevance to situations where women migrants may have been victims of trafficking. The Committee also notes that women migrant workers may become victims of trafficking due to varying degrees of vulnerability, arising from their migration status and/or the precariousness of their positions as workers. It is careful to avoid general presumptions of vulnerability, however, and specifically limits the scope of the Recommendation to low-income precarious work.

51 *Osman v. Denmark* (n 48) at para. 63.

52 *Osman v. Denmark* (n 48) at para. 64.

53 *Osman v. Denmark* (n 48) at para. 73.

54 See *General Recommendation No. 26 on women migrant workers*, UN Doc CEDAW/C/2009/WP.1/R.

55 *General Recommendation No. 26 on women migrant workers* (n 54) para. 3.

Limitations on the power of states to remove trafficked persons are recognized through the safe and 'preferably voluntary' return standard set out in the Palermo Protocol and replicated in regional and domestic legal instruments.[56] Access to asylum or complementary forms of protection may also herald the possibility of a more durable long-term solution recognizing a right of trafficked persons to remain in a destination state. States are required to ensure that trafficked persons are informed of asylum procedures and possibilities of complementary protection, where available. The Palermo Protocol itself makes reference to rights, obligations, and responsibilities arising under international refugee law.[57] The Council of Europe Anti-Trafficking Convention specifically refers to the right to seek and to enjoy asylum, and to the requirement that all states parties ensure that victims of trafficking have access to appropriate and fair asylum procedures.[58] The 2011 EU Directive requires states to ensure that victims have access to information about recovery and reflection periods and to information on the possibility of accessing international protection.[59] In 2006, the UNHCR published its guidelines on the application of the 1951 Convention Relating to the Status of Refugees to victims of trafficking and persons at risk of being trafficked.[60] The Guidelines explicitly recognize that not all trafficked persons may be entitled to a grant of asylum and note that all elements of the refugee definition must be satisfied in order to secure asylum. Herein lies the difficulty as problems of 'fit' frequently arise for claims of gender-related persecution. In the context of human trafficking, the difficulty of establishing the required nexus with a Convention ground may be compounded by the need to establish a failure of state protection and continuing risks.

The difficulties of securing access to asylum are well documented, as the categories of refugee law and other forms of complementary protection continue to limit the recognition of protection needs.[61] Problems of establishing credibility arise, in particular, for victims of sex trafficking who may find themselves in a double bind, their claims encountering the suspicions that attach to claims of sexual violence linked to the commercial sex industry on the one hand, and by generalized hostilities towards irregular migrants, on the other hand.

[56] See Art. 8(2).

[57] See Art. 14(1). There is now a substantial body of case law recognizing trafficked persons as coming within the scope of the refugee definition. See *Secretary of State for the Home Department v. Dzhygun* (2000) Immigration Appeal Tribunal Decision 00 TH 00728 (the group being women from Ukraine forced into prostitution against their will); *Miss AB v. Secretary of State for the Home Department* (2003) Immigration Appellate Authority decision CC/64057/2002 (the group consisting of girls trafficked from West Africa); *Appellant v. Secretary of State for the Home Department* (2003) UKIAT 00023 (the group consisting of women from the north-east of Albania); *Petition of Olga Shimkova*, Outer House, Court of Session, 23 December 2003 (the group consisting of women trafficked from Ukraine).

[58] Council of Europe Convention on Action against Trafficking in Human Beings (n 26) at Art. 14.

[59] Directive 2011/36/EU of the European Parliament and of the Council, n 27, Art. 11(6).

[60] See UN High Commissioner for Refugees, The Application of Article 1.A(2) of the 1951 Convention and/or the 1967 Protocol Relating to the Status of Refugees to Victims of Trafficking and Persons at Risk of Being Trafficked (2006), UN Doc HCR/GIP/06/07.

[61] See S. Mullally, 'Domestic Violence Asylum Claims and Recent Developments in International Human Rights Law: a Progress Narrative?' 60 *ICLQ* (2011) 459.

Part II of this chapter examines the challenges faced by refugee women seeking to 'fit' into the inherited categories of refugee law and questions the transformative potential of the expanding body of gender asylum law.

II. Gender Asylum Law: Providing Transformative Remedies?

Writing more than a decade ago, Deborah Anker pointed to the potential of expanding human rights standards to transform the practice of refugee law.[62] Grounding the interpretation of refugee law in a human rights paradigm, she argued, has the potential to internationalize refugee law practice. In the context of the evolving practice of gender asylum law, human rights activism on women's human rights, gender, and sexuality law has been crucial in securing recognition of gender-related persecution. Such recognition has been uneven, however. Landmark cases including *Shah and Islam*,[63] *HJ and HT*,[64] *Khawar*,[65] *Kasinga*,[66] and *Fornah*[67] have pushed the boundaries and extended the limits of refugee law. Empirical research suggests that positive decisions recognizing gender-related claims increased following these cases, at least in some jurisdictions.[68] The UNHCR has revised its gender guidelines, its guidelines on sexual orientation and on particular social group asylum claims, drawing on the practice of diverse jurisdictions to reassert the relevance and transformative potential of refugee law.[69] It continues to assert that gendered violations of human rights fall within the scope of the refugee definition and the protections of the 1951 Convention. As the 2002 UNHCR gender guidelines note, the analysis of sex and gender in the context of refugee law has been expanded through the practice of states, the case law of domestic courts, and academic literature.[70] This expansion has occurred in parallel to, and has been assisted by, developments in international human rights law and through the

[62] D. Anker, 'Refugee Law, Gender, and the Human Rights Paradigm', 15 *Harvard Human Rights Journal* (2002) 133.

[63] *Islam (A.P.) v. Secretary of State for the Home Department, Regina v. Immigration Appeal Tribunal and Another Ex Parte Shah (A.P.)* (Conjoined Appeals), [1999] 2 AC 629, [1999] 2 All ER 545.

[64] *HJ (Iran) v. Secretary of State for the Home Department (Rev 1)*, [2010] Imm AR 729, [2011] 1 AC 596, [2010] 3 WLR 386, [2010] UKSC 31.

[65] *Minister for Immigration & Multicultural Affairs v. Khawar* [2000] FCA 1130, per Lindgren J, para. 160.

[66] *In re Kasinga*, Interim Dec. 3278 (B.I.A. 1996).

[67] *SSHD v. K* and *Fornah v. SSHD*, [2006] UKHL 46, [2007] 1 AC 412, [2007] 1 All ER 671, [2006] 3 WLR 733.

[68] C. Dauvergne and J. Millbank, 'Forced Marriage as a Harm in Domestic and International Law' 73 *Modern Law Review* (2010) 57.

[69] See UNHCR, Guidelines on International Protection No. 2: 'Membership of a Particular Social Group' Within the Context of Art. 1A(2) of the 1951 Convention and/or its 1967 Protocol Relating to the Status of Refugees, UN Doc HCR/GIP/02/02, adopted 7 May 2002; UNHCR Guidance Note on Refugee Claims Relating to Sexual Orientation and Gender Identity, 21 November 2008; available at: <http://www.unhcr.org/refworld/docid/48abd5660.html>.

[70] Guidelines on International Protection No. 1: Gender-Related Persecution within the context of Art. 1A(2) of the 1951 Convention and/or its 1967 Protocol relating to the Status of Refugees, UN Doc HCR/GIP/02/01.

jurisprudence of the ad hoc international criminal tribunals and the Rome Statute of the International Criminal Court. It is UNHCR's position that the refugee definition, 'properly interpreted', includes gender-related claims and that further amendment is not necessary in order to recognize the gender dimension of persecution.[71] Yet, as the UNHCR Guidelines also note, women continue to face difficulty in bringing gender-related claims within the scope of refugee law.

A. Recognizing persecution: the continuing significance of public/private divides

Gender-related asylum claims unsettle the boundaries and categories of refugee law and other forms of complementary protection. Fitting into the institutional frameworks and policy agendas of refugee law is not easy. Fauziya Kasinga or Rodi Alvarado were not in the minds of the drafters of the 1951 Convention. The sexed subject of refugee law was the paradigmatic political dissident fleeing the imposition of restrictions on freedoms of assembly, expression, or religion. Persecution occurred in the public sphere and political activity was defined by engagement with the traditional structures of state authority. Although Eleanor Roosevelt commented that human rights begin in 'small places' close to home, international refugee law was not intended to capture those harms that occur in such small places at the hands of non-state actors. Expanding the boundaries of refugee law has required transforming ambiguous legal categories such as that of the particular social group, drawing on developments in international human rights law that have belatedly recognized the responsibility of states for systemic gender-related harms and demonstrating the relevance to refugee law of states' failures to protect against such harms.

In 2009, the Special Rapporteur on Violence against Women recognized that 'work remains to be done to establish gender as independent grounds for claiming asylum as a refugee'.[72] The Council of Europe Convention on Preventing and Combating Violence against Women and Domestic Violence requires parties to take the necessary legislative or other measures to ensure that gender-based violence against women may be recognized as a form of persecution within the meaning of the 1951 Convention and as a form of serious harm that may support a claim to subsidiary protection.[73] This provision builds on incremental developments within EU asylum law, which have included some recognition of gender-related persecution. The 2004 EU Qualification Directive provided that acts of persecution can, inter alia, take the form of acts of a gender-specific nature.[74] It also recognized that

[71] Guidelines on International Protection No. 1 (n 70) at 3, para. 6.

[72] Y. Ertürk, *15 years of the United Nations Special Rapporteur On Violence Against Women, Its Causes and Consequences* (2009).

[73] Council of Europe Convention on Preventing and Combating Violence against Women and Domestic Violence, Art. 60(1).

[74] European Council Directive 2004/83/EC, OJ 2004 L 304, 29 April 2004, on minimum standards for the qualification and status of third country nationals or stateless persons as refugees or as persons who otherwise need international protection and the content of the protection granted, Art. 9(2)(f).

non-state actors may constitute actors of persecution, where there is a failure of state protection. No further guidance on gender-related claims was given by the Directive, and so the practice of states has varied considerably. As is discussed later in this chapter, demonstrating a failure of state protection may be difficult, however. Where human rights violations occur in the private, domestic sphere, the evidence required to support an asylum claim may not be easily attained. The recast Qualification Directive does little to improve the gender dimension of asylum determination processes,[75] despite extensive advocacy campaigns from the European Women's Lobby, ILGA-Europe, and other NGOs,[76] and detailed recommendations on gender-related amendments from the LIBE Committee.[77] Inconsistencies in the interpretation and application of the Directive at domestic level are likely, therefore, to persist.

A recent study of asylum claims in Europe highlighted the difficulties that persist in securing recognition of gender-related harms as persecution. Combined with the problem of identifying the requisite nexus with a Convention ground, the problems faced in bringing gender claims within the scope of the refugee definition have meant that seeking subsidiary protection may be a more productive avenue to protection. The UNHCR gender guidelines note that female asylum applicants may face forms of persecution specific to their sex, including forms of sexual violence, dowry-related violence, female genital mutilation (FGM), domestic violence, and trafficking. At domestic level, such gender-related harms are not always recognized as persecution, however. In France, for example, asylum claims related to FGM are more likely to lead to a grant of subsidiary protection. Past experience of FGM may not always be recognized as persecution in and of itself, and future risks may be assessed differently depending on age or existence of other 'exotic' elements to the claim such as forced marriage. Similarly, domestic violence is often more likely to be defined as serious harm rather than as persecution for the purposes of a grant of asylum.[78] Fitting into the inherited categories of refugee law presents hurdles to gender-related claims that do not surface in the same way in the more porous concept of subsidiary protection.

As Edwards has noted, violence against women is 'exceptionalised' in international human rights law, as are the remedies for the harms caused.[79] Given the absence of explicit prohibitions of violence against women in core international human rights treaties, additional tests to identify the cause of the violent act are applied so as to trigger the application of sex discrimination or torture

[75] See Asylum Aid, *Gender-Related Asylum Claims in Europe* (2012).

[76] Asylum Aid (n 75) 40.

[77] Council of the European Union, Proposal for a Directive on minimum standards for the qualification and status of third country nationals or stateless persons as beneficiaries of international protection and the content of the protection granted (recast)—Examination of draft compromise text, 12337/1/11 REV 1; available at: <http://www.statewatch.org/news/2011/jul/eu-council-qualification-tcn-12337-rev1-11.pdf>.

[78] See, eg, in France CNDA, *BA*, no. 09 023 070, 17 November 2010, cited in Asylum Aid (n 75) at 46.

[79] A. Edwards, 'Violence against Women as Sex Discrimination: Judging the Jurisprudence of the United Nations Human Rights Treaty Bodies', 18 *Texas Journal of Women and the Law* (2008) 101.

prohibitions.[80] This step of building the cause of the act into the definition of the prohibited act is not one that is required in other areas of international human rights law.[81] It is a step that reflects the continuing reluctance to recognize violence against women as a human rights violation, in and of itself.[82] These additional hurdles that are found in the practice of human rights law recur in the everyday practice of refugee law. Although significant progress has been made in naming gender-related harms as persecutory, in practice, beyond the leading cases of selected jurisdictions, studies on gender asylum claims reveal continuing difficulties in securing a grant of asylum. The moment of crisis, of rupture, that continues to shape our understanding of human rights violations may not be present in a gender-based asylum claim. The 'continuum of violence' that often defines the experiences of refugee women does not fit easily in refugee law's tests for persecutory harms and failures of state protection. This continuum stretches from the 'gender violence of everyday life, through the structural violence of economic systems that sustain inequalities and the repressive policing of dictatorial regimes, to the armed conflict of open warfare'.[83] At the same time, while such a continuum may be part of the structure of a refugee woman's life, violence may also be experienced as a 'shattering experience of discontinuity',[84] regardless of the inequities of the everyday. Refugee law is not well equipped to capture the complexities of such experiences or the multi-dimensional nature of suffering endured.

B. Definitional problems and the requirements of 'fit'

Overcoming such exclusions and marginalization in the application of the refugee definition poses many hurdles. A gendered lens has long shaped both definitions of persecution and acknowledgment of the nexus with Convention grounds. Recognizing the links requires a questioning of the gender of refugee law concepts, and of the limits of accepted definitions of the political. Both the *Shah and Islam*[85] and the *Matter of R-A-*[86] cases highlight the difficulties of establishing a nexus with Convention grounds. In *Shah and Islam,* the claim of persecution on grounds of political opinion was dismissed as being 'unsustainable'[87] despite the Court's finding that discrimination against women in Pakistan was institutionalized in

80 See generally, C. A. MacKinnon, 'Equality Remade: Violence Against Women', in MacKinnon (n 19) at 105.

81 Edwards (n 79).

82 Edwards (n 79).

83 W. Giles and J. Hyndman, 'Introduction', in W. Giles and J. Hyndman (eds), *Sites of Violence: Gender and Conflict Zones* (2004) 3, at 19.

84 M. Walker, 'Gender and Violence in Focus: A Background for Gender Justice in Reparations', in R. Rubio-Marín (ed.), *The Gender of Reparations: Unsettling Sexual Hierarchies While Redressing Human Rights Violations* (2009) 29.

85 *Islam (A.P.) v. Secretary of State for the Home Department, Regina v. Immigration Appeal Tribunal and Another Ex Parte Shah (A.P.),* n 63.

86 *Matter of R-A-*, 22 I&N Dec. 906 (BIA 1999), vacated, 22 I&N Dec. 906 (A.G. 2001), remanded, 23 I&N Dec. 694 (A.G. 2005), remanded, 24 I&N Dec. 629 (A.G. 2008). See K. Musalso, 'Matter of R-A-: An Analysis of the Decision and its Implications', 76 *Interpreter Releases* (1999) 1177.

87 *Islam (A.P.) v. Secretary of State for the Home Department, Regina v. Immigration Appeal Tribunal and Another Ex Parte Shah (A.P.),* n 63, per Lord Steyn.

the law and practice of the state itself. This finding reveals again the difficulties of capturing women's human rights claims within the Convention's political opinion ground. Lord Hoffman acknowledged the threat of violence to the claimants from their husbands, but described this as 'a personal affair, directed against them as individuals'.[88] It was only through the additional recognition of the absence of state protection that 'the otherwise private violence' was defined as coming within the meaning of the 1951 Convention.

Having dismissed political opinion as a possible nexus, much of the debate before the House of Lords turned on how to define the particular social group. Ultimately, the court found by a majority (Lord Millet dissenting), that 'women of Pakistan' or 'women who had offended against social mores or against whom there were imputations of sexual misconduct', could form a particular social group within the meaning of the Convention.[89] A systematic failure of state protection was identified recognizing that the state's failure to meet its obligations of due diligence to prevent intimate violence can represent, in Macklin's words, 'an uncoordinated yet highly efficient matrix of inertia, consolidated at all loci of the criminal justice system'.[90]

Defining a particular social group was also to prove problematic in the *Matter of R-A-* proceedings. In that case, the Board of Immigration Appeals found that the respondent had not shown that 'Guatemalan women who have been involved intimately with Guatemalan male companions, who believe that women are to live under male domination' is a group that is recognized and understood to be a societal faction, or is otherwise a recognized segment of the population within Guatemala.[91] The size of the potential social group, and the concomitant consequences of rising numbers of asylum applicants was clearly to the fore in the Board's decision. As the UNHCR and others noted, however, other Convention grounds are not restricted in this way, and jurisprudential authorities did not support such a finding.[92] The UNHCR, in its advisory opinion on the case, had argued that Ms Alvarado could be identified as a member of a particular social group because of her sex, her marital status and her position in a society that condones discrimination against women.[93] Having sought the protection of the state and having complained of her abuse, she could be identified as a woman who had 'transgressed social mores' in a society where women were 'expected to accept their fate'. This view was not heeded, however.

[88] *Islam (A.P.) v. Secretary of State for the Home Department, Regina v. Immigration Appeal Tribunal and Another Ex Parte Shah (A.P.)*, n 63, per Lord Hoffman.

[89] *Islam (A.P.) v. Secretary of State for the Home Department, Regina v. Immigration Appeal Tribunal and Another Ex Parte Shah (A.P.)*, n 63 at 645, 655, 658–9.

[90] A. Macklin, 'Refugee Women and the Imperative of Categories', 17 *Human Rights Quarterly* (1995) 213, at 234.

[91] *In the Matter of R-A-*, n 86, at 918.

[92] See UNHCR, Re: Matter of Rodi Alvarado Peña (A73-753-922), Advisory Opinion on International Norms: Gender-Related Persecution and Relevance to 'Membership of a Particular Social Group' and 'Political Opinion', 9 January 2004, at 3; available at: <http://cgrs.uchastings.edu/campaigns/alvarado.php#advocacy>.

[93] UNHCR, Re: Matter of Rodi Alvarado Peña (n 92) at 9.

Difficulties were also encountered in identifying a nexus with the political opinion ground. In a majority decision, the Board found that Rodi Alvarado had not succeeded in establishing that the violence she had endured was the result of her political opinion, or imputed political opinion, as to her gender role and status as a spouse. As was noted in subsequent submissions on the case, and in the dissenting opinion, the Board's rejection of the political opinion ground seemed to contradict its own statements on the nature of the abuse suffered in the case, and the repeated links made by Ms Alvarado's spouse to her status and role as a woman.[94] The political context within which domestic violence occurs with impunity was highlighted by the dissent in the *R-A-* case.[95] It was precisely this context of domestic violence that was set aside by the majority opinion of the Board, however.

In the *Fornah* case,[96] the House of Lords addressed the applicability of the social group ground to gender asylum cases, this time in the context of female genital mutilation. Situating the case within the broader context of gender discrimination, Lord Bingham distinguished the particularity of the relevant group, either 'women of Sierra Leone' or 'intact or uninitiated women and girls who are in tribes in Sierra Leone which practise FGM'.[97] He concluded that the distinguishing feature of the group in this case was not the persecution complained of, but rather the 'position of social inferiority as compared with men'[98] within which women in Sierra Leone found themselves. As the *Fornah* case illustrates, the process of 'fitting' an asylum claim into the refugee definition may also bring with it the risk of essentializing the position of all women in a particular society. It is a risk that is particularly evident when women's claims are constrained within the parameters of the particular social group ground. The asylum adjudication process is sometimes criticized as positing a 'victim subject', denied of agency and defined by patriarchal forces of religion and culture,[99] with limited attention paid to the historical, socio-economic, and cultural specificities that shape experiences of gender discrimination, and that fragment the categories of gender and women. The categories of refugee law reinforce such tendencies. More nuanced presentations of gendered persecution risk falling victim to the all-encompassing requirements to demonstrate a failure of state protection, the absence of an internal protection alternative, or the requirement to identify a social group. And so 'women of Pakistan' or 'women of Sierra Leone' become a social group in the quest to make an asylum claim 'fit' with refugee law's categories.[100] As a result of these legal gymnastics, refugee women often find themselves in a

[94] See Harvard Immigration and Refugee Project, Brief of Amici Curiae in Support of Affirmance of Decision of the Immigration Judge in Re R-A- A73-753-922, at 42.

[95] *Matter of R-A*, n 86, at 925.

[96] *SSHD v. K* and *Fornah v. SSHD*, [2006] UKHL 46, [2007] 1 AC 412, [2007] 1 All ER 671, [2006] 3 WLR 733.

[97] *SSHD v. K* and *Fornah v. SSHD* (n 96) per Lord Bingham of Cornhill, [2006] UKHL 46, para. 31.

[98] *SSHD v. K* and *Fornah v. SSHD* (n 96), per Lord Bingham of Cornhill, [2006] UKHL 46, para. 31.

[99] R. Kapur, 'The Tragedy of Victimization Rhetoric: Resurrecting the "Native" Subject in International/Post-Colonial Feminist Legal Politics', 15 *Harvard Human Rights Journal* (2002) 1.

[100] See *Secretary of State for the Home Department v. ZH (Women as Particular Social Group) Iran*, CG [2003] UKIAT 00207, in which women in Iran were found not to constitute a social group.

double bind.[101] In presenting a claim for protection, it becomes necessary to position the asylum applicant as an abject victim, powerless in the face of the coercive powers of state or non-state actors. The gendered stereotypes of third-world women are thereby reinforced.[102]

The racial 'othering' of the asylum applicant raises further difficulties in securing recognition of the asylum claim, as presumptions concerning the extent of gendered harms in a country or region of origin reinforce the view that to recognize a claim for asylum would potentially open the floodgates to such claims.[103] Asylum adjudicators as 'internationalist gatekeepers' are keenly aware of migration control imperatives and not immune to the 'migration panics' that so frequently circulate in the global north. Against this background, despite the expansion of concepts of due diligence, persecution, and social groups, gender-related asylum claims continue to face procedural and substantive hurdles to making their arguments heard.

C. On persecutory harms and 'being discreet'

The recent decisions of the High Court of Australia and the UK Supreme Court in the *S395*[104]and *HJ and HT*[105] cases, rejecting the application of the discretion test to sexual-orientation asylum claims reveal how troubled the fixed categories of refugee law are by the appearance of gender and sexuality. The *HJ and HT* case involved two gay men, HJ, an Iranian national, and HT, a Cameroonian national. Both men, the Supreme Court noted, were 'practising homosexuals'. At issue was the test to be applied when considering an application for asylum based on sexual orientation and membership of a particular social group. As with other gender- and sexuality-related asylum claims, the difficulties highlighted in this case link directly to the ambiguities surrounding the particular social group ground, its 'catch-all' potential, and its ad hoc deployment to remedy the gaps in the 1951 Convention definition. The specific question before the Supreme Court was whether the so-called 'discretion test', stated by Maurice Kay LJ in *J v. Secretary of State for the Home Department*,[106] and applied in this case to the claims of HJ and HT, was correct. Specifically, the test required assessment of whether

> 'discretion' is something that the appellant can reasonably be expected to tolerate, not only in the context of random sexual activity but in relation to 'matters following from, and relevant to, sexual identity' in the wider sense.[107]

[101] See Macklin, n 90, at 263–4.

[102] See A. Sinha, 'Domestic Violence and U.S. Asylum Law: Eliminating the "Cultural Hook" for Claims Involving Gender-related Persecution', 76 *NYU Law Review* (2001) 1562.

[103] See Dauverne and Millbank (n 68).

[104] *Appellant S395/2002 v. Minister for Immigration & Multicultural Affairs (S395)* [2003] 216 CLR 473.

[105] *HJ (Iran) v. Secretary of State for the Home Department (Rev 1)* (n 64).

[106] [2007] Imm AR 73. [107] [2007] Imm AR 73, n 106, per Maurice Kay LJ, para. 11.

Rejecting the test applied by Maurice Kay LJ, Lord Hope described the term 'discretion' as 'euphemistic'. It failed, he said, to tell the whole truth of what was required by the test—not discretion but concealment.[108] Requiring such concealment, the Court found, established a form of 'secondary persecution'[109] in response to the primary persecution and failed to recognize the right of an applicant to live 'openly and freely'[110] as a gay man or a lesbian woman. Ultimately, the 'discretion test' was found by the Supreme Court to be 'wrong in principle, unworkable and inconsistent with Article 1(A)2 of the Convention'.[111] To require an asylum applicant to live 'discreetly' was, Lord Roger held, 'unacceptable'. It involved requiring the applicant to deny or hide 'precisely the innate characteristic which forms the basis of his claim for persecution'.[112] The Supreme Court distinguished between those individuals who choose to live discreetly to avoid 'social pressures' from those who were required to live discreetly because of the 'material fact' of a risk of persecutory harm.[113] Previous decisions applying the discretion test, including that of the Court of Appeal in this case, were found to be based on a misunderstanding of the Australian High Court's findings in *S395*.

S395 was a case before the Australian High Court, involving two gay men from Bangladesh, who claimed to be at serious risk of persecution because of their sexual orientation. Rejecting their applications for asylum, the Refugee Review Tribunal found that the men had lived together for four years at various places in Bangladesh and had not encountered anything more than minor problems. The shunning, gossip, and taunts that they had experienced from family members and neighbours were not viewed as constituting serious harm. The men had 'conducted themselves in a discreet manner', and there was no reason to believe that they would not do so again if returned home now.[114] The High Court found that the Refugee Review Tribunal, in rejecting the applicants' asylum claims, had erred in law by 'impliedly dividing homosexual men into two particular social groups—discreet and non-discreet homosexual men'. The Court also found that the Tribunal had erred by failing to consider whether a requirement of 'being discreet' in order to avoid serious harm, in itself, constituted persecution.[115]

In a series of cases involving persecution claims linked to sexual orientation, the courts had decided that the capacity of an asylum applicant to avoid persecutory harm was relevant to the assessment of risk being faced. This approach to risk assessment had been rejected in the context of asylum claims linked to political opinion.[116] It had persisted, however, in sexual-orientation-related claims,

[108] *HJ (Iran) v. Secretary of State for the Home Department (Rev 1)* (n 64).
[109] *HJ (Iran) v. Secretary of State for the Home Department (Rev 1)* (n 64) para. 75 per Lord Roger.
[110] *HJ (Iran) v. Secretary of State for the Home Department (Rev 1)* (n 64) para. 78 per Lord Roger.
[111] *HJ (Iran) v. Secretary of State for the Home Department (Rev 1)* (n 64) para. 81 per Lord Roger.
[112] *HJ (Iran) v. Secretary of State for the Home Department (Rev 1)* (n 64), per Lord Roger, at paras 75–76.
[113] *HJ (Iran) v. Secretary of State for the Home Department (Rev 1)* (n 64). paras 61–62.
[114] *Appellant S395/2002 v. Minister for Immigration & Multicultural Affairs (S395)*, n 104, para. 30 per McHugh and Kirby JJ.
[115] *Appellant S395/2002 v. Minister for Immigration & Multicultural Affairs (S395)*, n 104, para. 18.
[116] *Win v. Minister for Immigration and Multicultural Affairs* [2001] FCA 132.

suggesting a failure to recognize sexuality and sexual orientation as integral to human personhood. There is also a suggestion of 'burden-sharing' implicit in the imposition of the discretion test—that is, that the asylum applicant should take some responsibility for ensuring that she or he avoids persecution by 'being discreet'. By not 'being discreet', the implication here is that the asylum seeker may have provoked the persecutory harm complained of, and therefore bears some culpability. Choosing to reject this gendered line of reasoning, the Court concluded that the use of the terms 'discretion' and 'being discreet' may obscure more than they illuminate. A test requiring a gay or lesbian asylum seeker to 'take reasonable steps to avoid persecutory harm' was, they said, 'wrong in principle and should not be followed'.[117]

Already, the ripples of these decisions have been felt across many jurisdictions and in leading commentaries on refugee law. Hathaway and Pojboy, in a wide-ranging critique of the decisions, challenge the courts' failures to 'draw lines' to distinguish between integral and peripheral activities linked to gender identity, or between exogenous and endogenous harms.[118] Their critique, however, overlooks the difficulties in making such distinctions and, perhaps more seriously, ignores the very real risk of exogenous harms occurring regardless of an individual's way of life, activities, or the existence or otherwise of 'precipitating behaviour'. Control over such risks of persecution is rare. That it has taken so long for the discretion test to be finally rejected in sexual orientation asylum claims and that this rejection has led to such anxiety from leading refugee law scholars tells us much about the slow pace of reform in the practice of asylum law. It also highlights the many and varied hurdles that must be surmounted when seeking to add asylum claims 'in'. Hathaway and Pojboy criticize the judgments in these cases for what they describe as a 'fundamental distancing' from the framework of non-discrimination for analysing persecution, and an abandonment of the nexus requirement.[119] Distinguishing between identity and behaviour, between core and peripheral activities, is a process that is fraught with tensions, however, and allows multiple points at which the biases, misperceptions, and cross-cultural misunderstandings of asylum adjudicators are likely to close off persecution claims. As Millbank notes, the more marginal a group is, in legal or social terms, the more likely that what is experienced as core by members of that group, will be *deemed* marginal by adjudicators.[120]

Accepting that 'being discreet' could potentially avoid persecutory harms, and thereby resolve the state of its 'duty of hospitality' in the asylum context, allowed the status quo to go unchallenged. That the discretion test, or requirement of 'being discreet' could have persisted until very recently in asylum jurisprudence reveals just

117 *Appellant S395/2002 v. Minister for Immigration & Multicultural Affairs (S395)*, n 104, para. 50, per McHugh and Kirby JJ.

118 J. Hathaway and J. Pobjoy, 'Queer Cases Make Bad Law', 44 *NYU Journal of International Law & Politics* (2012) 315, at 388.

119 Hathaway and Pobjoy (n 118).

120 J. Millbank, 'The Right of Lesbians and Gay Men to Live Freely, Openly, and on Equal Terms Is Not Bad Law: A Reply to Hathaway and Pobjoy', 44 *NYU Journal of International Law & Politics* (2012) 497.

how slow the process of law reform can be, particularly when relying on adjudicative processes. In practice, the discretion test ensured that the promise of protection held out by asylum law did not typically apply to everyone, but rather to 'everyone the same'.[121] Unfamiliar claims, from gay men or lesbian women, who did not fit the refugee norm, faced many additional hurdles in securing recognition. This is what MacKinnon has called the equality of the Enlightenment, where recognition and survival depends on meeting the dominant standard and 'keeping your head low keeps you alive'.[122] The refusal to acknowledge that forced adherence to heteronormativity—in one's way of life and intimate relationships—may constitute persecution in itself, highlights the underlying gender of asylum law in practice.

D. The asylum process: the 'wrong' kind of victim?

Many of the challenges that are now faced by asylum applicants lie beneath the surface, less likely to raise the grand conceptual debates that for so long preoccupied asylum adjudicators. Instead, it is now the lower-level preoccupations with credibility, availability of state protection, and internal relocation alternatives that function as the primary gatekeepers in asylum adjudication. Procedural and evidentiary hurdles present significant barriers to gender asylum claims. The expanding use of accelerated determination procedures in particular raises further difficulties in accessing regular asylum processes. Refugee women face particular difficulties in establishing credibility, despite more than a decade of gender guidelines on international protection standards and procedures. As Munro has argued, improved practices within the criminal justice system relating to gender-related violence have not yet been transferred to asylum services or to the asylum adjudication process.[123] The disparities in practice as between criminal justice and the asylum system are evident, for example, in how late disclosure of domestic violence allegations is received.[124] In the asylum system, late disclosure can bring into question the reliability of the evidence submitted and the credibility of the applicant. Narrative inconsistencies, calm demeanour, or late disclosure of evidence are often viewed negatively in assessing the credibility of the asylum applicant.[125] Findings of lack of credibility persist, even in the face of reliable expert evidence.[126]

[121] See I. M. Young, 'Polity and Group Difference: A Critique of the Ideal of Universal Citizenship', in R. Beiner (ed.), *Theorizing Citizenship* (1995).

[122] MacKinnon (n 19) at 106.

[123] See Asylum Aid, *The rights of women seeking asylum: a charter/Explanatory notes* (2009); available at: <http://www.asylumaid.org.uk/pages/charterbackground.html>.

[124] See H. Baillot, S. Cowan, and V. Munro, 'Seen but Not Heard? Parallels and Dissonances in the Treatment of Rape Narratives across the Asylum and Criminal Justice Contexts', 36 *Journal of Law and Society* (2009) 195. Baillot et al. discuss a range of measures designed to facilitate and support disclosure of rape within the criminal justice process, at 207.

[125] *AS (Pakistan) v. Secretary of State for the Home Department* [2007] EWCA Civ 703, 21 June 2007, involving a domestic violence claim, in which it was found that inconsistencies in the applicant's testimony can lead to a finding of lack of credibility.

[126] See *VH (Malawi) v. Secretary of State for the Home Department* [2009] EWCA Civ 645, 2 July 2009.

Negative findings on credibility can lead to asylum claims being diverted through accelerated procedures, with reduced time limits and rights of appeal, an outcome that stands in marked contrast to the reforms that have been made in the operation of criminal justice systems in addressing crimes of gender-related violence. The opportunities for women to recount their own narratives, an important step in disclosing intimate harms, are seriously constrained by the limits and forms imposed by the asylum process and the constant return to the categories of refugee law. Assumptions as to appropriate victim behaviour may also hinder credibility assessments or a willingness to acknowledge the severity of the risk faced. Such assumptions can be particularly problematic in the context of intimate partner violence, where a woman's previous conduct in remaining within an abusive relationship or seeking to limit the sanctions imposed by law enforcement bodies may not fit well with the expectations of 'discontinuity' and rupture that attend asylum claims.[127]

Disclosure and reporting of gender-related harms, particularly sexual violence, requires a 'leap of faith' on the part of the asylum applicant. It requires a safe, non-judgmental environment, in which there is a possibility of trust and the potential of refuge.[128] Such trust can be difficult to secure in the asylum context, where adjudicators may be preoccupied with factual details concerning country of origin information, travel routes, or alternative protections sought by the applicant. Access to the regular asylum procedure will depend on overcoming initial checklists concerning routes of travel, documentation of identity and status, and 'fit' with complex legal categories. As transitional justice scholars have told us, responses to mass atrocities including sexual and other forms of intimate violence may include silence and repression of the trauma endured. The choice of silence may reflect an exercise of agency, not simply a failure to speak on the part of an abject victim. Such choices are not available, however, in the asylum context where the applicant's testimony may be the primary or only evidence of the harm endured. Given that gender-related persecution may touch deeply on the affective realm, the obstacles to disclosure and to consistent and coherent narratives are many.

III. Migrant Domestic Workers: The Significance of Place

Domestic work, the provision of caring work in the intimate, domestic sphere, is work that is predominantly undertaken by women and increasingly by women migrant workers.[129] The expected reduction in demand for paid domestic workers in Europe and elsewhere has not materialized, leading some to ask whether the

[127] Baillot et al. (n 124). [128] Baillot et al. (n 124) at 207.

[129] Art. 1 of the International Labour Organization (ILO) Domestic Workers Convention defines domestic work as 'work performed in or for a household or households' and a domestic worker as 'any person engaged in domestic work within an employment relationship', excluding those who perform domestic work 'only occasionally or sporadically and not on an occupational basis'. Art. 1, Convention Concerning Decent Work for Domestic Workers, International Labour Organization, adopted at the 100th session of the International Labour Conference, Geneva, 2011.

emergence of 'global care chains' should be assessed as a major defeat for the feminist movement or as 'unfinished business'.[130] Combined with the increased involvement of women in paid employment, the retreat from welfare state supports in Europe and elsewhere has produced care sectors of economies that are increasingly reliant on the outsourcing of intimate, reproductive labour.[131] Reproductive activities (that is, labour activities needed to sustain the productive labour force, including cleaning, care taking of the elderly, children, and other dependants) have become increasingly commodified,[132] resulting in the employment of paid domestic workers in many households.[133] A range of factors have contributed to the demand for domestic labour in the European context, including population ageing, changing household structures, increasing female participation in the labour market, difficulties in reconciling work and family responsibilities, and the availability of a flexible, low-cost, female (and mainly migrant) work force.[134]

Global capitalist relations between north and south are directly implicated in the inequalities and abuses experienced by migrant domestic workers. The structured inequalities built on these relations frequently mirror the relations between colonizer and the colonized, but are not limited either geographically or politically to these sets of relations. The abuse and enslavement of migrant domestic workers in the Arabian Gulf region, as well as in many parts of the global south, is evidence of the wider scope of such human rights abuses. As many parts of the global south have not developed welfare-state supports or have not been permitted to because of the conditions imposed by international financial institutions, reliance on paid domestic work continues as limited resources are made available to support the care of dependants.

For migrants the significance of place is always present. For migrant domestic workers, employed in domestic households, the significance of place is not only linked to the position of living in exile, it extends also to everyday questions of working conditions, security, and status. The significance of place, of the household as a realm within which different tests of justice (or none) apply, is not new. In the field of international law, it is an argument that has frequently delayed the expansion of human rights standards to the gendered domain of the private domestic sphere. The gendered divisions between the public and the private that continue to shape women's legal subjectivity are directly implicated in the precarious position of domestic workers. Exclusions and exemptions that operate in employment laws, in laws and policies on access to social security, in immigration and

[130] H. Lutz, 'Gender in the Migratory Process', 36 *Journal of Ethnic and Migration Studies* (2010) 1647, at 1652.

[131] Lutz (n 130) at 1654; B. Anderson, *Doing the Dirty Work? The Global Politics of Domestic Labour* (2000).

[132] S. Parrenas, 'Migrant Filipina Domestic Workers and the International Division of Reproductive Labour', 14 *Gender & Society* (2000) 560.

[133] H. Lutz, 'At your Service Madam! The Globalization of Domestic Service' 70 *Feminist Review* (2002) 89. See also M. Galotti, The *Gender Dimension of Domestic Work in Western Europe* (2009), in particular at 9–13.

[134] Galotti, (n 133), in particular at 9–13.

citizenship laws and in the scope of diplomatic immunity protections, reinforce the invisibility and constructed vulnerability of domestic workers. These exclusions take the form and shape of de-juridifications that seek to limit the application of transformative norms to domestic work.

A. Human rights standards: remedying the decent work deficit?

The 'decent work deficit' that has characterized domestic work includes low wages, volatile and unpredictable working hours, limited access to social security, and an ambiguous employment status.[135] More extreme types of exploitation and abuse to which domestic workers may be subjected include forced labour or trafficking. Migrant domestic workers, particularly those in an irregular situation, are particularly vulnerable to such risks. The UN Special Rapporteur on Contemporary Forms of Slavery, in her 2010 report to the Human Rights Council, identified a 'net of dependency factors' that prevent domestic workers from leaving situations of exploitation, many of which include constructed vulnerabilities linked to migration status.[136] The exploitation of migrant domestic workers is often presented by states as the action of an aberrant and abusive individual employer. The role played by migration law in creating the conditions within which such exploitation occurs and often goes unchecked, is not acknowledged. Not only does migration law reinforce the unequal power relations between migrant domestic workers and their employers, it also provides unscrupulous employers with mechanisms of control that they might not otherwise have.[137]

In the angst and anxieties played out in feminist commentary on domestic work and advocacy for decent work standards, questions remain as to whether domestic work can move beyond its legacies of slavery, exploitation, and abuse. Is the search for decent work standards misguided? Can law reform initiatives and expanding human rights norms produce transformative remedies? To some commentators the movement to establish decent work standards for domestic work is misguided, given the historical legacy of low status, low pay, and abuse. Legal reforms and standards may not fully account for the wider 'realm of indignities' experienced by domestic workers, or the dynamics of power played out on 'concrete historicized bodies' that are racialized, gendered, or classed.[138] Blackett and others, however, have argued that the notion of decent work, despite recognized limitations, continues to hold out potential to improve the lives of many domestic workers and

[135] M. Tomei, 'Decent Work for Domestic Workers: Reflections on Recent Approaches to Tackle Informality' 23 *Canadian Journal of Women & Law* (2011) 186, at 187. See also A. D'Souza, *Moving Towards Decent Work for Domestic Workers: An Overview of the ILO's Work* (2010), 19.

[136] Report of the Special Rapporteur on contemporary forms of slavery, including its causes and consequences, Gulnara Shahinia, UN Doc A/HRC/15/20, (18 January 2010), para. 47.

[137] B. Anderson, 'Migration, Immigration Controls and the Fashioning of Precarious Workers', 24 *Work, Employment & Society* (2010) 300, 312.

[138] A. Blackett, 'Introduction: Regulating Decent Work for Domestic Workers', 23 *Canadian Journal of Women & Law* (2011) 1, at 43, citing E. Gutiérrez-Rodriguez, *Migration, Domestic Work and Affect: A Decolonial Approach on Value and the Feminization of Labor* (2010) 6.

more generally to provide 'an important corrective to abstract articulations (and applications) of rights'.[139]

Human rights law has somewhat belatedly begun to address the structured inequalities and exclusions that structure the domain of domestic work. As in other areas of international law, it is primarily the moments of crisis—incidents of human trafficking, slavery, or forced labour—that have captured the attention of human rights law. The 'everyday' of workplace exploitation, exclusion from the protections of employment protections, social security, and precarious migration status, have attracted less attention. Recent standard-setting initiatives have attempted to address this gap and have included the adoption of the landmark 2011 ILO Convention Concerning Decent Work for Domestic Workers,[140] a General Recommendation from the UN Committee on the Elimination of All Forms of Discrimination Against Women (CEDAW) on Women Migrant Workers,[141] and a General Comment from the UN Committee on Migrant Workers and their Families on Migrant Domestic Workers.[142] Against the background of this 'justice cascade',[143] however, migration laws continue to limit the cosmopolitan promise of human rights law. Migration status adds yet another axis of discrimination and constructed vulnerability to the status of domestic workers as domestic work is increasingly carried out by migrant women. States remain reluctant, however, to recognize this role or to acknowledge the 'dissensus' that arises between 'border norms' and human rights law.[144]

B. The migration nexus

The UN Committee on Migrant Workers in its General Comment on migrant domestic workers outlines the specific role that immigration law plays in the production of vulnerability.[145] Overly restrictive immigration laws, the Committee notes, lead to higher numbers of migrant domestic workers who are undocumented or in an irregular situation, and thus particularly vulnerable to human rights

[139] Blackett (n 138) at 44, citing Blackett, 'Situated Reflections on International Labour Law, Capabilities, and Decent Work: The Case of Centre Maraîcher Eugène Guinois', (Hors-série) *Revue québécoise de droit international* (2007) 223, at 242.

[140] Convention Concerning Decent Work for Domestic Workers, International Labour Organization, adopted at the 100th session of the International Labour Conference, Geneva, 2011.

[141] Committee for the Elimination of All Forms of Discrimination Against Women, *General Recommendation No. 26 on Women Migrant Workers*, UN Doc CEDAW/C/2009/WP.1/R (2008), 5 December 2008.

[142] Committee on the Protection of the Rights of All Migrant Workers and Members of Their Families, *General Comment No. 1 on Migrant Domestic Workers*, UN Doc CMW/C/GC/1 (2011), 23 February 2011.

[143] This term is borrowed from K. Sikkink, *The Justice Cascade: How Human Rights Prosecutions Are Changing World Politics* (2011).

[144] Bosniak (n 4).

[145] Committee on the Protection of the Rights of All Migrant Workers and Members of Their Families, *General Comment No. 1 on Migrant Domestic Workers* (n 142) at paras 21, 22, and 27 in particular.

violations.[146] Similar vulnerabilities arise where migration laws tie a worker's migration status to the continued sponsorship of a particular employer, with the result that domestic workers may risk deportation if they leave an abusive employment relationship.[147] Migration status and immigration laws may also limit access to remedies and the effective exercise of human rights, including rights to family reunification. Where visa or work permit permissions impose limits on access to public funds, rights to education, healthcare, and housing remain illusory.[148] The difficulties that arise in accessing legal remedies, even where available, is specifically highlighted by the CEDAW Committee, which has noted that migrant domestic workers are 'scarcely ever out of sight of their employers' and so may face difficulties even registering with their embassies or filing complaints.[149] The role played by migration law in limiting access to rights protections is not of course unique to the sphere of domestic work.[150] The difficulties encountered by domestic workers are exacerbated, however, by their positioning at the intersections of many overlapping axes of discrimination and the constructed invisibility and isolation of their work.[151]

The obstacles to claiming rights are many, particularly for migrant domestic workers whose status may be tied to that of their employer, their presence within the territory of the state dependent on the goodwill of an unscrupulous employer, or perhaps irregular/illegal. The isolated and privatized nature of domestic work also limits the emergence of 'contact zones' within which alternative legalities may be presented. Migration laws create further barriers, given the absence of a firewall between the punitive and disciplinary functions of immigration controls and the operation of employment, social security, or wider human rights protections.

The links between limited opportunities for legal migration for domestic workers and the high level of irregularity in the sector have been emphasized by the EU Fundamental Rights Agency, among others.[152] Irregularity, as it notes, leads to high levels of insecurity, producing susceptibility to exploitation and difficulties in accessing rights protections.[153] The nexus between access to safe migration routes, obligations of due diligence, and compliance with human rights standards is rarely acknowledged by states, however. Neither are the wider policy challenges of opening borders and increasing migration opportunities. In response to concerns of abuse and exploitation of migrant domestic workers, it is open to states to

[146] Committee on the Protection of the Rights of All Migrant Workers and Members of Their Families, *General Comment No. 1 on Migrant Domestic Workers* (n 142) at para. 21.

[147] Committee on the Protection of the Rights of All Migrant Workers and Members of Their Families, *General Comment No. 1 on Migrant Domestic Workers* (n 142) at para. 21.

[148] See, generally, S. Spencer and J. Pobjoy, *The Relationship between Immigration Status and Rights in the UK: Exploring the Rationale* (2011).

[149] Committee for the Elimination of All Forms of Discrimination Against Women, *General Recommendation No. 26 on Women Migrant Workers* (n 141) at para. 21.

[150] Anderson (n 137) at 303.

[151] See written comments submitted by Interights to the European Court of Human Rights (pursuant to leave granted by the President of the Chamber in accordance with Rule 44§2 of the Rules of Court) in *Kawogo v. UK* (Appl. No. 56921/09) at para. 18.

[152] EU Fundamental Rights Agency, *Migrants in an irregular situation employed in domestic work: Fundamental rights challenges for the European Union and its Member States* (2011).

[153] EU Fundamental Rights Agency (n 152) at 19.

respond by expanding immigration controls. As Dauvergne notes, '[o]nce an argument is shifted to the terrain of rights, the right of the nation to shut its borders tends to overshadow the rights claims of individuals'.[154] The 'deportability' of the alien persists as a constant threat to the claiming and enjoyment of rights. Retreat to sovereign territorial prerogatives to justify the imposition of migration restrictions, is frequently accompanied by the normative reemergence of protective measures particularly concerning migrant women (often grouped together with children as a vulnerable group). The protective impulse is deployed by states to support the imposition of immigration restrictions. It does not typically extend, however, to challenging the continuum of exploitation that defines the everyday sphere of domestic work or the closing of migration pathways which, in turn, increases the *precarité* of migrant domestic workers.

C. Positive obligations, due diligence: expanding the scope of human rights protections

In *Siliadin v. France*, the European Court of Human Rights recognized that Article 4 ECHR could give rise to positive obligations for states.[155] The case, and particularly the proceedings at domestic level, highlight the difficulties that courts encounter in demarcating exploitative work in the domestic sphere. The applicant, a Togolese domestic worker, Siwa-Akofa Siliadin, complained that French criminal law 'did not afford her sufficient and effective protection against the "servitude" in which she had been held, or at the very least against the "forced and compulsory" labour which she had been required to perform'.[156] The Court concluded that Siliadin, who was fifteen years old when she was brought to France on a tourist visa, had been held in servitude within the meaning of Article 4 of the ECHR and that she had also been subjected to forced labour.[157]

A key question that had arisen in the *Siliadin* case in the domestic legal proceedings was the question of how to demarcate the boundaries of everyday intimate labour in the domestic sphere from working conditions that constituted treatment contrary to Article 4. In domestic legal proceedings, the French Civil Court of Appeal, in concluding that exploitation had taken place, was anxious to clarify that Siliadin was not a member of the family and was not treated as such. The public tests of rights compliance could, therefore, begin to be applied. In contrast (or perhaps not), the European Court of Human Rights found that Siliadin had not been subject to working conditions that were 'incompatible with human dignity', these conditions 'being the lot of many mothers'.[158] The presumption that the usual standards of human dignity could not apply served to distinguish domestic work as 'work like no other'.

[154] C. Dauvergne, *Making People Illegal: What Globalization Means for Migration and Law* (2008) 27.
[155] [2006] 43 EHRR 16. [156] [2006] 43 EHRR 16 at para. 3.
[157] [2006] 43 EHRR 16 at paras 121, 122, and 129. [158] [2006] 43 EHRR 16 at para. 44.

The isolation and belief that one's situation cannot be changed was identified as critical to the definition of servitude in *C.N. and V. v. France*, a case involving two sisters, originally from Burundi, who were living with relatives in Paris following the death of their parents in Burundi's bloody civil war.[159] The impugned legal framework remained the same as that addressed by the Court in *Siliadin* and the Court again found France to have failed to meet its positive obligations under Article 4. In *C.N. and V.*, both sisters were required to undertake extensive domestic work and the older sister, C.N., was also required to undertake care work for the disabled son of her relatives, including working at night. The Court found France to have violated its positive obligations under Article 4 with respect to the elder sister. The younger sister V. was allowed to attend school, developing social networks that were ultimately central to the Court's finding that no violation of the Convention had occurred with respect to her situation. The Court's reasoning in this case, as in *Osman*, shows limited evidence of engaging with the intersections of age, gender, and 'race' that are pertinent to the treatment endured by both girls in this case and that are particularly relevant to the issue of intra-familial abuses, including violations of Article 4.

Differing assessments of credibility and of the significance of the harms endured by migrant domestic workers can be seen in the case of *C.N. v. United Kingdom*.[160] The Court's judgment on the meaning of servitude is an important one. It recognizes 'domestic servitude' as a specific offence, distinct from trafficking and exploitation, 'which involves a complex set of dynamics, involving both overt and more subtle forms of coercion, to force compliance'.[161] Drawing on *Ranstev*, the Court noted that a duty to investigate was triggered wherever a 'credible suspicion' existed that rights protected by Article 4 had been violated. In this case, the Court was particularly critical of the failure to interview key actors, including a private recruitment agent. The case illustrates the challenges that face migrants in engaging with law enforcement bodies, and the role that assessments of credibility can play in limiting migrants' access to a legal remedy. Problems of establishing credibility arise, in particular, for migrant women who may find themselves in a double bind, their claims encountering the suspicions that frequently attach to gendered subjects of law on the one hand, and generalized hostilities towards irregular or temporary migrants, on the other hand.

The obligations of effective deterrence that arise from forced labour and trafficking prohibitions are enshrined in several international and regional instruments, including CEDAW,[162] the International Covenant on Civil and Political Rights,[163] the Palermo Protocol,[164] and the Council of Europe Convention on Action Against Trafficking.[165] The European Court of Human Rights has

159 (2012) ECHR, Appl. No. 67724/09, judgment of 11 October 2012.

160 (2012) ECHR, Appl. No. 4239/08, judgment 13 November 2012.

161 See (2012) ECHR (n 160) at para. 80.

162 See n 18.

163 International Covenant on Civil and Political Rights (1966), 999 UNTS 171.

164 Protocol to Prevent, Suppress and Punish Trafficking in Persons, Especially Women and Children, supplementing the United Nations Convention against Transnational Organized Crime (2000).

165 Council of Europe Convention on Action against Trafficking in Human Beings (2005), 197 CETS.

repeatedly recognized that a state's positive obligations under the Convention go beyond the imposition of criminal sanctions and include policing and operative measures. Such obligations have been recognized, in particular, in the context of domestic violence. Human rights law's engagement with domestic violence shares key features with its late arrival to the everyday exploitation experienced by domestic workers. In common is a reluctance to intervene in family relationships or 'family-like' relationships. It is moments of crisis only—most likely of extreme physical abuse—that are likely to trigger the application of human rights norms. Fitting states' positive obligations to prevent domestic violence into human rights law has been a slow and painful process, but one that has gained some momentum in recent times.

In *Opuz v. Turkey*, the European Court of Human Rights, for the first time in Strasbourg case law, linked states' obligations to combat domestic violence to Article 14 ECHR non-discrimination requirements.[166] The *Jessica Lenahan* case before the Inter-American Commission on Human Rights,[167] the *Campo Algondero* case[168] before the Inter-American Court of Human Rights, and others, similarly point to the non-discrimination nexus. Given that the majority of domestic workers are women and many are immigrants, a similar nexus between migration law, positive obligations, and non-discrimination norms arises. Making the discrimination claim, within the limits of current anti-discrimination law frameworks, is not an easy one, however, and faces many obstacles, particularly when the requirement to identify an appropriate comparator arises.

D. Intersectionality: 'race', gender, and migration status

As Crenshaw has noted, 'the intersections of racism and sexism ... cannot be captured wholly by looking at the race or gender dimensions separately'.[169] Addressing the intersections of both expands the possibilities of human rights law's potential to address discrimination. Migration status, however, is often excluded from the scope of race discrimination prohibitions and is frequently ignored in analyses of discrimination that adopt a 'nationally insular approach'.[170] Notably, the reluctance to extend non-discrimination norms to the migration context is evident even in the Migrant Workers Convention, which does not include migration status in the list of non-discrimination prohibitions. In the practice of UN human rights treaty bodies, including the Migrant Workers Committee, however, the significance of migration status as relevant to questions of racial and gender discrimination is increasingly probed, despite apparent textual

166 Appl. No. 33401/02, judgment of 9 June 2009.

167 *Jessica Lenahan (Gonzales) et al. v. United States*, IAComHR (2011), Case 12.826, Report No. 80/11, 21 July 2011.

168 *González et al. ('Cotton Field') v. Mexico*, IACtHR (2009) Series C, No. 205, Judgment of 16 November 2009.

169 K. Crenshaw, 'Mapping the Margins: Intersectionality, Identity Politics, and Violence Against Women of Color', 43 *Stanford Law Review* (1991) 1241, at 1241.

170 Bosniak (n 4) at 144, n 23.

exclusions from the treaty standards themselves.[171] As Bosniak notes, the category of immigration status is appearing with more frequency in various 'catalogues of subordination axes'.[172] In the ECHR context, the potential of Article 14 to address the intersections of gender and race discrimination remains to be realized. The gradual expansion of indirect discrimination prohibitions suggests possible strategies for such challenges.[173]

The Inter-American Court of Human Rights advisory opinion on *Undocumented Migrants*[174] highlights the potential—and the limits—of pursuing an equality/non-discrimination argument. The Court rejected the distinction between documented and undocumented workers as a legitimate one, for the purposes of justifying differential treatment. The difficulties of advancing this position can be seen, however, in the reluctance of states to ratify the UN Convention on the Rights of Migrant Workers and their Families. Particularly, migrant-receiving countries of the global north have signed and ratified the Convention in very small numbers. The Convention itself retains distinctions between the rights afforded to regular and irregular migrant workers, ultimately providing lesser safeguards than in general human rights treaties. Against this background of state resistance, progressing equality and non-discrimination arguments is challenging.

IV. Concluding Remarks

Given the normative basis of international human rights law, it is fitting that its application to non-citizens is now explicitly acknowledged. Arendt's categorization of citizenship as 'the right to have rights', if we presume a narrative of progress, would no longer seem to hold true as human rights bodies, from the CEDAW and CERD Committees to various UN special procedures, affirm the applicability of human rights standards to non-citizens. The inclusion of those who are strangers to the state in the panoply of human rights obligations disrupts the settled boundaries and imaginaries of state sovereignty, bringing to the fore the promised universalism of human rights norms and their transformative potential. As with any totalizing movement, however, there is always a remainder which is not addressed. Gender continues to play a significant role in determining who is included and who remains at the limits of such human rights protections. State laws, whether applying to the trafficked person's claims to be here and to remain, or assessing the validity of an asylum claim, impact upon gendered and sexed subjects of law. The precariousness of one's claim and migration status is shaped by many intersecting axes—of gender, sexuality, ethnicity, nationality, and socio-economic status. The transformation and expansion of human rights norms are belatedly addressing the limits of asylum

[171] Committee for the Elimination of All Forms of Racial Discrimination, *General Recommendation No. 30 on Discrimination against Non-Citizens*, 10 January 2004.

[172] Bosniak (n 4) at 11.

[173] *D.H. and Others v. the Czech Republic*, ECHR (2006) Appl. No. 57325/00, 7 February 2006.

[174] *Juridical Condition and Rights of Undocumented Migrants, Advisory Opinion OC-18 of September 17, 2003*, IACtHR (2003) Series A, No. 18.

and migration laws. Egregious human rights violations such as human trafficking, domestic violence, and sexual-orientation-related persecution, have until recently been unable to fit the structures and forms of inherited doctrines of human rights law. It is important to question why this is so and whether the process of adding in gender has been or can be a transformative one. As the earlier discussion on laws relating to human trafficking reveals, there are limits to the reform processes that have taken place to date.

Human rights advocates seek to mobilize law to prevent and to respond to the egregious human rights violations that occur in the context of human trafficking. It is important to reflect also, however, on the potential for law to be complicit in reinforcing gender inequalities and in limiting migrant women's agency. This potential is particularly relevant in the context of human trafficking measures, where the tendency to slide into protective measures is ever present and frequently works against the empowerment of trafficked women as full subjects of human rights law.[175] The concern to respond to women's apparent vulnerability continues to be a core motivating impulse in the anti-trafficking movement, both at national and international levels. The normative re-emergence of this protective impulse may limit the trafficked woman's agency and mobility and may also lend support to the creeping expansion of the criminal law and of immigration control agendas.

As in other areas of the law, the responses of states to egregious human rights violations remain preoccupied with prosecution and the expansion of criminal justice responses. Anti-trafficking policy and legislative reforms are replete with commitments to tackle the root causes of human trafficking. However, limited access to safe migration routes, a key factor in vulnerability to human trafficking, is rarely addressed in such reforms. States remain reluctant to acknowledge the link between precarious immigration status and vulnerability to human trafficking. Where it is acknowledged, it is more likely to provoke a protectionist response from states rather than an expansion of migration options. Access to secure immigration status would mitigate one of the significant causes of vulnerability of the trafficked person. That it would not resolve it completely 'speaks to the multiple sources of the disempowerment that generate the migrant woman's vulnerability, including sex, nationality, class and race/ethnicity'.[176]

Presuming, however, as I have argued, that the ideological capture of feminist agendas is not complete, the question that requires constant scrutiny is whether human rights norms are successfully pushing back, opening up possibilities for an emancipatory politics of gender equality in the context of migration. The potential for transformative steps can be seen in the *Rantsev* judgment, in the continuing push to recognize the rights claims of trafficked persons. States remain reluctant to remedy the fundamental irregularity of the trafficked person's presence; this expansion of the human rights remedies available would further challenge the links between sovereignty, territory, and presence. This reluctance is evident also in

[175] See D. Otto, 'Lost in Translation: Re-scripting the Sexed Subjects of International Human Rights Law', in A. Orford (ed.), *International Law and its Others* (2006) 318.

[176] See Macklin (n 36) at 495.

the expansion of gender asylum law. Yet, despite the continuing resistance of states, and despite the myriad hurdles that have to be overcome to fit the structures of asylum law, significant changes have occurred in practice. Transforming migration and asylum law requires more, however, than a process of 'adding in' or a gradual expansion of existing categories of law. It will require moving international and state law beyond a crisis governance response and shifting instead to a concern with everyday harms. Recognizing the migration nexus will also require acknowledging that remedying those harms entails acceptance of claims to be here and to remain.

[8]

Revisiting the Meaning of Marriage: Immigration for Same-Sex Spouses in a Post-*Windsor* World

*Scott Titshaw**

I. INTRODUCTION

As U.S. states and foreign nations began recognizing same-sex marriages over the last dozen years, the anti-gay definitions of "marriage" and "spouse" in Section 3 of the Defense of Marriage Act ("DOMA") rendered those marriages invisible for immigration purposes. Thousands of U.S. citizens were left with a cruel choice between country and family: Remain alone in the United States or start anew with spouses and stepchildren abroad.[1] Other couples did not qualify to emigrate *anywhere* together, leaving them no choice at all.[2] DOMA also devastated children. Not only might they be separated from one parent, but their own immigration or even

---

* Associate Professor at Mercer University School of Law. I thank Vickie Neilson for reviewing an early manuscript, and I thank everyone at Immigration Equality, past and present, for all the work they've done for binational same-sex couples and their children.

1. Scott Titshaw, *The Meaning of Marriage: Immigration Rules and Their Implications for Same-Sex Spouses in a World Without DOMA*, 16 WM. & MARY J. WOMEN & L. 537, 539–40 (2010).

2. Many countries restrict immigration to immediate family members of citizens, highly skilled workers, the well-heeled, and refugees from state persecution. Thus U.S. citizens, whose foreign spouses were not from countries recognizing lesbian and gay relationships do not all qualify to emigrate, even if they were willing to leave their homes and jobs.

citizenship status often hinged on definitions of terms like "stepchild" and "born in wedlock."[3]

When the Supreme Court struck down Section 3 of DOMA in *United States v. Windsor*,[4] it eliminated a categorical barrier to immigration for thousands of families. Yet *Windsor* was not an immigration case, and the Court's opinion did not address at least three resulting immigration questions: What if a same-sex couple legally marries in one jurisdiction but resides in a state that does not recognize the marriage? What if the couple is in a legally-recognized "civil union" or "registered partnership"? How about children born to spouses or registered partners in same-sex couples: will they be recognized as "born in wedlock" for immigration purposes?

The Obama administration appears to have answered the first question, concluding that same-sex spouses who celebrate their marriage in a jurisdiction where it is valid are married for immigration purposes, even if they reside in a state where it is not valid. In the context of immigration law, this uniform place-of-celebration rule rests on firm legal, precedential, and policy ground. As described below, the last two questions have not been resolved.

II. A UNIFORM PLACE-OF-CELEBRATION RULE

The terms "marriage" and "spouse" are scattered liberally throughout the Immigration and Nationality Act ("INA"), determining eligibility for everything from family-based immigrant visas to waivers of deportability and bars on admission.[5] In fact, the vast majority of U.S. immigration is based on such close family relationships.[6] This is no accident. Family unification has been the bedrock principle of U.S. immigration policy and law for a very long time.[7]

Because the stakes are so high, federal immigration authorities closely examine *individual* marriages, deeming them bona fide only if they were not entered for the purpose of obtaining immigration benefits.[8] However, the INA is largely silent about what *categories* of

3. *See* Scott Titshaw, *A Modest Proposal: to Deport the Children of Gay Citizens, & etc.: Immigration Law, the Defense of Marriage Act and the Children of Same-Sex Couples*, 25 Geo. Immigr. L.J. 407, 411, 415–20 (2011).

4. 133 S.Ct. 2675 (2013).

5. Titshaw, *supra* note 1, at 547–49.

6. *Id.* at 546–47.

7. Stephen H. Legomsky, *Rationing Family Values in Europe and America: An Immigration Tug of War Between States and Their Supra-National Associations*, 25 Geo. Immigr. L. J. 807, 808 (2011).

8. 8 U.S.C. §1186a. Same-sex spouses now must demonstrate these same *bona fides*.

marriage it will recognize for immigration purposes. Immigration authorities and judges have relied, therefore, on state and foreign family law to determine whether a disputed type of marriage or divorce is valid for immigration purposes.[9] The U.S. Supreme Court has recognized that such federal reliance on state family law is appropriate since "there is no federal law of domestic relationships, which is primarily a matter of state concern."[10] But *which* state law applies when married couples cross state lines?

In the case of same-sex marriage, President Obama has made his policy preference clear: "If you've been married in Massachusetts and you move someplace else, you're still married, and . . . under federal law you should be able to obtain the benefits of any lawfully married couple."[11] Although he also recognized that such a uniform place-of-celebration rule may not be legally possible in all federal contexts,[12] his Administration has now adopted that rule in the context of federal immigration law.

The Department of State has clearly announced: "If your marriage is valid in the jurisdiction (U.S. state or foreign country) where it took place, it is valid for immigration purposes."[13] U.S. consulates abroad will apply this place-of-celebration rule even for couples planning to reside in a state that will not recognize their marriage.[14]

The Justice Department's Board of Immigration Appeals ("BIA") has published an opinion recognizing the validity of a New Jersey couple's same-sex marriage, focusing solely on the law of Vermont where it was celebrated.[15] The Department of Homeland Security's U.S. Citizenship and Immigration Service ("USCIS") has also issued guidance recognizing this uniform place-of-celebration rule,[16] and two of the first same-sex marriage cases it approved involved Florida and Colorado couples married in New York and Iowa.

---

9. *See* Titshaw, *supra* note 1, at 564–79.

10. De Sylva v. Ballentine, 351 U.S. 570, 580 (1956) (focusing on state domestic law to determine whether a child was "legitimate" and, therefore, covered by the term "children" under federal copyright law).

11. Chris Johnson, *Obama Talks DOMA, gay rights in Africa,* WASH. BLADE, June 27, 2013, http://www.washingtonblade.com/2013/06/27/in-africa-obama-talks-doma-gay-rights/.

12. *Id.* ("But I'm speaking as a President, not a lawyer.").

13. *U.S. Visas for Same-Sex Spouses: FAQs for Post-Defense of Marriage Act,* http://travel.state.gov/visa/frvi/frvi_6036.html .

14. *Next Steps on DOMA – Guidance for Posts* (unclassified state 00112850) (Aug. 2013), http://travel.state.gov/pdf/Next_Steps_On_DOMA_Guidance_For_Posts_August_2013.pdf.

15. Matter of Zeleniak, 26 I&N Dec. 158 (BIA 2013).

16. In early August, USCIS replaced more ambiguous initial guidance with clearer language favoring a uniform place-of-celebration focus. *Implementation of the Supreme Court Ruling on the Defense of Marriage Act FAQ* (Aug. 2, 2013),

The uniform place-of-celebration rule for recognizing same-sex marriage comports with the expectations of both Democratic and Republican lawmakers who recently dodged an amendment to recognize same-sex partners under the Senate's comprehensive immigration reform bill by arguing that DOMA's judicial demise would eliminate immigration inequality for all married same-sex couples.[17] It is also consistent with well-established guidance on marriages involving transgender spouses under the INA.

Until *Windsor* struck down DOMA's federal rejection of same-sex marriages, transgender spouses were required to demonstrate that their unions qualified as valid different-sex marriages under state law. Both the Bush and Obama administrations have focused on the place of marriage celebration to make that determination, although some states of domicile would not recognize gender reassignment for marriage or other purposes.[18] The USCIS even allows fiancé(e) petitioners who indicate a specific intent to marry in a jurisdiction where the marriage would not be valid "the opportunity to submit . . . an affidavit attesting that the intended marriage will take place in a jurisdiction where" it will be valid for immigration purposes.[19]

There is some older authority refusing to recognize marriages of close relatives and biracial couples for immigration purposes due to strong public policy objections by the couples' state of domicile.[20] One scholar has suggested the old-fashioned concept of marital domicile on which these exceptions were based no longer fits an age of increased mobility and spousal equality.[21] In any event, the relevant published opinions are distinguishable from modern same-sex marriage cases since the exceptions they recognized were based on enforced state criminal statutes prohibiting cohabitation or evasion of state law.[22]

---

http://www.uscis.gov/portal/site/uscis/menuitem.eb1d4c2a3e5b9ac89243c6a7543f6d1a/?vgnextoid=2543215c310af310VgnVCM100000082ca60aRCRD&vgnextchannel=2543215c310af310VgnVCM100000082ca60aRCRD .

17. Ryan Lizza, *What the DOMA Decision Means for Immigration Reform,* The New Yorker, June 26, 2013, http://www.newyorker.com/online/blogs/newsdesk/2013/06/what-the-doma-decision-means-for-immigration-reform.html.

18. Matter of Lovo-Lara, 23 I & N Dec. 746 (BIA) (2005); USCIS Adjudicator's Field Manual § 21.3(a)(2)(J) [hereinafter *A.F.M.*].

19. *A.F.M., supra* note 18, at § 21.3(a)(2)(J).

20. Scott Titshaw, *supra* note 1, at 565–73 (2010); *See also e.g., A.F.M., supra* note 18, at §§ 21.3(a)(2)(C). Some valid state marriages would also be invalid for immigration purposes due to an express federal public policy objection such as the bar on admissibility of practicing polygamists, 8 U.S.C. §1182(a)(10)(A), as same-sex marriages were invalid under the federal policy of DOMA §3 before *Windsor*.

21. Kerry Abrams, *Marriage and Immigration – Which State's Law Applies?,* http://www.concurringopinions.com.

22. Titshaw, *supra* note 1, at 565–73.

Similar criminal treatment of same-sex cohabitation or out-of-state marriage would likely be invalid after *Lawrence v. Texas*.[23]

In addition to its consistency with precedent, a uniform place-of-celebration rule implements immigration law's bedrock principle of family unification. It would substantially undermine this principle if qualification for married couples to enter the United States and live together turned on the U.S. citizens' state of residence. Imagine a federal immigration system that only allowed a U.S. citizen to live with her foreign national wife and stepchild if she moved from Tennessee to a state that respects her marriage. Such hyper-federalism would result in a new, interstate version of the dilemma previously faced by same-sex, binational couples under DOMA: Tennesseans would have to choose between life alone in Tennessee or starting anew with their families in another state. This would undermine the freedom of interstate movement and the concept of national citizenship embodied in the Fourteenth Amendment for U.S. citizens with same-sex, foreign partners.

An immigration rule that conditions recognition of same-sex marriages on states of residence would also dramatically restrict interstate and international commerce, even in cases not involving U.S. citizens. Entrepreneurs and employers would have to consider the marriage law of worksite locations as a significant factor in determining where to locate or to base married lesbian and gay employees. (Of course, this issue would arise outside the immigration context as well, but other missing benefits would not directly prohibit married couples from living together in the same state.)

Although the majority opinion in *United States v. Windsor* included a great deal of language about Section 3 of DOMA undermining states' traditional authority over family law, federalism was not its ultimate rationale. In the end, Justice Kennedy found it "unnecessary to decide whether the federal intrusion on state power is a violation of the Constitution because it disrupts the federal balance" since DOMA presents discrimination of an unusual character and thereby "violates basic due process and equal protection principles" guaranteed by the Fifth Amendment.[24] On this point, the opinion echoed the refrains of equality, personhood and dignity in choice of intimate and familial relationships that featured prominently in Justice Kennedy's opinions in *Lawrence v. Texas* and *Romer v. Evans*.[25] These ideas also support a unified place-of-celebration rule for marriage validity. As Justice Scalia points out in dissent, *Windsor*

23. 539 U.S. 558 (2003) (holding Texas's homosexual sodomy law unconstitutional).

24. *Windsor*, 133 S.Ct. at 2692.

25. *Id.* at 2694--95.

also supports a constitutional requirement of full marriage equality for same-sex couples.[26] While the Court has not yet taken that step, it has made clear that government policies discriminating against same-sex couples raise serious constitutional issues. This is significant because the Court has held that ambiguities in an immigration statute should be interpreted so as to avoid " 'serious doubt' as to its constitutionality.' "[27] A uniform place-of-celebration rule would avoid such doubts.

III. *ADAMS V. HOWERTON* IS DEAD

In 1982, the Ninth Circuit decided *Adams v. Howerton*,[28] a fluke of a case, which has been cited repeatedly over the last thirty years, largely because of its flukishness. Decided fourteen years before DOMA was enacted and twenty years before any U.S. state actually recognized same-sex marriage, *Adams* discounted the state Attorney General's opinion that Colorado same-sex marriages were not valid in that state, and proceeded to hold that a U.S. citizen's "marriage" to another man would not qualify for immigration purposes even if it were valid.[29] Of course, that case was the last word on a hypothetical issue based on a premise (a valid same-sex marriage under state law), which would not exist for another two decades. Despite repeated attempts to resuscitate it, including a recent *New York Times* op-ed,[30] *Adams* is dead and should remain so.[31]

The reasoning of *Adams* was originally a three-legged stool, but now it has no leg left to stand on. The Ninth Circuit held that the Adams-Sullivan marriage could not be valid under federal immigration law for three reasons: (1) immigration statutes at the

26. *Windsor*, 133 S.Ct. at 2709—10 (Scalia, J., dissenting).

27. Zadvydas v. Davis, 533 U.S. 678, 689 (2001)(citing Crowell v. Benson, 285 U.S. 22 (1932)).

28. 673 F.2d 1036 (1982), *cert. denied* 102 S.Ct. 2393 (1982).

29. *Id.*

30. Aberto R. Gonzales & David N. Strange, *What the Court Didn't Say*, N.Y. TIMES, July 18, 2013, at A23.

31. In addition to its specific holding, a much-cited two-part general test of marriage validity described in *Adams* also seems to have been replaced by recognition of a more useful three-part test, even in the Ninth Circuit. *See* Agyeman v. INS, 296 F. 3d 871 n.2 (9th Cir. 2002) (looking at (1) legal validity; (2) bona fides; and (3) no public policy exception); *see also* Titshaw, *supra* note 1 at 550–53 (distilling the test employed by courts as (1) validity where celebrated; (2) state or federal categorical public policy exceptions; and (3) bona fides of the particular marriage in question). If immigration authorities extended the uniform place-of-celebration rule to all marriage contexts, only federal public policy exceptions would remain relevant. But there is still an argument that marriages recognized in *no* U.S. state (e.g., minors under the age of thirteen or polygamists) would not be valid under the INA, even without an express *federal* policy on point.) *See* Titshaw, *supra* note 1, at 570.

time barred admission into the United States of foreign "sexual deviants" such as homosexuals, expressing a clear federal policy incompatible with same-sex marriage; (2) the court was deferring to Immigration and Naturalization Service interpretation of the INA to reject such marriages; and (3) Congress did not intend to deviate from the "ordinary, contemporary, common" dictionary definition of "marriage" in order to benefit same-sex spouses.[32]

The first two rationales originally provided a valid basis for the decision in *Adams*. Yet they are no longer valid. The first rationale was superseded in 1990, when Congress repealed the "sexual deviant" ground of inadmissibility. The second rationale actually favors same-sex spouses now that immigration officials have begun recognizing their marriages.

The third rationale in *Adams* was always misguided, but that was difficult to see from a vantage point two decades away from actual state-sanctioned, same-sex marriage. At the time, the Court's unprecedented construction of a specifically anti-gay, federal definition of marriage (inferred from Congressional silence) coincided with the law in all fifty states. If one did not squint too hard, it appeared that *Adams* was merely following the customary practice of deference to state family law definitions. But the advent of state same-sex marriage two decades later cleared the fog. In a time when some, but not all states recognize same-sex marriage, Congressional silence more logically implies the intent to follow longstanding precedent and look to state family law.

Even if one employed the *Adams* court's approach of examining dictionary definitions of "marriage" to determine its meaning, one could find a new answer. Widespread movement toward marriage equality in the U.S. and other English speaking countries has altered the common meaning of "marriage" so that many dictionaries now expressly include same-sex couples within their definitions.[33]

In a world without *Adams* or DOMA, the Obama administration has appropriately clarified the spousal choice-of-law issue in favor of a uniform place-of-celebration rule, but it has not completely resolved the other two immigration questions posed in the second paragraph of this essay: How will civil unions or registered partnerships be treated? How about children born to spouses or registered partners in same-sex couples?

32. *Adams*, 673 F.2d at 1040.

33. *See e.g.*, MERRIAM-WEBSTER, http://www.merriam-webster.com/dictionary/marriage (Definition: (a) (1): the state of being united to a person of the opposite sex as husband or wife in a consensual and contractual relationship recognized by law (2): the state of being united to a person of the same sex in a relationship like that of a traditional marriage.).

IV. CHILDREN OF SAME-SEX SPOUSES AFTER *WINDSOR*

United States v. Windsor allows recognition of many parent-child relationships that were invisible under Section 3 of DOMA. Because the definition of "stepchild" in the INA expressly references the "marriage creating the relationship,"[34] lesbian and gay stepparents presumably did not count under DOMA. Now the State Department will recognize these stepparents for immigration purposes.[35] Children born to married same-sex parents should also be recognized as "born in wedlock" for immigration purposes.[36] However, the State Department has drawn the opposite conclusion with regard to U.S. citizenship transmission upon birth abroad.

Questions of immigration and citizenship are based on different titles of the INA with different definitions of "parent" and "child."[37] And the State Department takes an extremely limited view of parent-child relationships in the context of automatic citizenship upon birth abroad, requiring a genetic link between a child and her U.S. citizen parent.[38] As an increasing number of modern families use assisted reproductive technology to conceive children, this leads to absurd and harsh results. If a U.S. citizen and her Brazilian wife have a child abroad, the child's citizenship would depend entirely upon whose egg was fertilized, even if the U.S. citizen carries and gives birth to her wife's genetic child. This approach also applies to different-sex spouses: If a U.S. citizen wife gives birth abroad to a baby conceived *in vitro* using a donated egg and the sperm of her foreign national husband, that child is not a citizen. This can result in long delays, permanent family separation, and even stateless children.

The State Department's genetic fixation even extends to categorizing children whose "*genetic* parents were not married at the time of birth" as "born out of wedlock" for citizenship transmission purposes.[39] This includes children of different-sex married couples who use donated eggs or sperm. It includes *all* children born to same-sex spouses, even after *Windsor*.

34. 8 U.S.C. § 1101(b)(B).

35. *FAQs for Post-DOMA*, *supra* note 13.

36. *See* 8 U.S.C. § 1101(b)(A); Scott Titshaw, *Sorry Ma'am, Your Baby is an Alien: Outdated Immigration Rules and Assisted Reproductive Technology*, 12 FLA. COASTAL L. REV. 47, 118 (2010).

37. *Compare* 8 U.S.C. § 1101(b) (defining "child" and "parent" for purposes of immigration under INA Titles I and II) *with* 8 U.S.C. § 1101 (c)(1) (defining them for purposes of Title III).

38. *See* Titshaw, *supra* note 36, at 102–05; *see also* 7 FAM §§1131.4-1 and 1131.4-2 (focusing on the source of eggs and sperm to determine birth out of wedlock).

39. 7 Foreign Affairs Manual § 1445.5-7(a) (categorizing such children under 8 U.S.C. § 1409, which covers those "born out of wedlock") (emphasis added).

Only the strongest legal rationale would justify such discrimination against children of same-sex marriages now that those marriages provide immigration benefits to the parents. Yet, there is no such rationale.

The Ninth Circuit Court of Appeals has rejected the State Department's genetic essentialist approach to citizenship acquisition. It focuses instead on state or foreign family-law to determine whether a child was "born out of wedlock."[40] Children born "out of wedlock" fall under INA § 309, which expressly requires a "blood relationship" for citizenship transmission, while section INA §301 is silent on that issue. Reasoning that Congress meant this distinction, the court refused to require a "blood relationship" for citizenship transmission from a married U.S. citizen to a child born abroad to him and his wife, the child's biological mother. This textual analysis is based on well-established cannons of statutory construction. The State Department's approach, on the other hand, seems to stem from a literal translation of *jus sanguinis* (law of the blood),[41] a term derived not from the INA, but from sixth-century scholars who drafted the Justinian Code, a highly unlikely source for analyzing the results of *in vitro* fertilization.

The Ninth Circuit's approach also constitutes better policy. It avoids arbitrary and cruel distinctions, promotes the fundamental INA policy of family unification, and results in fewer stateless children. It is also more consistent with Supreme Court opinions in *Windsor* and other cases, which focus on state law to determine family statuses not expressly defined by federal statute.[42]

Unfortunately, since the State Department decides most cases of citizenship transmission upon birth abroad, its misguided approach continues to create arbitrary and unfair results. However, this approach is not required by statute, and the State Department is currently reconsidering it.[43] In the meantime, *Windsor* will allow many families to immigrate together to the United States based on stepparent-stepchild relationships while awaiting clarification of the citizenship issue.

40. *See* Solis-Espinoza v. Gonzales, 401 F.3d 1090 (9th Cir. 2005); Scales v. INS, 232 F.3d 1159 (9th Cir. 2000). These Ninth Circuit cases dealt with the children of old-fashioned non-marital sexual relationships, but the court expressly rejected the State Department's genetic relationship requirement for U.S. citizenship transmission to children born in wedlock, and its reasoning is even stronger in the context of planned pregnancies using assisted reproductive technology.

41. *See* 7 Foreign Affairs Manual § 1111(a)(2); *Id.* § 1131.1-1(a).

42. *See* United States v. Windsor, 133 S.Ct. 2675, 2690-93 (2013); Sylva v. Ballentine, 351 U.S. 570, 580 (1956).

43. *See* 7 Foreign Affairs Manual §1441.1(e) (added May 3, 2013) (indicating that State is reviewing its policy on reproductive technology and citizenship).

V. CIVIL UNIONS AND OTHER NON-MARITAL RELATIONSHIPS

The State Department has announced that it will not "at this time," consider civil unions or domestic partnerships as "marriages."[44] This may change upon further consideration since it already recognizes cohabitation as "the functional equivalent of marriage" for some purposes if "[l]ocal laws recognize such cohabitation as being fully equivalent in every respect to a traditional legal marriage."[45] Immigration officials might at least extend spousal recognition to legally registered couples in jurisdictions that define partners in civil unions as "spouses."[46]

The uniform place-of-celebration standard allows most couples to travel and marry elsewhere and then qualify for spousal immigration benefits even if they reside in non-recognition states.[47] Therefore, many couples in civil unions or domestic partnerships now need only marry to qualify.

Yet it is too late for some partners in legal, non-marital unions to marry. The widow of a U.S. citizen normally qualifies for permanent residence in the United States.[48] If a California domestic partner died before *Windsor* was decided, however, it is too late for marriage.[49] Perhaps immigration officials will recognize marriage-like civil unions in such compelling circumstances.

A child's "birth out of wedlock" and resulting immigration disadvantages may also be impossible to cure through a subsequent marriage. There is, however, a strong argument for treating children born into civil unions and other legal relationships carrying presumptions of parenthood as "born in wedlock" under the INA. The choice is binary, aimed solely at a "yes" or "no" answer regarding whether a parent-child relationship exists. The terms are not defined in the INA. Where state family law answers the question "yes," with all related legal rights and duties, federal recognition seems more appropriate than the alternative.[50]

---

44. *FAQs for Post-Defense of Marriage Act, supra* note 13.

45. 9 Foreign Affairs Manual §40.1 N1.2.

46. *See e.g.,* N.J. STAT. ANN. § 37: 1-33 (2013)(expressly defining the terms "spouse" and even "marriage" under state law to cover civil union relationships.).

47. Given the "public charge" basis for inadmissibility, 8 U.S.C. §1182(4), it is unlikely many otherwise-qualified couples will not be able to afford the trip.

48. *See* 8 U.S.C. 1151(b)(2)(A)(i).

49. The right to marry ends at death except in France, which allows posthumous marriage for some purposes. Kirsten Rabe Smolensky, *Rights of the Dead,* 37 HOFSTRA L. REV. 763, 780 (2009).

50. *See* Nancy D. Polikoff, *A Mother Should Not Have to Adopt Her Own Child: Parentage Laws for Children of Lesbian Couples in the Twenty-First Century,* 5 STAN. J. CIV. RTS. & CIV. LIBERTIES 201, 214 – 217, 257 n. 238 (2009) (describing current presumptions of parentage and

If the State Department someday recognizes children born to same-sex spouses for automatic citizenship purposes, the issue of birth "out of wedlock" could be determinative in that context as well. The binary statutory choice regarding automatic citizenship is between birth "out of wedlock" and everything else (rather than birth "in wedlock"), making the argument for recognition even stronger.[51]

Thanks to the Supreme Court, immigration authorities have been able to catch up with modern family-law and the reality of same-sex spouses. Now it is time for them to catch up with the realities of relationships between same- and different-sex parents and their children conceived through assisted reproductive technology.

---

problematic ambiguities regarding rebuttal as well as the District of Columbia law stating that "[a] child born to parents in a domestic partnership shall be treated for all legal purposes as a child born in wedlock.").

51. *See* Titshaw, *supra* note 3, at 483-84 (arguing for such recognition based on the textual distinction between the two alternative provisions for citizenship transmission upon birth abroad under 8 U.S.C. §§1401 and 1409).

[9]

Arendt's Children: Do Today's Migrant Children Have a Right to Have Rights?

Jacqueline Bhabha[*]

ABSTRACT

Large numbers of child migrants today—here referred to as "Arendt's children"—are functionally stateless, whether or not they have a legal nationality. The fundamental rights to protection, family life, education, and health care that these children have, in theory, under international law are unenforceable in practice. Moreover, their access to state entities willing and able to protect them is tenuous at best. This article surveys the obstacles to rights enforcement across a range of jurisdictions and contexts. It argues that, given their disenfranchised and precarious situation, these children have a stronger claim than has so far been acknowledged to effective advocacy and enforcement of their human rights within the states where they live.

> [I]t turned out that the moment human beings lacked their own government and had to fall back upon their minimum rights, no authority was left to protect them and no institution was willing to guarantee them . . . [What was] supposedly inalienable, proved to be unenforceable.[1]

* *Jacqueline Bhabha* is the Jeremiah Smith, Jr. Lecturer in Law at Harvard Law School. She is also a lecturer in public policy at the Harvard Kennedy School. She directs Harvard's University Committee on Human Rights Studies. The author of numerous articles on refugee protection, migration, and asylum, she is working on a book on child migrants. Prior to working in the academy, she was a practicing human rights lawyer in the United Kingdom.

I am grateful to Dr. Natalie Mooten and Trevor Bakker for superb research and editorial assistance. I am also grateful to commentators at a conference on human rights at CRASSH, Cambridge University, and at Duke University's seminar on asylum.

1. Hannah Arendt, The Origins of Totalitarianism 291–92, 293 (1966).

I. INTRODUCTION

With characteristic foresight, Hannah Arendt recognized the fundamental human rights challenge of our age: supposedly "inalienable" rights are unenforceable for individuals who "lack . . . their own government." To "lack one's own government" is a status neither precise nor transparent. At a minimum, though, it includes the situation captured by the definition of statelessness in international law: a person is stateless if "not considered as a national by any State under the operation of its law."[2] The international community has acknowledged Arendt's insight about the perils of this situation by enshrining and widely supporting three interrelated principles: the right to a nationality,[3] the right to a legal identity,[4] and the obligation to reduce child statelessness.[5] Yet, over half a century since Arendt wrote about the unenforceability of human rights, and despite the proliferation of human rights institutions, regional agreements, diasporic identities, and celebrations of global citizenship, child statelessness appears to be a growing problem.

In 2006, the United Nations High Commissioner for Refugees (UNHCR) announced that 5.8 million people were stateless.[6] Even though this figure is already more than double the number identified in any prior year, UNHCR emphasized that "the *real total* is believed to be nearer 15 million."[7] The disjuncture between the two figures is revealing. The first represents those who are technically stateless— people who do not have a nationality according to the international law definition cited above. But, those in the second group (nearly three times the size of the first according to UNHCR) also "lack their own government" in Arendt's sense: they are *de facto* or functionally stateless, unable to enforce rights that are supposedly inalienable. A peculiarly disenfranchised population that clearly illustrates this functional statelessness and its dire consequences is the subset of child migrants who lack their own

2. Convention Relating to the Status of Stateless Persons, *adopted* 28 Sep. 1954, art. 1(1), 360 U.N.T.S. 117 (*entered into force* 6 Jun. 1960).
3. Universal Declaration of Human Rights (UDHR), *adopted* 10 Dec. 1948, G.A. Res. 217A (III), U.N. GAOR, 3d Sess. (Resolutions, pt. 1), at 71, art. 15, U.N. Doc. A/810 (1948), *reprinted in* 43 Am. J. Int'l L. 127 (Supp. 1949).
4. International Covenant on Civil and Political Rights, *adopted* 16 Dec. 1966, G.A. Res. 2200 (XXI), U.N. GAOR, 21st Sess., Supp. No. 16, art. 16, U.N. Doc. A/6316 (1966), 999 U.N.T.S. 171 (*entered into force* 23 Mar. 1976).
5. Convention on the Rights of the Child (CRC), *adopted* 20 Nov. 1989, G.A. Res. 44/25, U.N. GAOR, 44th Sess., Supp. No. 49, arts. 6, 7, U.N. Doc. A/44/49 (1989) (*entered into force* 2 Sept. 1990), *reprinted in* 28 I.L.M. 1448 (1989).
6. U. N. High Comm'r for Refugees (UNHCR), Statistical Yearbook 2006: Trends in Displacement, Protection and Solutions 7 (Dec. 2007), *available at* http://www.unhcr.org/statistics/STATISTICS/478cda572.html (figures disaggregated for child statelessness are not available).
7. UNHCR, Protecting Refugees & the Role of UNHCR 2007–08, at 31 (Sept. 2007), *available at* http://www.unhcr.org/basics/BASICS/4034b6a34.pdf (emphasis added).

government. I will call this population Arendt's children. This article explores their ambiguous position between inalienable and unenforceable rights. It inquires what it means—to invoke Arendt again—to assert that these migrant children, like all children, have a right to have rights. First, it discusses what statelessness means for children today and how legal and functional statelessness impinge on their lives. It enquires into the rights that children are entitled to as a matter of law and contrasts this with the enforcement capabilities of states in practice. It also examines the effect of treaty ratification on rights realization and investigates particular areas of relevant policies such as age determination and information gathering. The discussion then turns to the consequences of rights denial, including detention and expulsion, and the efficacy of litigation as a rights enforcement strategy. Migrant children's access to economic and social rights, particularly education and health care, is reviewed. Finally, the article investigates what is required to reduce the functional statelessness of migrant children, concluding with a discussion of whether Arendt's children can be considered citizens and the consequences of their compromised status.

II. STATELESSNESS FOR CHILDREN TODAY

The above-cited definition of a stateless person in international law is straightforward. It divides the universe into two groups of people—those who are "considered nationals" by a state and those who are not. But the reality of child statelessness today is anything but straightforward. The unenforceability of fundamental rights related to nationality impinges on a heterogeneous group of children that includes undocumented immigrants, "irregular" migrants, and trafficking victims. By some accounts, the group also includes children whose birth is never registered and who therefore lack a legal identity or the ability to prove one—a group that encompasses approximately forty percent of annual births globally.[8] One can argue that it also includes some citizens,[9] who are at least functionally or potentially

8. The UNICEF Innocenti Research Center cites an estimate that 36 percent of all births are unregistered. Innocenti Research Ctr., UNICEF, Birth Registration and Armed Conflict 2 (2007), *available at* http://www.unicef-irc.org/publications/pdf/insight-br-eng.pdf. In some countries, the figures of unregistered births are even higher; in Bangladesh, for example, only 7–10 percent of children have their birth registered. Asian Dev. Bank, Legal Identity for Inclusive Development vii (Caroline Vandenabeele & Christine V. Lao eds., June 2007).
9. Others have also explored the statelessness of some groups of citizens. Audrey Macklin has an interesting discussion of the internally displaced person (IDP) as the embodiment of "the citizen without a state." Audrey Macklin, *Who is the Citizen's Other? Considering the Heft of Citizenship*, 8 Theoretical Inquiries in L. 333, 353 (2007).

stateless.[10] Many terms are used to describe members of this population, including "semi-citizens,"[11] liminal or "in between citizens,"[12] and "alien citizens."[13] The group is fluid and dynamic. Child migrants who begin their journeys or residences "statefully" (to coin a phrase) with regular visitor, asylum seeker, or student status, for example, can become irregular by overstaying or otherwise failing to comply with the restrictive requirements of their visas. By doing so, they may lose access to key state protections. Conversely, children who start their journeys as irregular migrants occasionally acquire lawful status through changes in domestic law (e.g., amnesty), in their personal situation (e.g., marriage), in their legal position (e.g., successful asylum application), or in their nationality through international treaties (e.g., the redrawing of state boundaries)—and thereby join the "state people" that Arendt described.[14]

III. WHO ARE ARENDT'S CHILDREN? THE DEFINITIONAL ISSUE

Despite their differences in legal status, location, gender, race, religion, nationality, and class, in my conception, Arendt's children all share three defining characteristics: they are minors;[15] they are, or they risk being, separated from their parents or customary guardians; and they do not in fact (regardless of whether they do in law) have a country to call their own because they are either noncitizens or children of noncitizens. Therefore, the group includes children in a variety of circumstances: migrant children who have traveled alone across borders, first-generation citizen children whose immigrant parents have been deported, citizen or migrant children living in so-called "mixed status" or "undocumented" families, and unregistered or stateless children living in the country of their birth with their immigrant parents.[16] However, it does not include stateless children living in their

10. What was true for the interwar and postwar periods described by Arendt is still true today: "the number of potentially stateless people is continually on the increase." Arendt, *supra* note 1, at 279.
11. A suggestive and helpful term which I explore below and owe to personal communications with Elena Rozzi.
12. Cecilia Menjivar, *Liminal Legality: Salvadoran and Guatemalan Immigrants' Lives in the United States*, 111 Am. J. Soc. 999 (2006); Karen Cebulko, Documented, Undocumented and Somewhere "In-Between": The Effects of Documentation Status on Children of Brazilian Immigrants (unpublished paper, on file with author).
13. Mae Ngai, Impossible Subjects: Illegal Aliens and the Making of Modern America 2 (2004).
14. Arendt, *supra* note 1, at 270.
15. I use the term "minor" interchangeably with the term "child," and follow the definition of a child in Article 1 of the 1989 UN Convention on the Rights of the Child: "a child means every human being below the age of eighteen years unless, under the law applicable to the child, majority is attained earlier." CRC, *supra* note 5, art. 1.
16. Laura van Waas, Is Permanent Illegality Inevitable? The Challenges to Ensuring Birth Registration and the Right to a Nationality for the Children of Irregular Migrants: Thailand and the Dominican Republic (2006), *cited in* Laura van Waas, *The Children of Stateless Migrants: A Stateless Generation?*, 25 Netherlands Q. Hum. Rts. 437 (2007).

country of origin with their parents, such as the tens of thousands of Russian children denied citizenship in Estonia and Latvia after independence from the Soviet Union[17] because there is no risk of separation from their families. Nor does the category include "left behind" children who receive remittances from parents who have migrated abroad for work. These children may be cared for by grandparents or other relatives, and will typically have access to all the state services available to children in the community. However, "left behind children" whose parents have fled as refugees and whose home communities are decimated certainly fall within the category of "Arendt's children"—lacking familial or effective state protection, they too have no country to call their own.

Therefore, although "Arendt's children" is a broad category that includes disparate populations, it is not synonymous with some common classifications of vulnerable migrant children. It includes children living in families; thus it is broader than the widely-used category "unaccompanied or separated children," which encompasses citizen, unauthorized, and stateless children.[18] The term is also more inclusive than the categories "child asylum seekers" or "child refugees." Because it requires children not to have a country they can call their own, it excludes unregistered children (those whose births have not been officially registered and who are thus not "seen" by the state) living with their families in their own home countries.[19]

When combined, each of the three characteristics that define Arendt's children brings with it the potential for some kind of rightlessness. First, children are disproportionately represented among the world's poor.[20] Second, children who are separated or unaccompanied face a far greater risk of abuse, exploitation, or neglect than their accompanied counterparts.[21] Finally, being functionally stateless, whether by virtue of "alienage" or familial noncitizen status, also brings with it economic, social, and psychological dangers.[22] For Arendt's children, burdened with this triple disadvantage, the

17. James R. Hughes, *"Exit" in Deeply Divided Societies: Regimes of Discrimination in Estonia and Latvia and the Potential for Russophone Migration*, 43 J. Common Market Stud. 739 (2005).
18. Or the European equivalents, *"minori stranieri non accompagnati"* in Italy, *"mineurs etrangers isolés"* in France, and *"menores o niños separados"* in Spain, for example.
19. Indeed, recent research shows that the fact of non-registration does not, per se, preclude access to certain key state services, such as vaccination and primary education. *See* Asian Dev. Bank, *supra* note 8, at 5–6.
20. UNICEF, Poverty Reduction Begins with Children 2, 41 (Mar. 2000), *available at* http://www.unicef.org/pub_poverty_reduction_en.pdf.
21. In the case of armed conflict, it is true that unaccompanied children are more likely to suffer harm than are accompanied children, according to UN reports. *See Impact of Armed Conflict on Children, Report of the Expert of the Secretary-General, Ms. Grac'a Machel*, U.N. GAOR, 51st Sess., Provisional Agenda Item 108, ¶¶ 67–69, U.N. Doc. A/51/306 (1996).
22. *Id.* UNICEF agreed with the report: "Of the millions of children displaced by war, unaccompanied children are at the greatest risk. They are the likeliest to lack the most basic

risk of some form of rightlessness is stark and the effect is marked, even in wealthy, industrialized, democratic states that generally celebrate children's rights to protection and autonomy.

Consider, for example, the 1.8 million unauthorized[23] children currently living in the United States.[24] They live with the daily threat of raids by the immigration authorities. Contact with state authorities in schools or hospitals may lead to unwanted inquiries into their status. Educational aspirations for college and university are forcibly truncated at the end of high school, irrespective of academic performance. They enjoy, at best, a partial or fractured citizenship; they may perceive their situation as living *between* rather than *within* states, despite the seamless division of the earth's territory into states—they can never fully belong where they are. The same is true of the thousands of Roma children living and working on the streets of Europe's capitals. Despite their EU citizenship, they are effectively disenfranchised, sometimes even confined to destitution in segregated "nomad camps." Sixty years after the signing of the 1948 Universal Declaration of Human Rights (UDHR), nearly twenty years after the near universal ratification of the 1989 UN Convention on the Rights of the Child (CRC), and several generations into what Louis Henkin has memorably called an "age of rights,"[25] these children's right to have rights is tenuous at best and frequently unenforceable in practice.

An inquiry into what their "right to have rights" consists of can be broken down into two more specific questions. First, to what social protections and services are these children entitled as a matter of public policy and law? Or, phrased differently, when do they have a right to have rights? Second, what does their social membership deliver to them in practice? What indicators do states use to define social membership, and what are the consequences of these choices? For states to act like states, they have to see and categorize like states.[26] In other words, they have to establish workable classifications among a diverse population. But historically, most states have overlooked or looked away from the needs of this group.

---

means of survival and to have their rights violated, the likeliest to be killed, tortured, raped, robbed and recruited as child soldiers." UNICEF, Information: Impact of Armed Conflict on Children, *available at* http://www.unicef.org/graca/alone.htm.

23. Many nouns and adjectives are used to describe individuals who lack a legal migration status: alien, immigrant, migrant, entrant, noncitizen, foreigner, illegal, unlawful, irregular, and undocumented. The term "unauthorized migrant" will be preferred here, where accurate ("undocumented" may not be, e.g., for those who overstay visas), over more value-laden alternatives.

24. Jeffrey S. Passel, The Size and Characteristics of the Unauthorized Migrant Population in the US: Estimates Based on the March 2005 Current Population Survey 8 (Mar. 2006), *available at* http://pewhispanic.org/files/reports/61.pdf.

25. Louis Henkin, The Age of Rights (1990).

26. James C. Scott, Seeing Like a State: How Certain Schemes to Improve the Human Condition Have Failed 76–83 (1998).

IV. DO ARENDT'S CHILDREN HAVE A RIGHT TO HAVE RIGHTS? POLITICAL PRONOUNCEMENTS

In the political domain, no consensus exists on whether Arendt's children have a right to have rights, even at the level of abstract entitlement. Progressive and official spokespersons may agree with the European Commission's statement that "children are vested with the full range of human rights" and that states are obliged to "[give] all children equal opportunities, regardless of their social background."[27] They may also agree with the famous 1982 US Supreme Court ruling in *Plyer v. Doe* that unauthorized migrant children were people "in any ordinary sense of the term" and therefore entitled to state-funded education.[28] Many commentators, however, have challenged this liberal assumption of social inclusiveness, arguing against automatic access to welfare benefits and basic public goods. According to a senior US immigration officer, unaccompanied child asylum seekers are "run-aways or throw-aways," petty criminals in the making.[29] Because of their harsh backgrounds and their different conceptions of the roles of adults and children, the argument goes, these young migrants are not like "our children," and there is no reason not to treat them like adults. Tom Tancredo, Republican Congressman from Colorado, echoes this perspective from a more instrumental standpoint: "Denying social services to them is something you have to do to stop the magnet effect that all of these combined things have, the health care, free schooling. This is all a magnet that draws people into this country and I'm trying to demagnetize it."[30] Some scholars have questioned the legitimacy of their social membership, which effectively challenges the rights claims advanced by citizen children born to unauthorized migrants. For example, Peter Schuck has argued:

> If mutual consent is the irreducible condition of membership in the American polity, questions arise about a practice that extends birthright citizenship to the native-born children of such illegal aliens. . . . [I]f the society has refused to consent to [the parents'] membership, it can hardly be said to have consented to that of their children who happen to be born while their parents are here in violation of American law.[31]

27. *Communication from the Commission: Towards an EU Strategy on the Rights of the Child*, ¶ 1.1, COM (2006) 0367 (4 July 2006).
28. Plyer v. Doe, 457 U.S. 202 (1982).
29. Jacqueline Bhabha, *Minors or Aliens? Inconsistent State Intervention and Separated Child Asylum-Seekers*, 3 Eur. J. Migration & L. 283, 295 (2001).
30. Brian Padden, *Health Care for Illegal Immigrants in USA Remains Point of Contention*, VOA News, 28 Apr. 2006.
31. Peter H. Schuck, Citizens, Strangers and In-Betweens: Essays on Immigration and Citizenship 212 (1998).

This perspective is not the preserve of US nativism. According to the premier of the Canary Islands, Adán Martín Menis, the Moroccan migrant children arriving alone on Spanish territory should not be protected, but rather treated like adults and detained or returned to their country of origin.[32]

Unlike judges, politicians, or scholars, state functionaries are not permitted to publicly declare their views, but their actions often speak louder than words, indicating that their beliefs mirror the opinions of some of the most rights-averse public spokespersons. Border patrol and immigration officials are perhaps the most notorious. Consider the behavior of UK immigration officers toward child migrants: in 2004, as many as 43 percent of those applying for asylum as unaccompanied or separated children had their cases "age disputed," and while authorities examined further age evidence, the applicants were denied additional child protections. Many of these children ended up in detention alongside adults in such harsh conditions that, on 26 January 2007, British Home Secretary John Reid admitted publicly that the government had been operating an unlawful policy towards child asylum seekers.[33] In this light, the European Commissioner for Human Rights was perhaps too generous when he said:

> [D]ecision-making politicians appear sometimes to be confused about how to treat migrant children. On the one hand, they state their full support of the idea that children do have rights and also recognize that our aging continent will need migration, not least young migrants. On the other hand a number of them appear not to be able to draw the *necessary conclusions* [about the rights of migrant children].[34]

Other public employees working away from the border evince similar attitudes and the same inability to draw "the necessary conclusions." Despite court rulings condemning French police violence against migrants,[35] brutality against migrant children persists. In the words of an unauthorized, homeless fifteen-year-old Romanian living on the streets of Paris, "It was eleven at night. Four police cars came after us. I did eighteen hours of detention. They don't touch your face, they beat you in the ribs, on the legs, the feet, everywhere."[36] Officials working outside immigration and law enforcement, including those in the welfare departments, also question the legitimacy of migrant children's basic rights claims. A recent study of asylum-seeking children in the United Kingdom produced the following case study:

---

32. Liz Fekete, They Are Children Too: A Study of Europe's Deportation Policies 14 (2007).
33. *Asylum Seekers Policy "Unlawful,"* BBC News, 26 Jan. 2007, *available at* http://news.bbc.co.uk/2/hi/uk_news/politics/6302919.stm.
34. Thomas Hammerberg, Comm'r for Human Rights, Council of Europe, Address at the Save the Children Sweden Conference (20 Mar. 2007) (emphasis added).
35. *See* Selmouni v. France, App. No. 25803/94, 29 Eur. H.R. Rep. 403 (1999) (emphasis added). Cases before the European Court of Human Rights are available at http://echr.coe.int/echr/en/hudoc.
36. Marine Vassort, Paroles d'Errance 13 (2006) (author's translation).

> "Y" was a 16-year-old boy from Chad. He claimed asylum on a Friday and the Asylum Screening Unit in Croydon told him that they did not believe that he was a child. It referred him to the Refugee Council's Children's Panel in Brixton. The Panel referred him on to the local social services department, who had closed their offices by the time he arrived there. He returned to the Refugee Council to discover that it too was closed. He spent the weekend living on the street.[37]

Access to basic shelter, subsistence level welfare payments, and in-kind benefits is as fundamental to modern conceptions of rights in general, and children's rights in particular, as is protection from physical violence. The same is true for access to such social and economic rights as education and health care, as the Committee on the Rights of the Child has frequently noted in its concluding observations on states parties' periodic reports.[38] Yet here too, public officials operate under personal codes of conduct that translate into dramatic rights denials. Sylvia da Lomba has remarked, "Curtailments of social rights for irregular migrants in host countries have become essential components of restrictive immigration policies. . . . The threat of destitution as a deterrent against irregular migration generates acute tensions within host states between immigration laws and human rights protections."[39] Consider this Spanish case:

> Sixteen-year-old 'Abd al Samad R. has been in Ceuta [an autonomous Spanish city located on the Moroccan coast] for about five years, including two and a half years living at the San Antonio Center. While at San Antonio he was diagnosed as suffering from renal disease, a potentially life-threatening medical

37. Jacqueline Bhabha & Nadine Finch, Seeking Asylum Alone: Unaccompanied and Separated Children and Refugee Protection in the U.K. 56 (Nov. 2006), *available at* http://www.ilpa.org.uk/seeking%20asylum%20alone.pdf.
38. In response to the Belgian report, the Committee commented: "The Committee is concerned at . . . the disparities in the enjoyment of economic and social rights, particularly health and education, experienced by . . . non-Belgian children, including unaccompanied minors." *Consideration of Reports Submitted by States Parties Under Article 44 of the Convention: Concluding Observations of the Committee on the Rights of the Child: Belgium*, U.N. ESCOR, Comm. on Rts. of the Child, 30th Sess., ¶ 18, U.N. Doc. CRC/C/15/Add.178 (2002). Regarding Denmark, "the Committee notes that all children who have had their asylum requests rejected but who remain in the country have had their rights to health care and education provided de facto but not de jure." *Consideration of Reports Submitted by States Parties Under Article 44 of the Convention: Concluding Observations of the Committee on the Rights of the Child: Denmark*, U.N. ESCOR, Comm. on Rts. of the Child, 8th Sess., ¶ 14, U.N. Doc. CRC/C/15/Add.33 (1995). Concerning Italy, the Committee criticized the state's "insufficient data in some areas covered by the Convention," and it expressed concern over "the disparities in the enjoyment of economic and social rights, particularly in the fields of health, social welfare, education and housing, experienced by . . . Roma Children, non-Italian children, including unaccompanied minors." *Consideration of Reports Submitted by States Parties Under Article 44 of the Convention: Concluding Observations of the Committee on the Rights of the Child: Italy*, U.N. ESCOR, Comm. on Rts. of the Child, 32d Sess., ¶¶ 16, 20, U.N. Doc. CRC/C/15/Add.198 (2003).
39. Sylvia da Lomba, *quoted in* Ryszard Cholewinski, Irregular Migrants: Access to Minimum Social Rights 17 (2005).

condition, and he received medical treatment. Then, in October 2001 he was told to leave San Antonio, apparently for disciplinary infractions. When we interviewed 'Abd al Samad on November 8, 2001, he was living with a group of other children and youth in makeshift hovels squeezed between a breakwater and piles of ceramic tiles and other building supplies. He had received no medical treatment since leaving San Antonio, although he was frequently in severe pain. "The pain comes often, when it is cold, or when someone hits me," he said. "I tried to go to the hospital when I was in pain but they wouldn't admit me. *They won't accept you at the hospital unless some one from San Antonio comes with you.* When the pain comes I can't move so who will come to take me to the hospital?"[40]

Without official confirmation of the child's social entitlements, he remained outside the categories established by the state—in effect not a person before the law. These exclusionary attitudes were translated directly into rightlessness. The acute risks to which this willful exclusion, combined with the fear of detection as an irregular migrant by state officials, can give rise were noted by the European Court of Human Rights in the case of *Siliadin v. France*. In this case, an unaccompanied child from Togo, "unlawfully present in [France] and in fear of arrest by the police . . . was . . . subjected to forced labour . . . [and] held in servitude," compelled to carry out housework and child care for fifteen hours a day without holidays.[41] The Court commented that the applicant "was entirely at [her employers'] mercy, since her papers had been confiscated . . . [S]he had no freedom of movement or free time. As she had not been sent to school . . . the applicant could not hope that her situation would improve."[42] Irregular migration status increases the risk of invisibility and thus gross rights violations. As the Court pointed out, states parties must recognize this serious risk and act "with greater firmness . . . in assessing the infringements of the fundamental values of democratic societies."[43] In other words, according to the Court, states have an obligation to "see"[44] Arendt's children—willful and selective blindness is not a legitimate option.

40. Human Rights Watch (HRW), Nowhere to Turn: State Abuses of Unaccompanied Migrant Children by Spain and Morocco (May 2002), *available at* http://www.hrw.org/reports/2002/spain-morocco/spnmorc0502.pdf (emphasis added).

41. Siliadin v. France, App. No. 73316/01, ¶¶ 118–21, 2005–VII Eur. Ct. H.R. 333 (2005).

42. *Id.* ¶¶ 126–28.

43. *Id.* ¶ 121.

44. James Scott discusses the tension between these two state approaches to categorizing the complexities of social reality by simplification and what he calls "seeing like a state," writing that "our ideas about citizenship, public-health programs, social security, transportation, communication, universal public education, and equality before the law are all powerfully influenced by state-created, high-modernist simplifications . . . [but] [w] hat has proved truly dangerous to us and to our environment . . . is the *combination* of universalist pretensions of epistemic knowledge and authoritarian social engineering." James C. Scott, Seeing Like a State: How Certain Schemes to Improve the Human Condition Have Failed 339–40 (1999).

V. DO ARENDT'S CHILDREN'S HAVE A RIGHT TO HAVE RIGHTS? THE LEGAL FRAMEWORK

If *public policy* approaches to the rights claims of Arendt's children differ, does *the law* offer a clearer answer? What does it mean for a rights claim to be asserted by or on behalf of Arendt's children? There are at least three correct, yet mutually contradictory, answers to the question: "Do Arendt's children have a right to have rights?" The first answer is an unqualified "yes"; the second, a resounding "no"; and the third, a cautious, even diffident "sometimes," "perhaps," or "it depends." Each answer finds support in the empirical record, though regrettably this is somewhat of an "evidence-free zone." The paucity of statistics and official data makes individual vignettes useful.

In a straightforward sense, Arendt's children have human rights: the normative framework of positive international human rights law encompasses all children. The UDHR, the founding document of modern international human rights, unequivocally states: "Everyone is entitled to all the rights and freedoms set forth in the Declaration, without distinction of any kind such as . . . social origin, . . . birth or other status."[45] Indeed, all thirty articles in the UDHR are age-neutral except Article 16, which articulates the right to marry and found a family. They are addressed to "everyone" (e.g., "Everyone has the right to life, liberty and security of person.")[46] or "no one" (e.g., "No one shall be subjected to torture or to cruel, inhuman or degrading treatment or punishment.").[47] They contain no minimum age requirement, no developmental maturity criterion, no citizenship, or even "legality" requirement. Undocumented and noncitizen children seem to fall clearly within the scope of universal protection.

Apart from a single reference in the UDHR to children's special needs for protection within the article proclaiming the right to health,[48] there is no acknowledgment of children's distinctive status. The approach of the UDHR is to mandate nondiscrimination, rather than to directly promote substantive equality. Because of this approach, as with women's rights, civil society pressure to promote children's rights led to the formulation of a subject-specific convention. If the drafting of the UDHR signaled a general, though implicit, acknowledgment that children's rights were human rights, because all children are part of the "human family," then the CRC expanded the normative perspective to promote awareness of children's agency and individuality. If

45. UDHR, *supra* note 3, art. 2.
46. *Id.* art. 3.
47. *Id.* art. 5.
48. "Motherhood and childhood are entitled to special care and assistance. All children, whether born in or out of wedlock, shall enjoy the same social protection." *Id.* art. 25(2).

the UDHR laid the foundation for acceptance of Arendt's children's human rights vis-à-vis the state, then the CRC, albeit cautiously, added the platform for these children to assert their human rights vis-à-vis their families,[49] their teachers,[50] and their communities.[51]

Formally, this exercise in international norm-building and standard-setting resulted in spectacular success, proving that even detailed and expansive articulations of children's rights were acceptable across continents, cultures, and religions. Indeed, as the Child Rights Information Network website proudly proclaims:

> Since its adoption in 1989 after more than 60 years of advocacy, the United Nations Convention on the Rights of the Child has been ratified more quickly and by more governments (all except Somalia and the US) than any other human rights instrument. This Convention is also the only international human rights treaty that expressly gives non-governmental organisations (NGOs) a role in monitoring its implementation (under Article 45a). The basic premise of the Convention is that children (all human beings below the age of 18) are born with fundamental freedoms and the inherent rights of all human beings.[52]

Even those who criticize aspects of the twentieth century children's rights movement, particularly as a dispute resolution framework, concede that this rights-based approach provides a crucial baseline for relations between children and states.[53] International moves have been followed by regional adoption of similar principles, most vigorously in Europe, where children's rights are not only recognized in the European Charter of Fundamental Rights,[54] but also identified by the European Commission as one of its main strategic objectives between 2005 and 2009.[55]

This discussion shows that, formally, there could be no clearer affirmative answer to the question posed above. A central feature of positive international human rights law is children's rights, including those of Arendt's children. This leads to other aspects of the international human rights machinery: regular reports by states parties to the Committee on the Rights of the Child (the

49. For an example of the careful balancing act between children's and parental rights engaged in by the CRC, see CRC, *supra* note 5, art. 14(1), (2). Not only are states parties required to respect the child's freedom of thought, conscience, and religion, but also the rights and duties of parents to provide direction to the child.
50. "States Parties shall take all appropriate measures to ensure that school discipline is administered in a manner consistent with the child's human dignity." *Id.* art. 28(2).
51. "States Parties shall take all effective and appropriate measures with a view to abolishing traditional practices prejudicial to the health of children." *Id.* art. 24(3).
52. Child Rights Information Network, Convention on the Rights of the Child, *available at* http://www.crin.org/resources/treaties/CRC.asp?catName=International+Treaties&flag=legal&ID=6.
53. *See* Martin Guggenheim, What's Wrong with Children's Rights xi (2006).
54. Charter of Fundamental Rights of the European Union, art. 24, 2000 O.J. (C 364) 1.
55. *Communication from the Commission, supra* note 27.

treaty body overseeing the CRC); investigations of child-specific human rights violations by UN special rapporteurs, other internationally appointed experts, and domestic human rights institutions; recitation of children's international legal rights in both domestic and international migration and social welfare policy; the preparation of general comments on detailed aspects of Arendt's children's rights by the CRC Committee;[56] and the opportunity to challenge state practices affecting Arendt's children through litigation.[57]

But the fact of near universal and speedy ratification of the CRC does not, in and of itself, prove that Arendt's children's rights are enforced as effectively as general, adult human rights set out in less universally ratified treaties, or that children enjoy greater protection of their human rights after the CRC's ratification than before. For one thing, there is a major gap in the near universal ratification of the Convention: despite having signed the CRC, the United States has not ratified it, so it has a limited obligation to bring its domestic law into conformity. This rightlessness in law reveals itself in practice:

> "You are a nobody in society," commented an undocumented Brazilian youth in Boston to a researcher; another respondent confirmed this: "You are already a minority, and already treated differently. Imagine people finding out you were an illegal minority? None of my friends ever knew. I probably wouldn't have had the ones I had if they had known."[58]

Even in states that have ratified the CRC, the situation is less than encouraging. Several states have entered broad reservations that exonerate them from applying many of the articles to noncitizen children.[59] Moreover, if the gap between theory and practice, between the normative framework and concrete enforcement, is notorious in law as a whole, then it is particularly egregious within the human rights field. For children who generally depend on intermediaries to secure their rights and who may lack the skills and political status necessary to protest rights violations, the problem of implementation is heightened. The UN Special Rapporteur on the human rights of migrants has complained that

---

56. *See General Comment No. 3: HIV/AIDS and the Rights of the Children*, U.N. ESCOR, Comm. on the Rts. of the Child, 32d Sess., U.N. Doc. CRC/GC/2003/3 (2003); *General Comment No. 4: Adolescent Health and Development in the Context of the Convention on the Rights of the Child*, U.N. ESCOR, Comm. on the Rts. of the Child, 33d. Sess., U.N. Doc. CRC/GC/2003/4 (2003).
57. Nsona v. Netherlands, App. No. 23366/94, 1996–V Eur. Ct. H.R. 1979; Mayeka v. Belgium, App. No. 13178/03, 2006–XI Eur. Ct. H.R.
58. Cebulko, *supra* note 12, at 11–12.
59. Examples include Brunei Darussalam, Djibouti, and Liechtenstein (reservation to Article 7); and Switzerland (reservation to Articles 7 and 10). U.N. High Comm'r for Human Rights, Declarations and Reservations, Convention on the Rights of the Child, *available at* http://www.unhchr.ch/html/menu3/b/treaty15_asp.htm.

> accompanied and unaccompanied children are often detained in punitive conditions, deprived of the care, protection and rights to which they are entitled under the Convention on the Rights of the Child and other international human rights norms, including the right to education, physical and mental health, privacy, information, and rest and leisure, among others.[60]

A recent case illustrates the huge gap between rights guarantees and deliverables in practice. It highlights a critical, child-specific issue—the indispensability of adult intermediaries as conduits to children's rights—and the vacuum between international law mandates and domestic realization of effective access to such rights mediators.

> Amnesty International has spoken to "John" who arrived in Italy as an unaccompanied minor fleeing a life as a child soldier . . . After arriving on Lampedusa, he was taken to a detention centre and ordered to get undressed for a body check. He told them that he was only 16 years old, yet he was detained at the Lampedusa centre for 2 days where he slept in a room with 6 adult men. He was later transferred to another centre in southern Italy where he had to share a room with 12 adults for a month. "John" eventually found accommodation in a reception centre for minors. However, 5 months after his arrival in Italy, a guardian had still not been appointed to represent him.[61]

This situation is not a small oversight. It is a pervasive institutional fact, the subject of general comments by the Committee on the Rights of the Child, of complaints and testimony before the US Congress, and of numerous advocacy reports and briefs. The absence of guardianship and representation neutralizes a child's claim to special treatment and obliterates social acknowledgment of his or her rights, including child asylum seekers' claims to international protection as a refugee. In other words, the absence of a person who acts "*in loco parentis*" and of an advocate who is charged with unlocking the protective promises contained in statutes essentially fixes Arendt's children in their radical otherness. It guarantees functional statelessness across key dimensions of social and economic need. It also undermines the holistic scope of rights claims by reducing the ability of a class of rights bearers to exercise their formal entitlements. Indeed this radical otherness, this deracination from the "normal" structures of a society, can even threaten one's basic claim to human dignity, and return one to the "nakedness of being human," a nakedness no longer abstract but frighteningly concrete. The world is sadly familiar with this scenario: in the refugee

60. *Specific Groups and Individuals: Migrant Workers, Report of the Special Rapporteur Ms. Gabriela Rodríguez Pizarro*, U.N. ESCOR, Comm'n on Hum. Rts., 58th Sess., Provisional Agenda Item 14(a), ¶ 47, U.N. Doc. E/CN.4/2003/85 (2002).

61. Amnesty Int'l, Invisible Children: The Human Rights of Migrant and Asylum-Seeking Minors Detained upon Arrival at the Maritime Border in Italy (Feb. 2006), *available at* http://web.amnesty.org/library/index/engEUR30001 2006.

camps in Chad, the internally-displaced person camps in Darfur, the HIV/AIDS orphanages in Ethiopia. But in the heart of Europe? In the middle of London? Global mobility and desperation are removing the comfortable distance of geographical separation and importing the challenge of translating children's rights into human rights onto our doorsteps.[62] Paraphrasing Arendt, one might want to argue that the "heart of darkness" representing Europe's imperial plunder of Africa has now struck home, revealing the brutal hand of the imperial state toward noncitizens within its own borders.[63] The following is the experience of a young girl, interviewed in 2005, who found herself alone and unaccompanied in the United Kingdom.

> L was a female asylum seeker from Guinea who fled after being imprisoned and tortured with her mother and brother on account of her father's political activities. The Asylum Screening Unit disputed her age and her local authority told her that it would not support her until she obtained medical confirmation of her age and the Immigration and Nationality Directorate accepted that she was a minor. She commented, "Social services treated me like a dog . . . because the Home Office said I was not under 18. They just told me to go away. I was so sad. *They need to treat people as humans* and give them food and shelter.[64]

L is one of an estimated 100,000 separated children living in Europe,[65] all facing daily hardships in the struggle to survive.

Unaccompanied children are not the only ones who have experienced this radical rightlessness. Arendt's children living with their parents also routinely experience serious infringements of the fundamental protections established by international standards. Some of these infringements arise out of brutal or mindless deportation policies. Consider the following case: in 2002, the European Court of Human Rights promoted a friendly settlement between Italy and a gypsy family of unknown nationality, which included a child with Down Syndrome who had recently undergone heart surgery. The family was rounded up at gunpoint in the middle of the night from a travelers' camp near Rome because they lacked residence permits, and they were deported to Sarajevo. Eventually, in response to allegations of inhuman treatment, Italy revoked the deportation orders and, on humanitarian grounds, allowed the family to remain in the country and the child to benefit from

---

62. Recall Arendt's reflection on an identical problem in a different historical moment:

> The full implication of this identification of the rights of man with the rights of peoples in the European nation-state system came to light only when a growing number of people and peoples suddenly appeared whose elementary rights were as little safeguarded by the ordinary functioning of nation-states in the middle of Europe as they would have been in the heart of Africa.

Arendt, *supra* note 1, at 291.

63. Seyla Benhabib, The Rights of Others 52 (2004).
64. Bhabha & Finch, *supra* note 37, at 60 (emphasis added).
65. Terry Smith, Separated Children in Europe Programme, Separated Children in Europe: Policies and Practices in European Union Member States: a Comparative Analysis 5 (2003).

Italian medical care.[66] Six years later, the Court is dealing with a similar case in the United Kingdom: a three-year-old child with a serious kidney disorder, who was born in the United States but "has lived almost her entire life in London" with her asylum seeker mother, was issued deportation papers to the United States, even though she has no relatives there.[67]

Other infringements, conversely, are caused by detention policies that fail to take into account the needs of young children. For example, the Human Rights Committee, the treaty body overseeing implementation of the International Covenant on Civil and Political Rights, has ruled against past Australian practice in this area, criticizing the prolonged detention of families because of severe consequences for the health of detained children. In the *Bakhtiyari* case, for example, the Committee observed that the "children have suffered demonstrable, documented and on-going adverse effects of detention" and ordered the release of the mother and the children and payment of compensation to the family.[68] A UK case involving the detention of a single-parent family consisting of a mother and two children, aged five and two, led to serious health consequences for both children, resulting in serious weight loss and eventual hospitalization of the two-year-old.[69]

The right to rights has frayed at the margins. Was Arendt's deep pessimism about the international system an accurate and sober reflection on the inevitable primacy of the nation-state? Or, to quote Seyla Benhabib, can one find a way out from the conclusion that Arendt's "moral cosmopolitanism founders on [her] legal and civic particularism,"[70] a conclusion that seems to undercut the whole project of post-war human rights. So, to return to the heart of the matter, in what sense do these children have rights?

VI. MAKING LAWS VERSUS MAKING A DIFFERENCE: THE ENFORCEMENT GAP

Formulating and passing laws, despite its complications and protracted frustrations, is probably the easiest step in the journey from aspirational principle to practical realization. Indeed, some argue that states knowingly sign on to human rights instruments without any serious political commitment to changing their practices, precisely because they realize that there is so little accountability and that the diplomatic kudos of signing is not offset by any

66. Sulejmanovic v. Italy, App. Nos. 57574/00, 57575/00 (2002).
67. Robert Verkaik, *Battle to Halt Deportation of Girl, 3, Puts Spotlight on UK Asylum Policy*, INDEPENDENT (U.K.), 2 Jan. 2008, at 10.
68. *Communication No. 1069/2002 (Bakhtiyari v. Australia)*, U.N. ESCOR, Hum. Rts. Comm., 79th Sess., ¶¶ 9.7, 11, U.N. Doc. CCPR/C/79/D/1069/2002 (2003).
69. Liz Fekete, *Detained: Foreign Children in Europe*, 49 RACE & CLASS 93, 100–01 (2007).
70. BENHABIB, *supra* note 63, at 66.

corresponding costs for non-enforcement.[71] The examples discussed above certainly illustrate the "law-to-practice-translation" failures.

Proving the impact of treaty making and monitoring on rights enforcement is not easy. Nor is it as clear as some assume that these are self-evidently good mechanisms for increasing the political will to secure change. As a scholar pertinently reflected, "What if claims made in the name of universal rights are not the best way to protect people?"[72] The amount of time spent on treaty ratification and legal strategies might divert effort from more concrete and specific approaches to rights enforcement.[73] On the other hand, it might be a key factor in limiting the scope of rights violations by states and strengthening public accountability. Assessing the relative impact of such strategies is a complex matter. Expert opinions on the topic are divided between the radical skeptics, who argue that "the costs and the benefits of [treaty ratification] are very small,"[74] and the human rights triumphalists, who see treaty ratification as a crucial piece of rights enforcement. The different assessments often reflect differing analytic methodologies, with qualitative studies portraying a more optimistic account of the impact of human rights advocacy than quantitative assessments.[75] A recent systematic survey of human rights convention ratifications, including the CRC, and the subsequent state practice concludes that:

> [O]nce made, formal commitments to treaties can have *noticeably positive consequences*. . . . Treaties signal a seriousness of intent that is difficult to replicate in other ways. They reflect politics, but they also shape political behavior, setting the stage for new political alliances, empowering new political actors, and heightening public scrutiny.[76]

What are the "noticeably positive consequences" for Arendt's children? The picture is mixed. To ascertain whether abstract rights—to protection, refugee status, and care—are translated into practice, one has to look beyond the generality of domestic law toward implementing policies, procedures, and practices. This approach is the only way to test the efficacy of general rights claims. On the one hand, one can point to the development of rights-respecting policies, which clearly reflect the thinking contained in the CRC, particularly in Articles 3 (establishing the primacy of the "best

71. *See generally* Oona Hathaway, *Do Human Rights Treaties Make a Difference?*, 111 Yale L.J. 1935 (2002).
72. Kenneth Cmiel, *quoted in* Emily Haffner-Burton & James Ron, Can the Human Rights Movement Achieve its Goals? (2004) (unpublished manuscript, on file with author).
73. For an interesting critique of the legal approach to rights enforcement, see Gerald N. Rosenberg, The Hollow Hope: Can Courts Bring About Social Change? (2d ed. 1991).
74. Jack L. Goldsmith & Eric A. Posner, The Limits of International Law 132 (2005).
75. Haffner-Burton & Ron, *supra* note 72.
76. Beth Simmons, Mobilizing for Human Rights: International Law in Domestic Politics 2 (2009).

interests of the child" principle) and 22 (requiring states parties to the CRC to "take appropriate measures to ensure that a child who is seeking refugee status . . . receive[s] appropriate protection and humanitarian assistance."[77] For example, if one compares different destination states' treatment of child asylum seekers and plots it against human rights obligations, some common deficiencies and interesting differences can be observed.

As discussed, many states fail to provide comprehensive guardianship and effective legal representation to unaccompanied or separated child migrants, despite unambiguous calls for these protections by the Committee on the Rights of the Child.[78] In the United States, for example, neither publicly funded legal representation nor access to guardianship or any form of individualized and consistent mentorship exists. Even six-year-old Cuban survivor Elian Gonzalez, whose case provoked vigorous legal sparring between interested adult parties with divergent views of Elian's best interests, lacked legal representation or guardianship, independent from his adult interlocutors.[79] In the United Kingdom, Arendt's children are entitled to publicly funded legal representation, but no system of guardianship exists. By contrast, in other EU states, such as Germany, Belgium, Spain, and France, domestic legislation or regulations stipulate guardianship for these children, though the practical impact of these provisions is unequal and inconsistent.[80] Two other areas of policy that impinge on decision making regarding Arendt's children, age determination and child interviewing procedures, also reflect divergent state practice.

An effective, reliable, and consistent mechanism for ascertaining the age of an applicant is obviously a necessary condition precedent for protecting children's rights; without it, child-specific protections will not reach their intended recipients. Yet despite years of advocacy, no such mechanism is uniformly in place. In the United States, the Netherlands, and Australia, for example, to establish whether the migrant applicant is under eighteen, and therefore entitled to child-specific procedures, the state relies on mechanistically implemented physical tests—dental, wrist, or clavicle X-rays, or rule of thumb personal assessments. Generally, these mechanisms yield results that ignore the physical variability of children from different social, economic, and ethnic backgrounds.[81] By contrast, in the United Kingdom, a holistic test

---

77. CRC, *supra* note 5, arts. 3, 22.
78. *General Comment No. 6: Treatment of Unaccompanied and Separated Children Outside Their Country of Origin*, U.N. ESCOR, Comm. on the Rts. of the Child, 39th Sess., ¶ 24, U.N. Doc. CRC/GC/2005/6 (2005).
79. *See* Comment, *US Court of Appeals for the 11th Circuit:* Elian Gonzalez v. Reno *(1 June 2000)*, 12 Int'l J. Refugee L. 430 (2000).
80. Daniel Senovilla Hernández, Report on Treatment of Unaccompanied Child Asylum Seekers in Europe 40–41 (May 2008) (prepared for Migrinter International Conference) (paper on file with author).
81. Jacqueline Bhabha & Mary Crock, Seeking Asylum Alone: Unaccompanied and Separated Children and Refugee Protection in Australia, the U.K., and the U.S. 82–85 (2006).

has been developed (though not yet implemented) in response to persistent advocacy on the topic.[82] This is an example of a rights-respecting approach approved by the courts,[83] which takes into account the child's "best interests" and his or her own views.[84] The holistic test creates a psychologically and socially nuanced tool for assessing age, which complements the raw indicators of physical development. Decision makers function with the social constructs embedded in their society—because childhood is one such construct, they need to unpack its elements to effectively map its categories and its relationship to chronological age onto subjects with novel backgrounds. As the UK Royal College of Paediatrics and Child Health points out:

> [A]ge determination is extremely difficult to do with certainty . . . [it] is an inexact science and the margin of error can sometimes be a much as 5 years either side. . . . Estimates of a child's physical age from his or her dental development are [only] accurate to within + or – 2 years for 95% of the population.[85]

Until recently, government officials have frequently ignored this statistic. According to one study, 50 percent of asylum applicants who were age disputed turned out to be minors; as a result, they were denied the child-specific protections they should have been accorded during the investigative process. A child asylum seeker "reported becoming very upset when immigration staff were rude and kept laughing at him when he showed them his birth certificate and said that he was 16."[86] Others have endured prolonged periods in detention until authorities accepted their original claim to be children. A holistic policy obligates the state official undertaking the age assessment to not rely solely on the child's physical appearance, but instead to consider his or her demeanor, ability to interact with adults, cultural background, social history, life experiences, educational history, as well as the views of foster caregivers, residential workers, teachers, and interpreters. This approach is a good way to explore whether someone is a child and to afford him or her a meaningful right to have rights. Regrettably, despite the open opposition of the British Dental Association, the UK government still has not implemented a holistic test, and instead is considering the use of dental X-rays to ascertain the age of asylum seekers.[87]

A complex set of questions arises regarding the merits of different strategies used to elicit information from Arendt's children. Adversarial interroga-

82. For a general discussion of age determination within the UK asylum system, see Bhabha & Finch, *supra* note 37, at 55–65.
83. R v. London Borough of Merton, [2003] EWHC 1689 (Admin).
84. CRC, *supra* note 5, arts. 3, 12.
85. Royal College of Paediatrics and Child Health, The Health of Refugee Children: Guidelines for Paediatricians ¶¶ 5.6, 5.6.3 (1999).
86. Bhabha & Finch, *supra* note 37, at 56, 57.
87. Andy Tate, *X-Ray Verdict Put on Hold*, Dentistry (U.K.), 21 Dec. 2007, *available at* http://www.dentistry.co.uk/news/news_detail.php?id=915.

tions, such as those conducted in the United States and Australia for asylum-seeking children, undoubtedly run counter to the children's best interests, particularly when interrogations are conducted in alienating settings such as formal courtrooms or detention centers. On the other hand, does the practice of states such as Canada and the United Kingdom, which refrain from any direct questioning by immigration authorities and prefer written submissions by legal representatives resulting from multiple, child-friendly interviews, prevent children from having a voice? How should states construe the child rights principle that "the child . . . capable of forming his or her own views [should have] the right to express those views freely in all matters affecting the child"?[88] Indirect representation of young children's views by advocates and guardians may be preferable to an obligation to appear before formal a decision maker. Older children, however, may benefit from the opportunity to directly express their views in a non-adversarial setting, particularly if they are afforded competent advice in preparing for the interview. Recent developments in participatory child rights, which emphasize the importance and impact of direct child engagement,[89] may lead to different conclusions than those from the more protective approach, which substitutes an adult's voice for that of the child. The dramatic impact of first person narratives by some of Arendt's children illustrates the point.[90] No sustained debate on the merits of these differing approaches has taken place within the advocacy or policy communities, nor is it clear which outcome is more in accordance with a child rights mandate. The issue illustrates the challenges of translating Arendt's children's rights in law into rights in practice, a challenge that is not only political but also conceptual. As this example illustrates, crafting the right to have rights for various children, who are confronting imponderable variables in unfamiliar surroundings, is not a mechanistic rolling out of pre-established entitlements but an evolving toolkit of strategies specifically tailored for change. Efforts to overcome these rights challenges are in their infancy.

---

88. CRC, *supra* note 5, art. 12.

89. *See, e.g.*, Gerison Lansdown, Int'l Inst. for Child Rights & Dev., Evolving Capacities and Participation (n.d.), *available at* http://web.uvic.ca/iicrd/graphics/CIDA%20CAP%20Report%20%20-%20Evolving%20Capacity%20and%20Participation.12.03.pdf (prepared for the Canadian International Development Agency Child Protection Unit).

90. Women's Comm'n for Refugee Women & Children, Prison Guard or Parent?: INS Treatment of Unaccompanied Refugee Children (May 2002), *available at* http://www.womenscommission.org/pdf/ins_det.pdf; Austl. Human Rights Comm'n, A Last Resort? National Inquiry into Children in Immigration Detention (2004), *available at* http://www.hreoc.gov.au/human_rights/children_detention_report/index.html.

VII. OUTCOMES OF RIGHTLESSNESS: ARENDT'S CHILDREN IN THE SPACE OF EXCEPTION

A balance sheet of the right to have rights for Arendt's children caught up in asylum adjudication in developed states yields mixed outcomes. On the one hand, children's rights in international law have had some influence on the formulation of state policies and practices in some of the countries examined, for example, with respect to holistic age determination procedures or appointments of guardians. These rights also have found their way into the adjudication of children's asylum cases through the development of the notion of child-specific persecution—gang violence, child abuse, forced marriage, recruitment as child soldiers[91]—as a strategy for applying to children the more generic concept of "well founded fear of persecution" that defines a refugee in international law.[92]

Yet, the predictability and uniformity of treatment that one would expect of a rights-respecting regime is still largely absent. In addition to the lack of a comprehensive guardianship system for Arendt's children and the devastating consequences that brings for successful realization of legal rights or social acculturation, there is the more generalized and pervasive climate of suspicion that permeates developed states' approaches to Arendt's children. For example, in the United Kingdom, this climate of suspicion results in extraordinarily high refusal rates for child asylum applications—only 2 percent granted in 2004 and 5 percent in 2005.[93] The lack of a rights-respecting framework has also led to policies of forcibly returning children to their countries of origin, even when no best interest assessment has taken place. Plans to implement such a system in Albania are reported to be well advanced.[94] But the most serious and lingering problem is that many of Arendt's children end up in detention—whether, as in the United Kingdom, because their age is disputed or because this is the policy of the destination country. Detention has devastating effects on children, not only because of its harshness and inappropriately punitive impact but also because of the indeterminacy and isolation that accompany it. It is the clearest example of the consequences of functional statelessness and of the impact this status has on rights access. For some children, detention in developed destination states follows refugee camp life or the rigors of street life in their regions of origin. This is the experience of a child held in a US "secure facility" who had a pending asylum claim:

---

91. Bhabha & Crock, *supra* note 81, at 159.
92. Convention Relating to the Status of Refugees, *supra* note 2.
93. Bhabha & Finch, *supra* note 37, at 127.
94. *Id.* at 136–37.

> My first couple of days there, I didn't like it. . . . I couldn't sleep. At 5 a.m. when they opened the cells for us to take showers, there was a table with clothes assigned to us by name. It didn't take into account our size, so I got shoes that didn't even fit me. . . . The rights we had in this facility depended on what color our shirt was. After three days, I had a gray shirt and the right to sit and eat with others. . . . I asked if I could call my family, but they told me not until I had been there for 25 days was I allowed to make a call. . . . Sometimes at night when it became very hot—they left the lights on—we would take off our shirts. We would be yelled at because they wanted us to wear our shirts so they would know what color they were and what privileges we had.[95]

Across the Atlantic, in the southern Mediterranean, pressures to rigidly enforce immigration control in a security driven political environment lead to similarly coercive situations. North African children trying to escape from the child immigration detention in Spain have reported being hit by the staff when caught, as described by a thirteen-year-old Moroccan boy to Human Rights Watch:

> One time we escaped, three of us, when a boy took a piece of metal and broke the door [of the punishment room]. One of the older boys caught us and hit us. They took us and put us in another room and locked the door and then [one of the educators] came and hit us with a baton like the police use. He hit me on the head and the face and leg.[96]

These arbitrary detention processes, apparently beyond the reach of domestic structures of accountability or the international oversight of monitoring bodies, such as the Committee on the Rights of the Child, function according to a completely different metric of "rights." The situation recalls Giorgio Agamben's provocative analogy between the treatment of refugees in camps and the archetypal experiment of encampment, the concentration camp: "The paradoxical status of the camp as a space of exception must be considered. The camp is a piece of land placed outside the normal juridical order, but it is nevertheless not simply an external space. . . . The camp is thus the structure in which the state of exception—the possibility of deciding on which founds sovereign power—is realized *normally*."[97] This is the extreme situation of rightlessness—the normalized state of exception—which governs the status of Arendt's children in detention centers at the periphery of Europe or in the heart of the US desert. Like children detained in airport facilities or border lockups, these children, though firmly within the confines of the state, nevertheless exist in a liminal space outside it.

---

95. Jacqueline Bhabha & Susan Schmidt, Seeking Asylum Alone: Unaccompanied and Separated Children and Refugee Protection in the U.S. 88 (2006).
96. HRW, *supra* note 40, at 15.
97. Giorgio Agamben, Homo Sacer: Sovereign Power and Bare Life 169–70 (Daniel Heller-Roazen trans., 1998).

If human rights in general, and children's rights in particular, are essentially about redistributing political justice and social/economic resources in favor of the disadvantaged, then the most effective and visible positive outcome is a treaty that gives individuals the right to challenge state failure to implement their rights by bringing a case before a court. The CRC does not afford this opportunity, but other human rights treaties do, and in the process of using them, advocates make reference to the children's rights principles of the CRC. Of course, the Moroccan children in Ceuta, off the African Mediterranean coast, or the sub-Saharan children on Lampedusa, off the coast of Italy, have no access to effective legal representation. That is what the normalized state of exception is—a space outside the law. But some of Arendt's children have managed to capitalize on their rights by using human rights instruments and courts. These litigation successes provide some support for the general claim that these children can assert a right to rights. Retrospectively, at least, gross violations that come to light are recognized as such. Sometimes legal strategies do appear to deliver a right to rights.

VIII. AN EXAMPLE: TABITHA—THE TIP OF AN ICEBERG

The recent case of Tabitha Kaniki Mitunga, a five-year-old citizen of the Democratic Republic of Congo (DRC) who found herself alone in Belgium, is emblematic. Tabitha is one of the many thousands of Arendt's "left behind" children.[98] Her mother fled the DRC as a refugee after Tabitha's father was killed, and Tabitha continued to live in the DRC with relatives while her mother sought asylum in Canada. Once her mother was able to legally bring Tabitha to join her, she asked her brother, a Dutch national living in the Netherlands, to collect the child. At the airport in Brussels, despite her age, Tabitha was separated from her Dutch uncle, who tried unsuccessfully to claim that he was her father in order to keep her with him. Because she was traveling without documents, Belgian authorities detained her in the remand center near the airport, where she spent two months in the presence

98. This is a category that applies to a very diverse group of children whose parents leave home in search of work or safety, often planning to reunify by returning home or sending for their children to join them. As stated above, not all "left behind" children are functionally stateless; those whose parents are migrant workers sending back remittances and eventually planning to return may be in a relatively satisfactory situation. (The picture is complex, and the evidence on the impact of parental migration on children left behind shows that while some groups benefit from the enhanced income and related opportunities, others suffer from isolation, lack of supervision, and other difficulties.) However, children whose parents are refugees and who are left behind pending family reunification are likely to be marginalized by the home state and to lack access to protection and fundamental rights. In this sense, they too can be considered "Arendt's children."

of unknown adults. During this time, her frantic mother tried to secure her release, and lawyers applied (without receiving any response from the authorities) for her to be placed in foster care. Eventually, the child was deported back to the DRC with no investigation into the suitability of arrangements for receiving her. No guardian was appointed, but an air hostess was assigned to look after her on the return flight, and a DRC official took charge of the child only after she waited six hours at the Kinshasa airport.

Tabitha's ordeal illustrates the effect of functional statelessness on migrant children when the state lacks a safety net of rights-respecting procedures. Without the automatic appointment of a guardian to represent Tabitha's legal rights, Belgium (the capital seat of the European Union) functioned as a state of exception, beyond the pale of the law. Considering that there are approximately 100,000 unaccompanied or separated Arendt's children presently in Europe, a high likelihood exists that others are exposed to comparable treatment. Fortunately, because of Tabitha's competent and vigilant mother, her case came to light and eventually found its way to Europe's highest human rights court. In October 2006, the European Court of Human Rights commented on the gratuitous *vide juridique* or legal vacuum in which the Belgian authorities' action had placed Tabitha, criticizing the prolonged and abusive detention, and ruled that Tabitha's treatment by the Belgian authorities amounted to "inhuman treatment," a violation of Article 3 of the ECHR.[99] The Court also found Belgium in violation of several other articles of the ECHR.[100] Breaking with the European Court's custom of low financial awards, it awarded Tabitha and her mother a total of €35,000 in addition to reimbursement of their significant legal costs.

Like thousands of other undocumented migrants per year, Tabitha had been detained in Belgium's notorious no man's land detention facilities for several months. As a result of this case, changes have been made to Belgian law, which now prohibits the detention of unaccompanied child migrants and requires the appointment of a guardian in each case,[101] propelling Belgium from one of the least to one of the most rights-respecting EU states for Arendt's children.

---

99. Mayeka v. Belgium, App. No. 13178/03, 2006–XI Eur. Ct. H.R.

100. *Id.* ¶¶ 87, 105, 114. *See* European Convention for the Protection of Human Rights and Fundamental Freedoms, *opened for signature* 4 Nov. 1950, arts. 3, 5(1), 5(4), 8, 213 U.N.T.S. 221, Europ. T.S. No. 5 (*entered into force* 3 Sept. 1953).

101. Programmawet of 24 Dec. 2002, Voogdij over niet-begeleide minderjarige vreemdelingen [Program Law of 24 Dec. 2002, Guardianship on the Unaccompanied Foreign Minors], Title XIII, Ch. 6 (Belg.). Belgian law allows undocumented migrants to be detained for five months without charge or other legal procedures. Each time the migrant resists removal or deportation, the clock restarts. As a result, many migrants endure long periods in this state of exception, including the 1,000 to 2,000 unaccompanied minors who arrive in Belgium each year. *See* Platforme Mineurs en Exile, *available at* http://www.mena.be.

Tabitha's case can be contrasted with a 1996 decision of the European Court, *Nsona v. Netherlands*,[102] in which the Court considered the applicability of the European Convention to the typical circumstances of Arendt's children for the first time. In that case, the Court criticized the speedy removal of a nine-year-old girl from the Netherlands, via Zurich, back to Zaire, and the Dutch government's willingness to hand over all responsibility for her welfare to others, especially the airline, once she left Dutch soil.[103] However, the Court did not go so far as to find a violation of the ECHR. It held that the arduous journey that the child endured, mostly unaccompanied and including time spent in airport nurseries and with unknown airline officials, was unsatisfactory but did not rise to the level of "inhuman or degrading treatment" required by Article 3 of the ECHR. The Court appears to have penalized the child for the fact that her aunt initially attempted to secure her entry into the Netherlands by means of deceit (using a falsified passport) and yet exonerated the member state for removing her without adequately inquiring into the circumstances that awaited her in Zaire. Like the European Commission on Human Rights, which heard the case prior to its referral to the full Court, perhaps the European Court justices were more concerned by the policy implications of appearing to approve irregular means of securing the admission of unaccompanied child migrants into destination states[104] than by the lack of attention to children's best interest considerations by governments seeking to remove them.

Tabitha's case illustrates the powerful reach of the law, while at the same time highlighting its partial impact. Once the state of exception was subjected to the full scrutiny of the legal mainstream, previously "binding obligations" were translated into new legal provisions, guaranteeing their implementation. On their own, the obligations had proved toothless. Many children, first detained in harsh conditions on the Canary Islands,[105] the island of Lampedusa,[106] and in Malta and Cyprus, and then summarily returned to their home countries without any best interest assessment, would benefit from the implementation of this judgment on their behalf. Other court decisions are relevant to their circumstances as well. For example, the European Court held in 2002:

> As regards the types of "treatment" which fall within the scope of Article 3 of the Convention, the Court's case-law refers to "ill-treatment" that attains a minimum

102. Nsona v. Netherlands, App. No. 23366/94, 1996–V Eur. Ct. H.R. 1979
103. *Id.* ¶ 103.
104. Ursula Kilkelly, Nsona v. the Netherlands: *The Treatment of Minors and the European Convention on Human Rights*, 8 Int'l J. Refugee L. 640, 646 (1996).
105. *Canary Islands Face Migrant Crisis*, Al Jazeera, 26 July 2007, *available at* http://english.aljazeera.net/NR/exeres/14F3FEC3-052C-4D6B-B969-0AE7059A9D3F.htm.
106. *See, e.g.*, Rutvica Andrijasevic, *Lampedusa in Focus: Migrants Caught Between the Libyan Desert and the Deep Sea*, 82 Feminist Rev. 120 (2006).

level of severity and involves actual bodily injury or intense physical or mental suffering. *Where treatment humiliates or debases an individual, showing lack of respect for, or diminishing, his or her human dignity or arouses feelings of fear, anguish or inferiority capable of breaking an individual's moral and physical resistance, it may be characterised as degrading and also fall within the prohibition of Article 3.* The suffering which flows from naturally occurring illness, physical or mental, may be covered by Article 3, where it is, or risks being, exacerbated by treatment, whether flowing from conditions of detention, expulsion or other measures, for which the authorities can be held responsible.[107]

This statement is a challenge to the human rights advocacy community.

IX. SOCIAL AND ECONOMIC RIGHTS: TO HAVE AND NOT TO HAVE

As a matter of domestic and international law, Arendt's children are entitled to protection from torture and from cruel, inhuman, or degrading treatment or punishment, along with other civil and political harms. As the discussion above has demonstrated, enforcing these protections has not always been possible in practice. Arendt's children are also entitled to several fundamental economic and social rights. With these rights, however, the picture is more complex than it is for civil and political rights. States' implementation of economic and social rights is more divergent, and, until very recently, little attention was paid to the ability of Arendt's children to access these rights. As the number of Arendt's children has grown, their length of residence as independent or unaccompanied child migrants has increased, and the determination of destination states to remove them to their countries of origin has escalated. Therefore, the access of Arendt's children to effective economic and social rights protections has become a central concern.

Discriminatory attitudes lead to exclusionary pressures to reduce these children's access to basic child protections in different ways. Interestingly, in some countries such as Denmark, this has resulted in de jure differences in eligibility for health care, which are not followed in practice by health care providers.[108] More common is the converse situation, where legal entitlements are unrealized in practice, sometimes for the reasons already discussed. For example, in December 2007, the UK government announced plans to pilot

107. Pretty v. U.K., App. No. 2346/02, 35 Eur. H.R. Rep. 1, ¶ 52 (2002) (emphasis added) (citations omitted).

108. For example in February 1995, the CRC Committee commented, in its final observations on the report submitted by Denmark, that rejected child asylum seekers still in the country had "their rights to health care and education provided de facto but not de jure." *Concluding Observations of the Committee on the Rights of the Child: Denmark*, *supra* note 38, ¶ 18. The Committee considered this situation "not fully compatible with the provisions and principles of articles 2 and 3 of the Convention." *Id.* ¶ 14.

a new, improved scheme for children under state care, which would allow them to remain in foster care until age twenty-one, but at the same time it proposed measures to place unaccompanied minors in more independent living from the age of sixteen. As a member of the House of Lords remarked, "Sadly, the proposition appears to have more to do with preparing the child for removal than with meeting the young person's needs."[109] Moreover, there is alarming evidence of children being trafficked to work under exploitative conditions,[110] begging or prostituting themselves on the streets of Western cities, and lacking access to education, shelter, or adequate health care.[111] At the same time, the desperation of many of Arendt's children to leave their home countries and indigent families and try for a better life with the possibility of education or employment elsewhere complicates the simple (sometimes convenient) official assumption that their "best interests" are automatically served by returning them to their countries of origin.[112] Widespread child abuse, grinding poverty, and lack of opportunities must surely compel the immigration and welfare officials making child repatriation decisions to question their assumptions and engage in individualized, evidence-based best interest assessments tailored to the circumstances of each case. As Arendt remarked with prescience half a century ago, "Nonrecognition of statelessness always means repatriation, *i.e.*, deportation to a country of origin."[113] A first-person account of the serious push factors driving a fifteen-year-old Romanian to leave home follows:

> I was the youngest of all my brothers. I did nothing there. . . . At ten, I was all alone. My brothers, they had all left, traveled to Germany, Austria, Italy. . . . I was all alone. I did nothing. So I said: "I have nothing here." My father and mother, what could they say to me? My father, he has a farm. I had to work with him. Are you mad? . . . My father came to me from time to time, slapped me around the head. "Wait. Leave me alone! I'm going." That's how it started. "I'm leaving home."[114]

The reality of poverty, child abuse, and lack of opportunities reinforces the determination to exit, to make a bid for adventure, to "put some air in

109. Maria Ahmed, *Peers Want Equal Status for Asylum-Seeking Children*, Communitycare.co.uk, 6 Dec. 2007, *available at* http://www.communitycare.co.uk/Articles/2007/12/06/106693/peers-want-equal-status-for-asylum-seeking-children.html.
110. Save the Children Italia, L'Identificazione dei minori vittime di tratta e sfruttamento [The identification of child victims of trafficking and exploitation] (draft report, on file with author).
111. For an excellent collection of first person narratives by children in these circumstances in France, see Vassort, *supra* note 36.
112. I am grateful to Elena Rozzi for drawing my attention to this issue and usefully illuminating it in her unpublished article, La valutazione dell'interesse del minore nella scelta tra accoglienza in Italia e rimpatrio [The evaluation of the best interests of the child in the choice between residence in Italy and removal] (May 2008).
113. Arendt, *supra* note 1, at 279.
114. Vassort, *supra* note 36, at 11 (author's translation).

your head,"[115] even if the journey is known to be arduous, the risks great, and the guarantees of success minimal.

> Every day in the port of Tangiers, at any time of the day or night, a fierce battle takes place; like a flock of birds, dozens of children try to squeeze into a trailer, a container or some other vehicle, with the sole objective of reaching Europe. The police pursue them relentlessly, and beat them up if they catch them. . . . They persist, constant, another time. . . . Some have made the return journey several times.[116]

And the numbers show no signs of abating. According to the authorities in the Canary Islands, for example, from 346 children arriving unaccompanied on the island in 2003, the number grew to 829 in 2006 and reached 931 by December 2007.[117] Some have called this increasing flow of child and teenage exiles, this flight from the hopelessness of "ados,"[118] a "third wave" of contemporary migration, following the mid-twentieth century migration led by single men and the later pattern of mass female migration.[119] Certainly, the decision to leave home in search of opportunity and livelihood complicates the child protection challenge facing law enforcement and welfare agencies. Because their migration is fueled by a desire to work, large numbers of Arendt's children placed in open child welfare shelters or institutions leave shortly after their placement. For example, the Caritas reception center for migrant youth in Rome reported in 2005 that about 80 percent of accommodated minors left without authorization.[120] Like previous generations of

---

115. "Tu vas rester ici comme un paysan? Ors un peu. Va voir d'authres pays. Mets de l'air dans ta tete. Meme si on n'arrive pas la premiere fois, on va arriver un jour." *Id.*
116. El Mirador De Tánger, A los niños les mataron los pájaros (19 Dec. 2007), *available at* http://blogs.20minutos.es/oriente-occidente/post/2007/12/19/a-niaaos-les-mataron-paajaros (author's translation, with thanks to Ana Colbert). *See generally* Col·lectiu DRARI d'Investigació Acció Participativa pels Drets de l'Infant, *available at* http://www.DRARI-Col-lectiu-IAP-Drets-Infant.blogspot.com.
117. Dory Merino, *Canarias alcanza la cifra récord de 931 menores extranjeros acogidos en centros*, El Día (Islas Canarias), 12 Dec. 2007.
118. French patois abbreviation of "adolescents."
119. "Il y a eu la première vague des migrants dans les années 60, des hommes seuls. Puis, les femmes ont rejoint les hommes, c'est la 2ème vague. Voici aujourd'hui la 3ème vague : les jeunes, enfants ou ados. Ils sont toujours plus nombreux à s'exiler seuls vers une vie qu'ils imaginent meilleure. Ils ont le plus souvent entre 15 et 18 ans, mais ils sont aussi âgés parfois d'à peine 10 ou 12 ans." ["There was the first wave of migrants during the sixties, single men. Then, women joined the men, that was the second wave. Today we have the third wave: young people, children or adoloscents. There are always more of them, exiling themselves towards a life they imagine will be better. They are usually between 15 and 18, but sometimes they are only 10 or 12".] Television Suisse Romande, *L'Exil a 15 Ans*, 21 Dec. 2007, *available at* http://www.DRARI-Col-lectiu-IAP-Drets-Infant.blogspot.com (author's translation).
120. Progetto Equal Palms, "Percorsi di accompagnamento al lavoro per minori stranieri non accompagnati," Pratiche di Accoglienza I: Aggancio, inserimento, mediazione e rimpatrio 7 (author's translation).

unwanted but ultimately employable migrants,[121] these children frequently end up in the most exploited occupations, such as agricultural laborers, factory hands, prostitutes, or petty criminals, when other options are not available. To use Mae Ngai's phrase, they constitute an imported "proletariat outside the polity."[122] Save the Children Italy has described the recruitment conditions of some of these children: Adolescent and post-adolescent males of Maghreb and sub-Saharan origin employed in the agricultural sector for primarily seasonal work, particularly in Puglia, Calabria, and Sicily. Normally the employer uses recruiters (called corporals) to make daily contact with the workers (including the minors) for work in the black economy at wages far below union rates and without required security guarantees. In addition, the "corporal" normally supervises the conduct of work, using extreme verbal insults which undermine the workers' dignity to accelerate the pace of work as much as possible (preventing breaks or pauses, even in very adverse weather conditions) and demands from each worker a percentage of daily earnings. The contact between the recruiter and the minor takes place in public places where the workers gather every morning waiting for the "corporal," who only offers work on a daily basis.[123]

Again a complex "best interest" calculus arises, one not yet adequately explored by officials and advocates engaged in the issues. Some state authorities, in the United States and Belgium[124] for example, have resorted to locked shelters to prevent the escape of unauthorized child migrants. This detention is also justified by a concern to protect the minors from traffickers or other sources of exploitation. Detention for protection is a suspect approach, discredited in most situations: victims of domestic abuse and children at risk of abduction are not incarcerated. One therefore can only wonder whether immigration control mandates contribute significantly to these policy choices. On the other hand, those such as the Italian and Spanish authorities, who do not detain unauthorized child migrants, acknowledge that a best interest calculation might justify more stringent supervision measures, as large proportions of at-risk children, many suspected of having been

121. An interesting comparison, from a quite different time and place, can be made with Filipino migrants to the United States in the 1920s: "Despite official efforts to discourage Filipinos from traveling to the United States, migration increased dramatically in the late 1920s. . . . In California, Filipinos, along with Mexicans, became the mainstay of migratory agricultural labor." Ngai, supra note 13, at 103–04.

122. *Id.* at 13.

123. Salvatore Fachile, Save the Children Italia, L'Identificazione dei Minori Vittime di Tratta e Sfruttamento (2007); Save the Children Italia, Programma AGIS 2005–Development of a Child Rights Methodology to Identify and Support Child Victims of Trafficking, JLS/2005/AGIS/045, at 31–32 (2007).

124. Personal communication with Gaelle Buysschaert, Belgian Representative, Belgium UNICEF National Committee Meeting: Children on the Move (29–30 Nov. 2007). UNICEF Belgium, personal communication, Zurich meeting.

trafficked, disappear from state provisions within days of being placed.[125] There is an acute tension between the infantilization of autonomous youth making decisions in suboptimal situations and the dereliction of duty toward exceedingly vulnerable child populations liable to severe abuse. Moreover, even if it were possible for destination states to establish that repatriating the child would be in his or her best interests, the country of origin may pose obstacles. Senegal, for example, has recently refused to accept the return of some of its irregular minor migrants because lack of birth registration and adequate documentation makes it impossible for the Senegalese authorities to confidently reunite them with their families.[126] Arendt's children's functional statelessness converts them into virtual citizens from the perspective of the home country and into stateless illegals from that of the host state.

Despite these impediments, international law clearly establishes a limited set of economic and social rights that are binding on states, even for their most "impossible subjects," to use Ngai's haunting term. Among these obligatory rights, two are key for Arendt's children: (1) "primary education shall be compulsory and available free to all," and (2) there should exist recognition of everyone's right to "the enjoyment of the highest attainable standard of physical and mental health."[127] States have interpreted their obligations in different ways.

X. A COMPARATIVE EDUCATION SNAPSHOT

As a matter of widely respected international law, primary education must be compulsory and freely available to all children, irrespective of their status. States also are encouraged to make secondary education accessible to all.[128] Preschool and tertiary education do not fall within the scope of these protections. Most states have established comprehensive entitlements for Arendt's children that match those of domestic children and mirror the obligations set out in international law.[129] This is certainly true in the European Union,

125. Ireland has faced a similar problem. Over the last seven years, 388 children placed in the care of the Irish authorities as suspected victims of trafficking have gone missing and have never been traced. Stanislaus Kennedy, *Who Cares About the Disappeared Children?*, Irish Times, 23 May 2008, *available at* http://www.irishtimes.com/newspaper/opinion/2008/0523/1211461644896.html.

126. Dory Merino, *Senegal tiene dificultades para aceptar a sus menores acogidos en Canaria*, El Dia (Islas Canarias), 31 Dec. 2007.

127. International Covenant on Economic, Social and Cultural Rights (ICESCR), *adopted* 16 Dec. 1966, G.A. Res. 2200 (XXI), U.N. GAOR, 21st Sess., Supp. No. 16, arts. 13(2)(a), 12(1), U.N. Doc. A/6316 (1966), 993 U.N.T.S. 3 (*entered into force* 3 Jan. 1976); CRC, *supra* note 5, art. 24.

128. ICESCR, *supra* note 127, arts. 2(2), 13; CRC, *supra* note 5, art. 28.

129. For a survey of six EU member states, see Daniel Senovilla Hernández, *supra* note 80, at 38.

where member states are signatories to the CRC. For example, all migrant minors in Italy, whether authorized or not, enjoy the same legal right/obligation to attend compulsory education as the domestic population,[130] as do those in Spain, France, the United Kingdom, Belgium, and Germany. In practice, however, access to educational facilities may be problematic for a variety of reasons. Sometimes parents require children to work, preventing them from attending school. This is true of Roma children, many of whom are now to be found begging, cleaning car windows, or prostituting themselves on the streets of large cities. "Roma children from Romania are led into prostitution [in Italy] by adults, often belonging to the same family, who in addition to being responsible for organizing and running their work, keep all the earnings."[131]

Others are victims of trafficking, some in conditions of absolute servitude where their movements are closely controlled by their exploiters. Yet others, destitute and living on the streets, have little access to public services and facilities, such as schools, welfare support, and health care. A young, undocumented Albanian migrant in France describes how this happens:

> The best thing is school. Yes, school. In Tirana, I did well in school, I spoke Italian, English, Albanian. I also speak a bit of Turkish. I had good grades. Then, because of my family problems—I am a bit sensitive, I can't stand misery—I was forced to leave home. I never imagined I'd end up in France, because already in school French was difficult and I didn't like it. . . . Then I said to myself, this is my fate, you've got make the best of it and move on. When my family problems started—my mother had problems with my father—I couldn't go to school. I was good but I just couldn't go to school at all. If you don't go to school, you just hang around in the street; if you hang around without money, you end up stealing, and you'll be picked up and land in trouble. No one wants to steal, I just decided to leave. I didn't speak a word of French when I arrived . . . no papers; it'll be a stroke of luck if I am allowed to stay.[132]

Despite the existence of a general right to education for migrant children, obstacles to securing it in practice are common. The situation in Poland illustrates this point. According to the 2005 Amendment to the Act on Educational Systems, children of foreigners have the right to education in Poland, and schooling is obligatory until the age of eighteen. As a result, children of parents whose status has become "irregular" (e.g., through the overstaying of visas, a failure to prolong a permit, or overdue tax payments) can enroll in public primary schools without any obstacles. However, other categories of Arendt's children in Poland do not have such access. Children of asylum seekers and individuals granted "tolerated stay permits" are granted the right

---

130. Consolidated Text 286/98 on Immigration, art. 19, § 2(a) (Italy).
131. Fachile, *supra* note 123, at 15.
132. Vassort, *supra* note 36, at 46–47 (author's translation).

to education on similar conditions as Polish citizen children as long as they pass a Polish language test before being enrolled. Undocumented children have access to public schools but have to pay appropriate fees.[133]

Because the United States has not ratified the International Covenant on Economic, Social and Cultural Rights, or the CRC, international law does not impose obligations on the US government regarding core social and economic rights. Nevertheless, as a result of a leading US Supreme Court case decided in June 1982,[134] all children in the United States, whatever their status, are entitled to state-funded public education for primary and secondary schooling. A statement by Justice Brennan in that case carries considerable contemporary relevance: "It is difficult to understand precisely what the State hopes to achieve by promoting the creation of a perpetuation of a subclass of illiterates within our boundaries, surely adding to the problems and costs of unemployment, welfare, and crime."[135] Interestingly, the Court also argued that "charging tuition to undocumented children constitutes a ludicrously ineffectual attempt to stem the tide of illegal immigration."[136] Despite a virulent resurgence of nativism in the United States and a dramatic increase in the population of undocumented migrants,[137] it appears that a majority of the US population still support this inclusive policy,[138] which may benefit the approximately 7,000 unaccompanied migrant children entering the United States each year.[139] However, the current climate of growing immigration enforcement detracts from this positive legal framework and

133. Zorana Medarič & Andreja Kopitar (Daphne/European Comm'n), The Risk Group of Unaccompanied Minors: Protection Measures in an Enlarged European Union, Country Report: Poland 18 (2007). This follows Council Framework Decision 629/JHA, 2002 O.J. (L 203) 1, and Council Directive 2004/81/EC, 2004 O.J. (L 261) 19. *See also* Polskie Forum Migracyjne, *available at* http://www.forummigracyjne.org/pl/aktualnosci.php?news=78&wid=26.

134. The US Supreme Court held in 1973, in *San Antonio Independent School District v. Rodriguez*, 411 U.S. 1 (1973), that education was not a human right. Following this ruling, the Texas education code was amended to allow school districts to charge tuition for undocumented children in primary and secondary schools. Michael A. Olivas, Plyler v. Doe, *the Education of Undocumented Children, and the Polity, in* Immigration Stories 197, 198–202 (David A. Martin & Peter H. Schuck eds., 2005). Nine years later, the Supreme Court revisited the question and reversed in the key case of *Plyler v. Doe*, 457 U.S. 202 (1982).

135. *Plyler*, 457 U.S. at 230.

136. *Id.* at 228.

137. The current undocumented population is estimated at an all time high of between 11.5 and 12 million, of which an estimated 1.8 million are under eighteen. Passel, *supra* note 24, at 2, 8.

138. A March 2006 survey by the Pew Research Center found that 71 percent of Americans support allowing the children of illegal immigrants to attend public schools. Pew Research Ctr. for the People & the Press, America's Immigration Quandary 26 (2006), *quoted in* Note, *Federal Funding for Newcomer Schools: A Bipartisan Immigrant Education Initiative*, 120 Harv. L. Rev. 799, 813 (2007).

139. National Center for Refugee and Immigrant Children, *available at* http://www.refugees.org/article.aspx?id=1260.

impacts the rights of Arendt's children. Evidence reveals that the escalation of workplace raids and arrests in particular[140] is having an impact, not only on family unity (with increasing numbers of deportations) and family security (with growing fear, trauma, and anxiety) but also on children's education. Although no systematic research exists, reports suggest that fear of further searches and arrests has led to declining school attendance in several school districts in North Carolina.[141]

XI. THE CHALLENGE OF SECURING HEALTH CARE[142]

Similar to the right to education, as a matter of international law, all children are theoretically entitled to comprehensive health care on par with the domestic population.[143] The European Court of Human Rights has even held that denial of the right to health for irregular migrants may constitute a violation of Article 3 of the European Convention, which prohibits inhuman and degrading treatment: "The suffering which flows from naturally occurring illness, physical or mental, may be covered by Article 3, where it is, or risks being, exacerbated by treatment, whether from *conditions of detention, expulsion or other measures*, for which the authorities can be held responsible."[144]

In practice, however, the health needs of some of the most vulnerable groups, including undocumented children, are elusive. This makes catering to them very challenging for policymakers and health care providers. In some cases, problems arise because of discriminatory or administrative barriers. There are reports of irregular children living outside shelters or reception centers in Spain who have been denied treatment because they do not have documents and are not accompanied by official caregivers.[145] As stated earlier, the British government shocked observers by ordering the removal of an unaccompanied three-year-old child with a serious kidney disorder while her mother was in immigration detention. The child, a US citizen, was informed that she was ineligible for medical treatment because she was an alien. The European Court granted an injunction to prevent the

140. Arrests have risen from 445 in FY 2003 to over 5000 in FY 2008. U.S. Immigration and Customs Enforcement, U.S. Dep't of Homeland Security, Fact Sheet: Worksite Enforcement (25 Nov. 2008), *available at* http://www.ice.gov/pi/news/factsheets/worksite.htm.

141. *See generally* Elizabeth de Ornellas, *Immigrants Feel the "Shadow of Fear,"* Daily Tar Heel, 30 Oct. 2007, *available at* http://www.dailytarheel.com/2.3568/1.160005.

142. I am extremely grateful to Dr. Natalie Mooten for her meticulous research assistance with this section.

143. CRC, *supra* note 5, art. 24.

144. Pretty v. U.K., App. No. 2346/02, 35 Eur. H.R. Rep. 1, ¶ 52 (2002) (emphasis added).

145. HRW, *supra* note 40, at 2.

child's removal pending an investigation of the case.[146] In many other cases, Arendt's children fail to secure necessary health care because of language or other cultural barriers or because they are unable to comply with other administrative requirements. In some cases, the denial of access to health care is a consequence of domestic legal restrictions, like in Europe, where "there is a growing tendency . . . to restrict access to health care for undocumented migrants and to reinforce the link between access to health services and immigration control policies."[147]

EU member states have adopted a broad range of approaches to providing health care for undocumented populations including children. The spectrum includes policies in Austria and Sweden, which generally require payment for treatment (with some exceptions, including treatment for rejected child asylum seekers), to those in Hungary and Germany, where limited free health care is available, but public personnel have an obligation to inform the authorities about undocumented patients. It also encompasses policies in France, Belgium, and the Netherlands, where undocumented migrants are treated in the mainstream health care system, although a parallel administrative/financial system exists for them. The most protective country is Spain where, despite practical gaps and obstacles, the spirit of the law and much of the practice is generally inclusive.

There are, however, some exceptions to this broadly satisfactory situation. Undocumented children in Ceuta (the Spanish enclave on the northern coast of Morocco) are entitled to health care if they can produce a government-issued health card. The procedure for obtaining a health card makes children completely dependent on the supervisory state officials; identification data has to be verified by social service officials before the document can be issued. According to a Human Rights Watch report:

> Ala gives his age as thirteen but he looks younger. When he arrived in Ceuta in the last quarter of 2000, police took him to the Mediterraneo Center, a residential center for children age ten and younger. Though he spent three months at the center before running away he was never issued with a health card. Staff refused to readmit him to the center and he lived on the streets, sniffing solvents and developing several serious health problems. Doctors in the health clinic refused to treat him because he lacked a health card. When HRW interviewed the child a year after he arrived in Ceuta, "he was not receiving medical care and was visibly ill."[148]

In Italy, children over age six without a residence permit are not entitled to anything except emergency health care and inpatient care for contagious

146. Verkaik, *supra* note 67.
147. Eve Geddie, Christina Oikonomou & Michele LeVoy, PICUM, Access to Health Care for Undocumented Migrants in Europe 7 (Nov. 2007).
148. HRW, *supra* note 40, at 20.

diseases.[149] In some cases, even these restrictive entitlements are violated. Thus, according to a report by Médecins du Monde: "In some regions, like Lombardia, children have to pay tickets because pediatricians are wrongly categorized as secondary health care."[150] Moreover, NGOs report significant regional disparities in the provision of health care; in the major cities and where NGO organization is strong, access is easier and standards are higher.

Limiting health care to emergency or urgent care, while narrower than the scope of protection envisaged in the CRC, is in conformity with the position set out in the International Convention on the Protection of the Rights of All Migrant Workers and Members of Their Families (CMW):

> Migrant workers and members of their families shall have the right to receive any medical care *that is urgently required* for the preservation of their life or the avoidance of irreparable harm to their health on the basis of equality of treatment with nationals of the State concerned. Such emergency medical care shall not be refused them by reason of any irregularity with regard to stay or employment.[151]

However, by limiting health care for irregular migrants to emergency treatment, the CMW seems to establish "narrower [protection of social rights] than corresponding rights afforded to *all persons, including those without legal status,* in general international human rights law as interpreted by the competent treaty bodies."[152] The Parliamentary Assembly of the Council of Europe has identified problems that arise from this restrictive approach:

> Irregular migrants, as they are often in a vulnerable situation, have a particular need for the protection of their human rights, including basic civil, political, economic and social rights . . . [S]tates should seek to provide *more holistic care,* taking into account, in particular, the specific needs of vulnerable groups such as children.[153]

Moreover, the interpretation of what counts as "emergency medical care" is inconsistent and ad hoc, both between and within states. The European Committee of Social Rights, the body responsible for monitoring the application of the European Social Charter of the Council of Europe, decided that

---

149. *Id.* at 52.
150. *Id.* at 55.
151. Convention on the Protection of the Rights of All Migrant Workers and Members of Their Families, *adopted* 18 Dec. 1990, U.N. GAOR, 69th plenary mtg., art. 28, U.N. Doc. A/RES/45/158 (1990) (*entered into force* 1 July 2003) (emphasis added).
152. Ryszard Cholewinski, Protection of the Human Rights of Migrant Workers and Members of Their Families Under the UN Migrant Workers Convention as a Tool to Enhance Development in the Country of Employment 14 (2005), *available at* http://www2.ohchr.org/english/bodies/cmw/docs/cholewinski.doc (emphasis added).
153. Parliamentary Assembly of the Council of Europe Resolution 1509, Human Rights of Irregular Migrants, ¶¶ 5, 13.2 (2006).

a 2002 French law about the rights of undocumented migrants to health care was not sufficiently precise in its use of the term "emergencies and life-threatening conditions." It concluded that the law violated access to health care, especially for irregular children, by restricting its use to emergency and life-threatening conditions.[154] It also has refused to limit medical care to Arendt's children, holding that France had violated the European Social Charter's guarantee of care and assistance to all children: "[L]egislation or practice which denies entitlement to medical assistance to foreign nationals, within the territory of a State Party, even if they are there illegally, is contrary to the Charter."[155] In short, state services do not yet uniformly reflect legal entitlements to economic and social rights for Arendt's children.

XII. ARE CHILDREN CITIZENS?

Tabitha's abusive and traumatic separation from her family by the Belgian authorities, the Albanian boy's lack of access to schooling in France, and the unaffordable health care for migrant children in northern Italy, illustrate some of the many obstacles to rights enforcement that confront Arendt's children. In Tabitha's case, the absence of a responsible adult compounded the disadvantages she faced as a noncitizen, with no country to call her own. The Albanian child could not re-enroll himself in school once he left Tirana; migrant children in Italy have no right to register for the National Italian Health Service and consequently depend on NGOs if their cases fall outside the limited exceptions in domestic law. None of these problems would have arisen had these children been citizens. But, as I suggested earlier, not all of Arendt's children are noncitizens. Citizen children can also find themselves summarily separated from family members, helpless in the face of serious human rights violations. To some extent, this is because the epiphany that took place in the realization and centralization of women's rights following the Bosnian War, the Vienna and Beijing Human Rights conferences, and the concerted and effective activism of a global women's movement, has no equivalent in the children's rights field. As a result, it is not an exaggeration to claim that, in many spheres—geographic, socioeconomic, and normative—children's rights do not translate into effective human rights. In fact, children are disproportionately disadvantaged and neglected with respect to similarly situated adults,[156] as the evidence presented above

154. PICUM, Council of Europe on Health Care for Undocumented Migrants (Mar. 2005), *available at* http://www.picum.org/HOMEPAGE/BreakingNews1.htm.

155. *See* Int'l Fed'n of Human Rights v. France, Complaint No. 14/2003, ¶ 32, *available at* http://www.coe.int/t/dghl/monitoring/socialcharter/complaints/cc14merits_en.pdf.

156. In the United States, The Nation's Food Bank Network provides "emergency" service for 24 to 27 million people each year. About 36 percent of them are under the age of

suggests. Law enforcement is carried out by adults and the lack of a child-centered focus needs to be specifically targeted. Consider the slow progress towards recognition of women's rights, which stemmed largely from the male-dominated perspective in law enforcement, an instructive precedent for child rights advocates today.

Moreover, as with women, claims arising out of the special, unique circumstances of children have been neglected. For example, because children's agency in migration generally is not acknowledged, children are considered dependent rather than independent; in other words, the concept of "the child" as an autonomous entity does not exist in immigration law.[157] This reality has some perverse consequences: migrant children traveling alone are more likely to have an illegal status than adults because the law does not accommodate their independent migration. Even citizen children can find themselves functionally stateless within their own country. This seemingly paradoxical situation is the product of two distinctive child characteristics: their prolonged, enforced dependency and their political and legal disenfranchisement.

A clear illustration of this situation can be found in the child's "citizenship deficit." In what sense is a child a "real" citizen?[158] He or she cannot vote or stand for public office. In many countries, a child cannot use his or her citizenship to guarantee continued family life at home. A child's citizenship does not block the deportation, removal, or summary arrest of a noncitizen parent. In other words, it does not protect the child against de facto or constructive deportation. As Bosniak has pointed out, citizenship turns out to have an ambiguous, hybrid, even inconsistent meaning: citizenship status does not convey citizenship rights.[159] Noncitizen adults have the right to permanent residence and access to welfare benefits, irrespective of citizenship—a citizenship right by most accounts. By contrast, citizen children (who have status) lack one of the cardinal rights of citizenship, non-deportability, in the sense just described.[160]

The difference between American and European legal protections also evidences an obstacle to rights enforcement. Because an international hu-

---

eighteen. Almost all recipients are US citizens. America's Second Harvest, Hunger Study 2006, *available at* http://www.hungerinamerica.org/key_findings/.

157. *See generally* David B. Thronson, *Choiceless Choices: Deportation and the Parent-Child Relationship*, 6 Nevada L.J. 1165 (2006).

158. Jacqueline Bhabha, *"The Mere Fortuity of Birth?" Children, Mothers, Borders, and the Meaning of Citizenship*, *in* Migrations and Mobilities: Citizenship, Borders, and Gender 187 (Seyla Benhabib & Judith Resnick eds., 2008).

159. Linda Bosniak, The Citizen and the Alien: Dilemmas of Contemporary Membership 14, 30, 37, 38 (2006).

160. Technically, of course, citizen children are not deportable, any more than any other citizen, but the deportability of noncitizen parents nullifies this important protection for affected children.

man rights regime does not oversee the US immigration control system, its exclusionary impetus is much less qualified by rights concerns. The European system, by contrast, has been shaped by the supervision of the European Court of Human Rights. The US test for families resisting deportation on the basis of a child's best interest in staying home allows far less leeway. Whereas citizen adults generally have the right and the ability to bring and keep their noncitizen dependents in their home country, citizen children have no such equivalent right; thus the right to respect for family life is asymmetric.[161] Where noncitizen parents of citizen children face removal or deportation (3 million US children have undocumented parents),[162] their children's citizenship generally does not afford any legal protection.[163] In other words, children's ties to their home country are considered less legally significant than those of adults. Whether this policy is based on a principled presumption of infantile adaptability, or on a pragmatic calculus about the dangers of encouraging reproductive behavior for immigration status, does not matter. The US test is particularly harsh: unless it can be shown that there is "exceptional and extremely unusual hardship"[164] affecting the citizen child, the parent(s) will be removed.[165] The "usual" compassionate factors, such as radical disruption of schooling, linguistic difficulties, loss of kinship and friendship networks, decline in standard of living, and unfamiliarity with new surroundings, are not sufficient to protect family unity. Exceptional situations, such as rare medical conditions untreatable away from the child's home country, are the only impediments to deportation. In normal cases, therefore, the child is forced to confront the Hobson's choice between home and family.

The fallout of a recent immigration raid on a factory in southern Massachusetts starkly illustrates the rightlessness of the citizen child and how he or she becomes one of Arendt's children. Similar raids, both in workplaces and within the homes of migrant workers, have since taken place on a regular basis. On 6 March 2007, the US Department of Homeland Security raided an equipment and clothes factory after months of prior undercover investigation and arrested 361 low-paid workers, who were then taken by plane to detention centers in Texas.[166] These events traumatized several hundred US citizen children whose parents were involved. Most of the arrested

161. Thronson, *supra* note 157.
162. Passel, *supra* note 24, at 8.
163. *See generally* The Urban Inst., Paying the Price: The Impact of Immigration Raids on America's Children (2007).
164. 8 U.S.C. § 1229b(b)(1)(D) (2006).
165. Recognition of the severity of the US test and its devastating fallout for US citizen children led to the proposal of the Child Citizen Protection Act, introduced in Congress in March 2006 by Congressman Jose Serrano.
166. Jason Szep, *Workers Sue U.S. Factory After Immigration Raid*, Reuters, 15 May 2007.

workers were young Guatemalan women, many single parents. Among the predictable fallout of the raid was the hospitalization of a seven-month-old US baby, dehydrated because of separation from the breast-feeding mother, and a distraught US seven-year-old, who returned home from school to find no trace of his mother. Though many of the women eventually were released from detention pending determination of their cases, the citizenship of their children will have no effect in retaining them in the United States, just as it did not prevent the parents' unnecessary and summary incarceration.

Within Europe, the test for resisting deportation of parents of citizen children is not quite as harsh because European human rights law has tempered some of the draconian policies of member states. Article 8 of the ECHR affords everyone the right to respect for their "private and family life, [their] home and . . . correspondence." It also requires states not to interfere with the exercise of this right except where this is "necessary in a democratic society." Whereas the asymmetry between adults and children in regards to the impact of citizenship on family reunion still exists—adults can bring dependents to join them, but children cannot bring relatives on whom they are dependent to join them—states are required to balance the competing interests of the state in enforcing immigration control and in protecting the individual's right to respect for his or her family life.[167]

But, the relative rightlessness of Arendt's children regarding family reunion still persists in Europe. As a rule, states tend to look at retrospective ties to place rather than at prospective disadvantages to which loss of place may lead; so the impact of the loss of ties, familiarity with societal norms and customs, education, and language skills on older children is weighed more heavily than are the similar impacts on younger children. And yet the place of residence has a pervasive influence even for very young children; it affects children's life expectancy, their physical and psychological development, material prospects, and general standard of living. The fact of belonging to a country fundamentally affects a child's family and private life, during childhood and beyond. Yet children, particularly young children, are often considered parcels that move easily across borders with their parents and without particular cost. They inexorably become children with no country to call their own.

A particularly interesting development concerns Romanian child migrants within the European Union.[168] Since the entry of Romania into the European Union on 1 January 2007, nearly all Romanian citizens within it have become de facto non-deportable. As Elena Rozzi points out,[169] this

167. *See e.g.*, Berrehab v. Netherlands, App. No. 10730/84, 11 Eur. Ct. H.R. (ser. A) 322 (1988).
168. I am completely indebted to Elena Rozzi for the thoughts and material set out in this paragraph.
169. Personal communication from Elena Rozzi (5 May 2008) (on file with the author).

community status can be considered a form of "semi-citizenship" ("*semi-cittadinanza*") because, even though it does not automatically afford EU citizens access to citizenship of the EU host state, it does severely limit their chances of being deported. Unless public order or security justifies it, or the EU citizens cannot demonstrate the ability to support themselves without reliance on public funds after an initial three months' stay, all EU citizens have an indefinite right to remain in any EU state. This has complex and somewhat paradoxical impacts on the protection of some of the most exploited Romanian child migrants. Save the Children Italy has found that young Romanian prostitutes have been much more difficult to include in social protection programs since their immigration "regularization" because they no longer need to obtain a residence permit to avoid the risk of deportation or removal.[170] Semi-citizenship thus perversely emancipates these Arendt's children from the social support networks with which they might otherwise be forced into contact. This in-between state, both legal and rightless, recalls other such liminal legal positions—of alien citizens, invisible children, and missing girls.

This depletion of children's citizenship, and disregard for the destructive impact of constructive deportation on their lives, are serious indicators of the lack of rights, a lack that sharply distinguishes children from adults. Family reunion is one of the bedrocks of contemporary immigration policy—the major source of legal immigration—and yet children are afforded no independent access to it; as with women in an earlier era, they are assumed to be dependent entities that follow rather than bring in a family. An intention to use a child's immigration status as a basis for adult migration is routinely dismissed as illegitimate, a deceitful abuse of the child as an "anchor." This asymmetry is one example of radical rightlessness for children. In an age of global migration and increased scrutiny of the position of migrants, protection from the possibility of deportation is one of, if not the, cardinal attributes of citizenship. Yet for Arendt's children, this salient citizenship benefit, one of the few that children are theoretically entitled to, is compromised.

XIII. CONCLUSION

Arendt's children regularly live their lives in the zone of exception. Where advocacy is weak, the rights holder weaker still, and political will absent, de facto rightlessness is the norm. Human rights instruments, however, have provided a framework for advancing claims for conceptualizing these children's entitlements apart from the approaches of law enforcement officials and politicians. In some cases, they also have fueled redistribution of

---

170. Progetto Equal Palms, *supra* note 120.

resources and protections, as in the case of Tabitha's claim to family reunion in Canada, expansions in some US jurisdictions of the notion of persecution in refugee law to include child-specific persecution, and European advances in children's asylum processing. More often, the rights enumerated are imperfect or inchoate rights awaiting realization. Children's rights are human rights, but they need much more thought, effort, and political will to function as the tools they were designed to be. As the discussion on the merits of requiring direct interviews of child asylum seekers by state officials demonstrates, the connection between human rights provisions and policies that actually respect rights must be crafted, not assumed. We have developed parts of the initial toolkit and have left it for children—migrant children, stateless children, Arendt's children—to use effectively. Yet when these children choose to further their chances of effectively buttressing their abstract claims to rights, whether by migrating across borders *sua sponte* or escaping from punitive detention "shelters" to create independent living situations, they are punished. They are forcibly returned "home" to their country of origin or are denied access to basic public services.

By virtue of both international law and domestic regulations, the system entitles undocumented migrant children to primary education and health care, even though they lack legal residency status. Their undocumented status does not render them officially rightless.[171] For example, foreign nationals generally have rights to public education enshrined in domestic law. Yet, as several of the case studies have demonstrated, in reality, Arendt's children lack access to services because entitlement depends on production of a government-issued document, which migrant children are not given. So the state still retains the monopoly of determining eligibility, despite the universalist aspirations of the human rights tradition.

These children are not rightless because they are disqualified by their age, as is the case for citizen children seeking family reunion, nor are they rightless because they are not recognized as persons before the law, as is the case for children whose birth is not registered. Rather they are rightless because the structures of inequality embedded in society are not adequately corrected by the available resources. This situation is not going to be rectified by the denigration of rights favored by some radical skeptics[172] any more than

171. CRC, *supra* note 5, art. 24; ICESCR; *supra* note 127; Convention Against Discrimination in Education, *adopted* 14 Dec. 1960, 429 U.N.T.S. 93 (*entered into force* 22 May 1962). The Committee on Economic, Social and Cultural rights has interpreted the principle of non-discrimination to extend "to all persons residing in the territory of a State part, including non-nationals, and irrespective of their legal status." *General Comment No. 13: The Right to Education*, U.N. ESCOR, Econ., Soc. & Cult. Rts. Comm., 21st Sess., ¶ 34, U.N. Doc. E/C.12/1999/10 (1999). For domestic Spanish law, see Organic Law 4/2000 of Jan. 11, Regarding the Rights and Freedoms of Foreign Nationals Living in Spain and Their Social Integration, as amended by Organic Law 8/2000 of 22 Dec.

172. *See, e.g.*, David Kennedy, *When Renewal Repeats: Thinking Against the Box*, *in* Left Legalism/Left Critique 373 (Janet Halley & Wendy Brown eds., 2002).

by gratuitous recitation of human rights treaty provisions. Clearly Arendt's children depend more on naming, shaming, and aggressive mobilization of advocacy strategies than the general population of children who have parents or fellow citizens watching out for them. Bottom-up mobilization is essential for the success of top-down litigation because without the former the latter is trumped by nativist and xenophobic sentiments, particularly in a post-9/11 climate of suspicion. Thus rights believers have their work cut out for them as opinion-formers, whistle-blowers, and concerned members of civil society. Most of all, they have an obligation to raise and stimulate discussion of the difficult and contentious issues that arise in actualizing migrant children's right to have rights. They need to address the ambivalence that policymakers feel, torn between sympathy and hostility, between a concern to protect and a pressure to punish, rather than minimize or ignore it. Human rights instruments will never deliver on their aspirations without the political honesty and the mobilizing muscle that transform them into live demands. Alas, there are no short-cuts to justice.

[10]

Of Relative Rights and Putative Children: Rethinking the Critical Framework for the Protection of Refugee Children and Youth

MARY E CROCK*

Abstract

This article is about a complex policy problem for governments everywhere: the phenomenon of children and young people presenting as forced migrants, either alone or in the company of responsible adults. The special vulnerability of children in situations of displacement is apparent and (typically) is readily acknowledged. Rather than responding directly and simply to the needs of the embodied child, however, governments have found serial justifications for denying protection and for adopting policies that harm, rather than help, the children in question. Using as a case study Australia's recent response to children presenting as unauthorised maritime arrivals ('UMA'), the article explores the discourses that have developed to deny children rights that are enshrined in international law. I argue that these have centred around three disabling ideas. The first is that the rights of children are compromised by their standing relative to the rights and interests of adults. The second is that the rights of refugee children and youth are affected by their status as non-citizens or aliens. This is because rights vested under international law will only have meaning if 'enabled' by domestic law. The third challenge to the notion of rights in refugee children and youth revolves around the perceived imperative that countries adopt measures to deter irregular migration. The idea is that policies must be set so as to deter adults from placing refugee children and youth in situations of peril by sending them alone in search of asylum. The protection of the *putative* child is invoked in defence of policies that are acutely harmful to embodied children. In Australia's case, examples of such policies are found in the mandatory detention of undocumented refugee children and youth and the decision to deflect UMA children and youth to regional processing centres on Nauru and Papua New Guinea's Manus Island. Without denying the difficulties governments face in these matters, I argue that Australia's laws and policies have now reached a tipping point. The very concept that refugee children and youth might be rights bearers has been put in question.

I The Challenge

Children presenting as forced migrants — most particularly children seeking asylum without the protection of a responsible adult — pose intractably difficult policy problems. The reasons young people end up in situations of forced displacement are as varied as the

---

* Professor of Public Law, University of Sydney. The author wishes to thank Hannah Martin for research assistance; Judy Cashmore, Yanghee Lee, Ron McCallum, Mary Anne Kenny and Ben Saul for comments on drafts of the article. Thanks also to Kate Pope and Kate Constantinou for supplying statistical data. Research for this article was undertaken with the support of the Australian Research Council, Linkage Project LP100200596 'Small Mercies, Big Futures: Enhancing Law, Policy and Practice in the Selection, Protection and Settlement of Refugee Children and Youth'. The views expressed in this article are those of the author alone and full responsibility is taken for any errors that remain.

world's evils, and equally as complex. Children can be part of a mass exodus. They can be the victims of vile criminal activities. They can be pawns in complex strategies devised by adults desirous of achieving immigration outcomes for either or both children and their families. In whatever circumstances they arrive, children are the most vulnerable of migrants. They are unusually susceptible to injury in situations of unrest or disaster (natural or humanitarian).[1] They are particularly ill-equipped to deal with the complexities of legal processes in navigating the protection pathways available under international and domestic law. On the other side, there is evidence that parents and responsible adults will target countries perceived to be generous in their reception of immigrant children.[2] Often placed in situations of great peril, these young migrants are referred to in policy circles as 'anchor' children. Governments everywhere struggle when required to accommodate the needs of children within regimes directed at border control and irregular migration.[3] Australia's experience has led the government in this country to adopt policies and propose law reforms that the government itself acknowledges are detrimental to the interests of the children affected, on the presumption that punitive measures are the only way to deter irregular migration (including irregular migration by children themselves).

The central argument in this article is that there has been a tendency in the Australian case to subscribe to theories about children in forced migration that both deny the complexity of the phenomenon and fail to provide useful frameworks for finding solutions. More specifically, I contend that the approach adopted in this country has led to a regressive tendency to objectify the child migrant — and to deny to children altogether their legal status as rights bearer under international law.

The challenges refugee children and youth face in asserting the rights conferred at law (international and domestic) are threefold. First, in practice, these children are rarely considered as rights bearers in isolation from the adults who dominate the family collective. Here, the rights of the children are perceived to be qualified by the relative rights of the responsible adults who are associated with children by relationship or responsibility. When parents are characterised as irregular migrants, as security risks, or are themselves subjected to deterrent measures such as interdiction and deflection to a third country, children are often the collateral damage to decisions made about adults' status.

Second, the refugee child's status as rights bearer qua child is seen as subservient to the child's status as a non-citizen or alien. Australia's migration laws are quite express[4] in the stipulation that immigration law and policy — particularly as it relates to control and enforcement — has precedence over any other applicable law and policy. Nowhere is this

---

1 For a discussion of the disproportionate number of children affected by the Boxing Day tsunami in 2004, see UNICEF, 'UNICEF Launches $144.5 Million Appeal' (Press release, 6 January 2005) <http://www.unicef.org/media/media_24707.html >.

2 This fact is borne out in Australia's experience, with the number of unaccompanied children presenting as irregular maritime arrivals jumping from eight in 2008 to 848 in 2012. See statistics supplied by Department of Immigration and Citizenship ('DIAC'), email to the author from Ms Katie Constantinou dated 26 November 2012, reflecting statistics as at 23 November 2012.

3 See Mary Crock, *Seeking Asylum Alone: A Study of Australian Law, Policy and Practice Regarding Unaccompanied and Separated Children* (Themis Press, 2006); Mary Crock and Jacqueline Bhabha, *Seeking Asylum Alone: Unaccompanied and Separated Children and Refugee Protection in Australia, the UK and the US* (Themis Press, 2007).

5 This is all the more so since the August 2012 amendments to the *Immigration (Guardianship of Children Act) 1946* (Cth), discussed further below.

as apparent as in laws and policies mandating the detention of children and youth presenting as undocumented asylum seekers.

As I have argued elsewhere,[5] Australians clearly understand the notion of obligation under international law, in particular the principle that refugees should not be *refouled* or returned to a place where they face persecution for a Convention reason.[6] However, there is mounting evidence that we do not accept that this obligation might vest a correlative right in persons in respect of whom obligations are owed. This is most particularly the case when the persons asserting rights are minors. Australia's position on these matters is apparent in the policy and laws enacted by its federal Parliament and by the way in which these laws have been interpreted by its highest courts. Subscribing to the dualist approach to international law,[7] both Parliament and the courts have made it plain that it is Australia's domestic laws that will dominate in the event of inconsistency with obligations assumed under international law.[8]

The third problem facing refugee children and youth aspiring to assert rights is what I identify as 'deterrence' theory.[9] This results in the figurative disembodiment of the refugee child by shifting the protective focus from the actual child to the 'putative' child. Deterrence measures play out as harsh and punitive policies that range from interdiction and deflection to a third country, mandatory immigration detention, denial of rights to education and of opportunities for family reunification. Deterrent measures are predicated on the notion that the harsh treatment of the embodied child is necessary so as to prevent harm to and the abuse of future children (the putative children). The imperative to deter is found in the harms befalling children caught up in the processes of irregular migration in general — and of irregular maritime travel in particular. The argument is that generous policies towards children presenting as forced migrants act as a pull factor, encouraging others to send their children in search of protection (or a better life). For example, in 2011, then Minister Chris Bowen used the dangers for children inherent in irregular maritime migration as a primary justification for deflecting unauthorised maritime arrivals ('UMAs') to Malaysia[10] — a country not party to the *Refugee Convention*, which was known to be a place where refugees suffered hardship and abuse of human rights. He said:

> I think the overriding obligation is to stop unaccompanied minors risking their lives on that dangerous boat journey to Australia. The overriding obligation is to say to

5 See Mary Crock, 'Shadow Plays, Shifting Sands and International Refugee Law: Convergences in the Asia Pacific' (2013) *International and Comparative Law Quarterly* (forthcoming).

6 See *Convention Relating to the Status of Refugees*, opened for signature 28 July 1951, 189 UNTS 150 (entered into force 22 April 1954) Art 1A(2) ('*Refugee Convention*') as amended by the *Protocol Relating to the Status of Refugees*, opened for signature 31 January 1967, 606 UNTS 267 (entered into force 4 October 1967).

7 See Gillian Triggs, *International Law: Contemporary Principles and Practices* (LexisNexis Butterworths, 2006) 105 [3.4], 142–3 [3.65].

8 See *Al-Kateb v Godwin* (2004) 219 CLR 562; Hilary Charlesworth et al, 'Deep Anxieties: Australia and the International Legal Order' (2003) 25 *Sydney Law Review* 423.

9 Mary Crock and Daniel Ghezelbash, 'Do Loose Lips Bring Ships? The Role of Policy, Politics and Human Rights in Managing Unauthorised Boat Arrivals' (2010) 19 *Griffith Law Review* 238.

10 The 'Arrangement' with Malaysia involved sending 800 UMAs to that country in exchange for 4000 refugees from Malaysia: *Arrangement between the Government of Australia and the Government of Malaysia on Transfer and Resettlement*, signed 25 July 2011 ('Arrangement'). See the discussion at Part 4 below.

parents, 'Do not risk the lives of your children to get the prospect of a visa in Australia'.[11]

This article begins, in Part II, with a brief overview of how the United Nations *Convention on the Rights of the Child*[12] and other international instruments that have shaped juridical conceptualisations of the child as legal person. While there has never been a time in human history when the international legal frameworks for the protection of refugee children have been stronger, a gulf has opened between international principle and domestic practice. Australian is presented in Part III as a case study demonstrating how the relativities of rights affect refugee children and youth in two areas of human rights law: the right to family life and the right to personal freedom and integrity of the person (infringed by immigration detention). In each instance it will be seen that the denial of children's fundamental rights is often accompanied by the invocation of deterrence as a policy motivation.

There follows, in Part IV, a study of policies adopted by Australia that plainly conflict with the rights of refugee children and youth to basic protection. With the spike in UMAs that followed the defeat of the so-called 'Malaysian Solution',[13] the government convened an 'Expert Panel' to devise a circuit breaker that would stop the flow of refugee boats to Australia.[14] For UMA children and youth, the change with the most serious ramifications was the decision in August 2012 to re-open 'offshore' processing centres on Nauru and on Papua New Guinea's (PNG's) Manus Island as deterrents. The 'regional processing' regime has the effect of deflecting asylum seekers to these countries, which then assume legal responsibility for all aspects of status determination, care and resettlement. In July 2013, this policy was hardened further by the announcement that all UMAs were to be *resettled* (permanently) in PNG.[15] A new conservative government, elected in September 2013, looks set to continue with the central tenets of this policy. It is a central feature of the scheme that it should cover all irregular maritime migrants, irrespective of their point of contact with Australia[16] and (in principle) irrespective of age and vulnerability. The Minister, acting personally and pursuant to a 'non-compellable, non-reviewable' discretion, is the only actor empowered to exempt individuals from the scheme.[17] The deflection policies reflect, once again, the relativities that plague refugee children and youth as rights bearers. They also embody the theory that irregular migrants can and should be deterred through the adoption of punitive policies.

11 See Julia Gillard PM and Chris Bowen MP, Minister for Immigration and Citizenship, 'Samantha Stosur, Asylum Seekers, Malaysia Agreement' (Transcript of joint press conference, Canberra, 8 August 2011).

12 *Convention on the Rights of the Child*, opened for signature 20 November 1989, 1577 UNTS 3 (entered into force 2 September 1990); ratified by Australia 17 December 1990 ('CRC').

13 See *Plaintiff M70/2011 v Minister for Immigration and Citizenship* (2011) 244 CLR 144 ('*Plaintiff M70*'), discussed in Mary Crock and Mary Anne Kenny, 'Rethinking the Guardianship of Refugee Children after the Malaysian Solution' (2012) 34 *Sydney Law Review* 437.

14 Angus Houston, Paris Aristotle and Michael L'Estrange, *Report of the Expert Panel on Asylum Seekers*, (Department of Immigration and Citizenship ('DIAC'), August 2012) ('*Houston Report*') <http://expertpanelonasylumseekers.dpmc.gov.au/>.

15 See ABC News, 'Asylum Seekers Arriving in Australia by Boat to be Resettled in Papua New Guinea', *ABC News* (online), 20 July 2013 <http://www.abc.net.au/news/2013-07-19/manus-island-detention-centre-to-be-expanded-under-rudd27s-asy/4830778>.

16 See *Migration Amendment (Unauthorised Maritime Arrivals and Other Measures) Act 2012* (Cth).

17 *Migration Act 1958* (Cth) s 198AE ('*Migration Act*').

I conclude by acknowledging the challenges posed by asylum-seeker children and youth. In so doing, I urge a return to the central tenets of the international legal principles which have done more than anything else to bolster the identity of the migrant child as a legal person both deserving of protection and worthy of respect.

II Legal Frameworks and Refugee Children and Youth

Today, there is little novelty in the idea that children should be regarded as 'rights bearers' in law — not as adults in miniature, but as individuals with separate identities and distinct needs and characteristics.[18] The CRC, done at Geneva in 1989, is the most widely accepted of all UN human rights conventions. It built on earlier human rights conventions[19] and epitomises the evolutionary change that has occurred in attitudes to children and to childhood.[20] The CRC demands that children be seen as 'subject of rights, who (are) able to form and express opinions, to participate in decision-making processes and influence solutions'.[21] Viewing children's rights through the human rights framework has moved children from 'objects' to 'subjects'.[22] The idea of 'children's rights' as 'human rights' promotes an approach to children centred on the *personhood* of children. Children have rights not because of their particular vulnerabilities, but simply because they are human beings who deserve the kind of dignity and respect that the rhetoric of human rights signals. Children are rights holders even in instances where the child may lack capacity to exercise rights autonomously.[23]

For its part, the Committee responsible for the oversight of the CRC has demonstrated a keen awareness of the particular vulnerabilities of children in situations of forced migration, issuing General Comments on the protection of unaccompanied and separated refugee children and youth.[24] The CRC has also been recognised by the United Nations High Commissioner for Refugees ('UNHCR') as the normative framework that should be adopted for the treatment of refugee children and youth.[25]

---

18 Jacqueline Bhabha and Wendy Young, 'Not Adults in Miniature: Unaccompanied Child Asylum Seekers and the New US Guidelines' (1999) 11 *International Journal of Refugee Law* 87.

19 See *International Covenant on Civil and Political Rights*, opened for signature 16 December 1966, 999 UNTS 171 (entered into force 23 March 1976 except Art 41 which came into force 28 March 1979) ('ICCPR'); *Convention against Torture and Other Cruel, Inhumane and Degrading Treatment or Punishment*, opened for signature 10 December 1984, 1465 UNTS 85 (entered into force 26 June 1987) ('CAT') .

20 See Philip Alston and John Tobin, *Laying the Foundations for Children's Rights: An Independent Study of some Key Legal and Institutional Aspects of the Impact of the Convention on the Rights of the Child* (UNICEF, 2005) 3ff <http://www.unicef-irc.org/publications/pdf/ii_layingthefoundations.pdf>, 3ff.

21 Maria Santos Pais, 'Child Participation and the Convention on the Rights of the Child' in Rakesh Rajani (ed) *The Political Participation of Children*, (Harvard Center for Population and Development Studies, 2000) 3, 4.

22 See Mary Ann Mason, *From Father's Property to Children's Rights: The History of Child Custody in the United States* (Columbia University Press, 1994).

23 David Thronson, 'Kids Will Be Kids? Reconsidering Conceptions of Children's Rights Underlying Immigration Law' (2002) 63 *Ohio State Law Journal* 979, 986–7.

24 Committee on the Rights of the Child, General Comment No 6: Treatment of Unaccompanied and Separated Children Outside Their Country of Origin, 39th sess, UN Doc CRC/GC/2005/6 (2005).

25 See UNHCR Policy on Refugee Children, Executive Committee of the High Commissioner's Programme, 44th Sess, Subcommittee of the Whole on International Protection, 23rd meeting, EC/SCP/82, 6 August 1993, [17].

More recent human rights treaties — most notably the *Convention on the Rights of Persons with Disabilities*[26] — accept and reinforce the personhood of children, including those with disabilities. The CRPD echoes the CRC in its core provisions, making no less than 36 mentions of children within its 50 articles. These constitute more references to children than any other human rights treaty apart from the CRC.[27]

The two most critical achievements of the CRC are those that have become known as the 'best interests' principle in art 3, and the notion that children should have the right to participate in all decisions affecting their future (art 12).[28] Article 12(1) of the CRC states that a child who is capable of forming his or her own views has the right to express those views freely 'in all matters affecting' him or her: 'those views of the child being given due weight in accordance with the age and maturity of the child'.[29]

Child-centred approaches involve using techniques to find out children's perspectives, including taking into account these differences and children's relative lack of power in society due to the fact that they communicate differently from adults. This places children as active subjects in the centre of decision-making processes, not as incompetent objects of their parents.[30] This rights-based approach was endorsed by the UNHCR Executive Committee in its Conclusion on Children at Risk. In this document, the Committee articulated a series of principles to underpin any strategies and actions taken by government. These include the primacy of the child's right to protection and assistance; the 'best interests' principle and the importance of adopting a rights-based approach.[31]

For children and young people displaced by conflict or disaster, the CRC provides a protective blueprint that should, in principle, cover almost every eventuality.[32] Article 2 makes it clear that the CRC applies to all children, irrespective of their legal status under domestic law. Article 20 calls for the provision of special protection and assistance for children 'temporarily or permanently deprived of [their] familial environments'. Perhaps most significantly, art 22 makes it clear that the protections available at law to children recognised as refugees should apply in equal measure to asylum-seeker children (that is, those whose status as refugees remains to be determined). The CRC therefore stands out from other instruments in that the phrase 'refugee children' is used to cover both recognised refugees and asylum seekers who are children.[33] The CRC also echoes other

---

26 See *Convention on the Rights of Persons with Disabilities*, opened for signature 30 March 2007, 2515 UNTS 3 (entered into force 3 May 2008) ('CRPD'); *Optional Protocol to the Convention on the Rights of Persons with Disabilities*, opened for signature 30 March 2007, 46 ILM 443 (entered into force 3 May 2008). The text of both instruments is available on the website of the Office of the High Commissioner for Human Rights: <http://www.ohchr.org/EN/HRBodies/CRPD/Pages/ConventionRightsPersonsWithDisabilities.aspx>.

27 See Ron McCallum and Hannah Martin, 'Comment: The CRPD and Children with Disabilities' (2013) 20 *Australian International Law Journal* 17 (in this mini symposium).

28 See CRPD art 7(2): 'in all actions concerning children with disabilities, the best interests of the child shall be a primary consideration'.

29 CRC art 12(1); see also CRPD art 7(3).

30 Jo Boyden and Judith Ennew (eds) *Children in Focus: a Manual for Participatory Research with Children*, (Save the Children, 1997).

31 See UNHCR, *Conclusion on Children at Risk, No 107 (LVIII), 2007* (5 October 2007), UNHCR Refworld <http://www.unhcr.org/refworld/docid/471897232.html>.

32 See also CRPD art 11.

33 CRC art 22; see also Mary Crock, 'You Have to be Stronger than Razor Wire: Legal Issues Relating to the Detention of Refugees and Asylum Seekers' (2002) 10 *Australian Journal of Administrative Law* 33.

instruments condemning and prohibiting human trafficking.[34] Regarding detention, art 37 of the CRC calls on states to detain children only as a last resort and for the shortest possible time, providing also for children in detention to be given access to legal assistance and the right to challenge their detention.

III Relative Rights

In developed countries like Australia, a strong civil society has seen the central tenets of the CRC promoted in many areas of practice,[35] even if state and federal governments have been reluctant to enshrine the Convention in domestic law. The days when children were viewed as the *property* of their parents — where adults were clearly and uniquely the rights holders — may have passed for citizen children.[36] Whether the CRC has had the effect of fully enfranchising *migrant* children as legal actors is another question. At one level, the notion that the welfare of the child should be a primary consideration in all matters concerning all children is well entrenched in both popular and governmental discourses — especially in the areas of family law and child protection.[37] At another, migrant children continue to struggle across a range of indicators. In this part, two aspects of international human rights law that offer key protections for children are considered: the right to family life,[38] and the principle that children should not be subjected to arbitrary or prolonged detention.[39] Australian law, policy and practice have been slow in both areas to recognise rights in migrant children. Where children are most valued is in their relationship with responsible adults. Children presenting as primary applicants do not fare as well. They suffer from both their inferior position in a created hierarchy of rights and in their characterisation as pawns in an adult game where the immigration objectives of the adults are the main concern.

A *The right to family*

In this section, I will illustrate the right of the migrant child to family life in two contexts. The first concerns sponsorship in family reunification cases. The second issue of central concern to migrant children and youth is the separation of family engendered by deportation or removal.

---

34 CRC art 34; Protocol to Prevent, Suppress and Punish Trafficking in Persons, Especially Women and Children, supplementing the United Nations *Convention Against Transnational Organised Crime* (Palermo Protocol) GA Res 55/25, UN GAOR 55th sess, 62nd plen mtg, Annex II, Agenda Item 105, UN Doc A/RES/55/25 (8 January 2001), opened for signature 15 November 2000 (entered into force 25 December 2003); see also the Optional Protocol to the *Convention on the Rights of the Child* on the sale of children, child prostitution and child pornography, UN Doc A/RES/54/263, opened for signature 25 May 2000, 2171 UNTS 227 (entered into force 18 January 2002).

35 See generally Geoff Monahan and Lisa Young, *Children and the Law in Australia* (LexisNexis, 2008).

36 See, eg, Anne Lawrence, *Principles of Child Protection: Management and Practice* (Open University Press, 2004) 41. In Australia, the construction of the 'welfare child' emerged in the late 19th century.

37 See also Nicola Ross, 'Images of Children: Agency, Art 12 and Models for Legal Representation' (2005) 19 *Australian Journal of Family Law* 94.

38 ICCPR arts 17, 23 (1)–(2), 24; CRC arts 8, 9, 10; CRPD art 23; *International Covenant on Economic, Social and Cultural Rights*, opened for signature 16 December 1966, 993 UNTS 3 (entered into force 3 November 1976) art 10.

39 See ICCPR arts 9, 10; CAT art 16; CRC art 37(b), (d); CRPD arts 14, 17. See also *Refugee Convention* art 31.

Sponsorship Disparities

The reification of children is seen most strongly in the disparity between the rights bestowed on migrant parents to create and maintain family life and those vested in migrant children. No limits are placed on the number of dependent children[40] and orphaned relatives[41] that migrant parents can sponsor upon settlement in Australia.[42] Although the adoption of foreign children can be very difficult,[43] Australia's laws and policies are justified on the basis of protective principles enshrined in the Hague Conventions on Child Abduction.[44]

Where children seek to sponsor parents or family members, however, the situation is dramatically different. Minor children are not permitted to sponsor working age parents from within Australia (the parents must be overseas).[45] Moreover, strict quotas apply to the number of parents who may be granted visas each year. While children who can afford to pay can get priority treatment for some parents,[46] children from disadvantaged backgrounds face impossible odds in the 'non-contributory' stream. Obstacles that have been introduced include a 'balance of family' test, requiring the nominated parents to have more children permanently resident in Australia than in any other country.[47] This is a particular problem for unaccompanied refugee children and youth from the world's most troubled countries: many come from large families and are often the only family member to have been sent abroad in search of protection. The quotas set for 'non-contributory' parent migration mean that the wait for parents can extend well over a decade.[48] As Jacqueline Bhabha has observed, it is an example of 'radical rightlessness' that there is asymmetry between parents whose ability to migrate with their children is virtually unlimited and children who cannot sponsor their parents.[49] When children are denied access to family reunion, she notes, 'they are assumed to be dependent, entities that follow rather than bring in a family'. Bhabha's research shows that Australia is not alone in limiting family reunion in this way or in dismissing child-led migration as illegitimate.

Until August 2012, the situation was brighter for unaccompanied children granted protection in Australia as refugees. A component of the offshore humanitarian program was set aside for 'split family' applications. Over the years, unaccompanied refugee minors were able to sponsor their families to join them in Australia under this scheme. The sharp rise in unaccompanied children presenting as UMAs after 2008,[50] however, raised concerns about the chain migration effect of allowing these children open access to family

---

40 See *Migration Act* s 87(1) and (2); Mary Crock and Laurie Berg, *Immigration, Refugees and Forced Migration: Law, Policy and Practice in Australia* (Federation Press, 2011) ch 8 [8.03].

41 See *Migration Regulations 1994* (Cth) sch 2 subcll 117, 837, Crock and Berg, above n 40, [8.21]ff.

42 See also Crock and Berg, above n 40, ch 8.2; Mary Crock, Mary Anne Kenny and Fiona Allison 'Children and Immigration and Citizenship Law' in Monahan and Young, above n 35, 238.

43 See *Migration Regulations 1994* (Cth) sch 2 subcll 102, discussed in Crock and Berg, above n 40, [8.18] ff.

44 See *Convention on Protection of Children and Cooperation in Respect of Intercountry Adoption*, opened for signature, 29 May 1993 (entered into force 1 May 1995). Australia ratified the Convention in 1998. See Crock and Berg, above n 40, ch 8.2.3.

45 See *Migration Regulations 1994* (Cth) sch 2, subcl 103; Crock and Berg, above n 40, ch 8.3.

46 See *Migration Regulations 1994* (Cth) sch 2 subcl 143; and Crock and Berg, above n 40, ch 8 [8.34].

47 See *Migration Regulations 1994* (Cth) reg 1.05; sch 2 subcll 103.213, 143.213; Crock and Berg, above n 40, ch 8 [8.35].

48 See Crock and Berg, above n 40, ch 8 [8.32].

49 Jacqueline Bhabha, 'Arendt's Children: Do Today's Migrant Children Have a Right to Rights?' (2009) 31 *Human Rights Quarterly* 410, 449.

50 Statistics provided by DIAC in November 2012 suggest that the number of arrivals went from eight in 2008 to 848 in 2012. Document provided to the author on 27 November 2012, available on request.

reunification. As well as the risk of overwhelming the humanitarian program, the concern was that the children were being used increasingly as 'anchors' to achieve migration outcomes for their families. The Explanatory Statement to the amending regulations justified the interference to the children's right to family life by reference to both the relativities of the rights vested in children and the need to deter parents from sending their children on dangerous sea voyages. Stressing that arts 17 and 23 of the ICCPR do not confer direct rights to enter a country, it reads:

> As refugees are unable to return to their country of origin, if family reunification is not available there is the potential that some refugees may be permanently separated from their family. However, Australia considers that changes to family reunification do not amount to a separation of the family as there has been no positive action on the part of Australia to separate the family. An [UMA] becomes separated from their family when they choose to travel to Australia without their family. To this end, Australia does not consider that Articles 17 and 23 are engaged. Even if Articles 17 and 23 were engaged, the change does not seek to remove the ability of [UMAs] in Australia to achieve family reunification; it simply places [UMAs] on an equal footing with all other Australian citizens and permanent residents wanting their family to join them in Australia. Australia considers that this is a necessary, reasonable and proportionate measure to achieve the legitimate aim of preventing [UMAs] from making the dangerous journey to Australia by boat.[51]

The Memorandum goes on to acknowledge that unaccompanied refugee children and youth can face impossible obstacles in achieving family reunification through the regular family migration stream (due to the balance of family test, costs and delays). However, the restriction is justified as proportionate — again on the basis of protecting the putative child from the perils of ocean voyages.[52]

Interestingly, this is the approach to sponsorship and family reunion that has been favoured by the United States (US) government with the visa program devised for immigrant children if a US family court has found that reunification with at least one parent is not viable due to abuse, neglect or abandonment and it is not in their best interests to return to their country of origin.[53] The Special Immigrant Juvenile Status ('SIJS') operates to grant unaccompanied migrant children a direct path to permanent residence if the application is complete before the child turns 21 and if that child remains unmarried.[54] Although more generous in some respects than the treatment of persons

---

51 Explanatory Statement to Migration Amendment Regulation 2012 (No 5), Select Legislative Instrument 2012 No 230 (Cth) 1–2.

52 Ibid 2.

53 *Immigration and Nationality Law Act* 8 USC § 1101(a)(27)(J). The first version of the statute required that the child had no parent available; in 2008, the statutory language was amended to protect children if reunification with one or both parents was not viable. The *Trafficking Victims Protection and Reauthorization Act* of 2008, Public Law 110-457, 122 Stat 5044.

54 See Ombudsman for US Citizenship and Immigration Services, *Recommendation: Special Immigrant Juvenile Status Adjudications: An Opportunity for Adoption of Best Practices*, 15 April 2011, Department of Homeland Security <http://www.dhs.gov/xlibrary/assets/Citizenship-and-Immigration-Services-Ombudsman-Recommendation-Special-Immigrant-Juvenile-Adjudications.pdf>

granted asylum as *Refugee Convention* refugees, its major drawback is that SIJS children face a lifetime ban on sponsoring family for migration to the US.[55]

Deportation and Removal

Children also face considerable problems in trying to retain a semblance of family life where a parent falls foul of Australia's migration laws. The children of temporary residents are treated at all stages as adjuncts to their parents, even if they are born in Australia.[56] They are subject to removal if a parent is deported.[57] The citizen children of Australian permanent residents are technically immune from removal. However, where a non-citizen parent is convicted of a serious crime, the interests of such children will not guarantee that their parent is given lenient treatment. Where the parent is the only available caregiver, citizen children can face either de facto exile or state care.

The effect of the CRC on this aspect of Australian immigration law was first considered by the High Court in the 1995 case of *Minister for Immigration and Ethnic Affairs v Teoh*.[58] The High Court recognised that Australia's ratification of the CRC gave rise to an entitlement of sorts that the best interests of children will be a primary consideration in relation to decision-making in the immigration context.[59] The case became something of a cause célèbre because it concerned the non-citizen father of seven Australian-citizen children. The man's deportation on messy drug offences placed the children at risk of a lifetime of state care. The High Court majority ruled that Mr Teoh had been denied procedural fairness because he had not been given an adequate hearing on the issue of whether his deportation was in the 'best interests' of his seven children. The Court's use of the principle enshrined in art 3 of the CRC was regarded as radical for two reasons. The first was that the majority had ascribed meaning to human rights principles that had not been expressly incorporated into Australia's domestic laws. Second, just as controversially, the majority was seen to be upholding in the *children* the right to family life.[60]

One reason that the *Teoh* decision raised great controversy lies in the sense of hierarchy that has developed in the discourse on international human rights. Article 2 of the CRC notwithstanding, migrant children are seen as migrants first and children second. As such, any rights vested in them by law must be relative — first to the right of the state to control immigration and thereafter to the rights and status of their parents. The dissonance between the discourse on children's rights in theory and the response generated by attempts to assert rights by or on behalf of a migrant child in practice was more than apparent in the aftermath of the High Court ruling in *Teoh*. The then Attorney General joined with the Minister for Foreign Affairs to issue a statement to the effect that the signature and ratification of an international instrument should not be taken to create any

---

55 See Jacqueline Bhabha and Susan Schmidt *Seeking Asylum Alone: Unaccompanied and Separated Children and Refugee Protection in the US* (Themis Press, 2006) 51–4.

56 *Australian Citizenship Act* 2007 (Cth) s 12(1)(a). See Kim Rubenstein, *Australian Citizenship Law in Context* (LawBook, 2002) 90.

57 See *Migration Act*, s 140.

58 (1995) 183 CLR 273 ('*Teoh*').

59 Ibid 291–2 (Mason and Deane JJ). Note, however, that *Teoh* dealt with issues of procedural fairness, and did not *guarantee* any child a right to have their best interests taken into account as a 'primary consideration' in decision-making. The precedential value of the case has also been questioned: See *Re Minister for Immigration and Multicultural Affairs; Ex parte Lam* (2003) 214 CLR 1.

60 See CRC arts 9, 10; ICCPR arts 17, 23.

expectations or entitlements in domestic law, absent enabling legislation. This was followed by legislation to similar effect which was ultimately not pursued[61] — in part because a change in the composition of the High Court saw a retreat by the judiciary from the stance taken in *Teoh*.[62]

In fact, the approach taken by the majority in *Teoh* fell out of fashion not just in respect of its treatment of the CRC. In subsequent cases virtually every attempt to invoke international legal obligations to defend the human rights of refugee children has failed. While these have included attempts to give content to the Immigration Minister's role as guardian of unaccompanied refugee children,[63] it is to the most egregious of these cases that we now turn.

B *The Detention Cases*

The second area where refugee children and youth have suffered serious harm in spite of protections spelled out in international human rights law, is in immigration detention.[64] Ironically, Australia began the practice of detaining children presenting as UMAs in 1989,[65] the very year that the CRC was made. The policy was enacted into laws[66] that survived a constitutional challenge in 1992 on arguments that gave first voice to justifications for the denial of rights that persist to this day. First, the detention of UMAs was framed (somewhat disingenuously) as voluntary in nature on the basis that Australia was merely exercising its sovereign right to prevent undocumented migrants from entering the country. It was said that the asylum seekers (then from Cambodia) were free to leave at any time; they were just not at liberty to enter Australia in the absence of government permission.[67] It followed from this that the detention process did not require the involvement of courts because its function was preventative rather than punitive. The characterisation of immigration detention centres as three-walled prisons, with asylum seekers free to go anywhere but into Australia, featured again in the *Tampa* litigation of 2001.[68] This was so even though the Human Rights Committee had expressly denounced this justification of Australia's laws.[69]

---

61 See Administrative Decisions (Effect of International Instruments) Bill 1995 (Cth) s 5. The Bill lapsed with the prorogation of Parliament in 1996, was resurrected by the Coalition government in 1999 but ultimately was not put to a vote.

62 See *Re Minister for Immigration and Multicultural Affairs; Ex parte Lam* (2003) 214 CLR 1 33–4 [102]. For a commentary on this case, see Wendy Lacey, 'A Prelude to the Demise of *Teoh*: The High Court Decision in *Re MIMA; Ex parte Lam*' (2004) 26 *Sydney Law Review* 131.

63 See Mary Crock, 'Lonely Refuge: Judicial Responses to Separated Children Seeking Refugee Protection in Australia' (2005) 22(2) *Law in Context* 120; Crock and Kenny, above n 13.

64 See, eg, Zachary Steel, et al 'Psychiatric Status of Asylum Seeker Families Held for a Protracted Period in a Remote Detention Centre in Australia' (2004) 28(6) *Australian and New Zealand Journal of Public Health* 23.

65 For an account of this period see Mary Crock (ed) *Protection or Punishment: The Detention of Asylum Seekers in Australia* (Federation Press, 1993).

66 See *Migration Amendment Act 1992* (Cth); discussion in Crock and Berg, above n 40, ch 16.2.3.

67 See *Chu Kheng Lim v Minister for Immigration, Local Government and Ethnic Affairs* (1992) 176 CLR 1, 31–2 ('*Chu Zheng Lim*'); Crock and Berg, above n 40, ch 3.3.2.

68 See *Ruddock v Vadarlis* (2001) 110 FCR 491, 548 ('*Vadarlis*').

69 See *A v Australia*, Communication No 560/1993, CCPR/C/59/D/560/1993 (30 April 1997); and *Amuur v France* (1992) 22 EHRR 533. On this point, see Crock, above n 33, 49.

In both *Chu Kheng Lim*[70] and *Vadarlis*,[71] however, the critical findings of the court turned on the relative status of the asylum seekers in question. As constitutional aliens, any rights they might have held under international law were subject to their status under Australia's domestic laws. Without visas, they had no (domestic) right to enter the country and, ipso facto, no right to freedom. This point was made in the opening statement by Heydon J in *Plaintiff M47/2012 v Director General of Security*:

> During oral argument in *Al-Kateb v Godwin*, McHugh J asked counsel for the appellant: 'How can you claim a right of release into the country when you have no legal right to be here?' Most of the plaintiff's arguments in this case were directed to that penetrating question. The plaintiff denied its premise, and denied the answer which the question expected.[72]

Heydon J found himself a dissentient in the Court's findings on the validity of the legislation that condemned the plaintiff to indefinite detention.[73] However, his Honour was not alone in his assumption that the assertion of rights by the non-citizen must always be qualified before the superior power of the sovereign state.

The politics surrounding the first detention cases was so raw that little or no attempt was made to characterise the government's actions as humanitarian in intent; the discourse on deterrence was simply about securing Australia's borders.[74] By 1994, more than 40 babies had been born to the asylum seekers from Cambodia over more than four years spent in detention under a Labor government. During the years of conservative Coalition rule, the number of children in immigration detention peaked at 918 in 2000–01.[75]

The first decade of the new millenium saw a series of cases in which an increasingly conservative High Court reiterated and reinforced the relativities in the human rights of refugee children and youth. All involved attempts to invoke principles of international law to override or modify the statutory regime that had developed mandating the detention of asylum seekers pending the grant of a visa.[76] No concessions were made for asylum-seeker children, notwithstanding earlier changes to the law that could have facilitated release into the community.[77]

The first of these cases involved an attempt by the Family Court of Australia to order the Minister for Immigration to release from detention the Bahktiyari children, whose

---

70 (1992) 176 CLR 1; see Mary Crock, 'Climbing Jacob's Ladder: The High Court and the Administrative Detention of Asylum Seekers in Australia' (1993) 15 *Sydney Law Review* 338.

71 See *Ruddock v Vadarlis* (2001) 110 FCR 491, 548.

72 See *Plaintiff M47/2012 v Director General of Security* (2012) 86 ALJR 1372, 1422 [228].

73 Ibid 1396–7 [71] (French CJ); 1416 [191]–[192] (Hayne J); 1455 [399] (Crennan J); 1463–4 [447], 1465 [458] (Kiefel J). Compare Heydon J's dissent 1439–42 [315]–[327] . See also 1406–7 [135]–[138] (Gummow J); 1471 [489] (Bell J) who agreed on this point.

74 See Senator Jim Kiernan, 'Defend, Deter, Deny' in Crock, above n 65, ch 4; Australian Broadcasting Commission, 'To Deter and Deny', *Four Corners*, 15 April 2002 (Debbie Whitmont) <http://www.abc.net.au/4corners/archives/2002a_Monday15April2002.htm>.

75 See Human Rights and Equal Opportunity Commission ('HREOC'), *A Last Resort? National Inquiry into Children in Immigration Detention* (HREOC, 2004) 65, 76.

76 For an account of the history and operation of these provisions, see Crock and Berg, above n 40, ch 16.

77 See *Migration Act*, s 72 which introduced the concept of the 'eligible non-citizen', in response to the Human Rights Committee's criticisms of Australia in *A v Australia*. See the discussion in Crock and Berg, above n 40, ch 4.4.

parents were at the centre of a bitter and protracted dispute over their status as refugees.[78] In 2003, a majority of the Full Family Court made history when they asserted that s 67ZC of the *Family Law Act 1987* (Cth) and the injunction powers conferred by s 68B of the same Act empowered that Court to make orders for the welfare of children held in immigration detention.[79] Nicholson CJ and O'Ryan J (Ellis J dissenting) held that if a trial judge found that the continued detention of the children was unlawful, then the Court had the power to order the Minister to release the children.[80]

In the Full Family Court, Nicholson CJ and O'Ryan J ruled that s 67ZC of the *Family Law Act* empowers the Court to make orders relating to the welfare of children, and in doing so prescribes that the Court have regard to the best interests of the child as the paramount consideration. Section 68F then provides guidance as to how a court is to determine the best interests of a child and includes matters such as the need to protect the child from physical or psychological harm. Their Honours found that the injunction power of the Court conferred by s 68B is an aid to the exercise of the Court's jurisdiction in relation to children.[81] Their Honours described these welfare provisions as conferring something akin to the parens patriae jurisdiction of state and territory courts.[82]

The High Court made short work of the Full Family Court's attempts to give primacy to the notion of the children's rights to protection and to treatment respectful of their welfare.[83] The Court made it clear that the welfare jurisdiction of the Family Court within a state is confined to the extent of any explicit reference of legislative power from the states to the federal legislature.[84] It struck down the majority's ruling that the original conferral of welfare jurisdiction on the Family Court in respect of children of marriages was without limitation.[85] Just as importantly, the High Court rejected the lower court's findings that its jurisdiction had been extended to cover asylum-seeker children by Australia's accession to the CRC.[86] The children remained in detention because of their alienage: they were migrants first and children second. Absent express changes to the jurisdiction of the Family Court, the advent of the CRC did not have the effect of extending the powers of that Court to adjudicate on matters involving refugee children.

There followed, in 2004, four cases in which the High Court made it clear that international human rights law must cede before the superior status of domestic

78 The family was eventually removed from Australia, despite a ruling of the Human Rights Committee condemning Australia's treatment of the family. See *Ali Aqsar Bakhtiyari and Roqaiha Bakhtiyari v Australia*, Communication No 1069/2002: Australia, CCPR/C/79/D/1069/2002 (6 November 2003).

79 See *B v Minister for Immigration and Multicultural and Indigenous Affairs* (2003) 173 FLR 360 ('*B v MIMIA*')

80 Following submissions on the deleterious effect detention was having on the children, the Family Court went on to order the release of the Bakhtiyari children.

81 *B v MIMIA* (2003) 173 FLR 360, 387 [132]–[133].

82 Ibid [134].

83 *Minister of Immigration and Multicultural and Indigenous Affairs v B* (2004) 219 CLR 365 ('*MIMIA v B*').

84 In the case of South Australia, the only such reference of power occurred in 1987 and was confined to matters relating to the maintenance of ex-nuptial children.

85 See, eg, *MIMIA v B* (2004) 219 CLR 365, 384 [24]–[52] (Gleeson CJ and McHugh J).

86 Nicholson CJ and O'Ryan J had relied on the *Teoh* decision to hold that the Convention was not merely 'aspirational' in its effect. According to their Honours, the reference to the 'best interests of the child' principle in s 67ZC of the *Family Law Act 1975* (Cth) contained sufficient specificity to require the behaviour of decision-makers to reflect that principle. They ruled (with Ellis J dissenting) that it was strongly arguable that at least part of the intent of the introduction of s 67ZC in 1995 was to extend its protection to all children as required by arts 3(2) and 19 of the CRC and not just children of a marriage. See *B v MIMIA* (2003) 173 FLR 360, 410 [287]. Cf Kirby J *MIMIA v B* (2004) 219 CLR 365, 408–9 (Kirby J).

immigration laws expressed in plain terms of statutory intendment. The first two cases involved failed asylum seekers who remained in detention by reason of the fact that no other country would take them.[87] The third involved asylum seekers detained in very poor conditions who argued that the terms of their incarceration impermissibly converted what was administrative or 'preventative' detention into something punitive.[88]

The last case was brought on behalf of the four Sakhi children[89] and also involved an argument that the mandatory detention provisions in the *Migration Act* were unconstitutional. The assertion was that a scheme mandating the detention of children without consideration of anything other than their immigration status had to be punitive — and therefore a matter within the province of the judicial power of government — requiring the involvement of courts. Unlike adult asylum seekers, the Sahki children could not be said to be 'voluntary' detainees because they had no power to elect to leave the country. Because they were children, counsel also argued that the children could not be said to pose a threat to Australia. Hence, arguments about the validity of preventive detention should fail. While the High Court split in the other cases, it was unanimous in *Re Woolley; Ex parte Applicants 276/2003*.[90] The identity of the applicants as children could not transform (lawful) administrative detention into (unlawful) punishment.[91] The Court ruled that in determining the constitutionality of an enactment, it could have regard only to the purpose of the legislation and not to its effect. Again, the Court made it plain that in spite of Australia's accession to the CRC, migration law will prevail in determining the treatment received by asylum-seeker children. The human rights of the Sakhi children as children were sublimated to their status as irregular migrants. In practice, this meant that they had no rights at all.

In the year that the High Court delivered judgment in the four detention cases, the Human Rights Commission released a 925-page report on children in immigration detention that roundly condemned the Australian government's policies and practices.[92] Having 'won' its battles in the High Court, one year later the government moved to amend the *Migration Act* so as to bring the legislation more in line with the language of the CRC. Section 4AA now provides that, as a matter of principle, children should be detained as a last resort.[93]

The relativity approach to the human rights of asylum seekers has found expression in more recent detention cases, most notably in the High Court's consideration of legislation conferring on Australia's security agency an effective power to veto the grant of a visa to persons recognised at law as 'Convention' refugees. In practice, an adverse security

---

87 See *Al-Kateb v Godwin* (2004) 219 CLR 562; *Minister for Immigration and Multicultural and Indigenous Affairs v Al Khafaji* (2004) 219 CLR 664.

88 See *Behrooz v Secretary, Department of Immigration and Multicultural and Indigenous Affairs* (2004) 219 CLR 486 ('*Behrooz*').

89 See *Re Woolley; Ex parte Applicants M276/2003* [2004] HCATrans 2 (3 February 2004).

90 (2004) 225 CLR 1.

91 Ibid 32 [82] (McHugh J), This argument was used in *Behrooz* to support the contention that in some circumstances it can be 'lawful' for a person to escape from custody. *Behrooz v Secretary DIMIA, SHDB v Godwin, MIMIA v Al Khafaqi* [2003] HCATrans 456, 458 (12–13 November 2003).

92 See HREOC, *A Last Resort? National Inquiry into Children in Immigration Detention* (HREOC, 2004).

93 The provision nevertheless narrows the concept of detention and makes no mention of the period spent in detention. It reads:

(1) The Parliament affirms as a principle that a minor shall only be detained as a measure of last resort.

(2) For the purposes of subsection (1), the reference to a minor being detained does not include a reference to a minor residing at a place in accordance with a residence determination.

clearance has meant that these refugees are condemned to indefinite detention. Children have once again been harmed as collateral damage.[94]

It is not just the children of the refugees found to be security risks who have remained in immigration detention for prolonged periods of time. In spite of a concerted push, after 2008, to reduce the length of time children and families spend in detention,[95] by May 2013 there were 1731 children (aged under 18 years old) in immigration detention facilities and alternative places of detention.[96] As explored in the following part, the reasons for this lie in the toxic mix of ideas surrounding the relativities of rights vested in refugee children and youth and the notion that punitive policies can be effective to deter irregular maritime migration.

IV Deterrence Theory and the Right to Basic Protection

The third area where refugee children and youth have emerged as collateral damage is in the struggle to halt irregular maritime migration through the institution of direct, *physical* deterrent measures in the form of interdiction and deflection. As noted earlier, the centrepiece of recent initiatives in Australia has been the establishment of a 'regional processing' regime, which this time involves the transfer of UMAs to a foreign country for all aspects of the asylum process. The history of Australia's involvement in such schemes is recounted elsewhere.[97] For present purposes it suffices to note that the various schemes have all involved measures that sit uneasily with Australia's obligations under international law.

Nauru and Manus Island were first used for processing the refugee claims of asylum seekers seeking protection in Australia in 2001. On that occasion, a conservative federal government went to some lengths to argue that the regime was compliant with Australia's obligations not to *refoule* or send back refugees to countries where they would face persecution for Convention reasons.[98] The legislative scheme paid lip service to the idea that the 'offshore' country to which asylum seekers were deflected should be party to the *Refugee Convention* and other human rights treaties.[99] Created at the height of the shock effect generated by the terrorist attacks of 11 September 2001, the regime survived the few legal challenges that were made, one of which involved an unaccompanied child.[100] It was a

---

94 On 15 October 2012 Australia held in detention seven children on grounds that their parents had recieved adverse security assessments. No minors currently have adverse security assessments against them; there was one, but he has now turned 18: Evidence given to Legal and Constitutional Affairs Legislation Committee, Parliament of Australia, Canberra, 15 October 2012, 132 (Martin Bowles, Acting Secretary, DIAC).

95 For a discussion of the scheme establishing Alternative Places of Detention, see Crock and Kenny, above n 13.

96 See DIAC, *Immigration Detention Statistics Summary*, 31 May 2013 <http://www.immi.gov.au/managing-australias-borders/detention/facilities/statistics/>.

97 See Crock, above n 5.

98 See Department of Immigration, Multicultural and Indigenous Affairs ('DIMIA'), *Interpreting the Refugees Convention* (DIMIA, 2002), which contains a lively defence of the lawfulness of the first Pacific Solution. See also Crock and Berg, above n 40, ch 4.3.3.

99 See *Migration Act* s 198A.

100 See *Ruddock v Vadarlis(No 2)* (2001) 115 FCR 229; *P1/2003 v MIMIA* [2003] FCA 1029; *Plaintiff P1/2003 v Ruddock* (2007) 157 FCR 518; and the decisions of McKerracher J in *Sadiqi v Commonwealth* [2008] FCA 1262 (18 August 2008); *Sadiqi v Commonwealth (No 2)* (2009) 181 FCR 1; and *Sadiqi v Commonwealth (No 3)* [2010] FCA 596 (11 June 2010). See the discussion of these cases in Crock and Kenny, above n 13.

package of measures[101] that did indeed stop UMAs for a period, but at great cost — to the refugees affected and to Australia in both financial[102] and psycho-social terms.[103] Unaccompanied and separated refugee children were particularly susceptible to harm.

Between 2001 and 2003, 55 unaccompanied UMA children were sent to these Nauru and Manus Island. Leaving to one side the very harsh conditions experienced, the greatest concern raised by this first 'Pacific Solution' is that some of the children affected were denied access to basic protections to which they should have been entitled. There is evidence that at least some of the children should not have been sent to Nauru or Manus Island in the first place — the date of their arrival in Australia meant that they should not have been caught by the change of law.[104] Without access to any form of advice or assistance, however, the children were powerless to assert their rights. More worryingly, of the 55 sent to Nauru, 32 were returned (voluntarily) to their countries of origin, their refugee claims having been rejected. Subsequent research suggests that some of the children were subsequently killed and that many left again in search of safety.[105] These statistics stand in sharp contrast to the (compatriot) unaccompanied children whose refugee claims were processed on mainland Australia around the same time. Of 290 unaccompanied children who sought asylum in Australia between 1 July 1999 and 28 February 2003[106] all were ultimately allowed to stay in the country.[107]

The experience of the children caught up in the Pacific Solution underscores the importance of process for the identification and protection of *Refugee Convention* refugees. The available evidence is that children left without assistance invariably fare worse in asylum processes than those who are represented.[108] The first regime established on Nauru and Manus Island was modelled on the processes employed by the UNHCR in its field operations. However, while the UNHCR's operations are driven most often by lack of resources, asylum seekers on Nauru were denied access to any outside assistance as a matter of principle.[109]

---

101 The strategy had four elements: the 'excision' from Australia's 'migration zone' of the offshore territories where maritime asylum seekers were making landfall; the interception of UMAs and their deflection to foreign countries; the 'push-back' of boats to Indonesia; and the grant of temporary protection to UMAs recognised as refugees. The legislative scheme was built around the following statutes: *Border Protection (Validation and Enforcement Powers) Act 2001* (Cth); *Migration Amendment (Excision from Migration Zone) Act 2001* (Cth); *Migration Amendment (Excision from Migration Zone)(Consequential Provisions) Act 2001* (Cth).

102 For an account of the cost of these strategies, see Crock and Ghezelbash, above n 9, 258–9.

103 The intense focus on UMAs over this period coincided with unprecedented aggression within Australia towards visible minorities. This played out in the targeting of persons thought to be irregular migrants, with more than 240 wrongful arrests, detentions and even deportations. This was also the era of the worst interracial rioting seen in Australia for many years. See Crock and Ghezelbash, above n 9, 276.

104 This allegation was put to the author by one unaccompanied minor brought to Australia from Nauru in 2002 as a 'transitory person'. See Crock, above n 3, 77.

105 Edmund Rice Centre, *Deported to Danger : A Study of Australia's Treatment of 40 Rejected Asylum Seekers* (Research Report, Edmund Rice Centre for Justice & Community Education in cooperation with the School of Education, Australian Catholic University, 2004) <http://www.erc.org.au/index.php?module=documents&JAS_DocumentManager_op=downloadFile&JAS_File_id=208>.

106 See Crock, above n 3, 39.

107 It should be noted that the children sent to Nauru and Manus Island shared very similar backgrounds and stories to those who made it to mainland Australia. It should be noted here that the children sent to New Zealand in the wake of the *Tampa* Affair were all granted permanent protection within weeks of arrival. See Crock, above n 3, 77

108 See Crock, above n 3, 147–8; Jaya Ramji-Nogales et al, *Refugee Roulette: Disparities in Asylum Adjudication and Proposals for Reform* (New York University Press, 2009).

109 During the early years of the Pacific Solution no one was allowed access to the camps on Nauru and Manus Island. Refugee advocates were denied visas to enter the country. In 2006, these policies were reversed. Migration agent

If public opinion finally turned against the mandatory detention of children in 2005,[110] by 2008 the newly-elected Labor party was ready to acknowledge that the regime established on Nauru was an embarrassment — and plainly in breach of Australia's international legal obligations. Then Shadow Minister Julia Gillard said:

> Labor will end the so-called Pacific solution — the processing and detaining of asylum seekers on Pacific islands — because it is costly, unsustainable and wrong as a matter of principle.[111]

As detailed elsewhere,[112] the politics of irregular maritime migration worked to dissuade the Labor government from making a clean break with the policies of its conservative predecessor. It abolished neither the policy of mandatory detention nor the rubric of offshore processing. The rights of the child were sublimated to the electoral interests of the government, even if the rhetoric adopted on this occasion centred on the imperative of adopting deterrent measures in the interests of 'saving lives at sea'.

Labor's first attempt to establish a regional processing framework, as the new-look deflection process was termed, relied on the same legislation used to support the first Pacific Solution. It was negotiated in May 2011 and promoted as a product of the so-called 'Bali Process'.[113] The *Arrangement between the Government of Australia and the Government of Malaysia on Transfer and Resettlement* was expressed not to be legally binding on either party, a fact that was later to trouble the High Court greatly because of the dissonance it created with the terms of the *Migration Act*.[114] It was to involve the transfer to Malaysia of 800 asylum seekers who arrive in Australia as UMAs. In exchange, Australia agreed to take in 4000 refugees residing in Malaysia under the care of the UNHCR. The scheme was one that the Minister insisted had to include unaccompanied UMA children if it was to have the effect of deterring parents from risking the lives of their children.[115] So it was that Plaintiff 106 was chosen to be among the first UMA asylum seekers to be transferred to Malaysia, a country where refugees, including children,[116] were known to be subjected to

---

Marion Le was given access to those who remained on Nauru. With her assistance, the remaining inmates lodged appeals and were all accepted as refugees and resettled in Australia. See Michael Gordon, *Freeing Ali* (University of New South Wales Press, 2005).

110 Pressure from government backbenchers led to softening of the detention policy and changes to the *Migration Act* in June 2005. See Crock and Berg, above n 40, [16.17].

111 Commonwealth, *Parliamentary Debates*, House of Representatives, 13 May 2003, 14006 (Julia Gillard).

112 See Mary Crock, 'First Term Blues: Labor, Refugees and Immigration Reform' (2010) 17 *Australian Journal of Administrative Law* 1; Crock and Ghezelbash, above n 9.

113 See *The Bali Process* <http://www.baliprocess.net/>. In recent years, regional consultative processes have been established in most regions of the world. See Alexander Betts, *Global Migration Governance* (Oxford University Press, 2011) 18; Mary Crock and Daniel Ghezelbash, 'Secret Immigration Business: Policy Transfers and the Tyranny of Deterrence Theory', in Savinder Singh (ed), *The Ashgate Research Companion to Migration Theory and Policy* (Ashgate, 2013).

114 *Plaintiff M70/2011 v Minister for Immigration and Citizenship* (2011) 244 CLR 144 ('*M70*').

115 Australian Broadcasting Commission, 'Children Part of Refugee Swap: Bowen', *Lateline*, 2 June 2011 (Tony Jones) <http://www.abc.net.au/lateline/content/2011/s3234302.htm>.

116 Adrian Edwards, *UNHCR Calls for Proper Safeguards for Children Being Returned to Malaysia by Australia* (3 June 2011) United Nations High Commissioner for Refugees <www.unhcr.org/4de8bb8d9.html>.

detention and exploitation.[117] The campaign that followed caused embarrassment of the governments of both Malaysia and Australia.[118]

In the result, the 'Arrangement' with Malaysia did not survive a challenge in the High Court. Absent the shock factor that prevailed in 2001,[119] one decade later the Court was not prepared to accept the assertion that the declaration of a country under s 198A of the *Migration Act* should be regarded as a legislative act and an inappropriate subject for judicial review. The majority ruled that s 198A(3) of the *Migration Act* established a series of jurisdictional facts, the satisfaction of which was required for the lawful declaration of a country as a regional processing country.[120] The declaration was struck down because Malaysia did not meet the objective criteria outlined. It is not a party to the *Refugee Convention* and Protocol and did not in fact have a record sufficient to satisfy an objective observer that it would be able to safeguard the human rights of UMAs sent to it for processing and resettlement as refugees.

The failed Arrangement with Malaysia was interesting in that, at least on its face, the scheme tried to be consistent with human rights standards.[121] It is just that neither country wanted the applicable framework to be legally binding. The situation facing the unaccompanied UMA children was particularly serious, as the guardianship arrangements pertaining in Australia would not have applied in Malaysia.[122] In the *Malaysian Declaration Case*, the High Court did not address the broader question of who should care for children transferred to Malaysia. However, it did rule that the Minister in the instant case had failed to comply with the terms of his own domestic legislation by choosing Plaintiff 106 (the minor plaintiff) for transfer without certifying that the action was in the child's best interests.[123]

---

117 Amnesty International *Abused and Abandoned: Refugees Denied Rights in Malaysia,* (Report, Amnesty International, 20 June 2010) <http://www.amnesty.org/en/news-and-updates/report/refugees-malaysia-arrested-abused-and-denied-right-work-2010-06-16>.

118 See, eg, Australian Broadcasting Commission, 'PM Defends Malaysia's Treatment of Refugees', *News,* 27 October 2011 <http://www.abc.net.au/news/2011-10-27/pm-defends-malaysias-treatment-of-refugees/3604674>; Al Jazeera, 'Australian and Malaysia Sign "Refugee" Deal', 25 July 2011 <http://www.aljazeera.com/news/asia-pacific/2011/07/20117254439553573.html>.

119 For an analysis of the effect of these events, see Naomi Klein, *The Shock Doctrine: The Rise of Disaster Capitalism* (Penguin, 2008).

120 See *M70* (2011) 244 CLR 144, 194 [109]; 201–202 [135] (Gummow, Hayne, Crennan and Bell JJ); cf 180 [58] (French CJ).

121 For example, the Arrangement provides that the government of Australia would conduct pre-screening assessments 'in accordance with international standards' prior to any transfer from Australia to Malaysia. See the Arrangement, cl 9(3). This would include an assessment of Australia's obligations under the CRC: see DIAC, Submission no 13 to the Senate Legal and Constitutional References Committee, *Inquiry into Australia's Arrangement with Malaysia in Relation to Asylum Seeker*, 11 October 2011 [59]. The Arrangement stipulates (at cl 8) that those transferred from Australia to Malaysia should be 'treated with dignity and respect and in accordance with human rights standards' and that '[s]pecial procedures will be developed and agreed to by the Participants to deal with the special needs of vulnerable cases including unaccompanied minors'. Australia was also to meet the costs relating to ensuring the health and welfare of the transferees: cl 9(1)(c).

122 The previous Minister for Immigration argued that his guardianship of those unaccompanied children transported under the 'Pacific Solution' ceased upon their arrival at the 'declared countries' of Nauru and Papua New Guinea ('PNG'). See Senate Legal and Constitutional Affairs Committee, *Inquiry into the Migration Legislation Amendment (Further Border Protection Measures) Bill 2002* [5.60].

123 *Immigration (Guardianship of Children) Act* 1946 (Cth) s 6A(1) ('*IGOC Act*') requires the Minister to consent in writing before a non-citizen child can be removed from Australia. The majority ruled that a declaration, in the form of Memorandum of Understanding comprising an 'Arrangement' with Malaysia, did not constitute the written consent required by the *IGOC Act*. This meant that removal of Plaintiff M106 would be unlawful. See *M70* (2011) 244 CLR 144, 203 [143] (Gummow, Hayne, Crennan and Bell JJ).

The very domestic focus of the High Court's ruling in *M70* underscores the extent to which the legal discourse on refugees in Australia has come to avoid the high road of international legal principle — and indeed the notion that refugees might be rights holders. Instead of responding to the criticisms of its laws and policies in a manner that is respectful of Australia's obligations under international law, the government opted for an even more extreme response. On this occasion, they were supported by the conservative opposition as well as by an electorate ever sensitive to the issue of irregular maritime migration.[124]

In responding to the surge in UMAs following the defeat of the Malaysian Solution policy,[125] the Australian government used the recommendations of its Expert Panel[126] to justify legislation that repealed s 198A of the *Migration Act*.[127] The replacement scheme allows for the establishment of regional processing, ostensibly free from the constraints of judicial oversight by any Australian court. UMA asylum seekers are liable to removal to Nauru and PNG's Manus Island where their status as refugees will be determined by officials in those countries, under Nauruan and PNG laws respectively. It is a central tenet of the Expert Panel's 'no advantage test' that asylum seekers processed under the regional scheme should face the same sort of delays experienced by other refugees in the region. Given the huge variation in the experiences in the region, it is difficult to know just what is envisaged by this so-called principle.[128] Amendments to the *Immigration (Guardianship of Children) Act 1946* (Cth) make explicit the cessation of Ministerial responsibility for unaccompanied non-citizen children who are transferred to a regional processing centre.[129] The *Migration Act* was amended further in 2013 to extend the operation of provisions that prevent UMAs intercepted in offshore territories such as Christmas Island from seeking protection in Australia. The 'excision' of these territories from Australia's migration zone in 2001 has meant that UMAs apprehended at these locations can only claim asylum in Australia if the Minister exercises a personal, 'non-compellable, non-reviewable' discretion to 'lift the bar' on applications. The operation of these so-called 'excision' provisions now apply also to mainland Australia. This means that no UMA is eligible to seek asylum in

---

124 On this point, see Mary Crock, 'Alien Fears: Politics and Immigration Control' (2010) 2 *Dialogue* 20-31.

125 Department of Immigration, Answer to Question Taken on Notice, Budget Estimates Hearing, 21-2 May 2012, BE12/0262, <http://www.aph.gov.au/Parliamentary_Business/Committees/Senate_Committees?url=legcon_ctte/estimates/bud_1213/diac/BE12-0262_Attachment.pdf>. The government has been reticent to release statistics on boat arrivals and clear statistics are hard to find. The Deputy Secretary, Policy and Program Management Group, DIAC, gave evidence to a Parliamentary Committee in December 2012 that the 'ballpark number' of arrivals in the 2012 calendar year was around 8000 irregular maritime arrivals: Evidence to Parliamentary Joint Committee on Human Rights, Parliament of Australia, Canberra, 17 December 2012, 5 (Wendy Southern). The Department's annual statistical publication gives a figure of 7379 UMAs screened in to the RSD process, a figure which certainly does not capture the actual number of boat arrivals (DIAC, Asylum Trends Australia: 2011–12 Annual Publication, DIAC, 2012 <http://www.immi.gov.au/media/publications/statistics/asylum/_files/asylum-trends-aus-annual-2011-12.pdf> 25.

126 See ABC News, above n 15.

127 See *Migration Legislation Amendment (Offshore Processing and Other Measures) Act 2012* (Cth). The government had earlier introduced two Bills into Parliament: the Migration Legislation Amendment (Offshore Processing and Other measures) Bill 2011 (in September 2011); and the Migration Legislation Amendment (The Bali Process) Bill 2012 (rejected by the Senate in June 2012).

128 Letter from Antonio Guterres to Chris Bowen, 5 September 2012, <http://unhcr.org.au/unhcr/images/120905%20response%20to%20minister%20bowen.pdf>.

129 *Immigration (Guardianship of Children) Act 1946* (Cth) especially s 8(3) as amended by *Migration Amendment (Regional Processing and Other Measures) Act 2012* (Cth) sch 2 items 1–8.

Australia without a special ministerial dispensation. They are liable to be processed in a Regional Processing Country[130]

The Memoranda of Understanding with Nauru and PNG echo the Arrangement with Malaysia by confirming that the scheme is not dependent on the observation of international legal obligations. For its part, Nauru has now enacted the *Refugees Convention Act 2012* (Nauru)[131] and it has amended its *Immigration Regulations 2000* to create a special 'Australian Regional Processing' visa regime which includes a merits review process. In practice, the entire scheme will be run by Australians and for Australia. Nauru does not have the capacity to either design or run either status determination processes or appeals. In December 2012, after the transfers (not including transfers of unaccompanied minors) to Nauru began, the Nauru Parliament passed the *Asylum Seekers (Regional Processing Centre) Act 2012* (Nauru).[132] As well as regulating the operation of the Regional Processing Centres, the Act makes the Minister for Justice, Customs and Border Patrol (or his/her delegate) the automatic and exclusive guardian of any unaccompanied minors transferred to Nauru.[133] Until this Act was passed, there was no meaningful framework for the legal protection of transferred children.[134] Now, Nauru's protections for children are stronger than Australia's. Whereas the CRC has never been fully implemented and has been given scant recognition in Australian law,[135] s 14 of the recent Nauruan legislation affirms that 'It is the intention of Parliament that, in the treatment of a protected person[136] who is a child, regard must be had to the terms of the Convention of the Rights of the Child'.[137] It will still be a harsh sentence for a child who is sent to Nauru, but it is another of the great ironies of the government's scheme that there now a better framework for recognition of a child's international rights in Nauru than there is in Australia. Of course the problem is that the most critical decision — the decision to transfer — will have been made back in Australia, where the interests of the embodied child are not so protected. It seems that Australia is happy to write human rights into the legislation of other countries, but will not acknowledge these children as rights-bearers on our own territory.

---

130 See *Migration Amendment (Unauthorised Maritime Arrivals and Other Measures) Act 2012* (Cth). Presented as an important component of the Expert Panel's 'No Advantage' principle, the amendments will have the effect of creating two classes of asylum seeker in Australia: those who arrive by plane (and who generally present with some form of documentation) and those who arrive by boat without visas. The former group are given access to one of the most sophisticated refugee status determination systems in the world, with access to free assistance where required; oral hearings at both application stage and on appeal; and judicial review of the decisions made. Asylum seekers travelling by plane are generally not detained pending determination of their status as refugees. They are entitled to immediate permanent residence and to an array of assistance measures to settle them into their new country.

131 Nauru became a party to the Refugee Convention and Protocol by accession on 28 June 2011. It was not a party to these instruments when the Conservative Coalition established the first Pacific Solution.

132 Note that PNG does not have legislation to similar effect. PNG's *Child Welfare Act 1961* (PNG) does not readily map onto the circumstances of transferred children, and would at any rate require and order of the Children's Court to take effect (s 41).

133 *Asylum Seekers (Regional Processing Centre) Act 2012* (Nauru) s 15.

134 Nauru has a general guardianship Act (*Guardianship of Children Act 1975* (Nauru)) however this would have had no application to children transferred unless a local Nauruan took it upon themselves to apply for guardianship and obtained a Supreme Court order to that effect. Now that Act is relevant in that it sets out the powers that are vested in the Minister by virtue of the December 2012 legislation.

135 See generally John Tobin, 'The Development of Children's Rights' in Monahan and Young, above n 35, 23, 29–31 [2.7].

136 'Protected person' is the term the Act uses to describe people who have been brought to Nauru under the Australian *Migration Act*, see *Asylum Seekers (Regional Processing Centre) Act 2012* (Nauru) s 3(1).

137 *Asylum Seekers (Regional Processing Centre) Act 2012* (Nauru) s 14.

This is a scheme that sees Australia engaging in the wholesale abdication of its responsibilities as a party to both the *Refugee Convention* and a variety of international human rights instruments. If either Nauru or PNG establish inferior status determination processes, Australia could indeed become complicit in the indirect *refoulement* of refugees that as a matter of international law are squarely its responsibility. The arrangements also do nothing to safeguard the rights Convention refugees have to a whole range of protections beyond *refoulement.*[138] By making a blanket distinction between UMAs and asylum seekers travelling by plane, Australia is plainly in breach of art 31 of the *Refugee Convention*. This prohibits the penalisation of refugees who enter the territory of a state party without authorisation.[139] One might even argue that the whole regime constitutes a breach of the fundamental principle that parties to UN treaties should perform the obligations that they have undertaken in good faith.[140]

For the UMA children and youth selected for transfer to the regional processing countries, the only certainty is that the scheme will involve protracted periods of time living in conditions that will vary from poor to life threatening.[141] On this occasion, Australia has made little attempt to argue that it is acting in compliance with its obligations under international human rights law. The most basic rights of these children are being sacrificed in the name of deterrence. Once again, embodied children are being required to suffer in order to protect the putative children who might otherwise follow in their footsteps.

In Indonesia in October 2012, I met with a 10-year-old boy who was one of very few survivors following the sinking of a boat carrying more than 100 asylum seekers. The oldest child of a widowed mother, he had been sent abroad in search of safe haven with an uncle who perished in the shipwreck. The boy was placed briefly with a family of recognised refugees who left Indonesia to be resettled in New Zealand, moved to a shelter for unaccompanied asylum-seeker children and then taken in by another family. For this child, measures aimed at deterring the responsible adults in his life are light years away from the lived reality of his haunting desolation. The boy stands as a reminder of why the nations of the world came together in 1989 to create *rights* in refugee children — that is, in the child before us, not in the putative child.

---

138 See Michelle Foster and Jason Pobjoy, 'A Failed Case of Legal Exceptionalism? Refugee Status Determination in Australia's "Excised" Territory' (2011) *International Journal of Refugee Law* 23.

139 See Guy Goodwin-Gill, 'Article 31 of the 1951 *Convention relating to the Status of Refugees*: Non Penalisation, Detention and Protection', paper prepared for UNHCR Global Consultations, October 2001 <http://www.unhcr.org/419c778d4.html >.

140 See *Vienna Convention on the Law of Treaties*, opened for signature 23 May 1969, 1155 UNTS 331 (entered into force 27 January 1980) art 26.

141 Manus Island is a very high risk location for malaria and dengue fever: more than 90 per cent of the population of PNG as a whole is at high risk of Malaria. PNG is the highest risk country in the western Pacific region for Malaria, and Manus Island has the highest number of cases of malaria in the country: see World Health Organization, *World Malaria Report 2012* (2012), 161 <http://www.who.int/malaria/publications/country-profiles/profile_png_en.pdf>. Dengue fever presents a similarly high risk: Central Intelligence Agency, 'Field Listing: Major Infectious Diseases' *The World Factbook* (2012) <https://www.cia.gov/library/publications/the-world-factbook/fields/2193.html#>

Part IV
Migrant Workers

[11]

AT THE BORDER AND BETWEEN THE CRACKS: THE PRECARIOUS POSITION OF IRREGULAR MIGRANT WORKERS UNDER INTERNATIONAL HUMAN RIGHTS LAW

LAURIE BERG*

[This article aims to identify jurisprudence which advances the standards of treatment of unauthorised migrants in the context of often hostile domestic laws and political rhetoric. Due to its universalist and humanist underpinnings, many would consider international human rights law to be a natural source of rights protecting migrant workers. However, human rights doctrine takes a chequered approach to the protection of those living or working in a foreign state without visa authorisation. Even the Migrant Workers Convention *recognises states' sovereign prerogative over immigration control, and thereby fails to cater to the especially precarious position of irregular migrants who decline to assert their rights for fear of facing sanctions under immigration laws. It is argued that we need to look to regional judicial forums to find international legal doctrine which articulates a progressive legal framework robustly protective of irregular migrants' rights. This article canvasses jurisprudence in the regional Human Rights Courts in Europe and the Americas which succeeds, in different ways, at decoupling the absolute discretion of states to regulate border control from the substantive rights of irregular migrants once present in a host state.]*

CONTENTS

---

* BA (Hons), LLB (UNSW); LLM (NYU); PhD candidate, School of Law, University of Sydney and recipient of the Lionel Murphy Postgraduate Scholarship for 2006. The author would like to thank Associate Professor Mary Crock, Azadeh Dastyari, Samantha Newman, Katherine Fallah, the participants at the Australian and New Zealand Society of International Law Postgraduate Students Workshop and the Sydney University Postgraduate Law Students Workshop, and the two anonymous referees for their comments. Thanks to Cindy Cross for everything else. Any errors remain, of course, the author's own.

I INTRODUCTION

International migration featured high on the United Nations' agenda in 2006, when, on 14 and 15 September, government delegations from around the world met for the UN General Assembly's High-Level Dialogue on International Migration and Development.[1] This same year saw hundreds of thousands of people lining the streets of Los Angeles with placards proclaiming 'no human is illegal'.[2] Clearly, international migration has become the subject of urgent policy debate within many countries and at the international level. It is equally evident that no single issue is more contentious than that of the movement of people without state authorisation, described in international parlance as 'irregular migration'.[3]

As the Australian Government attempts to guard against the entry of asylum seekers arriving by boat,[4] even 'fortress Australia'[5] is not insulated from irregular (or 'undocumented') migrants. In December 2005, there were approximately 46 400 visa overstayers in Australia,[6] together with an unknown number of non-citizens present in Australia with valid visas who were working in breach of their visa conditions.[7] In current Australian public debate, as in most Western countries, irregular migrants are maligned as 'economic migrants'[8] — less deserving even than refugees because the circumstances precipitating their arrival in Australia are not considered to found a legitimate claim to stay on

---

1 See *Summary of the High-Level Dialogue on International Migration and Development, Note by the President of the General Assembly*, UN GAOR, 61st sess, Agenda Item 55(b), UN Doc A/61/515 (13 October 2006).

2 Not in Our Name Steering Committee, *No Human is Illegal!* (2006) <http://www.notinourname.net/archive/immigrant-justice-10apr06.htm> at 18 May 2007.

3 See, eg, Global Commission on International Migration, *Migration in an Interconnected World: New Directions for Action* (October 2005) 32, available from <http://www.gcim.org> at 18 May 2007; *Summary of the High-Level Dialogue on International Migration and Development, Note by the President of the General Assembly*, UN GAOR, 61st sess, Agenda Item 55(b), UN Doc A/61/515 (13 October 2006).

4 See, eg, Jewel Topsfield, 'Nauru Sets Six-Month Limit on Asylum Seekers', *The Age* (Melbourne, Australia) 20 March 2007, 6.

5 See Margo Kingston, 'Fortress Australia — The Implications', *The Sydney Morning Herald* (Sydney, Australia) 3 September 2001 <http://www.smh.com.au/articles/2003/11/26/1069522644875.html> at 18 May 2007.

6 Department of Immigration and Citizenship, Commonwealth of Australia, *Fact Sheet 86: Overstayers and People in Breach of Visa Conditions* (2007), available from <http://www.immi.gov.au> at 18 May 2007. In 1999, the Department of Immigration and Multicultural Affairs estimated that half of all 'unlawful non-citizens' were engaged in paid employment: Department of Immigration and Multicultural Affairs, Commonwealth of Australia, *Review of Illegal Workers in Australia: Improving Immigration Compliance in the Workplace* (1999) 18.

7 Auditor-General, Australian National Audit Office, *Onshore Compliance — Visa Overstayers and Non-Citizens Working Illegally* (Audit Report No 2, 2004–05) [4].

8 See, eg, Paul Kelly, 'Australia Beyond 2001 — Towards a New National Project' (Speech delivered at the American Australian Association, New York City, US, 26 April 2002) [14] <http://www.americanaustralian.org/Corporate/pdf/speech_paul_kelly.pdf> at 18 May 2007; Rosie Goldsmith, 'Australia's Great Immigration Debate', *BBC News* (UK) 24 October 2001 <http://news.bbc.co.uk/1/hi/programmes/crossing_continents/asia/1613538.stm> at 18 May 2007. See also Wendi Adelson, 'Economic Migrants and Political Asylum Seekers in the United Kingdom: Crafting the Difference' (2004) 1 *Michigan Journal of Public Affairs* <http://www.mjpa.umich.edu/uploads/Volume_1_Migrants_Article_Final.pdf> at 18 May 2007.

Australian soil.[9] As irregular migrants have not been extended the privilege of entry into Australian territory, enforcement plays a dominant role in political discourse.[10] Those who advocate for the rights of undocumented migrant workers are often blocked by the hold that the mantra of border control has on the popular psyche.

This article has the practical goal of identifying jurisprudence which advances the standards of treatment of unauthorised migrants in the context of often hostile domestic laws and political rhetoric. It is hoped that this article will fuel a more sophisticated public debate about the conceptual frameworks necessary to protect the rights of undocumented migrant workers. It is also envisaged that this research will contribute to the arsenal of advocates' tools as they challenge the prevailing view that decent treatment of migrants must always be sublimated to states' wide-ranging powers over their borders and immigrant admissions. Additionally, examples of laws insisting on decent treatment of irregular migrants may form the basis for a positive framework of rights protection of this vulnerable population by courts and law-makers.

Many would consider international law to be a natural source of rights protecting migrant workers, including those living or working without authorisation. This is because undocumented migrant workers have no access to domestic electoral processes in their states of employment, and often resist reporting exploitative living and working conditions to domestic authorities (or seeking judicial redress) for fear of attracting the attention of immigration enforcement authorities. International law, somewhat insulated from domestic debates over immigration policies, might therefore be better placed to provide positive guidance on the treatment of individuals who form part of the global movement of labourers, and who have no access to their own states for protection.

However, when one examines international human rights legal principles, the result is not progressive doctrine, but rather a deep uncertainty about the legal protections afforded to irregular migrants. As states parties jealously guard control of their territory and national membership, they have adopted UN Conventions which emphasise states' sovereign control over their borders, and their absolute prerogative to control admission and deportation of unauthorised migrants.[11] By and large, comprehensive human rights instruments do not explicitly include the protection of irregular migrants; moreover, they explicitly exclude this group from certain rights afforded to authorised immigrants or nationals of the state of residence.[12] When the *International Convention on the Protection of the Rights of All Migrant Workers and Members of Their Families*

9 See Adelson, above n 8, 1.

10 See, eg, the second reading speeches accompanying the passage of the *Migration Amendment (Employer Sanctions) Act 2007* (Cth): Commonwealth of Australia, *Parliamentary Debates*, Senate, 29 March 2006, 2–3 (Nick Minchin, Minister for Finance and Administration); Commonwealth of Australia, *Parliamentary Debates*, House of Representatives, 29 November 2006, 135–7 (Andrew Robb, Minister for Vocational and Further Education). See also *Review of Illegal Workers in Australia*, above n 6.

11 See below Part III(A).

12 Linda Bosniak, 'Human Rights, State Sovereignty and the Protection of Undocumented Migrants under the International *Migrant Workers Convention*' (1991) 25 *International Migration Review* 737, 739.

('*Migrant Workers Convention*')[13] entered into force, the inclusion of *all* migrant workers in the human rights corpus was acclaimed as an unprecedented affirmation of the dignity of undocumented migrants.[14] However, as will be explored in some detail below, the *Migrant Workers Convention* continues to allow states the absolute prerogative to pursue any immigration control policies they see fit. Linda Bosniak has argued that this deference to state interests means that the substantive rights afforded to irregular migrants may be unenforceable in practice.[15]

It seems that, in order to find international legal doctrine which mediates state sovereignty and migrants' rights with more regard to the needs of migrant workers, we need to look to regional judicial forums. Perhaps this is because these are still more distant from the influence of states and the overriding goal of preserving territorial sovereignty. Jurisprudence is emerging in regional human rights courts in Europe and the Americas which affirms the right of states to prohibit the entry of foreigners onto their sovereign territory, but also succeeds, in different ways, at decoupling the absolute discretion of states to regulate entry at the border from the substantive rights of irregular migrant workers once present in their countries of employment.[16]

I explore this argument in three stages. Part II begins with a brief outline of some of the bases upon which it has been asserted that undocumented workers are entitled to protection in their states of employment and redress for the exploitation they experience. I then discuss why international human rights law might appear at first to be a natural repository of checks on states' discretion when it comes to the treatment of irregular migrants.

Nevertheless, in Part III, I will proceed to demonstrate that a review of treaty standards — in both the comprehensive human rights instruments and the dedicated migrant-oriented *Migrant Workers Convention* — disclose a deep ambivalence towards the ability of undocumented migrants to enforce their rights. This ambivalence often allows sovereign discretion over immigration control policies to trump any of the few rights which irregular migrants do hold under these treaties. I suggest that states have intentionally drafted and endorsed treaties which accord a great deal of deference to the plenary power of governments to resist unauthorised entries.

Part IV then proposes that international or regional judicial tribunals may be better placed to articulate protective measures for irregular migrants, since they are further removed from the sovereign control of states. This contention is supported by an exploration of recent case law emanating from the European Court of Human Rights ('ECHR') and the Inter-American Court of Human Rights ('IACHR'). This case law recognises that irregular migrants hold substantive rights opposable against their host state and require states to sequester migrants' unlawful immigration status from their ability to claim these rights. This judicially mediated doctrine suggests different ways in which a uniquely vulnerable class of claimants may be empowered without totally abdicating states' traditional prerogative over immigration enforcement.

---

13 Opened for signature 18 December 1990, 2220 UNTS 3 (entered into force 1 July 2003).

14 Bosniak, above n 12, 740, 758.

15 Ibid 742.

16 See below Part IV.

II THE RIGHTS OF IRREGULAR MIGRANTS AND THE PROMISE OF HUMAN RIGHTS LAW

Irregular or undocumented migrants are people who work in a state of employment without authorisation.[17] To borrow from the internationally enshrined definition, irregular migrants may have entered without authorisation, be employed contrary to their visa stipulations, or have entered with permission but remained after their visas expired.[18] However, treaty definitions aside, it is difficult to address this topic without becoming mired in inflammatory and politically-charged terminology.[19] Individuals working in a foreign state without authorisation have been variously described as illegals,[20] criminal aliens[21] and unlawful non-citizens.[22] It has been observed that the 'collection of pejorative terms, racial slurs and denigrating epithets appear to have no end'.[23]

As an alternative, in 1994, the International Conference on Population and Development recommended the use of the term 'undocumented'.[24] However, this word does not 'cover migrants who enter the host country legally with tourist documents but later violate their conditions of entry by taking a job'.[25] In light of this, the International Symposium on Migration in Bangkok in April 1999 recommended use of the term 'irregular'.[26] This is intended to capture the fact that '[i]rregularities in migration can arise at various points — departure, transit, entry and return — and they may be committed against the migrant or by

---

17 *Migration in an Interconnected World*, above n 3, 32.

18 Article 5 of the *Migrant Workers Convention*, above n 13, states that migrant workers and members of their families:

> (a) Are considered as documented or in a regular situation if they are authorized to enter, to stay and to engage in a remunerated activity in the State of employment pursuant to the law of that State and to international agreements to which that State is a party;
>
> (b) Are considered as non-documented or in an irregular situation if they do not comply with the conditions provided for in subparagraph (a) of the present article.

19 See, eg, Kevin R Johnson, '"Aliens" and the US Immigration Laws: The Social and Legal Construction of Nonpersons' (1996–97) 28 *University of Miami Inter-American Law Review* 263, 279; Elspeth Guild, 'Who is an Irregular Migrant?' in Barbara Bogusz et al (eds), *Irregular Migration and Human Rights: Theoretical, European and International Perspectives* (2004) 3.

20 See, eg, Edward Barnes, 'Slaves of New York: How Crime and Mismanaged Laws Have Made the City the Biggest Magnet for Chinese Illegals', *Time* (New York City, US) 2 November 1998, 72 (discussing the situation of Chinese 'illegals' in New York); '"Illegals" to be Deported', *ABC News Online* (Australia) 29 June 2004, available from <http://www.abc.net.au> at 18 May 2007.

21 See, eg, Jerry Seper, 'Illegal Criminal Aliens abound in US', *The Washington Times* (Washington DC, US) 26 January 2004, A01.

22 See, eg, 'Suicidal Boy Didn't Need Psychiatrist, Court Told', *The Sydney Morning Herald* (Sydney, Australia) 28 July 2003 <http://www.smh.com.au/articles/2003/07/28/1059244548741.html> at 18 May 2007 (referring to a suicidal child as an 'unlawful non-citizen').

23 Jorge A Vargas, 'US Border Patrol Abuses, Undocumented Mexican Workers, and International Human Rights' (2001) 2 *San Diego International Law Journal* 1, 29.

24 International Labour Office, 'Towards a Fair Deal for Migrant Workers in the Global Economy' (Report VI presented at the International Labour Conference, 92nd sess, Report VI, Agenda Item 6, Geneva, 1–17 June 2004) 11.

25 Ibid.

26 Ibid.

the migrant'.[27] I adopt the descriptors 'undocumented', 'unauthorised' or 'irregular' migrant worker in an effort to avoid dehumanising language. Irregular migrants have committed mere administrative violations by breaking immigration laws in their country of employment. In the words of Judge Ramírez of the IACHR, '[w]hat should be an administrative description with well-defined effects becomes a "label" that results in many disadvantages and exposes the bearer to innumerable abuses'.[28] Catherine Dauvergne has remarked that the nomenclature of 'illegal' 'names the other not only as an outsider to a particular nation, but as an outsider to any nation. As such, the other is outside the law itself, and, in a word, illegal'.[29] In sum, it is imperative to avoid labels that suggest a lack of legal existence which is both discriminatory and counterfactual.

A *Arguments for the Need to Protect Irregular Migrants*

Living on the fringes of society, undocumented migrants assume an extremely precarious life within their states of employment. In many parts of the world, they are among the lowest paid and hardest worked employees in the workforce.[30] Due to their unlawful status, irregular migrants live in constant fear of removal, and are thus especially vulnerable to exploitation. The Special Rapporteur on the Human Rights of Migrants has reported abusive working conditions, such as extremely long hours without breaks, refusal to pay wages due, ill-treatment and confinement, which amount, in some cases, to forced labour.[31] States around the world tend to explicitly exclude irregular migrants from access to civil and labour rights and social benefits, adopting rhetoric which conflates immigrants and asylum seekers with criminals and terrorists. For example, shortly after the attacks of 11 September 2001, the former US Attorney-General John Ashcroft was heard to declare, '[l]et the terrorists among us be warned … If you overstay your visas even by one day, we will arrest you'.[32] It is, therefore, unsurprising that undocumented migrants often resist asserting the rights they are entitled to for fear of exposure to immigration authorities.

However, while their living and working conditions are marginal, the size of the irregular migrant worker population worldwide is certainly not. In 2005, an

---

27 Ibid.

28 IACHR, *Juridical Condition and Rights of the Undocumented Migrants (Advisory Opinion)* 18 (ser A) (2003) [11] (Concurring Opinion of Judge Ramírez).

29 Catherine Dauvergne, 'Making People Illegal' in Peter Fitzpatrick and Patricia Tuitt (eds), *Critical Beings: Law, Nation and the Global Subject* (2003) 83, 84.

30 Bosniak, above n 12, 737.

31 Jorge Bustamante, Special Rapporteur on the Rights of Migrants, *Report of the Special Rapporteur on the Human Rights of Migrants*, UN Doc E/CN.4/2006/73 (30 December 2005) [47].

32 Dan Eggen, 'Tough Anti-Terror Campaign Pledged; Ashcroft Tells Mayors He Will Use New Law to Fullest Extent', *The Washington Post* (Washington DC, US) 26 October 2001, A01.

estimated 191 million people were international migrants.[33] The International Labour Organization has calculated the number of 'economically active migrants' around the world at over 86 million.[34] Although precise data relating to clandestine activities is impossible to ascertain, current knowledge puts irregular migration for Europe at about 10–15 per cent of all cross-border movement.[35]

Clearly, some academics and many governments consider the prospect of extending substantial rights to irregular migrants extremely problematic.[36] It is outside the scope of this article to provide a fully-fledged argument for the robust protection of the rights of undocumented migrants. Nevertheless, a range of rationales for advancing the rights and dignity of irregular migrants shape the legal standards of protection that do exist in both domestic and international legal regimes. Just as influential are the tensions or presuppositions implicit in these rationales. For this reason, it is necessary, briefly, to canvass the grounds anchoring the promotion of the rights of undocumented migrants. These include normative arguments as well as those based on pragmatic expediency.

Human rights advocates predictably invoke the universal values underpinning the human rights regime.[37] Some point to the extreme social vulnerability of the undocumented migrant population, who undertake work ubiquitously described as the 'three Ds' — dirty, degrading and dangerous[38] — work that nationals and legal migrants avoid. The sectors which employ migrant workers are usually those where little or no regulatory activity upholds minimum safety, health and

---

33 UN Secretary-General, *International Migration and Development: Report of the Secretary-General*, UN GAOR, 60th sess, Agenda Item 54c, UN Doc A/60/871 (19 May 2005) [43]. The Commission on Human Security put the figure at 175 million, comprising 3 per cent of the world's population in 2000: Commission on Human Security, *Human Security Now* (2003) 41, available from <http://humansecurity-chs.org> at 18 May 2007. According to the International Organization for Migration, the total number of migrants in the world more than doubled between the years 1965 to 2000, from 75 to 175 million people. The projections for the future are that this total will continue to increase: International Organization for Migration, *World Migration 2003: Managing Migration — Challenges and Responses for People on the Move* (IOM World Migration Report Series, vol 2, 2003) 4–5.

34 International Labour Office, 'Towards a Fair Deal for Migrant Workers in the Global Economy', above n 24, [19].

35 Ibid [37]. See also Timothy Hatton and Jeffrey Williamson, 'What Fundamentals Drive World Migration?' (NBER Working Paper No 9159, National Bureau of Economic Research, Cambridge, Massachusetts, 2002) 3 <http://www.economics.harvard.edu/faculty/jwilliam/papers/w9159.pdf> at 18 May 2007.

36 In the view of Schuck and Smith, undocumented aliens entering a state's territory without consent are strangers to the social contract that binds the national community: Peter Schuck and Rogers Smith, *Citizenship without Consent: Illegal Aliens in the American Polity* (1985) 130–40. The Prime Minister of Australia, John Howard, evoked similar sentiments in his 2001 election slogan: 'We will decide who comes to this country and the circumstances in which they come': John Howard (Address delivered at the Federal Liberal Party Campaign Launch, Sydney, Australia, 28 October 2001).

37 See, eg, Gabriela Rodríguez Pizarro, Special Rapporteur on the Rights of Migrants, *Specific Groups and Individuals: Migrant Workers*, UN Doc E/CN.4/2004/76 (12 January 2004) [17].

38 Antoine Pécoud and Paul de Guchteneire, *Migration, Human Rights and the United Nations: An Investigation into the Low Ratification Record of the UN* Migrant Workers Convention (Global Migration Perspectives Series No 3, UN Educational, Scientific, and Cultural Organization, October 2004) 3.

working conditions that should ensure 'decent work'.[39] Those who articulate claims for migrants' rights on the basis of universal values tend to recall the particular concern that the international community has shown for groups experiencing extreme social vulnerability, including the undocumented.[40]

Other arguments in favour of promoting the rights of undocumented migrants rest on structural analyses of irregular migration flows. According to one such argument, many receiving countries welcome the physical labour of foreigners, but rigidly restrict the number of legally issued visas for blue-collar workers to migrate legally, making the existence of undocumented workers inevitable.[41] According to another, even while countries overtly combat clandestine immigration, irregular migration 'is often tacitly permitted or even encouraged [by governments and employers], just because illegals lack rights and are easy to exploit'.[42] Such encouragement may result from geopolitical and transnational economic dynamics based on older colonial patterns.[43] Alternatively, encouragement may take the form of permeable borders. Although states wield extensive authority under international law to control the entry of foreigners into their territory, in practice, states often fail to exercise this control.[44] Such failures to prevent the presence of tens of millions of irregular migrants around the world could be understood as tacit invitations to enter. Analytically, these contributions reject portrayals of irregular migrants as voluntary transgressors of state immigration laws,[45] and emphasise the complicity of receiving states and local employers in the entrance and continued presence of irregular migrants.

Others argue that irregular migrant workers are, in certain respects, de facto members of the national community by virtue of their social and cultural contributions.[46] Generally, the thrust of these arguments is that states and employers should not be entitled to benefit from the labour of irregular migrant workers without according them some degree of entitlement to participate in the political and social community, including access to fundamental rights and protections. Correspondingly, 'the community should keep its end of the unwritten compact by extending the undocumented legal recognition and certain basic rights'.[47]

Consequentialist arguments, on the other hand, seek to demonstrate that guaranteeing undocumented migrants' rights serves the interests of not only the

---

39 Ibid 3–4.

40 *Migrant Workers Convention*, above n 13, preamble.

41 Beth Lyon, 'New International Human Rights Standards on Unauthorised Immigrant Worker Rights: Seizing an Opportunity to Pull Governments Out of the Shadows' in Anne Bayefsky (ed), *Human Rights and Refugees, Internally Displaced Persons and Migrant Workers: Essays in Memory of Joan Fitzpatrick and Arthur Helton* (2005) 551, 552.

42 Stephen Castles and Alastair Davidson, *Citizenship and Migration: Globalization and the Politics of Belonging* (2000) 73.

43 Saskia Sassen, *Losing Control? Sovereignty in an Age of Globalization* (1996) 76–8.

44 Bosniak, above n 12, 737.

45 Sarah Paoletti, 'Human Rights for All Workers: The Emergence of Protection for Unauthorized Workers in the Inter-American Human Rights System' (2004) 12(1) *Human Rights Brief* 5, 5.

46 IACHR, *Juridical Condition and Rights of the Undocumented Migrants (Advisory Opinion)* 18 (ser A) (2003) [6] (Concurring Opinion of Judge Ramírez).

47 Bosniak, above n 12, 750. See Joseph Carens, 'Membership and Morality: Admission to Citizenship in Liberal Democratic States' in William Rogers Brubaker (ed), *Immigration and the Politics of Citizenship in Europe and North America* (1989) 31, 32–3, 43–4.

migrants, but those of the state and its citizens as well.[48] Enforcing minimum standards of working conditions, for example, wage rates, is thought to remove employers' incentives to seek out irregular migrant labour.[49] In the words of one long-time community advocate, refusing legal redress for abuses experienced by irregular migrant workers simply serves to

> embolden lawbreakers who prey on immigrants, frustrate civil and criminal law enforcement generally, undermine public safety and health, entrench undocumented immigrants in a caste hierarchy, and foster an underground economy that depresses the terms and conditions of employment for all workers.[50]

Naturally, there are policy-makers, politicians and community representatives who contest the suggestion that irregular migrants receive anything other than summary deportation. Normatively, some legal theorists and political philosophers have expressed the belief that national communities are constituted on the basis of shared values and culture, and that protecting this unique character requires communities to have absolute discretion over the admission of foreigners and the terms on which they are to be welcomed.[51] Others reject the notion of rights of membership, including protection of laws and access to forums to assert those rights, without the prior consent of the polity (whether manifested as an entry visa, a licence to permanently reside, or full citizenship).[52] In instrumental terms, many public opinion-shapers — from government policy-makers to tabloids — see rights as improper rewards for irregular migrants' violations of a state's territorial borders. Punitive immigration control measures, on the other hand, are believed to deter further irregular migration, thereby eliminating the potential for exploitation of irregular migrants.

48 See, eg, Owen Fiss 'The Immigrant as Pariah' (1998) 23 (October/November) *Boston Review* <http://bostonreview.net/BR23.5/Fiss.html> at 18 May 2007.

49 Secretary of State for the Home Department, *Human Trafficking* (Command Paper 6996, Government Reply to the Twenty-Sixth Report From the Joint Committee on Human Rights, session 2005–06, HL Paper 245, HC 1127, 19 December 2006) [13], available from <http://www.official-documents.gov.uk> at 18 May 2007.

50 Michael J Wishnie, 'Immigrants and the Right to Petition' (2003) 78 *New York University Law Review* 667, 670 (citation omitted).

51 Michael Walzer, *Spheres of Justice: A Defence of Pluralism and Equality* (1983) 32. Peter Schuck argues that:

> Since the ideal of nationhood first fired the human imagination, a country's power to decide unilaterally who may enter its domain, under what conditions, and with what legal consequences has been regarded as an essential precondition of its independence and sovereignty.

Peter Schuck, *Citizens, Strangers, and In-Betweens: Essays on Immigration and Citizenship* (1998), 19.

52 Schuck and Smith, above n 36, 131–40.

B *The Promise of Human Rights Law*

As mentioned above, the aim of this article is to furnish migrants' rights advocates with positive examples of jurisprudential practice in order to challenge the crude utilitarian premises of arguments opposing immigrants' rights. In this vein, Beth Lyon recently issued a call in the US for comparative work on the ways in which legal regimes affect unauthorised immigrant workers — the aim of such a comparison being the proposal of conceptual frameworks for transnational and regional bodies, and to directly influence national policy pertaining to the legal treatment of undocumented immigrant workforces.[53] In the face of inadequate domestic safeguards protecting individuals' rights, international human rights law holds much promise as a source of progressive standards. As will be explained, however, the ambivalence of the actual standards provided by human rights law belies this promise.

General principles of human rights law occupy an important place in legal strategies to constrain government abuse and the promulgation of unjust domestic laws. Among other ways in which sovereignty is being steadily eroded, many point out that nations are increasingly called to account for their actions politically and are occasionally also held to account legally. For example, Harold Koh has discerned a trend towards a transnational legal justice system in which the national and the international increasingly merge.[54] Those who share his vision point to the proliferation of human rights treaties since the end of the Second World War, and the evolution of international enforcement mechanisms as vital developments in this trend.

Faith in international human rights standards might seem even more natural in the context of an inherently transnational phenomenon such as immigration. Yasemin Soysal has expressed a strong belief in the growing impact of international human rights law on immigration policy. Soysal argues that there has been a reconfiguration of citizenship from a more particularistic notion based on nationhood to a more universalistic one based on personhood.[55] As a result, according to Soysal, immigrants are increasingly granted rights that used to belong solely to nationals, thereby heralding a new post-national model of membership short of citizenship, which 'derive[s] from transnational discourse and structures celebrating human rights as a world-level organizing principle'.[56] David Jacobson also links the failure of the state to control migration with the rise of an international human rights regime. In his view, 'the basis of state legitimacy is shifting from principles of sovereignty and national self-determination to international human rights'.[57]

Others are more cautious about the potential of international human rights law. Saskia Sassen argues that while external economic pressures and human

---

[53] Lyon, 'New International Human Rights Standards on Unauthorised Immigrant Worker Rights', above n 41, 571.

[54] Harold Hongju Koh, 'The United States Constitution and International Law: International Law as Part of Our Law' (2004) 98 *American Journal of International Law* 43, 56.

[55] Yasemin Soysal, *Limits of Citizenship: Migrants and Postnational Membership in Europe*, (1994) 1.

[56] Ibid 3.

[57] David Jacobson, *Rights Across Borders: Immigration and the Decline of Citizenship* (1996) 2.

rights may constrain some elements of restrictive executive control policies, such constraints do not limit states' discretion when dealing with undocumented migrants.[58] Others, like Christian Joppke, consider that excessive reliance on international standards downplays the complexity and diversity of domestic legal norms on the basis of which immigrants have been accorded rights.[59] Catherine Dauvergne adds that the enforcement of international human rights still depends upon a venue in which to lay claim to them,[60] displacing authority back to the domestic legal field. In relation to domestic litigation, it has been argued that the enforcement difficulties which plague international law meant that '[i]nternational human rights arguments are often seen as the advocates' last refuge, pulled out only when there is no other authority to cite'.[61] This observation seems equally astute in relation to the political arena of public domestic advocacy.

However, it is my contention that international law remains a crucial site for migrants' rights advocacy and should not lightly be discarded. First and most obviously, migrants are systematically sidelined from traditional domestic political channels. As a class of individuals, migrant workers almost invariably lack access to electoral processes. While many migrant workers are not prevented from participating in public aspects of democratic engagement (such as the news media, lobbying or protests), the degree of political pressure which migrants can exert is, nonetheless, greatly diminished by the very premise of popular sovereignty, which insists that democratic representatives must be accountable to an electorate comprised of citizens and excluding immigrants. Human rights law, on the other hand, does not depend on the same degree of political mobilisation of those who seek its protection.

Second, it is widely acknowledged that international human rights standards can have a persuasive influence on domestic laws and policies.[62] In particular, immigration policy may be especially conducive to this influence because it necessarily implicates a state's relationships with other states. The interests of foreign states in domestic immigration admissions can be seen in the recent lobbying of the Australian government by Pacific Island officials seeking an Australian temporary labour scheme allowing Islander workers to meet seasonal skills shortages in Australian agricultural sectors.[63] While the World Bank has drawn attention to the need to enhance regional development,[64] international human rights law has not yet been deployed to bolster this argument. Framing a

58 Sassen, above n 43, 56.

59 Christian Joppke, 'The Legal–Domestic Sources of Immigrant Rights: The United States, Germany, and the European Union' (2001) 34 *Comparative Political Studies* 339, 342.

60 Catherine Dauvergne, 'Sovereignty, Migration and the Rule of Law in Global Times' (2004) 67 *Modern Law Review* 588, 611.

61 David Cole, 'The Idea of Humanity: Human Rights and Immigrants' Rights' (2005–06) 37 *Columbia Human Rights Law Review* 627, 628.

62 Beth Lyon, 'The Inter-American Court of Human Rights Defines Unauthorized Migrant Workers' Rights for the Hemisphere: A Comment on Advisory Opinion 18' (2004) 28 *New York University Review of Law and Social Change* 547, 553.

63 Senate Employment, Workplace Relations and Education Committee, Commonwealth of Australia, *Perspectives on the Future of the Harvest Labour Force* (2006) [3.37].

64 World Bank, *At Home and Away: Expanding Job Opportunities for Pacific Islanders through Labour Mobility* (Report of the Poverty Reduction and Economic Policy Unit, 2006), available from <http://www.worldbank.org> at 18 May 2007.

denunciation of a state in terms of an international human rights violation may immediately capture the attention of foreign lawyers, foreign civil society and, possibly, also foreign governments. Such governments may have an interest in promoting the rights of their citizens abroad in a way that is not accomplished by reference to domestic law violations alone. It is therefore understandable that some who have witnessed abuses committed against undocumented migrant workers have urged lawyers to 'understand and make use of international human rights law to avoid further deprivation of migrant worker rights'.[65]

However, my argument is not that international human rights law *guarantees* a transformation of domestic laws and policies, and the lives of unauthorised migrants. This is because I support the scepticism of Critical Legal scholars that 'there are no safe havens, no areas of law — not jurisprudence, not moral philosophy, not constitutional law, not international law — where one will be embraced, where one will find wholehearted allies'.[66] Instead, my contention is that progressive formulations of international human rights principles can be a useful source of legal precedent for advocates seeking to secure social change and law reform. It is widely acknowledged that human rights doctrine holds great 'discursive power'[67] and 'symbolic impact'.[68] However, such doctrine will not hold any promise as a tool to improve the lives of irregular migrants, unless it is formulated in such a way as to prove itself equal to its aspirational origins and universalist framework.

III The Hesitant Approach of Human Rights Law to the Protection of Irregular Migrants

The coverage of migrants and irregular migrants under the principal human rights treaties has been the subject of much debate. The UN Special Rapporteur for the Subcommission on Prevention of Discrimination and Protection of Minorities recently noted that the architecture of international human rights is built on the premise that all persons, by virtue of their essential humanity, enjoy certain rights.[69] Furthermore, a number of commentators argue that a strong body of norms already exists to protect the rights of all individuals, including

65 Connie de la Vega and Conchita Lozano-Bastista, 'Advocates Should Use Applicable International Standards to Address Violations of Undocumented Workers' Rights in the United States' in Anne Bayefsky (ed), *Human Rights and Refugees, Internally Displaced Persons and Migrant Workers: Essays in Memory of Joan Fitzpatrick and Arthur Helton* (2005) 517, 549.

66 Richard Delgado and Jean Stefancic, 'Cosmopolitanism Inside Out: International Norms and the Struggle for Civil Rights and Local Justice' (1995) 27 *Connecticut Law Review* 773, 787.

67 T Alexander Aleinikoff, 'Between National and Post-National: Membership in the United States' (1999) 4 *Michigan Journal of Race and Law* 241, 254.

68 Kevin R Johnson, 'The Moral High Ground? The Relevance of International Law to Remedying Racial Discrimination in US Immigration Laws' in Berta Esperanza Hernández-Truyol (ed), *Moral Imperialism: A Critical Anthology* (2002) 285, 296.

69 David Weissbrodt, Special Rapporteur on the Rights of Non-Citizens, Committee on the Elimination of Racial Discrimination, *Progress Report on the Rights of Non-Citizens*, UN ESCOR, 54th sess, Provisional Agenda Item 5, UN Doc E/CN.4/Sub.2/2002/25 (5 June 2002) [11].

non-citizens.[70] However, recognition of the inalienable rights of all individuals in the immigration context seems to be systematically undermined by deference to states' control over immigration policy. This has produced a chequered approach to the treatment of migrants. Wide-ranging analyses of the treatment of migrants under the core international human rights treaties have been provided elsewhere[71] and are beyond the scope of this article. Nonetheless, the pervasive ambivalence toward the treatment of undocumented migrants under international human rights law is apparent in the *International Covenant on Civil and Political Rights* ('*ICCPR*').[72]

A *Irregular Migrants and the* International Covenant on Civil and Political Rights

The *ICCPR* is premised on the universality of human rights, making at times no distinction between the rights of citizens and non-citizens, nor distinctions based on immigration status.[73] For instance, art 2(1) states:

> Each State Party to the present Covenant undertakes to respect and to ensure to *all individuals within its territory and subject to its jurisdiction* the rights recognized in the present Covenant, without distinction of any kind, such as race, colour, sex, language, religion, political or other opinion, national or social origin, property, birth or other status.[74]

However, at the heart of the *ICCPR* lies a contradiction between territorial sovereignty and migrants' rights, evident for example in art 12, which provides:

> 1. Everyone lawfully within the territory of a State shall, within that territory, have the right to liberty of movement and freedom to choose his residence.
>
> 2. Everyone shall be free to leave any country, including his own.

The privilege accorded to territorial sovereignty in this article operates on two levels. First, art 12(2) epitomises the asymmetric character of the right of movement under international human rights law. At the same time as the provision recognises one aspect of a right to freedom of movement across boundaries (at least insofar as there is a right to leave a country) and the right of freedom of movement within a country, the Convention is silent on states' obligations to grant entry to foreigners. Similarly, art 12(4) of the *ICCPR* provides that '[n]o one shall be arbitrarily deprived of the right to enter his own country'. The UN Human Rights Committee ('HRC') — the body established under the *ICCPR* to monitor states parties' compliance with the Covenant — has issued an opinion that this implied prohibition on the right of a non-national to enter a country other than that of their nationality is subject to an exception for

---

70 Margaret L Satterthwaite, 'Crossing Borders, Claiming Rights: Using Human Rights Law to Empower Women Migrant Workers' (2005) 8 *Yale Human Rights and Development Law Journal* 1, 4.

71 See ibid; Ryszard Cholewinski, *Migrant Workers in International Human Rights Law: Their Protection in Countries of Employment* (1997).

72 Opened for signature 16 December 1966, 999 UNTS 171 (entered into force 23 March 1976).

73 Ibid preamble.

74 Ibid art 2(1) (emphasis added).

immigrants who hold long-term or permanent residence status.[75] The HRC thus accords the right to 'return to his country' to alien residents who have established 'close and enduring connections' to the relevant country,[76] although the exclusion of other non-nationals apparently remains.

Second, by explicitly linking the general right of freedom of movement to lawful immigration status, art 12(1) establishes the basis for a hierarchy of entitlements accorded to individuals on the basis of their immigration status, which extends to other rights related to presence in a foreign country. For instance, unlike lawful migrants, irregular migrants have no legal right to challenge their expulsion on any ground whatsoever. Article 13 of the *ICCPR* provides that aliens lawfully present in a state are entitled to procedural protections prior to being expelled, including review by a competent authority and the opportunity to submit reasons against the expulsion.[77] Unlike asylum seekers, irregular migrants are not immune from penalties for being present on foreign territory without authorisation on account of their illegal presence.[78] It has been remarked that this hierarchy of protection, which accords privilege solely on the basis of legal status, runs counter to a number of progressive national policies which accord rights not on the basis of an individual's immigration status, but according to the equities gained by virtue of being present on a state's territory.[79]

The logic of differential entitlements pervades even some of the most basic provisions of the *ICCPR*, such as its prohibition of discrimination. Article 26 provides:

> All persons are equal before the law and are entitled without any discrimination to the equal protection of the law. In this respect, the law shall prohibit any discrimination and guarantee to all persons equal and effective protection against discrimination on any ground such as race, colour, sex, language, religion, political or other opinion, national or social origin, property, birth or other status.

On its face, this non-discrimination provision is ambiguous in its extension to migrants as a class, since it prohibits discrimination on the basis of national and social origin or 'other status' without specifically addressing citizenship, alienage or immigration status. In an effort to address this uncertainty, the HRC, charged also with interpreting the *ICCPR*, has concluded that most of the provisions of the *ICCPR* generally apply to all persons in a state's territory,

---

75 HRC, 'General Comment No 27: Article 12 (Freedom of Movement)' in *Compilation of General Comments and General Recommendations Adopted by Human Rights Treaty Bodies*, UN Doc HRI/GEN/1/Rev.8 (8 May 2006) 213, 217.

76 Ibid.

77 However, these procedural rights may be denied to regular migrants if national security interests so require: *ICCPR*, above n 72, art 13.

78 See *Convention relating to the Status of Refugees*, opened for signature 28 July 1951, 189 UNTS 2545, art 31 (entered into force 22 April 1954). This protection is tied to the primary right of refugees, under art 33(1) of the Convention, not to be forcibly returned to a country 'where his life or freedom would be threatened on account of his race, religion, nationality, membership of a particular social group or political opinion'.

79 Susan Martin, 'The Legal and Normative Framework of International Migration' (Paper prepared for the Policy Analysis and Research Programme of the Global Commission on International Migration, September 2005) 9.

including aliens who are not legally present.[80] However, elsewhere, the HRC has concluded that 'not every differentiation of treatment will constitute discrimination, if the criteria for such differentiation are reasonable and objective and if the aim is to achieve a purpose which is legitimate under the Covenant'.[81] Further, national labour market regulation, national security, public order and public health and safety have been considered legitimate reasons to restrict the rights of foreigners.[82] As a result, some state practices that disproportionately impact upon non-citizens may not amount to discrimination if immigration status proves to be a relevant consideration. According to the same rationale, certain state practices will not be deemed 'arbitrary', and therefore contrary to law, as long as they are directed solely against migrants. For example, the prohibition in art 9(1) of 'arbitrary arrest and detention' cannot be read as prohibiting all detentions of irregular migrants. It is clear that states' border control powers alone provide a reasonable basis upon which to discriminate against irregular migrants.

It can be seen, therefore, that the international protection of undocumented migrants depends on a tension between the concerns of international human rights and states' territorial sovereignty. The doctrine of territorial sovereignty permits states to exercise exclusive control over their physical domain.[83] Certainly, this power is said to be subject to limitations imposed by international law, and human rights might be thought to operate here, as in other contexts, as a check on state sovereignty. However, when it comes to the treatment of non-citizens, human rights norms appear to give way to another incident of territorial sovereignty — the long-established principle of international law that gives states discretion over the reception and exclusion of aliens.[84] As Linda Bosniak has noted, when dealing with undocumented migrants, human rights interests contend not just with states' arguments about their jurisdictional authority over domestic affairs but also with this substantive aspect of sovereignty — states' expansive territorial powers, including their virtually uncontested authority to control the admission and exclusion of aliens and grant nationality — in effect, to prescribe the composition of the national community.[85]

---

80 HRC, 'General Comment No 15: The Position of Aliens under the Covenant' in *Compilation of General Comments and General Recommendations Adopted by Human Rights Treaty Bodies*, UN Doc HRI/GEN/1/Rev.8 (8 May 2006) 179, 179–80.

81 HRC, 'General Comment No 18: Non-Discrimination' in *Compilation of General Comments and General Recommendations Adopted by Human Rights Treaty Bodies*, UN Doc HRI/GEN/1/Rev.8 (8 May 2006) 185, 188.

82 Virginie Guiraudon and Gallya Lahav, 'A Reappraisal of the State Sovereignty Debate: The Case of Migration Control' (2000) 33 *Comparative Political Studies* 163, 168.

83 Lassa Oppenheim, *International Law: A Treatise* (Hersch Lauterpacht, 8th revised ed, 1955) vol 1, 286.

84 Ibid 675–6; Ian Brownlie, *Principles of Public International Law* (6th ed, 2003) 498.

85 Bosniak, above n 12, 752.

B *The Innovation Presented by the* Migrant Workers Convention

When the *Migrant Workers Convention* entered into force on 1 July 2003,[86] it was acclaimed as 'the most ambitious statement to date of international concern for the problematic condition of undocumented migrants'.[87] It covers both lawful and irregular migrants and provides the first international definition of 'irregular migrant workers'.[88] Furthermore, the *Migrant Workers Convention* expressly recognises that

> workers who are non-documented or in an irregular situation are frequently employed under less favourable conditions of work than other workers and that certain employers find this an inducement to seek such labour in order to reap the benefits of competition.[89]

The *Migrant Workers Convention* explicitly articulates a broad range of human rights for undocumented migrant workers and members of their families, far surpassing any protections afforded to them previously. Rights in Part III of the *Migrant Workers Convention* apply to all migrant workers, irregular as well as regular, and include: the right to enjoy treatment that is at least equal to nationals of the state of employment in respect of remuneration;[90] the right to enforce employment contracts against employers;[91] the right to join trade unions;[92] the right to emergency medical care;[93] and the right to basic education, regardless of a child's or parents' irregular status.[94] The *Migrant Workers Convention* emphasises that these rights apply to all migrant workers, irregular as well as regular and, further, that states parties are obliged to ensure that 'migrant workers are not deprived of any [of these] rights … by reason of any irregularity in their stay or employment'.[95]

However, lest it be thought that the *Migrant Workers Convention* rejects the doctrine of national sovereignty, the Convention does differentiate the rights accorded to undocumented and documented migrants. The protections due to all migrants (contained in Part III of the *Migrant Workers Convention*) fall short of broader protections owed to lawful migrants, which are separately enumerated in

86 *Migrant Workers Convention*, above n 13, art 87(1) (pursuant to the 20th ratification by Guatemala on 14 March 2003).

87 Bosniak, above n 12, 740.

88 Prior to the *Migrant Workers Convention*, a definition of 'migrant for employment' could be found in the *Convention (No 97) concerning Migration for Employment (Revised 1949)* opened for signature 1 July 1949, 120 UNTS 71, art 11 (entered into force 22 January 1952). The term 'migrant worker' was defined in the *Convention (No 143) concerning Migrations in Abusive Conditions and the Promotion of Equality of Opportunity and Treatment of Migrant Workers*, opened for signature 24 June 1975, 1120 UNTS 323, art 11 (entered into force 9 December 1978). At the regional level, there is a definition of migrant workers in the Council of Europe's *European Convention on the Legal Status of Migrant Workers*, opened for signature 24 November 1977, ETS 93, art 1 (entered into force 1 May 1983).

89 *Migrant Workers Convention*, above n 13, preamble.

90 Ibid art 25.

91 Ibid art 25(3).

92 Ibid art 26.

93 Ibid art 28.

94 Ibid art 30.

95 Ibid art 25(3).

Part IV. Unlike regular migrants, the undocumented have no rights to: liberty of movement;[96] family unity;[97] to form associations and trade unions;[98] or protection from abusive expulsions.[99] Strikingly, there is no general prohibition on discrimination on the basis of immigration status.[100]

States' concern to police their borders featured prominently in debates during the drafting of the *Migrant Workers Convention*,[101] making these concessions unsurprising. Indeed, even with the compromise to border protection offered by this tiered structure, the ratification record of the *Migrant Workers Convention* is extremely low in comparison with other UN human rights instruments.[102] This low ratification record has been identified as a major weakness of the *Migrant Workers Convention*.[103] Consequently, a great deal of attention has been directed to illuminating the obstacles to ratification of the *Migrant Workers Convention*.[104] Sending states are driven to protect their nationals living abroad and signing onto this convention forms part of that strategy. However, thus far, no major receiving state, including the US, Australia, or any European state, has ratified the *Migrant Workers Convention*, asserting that it is too ambitious.[105] Presumably, receiving states have baulked at the significant protections accorded to irregular migrant workers. However, it bears reflection that the distinction between sending states and receiving states can be quite fluid. Indeed, certain states parties to the *Migrant Workers Convention* were primarily sending countries at the time of ratification but increasingly have become points of

---

96 Ibid art 39.

97 Ibid art 44.

98 Ibid art 40.

99 Ibid art 56.

100 Ibid art 7.

101 Bosniak, above n 12, 756.

102 For example, the *International on Covenant on Economic, Social and Cultural Rights*, opened for signature 16 December 1966, 993 UNTS 3 (entered into force 3 January 1976) has, to date, 156 states parties; the *ICCPR*, above n 72, has 160 parties; and the *Convention on the Rights of the Child*, opened for signature 20 November 1989, 1577 UNTS 3 (entered into force 2 September 1990) has 193 parties. See Pécoud and de Guchteneire, above n 38, 6. It took 13 years for the *Migrant Workers Convention* to obtain the 20 ratifications necessary to enter into force. As of 18 May 2007, there were 36 state parties to the convention: Algeria, Argentina, Azerbaijan, Belize, Bolivia, Bosnia and Herzegovina, Burkina Faso, Cape Verde, Chile, Colombia, Ecuador, Egypt, El Salvador, Ghana, Guatemala, Guinea, Honduras, Kyrgyzstan, Lesotho, Libyan Arab Jamahiriya, Mali, Mauritania, Mexico, Morocco, Nicaragua, Peru, Philippines, Senegal, Seychelles, Sri Lanka, Syrian Arab Republic, Tajikistan, Timor-Leste, Turkey, Uganda and Uruguay.

103 Nicola Piper and Robyn Iredale, UN Educational, Scientific and Cultural Organization, *Identification of the Obstacles to the Signing and Ratification of the UN* Convention on the Protection of the Rights of All Migrant Workers — *The Asia-Pacific Perspective* (UNESCO Series of Country Reports on the Ratification of the UN *Convention on Migrants*, SHS/2003/MC/1 REV, October 2003) <http://unesdoc.unesco.org/images/0013/001395/139528E.pdf> at 18 May 2007.

104 See, eg, Pécoud and de Guchteneire, above n 38; Piper and Iredale, above n 103; Martin, above n 79.

105 Pécoud and de Guchteneire, above n 38, 8; Cholewinski, *Migrant Workers in International Human Rights Law*, above n 71, 201–2. As observed in 2000, 'no developed country has signed it, not even the most progressive countries in the area of international human rights legislation': IACHR, Special Rapporteurship on Migrant Workers and Members of their Families, *Second Progress Report of the Second Rapporteurship on Migrant Workers and Their Families in the Hemisphere*, OEA/Ser.L/V/II.111, Doc. 20 rev (16 April 2001) [69] <http://www.cidh.org/annualrep/2000eng/chap.6.htm> at 18 May 2007.

reception for migrants.[106] Morocco, for example, has become a major transit country for population flows from West Africa to Europe, which has resulted in the presence of a significant number of undocumented migrants within its borders.[107] Nevertheless, this is not the only barrier to the *Migrant Workers Convention*'s coverage of irregular migrant workers.

The apparent privileging of lawful migrant workers over unauthorised workers is not the only concession to states' traditional prerogative over border control. The *Migrant Workers Convention* repeatedly affirms the immigration-specific aspects of territorial sovereignty. It permits states parties to pursue immigration control policies that they see fit,[108] and requires them to take measures 'with a view to preventing and eliminating illegal or clandestine movements and employment of migrant workers in an irregular situation'.[109] Contracting states are explicitly not obliged to regularise the status of irregular migrant workers,[110] and it is made clear that undocumented immigrants are not exempted from 'the obligation to comply with the laws and regulations of any State of transit and State of employment',[111] which naturally include domestic laws against unauthorised entry, employment or residence.

From these provisions, Linda Bosniak has extrapolated that the *Migrant Workers Convention* navigates the conflict between human rights and state sovereignty by distinguishing between two different domains: state immigration power over admission and exclusion, and state treatment of migrants under other areas of the law.[112] When it comes to the admission and expulsion of aliens — the domain of the border — Bosniak argues that the conflict has been resolved in favour of states, as their interests in curbing irregular migration are affirmed, along with their sovereign prerogative over migrants' entry and exclusion.[113] Yet when it comes to migrants' rights in areas other than immigration, the *Migrant Workers Convention* requires states to protect the basic rights of undocumented migrants, even if the rights are not identical to those accorded to its citizens or lawful residents. Article 79 reflects this bifurcated approach:

> Nothing in the present Convention shall affect the right of each State Party to establish the criteria governing admission of migrant workers and members of their families. Concerning other matters related to their legal situation and treatment as migrant workers and members of their families, States Parties shall be subject to the limitations set forth in the present Convention.

During the drafting of the *Migrant Workers Convention*, delegates in a working group riven by divisions in this controversial area broadly agreed that it should not effectively force states parties to regularise the status of illegal migrant workers or grant an amnesty.[114] The delegates held that sovereign

---

106 Pécoud and de Guchteneire, above n 38, 6.
107 Ibid.
108 *Migrant Workers Convention*, above n 13, art 79.
109 Ibid art 68.
110 Ibid art 35.
111 Ibid art 34.
112 Bosniak, above n 12, 751–8.
113 Ibid 753.
114 Cholewinski, *Migrant Workers in International Human Rights Law*, above n 71, 191.

prerogative over immigration must remain intact.[115] The resulting *Migrant Workers Convention* attempts to strike this balance. It seeks to provide full assurance to states that their sovereign powers are not in jeopardy without frustrating the ultimate objective to guarantee human rights for migrants.

The trouble is that these two domains — regulation of entry, on the one hand, and substantive protections in other areas of law, on the other — are inextricably linked. The way in which the *Migrant Workers Convention* mediates this connection seriously limits its ability to provide effective protection to irregular migrants. Essentially, the problem is this: the provisions which protect states' sovereign prerogatives to control immigration are so wide-ranging that they end up infiltrating the domain of undocumented migrants' substantive protections in other areas of domestic law, thus effectively defeating their enforceability.

The way in which states' border control powers ultimately trump the rights provisions can be seen through the prism of the protection afforded by art 25(3) of undocumented migrants' legal and contractual rights with respect to employers. This provision purports to assure enforceable employment rights to irregular migrants, notwithstanding their irregular status, by prohibiting employers from evading their obligations to migrant workers 'by reason of any such irregularity'.[116] But if, in response to an undocumented employee's efforts to assert her rights an employer decides to notify the state's immigration officials, the state is free to prosecute the immigrant for violations of its immigration laws.[117] There is nothing in the *Migrant Workers Convention* which protects undocumented migrants from prosecution for immigration violations based on information obtained in the course of the migrants' exercise of their rights under the same Convention. As provided in art 34:

> Nothing in [Part III] of the present Convention shall have the effect of relieving migrant workers and the members of their families from ... the obligation to comply with the laws and regulations of ... the state of employment.

Similarly, when an irregular migrant worker asserts a right under the *Migrant Workers Convention* against a state party, the state is obliged under the Convention to facilitate the enjoyment of this right.[118] However, the state is simultaneously free under the *Migrant Workers Convention* to demand to know a migrant worker's immigration status which could lead to expulsion or punishment for immigration-related violations.[119]

In the Western world, the dictates of stringent border control seem so natural that we are accustomed to conceiving of migrants' rights as inevitably yielding to this state interest. Against this backdrop, the balance struck by the *Migrant Workers Convention* may appear fair. However, the *Migrant Workers Convention* handles this tension much more delicately when it comes to the rights of *authorised* migrant workers. Article 56 stipulates that 'expulsion shall not be resorted to for the purpose of depriving' authorised migrant workers of rights arising from their residence and employment. In so doing, it quarantines a

[115] Ibid 192–3.

[116] *Migrant Workers Convention*, above n 13, art 25(3).

[117] Ibid art 34. See also Bosniak, above n 12, 761.

[118] *Migrant Workers Convention*, above n 13, art 23.

[119] Bosniak, above n 12, 760.

state's discretion over migrant entry from the substantive obligations owed to migrants once they have entered the state. This approach is precisely what is needed to give effective protection to undocumented workers, but it is reserved for documented migrant workers only.

According to the doctrine of the *Migrant Workers Convention*, the relationship between undocumented migrants and the state at the border, in regulating entry and exclusion, infiltrates the relationship between them in the domain of substantive protections in other areas of domestic law. This barrier to enforcement seriously impairs the *Migrant Workers Convention*'s capacity to improve the social condition of undocumented migrants.

IV Seeking Out More Progressive Doctrine: The Regional Human Rights Courts

To be of practical benefit to irregular migrants, international human rights standards must quarantine a migrant's immigration status from his or her ability to seek effective protection under other areas of the law once in a state of employment. In a sense, this limitation is bound up in the strength of the doctrine of state sovereignty in the international arena. However, this outcome is not unique to international law. A great many domestic laws also allow the absolute discretion of states to regulate entry at the border to infect their treatment of irregular migrant workers once present in a country of employment. For instance, s 76 of the *German Foreigners Law* requires 'all public offices' to notify immigration officials of irregular migration status[120] — with the result that this lack of confidentiality discourages unauthorised immigrant workers from making wage claims to industrial tribunals.

The question remains whether any such separation is possible. It is significant that the *Migrant Workers Convention* was 'promulgated under the auspices of the UN', an institution which is comprised of individual states stridently committed to state sovereignty.[121] As we will see, the rights of undocumented migrants *have* been elaborated much more progressively in forums at a distance from the influence of states and the overriding goal of preserving sovereignty. In regional human rights courts, in Europe and the Americas, the absolute discretion of states to regulate entry at the border is being decoupled from the substantive rights of irregular migrant workers once present in their countries of employment.

Structurally, international or regional courts seem better placed than international treaty law to articulate standards that are responsive to the protection needs of migrants. An analogy may be drawn with domestic courts, which are often attributed a key role in the expansion of migrant rights due to

---

120 *Gesetz über die Einreise und den Aufenthalt von Ausländern im Bundesgebiet (Ausländergesetz — AuslG)*, vol 9, July 1990 (BGB1. I S. 1354) as amended by *Gesetz zur Änderung ausländer — und asylverfahrensrechtlicher Vorschriften*, vol 29, October 1997 (BGB1. I S. 2584) (*Aliens Act*).

121 Bosniak, above n 12, 765.

their insulation from democratic majority pressures.[122] Lacking citizenship, migrants are almost always excluded from direct access to parliamentary law reform through the traditional democratic route of voting.[123] While migrants may be free to assert rights through other forms of civic participation and political mobilisation, in any contest with the rights claims of citizens, elected representatives will almost invariably accord priority to their constituents.[124] After all, the very principle of popular sovereignty requires that the law respond to the will of citizens, as expressed through electoral processes and voiced through conflict between mobilised interest groups.[125] Democratically accountable governments are therefore susceptible to populist pressures that readily absorb racist and xenophobic sentiments.[126] Courts, on the other hand, to some extent, are 'less determined and more insulated both from concrete social interests and from political struggle taking place in other state institutions'.[127]

Judicially mediated doctrine can be seen to recognise the unique vulnerability of undocumented migrants and restrain states' immigration power. Both the ECHR and the IACHR have not only recognised that irregular migrants hold substantive rights vis-à-vis their host state but have also enjoined states to sequester migrants' unlawful immigration status from their ability to claim these rights. These two courts accomplish this in very different ways in the context of the relevant provisions of the regional human rights convention. Nevertheless, the bodies of jurisprudence are similar in that they both suggest ways to avoid the shortcoming of the *Migrant Workers Convention*, whereby the substantive protections offered to irregular migrants are apparently compromised by an inability to claim them.

A *European Jurisprudence on the Right to Family Life*

The Council of Europe was established in 1949 in response to the atrocities of the Second World War to promote unity, social and economic progress and

---

122 See Christian Joppke and Elia Marzal, 'Courts, the New Constitutionalism and Immigrant Rights: The Case of the French *Conseil Constitutionnel*' (2004) 43 *European Journal of Political Research* 823, 825; Joppke, 'The Legal–Domestic Sources of Immigrant Rights', above n 59, 340. See generally Charles Epp, *The Rights Revolution: Lawyers, Activists, and Supreme Courts in Comparative Perspective* (1998).

123 However, it is true that permanent residents, in certain states, have electoral rights and other political participatory rights traditionally reserved for citizens: see generally, Lisa García Bedolla, 'Rethinking Citizenship: Noncitizen Voting and Immigrant Political Engagement in the United States' (Paper presented at the Nation of Immigrants Conference, Berkeley Institute for Governmental Studies, University of California, May 2–3 2003); Virginia Harper-Ho, 'Noncitizen Voting Rights: The History, the Law and Current Prospects for Change' (2000) 18 *Law and Inequality* 271; Gerald L Neuman, 'We are the People: Alien Suffrage in German and American Perspective' (1992) 13 *Michigan Journal of International Law* 259; Jamin Raskin, 'Legal Aliens, Local Citizens: The Historical, Constitutional and Theoretical Meanings of Alien Suffrage' (1992–93) 141 *University of Pennsylvania Law Review* 1391.

124 Harper-Ho, above n 123, 295.

125 Raskin, above n 123, 1393.

126 Ibid 1464.

127 Alec Stone, as quoted in Virginie Guiraudon, 'Citizenship Rights for Non-Citizens: France, Germany, and the Netherlands' in Christian Joppke (ed), *Challenge to the Nation-State* (1998) 272, 301. See generally David Jacobson and Galya Benarieh Ruffer, 'Courts Across Borders: The Implications of Judicial Agency for Human Rights and Democracy' (2003) 25 *Human Rights Quarterly* 74, 75.

human rights in Europe.[128] The Council promptly created the *Convention for the Protection of Human Rights and Fundamental Freedoms* ('*European Convention*'), which was adopted in 1950.[129] The addition of Protocol 11 to the *European Convention* in 1998 dramatically changed the ECHR's structural system of enforcement.[130] Protocol 11 created an absolute right for individuals or non-governmental organisations to petition the ECHR[131] which has the power to issue decisions regarding *European Convention* violations and to order the offending state to pay compensation and costs to the applicant.[132] The ECHR may receive applications from 'any person, non-governmental organisation or group of individuals claiming to be the victim of a violation' committed by one of the contracting states.[133]

Notwithstanding this broad jurisdiction, the European human rights regime does not necessarily protect people regardless of the passport they hold. Under the *European Convention*, like the *ICCPR*, political rights are explicitly reserved for citizens.[134] From 1959, when the ECHR started functioning, until December 1993, fewer than a dozen decisions involved the civil rights of foreigners.[135] Nor has Europe promulgated any specialised protective standards for unauthorised migrant workers. The *European Social Charter*[136] protections for migrants and the *European Convention on the Legal Status of Migrant Workers*[137] in their terms apply only to the nationals of other contracting parties, who are, by definition, legally working as a matter of regional immigration law.[138] Ryszard Cholewinski has observed that the *Migrant Workers Convention* contains the 'minimum standard of treatment for illegal migrants in Europe, who are presently ignored by analogous European standards'.[139]

Yet, even though the ECHR has no express mandate to protect unauthorised immigrant workers, a body of jurisprudence bolstering the rights of migrants has

---

128 See *Statute of the Council of Europe*, opened for signature 5 May 1949, 87 UNTS 103, preamble, art 1 (entered into force 3 August 1949).

129 Opened for signature 4 November 1950, 213 UNTS 222 (entered into force 3 December 1953).

130 *Protocol No 11 to the Convention for the Protection of Human Rights and Fundamental Freedoms, Restructuring the Control Machinery Established Thereby*, opened for signature 11 May 1994, 2061 UNTS 12 (entered into force 1 November 1998).

131 *European Convention*, above n 129, art 34 places an obligation on the contracting states to allow individuals to bring complaints and obliges those states not to hinder applicants in seeking this right.

132 Ibid art 41.

133 Ibid art 34.

134 Ibid art 16.

135 Virginie Guiraudon, 'European Courts and Foreigners' Rights: A Comparative Study of Norms Diffusion' (2000) 34 *International Migration Review* 1088, 1096.

136 Opened for signature 18 October 1961, 529 UNTS 89 (entered into force 26 February 1965).

137 Opened for signature 24 November 1977, 1496 UNTS 3 (entered into force 1 May 1983).

138 Jan Niessen, 'Migrant Workers' in Asbjørn Eide, Catarina Krause and Allan Rosas (eds), *Economic, Social and Cultural Rights: A Textbook* (2nd revised ed, 2001) 389, 395–7, describing the *European Social Charter*, above n 136 and the *European Convention on the Legal Status of Migrant Workers*, above n 137. However, the European Committee of Social Rights has concluded that regardless of its apparent limited personal scope, the *European Social Charter* does apply to protect particularly vulnerable groups, including children of irregular migrants whose access to health care in France was restricted: European Committee on Social Rights, *Complaint No 14/2003: International Federation of Human Rights Leagues v France (Merits)* (8 September 2004).

139 Cholewinski, *Migrant Workers in International Human Rights Law*, above n 71, 200.

emerged. Among other areas, significant case law has developed around the application of art 8 of the *European Convention*, which protects the right to respect for private and family life:

> 1. Everyone has the right to respect for his private and family life, his home and his correspondence.
>
> 2. There shall be no interference by a public authority with the exercise of this right except such as is in accordance with the law and is necessary in a democratic society in the interests of national security, public safety or the economic well-being of the country, for the prevention of disorder or crime, for the protection of health or morals, or for the protection of the rights and freedoms of others.

Clearly, art 8 does not guarantee foreigners the right to a family home in their country of choice. As a recent International Labour Organisation report observes, states 'are not bound by any provision of international law to guarantee family reunification'.[140] In all of its decisions, the ECHR reaffirms that it does not forbid states from regulating immigration and details a number of legitimate reasons for states to restrict immigration, including the economic well-being of a country and threats to public order. These restrictions are applicable if 'necessary in a democratic society'.[141]

However, the ECHR *does* recognise that any exercise of immigration control must be compatible with art 8,[142] and has repeatedly found that the decision to expel a non-citizen may prima facie constitute an 'interference' with the right to respect for family life.[143] The Court then assesses the proportionality between the legitimate goal of a measure or a law, the means used to achieve this goal and the damage done to the individual as measured by the violation of *European Convention* rights.[144] In doing so, the Court considers both the individual's interest in 'respect for his private or family life' and the government's need to control disorder and crime.[145]

In balancing these interests, a number of considerations are taken into account. These include: the amount of time a non-national has lived in the deporting state; whether his or her family resides there; whether he or she has any ties to another state; and the effect of deportation on his or her family in the

140 International Labour Office, *Migrant Workers* (Report presented at the International Labour Conference, 87th sess, Report III(1B), Agenda Item 3, Geneva, June 1999) [473].

141 *European Convention*, above n 129, art 8(2).

142 See *Abdulaziz, Cabales and Balkandali v the United Kingdom* (1985) 94 Eur Court HR (ser A) 4. See also Ryszard Cholewinski, 'Family Reunification and Conditions Placed on Family Members: Dismantling a Fundamental Human Right' (2002) 4 *European Journal of Migration and Law* 271; P Van Dijk, 'Protection of "Integrated" Aliens against Expulsion under the *European Convention on Human Rights*' (1999) 1 *European Journal of Migration and Law* 293; Rut Rubio Marin and Rory O'Connell, 'The *European Convention* and the Relative Rights of Resident Aliens' (1999) 5 *European Law Journal* 4.

143 *Mehemi v France* (1997) VI Eur Court HR 1962, 1970; *Beldjoudi v France* (1992) 234 Eur Court HR (ser A) 6, 25–8; *Moustaquim v Belgium* (1991) 193 Eur Court HR (ser A) 4, 16 19.

144 *Djeroud v France* (1992) 194 Eur Court HR (ser A) 27, 35; *Lamguindaz v UK* (1993) 258 Eur Court HR (ser A) 95, 100–3; *Beldjoudi v France* (1992) 234 Eur Court HR (ser A) 6, 25–8. See also, *C v Belgium* (1996) III Eur Court HR 917, 922–5; *Nasri v France* (1996) 320 Eur Court HR (ser A) 14, 22–6.

145 See, eg, *Beldjoudi v France* (1992) 234 Eur Court HR (ser A) 6, 25–8.

deporting state.[146] The ECHR also considers the seriousness of any criminal offence committed by the applicant and the applicant's police record since the crime.[147] One line of authority also requires the Court to investigate whether the disruption or threat of disruption to family life is caused by an action or situation for which the persons concerned, and not the state, carry the primary responsibility.[148]

Due to these considerations, the case law developed in relation to art 8 has been developed most prominently in the context of long-term or permanent resident aliens. One of the first successful attempts to invoke art 8 in a deportation case was the challenge to expulsion brought by Mr Berrehab after his marriage dissolved and his residence permit was revoked.[149] The ECHR found that his expulsion would violate art 8(1) because it would interrupt settled access between father and child.[150] Although immigration control was an interference that was in accordance with the law and had the legitimate aim of preserving the country's economic well-being within the meaning of art 8(2), the Netherlands had failed to justify this expulsion as necessary in a democratic society.[151] As a result, it did not represent a fair balance between the public interest and the rights of the family concerned.[152]

Shortly thereafter, the European Commission of Human Rights issued a pronouncement on the application of art 8 to aliens, which was striking in its characterisation of the relationship between a non-citizen and his country of residence. In the case of *Djeroud*,[153] the Algerian applicant had been convicted of a series of serious offences in France and was issued with numerous deportation orders. Yet the European Commission of Human Rights upheld his complaint, attributing particular significance to his presence in France since infancy, notwithstanding his migrant status:

> Although *legally an alien*, the applicant has his family and social ties in France and the nationality which links him to Algeria, though a legal reality, *does not reflect his actual position in human terms*.[154]

This statement is remarkable in its willingness to look behind the applicant's legal immigration status and accord weight to his factual presence in a state of residence.

However, the ECHR has been far more hesitant to take this approach where the applicant's presence has been continually unauthorised. Until very recently, *Dalia v France* was one of the only judgments issued by the ECHR ruling on the applicability of art 8 to the exclusion of an irregular migrant.[155] In that instance,

146 *Mehemi v France* (1997) VI Eur Court HR 1962, 1971.

147 *Boultif v Switzerland* (2001) IX Eur Court HR 123, 132; *Mehemi v France* (1997) VI Eur Court HR 1962, 1970; *Bouchelkia v France* (1997) I Eur Court HR 50, 65.

148 Van Dijk, above n 142, 295–8. See, eg *Gül v Switzerland* (1996) I Eur Court HR 159, 175–6. But see 178–85 (Dissenting Opinion of Judge Martens).

149 *Berrehab v Netherlands* (1988) 138 Eur Court HR (ser A) 6.

150 Ibid 16.

151 Ibid.

152 Ibid.

153 *Djeroud v France* (1992) 194 Eur Court HR (ser A) 27.

154 Ibid 35 (emphases added); Jacqueline Bhabha, 'Belonging in Europe: Citizenship and Post-National Rights' (1999) 51 *International Social Science Journal* 11, 20–2.

155 *Dalia v France* (1998) I Eur Court HR 79, 92.

the Court found that the exclusion of Ms Dalia, an irregular migrant convicted of heroin trafficking, did not violate art 8. Although this result was disappointing for Ms Dalia, what is significant about this case was that her irregular status was not decisive. While unlawfully present in France, she had given birth to a son (a French citizen). The Court concluded that removing Dalia from a country where a close member of her family lived prima facie amounted to an interference in her family life.[156] Her unlawful status at the time did not affect this finding. Ms Dalia's case failed because of her inability to show, under art 8(2), that her deportation was not proportionate to a legitimate aim pursued in a democratic society. In light of her serious crime and her extensive social ties in Algeria, referring to 'her Algerian nationality [as] not merely a legal fact but reflect[ing] certain social and emotional links', the Court decided against her.[157]

The ECHR seemed to strike a delicate balance with regard to the significance of Ms Dalia's undocumented status. Ms Dalia's illegal presence was apparently irrelevant to the Court's consideration of the birth of her son in France and the prima facie interference that her removal would have on her relationship with him.[158] However, the Court refused to accord substantial weight to this relationship when it came to ruling on the second element of the art 8 test.[159] The reason for this is not clear. It may be that the Court simply considered that the applicant's relationship with her son was not so significant as to outweigh France's legitimate aim of removing a migrant with a criminal record. Indeed, the Court used very strong language when describing the social detriment caused by her drug-related offences.[160] On the other hand, it is possible that the Court was suggesting that states have a greater interest in expelling undocumented migrants than lawful migrants and that, had Ms Dalia been living in France with lawful immigrant status, her removal from her son would have been considered disproportionate to any legitimate aim advanced by France.

The precise content of a state's interest in controlling irregular migration was considered most recently in a decision concerning an application brought by Ms Solange Rodrigues da Silva, a Brazilian mother living and working illegally in the Netherlands, and her Dutch daughter, Rachael Hoogkamer. On 31 January 2006, the ECHR ruled unanimously that the refusal to grant Ms Rodrigues da Silva a residence permit amounted to a violation of her right to private and family life under art 8.[161]

In its submissions to the ECHR, the Government of the Netherlands had emphasised the national interests at stake.[162] Defending the refusal, the Netherlands had maintained, in particular, that the applicant, who was working illegally, did not pay taxes or social security contributions, and that there were ample European Union nationals or lawful migrants in the Netherlands to fill the

---

156 Ibid 89.
157 Ibid 91.
158 Ibid.
159 Ibid 92.
160 Ibid.
161 *Rodrigues da Silva and Hoogkamer v the Netherlands*, Application No 50435/99 (Unreported, European Court of Human Rights, Grand Chamber, 31 January 2006) ('*Rodrigues*').
162 Ibid [38].

job she was occupying.[163] On these bases, the Deputy Minister of Justice and the Regional Court of the Hague had both considered that the interests of the economic well-being of the country outweighed Ms Rodrigues da Silva's right to reside in the Netherlands — her daughter's state of nationality.[164]

Nevertheless, the ECHR held that Ms Rodrigues da Silva's expulsion would have far-reaching consequences on her family life with her young daughter and that it was clearly in Rachael's best interests for her mother to stay in the Netherlands.[165] After the relationship between Ms Rodrigues da Silva and Mr Hoogkamer had dissolved, custody of Rachael had been awarded to her father. This was decided on the basis that Rachael's interests were best served by remaining in the Netherlands and that there was no guarantee, due to Ms Rodrigues da Silva's irregular migration status, that her mother would be in a position to continue residing there to care for her.[166] The ECHR determined, as a result of this custody decision, that deporting Ms Rodrigues da Silva would sever almost all contact with Rachael, who would remain in the Netherlands. The fact that Rachael would not be able to live with her mother in Brazil loomed large in the Court's balancing test of the proportionality of the visa refusal decision.[167]

The ECHR then turned to the significance of Ms Rodrigues da Silva's irregular immigration status. At no point had Ms Rodrigues da Silva been entitled to a right of lawful presence in the Netherlands.[168] The Court took into account the fact that Ms Rodrigues da Silva and Mr Hoogkamer were both aware, from the outset of their relationship, that the continued existence of their family life within the Netherlands was precarious because of her illegal immigration status.[169] In the balancing test, it could be imagined that this would create an equity against Ms Rodrigues da Silva since this 'illegality was mainly the result of the first applicant's own actions, or lack thereof'.[170] However, the ECHR declined to take such an approach, holding instead that:

> Lawful residence in the Netherlands would have been possible on the basis of the fact that the first applicant and Mr Hoogkamer had a lasting relationship between June 1994 and January 1997. Although there is no doubt that a serious reproach may be made of the first applicant's cavalier attitude to Dutch immigration rules, this case should be distinguished from others in which the Court considered that the persons concerned could not have any time reasonably expected to be able to continue family life in the host country.[171]

The ECHR ultimately determined that:

> the economic well-being of the country does not outweigh the applicants' rights under Article 8, despite the fact that the first applicant was residing illegally in the Netherlands at the time of Rachael's birth. Indeed, by attaching such paramount

163 Ibid [17].
164 Ibid [17].
165 Ibid [43].
166 Ibid [12].
167 Ibid [41]–[44].
168 Ibid [43].
169 Ibid [39].
170 Ibid [34].
171 Ibid [43].

importance to this latter element, the authorities may be considered to have indulged in excessive formalism.[172]

It has been suggested that ECHR jurisprudence generally provides a valuable framework for the determination of the rights of irregular migrants, because, when a deportation places obstacles to the unity of a family, the margin of appreciation afforded to states in immigration control markedly narrows.[173] *Rodrigues da Silva and Hoogkamer v the Netherlands* represents a further conceptual advancement in judicial gloss on states' margin of appreciation when regulating illegal migration for three reasons. First, the applicants' challenge before the ECHR related not to a deportation order but to the Minister's refusal to grant residency. This means that, in finding in favour of the applicants, the ECHR held that irregular migrants' right to family life can engage a positive obligation to permit residence on the part of host states. Secondly, the judgment explicitly extends the entitlements of undocumented migrants to include family-based rights, where the *Migrant Workers Convention* had afforded the right to family unity to regular migrants alone.[174] Thirdly, the Court, in this case, approaches unlawful immigration status in a vein similar to *Djeroud*,[175] attributing value to Ms Rodrigues da Silva's factual presence in the Netherlands and her putative right to have regularised her situation in the past, rather than relying on her strict legal status alone.[176] To have fixed attention on her current immigration status would have been, in the words of the Court, to have engaged in 'excessive formalism'.[177]

In these ways, the ECHR has established standards which avoid the enforcement pitfalls of the *Migrant Workers Convention* framework. Rather than invoking formal rights which irregular migrants are unable to access for fear of detection, the jurisprudence concerning the *European Convention* provides that states may be obliged to grant full residence to undocumented migrants to safeguard their right to family unity.[178] Irregular status alone does not dislodge a reasonable expectation to be able to continue family life in the host country. By way of comparison, the human rights regime in the Americas, although taking a markedly different approach, also manages to protect migrants' rights, notwithstanding their unauthorised status.

B *The Inter-American Court of Human Rights*

In its *Advisory Opinion on the Legal Status and Rights of Undocumented Migrants* ('*Advisory Opinion*') of 17 September 2003, the IACHR ruled that

---

172 Ibid [44].

173 Nicholas Blake, 'Developments in the Case Law of the European Court of Human Rights' in Barbara Bogusz et al (eds), *Irregular Migration and Human Rights: Theoretical, European and International Perspectives* (2005) 431, 443.

174 *Migrant Workers Convention*, above n 13, art 44.

175 *Djeroud v France* (1992) 194 Eur Court HR (ser A) 27, 36.

176 *Rodrigues*, Application No 50435/99 (Unreported, European Court of Human Rights, Grand Chamber, 31 January 2006) [44].

177 Ibid.

178 See ibid.

international principles of non-discrimination provide workplace protections for undocumented migrant workers.[179]

The background to the *Advisory Opinion* was the 2002 US Supreme Court case of *Hoffman Plastic Compounds, Inc v National Labor Relations Board* ('*Hoffman Plastic*').[180] This case arose after José Castro, an irregular Mexican worker at a plastics factory in the US, was illegally fired for union organising.[181] The US National Labor Relations Board ('NLRB') held that the employer's decision to fire the worker had violated the applicable domestic labour protection laws.[182] A dispute then arose between the employer and the NLRB over the remedies — the employer argued that Mr Castro was not entitled to compensation for the time he missed work since he had not legally been entitled to work under immigration law.[183]

The Supreme Court ruled that Mr Castro's unlawful immigration status displaced his right to recover back pay for lost wages (which was the only direct remedy available to him for wrongful dismissal). In the Court's view, the imperatives of immigration enforcement justified this carve out in labour protections. Writing for the majority, Chief Justice Rehnquist stated that the NLRB could not order back pay for unperformed work which the worker could not lawfully have undertaken, because such remedies encourage illegal immigration.[184] On the other hand, the dissenting judgments took a more pragmatic approach. They pointed out that full remedies would actually further the objectives of immigration control by discouraging employers from hiring undocumented workers.[185] It was argued that equal enforcement of labour laws on par with the protections enjoyed by authorised workers would raise the cost for employers and thus reduce the economic incentive to hire undocumented workers.[186]

The Mexican Government responded to this decision through diplomatic channels, conveying its concern about the impact of the decision on Mexicans working in the US. The response provides an exceptional example of the deployment of international human rights strategies in shaping foreign policy, especially those related to international population flows. Mexico then sought an advisory opinion from the IACHR on the rights of undocumented workers, as

179 IACHR, *Juridical Condition and Rights of the Undocumented Migrants (Advisory Opinion)* 18 (ser A) (2003) 13.

180 535 US 137 (2002).

181 Ibid 149.

182 Ibid 152.

183 Ibid 149–50.

184 Ibid 150.

185 Ibid 158.

186 Ibid 155.

this was the only legal mechanism open to it.[187]. Since the US had not ratified the *American Convention on Human Rights* ('*American Convention*'),[188] the dispute could not fall within the contentious jurisdiction of the IACHR.

The *Advisory Opinion* has been described as 'a watershed' for undocumented migrants.[189] In a unanimous opinion, the Court found that the principles of equality and non-discrimination prohibit the denial of human rights to migrants on the basis of their immigration status.[190] Indeed, the Court concluded that non-discrimination norms have the status of *jus cogens*, or peremptory norms of international law.[191] This was the first time an international tribunal had reached this conclusion, which imposes obligations *erga omnes* on all states.[192] The IACHR acknowledged that governments have the sovereign right to deny employment to undocumented immigrants,[193] but held that, once an employment relationship is established, such workers are equally protected by human rights in the workplace.[194]

The decision was based partly on art 24 of the *American Convention*, which provides that '[a]ll persons are equal before the law. Consequently, all persons are entitled, without discrimination, to equal protection of the law', as well as arts 3(1) and 17 of the *Charter of the Organization of American States* (proclaiming human rights for all without discrimination); art 2 of the *American Declaration of the Rights and Duties of Man*[195] (equality before the law); arts 1,

---

187 IACHR, *Juridical Condition and Rights of the Undocumented Migrants (Advisory Opinion)* 18 (ser A) (2003) 1–4, 10. Note that the American Federation of Labor and the Congress of Industrial Organisations ('AFL-CIO') and the Confederation of Mexican Workers ('CTM') also filed petitions before the ILO in relation to this case, citing breaches of trade union rights under the *Convention (No 87) concerning Freedom of Association and Protection of the Right to Organize*, adopted 9 July 1948, 68 UNTS 17 (entered into force 4 July 1950) ('*ILO Convention No 87*'), the *Convention (No 98) concerning the Application of the Principles of the Right to Organise and to Bargain Collectively*, adopted 1 July 1949, 96 UNTS 257 (entered into force 18 July 1951) ('*ILO Convention No 98*') and the ILO Declaration on Fundamental Principles and Rights at Work: ILO, Committee on Freedom of Association, *332nd Report of the Committee on Freedom of Association* (GB288/7(Part I), 288th sess, November 2003) [551]. The ILO Committee on Freedom of Association has held that irregular migrants have the right to participate in union activities and are entitled to a meaningful remedy should that right be denied. The Committee concluded that the remedies remaining after *Hoffman Plastics* were 'likely to afford little protection to undocumented workers who can be indiscriminately dismissed for exercising freedom of association rights without any direct penalty aimed at dissuading such action': at [609]. See also, Paoletti, above n 45; Lyon, 'New International Human Rights Standards on Unauthorised Immigrant Worker Rights', above n 41, 556.

188 Opened for signature 22 November 1969, 1144 UNTS 123, art 62(3) (entered into force 18 July 1978). Any state party to the Organization of American States has a right to request an advisory opinion of the IACHR: art 64(1)–(2).

189 Paoletti, above n 45.

190 IACHR, *Juridical Condition and Rights of the Undocumented Migrants (Advisory Opinion)* 18 (ser A) (2003) 100.

191 Ibid.

192 Sarah H Cleveland, 'Legal Status and Rights of Undocumented Workers. Advisory Opinion OC-18/03' (2005) 99 *American Journal of International Law* 460, 462; Lyon, 'The Inter-American Court of Human Rights Defines Unauthorized Migrant Workers' Rights for the Hemisphere', above n 62, 587.

193 IACHR, *Juridical Condition and Rights of the Undocumented Migrants (Advisory Opinion)* 18 (ser A) (2003) 105–6.

194 Ibid 106.

195 Organization of American States, *American Declaration of the Rights and Duties of Man*, OAS Res XXX (1948).

2(1) and 7 of the *Universal Declaration of Human Rights* ('*UDHR*')[196] (the principles of human dignity, non-discrimination and equality before the law); and arts 2(1), 2(2), 5(2) and 26 of the *ICCPR* (general obligations to implement the Covenant with non-derogation and equality before the law, and without discrimination).[197]

The IACHR had earlier addressed the applicability of art 24 to non-nationals, distinguishing discrimination from the mere act of noting differences or factual inequalities.[198] In discerning whether differences in legal treatment amount to discrimination, the Court had suggested it would evaluate whether the differences are 'in themselves offensive to human dignity', or whether they had a 'legitimate purpose' that would not 'lead to situations which are contrary to justice, to reason or to the nature of things'.[199]

In the *Advisory Opinion*, the IACHR drew upon this principle of equality and non-discrimination, reiterating that states may, in accordance with art 24, grant some 'distinct treatment' between undocumented migrants and documented migrants, or between migrants and nationals.[200] However, expanding on its earlier dicta, the IAHCR maintained that the differential treatment is only permissible to the extent that it is 'reasonable, objective, proportionate and does not harm human rights'.[201] By way of concrete example, the Court acknowledged that states are permitted to distinguish between nationals and non-nationals in terms of who has the right to employment,[202] but once 'undocumented workers are engaged, they immediately become possessors of the labour rights corresponding to workers and may not be discriminated against because of their irregular situation'.[203] Migrant workers are entitled to workers' rights because these rights derive from the individual being engaged in renumerated work, regardless of the background context coloured by the individual's immigration status. States may not further their immigration policies by denying basic workplace protections to undocumented employees.

On its face, this prohibition on employment-related discrimination appears to go no further than the corresponding stipulation in the *Migrant Workers Convention*.[204] However, it constitutes a significant advancement for several reasons. First, the IACHR substantially enlarges the rights owed to undocumented migrant workers under the *Migrant Workers Convention*. It extends the obligation not to discriminate in regards to: the payment of fair wages for work performed; reasonable working hours; safe and healthy working

---

196 GA Res 217A, UN GAOR, 3rd sess, 183rd plen mtg, UN Doc A/RES/217A (III) (10 December 1948).

197 The IACHR's jurisdiction is exceptionally broad, extending not only to questions regarding the interpretation of the *American Convention*, above n 188, but also questions reliant on the interpretation of 'other treaties concerning the protection of human rights in the American states': art 64(1).

198 IACHR, *Proposed Amendments to the Naturalization Provision of the Constitution of Costa Rica (Advisory Opinion)* 4 (ser A) (1984) [56].

199 Ibid 15.

200 IACHR, *Juridical Condition and Rights of the Undocumented Migrants (Advisory Opinion)* 18 (ser A) (2003) 9, 100–2.

201 Ibid.

202 Ibid 106.

203 Ibid.

204 *Migrant Workers Convention*, above n 13, art 25.

conditions; social security; a right to rest and compensation; protection for women workers; judicial and administrative guarantees;[205] access to state health services; and contributions to state pension systems.[206] In contrast, the *Migrant Workers Convention* reserves several of these rights for regular migrants only.[207] No doubt in reference to the Supreme Court's judgment in *Hoffman Plastic*, Judge Ramírez especially emphasised the obligation to provide due process and unrestricted access to effective judicial remedies to migrant workers for violations of workplace rights:

> undocumented workers usually face severe problems of effective access to justice. These problems are due not only to cultural factors and lack of adequate resources or knowledge to claim protection from the authorities with competence to provide it, but also to the existence of norms or practices that obstruct or limit delivery of justice by the State. This happens because the request for justice can lead to reprisals against the applicants by authorities or individuals, measure of coercion or detention, threats of deportation, imprisonment or other measures that, unfortunately, are frequently experienced by undocumented migrants.[208]

Second, in a sweeping judgment, undocumented workers have gained non-discrimination protection based on a broad body of human rights law, including the *ICCPR* and the *UDHR*, rather than the poorly-ratified *Migrant Workers Convention*.[209] This was accomplished by the IACHR's reliance on the general principles of equality and non-discrimination and its determination that the applicability of these protections extend to unauthorised migrant workers, notwithstanding their 'definitional status as lawbreakers'.[210] Indeed, it has been observed that, as a result of the Court's opinion in this matter,

> whilst only eight of the thirty-five ... [Organization of American States] member states are parties to the ... [*Migrant Workers Convention*], those states which are not have at least been openly advised that they must in large part observe the obligations enshrined therein.[211]

Finally, the decision of the IACHR is explicitly geared towards ensuring the effective exercise of human rights by undocumented migrant workers on equal footing with all other workers in the state of employment. In this respect, it appears to go further than the *Migrant Workers Convention* by requiring that irregular migrants be able to enforce workplace rights without fear of immigration-related retaliation. This is a departure from the more nominal or formal approach that was the outcome of the uneasy compromise brokered in

205 IACHR, *Juridical Condition and Rights of the Undocumented Migrants (Advisory Opinion)* 18 (ser A) (2003) 108.

206 Ibid 108–9.

207 The *Migrant Workers Convention* accords only regular migrants rights to liberty of movement (art 39), family unity (art 44), to form a trade union (art 40) or protection from unreasonable expulsions (art 56). Strikingly, irregular migrants are afforded no general protection against discrimination on the basis of immigration status (art 7).

208 IACHR, *Juridical Condition and Rights of the Undocumented Migrants (Advisory Opinion)* 18 (ser A) (2003) 9, 100–2.

209 Ibid 107–9.

210 Lyon, 'New International Human Rights Standards on Unauthorised Immigrant Worker Rights', above n 41, 563.

211 Israel de Jesús Butler, 'Recent Advisory Opinions and Contentious Cases of the Inter-American Court of Human Rights' (2004) 4 *Human Rights Law Review* 125, 136.

drafting the *Migrant Workers Convention*.[212] According to the Court, when fear of deportation or denial of free public legal services to immigrants prevents immigrants from asserting their rights, the right to judicial protection is violated.[213] In particular, Judge Ramírez stated that governments should not sanction violations of immigration law with measures unrelated to the migratory offence:

> Non-compliance with migratory provisions would entail the relevant consequences, but should not produce effects in areas that are unrelated to the matter of the entry and residence of migrants.[214]

Here, the Court is de-coupling the protections necessary to alleviate the vulnerable position of undocumented migrants while working in their host state from the infraction against domestic law.

V Conclusion

Migrants who live or work without authorisation lead extremely precarious lives. Many migrants face structural barriers such as language difficulties or lack understanding about local institutions and laws.[215] However, irregular migrants occupy positions of even more extreme social vulnerability since they often work in undesirable jobs avoided by nationals and legal migrants, and live in constant fear of removal or possible prosecution as a result of their unlawful status.[216] In an effort to assist advocates to promote the rights of undocumented migrants, this article has identified bodies of jurisprudence developed by regional human rights courts which represent major conceptual advancements in the international standards of treatment of unauthorised migrants.

My purpose in canvassing progressive doctrine emanating from the case law of regional human rights courts is not to suggest that these forums guarantee redress for rights violations experienced by undocumented workers. Nor do I claim that litigation before these regional bodies signals the only way forward for advocates seeking to assist undocumented migrants in attaining justice. Just outcomes for claimants appearing before these international forums require enforcement mechanisms which do not yet exist at the international level. In the case of the IACHR, jurisprudence emanating from its advisory jurisdiction is not binding.[217] Indeed, the US has taken no steps to reinstate direct remedies for undocumented workers fired in violation of labour laws, as required by the IACHR pursuant to the *ICCPR*. In relation to the ECHR, the inconsistency of its case law has been disparaged as amounting to a 'lottery'.[218] In part, this is due to the source of the rights itself, art 8, which has been described as 'easily the most

212 See above Part III(B).

213 IACHR, *Juridical Condition and Rights of the Undocumented Migrants (Advisory Opinion)* 18 (ser A) (2003) 106.

214 Ibid 6.

215 Pécoud and de Guchteneire, above n 38, 3.

216 Bosniak, above n 12, 747.

217 Jo M Pasqualucci, 'Advisory Practice of the Inter-American Court of Human Rights: Contributing to the Evolution of International Human Rights Law' (2002) 38 *Stanford Journal of International Law* 241, 246.

218 Karen Reid, *A Practitioner's Guide to the* European Convention on Human Rights (1998) 280.

comprehensive yet obscure provision of the Convention'.[219] At the same time, it is a result of the case by case approach taken to art 8 cases, which has received a great deal of criticism from dissenting judges.[220] Moreover, although the ECHR's attention to immigrants' rights has encouraged a degree of legislative reform within member states,[221] the ECHR has no power to award anything other than compensation and costs — it cannot order the state to take, or refrain from taking, any particular action.[222]

Given the significant enforcement limitations of the international human rights system, much depends on whether and how advocates take up the discourse of rights. My aim in exploring the jurisprudence issuing from these regional bodies is to provide advocates with a language and a conceptual framework through which to engage states and international organisations. Opportunities for advocacy are many. Indeed, the Committee on Migrant Workers, established pursuant to the *Migrant Workers Convention*, will soon begin to issue general comments interpreting the precise contours of the obligations of states parties.[223] Since so many domestic legal systems rely on the doctrine of territorial sovereignty in determining the rights of migrants, the fact that this doctrine finds its source in international law makes domestic policy especially susceptible to developments in international law that restrict the prerogative of the sovereign.

This article has explored the ways in which both the ECHR and IACHR have significantly departed from the logic of international human rights law treaties by recognising that, in order to provide effective protection, the undocumented migrant's immigration status must be quarantined from his or her ability to claim substantive rights. Nevertheless, this acknowledgement poses a real challenge as to how to accomplish this objective. While both bodies of jurisprudence read down the significance of unauthorised immigration status in claiming certain substantive rights, they propose quite different conceptual frameworks.

The *Advisory Opinion* of the IACHR suggests that certain rights of undocumented workers should not be affected by their unlawful immigration status. It distinguishes immigration enforcement policies that violate the human rights of undocumented workers from those that do not. The IACHR observes that states may deny immigrants some political rights, regulate the entry and deportation of undocumented migrants, deny them permission to work and

219 Sally Frontman-Cain, 'Boultif v Switzerland: The ECHR Fails to Provide Precise Criteria for Resolving Article 8 Deportation Cases' (2003) 25 *Loyola Los Angeles International and Comparative Law Review* 323, 324.

220 Ann Sherlock, 'Deportation of Aliens and Article 8 ECHR' (1998) 23 *European Law Review: Human Rights Survey 1998* HR/62, HR/70. See, eg, *Beldjoudi v France* (1992) 234 Eur Court HR (ser A) 6 (Dissenting Opinion of Judge Pettiti).

221 French law was amended in 2003 to embrace the guarantee expressed in Article 8: Law No 2003-1119, enacted on 26 November 2003, JO of 27 November 2003, 20136. However, it has been pointed out that the law has become more restrictive in other ways: see Sophie Robin-Olivier, 'Citizens and Noncitizens in Europe: European Union Measures against Terrorism after September 11' (2005) 25 *Third World Law Journal* 197, 202.

222 Luke Clements, Nuala Mole and Alan Simmons, *European Human Rights: Taking a Case under the Convention* (2nd ed, 1999) 79.

223 See Committee on Migrant Workers, Office of the United Nations High Commissioner of Human Rights, *Monitoring the Protection of the Rights of All Migrant Workers and Members of Their Families* (2007) <www.ohchr.org/english/bodies/cmw/index.htm> at 18 May 2007.

regulate the entry and residence of guest workers in particular economic sectors.[224] However, once an employment relationship has been established, the migrant acquires rights as a worker irrespective of his or her irregular status in the state of employment.[225] When it comes to enforcing these protected workplace rights, the IACHR suggests the need for unauthorised workers to be guaranteed immigration confidentiality. In other words, according to the IACHR, undocumented workers have certain rights as workers notwithstanding their lack of status as members of the political community in their country of employment. Further analysis is required to structure a concrete basis for determining workplace rights which cannot be denied on the basis of migration status and those which can.

The ECHR takes a markedly different perspective by linking the rights held by irregular migrants to their standing as members of European state communities. Whereas the IACHR found that undocumented migrants lack membership status (and sought to quarantine this position from migrants' ability to enforce workplace protections), the ECHR ruled that migrants' constant presence and social ties create a de facto citizenship. Indeed, the equities gained by continuous presence and local family relationships may include a reasonable expectation to be able to continue family life in the host country.

Both bodies of jurisprudence suggest novel approaches which assist lawyers and policy-makers as they continue to evolve standards and remedies which offer effective protection against grave abuses of rights. Under both international law and domestic laws, these standards will inevitably grapple with the philosophical tensions raised by the presence of unauthorised migrants, including whether or not they are granted status as community members in the state of employment and whether or not that matters.

224 IACHR, *Juridical Condition and Rights of the Undocumented Migrants (Advisory Opinion)* 18 (ser A) (2003), 105, 119.

225 Ibid 108.

[12]

Numbers vs. Rights: Trade-Offs and Guest Worker Programs[1]

Martin Ruhs
ESRC Centre on Migration, Policy and Society (COMPAS), University of Oxford

Philip Martin
Department of Agricultural and Resource Economics, University of California at Davis

This paper examines the relationship between the number and rights of low-skilled migrant workers in high-income countries. It identifies a trade-off: Countries with large numbers of low-skilled migrant workers offer them relatively few rights, while smaller numbers of migrants are typically associated with more rights. We discuss the number-vs.-rights trade-off in theory and practice as an example of competing goods, raising the question of whether numbers of migrants or rights of migrants should get higher priority. There is no easy or universal answer, but avoiding an explicit discussion of the issue – as has been done in recent guest worker debates – can obscure an important policy choice.

INTRODUCTION

Although declared "dead" more than two decades ago (Castles, 1986), guest worker programs that admit migrant workers on a temporary basis to fill jobs in high-income countries are once again in vogue. The World Bank, the Global Commission on International Migration, the World Trade Organization's General Agreement on Trade in Services (GATS) Mode 4 negotiations, the International Organisation for Migration, and voices in both high-income and lower-income countries are calling for more temporary labor migration through new guest worker programs (*see* Winters *et al.*, 2003; GCIM, 2005; IOM, 2005; World Bank, 2005). The result should be "win-win-win" outcomes, as migrant workers win by earning higher wages abroad, migrant-receiving countries win with additional workers who expand employment and

[1]We are grateful to Bridget Anderson, Xiang Biao, Joseph Carens, Stephen Castles, David Coleman, Alan Gamlen, Nick van Hear, Marit Hovdal Moan, and Nicola Piper for helpful comments. Philip Martin also thanks the Economic and Social Research Council (ESRC) and the Social Science Research Council (SSRC) for a Visiting Fellowship at the Centre on Migration, Policy and Society (COMPAS), University of Oxford. For a previous and longer version of this paper, *see* Ruhs and Martin (2006).

economic output, and migrant-sending countries win via greater remittances and the return of workers who gained skills abroad.

Economic theory and experience confirm that moving workers from low-income to higher-income countries benefits migrants and raises global income while creating small net economic benefits in receiving countries, largely because the migrants hold down wages and prices (*see*, for example, Borjas, 1995; Freeman, 2006). For the US in the mid-1990s, a National Research Council report estimated that the net economic benefits of immigration ranged from $1 billion to $10 billion, meaning that US economic output was this much higher because of immigration (Smith and Edmonston, 1997). Proponents of immigration stressed the positive economic benefits of immigrants; opponents pointed out that a then $8 trillion economy expanding by 3 percent grows by $240 billion a year, or $10 billion in two weeks.

The new twist in proposals for more guest workers is the argument that low-income countries would benefit by sending more workers abroad. The World Bank estimated that moving an additional 14 million workers from low-income to higher-income countries would generate a global income gain of over $350 billion, exceeding the $300-billion gain from completing the Doha round of trade negotiations (World Bank, 2005). The press release accompanying the World Bank's Global Economic Prospects report for 2006 argued that more "managed migration programs, including temporary work visas for low-skilled migrants in industrial countries . . . would contribute to significant reductions in poverty in migrant sending countries, among the migrants themselves, their families and, as remittances increase, in the broader community." In its report to the Secretary-General of the United Nations, the Global Commission on International Migration recommended "carefully designed temporary migration programs as a means of addressing the economic needs of both countries of origin and destination" (GCIM, 2005:16).

If these recommendations are followed, we can expect a new wave of guest worker programs, increasing the number of migrant workers legally working outside their countries of origin. The new guest worker programs would, however, also involve restrictions of at least some of the rights of migrant workers. For example, by definition, guest workers have a time-limited right to residence and employment in the host country. Time spent in employment as a guest worker usually does not count or help a migrant earn permanent residence rights. Most guest worker programs restrict migrants to employment in certain sectors, do not allow migrants to freely change employers, and require them to leave the country if they lose their jobs. Under many proposals for new guest worker programs, migrants are also likely to have very restricted access to unemployment and welfare benefits and no right to family reunion.

All guest worker programs restrict the rights of migrant workers. However, the United Nations (UN) and the International Labour Organization (ILO) have enacted a number of international Conventions that outline a comprehensive set of rights for migrants, including the right to equal protections under labor laws, antidiscrimination laws, and family laws (for an overview, *see* Weissbrodt, 2003). For example, the International Convention on the Protection of All Migrant Workers and Members of their Families (ICMR), adopted by the General Assembly of the UN in 1990, sets out a very broad set of rights for migrants, including those living and/or working abroad illegally. The ICMR has become a cornerstone of the "rights-based approach" to migration advocated by many international and national organizations concerned with the protection of migrants (*see*, for example, ILO, 2005).[2] According to Grant, the essential elements of a rights-based approach include

> the observance of international human rights norms, including equality and non-discrimination, standard setting and accountability, the recognition of migrants as subjects and holders of rights, the participation of communities and the integration of a gender, child's rights and ethnic perspective. (2005:26)

With some international organizations calling for increasing the number of labor migrants, while others call for more migrant rights, this paper explores the relationship between migrant numbers and rights.[3] An understanding of this relationship is important for debates on guest workers as well as for more general discussions of labor immigration. Our basic argument is that there is a trade-off, *i.e.*, an inverse relationship between the number and rights of migrants employed in low-skilled jobs in high-income countries. The primary reason for this trade-off is that employer demand for labor is negatively sloped with respect to labor costs, and that more rights for migrants typically means higher costs. The result is that more migrants tend to be associated with fewer rights for migrants, and vice versa.

[2]There are also a number of other human rights conventions that protect all persons, including migrants. The 1966 International Covenant on Civil and Political Rights, for example, bans slavery and forced labor in Article 8. Article 12 grants persons lawfully in a state the "right to liberty of movement and freedom to choose his residence," a right routinely denied to guest workers because their lawful stay in the country depends on continued employment with a specific employer.

[3]Since the focus of this paper is on labor migration, we use the terms "migrants" and "migrant workers" interchangeably.

The paper has four parts. It begins with a discussion of the relationship between migrant numbers and migrant rights in theory. We distinguish between labor markets for skilled and low-skilled or unskilled migrant workers and argue that in high-income countries the demand for low-skilled migrant labor is downward sloping with respect to rights that have costs. The second part presents selected empirical evidence of the numbers-vs.-rights trade-off in the employment of migrants in low-skilled jobs.[4] We then briefly explore how the trade-off affects migrants and their countries of origin. The conclusion discusses the implications of our analysis for current debates about new guest worker programs. We argue that any informed normative position on guest worker programs and migrant rights needs to take account of the existence and potential impacts of the numbers-vs.-rights trade-off, including its consequences for migrants and their countries of origin.

We do not discuss the equally important question of whether and how guest worker programs are *feasible* in the sense that they can avoid the unintended consequences of the past. There is a substantial literature that discusses the "failures" and "policy lessons" of past temporary migration programs, especially of the Bracero program in the United States during 1942–1964 and the Gastarbeiter program in Germany during 1955–1973 (*see*, for example, Martin and Teitelbaum, 2001; Plewa and Miller, 2005; Abella, 2006; Castles, 2006; GAO, 2006; Martin *et al.*, 2006). Other studies propose policy principles and/or specific policy measures for avoiding past policy mistakes (*see*, for example, Martin, 2003; Schiff, 2004; Amin and Mattoo, 2005; Ruhs, 2006a). Although considerations of feasibility are obviously of paramount importance, the trade-off between numbers and rights that underlies all guest worker programs – and, as we argue in this paper, the employment of low-skilled migrants more generally – deserves equal attention.

NUMBERS AND RIGHTS IN THEORY

It is useful to conceptualize the numbers and rights of migrants employed in high-income countries as the outcome of the policies/actions of three key actors: states, employers, and migrants. At its core, the design of a labor immigration policy – including guest worker programs – requires states to make policy

[4]This formulation recognizes that many migrants working in low-skilled jobs in high-income countries are in fact skilled or even highly skilled in terms of their qualifications. This should be kept in mind whenever we talk about the demand for "low-skilled migrants," a formulation adopted in this paper for linguistic convenience.

decisions on parameters that include the *number* of migrants to be admitted; the *selection* of migrants (*e.g.*, by skill or nationality); and the *rights* that migrants are granted after admission. States' control over immigration is inevitably incomplete, and migration policies may be inconsistent and generate unintended consequences (*see*, for example, Joppke, 1998; Castles and Miller, 2003; Cornelius *et al.*, 2004). However, high-income countries can and do make decisions on the mechanisms that determine the numbers, selection, and rights of migrants in order to achieve certain policy objectives. These objectives can include goals such as maximizing economic growth and minimizing adverse distributional consequences; minimizing fiscal costs; maintaining social cohesion and national security; and/or complying with international human rights treaties and maintaining a certain minimum level of rights for all workers and residents (*see*, for example, the discussion in Spencer, 2003).

In their policy decisions on how to regulate the number and selection of migrants, states may assign employers varying degrees of control. At one extreme, states can – and many do – strictly regulate the maximum number of migrants legally admitted for employment purposes (*e.g.*, through annual quotas) and specify strict criteria for selection (*e.g.*, high-skilled migrants to be employed in the IT sector only). At the other extreme, states may have a "laissez faire" admissions policy that allows employers to determine how many and what types of migrants to employ. In this case, the total number of migrants admitted is simply the aggregate of the recruitment decisions of individual employers. The role assigned by the state to employers in regulating the number and selection of migrants will depend, to a large degree, on the extent to which the interests of individual employers match those of the state. For example, where labor immigration is perceived to have significant social costs that are carried by the state and society at large rather than by employers, the state will be unlikely to let employers decide freely on the number and selection of migrant workers.

Regardless of how admission and selection are regulated, nation-states always determine the rights – including the economic and social rights – that migrants are to be granted after admission. In the labor market, it is useful to think of migrants' (employment) rights as minimum standards that employers must satisfy (unless they choose to employ migrants "illegally," *i.e.*, outside the legal framework set by the state).

Importantly, the state can only provide the "framework conditions" within which the legal immigration and employment of migrants may occur. In the end, migrants will not be employed in high-income countries unless employers demand migrant labor and workers are willing to migrate and take up employment abroad at the conditions offered. This suggests that any discussion of the relationship between the number and rights of migrant workers must put employers and migrants at the heart of the analysis while taking account of the state's role in setting the framework conditions for labor immigration.

Given this simple conceptualization of labor immigration policy and the employment of migrants, what relationship can we expect between the number and rights of migrants employed in high-income countries? From an economic point of view, we can expect an important asymmetry in the relationship between the numbers and rights of skilled and low-skilled migrants.

The international market for skilled and highly skilled migrant workers is characterized by "excess" demand for labor, *i.e.*, a significant number of high-income countries are competing for a relatively small pool of highly qualified workers willing to migrate. As a result, qualified migrants are able to choose among competing destinations, and their choice of destination is likely to depend on both expected earnings and expected rights in destination areas. Consequently, countries and employers seeking to attract skilled workers are likely to offer them not only high wages but also substantial rights, generating a positive relationship between the number and rights of highly skilled migrants.

In contrast, the demand for low-skilled migrant workers is likely to be downward sloping with regard to migrants' rights. There is an almost unlimited supply of migrants willing to accept low-skilled jobs in high-income countries at wages and employment conditions significantly lower than those mandated by local laws and international norms. Migrants, whose "frame of reference" (Piore, 1979) is the labor market in their countries of origin, may not demand equal treatment in the labor markets of higher-income countries, especially if they plan a limited and relatively short spell of employment abroad.

From the employer's point of view, more employment rights for workers generally mean increased labor costs, generating a numbers–rights trade-off. This trade-off is familiar, as when employers oppose minimum wage increases because they assert that higher labor costs will mean fewer jobs. The analogy to migrants' rights is clear: if migrants have the "full rights" laid out in ILO and UN conventions, including the right to equal wages and all work-related benefits, their cost will be higher and fewer will be employed. On the other hand, more limited migrant rights may mean lower costs for employers and more migrants employed. In this sense, increasing the rights of migrants affects their employment in the same way that a higher minimum wage can reduce the number of jobs (for all workers, not just migrants). Of course, it needs to be added that not all rights create significant costs for employers, just as raising minimum wages does not always lead to reduced employment (*see* Card and Krueger, 1994; Neumark and Wascher, 2007). Nevertheless, it is clear that *significant* increases in labor costs will, ceteris paribus, encourage profit-maximizing employers to reduce the number of jobs on offer.

The numbers–rights trade-off described above rests entirely on the rational behavior of employers and workers, and can be expected to hold in any competitive labor market, regardless of the framework conditions set by the state. If the state stipulates a relatively high set of employment rights for low-skilled migrants, employer demand – and thus the number of migrants legally employed in low-skilled jobs – can be expected to be lower than what it would be if migrants had fewer rights.

There may also be a second factor, stemming from the interests and policies of the state rather than the actions of employers and workers, that helps to generate a negative relationship between the number of low-skilled migrants and their rights: the fiscal effects of immigration. The public finance impact of migrants, the balance between the taxes they pay and the cost of tax-supported services they receive, depends largely on their age, wages, and eligibility for and take-up of government benefits and public services (*see*, for example, Smith and Edmonston, 1997). Migrants with lower than average incomes, *i.e.*, those in low-skilled and low-wage jobs, tend to pay less in taxes and, because of their lower incomes, may be eligible for more government-funded services, especially if their families are with them. In order to minimize the fiscal costs of low-skilled migrants, high-income countries may be expected to limit migrant numbers or their access to welfare benefits.

To be sure, the state's interest in setting migrants' rights may be complex and will most likely be determined by a range of economic and noneconomic considerations that go beyond fiscal impacts. For example, states that make egalitarianism and/or compliance with international human rights norms key components of their national identity may be reluctant to restrict migrant rights. Restricting migrants' rights may also generate significant social costs, especially if the restrictions are long term and lead to the emergence of a large group of "second-class residents." These are potentially important considerations that may have an impact on how states establish and enforce migrant rights. Nevertheless, policies that lead to sustained fiscal losses are often politically unpopular and may be unsustainable in the long term, so it is reasonable to expect fiscal considerations to play an important and perhaps dominant role in the "politics" of migrant rights.

NUMBERS VS. RIGHTS IN PRACTICE

This section provides selective case-study evidence of the relationship between the number and rights of migrant workers in practice. It is important to note that when comparing countries of different sizes in terms of population and labor force, the analysis of "migrant numbers" needs to take account of the relative share of migrant workers in the labor force, rather than just absolute numbers. We do not present a comprehensive empirical test of the numbers-vs.-rights hypothesis. Our aim instead is to illustrate and indicate the relevance of the trade-off suggested by theory to motivate further research and empirical testing of the issue.

Because there is a global quest for talent (Kuptsch and Pang, 2006), high-income countries recognize the need to grant skilled migrants substantial rights in order to attract significant numbers. For example, Canada and Australia, two countries that have long been successful at attracting skilled migrants, grant qualified migrants permanent residence and the associated comprehensive set of rights immediately upon arrival (*see*, for example, Richardson and Lester, 2004). The UK's Highly Skilled Migrant Programme aims to attract qualified migrants by offering them the opportunity to migrate to the UK without a job offer and with the right to apply for permanent residence after five years of residence in the UK (Home Office UK, 2006a). Ireland is introducing a long-term residence status to attract migrants with scarce skills in short supply in the Irish economy (Department of Justice, Equality and Law Reform, 2006). In contrast, Germany's "Green Card" program for attracting IT workers from abroad offered a five-year work permit rather than permanent residency status, and attracted fewer than the 20,000 visas offered (for a discussion, *see* Kolb, 2005).[5]

In contrast, high-income country policies for regulating low-skilled labor immigration are typically characterized by a negative relationship between migrant numbers and rights. Singapore and many of the Persian Gulf States in the Middle East are examples of countries operating "high number – low rights" policies toward unskilled migrants. Both admit large numbers of migrants to fill low-wage jobs – migrants constitute over 95 percent of Kuwait's private sector workforce (Kuwait Institute of Banking Studies, 2006) and about 25 percent of Singapore's low-skilled workforce (Statistics Singapore,

[5]Following the failure of the Green Card system to attract significant numbers of highly skilled migrants, Germany passed a new immigration law in 2004 that provides for unlimited residence permits for highly qualified migrants and their families.

2006). However, in both Kuwait and Singapore, the protections of local labor laws do not apply to certain types of migrants, such as domestic workers. In Singapore, migrants employed in low-wage jobs are officially prohibited from co-habiting with or marrying a Singaporean resident, an effort to limit the costs of migrants by limiting settlement (*see* Piper and Iredale, 2003).

Bell and Piper (2005) contrasted the numbers-vs.-rights trade-off in Singapore and Hong Kong for domestic helpers with Canada's Live-in Caregiver program, which admits a small number of migrants to be in-home helpers but allows them to earn permanent residence after two years of employment. Bell and Piper note that "the choice, in reality, is between few legal openings for migrant workers with the promise of equal citizenship and many openings for migrant workers without the promise of citizenship" (Bell and Piper, 2005:209).

Although less extreme, trade-offs between numbers and rights of low-skilled migrants can also be observed in the labor markets and labor immigration policies of liberal democracies in Europe and North America. For example, in May 2004, the UK, Ireland, and Sweden granted workers from the eight Central European states ("A8 countries") that joined the EU in 2004 the right to enter and work. Sweden offered A8 workers full access to the social welfare system. In contrast, the right to work in the "flexible" labor markets of the UK and Ireland was accompanied by restrictions on migrants' access to unemployment and welfare benefits (*see* National Economic and Social Council of Ireland, 2006a; Ruhs, 2006b). By 2006, a million East European workers had migrated to work in the UK and Ireland after EU enlargement (Home Office UK, 2006b; National Economic and Social Council of Ireland, 2006b), but only 5,000 found jobs in Sweden in 2005 (*see* Doyle *et al.*, 2006; Tamas and Munz, 2006).

One of the reasons for the paucity of A8 migrants in Sweden is the tight regulation of Swedish labor markets, which gives migrant workers full employment rights and makes them as expensive as local workers. Most wages and benefits in Sweden are set via collective bargaining and, with most workers in unions, wages and benefits adhere to industry-wide standards. At the time of EU enlargement in 2004, Sweden introduced a number of measures aimed at preventing immigration from undermining existing labor market regulations and collective bargaining structures (Tamas and Munz, 2006). With effective labor-law compliance, there was little incentive for employers to hire A8 migrants to save money. The UK's and Ireland's relatively "low-rights" policies combined with flexible labor markets to attract large numbers of A8 migrants, while Sweden's "high-rights" policies were associated with far fewer A8 migrants.

Trade-offs between the number and rights of migrants can also be observed in the United States, which in 1996 elected to keep legal immigration high by restricting access to means-tested welfare benefits and adopting a one-strike-and-you're-out policy toward immigrants who committed felony crimes. The Commission on Immigration Reform, reacting to the perceived cost of providing tax-supported services to immigrants that led to approval of Proposition 187 in November 1994 in California,[6] urged Congress to reduce immigrant admissions but maintain immigrant access to social safety net programs (US Commission on Immigration Reform, 1995). Congress rejected this recommendation, and instead kept immigrant numbers high and reduced migrant access to benefits (*see* the discussion in Tichenor, 2002).

Irregular migration represents an extreme end of the numbers-vs.-rights spectrum, the place where high numbers are often associated with very few rights. In the US, for example, there are about seven irregular workers for each legal guest worker, and most are employed in low-skilled jobs (Passel, 2005). In the UK, estimates of irregular migrants range from 310,000 to 570,000, with a median estimate of 430,000, equivalent to about 0.7 percent of the UK population (Woodbridge, 2005). Most irregular migrants in the UK are thought to be working in low-wage jobs in agriculture and food processing, construction, the care sector, cleaning, and in hospitality. In both the US and UK, the debate over how to deal with irregular migration includes the argument that better enforcement of employment laws would reduce the demand for irregular migrant labor by raising its cost (*see*, for example, Abraham and Hamilton, 2006; Denham, 2006), suggesting a numbers–rights trade-off.

BALANCING NUMBERS AND RIGHTS: THE PERSPECTIVES OF MIGRANTS AND THEIR COUNTRIES OF ORIGIN

The trade-off between numbers and rights is generated by markets and politics in migrant-receiving countries, but it also has important implications for migrants and their countries of origin. Large numbers of migrant workers are employed in countries that severely restrict migrants' rights, suggesting that many workers are willing to accept fewer rights in exchange for higher wages. Of course, the mere presence of migrants in countries with "high numbers – low rights" policies does not mean that such policies are in the migrants' best

[6]The purpose of Proposition 187 was to deny illegal aliens and their children welfare benefits, nonemergency healthcare, and public education. Proposition 187 was approved by voters in California but later declared unconstitutional by a federal court (*see* Tichenor, 2002).

interests and therefore desirable. Nevertheless, the fact that migrants often pay significant recruitment fees to work in such countries highlights the need for a more explicit discussion of the choices that many workers in low-income countries face. Rights-based approaches to migration rarely discuss the agency of migrant workers, *i.e.*, their capacity to make rational and independent decisions when faced with limited options. Instead they often tend to treat migrants as victims of recruiters and smugglers rather than rational economic agents maximizing within constraints.

The numbers-vs.-rights trade-off also affects sending-country governments that have the dual and sometimes competing interests of, on the one hand, promoting the rights of their nationals abroad, and, on the other, maximizing the economic benefits from emigration. Some migrant-sending countries would like receiving countries to restrict the right of migrants to settle in order to maximize remittances and returns. For example, the Seasonal Agricultural Workers Program is based on a memorandum of understanding (MOU) between Mexico and Canada, under which seasonal workers have gone to Canada since 1974 (*see* Martin *et al.*, 2006). For most of the past three decades, only married men with children could participate, leaving their families behind and returning with evaluations in sealed envelopes that had to be delivered to Mexican authorities to avoid being dropped from eligibility lists for next season. Other migrant-sending countries are reluctant to ratify the ICMR for fear of losing jobs for their nationals abroad (Piper and Iredale, 2003).

The numbers-vs.-rights dilemma for sending countries was also highlighted during the WTO's GATS negotiations, which aim to liberalize the movement of "service providers." Mode 4 of the GATS involves the "movement of natural persons." Many low-income countries would like to see more Mode 4 movements, with India leading a group of countries demanding, inter alia, changes in high-income country policies that would open more doors for their nationals seeking to provide services. The goal is a "GATS visa" that would allow access to any WTO member country for one to three years (Chanda, 2001); refusal to allow entry and employment would be a reason to file a complaint with the WTO.

The numbers-vs.-rights trade-off becomes clear when dealing with wage parity for GATS service providers. ILO Conventions 97 and 143 call for migrant and local workers to receive the same wages for the same work. However, Chaudhuri *et al.* (2004:366) assert that equal wages would limit numbers: "Wage-parity . . . is intended to provide a nondiscriminatory environment, [but] tends to erode the cost advantage of hiring foreigners and works like a de facto quota." Chanda (2001:635) goes further, asserting that wage parity "negates the very basis of cross-country labor flows which stems from endowment-based cost differentials between countries." In other words, if GATS opened new channels for migrants, would they be paid wages equal to those of local workers, which may limit their numbers, or could migrants work for lower wages, which would presumably increase their numbers?

CONCLUSION: IMPLICATIONS FOR GUEST WORKER DEBATES

Governments that face public opposition to labor immigration often see guest worker programs – which, by design, increase migrant numbers but restrict migrant rights – as the best compromise between the extremes of no borders and no migrants. The arguments for legal guest worker programs as "middle path policies" that increase the number of migrants legally employed in high-income countries seem compelling. Employers argue they need guest workers because they cannot find local workers to fill vacant jobs at prevailing wages and working conditions, and many migrants want to fill these jobs because they will receive higher wages than at home. Sending countries can benefit from more guest workers via remittances and the return of migrants with new skills. With worries about integrating second- and third-generation foreigners, and about the fiscal and social costs of immigration more generally, receiving-country governments find it appealing to use guest worker programs to "borrow" workers from lower-wage countries, and to restrict the rights of migrants in order to minimize their costs.

Most recent discussions of new guest worker programs have been concerned with their feasibility, *i.e.*, whether and how to avoid past policy mistakes that have, among other things, led to the permanent settlement of what were supposed to be temporary workers. An equally fundamental but little discussed question that guest worker programs raise concerns the relationship between the numbers and rights of migrant workers in the global labor market.

This paper argues that the relationship between the number and rights of migrant workers employed in low-skilled jobs in high-income countries is characterized by a trade-off: countries with large numbers or shares of low-skilled migrant workers offer them relatively few rights, while smaller numbers of migrants are typically associated with more rights. The primary reason for this trade-off is that rights can create costs for employers, and rising labor costs are typically associated with a reduced demand for labor. A second reason stems from the political imperative in most high-income countries to minimize the fiscal costs of low-skilled immigration, either by keeping migrant numbers low or by restricting migrants' access to the social welfare system. Although we have not provided a comprehensive empirical test, we have given empirical examples that, in our view, provide convincing evidence of the relevance of the numbers-vs.-rights trade-off in practice.

In practice, migrants and migrant-sending countries often tolerate restrictions of migrant rights in order to gain legal access to low-skilled labor markets in higher-income countries. Of course, it does not automatically follow that restricting migrant rights under a guest worker program is a desirable policy from a normative point of view. Whatever the logic of the market and the interests of receiving countries, migrants, and their countries of origins, there may be strong normative arguments against restricting migrant rights. For example, Carens (2007:4) argues that, even if there is a trade-off between migrant numbers and rights, restricting the rights of migrants is always morally problematic "because they violate the state's own understanding of morally acceptable conditions of employment." In contrast, Bell and Piper (2005:214) suggest that unequal rights under a guest worker program could be morally justified if three conditions are met: (a) if they benefit migrant workers, as decided by migrant workers themselves; (b) if they create opportunities for people to improve their lives; and (c) if there are no feasible alternatives to (a) and (b).

We are not trying to determine where high-income countries should locate themselves on the numbers–rights spectrum. Instead, we argue in this paper that any normative and policy discussion of guest worker programs and migrant rights needs to carefully consider (as Carens (2007) and Bell and Piper (2005) have done) the trade-off between migrant numbers and rights, and its consequences for all sides, including the impacts on migrants and their countries of origin.

Most advocates and critics of more guest workers or a strict rights-based approach to labor migration have not dealt with the fundamental dilemma that inequality motivates the movement of people, but most norms call for equal treatment after arrival. Countries in which this equality norm is ignored have the most migrants ("high numbers–low rights policies"), as in the Middle East, while countries which adhere to the equality norm have fewer migrants ("high rights–low numbers" policies), as in Scandinavia. There is no easy or universal answer as to whether numbers or rights should get higher priority, but avoiding an explicit discussion of the numbers-vs.-rights trade-off altogether simply confuses the issue and can obscure an important policy choice.

REFERENCES

Abella, M.

2006 "Policies and Best Practises for Management of Temporary Migration." Paper prepared for the International Symposium on International Migration and Development, Turin, Italy, June 28–30.

Abraham, S., and L. Hamilton
2006 *Immigration and America's Future: A New Chapter.* Washington, DC: Migration Policy Institute. <http://www.migrationpolicy.org>.

Amin, M., and A. Mattoo
2005 "Does Temporary Migration Have to be Permanent?" World Bank Policy Research Working Paper, No. 3582, World Bank, Washington, DC.

Bell, D., and N. Piper
2005 "Justice for Migrant Workers? The Case of Foreign Domestic Workers in Hong Kong and Singapore." In *Multiculturalism in Asia.* Ed. W. Kymlicka and H. Baogang. Oxford: Oxford University Press. Pp. 196–223.

Borjas, G.
1995 "The Economic Benefits from Immigration." *Journal of Economic Perspectives* 9(2):322.

Card, D., and A. Krueger
1994 "Minimum Wages and Employment: A Case Study of the Fast-Food Industry in NJ and PA." *American Economic Review* 84:772–793.

Carens, J.
2007 "Live-in Domestics, Seasonal Workers, Foreign Students and Others Hard to Locate on the Map of Democracy." Mimeo.

Castles, S.
2006 "Guestworkers in Europe: A Resurrection?" *International Migration Review* 40(4):741–766.

———
1986 "The Guest-Worker in Western Europe—An Obituary." *International Migration Review* 20(4):764–778.

———, and M. Miller
2003 *The Age of Migration.* Basingstoke, UK and New York: Palgrave.

Chanda, R.
2001 "Movement of Natural Persons and the GATS." *World Economy* 24(5):631–654.

Chaudhuri, S., A. Mattoo, and R. Self
2004 "Moving People to Deliver Services: How Can the WTO Help?" *Journal of World Trade* 38(3):363–394.

Cornelius, W., T. Tsuda, P. Martin, and J. Hollifield
2004 *Controlling Immigration.* Stanford, CA: Stanford University Press.

Denham, J.
2006 "Immigrations' Real Frontline." Opinion piece in *The Guardian,* July 26.

Department of Justice, Equality and Law Reform
2006 "Scheme for an Immigration, Residence and Protection Bill." <http://www.justice.ie>.

Doyle, N., G. Hughes, and E. Wadensjo
2006 *Freedom of Movement for Workers from Central and Eastern Europe. Experiences in Ireland and Sweden.* Stockholm: Swedish Institute for European Policy Studies.

Freeman, R.
2006 "People Flows in Globalization." NBER Working Paper, No. 12315. Cambridge, MA: National Bureau of Economic Research, Inc.

Global Commission on International Migration (GCIM)
2005 *Migration in an Interconnected World: New Directions for Action.* Geneva: GCIM.

Government Accountability Office – United States
2006 *Foreign Workers, Information on Selected Countries' Experiences.* Report to the Chairman, Committee on the Judiciary, House of Representatives. Washington, DC: Government Accountability Office.

Grant, S.
2005 "International Migration and Human Rights." A paper prepared for the Policy Analysis and Research Programme of the Global Commission on International Migration (GCIM), Geneva.

Home Office UK
2006a "HSMP Guidance for Applicants under the Age of 28." <http://www.workingintheuk.gov.uk/working_in_the_uk/en/documents/all_forms.html>.

———
2006b "Accession Monitoring Report May 2004–June 2006." <http://www.homeoffice.gov.uk>.

International Labour Organisation (ILO)
2005 *ILO Multilateral Framework on Labour Migration. Non-binding Principles and Guidelines for a Rights-based Approach to Labor Migration.* Geneva: ILO.

International Organisation for Migration (IOM)
2005 *World Migration 2005.* Geneva: IOM.

Joppke, C., ed.
1998 *Challenge to the Nation-State: Immigration in Western Europe and the United States.* New York: Oxford University Press.

Kolb, H.
2005 "The German 'Green Card'." Policy Brief No. 3. Hamburg: Migration Research Group, HWWA.

Kuptsch, C., and E. Pang
2006 *Competing for Global Talent.* Geneva: International Institute for Labour Studies, International Labour Office (ILO).

Kuwait Institute of Banking Studies
2006 "Kuwait – Summary of Major Economic and Financial Indicators." <http://www.kibs.org/eco/ecokmain.htm>.

Martin, P.
2003 *Managing Labor Migration: Temporary Worker Programs for the 21st Century.* Geneva: Special lecture on migration, International Institute for Labor Studies, International Labor Organisation (ILO).

———, M. Abella, and C. Kuptsch
2006 *Managing Labor Migration in the Twenty-First Century.* New Haven, CT: Yale University Press.

———, and M. Teitelbaum
2001 "The Mirage of Mexican Guest Workers." *Foreign Affairs* 80(6):117–131.

National Economic and Social Council of Ireland
2006a *Managing Migration in Ireland: A Social and Economic Analysis.* A report by the International Organization for Migration for the National Economic and Social Council of Ireland, NESC Report No. 116. <http://www.nesc.ie>.

———
2006b *Migration Policy.* Report No. 115. <http://www.nesc.ie>.

Neumark, D., and W. Wascher
2007 "Minimum Wages and Employment: A Review of the Evidence from the New Minimum Wage Research." NBER Working Paper No. 12663. Cambridge, MA: National Bureau of Economic Research, Inc.

Passel, J.
2005 "Unauthorized Migrants. Numbers and Characteristics." Pew Hispanic Center, June 14. <http://pewhispanic.org/reports/report.php?ReportID=46>.

Piore, M.
1979 *Birds of Passage: Migrant Labor and Industrial Societies.* New York: Cambridge University Press.

Piper, N., and R. Iredale
2003 *Identification of the Obstacles to the Signing and Ratification of the UN Convention on the Protection of the Rights of All Migrant Workers. The Asia Pacific Perspective.* Paris: International Migration and Multicultural Policies Section, UNESCO.

Plewa, P., and M. Miller
2005 "Postwar and Post-Cold War Generations of European Temporary Foreign Worker Policies: Implications from Spain." *Migraciones Internacionales* 3(2):58–83.

Richardson, S., and L. Lester
2004 "A Comparison of Australian and Canadian Immigration Policies and Labor Market Outcomes." Report to the Department of Immigration and Multicultural and Indigenous Affairs, The National Institute of Labor Studies, Flinders University, September.

Ruhs, M.
2006a "The Potential of Temporary Migration Programmes in Future International Migration Policy." *International Labor Review* 146(1–2):7–36.

———
2006b "Greasing the Wheels of the Flexible Labor Market: East European Labor Immigration in the UK." COMPAS Working Paper No. 38. <http://www.compas.ox.ac.uk/publications/working_papers.shtml>.

———, and P. Martin
2006 "Numbers vs. Rights: Trade-offs and Guest Worker Programmes." COMPAS Working Paper No. 40. Oxford: COMPAS.

Schiff, M.
2004 "When Migrants Overstay Their Legal Welcome: A Proposed Solution to the Guest-Worker Program." IZA Discussion Paper 141. Bonn: Institute for the Study of Labor.

Smith, J., and B. Edmonston, ed.
1997 *The New Americans.* Washington, DC: National Academy Press.

Spencer, S.
2003 "Introduction." In *The Politics of Migration.* Ed. S. Spencer. Oxford: Blackwell. Pp. 1–25.

Statistics Singapore
2006 "Economic Characteristics." <http://www.singstat.gov.sg/keystats/annual/ghs/r1/chap3.pdf#search=%22nonresident%20labour%20force%22>.

Tamas, K., and R. Munz
2006 *Labor Migrants Unbound? EU Enlargement, Transitional Measures and Labor Market Effects.* Stockholm: Institute for Futures Studies.

Tichenor, D.
2002 *Dividing Lines. The Politics of Immigration Control in America.* Princeton, NJ: Princeton University Press.

US Commission on Immigration Reform
1995 *Legal Immigration, Setting Priorities.* <http://www.utexas.edu/lbj/uscir/exesum95.html>.

Weissbrodt, D.
2003 "Final Report on the Rights of Non-Citizens." U.N. Doc E/CN.4/Sub.2/2003/23. <http://www1.umn.edu/humanrts/demo/noncitizenrts-2003.html>.

Winters, A., T. Walmsley, Z. Wang, and R. Grynberg
2003 "Liberalising Temporary Movement of Natural Persons: An agenda for the Development Round." *World Economy* 26(8):1137–1161.

Woodbridge, J.
2005 "Sizing the Unauthorised (Illegal) Migrant Population in the United Kingdom in 2001." Home Office Online Report 29/05, London. <http://www.homeoffice.gov.uk/rds/pdfs05/rdsolr2905.pdf>.

World Bank
2005 *Global Economic Prospects 2006: Economic Implications of Remittances and Migration.* Washington, DC: World Bank.

[13]

The Invisible Worker

Lenni B. Benson[*]

> I am an invisible man. No, I am not a spook like those who haunted Edgar Allan Poe; nor am I one of your Hollywood-movie ectoplasms. I am a man of substance, of flesh and bone, fiber and liquids—and I might even be said to possess a mind. I am invisible, understand, simply because people refuse to see me. . . . That invisibility to which I refer occurs because of a peculiar disposition of the eyes of those with whom I come in contact. A matter of the construction of their inner eyes, those eyes with which they look through their physical eyes upon reality.[1]

Immigration law and policy are frequently discussed in political terms. In the United States our debate focuses on concepts of rights and membership in the American polity. We ask ourselves who should be admitted into our state and who should be allowed to remain. In part, we define our nation by setting boundaries that determine "who is in" and "who is out" of the nation. Far too often this debate ignores the invisible workers who reside in our country without formal immigration status.

Let us begin to think about the issues of immigration policy in another way. Let us, for a change, address the reality of how immigration law affects millions of this nation's residents, rather than assume the law's fair application. While the debate about immigration policy may seem particularly important at this moment, it is my contention that until we learn to understand the reality of the life of the undocumented person, we cannot develop nor implement our earnest reforms. As the quote above informs us, we must examine the "peculiar disposition" of our "inner eyes"

---

* Professor of Law and Executive Director, Justice Action Center, New York Law School. J.D., 1983, Arizona State University; B.S., 1980, Arizona State University. This paper is the text of remarks prepared for the Symposium "Work, Migration & Identity." I appreciate the comments of Professor Margaret Taylor, Judge Evan Wallach, and the assistance of Alice Youngbar and Brenda Cooke.

1 RALPH ELLISON, THE INVISIBLE MAN 3 (Modern Library, 1994) (1952) (emphasis in original).

if we hope to make the invisible seen.

Our existing immigration laws create a legal structure that in turn shapes and defines many essential social relationships. Legal definitions not only define who is a legal immigrant but also, by necessity, create the converse—the "illegal" or undocumented worker. These legal definitions go far beyond being mere labels, and instead become the building blocks of legal status, creating intentional and unintentional interactions with other laws such as criminal law, family law, tax law, and labor and employment law. These labels, and the power law conveys to labels, give rise to a class of invisible people: People who do not *fit* within the legal system (or who erroneously believe they do not fit within it), existing in an underground world—a world of invisible workers.[2]

The invisibility comprises two factors. First, it is difficult to see and measure people who do not want to be known to the government. Our legal concepts and structures contribute to that aspect of invisibility. Second, more abstract but equally powerful, we choose not to see these workers; they hide in plain sight. Let me explore both components of invisibility.

Counting the Invisible

First, let me examine the empirical or demographic problem. One of the enduring difficulties of forging immigration policy is gathering accurate or reliable empirical evidence of the numbers of foreign people in the United States. Even when people can be counted, accurately characterizing their status requires legal sophistication. We have a wide variety of legal status categories in the United States with complex rules and frequently altered criteria. It is not uncommon to find that an individual may not be able to fully articulate his or her own status.

More often, the potential of removal or deportation creates the incentive to hide and to avoid being counted or measured. While

---

2 The dual identity of undocumented workers is poignantly discussed by Professor Linda Bosniak as a "clash between membership and exclusion." Linda Bosniak, *Exclusion and Membership: The Dual Identity of the Undocumented Worker Under United States Law*, 1988 WIS. L. REV. 955, 1007 (1988); *see also* Kevin R. Johnson, *Los Olvidados: Images of the Immigrant, Political Power of Noncitizens, and Immigration Law and Enforcement*, 1993 BYU L. REV. 1139, 1221 (1993) (discussing the undocumenteds' unusual situation as "outsiders in this country unlawfully and, at the same time, present in society").

lawyers may understand that a census questionnaire will not lead to arrest by the Immigration and Naturalization Service (INS), the ordinary person may not distinguish one branch of government from another. Moreover, the false identity and document industry has grown rapidly since the 1986 statutory requirement that people prove they are authorized to work in the United States when they seek employment. Thus, distinguishing between the *documented* and the *falsely documented* adds an additional layer of complexity to the issue of counting people present in the United States.[3]

Let us assume that the economists, demographers, and other scientists who attempt to measure those present in our society without legal status have appropriate empirical methodology and can accurately measure the numbers of these people.[4] How many undocumented people are there? INS estimates range from four to six million people residing without legal status in the United States.[5] Using the high end of that estimate, approximately six

---

3 *See* GENERAL ACCOUNTING OFFICE, COMPTROLLER GENERAL OF THE UNITED STATES, SMUGGLERS, ILLICIT DOCUMENTS, AND SCHEMES ARE UNDERMINING UNITED STATES CONTROLS OVER IMMIGRATION GGD-76-83 (1976).

4 These empirical problems are fiercely debated. The inability to adequately account for the illegal migrant population is even a subject of the upcoming Population Association of America 2002 Annual Meeting Program, hosted by the Office of Population Research at Princeton University. *See* Population Association of America 2002 Meeting Program, 2002 Meeting Program Summary, http://paa2002.princeton.edu/programSummary.asp (last visited May 8, 2002); *see also* THE NEW AMERICANS: ECONOMIC, DEMOGRAPHIC, AND FISCAL EFFECTS OF IMMIGRATION 80–82 (James P. Smith & Barry Edmonston eds., 1997). The United States Census Bureau states unequivocally in a working paper discussing its estimates of undocumented people that "[r]esearchers have not agreed on how many unauthorized migrants were missed in the census." KEVIN E. DEARDORFF & LISA M. BLUMERMAN, EVALUATING COMPONENTS OF INTERNATIONAL MIGRATION: ESTIMATES OF THE FOREIGN-BORN POPULATION BY MIGRANT STATUS IN 2000, at 3 (U.S. Census Bureau Population Division, Working Paper No. 58, 2001), *available at* http://www.census.gov/population/www/documentation/twps0058.html. It is also important to know that the Census Bureau is not making specific inquiries about immigration status but is working with the number of "foreign born" and then using INS and Department of State estimates to determine who among these foreign born might be undocumented. U.S. Census Bureau, Immigration, http://www.census.gov/population/www/socdemo/immigration.html (last updated Dec. 28, 2001) (on file with the North Carolina Journal of International Law and Commercial Regulation).

5 INS, Illegal Alien Resident Population (Estimates of Undocumented Immigrant Population Residing in the United States: Oct. 1996), *at* http://www.ins.usdoj.gov/graphics/aboutins/statistics/illegalalien/illegal.pdf (last updated Dec. 2001) (estimating as of October 1996 that five million illegal aliens were in the United States, and given yearly growth rates in illegal immigration, this figure should have exceeded six million

million of the 285 million people in this country are undocumented,[6] representing approximately two percent of the population. That percentage seems small to me, but it represents people in addition to the approximate one million immigrants per year we have chosen to admit, and the more than one million temporary workers and students to whom we have also granted temporary legal admission.[7] So the number of undocumented, or "illegal," immigrants may be seen as very large relative to the actual limits we have set in the legal admission system.[8]

The reaction that "illegal" is too large in proportion to "legal" does not answer the question of whether there are distinctions among the undocumented population. Asked another way, do we really believe all undocumented people are alike? Our value judgment that the number is too high depends in part upon our view of the quality and nature of the ties these people have with our society. For some of us, one of the critical issues is whether these people are likely to one day obtain legal status. Our judgment may depend on the reasons why they have not previously obtained legal status.

Many of the six million undocumented people are close relatives of those admitted legally, although it is difficult to know exactly how many undocumented people are relatives. For example, the wife of a computer scientist from India may have come to this country on a tourist visa under which she was authorized to remain for six months. The scientist, a lawful permanent resident, then sponsors his wife for immigration, and the couple learns that the backlog for immigration ranges from six to eight years. This is because Congress has only assigned

---

in 2000).

6 The U.S. Census Bureau estimated the current U.S. population to be 284,796,887 on July 1, 2001. U.S. Census Bureau, Population Estimates, *at* http://eire.census.gov/popest/data/national.php (last updated Apr. 11, 2002).

7 Statistical Yearbook of the Immigration and Naturalization Service, 1999, *at* http://www.ins.gov/graphics/aboutins/statistics/TempExcel99/Table_38.xls (last visited May 8, 2002).

8 Of course, the six million undocumented immigrants did not enter in a single year. The INS estimates the undocumented population may increase by 275,000 people annually. While this number is potentially unreliable, this is the figure that should be compared to the annual permanent immigration rates. Illegal Alien Resident Population, *supra* note 5.

114,200 annual visas to this high demand immigrant category.[9] Choosing between waiting apart in separate countries or continuing their lives together in the United States, many choose to overstay their visitor visas and thus become one of those illegally present.

While recent statutory reforms have lessened the hardship of the long delay by allowing a temporary visa category and admitting those spouses and children who have been waiting more than three years, these changes are not yet widely known or understood in immigrant communities.[10] Contributing to these delays is the failure of the INS to adjudicate the family-based petitions. In November 2001, the Department of State was asked if it had found all of the people eligible for this new special nonimmigrant category. The official answer was that the Department knew it did not have a clear picture, but recent electronic database information transmitted from the INS revealed that the INS reported more than 122,000 [!] unadjudicated spouse petitions which had been pending at the INS for more than three years.[11] We must acknowledge that these types of delays are some of the "pull factors" that lead people to self-help or law violation. Such delays must also contribute to a loss of respect for the INS, which in turn can contribute to the perception that the visa laws themselves are unimportant.

There are other provisions of the immigration laws that make it

---

[9] Immigration and Nationality Act (INA) § 203(a)(2), 8 U.S.C. § 1153(a)(2) (2001).

[10] INA § 101(a)(15)(v), 8 U.S.C. § 1101(a)(15)(V) (2001) (providing a temporary visa for a lawful permanent resident's spouse and minor children who have been waiting at least three years for admission as immigrants if they filed petitions on or before December 21, 2001); *see also* Janice Luo et al., *The V Visa: A New Life Form, in* SELECTED FUNDAMENTALS OF IMMIGRATION LAW AND PRACTICE 117 (2001–2002).

[11] *Questions and Answers for American Immigration Lawyers Association Liaison Meeting with the Visa Office of the Department of State, October 26, 2001*, 21 IMMIGRATION LAW TODAY 59, 62 (Jan./Feb. 2002). Given that the quota for this category is 74,000 people per year, the delay in adjudication means that the current backlog of six to eight years is undercounted by nearly two years. The erratic and delayed adjudication merely contributes to the difficulty of understanding and predicting movement of our quota numbers. In a forthcoming article, I explore at length the structural and organizational problems in three federal agencies: the INS, the Department of State, and the Department of Labor, that combine and interrelate to create many of the process failures. *See* Lenni B. Benson, *Breaking Bureaucratic Borders: A Necessary Step to Immigration Law Reform*, 54 ADMIN. L. REV. 203 (forthcoming Winter 2002).

difficult to move from undocumented status to legal status. In 1996, Congress sought to create an incentive for people to comply with our immigration laws by creating a new penalty or ground of inadmissibility for people who have remained illegally in the United States.[12] Basically, the statute sought to prevent the reentry of those people who had overstayed or entered illegally and remained for six months or more. Unlawful presence triggered statutory exclusion for three years, and, if one remained unlawfully for more than one year, the bar increased to ten years. While the bar contains a potential waiver for the spouse and children of permanent residents and citizens, it is unclear how generously the waivers will be granted. Perhaps equally disturbing, it is impossible to know how long the INS will take to adjudicate a waiver application.[13]

In what was probably an inadvertent drafting error, the new ground of exclusion only applies to those people who have *departed* the United States.[14] Technically then, and as the INS applies the statute, if one does not depart the United States, regardless of the length of the overstay, one is not subject to this exclusion provision. Perversely, the statutory provision meant to encourage compliance with the law may have encouraged the opposite: People wait in the United States hoping for a method of legalizing or adjusting status rather than leaving the United States and triggering the bar. These hopes are not as irrational as they

---

12 INA § 212(a)(9)(B), 8 U.S.C. § 1181(a)(9)(B) (2001).

13 The unlawful presence bars are particularly difficult to understand because the INS has not yet issued any regulations interpreting the statutory provision or setting guidelines for the adjudication of the waivers. While there have been some interpretive policy memos from the INS General Counsel's office, this is an area that attorneys and immigrants alike find very confusing. GORDON ET AL., IMMIGRATION LAW AND PROCEDURE § 63.10[2][b] (2001).

14 INA § 212(a)(9)(B)(i), 8 U.S.C. § 1181(a)(9)(B)(i) (2001):

> Aliens unlawfully present. (i) Any alien . . . who—(I) was unlawfully present in the United States for a period of 180 days but less than 1 year, voluntarily departed the Untied States . . . prior to the commencement of proceedings under section 235(b)(1) . . . and again seeks admission within 3 years of the date of such alien's departure or removal, or (II) has been unlawfully present in the United States for one year or more, and who again seeks admission within 10 years of the date of such alien's departure or removal from the United States, is inadmissible.

Id.

may appear. Since the mid-1980s we have had at least five different statutory reforms that sought to regularize the status of millions of people.[15] The most recent program, named after its statutory reference, 245(i), allowed people who had a method of immigrating through a family or employer sponsor to pay a fine of $1,000 in order for the INS to overlook the period of unauthorized status, illegal entry, or unauthorized work which normally bars the adjustment of status for most classes of noncitizens.[16]

The last revival of the 245(i) program allowed anyone who filed an application for a visa petition or a labor certification (the necessary prerequisite measuring the availability of U.S. workers for a specific job offer required in most employment categories) to qualify for the benefits of the fine-based waiver. The Department of Labor alone received nearly 230,000 applications for labor certification during a four-month period.[17] The normal application rate for labor certification is approximately 65,000 to 80,000.[18] Surely this surge of applications is evidence of the hundreds of thousands of people who seek to regularize their status, and it suggests that for many of these people the obstacle was not the lack of a sponsor but the problem of prior illegal entry or overstay which would make them subject to the three or ten year bars.

Thus, we get glimpses of our invisible neighbors when our laws create opportunities for them to come out of the shadows. Some neighbors are family members; some are workers who employers would sponsor through our system. Not all "illegal aliens" are alike. Trying to measure the percentage and type of undocumented people in our country is extremely difficult because

---

15 For example, in 1986 we had two major legalization programs, one for people unlawfully present since 1982 (note that people lawfully present did not qualify) and one for those who demonstrated at least ninety days of labor in agriculture. INA § 210(a)(B)(i), 8 U.S.C. § 1160 (2001); *see* INA § 245, 8 U.S.C. § 1255 (2001). At this time Congress also moved the "registry" date from 1948 to 1972. Thus, people who entered the United States prior to 1972 are also allowed to apply for permanent residence under relaxed rules. INA § 249, 8 U.S.C. § 1259 (2001).

16 INA § 245(i), 8 U.S.C. § 1255(i) (2001).

17 Dale Ziegler, Director of the Alien Labor Certification Program of the Office of Workplace Security of the Department of Labor, Remarks at the 2001 Annual Conference of the American Immigration Lawyers Association (June 20, 2001) (notes on file with the author).

18 *See* Benson, *supra* note 11 (discussing the workload and processing times for alien labor certification from 1990 to 2001).

of these distinctions. Making evaluative judgments about the scope and magnitude of the problem requires assumptions built upon speculations that ultimately frustrate our vision.

Refusing to See the Invisible Worker

There is, importantly, a second type of invisibility. As Ralph Ellison reminds us, there are people we see, but *see through*.[19] Let us examine one industry where recent INS and congressional attention has focused on measuring labor shortages and the percentage of undocumented workers. Again, I wonder about the accuracy of such estimates,[20] but let us work with the information the government has provided. In 2000, the Department of Agriculture prepared a detailed report and announced that fifty-two percent of all agricultural workers in the United States were present without legal status.[21] I repeat, fifty-two percent. Now let us go back and consider what that means in terms of the large numbers. We estimate that less than two percent of our population are undocumented noncitizens. That number suggests it is difficult to find these people. But more than half of the workers in the agriculture industry are undocumented. Undocumented agricultural workers must be easy to see and easy to find and their impact on the economics of agriculture surely must be understood. Or is it? How visible is any agricultural worker? In your mind's eye can you see the hands and faces and laboring muscles of any agricultural worker? Do you even know what agricultural work is or are your impressions built solely upon *The Grapes of Wrath*[22] or the occasional trip to an apple farm or pumpkin field in the fall?[23]

---

19 ELLISON, *supra* note 1, at 3.

20 *See supra* note 4.

21 U.S. DEP'T OF LABOR, RESEARCH REPORT NO. 8, FINDINGS FROM THE NATIONAL AGRICULTURAL WORKERS SURVEY (NAWS) 1997–1998: A DEMOGRAPHIC AND EMPLOYMENT PROFILE OF UNITED STATES FARMWORKERS 22 (2000), *available at* http://www.dol.gov/asp/programs/agworker/report_8.pdf.

22 JOHN STEINBECK, THE GRAPES OF WRATH (Viking Press, 1939).

23 I grew up in rural Arizona on a citrus farm. We had a small farm of around fifteen acres and my family did most of the labor. Occasionally my parents hired teenagers from the local high school as part of a vocational education program for young farmers. Yet all around me were the large industrial citrus farms whose crops were contracted to large fruit corporations. Surely I saw the workers who cleared those crops or I saw their children. I cannot remember. I do not think I saw them. I did not live in town. We lived on our farm, but I assure you I did not know or truly see these workers.

So what do we do about this undocumented population and this agriculture industry, which is apparently so reliant on these workers? There are many congressionally proposed solutions.[24] Some focus on creating worker registries that will help farmers and agribusinesses find domestic workers; others focus on streamlining the temporary worker petitioning process for foreign workers. All of these proposed solutions are controversial for a number of reasons. Some people fear that the increase of guest-worker programs will lead to new permanent immigrants.[25] Others fear the impact on the impoverished domestic farm workers in the United States.[26] Still others appropriately worry about the abuse and suffering of the guest workers due to inadequate protection from unscrupulous labor contractors and employers.

Of course, invisibility of the worker is not a new problem and it is not limited to agriculture alone. That, in turn, adds to the complexity. What creates visibility and fairness in one industry may not be appropriate in another. These are complex problems for which solutions need to be found. However, today I am asking a different question: Can we really provide solutions when our understanding of the problem is limited by our vision of the reality of these people and their working conditions?

While several scholars, journalists, and advocates have tried to make visible the lives of both agricultural workers and other hidden workers in our society, in truth, most of us know very little about the invisible workers or the jobs they fill.[27] I practiced immigration law for twelve years. It was amazingly common for

---

I do not think it was my youthful blindness or my ignorance; perhaps I was surrounded by the children of these workers as we rode the bus to school. Instead, I suspect that even in what was a relatively small town at the time, the world of the agricultural worker and my world were segregated in many ways. Our lives did not intersect.

24 *See* Rain Levy Minns, Note, *Registry Systems for Foreign and Domestic Farmworkers in the United States: Theory vs. Reality*, 15 GEO. IMMIGR. L.J. 663 (2001).

25 *See* Philip Martin, *Guest Worker Programs for the 21st Century* (Apr. 2001), *at* http://www.cis.org/articles/2000/back400.html (on file with the North Carolina Journal of International Law and Commercial Regulation).

26 *See* Andrew Scott Kosegi, *The H-2A Program: How the Weight of Agricultural Employer Subsidies is Breaking the Backs of Domestic Migrant Farm Workers*, 35 IND. L. REV. 269 (2001).

27 *See, e.g.*, PETER KWONG, FORBIDDEN WORKERS: ILLEGAL CHINESE IMMIGRANTS AND AMERICAN LABOR (1997); ALEC WILKINSON, BIG SUGAR: SEASONS IN THE CANE FIELDS OF FLORIDA (1989).

an employer to contact me, and be it manufacturer, storeowner, rancher, or a family looking to hire a domestic worker; over and over I heard the same story:

"Generally, I think we have too many immigrants and too many illegals in this country, but Henry . . . Gen Li . . . Juan . . . is different. I can't manage without him."

"When she told me that she needed help with her immigration papers, why I thought of course I would help her. This is the kind of person who built this country."

It also was not uncommon for the employer to have worked with a particular employee for a number of years before learning that the worker lacked documents. Even more frequently, if the worker was white and from an English-speaking country, the employers assumed that immigration papers were "easy to obtain" or "no big deal" for their employee. This experience strongly suggests to me that most people in our country have little understanding of the immigration laws. Perhaps because we are used to meeting people from other countries, we assume all foreigners are legal immigrants. Of course, far too often, especially where the person is not white, the assumption is the person must be an immigrant and must prove legal status. For example, when employer sanctions were first established and employers had to verify the citizenship or work authorization of new hires, Puerto Ricans, United States citizens at birth, were frequently refused employment because they lacked a "green card."[28] A congressionally mandated study found that national origin and racial discrimination in the arena of employment increased by nineteen percent.[29]

Similarly, in my eight years of teaching, students repeatedly seem astonished as they begin to look around them and recognize that so many of the people they come across in everyday life may lack documents. I teach in New York City, a metropolitan area with a high percentage of immigrants. Even within this context, many of the students have never considered whether the workers they see in restaurants, delis, grocery stores, delivery trucks,

---

28 *See* United States v. Marcel Watch Corp., 1 OCAHO 988 (A.L.J. Morse, 1990).

29 United States General Accounting Office, *Immigration Reform—Employer Sanctions and the Question of Discrimination: Hearing Before the Senate Committee on the Judiciary*, 101st Cong. (1990), *available at* http://161.203.16.4/d24t8/140974.pdf.

cleaning services, or commuting in the subway are documented or undocumented. While I am glad my students are not trying to label workers by appearance or job title, my point is that we have largely chosen to ignore the issue of immigration status.

Let me give you a very poignant example. In the horrible months after the destruction of the World Trade Center, we would all agree that our media and government officials provided a tremendous amount of information about the dismantling of the rubble and the attempts to recover the bodies of those who perished. Volunteers came from all over the country, and residents and tourists flocked to try to observe the large machinery and workers at the site. Every day *The New York Times* published numerous stories about the recovery efforts at the site. In early January, a story broke that the potential pollution at the site and in the nearby buildings was much higher than had previously been reported by government officials.[30] Suddenly, people working near Ground Zero learned that they might have been exposed to lead, PCBs, asbestos, and other toxins.[31] Contractors had hired itinerant workers to clean the surrounding buildings and to remove debris from the site. Thus, when the city mobilized health care vans to come down to the site to start testing the blood and health of the workers, officials acknowledged that for the most part, they had no formal method of contacting and finding these workers because of their status. Here they are: invisible workers in the midst of one of the most public disasters in this country.

Why do we have this peculiar disposition not to see the people living and working among us? As I have suggested, in part it is because our social fabric conditions us not to "see" workers, and, especially for those of us with higher education or service industry jobs, we may be insulated from recognizing those who do a wide variety of work in our society. But I also think that part of the invisibility comes because we do not want to see. There is a basic tension in most of us that, although we treasure our sense of being Americans who treat all equally, and may feel comfortable applying legal labels in the abstract, when we are face-to-face with

---

30 *See* Kirk Johnson, *Studies Will Take Sept. 11's Measure In Health Effects*, N.Y. TIMES, Jan. 11, 2002, at B1.

31 *See* Paul H.B. Shin, *Migrant Cleanup Hires Ripped*, DAILY NEWS (New York), Jan. 12, 2002, at 7; Ralph R. Ortega, *Free Exams Offered to WTC-Area Laborers*, DAILY NEWS (New York), Jan. 15, 2002, at 8.

a human, at times we struggle and seek solace in determining that this person is a "good illegal" or a "worthy immigrant" or "doing a job no one else wants to do." I am not advocating that you reject your willingness to see that humanity; please don't mistake me. Instead, I am asking us to examine why we don't try harder to shape immigration laws and the *critical operation* of these laws to guarantee equal treatment and humanity.

Increased Visibility ≈ Increased Justice

As I have already suggested, I think a critical and under-recognized contributor to the visibility problem is the inability of the agencies charged with regulating immigration to function efficiently and in a transparent fashion. Both Congress and the executive branch are trying harder to reduce backlogs and achieve some of these goals. Recently, the House has proposed a large increase to the INS's budget to adjudicate backlogged petitions, and the INS has taken preliminary steps to improve customer service and set up an ombuds' office to try to resolve problems.[32] While I remain skeptical based on many years of observation of the problem, these are welcome steps in the right direction.

Equally important is a serious examination of how all workers are protected in our society and how under enforcement of our labor and safety laws contributes to the problem of undocumented workers in our society. This is not a novel idea. Many people who seek to find ways to protect the domestic workforce and lessen the incentives for employers to rely on undocumented labor have called for greater enforcement of our laws.[33] In a recent law review article exploring wage and hour enforcement in the agricultural industry, Rain Levy Minns reported that in the years she examined, about 0.108% of all farms had inspections, but the violation rate found where inspections were conducted was sixty-three percent.[34] However, it is obvious that we lack the political will to increase enforcement of our laws. There are several recent

32 INS, Fact Sheet: INS Restructuring Plan (Nov. 14, 2001), *at* http://www.ins.gov/graphics/publicaffairs/factsheets/restruct.htm (on file with the North Carolina Journal of International Law and Commercial Regulation).

33 Lori A. Nessel, *Undocumented Immigrants in the Workplace: The Fallacy of Labor Protection and the Need for Reform*, 36 HARV. C.R.-C.L. L. REV. 345 (2001).

34 Minns, *supra* note 24, at 688.

examples where the Department of Labor or the INS tried to increase enforcement in an industry and the political outcry quickly led to a slow down or stoppage of the investigations.

In my view, we cannot try to use the removal of aliens and employer sanctions to approach this problem. Instead, we should increase wage and hour and safety and health enforcement to ensure the safety of all workers.[35] We also have to couple these investigations with a guarantee that the information uncovered by the Department of Labor, the Occupational Safety and Health Administration, or other state agencies will not be turned over to the INS as fodder for large numbers of removals and deportations. I am not suggesting a moratorium on removals, but the INS has more than enough work effectuating the removals of the people already in its custody, many of whom are convicted of crimes or are apprehended through other enforcement mechanisms. In the past, these agencies have sometimes worked under Memoranda of Understanding that the investigations would not subject people to border enforcement.[36] In a number of states, the state attorneys general have used their offices to enforce wage and hour laws and obtain back pay for undocumented workers.[37] These types of investigations have also led industry organizations to try to provide greater education and guidance to employers about the requirements of our wage and hour laws. But these types of programs cannot be successful if the main witnesses are afraid of

[35] Unfortunately, as this article goes to press, the Supreme Court held that the National Labor Relations Board (NLRB) improperly awarded backpay to an undocumented alien who had been terminated by his employer for union organizing activity. *See* Hoffman Plastic Compounds, Inc. v. NLRB, 122 S. Ct. 1275 (2002) (5–4 decision). The NLRB had originally ordered the backpay in the belief that allowing an employer to escape this sanction because the worker was undocumented would seriously undermine the labor laws of the United States. The narrow majority of the Supreme Court concluded instead that awarding back pay would frustrate U.S. immigration policy. Obviously this problem requires congressional attention and I would urge Congress to think about the larger harm to all U.S. workers because this case and others like it may actually encourage the employment of undocumented workers.

[36] *See, e.g.*, INS, Memorandum of Understanding to Enhance Worksite Enforcement Sanctions and Labor Standards (Nov. 23, 1998), http://www.ins.usdoj.gov/graphics/publicaffairs/backgrounds/laborbg.htm (on file with the North Carolina Journal of International Law and Commercial Regulation).

[37] Greg Wilson, *Back Pay For Grocery Workers*, DAILY NEWS (New York), Nov. 21, 2001, at 69 (New York Attorney General); Ralph Ranali, *AG Aids Foreign Workers, Not INS*, THE BOSTON GLOBE, Apr. 1, 2001, at A1 (Massachusetts Attorney General).

immediate detention or removal from the United States.[38]

I am not naive enough to believe that federal or state prosecutions and investigations can really solve the economic and social conditions that lead employers to seek out or rely upon undocumented workers. An increase in these efforts to a reasonable level, a level that indicates our commitment to the labor and employment laws, will have a side benefit of helping us gather information about the real lives of the workers. It may also have the side benefits of reducing some of the incentives to hire undocumented people or increasing the opportunity to educate employers about using existing law to sponsor foreign workers.

In addition, we need to examine the complex mesh of our labor and employment laws and dismantle the obstacles for the undocumented to recover adequate remedies under the laws. We also need to recognize that government enforcement alone will never be sufficient, and thus we should create adequate incentives, such as attorneys' fees, to encourage private rights of action and litigation by those victimized.

I am not offering a silver bullet that will solve our "illegal immigration" problem. In fact, my premise is that there is no single solution and that our willful blindness coupled with the invisibility of the workers' lives make it impossible to fashion perfect political and legal solutions. Still, I urge that we remember that behind every legal label is a person. Let us do the humane thing. How must it feel to labor hard, to work without any safety net, to always be subject to the nightmare of the employer who refuses to pay, who may call the border patrol? When will we see this as demeaning and immoral treatment of people? So long as we seek comfort in the labels, we will have the invisible worker within our society. Of course, the invisible worker does not pay the cost alone. There are also costs to the children born to the undocumented, costs to the employer who tries to comply with the law and cannot compete with unscrupulous employers, and costs to the health and freedom of workers throughout our country. We all suffer when we support a legal regime where justice is blind because our society refuses to see.

---

38 *See* Nessel, *supra* note 33, at 393 (suggesting legal status for undocumented workers who testify against employers who violate wage and hour laws).

[14]

In Defence of the Migrant Workers Convention: Standard Setting for Contemporary Migration

Bernard Ryan[1]

Introduction

The International Convention on the Protection of the Rights of All Migrant Workers and Members of Their Families ('the Migrant Workers Convention') has had a difficult history. The adoption of a treaty on the subject of migrant workers was formally proposed by a General Assembly resolution of 17 December 1979.[2] As a result of differences of opinion between states of origin and destination, however, the final text was not endorsed by the General Assembly until 18 December 1990.[3] There was then a further lengthy period until the Convention came into force on 1 July 2003, once the requisite 20 ratifications had been obtained. Since then, ratification has proceeded slowly, with a total of 44 states having ratified by early 2011.

In contrast to the doubts that have often been expressed as to the value of the Migrant Workers Convention, this chapter will argue for its potential as a source of standards concerning international migration. Section 1 will consider the text of the Convention, and will show that it is a coherent instrument for the protection of migrants as a category. Section 2 will then consider the Convention in practice, arguing that its strength lies in a combination of two factors: the migration experiences of the states that have ratified it, and the interpretative work of the Committee on Migrant Workers since it was established on 1 January 2004. That combination enables the Convention to be an effective and authoritative source of standards on the treatment of migrants.

---

[1] Professor of Law, University of Kent. I am grateful to Ryszard Cholewinski, Virginia Mantouvalou and Eki Yemisi Omorogbe for their comments on the paper in draft.

[2] UNGA Resolution 34/172, 17 December 1979.

[3] UNGA Resolution 45/158, 18 December 1990.

1. The Migrant Workers Convention

The origins of the Migrant Workers Convention lie in the postwar period of high demand for migrant labour in the developed countries of Europe and North America. At the international level, standards on international migration were initially developed within the International Labour Organization. The Migration for Employment Convention (Revised), 1949 (No. 97) provided for the equal treatment of lawfully resident migrant workers.[4] More significantly, the Migrant Workers (Supplementary Provisions) Convention 1975 (No. 143) focused on irregular migration and employment. It required contracting states to take action against 'the organisers of illicit or clandestine movements of migrants for employment', and against 'those who employ workers who have immigrated in illegal conditions'.[5] That approach to irregular migration and employment was followed by calls from states of origin – led by Mexico and Morocco – for a new treaty that was more concerned with the interests of their nationals.[6] Because the ILO structures gave a greater say to 'industrialized' countries, the preference of states of origin was for such an instrument to be adopted through the United Nations General Assembly.

The debate over the Convention was initially quite polarized.[7] Seventeen developed Western countries had indicated their scepticism about the proposal for a Convention by abstaining on the General Assembly resolution setting up the working group in 1979.[8] When an initial draft Convention was presented in May 1981, with the support of five states of emigration, the most developed countries rejected it as 'a blank check for continued illegal migration'.[9] The intervention of a group of seven Southern European and Nordic states proved decisive, and the eventual text of the Convention reflected their broadly socially democratic approach to migration.[10] On the one hand, Part III of the Convention extended many human and labour rights to migrant workers and their families, irrespective of immigration status. On the other hand, irregular migrant and employment was discouraged, in two ways: Part

4 ILO Convention 97, Article 6.

5 ILO Convention 143, Article 3(b).

6 On the history of the Convention, see Roger Böhning, 'The ILO and the New UN Convention on Migrant Workers: The Past and Future' (1991) 25 *International Migration Review* 698–709, and Graziano Battistella, 'Migration and Human Rights: The Uneasy but Essential Relationship' in Paul de Guchteneire, Antoine Pécoud and Ryszard Cholewinski (eds), *Migration and Human Rights: The United Nations Convention on Migrant Workers' Rights* (Cambridge University Press, Cambridge, 2009) 47–69.

7 On the drafting of the Convention, see Juhani Lönnroth, 'The International Convention on the Rights of All Migrant Workers and Members of Their Families in the Context of International Migration Policies: An Analysis of Ten Years of Negotiation' (1991) 25 *International Migration Review* 710–36.

8 For the list, see Battistella, 'Migration and Human Rights', 54. This group of states included 12 West European states (Austria, Belgium, Denmark, Finland, France, West Germany, Iceland, Luxembourg, the Netherlands, Norway, Sweden and the United Kingdom) and five other highly developed states (Australia, Canada, Israel, New Zealand and the United States). Burma and Guatemala also abstained.

9 Böhning, 'ILO and the New UN Convention on Migrant Workers', 701. The 1981 draft was initially endorsed by Algeria, Mexico, Pakistan, Turkey and Yugoslavia, and later supported by Barbados and Egypt: Battistella, 'Migration and Human Rights', 55.

10 These were Finland, Greece, Italy, Norway, Portugal, Spain and Sweden.

IV of the Convention conferred certain rights solely on workers in a lawful position, while Part VI of the Convention – which is concerned with 'sound, equitable, humane and lawful conditions' in international migration – provided for measures to prevent irregular migration and employment.

These features of the Convention have in turn given rise to two frequent criticisms since it was negotiated: that it overlaps unnecessarily with other international instruments, and that it gives insufficient protection to irregular migrants. The rest of this section will address these criticisms, through a review of the content of the Convention.

Overlap

Criticism of the Migrant Workers Convention for overlapping unnecessarily with other instruments began even before the text of the Convention had been formally adopted. Writing in 1988, Roger Böhning observed, with reference to the International Covenant on Civil and Political Rights (ICCPR) and the International Covenant on Economic, Social and Cultural Rights (ICESCR), that Part III of the Convention 'almost entirely repeats textually the provisions of one Covenant or the other, which demonstrates that there was no need for a new convention in this respect.'[11] That line of criticism was developed in particular by James Nafziger and Barry Bartel, who argued in an article in 1991 that overlaps would 'obfuscate or obscure the enforcement of both the Convention and corresponding human rights instruments that are designed to protect everyone, including migrant workers.'[12] More recently, Vincent Chetail has remarked that, 'from a purely legal perspective, the added value of the ICMW is relatively limited given that most of its provisions simply restate – and sometimes specify – basic human rights which are already enshrined in other general instruments.'[13]

This line of criticism will be addressed here through an examination of the Convention's provisions on personal scope (Article 3) and non-discrimination (Article 7), and of the rights it recognizes for all migrant workers and their families (Part III of the Convention). It will be argued that overlaps of content are explicable in terms of the Convention's underlying objective of protecting migrants. Because of that objective, the rights-conferring provisions of the Convention either go beyond other instruments in significant ways, or else merit inclusion in the Convention because of their distinct relevance for migrants.

Personal scope

Article 2 of the Convention, which sets out its personal scope, gives a first example of its content going beyond other instruments.[14] It defines the term 'migrant worker' to mean 'a person who

---

11 Roger Böhning, 'The Protection of Migrant Workers and International Labour Standards' (1988) 26(2) *International Migration Review* 133–46, at 143.

12 James Nafziger and Barry Bartel, 'The Migration Workers Convention: Its Place in Human Rights Law' (1991) 25 *International Migration Review* 771–99, at 787.

13 Vincent Chetail, 'Review of *Migration and Human Rights: The United Nations Convention on Migrant Workers*' (2010) 22 *International Journal of Refugee Law* 677–82, at 679.

14 For an earlier discussion, see Ryszard Cholewinski, *Migrant Workers in International Human Rights Law: Their Protection in Countries of Employment* (Oxford University Press, Oxford, 1997) 149–52.

is to be engaged, is engaged or has been engaged in a remunerated activity in a State of which he or she is not a national.'[15] This definition may be contrasted in particular with the two ILO Conventions in the field. ILO Convention 97 applies to a 'migrant for employment', defined as 'a person who migrates or who has migrated from one country to another with a view to being employed otherwise than on his own account.'[16] The same formulation appears in ILO Convention 143, in order to define the category of 'migrant workers'.[17]

The definitions in the Migrant Workers Convention and the ILO Conventions have in common that they potentially cover workers whose stay and/or economic activity is irregular. In other respects, however, the Migrant Workers Convention's personal scope is far broader. One reason is that the Convention definition includes *all* foreign nationals who engage in remunerated activity, without it being necessary that they have migrated *for* employment. It therefore includes foreign national workers lawfully in a contracting state for other reasons, such as a family relationship, or who have never migrated, because they were born there. A second difference is that the Convention's focus on 'remunerated activity', rather than employment, means that both employees and the self-employed are included.[18] The inclusion of self-employment is of particular relevance to irregular migrants, who often work outside formal employment relationships. A third difference is the reference in the Convention to past economic activity, which ensures that the Convention applies to those who have previously engaged in economic activity in the state in question.

The broad personal scope of the Convention, going beyond current workers, was one of the criticisms of it made by Nafziger and Bartel in their 1991 article.[19] Yet it can equally be argued that the breadth of Article 2 is one of its strengths, as central to the Convention's potential as an instrument concerning migrants in general. We will see in this section how that potential has been reflected in Part III of the Convention, and in section 2, how it has been carried forward in the work of the Committee on Migrant Workers.

Non-discrimination clause

The Convention's non-discrimination guarantee is a second example of a provision that goes further than other instruments. Under Article 7, contracting states are obliged

> to respect and to ensure ... the rights provided for in the present Convention without distinction of any kind such as to sex, race, colour, language, religion or conviction, political or other opinion, national, ethnic or social origin,

[15] A number of exceptions are set out in Article 3: persons sent by international organizations and foreign states; investors; refugees and stateless persons; students and trainees; and seafarers and workers in offshore installations who are not authorized to reside and work in the state in question.

[16] ILO Convention 97, Article 11(1).

[17] ILO Convention 143, Article 11(1), which refers solely to the rights applicable to workers in a lawful position set out in its Part II. The provisions concerning irregular migration in Part I of that Convention are not governed by an express statement of personal scope.

[18] This is confirmed by Articles 2(2)(h) and 63, which specifically concern the self-employed.

[19] Nafziger and Bartel, 'Migration Workers Convention', 786.

nationality, age, economic position, property, marital status, birth or other status.

The breadth of this formulation is apparent from a comparison with the equivalent provisions in Article 2(1) ICCPR and Article 2(2) ICESCR.[20] Under each of those, contracting states undertake 'to respect and to ensure ... the rights recognized in the present Covenant, without distinction of any kind, such as race, colour, sex, language, religion, political or other opinion, national or social origin, property, birth or other status.' By comparison, Article 7 adds non-religious convictions, ethnic origin, nationality, age, economic position and marital status to the grounds of discrimination that are enumerated.[21] Among these, the inclusion of 'nationality' is of particular significance, as it reflects the Convention's character as an instrument concerning migration.

The inclusion of 'nationality' in Article 7 distinguishes the Migrant Workers Convention from other instruments. In the case of Article 2(2) ICESCR, the Committee on Economic, Social and Cultural Rights has had to read 'nationality' into the term 'other status'.[22] By comparison, the merit of the Convention's approach is that 'nationality' is referred to expressly, removing the need for it to be read into the Convention in this way. The inclusion of 'nationality' also differentiates the Convention from the International Convention on the Elimination of All Forms of Racial Discrimination (ICERD). Article 1(1) ICERD does not list 'nationality' as a form of 'racial discrimination', which instead covers 'any distinction, exclusion, restriction or preference based on race, colour, descent, or national or ethnic origin'. Moreover, Article 1(2) ICERD expressly states that the Convention does not address differentiation by states 'between citizens and non-citizens'. In contrast, the advantage of the Migrant Workers Convention is precisely that many of its provisions aim at securing the equal treatment of foreign nationals.

Civil rights in Part III

Part III of the Convention lists the rights that are applicable to *all* migrant workers and their families, irrespective of the lawfulness of their stay and/or employment. The criticism that the Convention overlaps unnecessarily with other instruments concerns in particular the civil rights listed in Part III, relative to the equivalent provisions of the ICCPR.[23] Can the inclusion of these rights nevertheless be justified?[24]

---

[20] See too the discussion in Cholewinski, *Migrant Workers in International Human Rights Law*, 155.

[21] This point is also made by Isabelle Slinckx in 'Migrants' Rights in UN Human Rights Conventions' in De Guchteneire, Pécoud and Cholewinski (eds), *Migration and Human Rights*, 122–49, at 146.

[22] Committee on Economic, Social and Cultural Rights, *General Comment No. 20: Non-discrimination in Economic, Social and Cultural Rights* (2 July 2009), UN Doc. E/C.12/GC/20, para. 30.

[23] The term 'civil right' is understood here to refer to individual freedoms and status rights that potentially apply to all persons. The term 'political right' is understood to refer to freedoms and protections that derive from an attachment to a particular state, or that concern political participation.

[24] Nafziger and Bartel, in 'Migration Workers Convention', also compare the civil rights set out in the Convention with the Universal Declaration of Human Rights. The ICCPR is taken as the sole reference point here, because it is a binding instrument.

A first point is that Part III of the Migrant Workers Convention includes two rights of direct relevance to migrants that are not set out in the ICCPR. One is the prohibition on confiscation or destruction of identity or immigration documents by anyone other than a public official acting with legal authority (Article 21). The other is the right to consular assistance 'whenever the rights recognized in the present Convention are impaired' (Article 23). The latter of these provisions is complemented by Article 65(2), in Part VI of the Convention, which obliges contracting states to 'facilitate the provision of adequate consular and other services' to migrant workers and their families.

Secondly, where there are overlaps of subject matter, the migration context is often reflected in stronger statements in the Migrant Workers Convention. Protection against expulsion offers a clear example. Article 13 ICCPR provides that a foreign national may be expelled only on the basis of decision reached in accordance with the law, that they should ordinarily be allowed to submit the reasons against the expulsion, and that there should be the possibility of review by a competent authority. By comparison, Article 22 of the Convention is stronger in its substance: collective expulsions are prohibited, expulsion decisions are required to be in a language the individual understands, a written decision setting out the reasons for the expulsion may be requested, and it should be possible to apply for the suspension of an expulsion while a legal challenge to it is pending. Moreover, there is a crucial difference in personal scope. Article 22 extends protection to *all* migrant workers and their family members, irrespective of the legality of their stay. By contrast, the benefit of Article 13 ICCPR is limited to foreign nationals 'lawfully in the territory of a State Party'.[25]

Many other illustrations may be given of stronger statements in the Convention, due to its concern with the position of migrants. Article 8(2) of the Convention states, 'Migrant workers and members of their families shall have the right at any time to enter and remain in their State of origin.' In presenting the right of entry and residence in absolute terms, Article 8(2) goes beyond the equivalent Article 12 ICCPR, which provides that a person may not be '*arbitrarily* deprived of the right to enter his own country'.[26] Another case is the provision for the right to liberty and security of the person in Article 16 of the Convention. It goes beyond Article 9 ICCPR in requiring that identity checks by state officials 'be carried out in accordance with procedure established by law', and in providing for access to consular assistance and for interpreters in proceedings concerning the legality of detention. A further example is Article 17 of the Convention, which requires that detention be lawful and legitimate. It goes beyond Article 10 ICCPR in providing that persons detained for violation of immigration rules 'shall be held, in so far as practicable, separately from convicted persons or persons detained pending trial', and in providing that migrants should not bear the cost of detention aimed at verifying compliance with immigration law.

Thirdly, even where the Convention is substantively similar to other instruments, the civil rights set out in Part III are likely to be of particular value to migrants. A good example is the provision in Article 29: 'Each child of a migrant worker shall have the right to a name, to registration of birth and to a nationality'. Other cases are the provisions in the Convention for

[25] This key difference between Article 22 ICRMW and Article 12 ICCPR was not referred to in the summary in Nafziger and Bartel, ibid., 791.

[26] Emphasis added. In their summary, Nafziger and Bartel did not refer to this key difference between Article 8 ICRMW and Article 12 ICCPR: ibid., 790.

freedom from slavery, servitude and forced labour, freedom of thought and religion, the right to a fair trial, the principle that criminal offences should not be retroactive, the rule against imprisonment for breach of a contractual obligation, and the right to freedom of association.[27] All of these rights are potentially of particular value for foreign nationals and their family members, simply because they may be in a weaker social or legal position than the established population of the state in question.

Economic and social rights in Part III

Criticisms concerning overlap also cover the economic and social rights of migrant workers and their families set out in Part III of the Migrant Workers Convention. In response, an initial point is that two economic and social rights listed in Part III do not appear in the ICESCR. One is the right not to be arbitrarily deprived of property.[28] The other is the right to transfer earnings, savings and personal property abroad when the period of residence comes to an end.[29]

The economic and social rights in Part III of the Convention are anyway quite different in content to their equivalents in the ICESCR. That is because the Convention provisions generally aim at equal treatment on grounds of nationality, whereas the ICESCR provisions concern the substance of the right at issue. For example, Article 25 of the Convention provides for equal treatment in remuneration and terms and conditions of employment, whereas Article 7 ICESCR provides for 'just and favourable conditions of work'. Article 27 provides for equal treatment in matters of social security, whereas Article 9 ICESCR sets out 'the right of everyone to social security'. Article 28 provides for equal treatment in respect of medical care that is urgently needed in serious cases, whereas Article 12 ICESCR articulates 'the right of everyone to the enjoyment of the highest attainable standard of physical and mental health'. Finally, Article 30 provides for equal access to schooling by migrants' children, as compared to 'the right of everyone to education' in Article 13 ICESCR.

This focus on equality of treatment is logical in an instrument that is concerned with the position of migrants, and not with the advancement of economic and social rights as such. Part III of the Convention need not imply a lower standard of protection, however. The reason is that the rights set out in the ICESCR are not absolute standards. Rather, the duty on a state party to the ICESCR is 'to take steps ... to the maximum of its available resources, with a view to achieving progressively the full realization of' those rights (Article 2(1) ICESCR). In practice, one consequence is that equal treatment is also a central principle within the ICESCR framework, including for foreign nationals. In the words of the Committee on Economic, Social and Cultural Rights, 'the ground of nationality should not bar access to Covenant rights' and 'the Covenant rights apply to everyone including non-nationals, such as refugees, asylum-seekers, stateless persons, migrant workers and victims of international trafficking, regardless of legal status and documentation.'[30]

---

27 Articles 11, 12, 18, 19, 20 and 26 ICRMW, respectively.

28 Article 15 ICRMW.

29 Article 32 ICRMW.

30 Committee on Economic, Social and Cultural Rights, *General Comment No. 20*, para. 30.

Irregular Migrants

The second line of criticism of the Convention has been that it gives insufficient protection to irregular migrants. This critique has two elements: that irregular migrants have fewer rights than those in a lawful position, and that they are vulnerable to expulsion. These two arguments are addressed in turn here.

Fewer rights

Part IV of the Convention confers a number of rights solely upon migrant workers and their family members 'who are documented or in a regular situation'. The distinction drawn within the Convention between the rights of irregular migrants and those of persons in a regular position led to Linda Bosniak's criticism in 1991 that, 'under the terms of Convention, the undocumented continue to enjoy institutionally-sanctioned second- (or third-) class status.'[31]

One point that may be made in response is that the Convention achieves a great deal *for* irregular migrants.[32] In three cases, protection is expressly extended to irregular migrants: Article 25 on equal treatment in employment, Article 28 on emergency medical care, and Article 30 on the schooling of children. More generally, the very fact that the Convention's rights are divided between two Parts itself removes any doubt as the application of Part III rights to irregular migrant workers and their families.

A second point is that many of the rights set out in Part IV concern the detail of immigration status, and as such are logically applicable only to 'regular' migrants. That is the case with several provisions concerning the movement and residence of migrants workers and their families: the right to temporary absence from the state in question (Article 38), the right to liberty of movement and residence throughout the territory (Article 39), and the principle that expulsion should not be intended to deprive a person of the benefit of their permission to reside or to work (Article 56(2)).[33] The same may be said of certain rights conferred on migrant workers: protection of the right of residence in the event of loss of employment (Article 51), free choice of employment after a maximum of five years (Article 52), equal protection in the event of loss of employment (Article 54), and equal treatment in the exercise of employed activity (Article 55). It is also true of requirements concerning migrants' family members: 'facilitation' of admission (Article 44), access to the labour market (Article 53), and 'favourable consideration' to their staying after the death of a migrant worker or the dissolution of a marriage (Article 50).

Criticism concerning the exclusion of irregular migrants is more persuasive in relation to Part IV rights that could in principle have been extended to them, but were not. One example is the right to participation in the political affairs in the state of origin, including the right to vote and to be elected there (Article 41). Another is the right to equal treatment

31 Linda Bosniak, 'Human Rights, State Sovereignty, and the Protection of Undocumented Migrants under the International Convention for the Protection of the Rights of All Migrant Workers and Members of Their Families' (1991) 25 *International Migration Review* 737–70, at 759.

32 For this point, see Slinckx, 'Migrants' Rights in UN Human Rights Conventions', 146–7.

33 Note that the right to liberty of movement and residence is also limited to those 'lawfully in the territory' in Article 12 ICCPR.

in education, vocational provision, housing, 'social ... services', access to cooperatives and self-managed enterprises, and in cultural life (Article 43). Other cases concern personal finances: exemption from import and export duties and taxes when international migration occurs, freedom to transfer earnings and savings to the state of origin or elsewhere, and equal treatment in taxation (Articles 46–8). The provision that expulsion should only be for reasons defined in national legislation (Article 56(1)) could logically apply to irregular migrants as well.

In two cases, indeed, the exclusion of irregular migrants from Part IV rights appears inconsistent with other international treaties. One case is the Convention's provision for trade union rights. Article 26 of the Convention (in Part III) recognizes three rights for *all* migrant workers: '(a) to take part in meetings and activities of trade unions ... with a view to protecting their economic, social, cultural and other interests', '(b) to join freely any trade union,' and '(c) to seek the aid and assistance of any trade union.' What it omits, however, is the right to *form* trade unions, which is instead recognized in Article 40 (in Part IV) solely for migrant workers in a regular situation. This non-recognition of the right of irregular migrant workers to form trade unions is inconsistent with Article 2 of ILO Convention 87 on the freedom of association, which provides that 'workers and employers, without distinction whatsoever, shall have the right to establish and ... to join organisations of their own choosing.'[34] The Migrant Workers Convention is also at odds with Article 22 ICCPR, which states that 'everyone shall have ... the right to form and join trade unions', and with Article 8 ICESCR, which refers to 'the right of everyone to form trade unions and join the trade union of [their] choice'.[35]

The second case is that of rights concerning healthcare. Article 28 of the Convention (in Part III) recognizes the right of all migrant workers and their family members to equal treatment in 'medical care that is urgently required for the preservation of their life or the avoidance of irreparable harm to their health.' A full right to equal treatment in 'access to ... health services' – extending to cases where medical treatment is not urgently required, or the consequences of its non-provision are not serious – is recognized by Article 43(1)(e) (in Part IV) only for migrants in a regular situation. This is contrary to the provision in Article 12 ICESCR for 'the right of everyone to the enjoyment of the highest attainable standard of physical and mental health', read in light of the equal treatment guarantee in Article 2(2) of that Convention (discussed above).[36]

[34] The Committee on Freedom of Association has confirmed that Article 2 of ILO Convention 87 applies to *all* workers, irrespective of their immigration status: see *Spain (Case No 2121)* (23 March 2001) Report of the Committee on Freedom of Association No. 327 (Vol. LXXXV 2002 Series B No. 1), paras 561–2 and *Republic of Korea (Case No 2620)* (18 December 2007) Report of the Committee on Freedom of Association No. 353 (Vol. XCII 2009 Series B No. 1), para. 788.

[35] The use of the term 'everyone' in these Articles implies that the regularity of stay or employment should be irrelevant to these rights: see Cholewinski, *Migrant Workers in International Human Rights Law*, 164.

[36] See Committee on Economic, Social and Cultural Rights, *General Comment No. 14: The Right to the Highest Attainable Standard of Health* (2000), para. 34. For a discussion, see Vincent Chetail and Gilles Giacca, 'Who Cares? The Right to Health of Migrants' in Andrew Clapham and Mary Robinson (eds), *Realising the Right to Health* (Rueffer, Zurich, 2009) 224–34.

Immigration policy and control

The Convention's acceptance of immigration control was a second reason for criticism of its treatment of irregular migrants by Bosniak in 1991. As she put it, 'the real problem with the Convention ... is that its provisions protecting states' sovereign prerogatives to control immigration will often effectively undermine or defeat the rights it provides to those migrants.'[37] On close examination, however, it appears that this critique overestimates the weight given to immigration policy and control within the Convention.

Consider first Article 68 of the Convention. It obliges states to 'collaborate with a view to *preventing and eliminating*' irregular movements of persons and the irregular employment of migrant workers, and to 'take all adequate and effective measures to *eliminate* employment ... of migrant workers in an irregular situation.'[38] Bosniak's interpretation of Article 68 was that it required states 'to undertake *control* measures to end the process of clandestine migration and the ... employment of irregular migrants including ... employer sanctions'.[39] The difficulty with this reading is that Article 68 does not use the language of 'control'. Its language of 'preventing' and 'eliminating' potentially covers both control measures and pre-emptive policies designed to remove the basis for irregular migration. Pre-emptive policies would generally be beneficial to migrants, including those who are, or would otherwise be, in an irregular position.

Policy on regularization is another example. Article 69(1) of the Convention sets out the general proposition that, 'when there are migrant workers and members of their families within their territory in an irregular situation', contracting states 'shall ... take appropriate measures to ensure that such a situation does not persist'. Bosniak's reading was that Article 69 required states 'to undertake control measures to end ... the presence ... of irregular migrants.'[40] In reality, control measures aimed at expulsion are only one option for state authorities, who may choose regularization instead.[41] Indeed, Article 69(2) expressly provides that states may 'consider the possibility of regularizing the situation of such persons', and requires that, where they do so, 'appropriate account shall be taken of the circumstances of their entry, the duration of their stay in the States of employment and other relevant considerations, in particular those relating to their family situation.' Bosniak also cited Article 35 of the Convention as evidence that 'contracting states are explicitly not obliged to regularize the status of irregular migrant workers.'[42] In fact, Article 35 provides only that 'nothing in *the present Part* of the Convention [i.e. Part III] shall be interpreted as implying ... regularization',[43] and is stated to be without prejudice to Part VI of the Convention, which includes Article 69.

Two further provisions of the Convention may be discussed more briefly. One is Article 34 of the Convention, which provides that '[n]othing in [Part III] of the Convention shall have the

37 Bosniak, 'Human Rights, State Sovereignty', 759.

38 Emphasis added.

39 Bosniak, 'Human Rights, State Sovereignty', 741, emphasis added.

40 Ibid., 741.

41 For example, De Guchteneire and Pécoud have noted that Article 69 'may be interpreted as an obligation to either expel or regularize undocumented migrants': Paul de Guchteneire and Antoine Pécoud, 'Introduction: The UN Convention on Migrant Workers' Rights' in De Guchteneire, Pécoud and Cholewinski (eds), *Migration and Human Rights*, 1–44, at 22–3.

42 Bosniak, 'Human Rights, State Sovereignty', 741.

43 Emphasis added.

effect of relieving migrant workers and the members of their families from ... the obligation to comply with the laws and regulations of any State of transit and the State of employment.' In Bosniak's analysis, this provision covered 'states' laws against unauthorized entry, employment or residence.'[44] Article 34 can also be read more narrowly, however, to require migrants to comply with the law *in general*, while obliging states to respect the substantive provisions of the Convention. The other is Article 79, which provides that 'nothing in the present Convention shall affect the right of each State Party to establish the criteria governing admission of migrant workers and members of their families.' Bosniak's characterization of Article 79 was that it permitted 'states parties to pursue the immigration *control* policies that they see fit'.[45] It would, however, be more accurate to say that Article 79 is concerned solely with the *criteria* for admission, and that it does not refer to states' immigration control methods.

The wider point is that the Convention does not give *carte blanche* to states in their immigration control systems. States remain free to have immigration policies, and to take immigration control measures in support of them. But the provision for an orderly approach to international migration in Articles 68 and 69 may equally imply acceptance of migration. Moreover, certain of the substantive rights of migrants – particularly those in Part III – may impact on immigration control measures applied to irregular migrants. We shall see in section 2 how this is an area in which the Committee on Migrant Workers has been especially creative in its interpretative work to date.

2. The Convention in Practice

Where section 1 considered the content of the Convention in the abstract, this section will consider its application in practice. The extent and pattern of ratification of the Convention are considered first, as these have been a particular area of doubt concerning its prospects. The section will then provide a detailed analysis of the work of the Committee on Migrant Workers to date.

Ratification

Forty-four states had ratified the Migrant Workers Convention at the time of writing (May 2011). Of these, the largest concentration by continent is in the Americas, where 17 out of 35 UN members have ratified the Convention.[46] There has also been extensive ratification in Africa, where 17 of 53 UN member states are parties, primarily in North and West Africa.[47] By

44 Bosniak, 'Human Rights, State Sovereignty', 741.

45 Ibid., emphasis added.

46 These are Argentina, Belize, Bolivia, Chile, Colombia, Ecuador, El Salvador, Guatemala, Guyana, Honduras, Jamaica, Mexico, Nicaragua, Paraguay, Peru, Saint Vincent and the Grenadines and Uruguay.

47 The full list of African states to have ratified is Algeria, Burkina Faso, Cape Verde, Egypt, Ghana, Guinea, Lesotho, Libya, Mali, Mauritania, Morocco, Niger, Nigeria, Rwanda, Senegal, Seychelles and Uganda.

contrast, only six Asian states of 43 UN members and only four European states out of 47 UN members have ratified, while none of the 14 UN members in Oceania have done so.[48]

The low level of ratification of the Convention has contributed to doubts as to its true value. Unfavourable comparisons have been drawn with other specific UN human rights instruments, including the Convention on the Elimination of Discrimination against Women (adopted in 1979), which had 186 parties at the time of writing, and the Convention on the Rights of the Child (adopted in 1989), which had 190, and with the Migrant Smuggling Protocol (adopted in 2000), which had 127 parties at the time of writing.[49] In itself, however, this relatively low level of ratification does not tell us whether the Convention has value for those states that are parties.

The lack of ratification by the major countries of immigration in Europe, North America and elsewhere has been seen as a further weakness. Writing in 2009, Paul de Guchteneire and Antoine Pécoud put it bluntly: 'no major state has ratified, which strongly diminishes the impact of the Convention.'[50] There is, however, a risk of what may be termed 'North-centrism' in discussion of the Convention. This bias is reflected in the extensive research (including by the present author) into obstacles to ratification in highly developed countries.[51] The danger is that scholarship on the Convention is blind to its potential *outside* the most developed group of states. It is striking in particular that the experience of countries that *have* ratified has remained largely unexamined in academic commentary to date.[52]

One reason why the Convention may have value as a source of standards for countries that have ratified is that many of those states have extensive experience of *emigration*. For example, the many Latin American states that have ratified are countries of origin, as are the North and West African states that have done so, the Philippines and Sri Lanka in Asia, and Albania and Turkey in Europe. States of origin that have ratified may have intended thereby to boost the Convention, in order to secure better treatment for their nationals in destination countries.[53] But the text of the Convention also places duties upon them. We shall see below that this latter aspect has been prominent in the work of the Committee on Migrant Workers to date.

---

48 The Asian states to have ratified are Kyrgyzstan, Philippines, Sri Lanka, Syria, Tajikistan and Timor Leste. The four European states to have ratified are Albania, Azerbaijan, Bosnia and Herzegovina and Turkey. (Membership of the Council of Europe has been used to define the category of 'European' state here.)

49 De Guchteneire and Pécoud, 'Introduction', 11–12, 24–5.

50 Ibid., 13. In the same collection, Carla Edelenbos expressed frustration at the 'absence of any major receiving country among the States Parties': 'Committee on Migrant Workers and Implementation of the ICRMW' in De Guchteneire, Pécoud and Cholewinski (eds), *Migration and Human Rights*, 100–121, at 119.

51 See, for example, Shirley Hune and Jan Niessen, 'Ratifying the UN Migrant Workers Convention: Current Difficulties and Prospects' (1994) 12 *Netherlands Quarterly of Human Rights* 130–41, and the studies on Canada, France, Germany, Italy and (by the present author) the United Kingdom in De Guchteneire, Pécoud and Cholewinski (eds), *Migration and Human Rights*.

52 For a similar observation, see Chetail, 'Review of *Migration and Human Rights*', 680. An exception is the chapter by Gabriela Díaz and Gretchen Kuhner, 'Mexico's Role in Promoting and Implementing the ICRMW' in De Guchteneire, Pécoud and Cholewinski (eds), *Migration and Human Rights*, 219–46.

53 See Battistella, 'Migration and Human Rights', 59.

Secondly, many states that have ratified the Convention have experienced significant levels of *transit migration*. The wider picture is that, since the mid-1980s, the most developed countries have taken a more rigorous approach to immigration control, including through tougher visa policies and the introduction of carrier sanctions. As a result, their neighbouring states have often faced an increase in arrivals by persons in transit. Among states that have ratified the Convention, this has been the case in particular for Mexico (mainly in relation to Central America), for Algeria, Egypt, Libya and Morocco (mainly in relation to sub-Saharan Africa) and Turkey (mainly in relation to Asian countries).[54] When those neighbouring states are parties to the Convention, they are bound by its terms in their treatment of transit migrants who are migrant workers or their family members.

Thirdly, a number of states that are parties to the Convention are migration *destinations* in their own right. Among the states that have ratified, Argentina and Libya stand out as countries – for quite different reasons – with long histories of inward migration for employment.[55] The emergence of a migrant population is also a feature of conditions in Chile, Ecuador and Uruguay.[56] More generally, all of the 'transit' countries and regions referred to above are potential destination countries, if those who initially intend to move on to North America or Western Europe elect to remain there.[57]

The relevance of the Convention to the migration experience of ratifying states has been recognized in the work of the Migrant Workers Committee. In its observations on the state reports submitted to it (see below), it has frequently noted that the state in question, in addition to being a state of origin, is also a place of transit and/or of destination. Statements of this kind have been included in the concluding observations concerning all five Latin American states considered to date (Bolivia, Colombia, Ecuador, El Salvador and Mexico), as well as three African states (Algeria, Egypt and Senegal) and two European states (Azerbaijan and Bosnia and Herzegovina). In three further cases, there has been partial recognition that the party was not merely a country of origin: Albania was described as a country of origin and transit; Mali was said to have difficulties in controlling irregular migration; and it was noted that Syria had recently experienced extensive migration as a result of the armed conflict in Iraq. Of the fifteen countries commented upon so far, only the Philippines and Sri Lanka have been characterized by the Committee as states of origin alone.

---

[54] See generally Manuel Ángel Castillo, 'Mexico: Caught between the United States and Central America' (Migration Information Source, April 2006) and Franck Düvell 'Crossing the Fringes of Europe: Transit Migration in the EU's Neighbourhood' (COMPAS Working Paper WP-06-33, 2006).

[55] See Maia Jachimowicz, 'Argentina: A New Era of Migration and Migration Policy' (Migration Information Source, January 2006) and Sara Hamood, *African Transit Migration through Libya to Europe: The Human Cost* (American University in Cairo, 2006) 17–19.

[56] See Agustín Escobar Latapí, *The Future of Migration Policies in the Americas* (IOM, Geneva, 2010) 7.

[57] See Michael Colyer and Hein de Haas, 'Developing Dynamic Categorisations of Transit Migration' (2011) 17 *Population, Space and Place* 468–81.

The Committee on Migrant Workers

The Committee on Migrant Workers is provided for in Article 72 of the Convention. It was established on 1 January 2004, six months after the Convention came into force. The distribution of its current 14 members broadly corresponds to the geographical spread of ratifications, with five American states (Ecuador, El Salvador, Jamaica, Guatemala and Mexico), five African states (Burkina Faso, Egypt, Morocco, Mali and Senegal), two Asian states (the Philippines and Sri Lanka), and two European states (Azerbaijan and Turkey).

The Convention provides for two optional procedures through which complaints may be brought to the Committee. Participating states may recognize the Committee's competence over interstate complaints (Article 76), and over complaints by 'individuals subject to its jurisdiction' who claim their rights have been violated by that state (Article 77).[58] Each of these procedures is to come into effect when ten states have accepted the competence of the Committee. At the time of writing, only Guatemala had made the necessary declaration with respect to Article 76, while only Guatemala and Mexico had done so with respect to Article 77. In addition, Turkey has declared that it will recognize the competence of the Committee 'at a later time'.

Accordingly, the Committee's most significant role to date has been its consideration of state reports, made under Article 73, on the 'legislative, judicial, administrative and other measures' taken to give effect to the Convention. A contracting state is to submit the first such report within one year of the entry into force of the Convention for it. Subsequently, reports should be submitted every five years, or 'whenever the Committee so requests'. By early 2011, 20 states had submitted initial reports to the Committee, and two states (Mexico and Ecuador) had reported a second time.[59] In total, 15 initial state reports, and both of the second periodic reports, had been the subject of concluding observations by the Committee.[60] As against that, 22 states had failed to submit a required initial report as of early 2011,[61] while a further four states had failed to submit second periodic reports that were due in 2009 or 2010.[62]

The rest of this section will offer an analysis of the Committee's interpretation of the Convention in its concluding observations. It will also discuss the Committee's only General Comment to date, on migrant domestic workers (General Comment No. 1, 2010).[63] Rather than an exhaustive summary, what will be provided is a thematic account of the major issues that

58 Article 77(2) makes it a precondition to the Committee's considering an individual complaint that 'the same matter has not been, and is not being examined under another procedure of international investigation or settlement'. This replicates the language of Article 5(2) of the First Optional Protocol to the ICCPR, which gives the Human Rights Committee jurisdiction over individual complaints.

59 The states that had submitted initial reports by the end of 2010 were: Albania, Algeria, Argentina, Azerbaijan, Bolivia, Bosnia and Herzegovina, Chile, Colombia, Guatemala, Ecuador, El Salvador, Egypt, Mali, Mexico, Paraguay, the Philippines, Senegal, Sri Lanka, Syria and Tajikistan.

60 At the time of writing, the reports by Argentina, Chile, Guatemala, Paraguay and Tajikistan had not been the subject of concluding observations.

61 Note that Guyana and St Vincent and the Grenadines each ratified the Convention during 2010, and were therefore obliged to submit an initial report only in 2011.

62 These were Bolivia, Egypt, El Salvador and Mali.

63 The only similar analysis of which the author is aware is the discussion of the Committee's first three sets of concluding observations in Edelenbos, 'Committee on Migrant Workers'.

have emerged, grouped under the following headings: the position of emigrants, the rights of immigrants, and immigration policy and control.[64]

The Position of Emigrants

As all of the states whose reports have been considered to date are countries of origin of migrants, the Committee's observations have frequently addressed their relationship with emigrant nationals.[65] It has focused on three topics in particular: the right to leave, the representation of nationals abroad, and political rights.

The right to leave

Article 8 of the Convention provides for the right of migrant workers 'to leave any State, including their State of origin'. The Committee relied upon Article 8 to question Ecuador's (2007) requirement that its nationals obtain an exit permit in order to leave the territory.[66] In addition, while not referred to explicitly, Article 8 was presumably the basis for the Committee's recommendation to Egypt (2007) that women should be able to obtain passports without the approval of a husband or male relative.[67]

The Committee has also taken the view that states ought not to criminalize irregular exit with the aim of deterring migrant smuggling. In its concluding observations on Algeria (2010), the Committee recommended reconsideration of a legislative proposal to criminalize departure other than through a border post, for which the proposed maximum penalty was a period of imprisonment of six months.[68] That recommendation was adopted with reference, not to Article 8, but to Part VI of the Convention, which concerns 'orderly' migration. The Committee also suggested that penalties were contrary to the Migrant Smuggling Protocol of 2000 (to which Algeria is a party), presumably because its Article 5 prohibits 'criminal prosecution' of migrants 'for the fact of having been the object of' smuggling.[69]

Representation of nationals abroad

The Committee has also supported the conclusion of bilateral arrangements by states of origin with states of employment. In the case of Sri Lanka (2009), it 'note[d] with interest the memoranda of understanding and bilateral agreements with major labour receiving

[64] The concluding observations will be cited below by giving the state name and the year of the document in which the observations were published.

[65] For a similar observation, see Edelenbos, 'Committee on Migrant Workers', 120–21.

[66] Ecuador, 5 December 2007, para. 22. In 2010, Ecuador reported that the exit permit requirement had been ruled unconstitutional, and that it was no longer in force: Ecuador: Second Periodic Report, 26 January 2010, para. 122.

[67] Egypt, 25 May 2007, paras 26–7.

[68] Algeria, 19 May 2010, paras 40 and 41. Details of the legislation are in 'Algeria: Comments by the State Party', 3 May 2010.

[69] In a written response, Algeria argued that its proposed legislation aimed to uphold human dignity and the right to life, and to prevent human trafficking: 'Algeria: Comments by the State Party', 3 May 2010.

countries'.[70] Similarly, the Committee welcomed Ecuador's (2010) signature of ten 'alliances and agreements' with other countries for the protection of its nationals abroad.[71] By contrast, the Committee called upon Egypt (2007) to negotiate with Gulf states for the abolition of legal arrangements there that gave sponsors personal control over its nationals.[72] Similar recommendations concerning the protection of migrant workers in Gulf states were made to Syria (2008) and to the Philippines (2009).[73] It may be added that the Committee has mainly based these observations on Part VI of the Convention, which aims at 'orderly' international migration.[74]

The Committee has also emphasized the importance of effective consular support for contracting states' nationals. One aspect of such support is the provision of assistance to migrant workers who have grievances arising out of their employment. The Committee recommended that the Philippines (2009) 'ensure that its embassy and consulate staff abroad are knowledgeable about the laws and procedures of the countries of employment of Filipino foreign workers'.[75] Similarly, it encouraged Sri Lanka (2009) to ensure that legal assistance was available to migrant workers in *all* its embassies and consulates, and that its labour welfare officers were knowledgeable about the labour laws and procedures of the country of deployment.[76] A second aspect of consular assistance that the Committee has highlighted is the timely provision of travel documents to their nationals who face expulsion from another country. Egypt (2007) and Bolivia (2008) have each been criticized for systematic failures in this regard.[77] These various observations have been made either under Part III of the Convention, or – in the sole case of Egypt – under Part VI. This implies that they were based on Article 23 and Article 65 of the Convention, respectively (see section 1, above).

Political rights

The Committee has also sought to promote compliance with the right of emigrant workers in a regular position to vote in elections in their state of origin (Article 41 of the Convention). Failures to respect this right in the state's electoral rules were identified in two cases: the Philippines (2009), which allowed the right to vote only to those who affirmed their intention to return within three years, and Albania (2010), which allowed voting to take place solely on its territory.[78] In seven other cases, the Committee has called for the contracting state to take steps to facilitate the practical exercise of the right to vote by its nationals abroad.[79]

70 Sri Lanka, 19 October 2009, paras 39–40.

71 Ecuador, 15 December 2010, para 5.

72 Egypt, 25 May 2007, paras 48–9.

73 Syria, 2 May 2008, para. 38; The Philippines, 22 May 2009, para. 32.

74 The observations on Sri Lanka, Egypt and Syria were made under Part VI. The observation concerning Ecuador was listed under 'positive aspects', without further elaboration. The observation on the Philippines was based on Part III.

75 The Philippines, 22 May 2009, para. 30.

76 Sri Lanka, 19 October 2009, para. 30.

77 Egypt, 25 May 2007, paras 46 and 47; Bolivia, 29 April 2008, para. 28.

78 The Philippines, 22 May 2009, paras 35–6; Albania, 26 November 2010, paras 31–2.

79 Mali, 31 May 2006, para. 7; Egypt, 25 May 2007, para. 43; Bolivia, 29 April 2008, para. 34; El Salvador, 4 February 2009, para. 35; Colombia, 22 May 2009, para. 34; Bosnia and Herzegovina, 3 June 2009, para. 30; Sri Lanka, 19 October 2009, para. 34.

The Rights of Immigrants

Given the focus of the Convention on the treatment of migrant workers and their family members, it is not surprising that the rights of immigrants have been central to the work of the Committee to date. The discussion here considers the Committee's comments in four areas: personal status, access to labour law, trade union rights, and social provision for irregular migrants.

Personal status

We saw above that Article 29 of the Convention confers 'the right to a name, to registration of birth and to a nationality' upon children. Relying upon that Article, the Committee has addressed recommendations to three states concerning the registration of births. It expressed its regret that children born in Egypt (2007) to migrant workers, whether in a regular or an irregular situation, were unable to obtain birth certificates.[80] It expressed concern at the number of children of migrants in Ecuador (2007) whose births were not registered 'either because their parents fail to register them for fear of being deported or because their registration is refused on the ground of the irregular status of one or both parents.'[81] Similarly, it expressed concern at refusals by many officials in Mexico (2011) to register the births of the children of irregular migrants, notwithstanding that they were Mexican citizens by birth.[82]

In a further case, the Committee addressed the right to a nationality. Having noted that only children with a parent domiciled in Colombia (2009) were eligible for Colombian nationality, it expressed concern that some children might remain stateless as a result. It therefore recommended that the state ensure the right of all children to a nationality, and that it proceed with its proposed accession to the 1961 United Nations Convention on the Reduction of Statelessness.[83]

Access to labour law

The Committee has interpreted the Convention to require that migrants have access to the protection of labour law both in theory and in practice. The starting point is that Article 25(1) of the Convention provides that 'migrant workers shall enjoy treatment not less favourable than that which applies to nationals of the State of employment' in respect of terms and conditions of employment. Article 25(2) makers clear that this guarantee of equal treatment applies within individual employment relationships, by providing that 'it shall not be lawful to derogate in private contracts of employment from the principle of equality of treatment'.

---

[80] Egypt, 25 May 2007, para. 34.

[81] Ecuador, 5 December 2007, para. 35.

[82] Mexico, 8 April 2011, para. 39.

[83] Colombia, 22 May 2009, paras 29–30. The 1961 Convention had not been ratified as of May 2011. Note that ratification would not imply an unlimited right to the nationality of the state of birth for those who are otherwise stateless. In particular, where a child born on the territory was born to foreign parents, Article 1 of the 1961 Convention permits parties to set a minimum age, up to 18, for an application, and to make the grant of nationality conditional upon the person's habitual resided in the territory for up to 10 years.

The Committee relied specifically upon Article 25 in criticism of Egypt (2007) for an apparent requirement of reciprocity before its Labour Code applied to legally employed foreign workers.[84] The Committee also referred to it in General Comment No. 1 (2010), when stating that migrant domestic workers 'should enjoy treatment not less favourable than that which applies to nationals of the State of employment'.[85]

The Committee's has also called for the inclusion of migrant domestic workers within labour law in its comments on Egypt (2007) and in General Comment No. 1 (2010).[86] In the case of Egypt, its observations were made under Part III of the Convention, without further explanation. In General Comment No. 1, it simply referred in general to 'equal protection under the law' as a conceptual basis for the inclusion of domestic workers within labour law, even though that principle does not appear in the text of the Convention. The Committee presumably did not refer to Article 25 in these observations because that Article requires the *equal treatment* of migrants, which may be thought to provide an insufficient basis to challenge the exclusion of an entire category of worker from some or all labour laws.

The Committee has also addressed the question of limited access to labour law protections by irregular workers. The background is that Article 25(3) of the Convention contains two propositions of relevance to their position – that irregularity may not be a ground for depriving migrant workers of equal treatment, and that 'employers shall not be relieved of any legal or contractual obligations' because of a worker's 'irregularity of stay or employment'. To date, the Committee has, however, relied upon this Article only by implication, preferring instead to base its remarks on the position of irregular workers under Article 83 of the Convention, which sets out a right to an effective remedy where Convention rights or freedoms are violated. In the case of Mexico (2006), the Committee expressed its concern at a legislative provision that allowed legal proceedings to be instituted by foreign nationals only if they were legally resident.[87] Lack of access by irregular migrant workers to an effective remedy was also the subject of Committee recommendations to Syria (2008), in relation to its labour commissions, and Algeria (2010), in relation to the courts in general.[88]

Finally, the Committee has sought to promote the practical effectiveness of labour law in relation to particularly vulnerable groups of workers. It recommended that the application of labour law standards be made effective for migrant domestic workers in Mexico (2006), Ecuador (2007 and 2010), El Salvador (2009), and in General Comment No. 1(2010), and for migrant workers in agriculture in Mexico (2006) and El Salvador (2009).[89] Among these cases,

[84] Egypt, 25 May 2007, paras 30–31. The Government's evidence was that the principle of reciprocity applied only to exemption from the requirement to obtain a work permit: see 'Egypt: Written Replies', 6 February 2007, 16–17.

[85] General Comment No. 1 on Migrant Domestic Workers (23 February 2011), UN Doc. CMW/C/GC/1, para. 38.

[86] Egypt, 25 May 2007, paras 38–9; General Comment No. 1, para. 38.

[87] Mexico, 20 December 2006, paras 25–6. In November 2008, Mexico's Supreme Court ruled that foreign workers were entitled to the protection of labour law, irrespective of their migration status, and, in 2010, the offending legislative provision was removed, so as to permit all legal claims by irregular migrants. See 'Mexico: Second Periodic Report', 14 January 2010, para. 29, and Mexico, 8 April 2011, para. 7(e).

[88] Syria, 2 May 2008, paras 25–6; Algeria, 19 May 2010, paras 16–17.

[89] Mexico, 20 December 2006, paras 33–4 and 37–8; El Salvador, 4 February 2009, paras 29 and 30; Ecuador, 5 December 2007, para. 38; Ecuador, 15 December 2010, para. 28; General

the Committee cited Article 25 only in relation to El Salvador (2009). Elsewhere, it has made these comments under general headings – Part IV of the Convention in the case of agricultural workers in Mexico (2006), 'conditions of work' in General Comment No. 1 (2010), and Part III of the Convention in the other cases.

Trade union rights

We saw in section 1 that trade union rights are provided for in two places in the Convention: Article 26 for all migrant workers, and Article 40 for migrant workers in a regular situation. To date, the Committee has relied upon Article 26 mainly in relation to irregular migrant workers. In the case of Albania (2010), it referred to Article 26 in criticizing a legal provision specifically excluding irregular migrant workers from joining trade unions.[90] In the case of Algeria (2010), it expressed its concern more generally that irregular workers did not 'effectively enjoy' a range of Convention rights, including the right to join trade unions in Article 26.[91] An exception – where Article 26 was recognized to apply to all workers – was the statement in General Comment No. 1 (2010) that 'the laws of States parties, particularly countries of employment of migrant domestic workers, should recognize the right of the latter to form and join organizations, regardless of migration status (article 26).'[92]

The Committee has by contrast shown itself more willing to identify a breach of Article 40. In some cases, this has been because of discrimination against foreign nationals in the law relating to trade unions. The Committee concluded that that the reservation of the constitutional right to form trade unions to citizens in Sri Lanka (2009) was a breach both of Article 40 and of the non-discrimination guarantee in Article 7.[93] It concluded that the Philippines (2009) was in breach of Article 40 in making the trade union rights of migrant workers subject to a condition of reciprocal treatment of its nationals.[94] In the case of Algeria (2010), the Committee identified a breach of Article 40 in the exclusion of migrant workers from the right to form trade unions.[95] On that occasion, it also expressed its concern at the non-exercise by lawful migrant workers of the right to engage in trade union activities under Part IV of the Convention, though without linking its observation to a specific Article.[96]

In four other cases, the Committee has criticized the exclusion of foreign nationals from official positions within trade unions. Mexico (2006, 2011), Ecuador (2007, 2010) and El Salvador (2009) all had blanket rules excluding foreign nationals from the leadership of trade unions. In each case, the Committee identified a breach of what it has termed 'the right to form, and to form part of the leadership of ... trade unions', guaranteed by Article 40.[97] In addition, the Committee recommended that Senegal (2010) remove its precondition to migrant

Comment No. 1, para. 41.

[90] Albania, 26 November 2010, paras 29–30.

[91] Algeria, 19 May 2010, para. 19.

[92] General Comment No. 1, para. 46.

[93] Sri Lanka, 19 October 2009, paras 25–6 and 31–2.

[94] The Philippines, 22 May 2009, paras 33–4.

[95] Algeria, 19 May 2010, paras 28–9.

[96] Ibid.

[97] See Mexico, 20 December 2006, para. 36. Similar observations are in Mexico, 8 April 2011, para. 46; Ecuador, 5 December 2007, para. 42; Ecuador, 15 December 2010, para. 42; and,

workers serving as trade union officials that there be a reciprocal agreement with the country of nationality.[98] This recommendation was made under Part IV of the Convention, and by implication was again based on Article 40.

It is significant that, in its comments on trade union rights to date, the Committee has preferred to rely upon Article 40, or Part IV more generally, even though the subject matter of its comments potentially falls within Article 26. For example, the non-participation of lawful migrant workers in trade union activities in Algeria (2010) touched on a matter expressly mentioned in Article 26 alone. Similarly, discrimination against foreign nationals in Sri Lanka, Algeria and the Philippines presumably entailed a denial not just of the right to form trade unions, but also of their Article 26 rights. Equally, the possibility for foreign nationals to be officials or leaders of a trade union could have been classed, not as an aspect of trade union formation, but as 'participation' in trade union activities. Much as with the Convention itself, therefore, the Committee has generally approached trade union rights in a manner that has avoided the fullest protection for irregular migrant workers.

Social provision for irregular migrants

Three of the provisions in Part III of the Convention referred to in section 1 are of particular relevance to state social provision for irregular migrants. Article 27 provides for the equal treatment of all migrant workers and their family members in the field of social security. Article 28 provides for access to urgent medical care, and expressly covers those whose residence or employment is irregular. Article 30 sets out the right of a child of a migrant worker to equality of access to education, and expressly precludes the irregularity of a parent's residence or employment, or of the child's own residence, from being a reason for denying a child access to schooling.

The Committee has invoked these Articles in relation to irregular migrant workers on four occasions. It called for compliance by Egypt (2007) with Article 30, because of its concern that 'the children of undocumented migrant workers do not have any access to the schooling system, whether public or private.'[99] It called for Ecuador (2007) to comply with Article 28, because of evidence that 'in practice migrant workers in an irregular situation and members of their families face difficulties in accessing the public health system.'[100] It called for Azerbaijan (2009) to comply with Articles 28 and 30, because of reports that irregular migrants and their family members did not have access to medical care in practice, and that the children of irregular migrants had difficulty obtaining access to education.[101] Finally, in the case of Algeria (2010), it listed both Article 27 on social security and Article 28 on medical care among the rights that irregular migrant workers did not 'effectively enjoy'.[102]

El Salvador, 4 February 2009, para. 32. In the case of El Salvador, the right to form part of the leadership was limited to its nationals by birth.

98 Senegal, 10 December 2010, para. 16.

99 Egypt, 25 May 2007, paras 36–7. The Committee also expressed its concern at the lack of access to public schools by the children of legal migrant workers.

100 Ecuador, 5 December 2007, paras 39–40.

101 Azerbaijan, 19 May 2009, paras 30–31.

102 Algeria, 19 May 2010, para. 19.

Immigration Policy and Control

We saw in section 1 that the Convention has been criticized for leaving too much scope for states' immigration policy and control. In practice, however, the Committee has taken a more robust view, and has identified ways in which immigration policies and control measures conflict with states' obligations under the Convention. Three issues are addressed here: the treatment of irregular migrants within immigration control systems, regularization, and the content of legal migration policy.

Treatment of irregular migrants within immigration control

An important subject addressed by the Committee concerning irregular migrants is the detention of those presumed to have breached immigration law. As we saw above, Article 17 of the Convention requires that those suspected of a breach of immigration laws should if possible be detained separately from those within the criminal justice system. The Committee has to date commented on three states' failures to respect the general principle: Mexico (2006), Ecuador (2007) and Senegal (2010).[103] In the case of Mexico, this recommendation was included under Part III without reference to a particular Article, while, in the other cases, Article 17 was referred to expressly.[104]

In addition, the Committee has twice criticized states for providing criminal sanctions for those who breach immigration law. The Convention does not expressly prohibit criminal penalties, and the Committee has not referred to any particular provision in support of these comments. One possible argument is that the sanction of *imprisonment* is prohibited by the requirement in Article 17 (above) to keep those who breach immigration law separate from those detained within the criminal justice system. That may explain the Committee's recommendation to Mexico (2006) – under the heading of 'General measures of implementation' – that it 'annul the classification of illegal entry into the country as an offence punishable by deprivation of liberty.'[105] Alternatively, *criminalization as such* might be thought incompatible with the effective exercise by irregular migrants of their rights under the Convention. That was the approach taken by the Committee when it called upon Algeria (2009) to ensure that migrant workers and their families were 'not deprived of any of the rights under the Convention which apply to all migrant workers, including those in an irregular situation', and to 'bring its legislation – which criminalizes irregular migration – into conformity with the Convention.'[106]

---

[103] Mexico, 20 December 2006, para. 28; Ecuador, 5 December 2007, para. 24; Senegal, 10 December 2010, para. 15.

[104] The recommendation concerning Ecuador referred to Article 17(3). Confusingly, however, that in relation to Senegal referred to Article 17(2). That may have been an error, as that provision is concerned with the rights of 'accused' persons, rather than those suspected of a breach of immigration law.

[105] Mexico, 20 December 2006, para. 15. In line with that recommendation, in its second report, Mexico informed the Committee that its legislation had been amended, so that breaches of immigration law had become the subject of fines alone, and could no longer give rise to a prison sentence: 'Mexico: Second Periodic Report', 14 January 2010, paras 136–7.

[106] Algeria, 19 May 2010, paras 18 and 21.

Regularization

The Committee has consistently taken the view that a procedure for regularization ought to be available as a solution to irregular status, at least where there are substantial numbers of irregular workers present on a state's territory. It has generally favoured Article 69 (discussed in section 1, above) as the basis for its comments on this subject. For example, it expressed its concern at reports that a high percentage of migrant workers in Azerbaijan (2009) were in an irregular position, and recommended 'appropriate measures, in accordance with the Convention, in particular with Article 69, to ensure that this situation does not persist, including the possibility of regularizing the situation of these migrant workers.'[107] Article 69 was also cited as the basis for recommending access to regularization for domestic workers in the General Comment on Migrant Domestic Workers (2010).[108] In addition, in the case of Senegal (2010) the Committee referred to both Articles 68 and 69, before recommending 'proactive and effective measures to ensure that migrant workers and members of their families do not remain in an irregular situation', and that any regularization mechanism should be 'accessible and expeditious'.[109] That joint reference to Articles 68 and 69 is especially significant, as it is in line with the view (discussed above) that these Articles may oblige states to take pre-emptive action to prevent irregular migration and employment.

The Committee has not relied upon Article 69 alone, however. In the cases of Mexico (2006) and Ecuador (2007, 2010), it recommended regularization as a means of social and labour market protection for female migrant domestic workers under Part III of the Convention.[110] Part III was also the heading for a recommendation to Ecuador (2010) to 'redouble its efforts to establish and implement a comprehensive migration regularization policy.'[111] Finally, in the case of Bolivia (2008), the Committee inexplicably addressed regularization under Part IV of the Convention, when recommending that an existing regularization procedure be strengthened, through reductions in fees and delays, and by allowing applicants to remain while a decision was taken.[112]

Content of legal migration policy

Despite the terms of Article 79, which allows contracting states to set admission criteria (see section 1), the Committee has made recommendations to states on several occasions concerning their legal migration policy. One key proposition it has advanced is that a state ought to design its legal migration policy so as to minimize the risks of irregular migration and employment. Azerbaijan (2009) issued work permits for up to one year at a time, which could be renewed up to four times, but then expected foreign workers to leave its territory for at least one year before reapplying. In response, the Committee observed that the 'burdensome and complex' nature of these procedures risked encouraging irregular migration, and recommended that

107 Azerbaijan, 19 May 2009, paras 44–5.

108 General Comment No. 1, para. 52.

109 Senegal, 10 December 2010, para. 23.

110 Mexico, 20 December 2006, para. 34; Ecuador, 5 December 2007, para. 38; Ecuador, 15 December 2010, para. 28.

111 Ecuador, 15 December 2010, paras 6, 33 and 34.

112 Bolivia, 29 April 2008, para. 32.

the state 'consider reviewing the existing restrictions on the renewal of work permits'.[113] On that occasion, its observations were based solely on the duty to implement the Convention (Articles 73 and 84), without reference to any substantive obligation. The Committee was more specific in General Comment No. 1 (2010) on migrant domestic workers, when it based a similar recommendation on Article 68 of the Convention:

> With a view to preventing irregular migration as well as smuggling and human trafficking, States parties should ensure that migrant domestic workers have access to regular channels for migration based on actual demand (Article 68).[114]

Here too, the Committee treated Article 68 as implying a duty to design policy pre-emptively, so as to minimize irregular employment.

A second reason for the Committee's interest in legal migration policy is discrimination against a particular nationality. Relying upon the general principle of non-discrimination in Article 7 of the Convention, the Committee expressed its concern at Ecuador's (2007 and 2010) requirement that Colombian nationals produce an official certificate to show that they do not have a criminal record.[115] In its view, this exclusive requirement risked contributing to the 'stigmatization and stereotyping' of Colombian nationals.[116] Discrimination against particular nationalities within immigration policy appears therefore to be inherently suspect under Article 7.

Thirdly, the Committee has commented on provision for family reunification. The background is the uncertain obligation upon states in Article 44(2) (referred to in section 1) to 'take measures that they deem appropriate ... to facilitate' the reunification of migrant workers with spouses, persons in 'a relationship that, according to applicable law, produces effects equivalent to marriage', and minor dependent unmarried children. Given the lack of specificity within this provision, it is significant that the Committee expressed its concern that Algeria's (2010) regulations on family reunification for migrant workers applied to spouses alone, and called upon it to bring its policy into line with Article 44.[117] The implication appears to be that a state must make *some* provision for the family members referred to in that Article.

Conclusion

This chapter has offered a broadly optimistic analysis of the Migrant Workers Convention as a source of standards for international migration. It started by arguing that criticisms of the Convention have for the most part been misplaced. The claim that the Convention unnecessarily duplicates provisions of other international human rights treaties underestimates the ways in

[113] Azerbaijan, 19 May 2009, paras 14–15.

[114] General Comment No. 1, para. 51.

[115] Ecuador, 5 December 2007, paras 19–20, and 15 December 2010, paras 25–6.

[116] Ecuador maintained its policy, arguing that it was necessary for reasons of public safety and public order: see 'Ecuador: Written Replies', 20 September 2010, para. 86.

[117] Algeria, 19 May 2010, paras 32–3. The Committee also referred to Article 4, which sets out a definition of family member for the purpose of the Convention as a whole.

which the Convention is a coherent instrument for the protection of migrants as a category. Similarly, the claim that the Convention gives insufficient protection to irregular migrants is at odds with the extensive protection it confers on that group, and reflects an over-interpretation of its provisions concerning immigration policy and control.

The chapter then showed how the potential of the Convention has been revealed in practice. The Convention is directly relevant to the circumstances of the states that have ratified it, as they all have experience as countries of origin of emigrants, while many have experience of immigration as transit and/or as destination locations. That argument was supported by a review of the work of the Committee on Migrant Workers to date.[118] In the first place, the Committee has served as a mechanism for calling attention to clear failures of implementation by the states that have ratified – e.g., in relation to representation of emigrant nationals, the denial of trade union rights to foreign nationals, or the exclusion of irregular migrants from social protection. Beyond that, the Committee has shown a certain creativity in interpreting the Convention in the face of current issues in the field of international migration. One example is its advancement of the proposition that the Convention requires that migrant domestic workers should be protected by labour law. Other examples have concerned policy relating to irregular migration, where the Committee has rejected criminal penalties for breaches of immigration law and for irregular exit, promoted regularization, and proposed that the duty to prevent irregular migration and employment may require adjustments to legal migration policy.

The overall conclusion to be drawn is that the Convention has a clear role in relation to the states that have ratified it, especially where those states engage with the Committee on Migrant Workers. Going forward, two initiatives appear desirable, in order to clarify the Convention's potential value. Firstly, research into the Convention ought to focus on the states that have ratified it, rather than – as hitherto – upon those that have not. Secondly, the Committee's approach to the protection of migrants would be more authoritative if it were more clearly and consistently linked to particular provisions of the Convention. Each of these steps may be thought critical in enhancing support for the Convention as a source of norms in the contemporary migration context.

References

Battistella, Graziano, 'Migration and Human Rights: The Uneasy but Essential Relationship' in Paul de Guchteneire, Antoine Pécoud and Ryszard Cholewinski (eds), *Migration and Human Rights: The United Nations Convention on Migrant Workers' Rights* (Cambridge University Press, Cambridge, 2009) 47–69.

Böhning, Roger, 'The ILO and the New UN Convention on Migrant Workers: The Past and Future' (1991) 25 *International Migration Review* 698–709.

[118] Slinckx has offered a similar assessment of the Committee's potential – 'the CMW ... offers an expert understanding of the specificities of the situation of migrants': Slinckx, 'Migrants' Rights in UN Human Rights Conventions', 149.

Böhning, Roger, 'The Protection of Migrant Workers and International Labour Standards' (1988) 26 *International Migration* 133–46.

Bosniak, Linda, 'Human Rights, State Sovereignty, and the Protection of Undocumented Migrants under the International Convention for the Protection of the Rights of All Migrant Workers and Members of Their Families' (1991) 25 *International Migration Review* 737–70.

Chetail, Vincent, 'Review of *Migration and Human Rights: The United Nations Convention on Migrant Workers*' (2010) 22 *International Journal of Refugee Law* 677–82.

Chetail, Vincent and Gilles Giacca, 'Who Cares? The Right to Health of Migrants' in Andrew Clapham and Mary Robinson (eds), *Realising the Right to Health* (Rueffer, Zurich, 2009) 224–34.

Cholewinski, Ryszard, *Migrant Workers in International Human Rights Law: Their Protection in Countries of Employment* (Oxford University Press, Oxford, 1997).

Colyer, Michael and Hein de Haas, 'Developing Dynamic Categorisations of Transit Migration' (2011) 17 *Population, Space and Place* 468–81.

De Guchteneire, Paul and Antoine Pécoud, 'Introduction: The UN Convention on Migrant Workers' Rights' in Paul de Guchteneire, Antoine Pécoud and Ryszard Cholewinski (eds), *Migration and Human Rights: The United Nations Convention on Migrant Workers' Rights* (Cambridge University Press, Cambridge, 2009) 1–44.

Díaz, Gabriela and Gretchen Kuhner, 'Mexico's Role in Promoting and Implementing the ICRMW' in Paul de Guchteneire, Antoine Pécoud and Ryszard Cholewinski (eds), *Migration and Human Rights: The United Nations Convention on Migrant Workers' Rights* (Cambridge University Press, Cambridge, 2009) 219–46.

Edelenbos, Carla, 'Committee on Migrant Workers and Implementation of the ICRMW' in Paul de Guchteneire, Antoine Pécoud and Ryszard Cholewinski (eds), *Migration and Human Rights: The United Nations Convention on Migrant Workers' Rights* (Cambridge University Press, Cambridge, 2009) 100–121.

Escobar Latapí, Agustín, *The Future of Migration Policies in the Americas* (IOM, Geneva, 2010).

Hune, Shirley and Jan Niessen, 'Ratifying the UN Migrant Workers Convention: Current Difficulties and Prospects' (1994) 12 *Netherlands Quarterly of Human Rights* 130–41.

Lönnroth, Juhani, 'The International Convention on the Rights of All Migrant Workers and Members of Their Families in the Context of International Migration Policies: An Analysis of Ten Years of Negotiation' (1991) 25 *International Migration Review* 710–36.

Nafziger, James and Barry Bartel, 'The Migration Workers Convention: Its Place in Human Rights Law' (1991) 25 *International Migration Review* 771–99.

Slinckx, Isabelle, 'Migrants' Rights in UN Human Rights Conventions' in Paul de Guchteneire, Antoine Pécoud and Ryszard Cholewinski (eds), *Migration and Human Rights: The United Nations Convention on Migrant Workers' Rights* (Cambridge University Press, Cambridge, 2009) 122–49.

Part V
Health and Disability

[15]

IMMIGRATION STATUS AND BASIC SOCIAL HUMAN RIGHTS: A COMPARATIVE STUDY OF IRREGULAR MIGRANTS' RIGHT TO HEALTH CARE IN FRANCE, THE UK AND CANADA

Sylvie Da Lomba*

Abstract

The article examines the constraints that irregular migrants' immigration status exerts on the realisation of their basic social human rights. To this end, the article focuses on the right to health care and undertakes a comparative study of irregular migrants' access to health care in France, the United Kingdom and Canada. The study shows that States perceive the conferment of social rights on irregular migrants as an erosion of the government's immigration power notwithstanding their characterisation as human rights. The resource-intensive nature of the right to health care further heightens States' reluctance to extend this right to irregular migrants. Yet compliance with international human rights law and respect for human dignity require that States reinstate personhood as a source of rights and therefore reassess the relevance of their immigration power.

1. INTRODUCTION

> 'The protection of strangers should constitute an important test for human rights since they do not claim protection as members of a family, clan, or nation, but as members of humanity.'[1]

International human rights law undertook a seminal conceptual reorientation in the post-World War II period by disentangling rights from citizenship and attaching rights to the person.[2] This reorientation, however, has not made one's legal status in

* Sylvie Da Lomba is a lecturer at the Law School of the University of Strathclyde, Glasgow, Scotland, the United Kingdom. All internet sites were last accessed on 15 January 2010.

1 Guiraudon, V., 'European courts and foreigners' rights: a comparative study of norms diffusion', *The International Migration Review*, Vol. 34, No. 4, 2000, pp. 1088–1125, at p. 1092.

2 Fletcher, G.P., 'Guantanamo disentangled? The US Supreme Court steps in: citizenship and personhood in the jurisprudence of war: Hamdi, Padilla and the detainees in Guantanamo Bay',

the nation-State redundant and migrants' immigration status remains the primary determinant of their rights in the host State. Recognising personhood as a source of rights, however, is critical to irregular migrants as their immigration status renders them ineligible for the rights host States confer on regular migrants.[3]

This article examines the respective significance of personhood and immigration status as sources of rights with a view to determining whether international human rights law may contribute to offsetting legal status divides in the nation-State. To this end, the article focuses on the question of basic social rights for irregular migrants who are settled in host States. Irregular migrants are foreign nationals who do not comply with immigration law requirements. Irregular migration covers a range of situations which include: clandestine arrival in the host State, stay beyond the permitted period of residence, or working without a permit or in a manner inconsistent with one's immigration status.[4] The term irregular migrant also covers people who enter on false papers, rejected asylum seekers who have exhausted their appeal rights and can no longer remain in the host State, and regularised migrants who fall back into an irregular situation.[5] The treatment of irregular migrants in the social sphere puts international human rights law and personhood as a source of rights to the test. It also raises the question of the relevance of immigration status to the realisation of basic social human rights. In order to examine these issues, this article looks at irregular migrants' access to health care in France, the United Kingdom (UK) and Canada.

Health care has been characterised as a basic necessity[6] and as such is recognised in international human rights law as a social right inherent in human dignity.[7] A comparative study of irregular migrants' access to health care in selected host States provides a cross-national basis for measuring the weight apportioned to immigration status and personhood as sources of rights. In particular, it provides a

Journal of International Criminal Justice, Vol. 2, No. 4, 2004, pp. 953–966, at p. 954.

3 For an analysis of the concept of personhood in relation to human rights, see, for instance, Griffin, J., *On Human Rights*, Oxford University Press, Oxford, 2008, pp. 33–37, 57–58 and 66–80.

4 Guild, E., 'Who is an irregular migrant?', in: Bogusz, B., Cholewinski, R., Cygan, A. and Szyszczak, E. (eds), *Irregular Migration and Human Rights: Theoretical, European and International Perspectives*, Martinus Nijhoff Publishers, Leiden/Boston, 2004, pp. 3–28, at p. 3.

5 Cholewinski, R., 'Identifying and clarifying concepts on "irregular migration"', 10th Regional Conference on Migration Current Perspectives and Strategies in Addressing 'Irregular' Migration, Singapore, 6–10 November 2006, available at: www.mfasia.org/mfaResources/RCholewinski-Concepts.pdf.

6 Arras, J.D., 'Retreat from the right to health care: the President's Commission and access to health care', *Cardozo Law Review*, Vol. 6, 1984–1985, pp. 321–345, at p. 323.

7 The right to health care is a core component of the right to health together with the underlying preconditions for health such as an adequate supply of food and nutrition and access to potable water and adequate sanitation; Committee on Economic, Social and Cultural Rights, General Comment No. 14 (2000), *The Right to the highest attainable standard of health*, UN Doc. E/C.12/2000/4, 11 August 2000, paras 4 and 11. For a comprehensive analysis of the content of the right to health, see Toebes, B.C.A., *The Right to Health as a Human Right in International Law*, Intersentia, Antwerpen, 1999, pp. 243–289.

basis for examining the extent to which the realisation of irregular migrants' basic social rights as recognised in international human rights law may be constrained by their immigration status in the host State. This comparative study also allows us to ascertain whether State-specific factors significantly mediate host States' responses to the question of basic social rights for irregular migrants or whether a common position may be identified.

The three jurisdictions under consideration, namely France, the UK and Canada, possess common characteristics that make a comparison of their respective approaches to irregular migrants' access to health care and their overall stance on the question of basic social rights for this population feasible. First, these are States which have comparable socio-economic structures and are amongst the wealthiest in the world.[8] Secondly, they are also amongst the States with the largest numbers of migrants.[9] Thirdly, France, the UK and Canada have all professed their commitment to international human rights law and its founding values and principles. Consequently, all three jurisdictions have been instrumental in relocating basic rights outside the nation-State. Finally, France, the UK and Canada have all publicly funded health care systems, although there are significant differences in the way their national systems operate. It is acknowledged that other States such as Spain or Germany share the same characteristics, but space constraints did not allow for greater inclusiveness. The choice of jurisdictions, however, provides a representative sample of host Western States and has the advantage of introducing a transatlantic element to the comparison that makes the study relevant beyond Europe. The focus on France, the UK and Canada is further justified by the fact that, in spite of their strong commonalities, their legal responses to irregular migrants' health care needs differ significantly.

Before engaging in a comparative study of irregular migrants' access to health care and examining the extent to which irregular migrants' immigration status may constrain the realisation of their basic social rights, and in particular the realisation of

8 All three States are members of the G8.

9 Estimated numbers of migrants for 2010 in France, the UK and Canada are respectively 6.7, 6.5 and 7.2 millions (International Organization for Migration, www.iom.int/jahia/Jahia/about-migration/facts-and-figures/regional-and-country-figures/cache/offonce). Data on irregular migrant numbers, however, is both scant and unreliable. In 2006, it was estimated that there were between 200,000 and 500,000 undocumented workers in Canada (39th Parliament, 1st Session, Standing Committee on Citizenship and Immigration, Evidence, 19 October 2006, 0950). The central estimate of the number of irregular residents in the UK at the end of 2007 was 618,000, with a range of 417,000 to 863,000; Gordon, I., Scanlon, K., Travers, T. and Whitehead, C., *Economic Impact on the London and UK Economy of an Earned Regularisation of Irregular Migrants to the UK*, LSE, London, April 2009, p. 6, available at: www.london.gov.uk/mayor/economic_unit/docs/irregular-migrants-report.pdf. The central estimate includes children born in the UK to irregular migrant workers. They add between 12 and 20 percent to the estimate (*idem*). In France, estimates vary between 200,000 and 400,000 for 2007; Van Eeckout, L., 'Régularisation: le travail, un espoir pour les sans-papiers' [Regularisation: work, some hope for undocumented migrants], *Le Monde*, 8 January 2008, www.lemonde.fr/a-la-une/article/2008/01/08/regularisation-le-travail-un-espoir-pour-les-sans-papiers_996908_3208.html.

their right to health care, we need to consider three preliminary issues. The first issue is concerned with the relevance of immigration status to migrants' treatment in the social sphere. To this end, section 2 looks at the citizen/migrant divide. The latter remains resilient in the political domain, but has subsided in the social sphere with social membership, and more specifically social rights originally predicated on citizenship, becoming accessible to migrants. Access to social membership, however, is contingent on migrants' immigration status in the host State. Consequently, membership in the national community remains outside the reach of irregular migrants. This second issue is considered in section 3. This section discusses the rationale for irregular migrants' location outside the national community and provides a critique of their exclusion from social membership and ensuing ineligibility for membership rights on account of their immigration status. The third preliminary issue, considered in section 4, focuses on irregular migrants and the welfare State. Welfare provision is instrumental in the realisation of basic social rights, including the right to health care. Inclusion in the redistribution of welfare, however, requires membership in the national community, which results in the exclusion of irregular migrants. Section 5 proceeds to examine irregular migrants' right to health care in international human rights law. A comparative study of irregular migrants' access to health care in France, the UK and Canada is undertaken in section 6. Finally, drawing on this comparative analysis, section 7 offers some conclusions on the interface between personhood and immigration status as sources of basic social rights for irregular migrants with a view to reconciling the exercise of the government's immigration power with international human rights law.

2. MIGRANTS' TREATMENT IN THE SOCIAL SPHERE: IMMIGRATION STATUS DOES MATTER

Immigration status remains characterised by the disabilities it entails.[10] Migrants' outsider status stems from the modern nation-State's construct of citizenship. National citizenship may be readily described as membership in the bounded national community. National citizenship serves an allocating function in the international order of nation-States in that it assigns individuals to a specific State.[11] Within the nation-State, national citizenship is construed as the common ground that binds members together. It aims to encapsulate members' privileged ties with and commitment to the national community and reflect their distinctive position *vis-à-*

10 Bosniak, L., *The Citizen and the Alien, Dilemmas of Contemporary Membership*, Princeton University Press, Princeton/Oxford, 2006, p. 9.

11 Miller, D., 'The ethical significance of nationality', *Ethics*, Vol. 98, No. 4, 1988, pp. 647–662, at p. 652.

vis the nation-State, which in turn validate their claim to citizenship rights. The latter include social as well as civil and political rights.[12]

> As a counterpart [to the benefits and rights they enjoy], citizens are expected to contribute to sharing the burdens or restrictions on their liberties that make the provision of these benefits [and rights] possible in the first place.[13]

As the primary bearers of citizenship duties,[14] national citizens are entitled to full citizenship rights and the distinctiveness of their status is seen as essential to the community-bonding function of national citizenship.[15]

National citizenship is both inclusive and exclusive: it brings members together but excludes others.[16] It distinguishes between citizens and non-citizens on account of the former's unique rapport to the nation-State: whilst citizenship assumes a very close bond with the nation-State, immigration status implies a more remote relationship. Consequently, migrants are not bestowed the full range of citizenship rights. Like citizenship, immigration status is a legal status that is accompanied by rights and duties. It seeks to embody migrants' position *vis-à-vis* the nation-State and purports to reflect their contribution to the national community, which in turn determines the citizenship rights they may be granted. However, not all citizenship rights are deemed distributable to migrants. Indeed, as the gap between citizens and migrants progressively closes in the social as well as the civil and economic domains, migrants remain excluded from political membership. Migrants' exclusion aims to safeguard the material and symbolic significance of national citizenship as a pact between State and citizen and preserve citizenship as the traditional basis of national membership.[17] As non-citizens, migrants are ascribed to another political community, that of the State of nationality. As a result, migrants' allegiance is deemed to lie primarily with that State and their political socialisation in their State of residence is regarded as too

---

12 This rights-based approach to citizenship is closely associated with T.H. Marshall. He developed a three-dimensional construct of national citizenship which, for the first time, involved the entitlement to and enjoyment of social rights alongside civil and political rights. See Marshall, T.H., *Citizenship and Social Class*, Cambridge University Press, Cambridge, 1950.

13 Rubio-Marín, R., *Immigration as a Democratic Challenge – Citizenship and Inclusion in Germany and the United States*, Cambridge University Press, Cambridge, 2000, p. 43.

14 Citizenship duties include obedience to the law, paying taxes, and military service. See, for instance, Janoski, T., *Citizenship and Civil Society, A Framework of Rights & Obligations in Liberal, Traditional, and Social Democratic Regimes*, Cambridge University Press, Cambridge, 1998, pp. 54–56.

15 Schauer, F., 'Community, citizenship and the search for national identity', *Michigan Law Review*, Vol. 84, No. 7, 1986, pp. 1504–1517, at p. 1516.

16 Brubaker, R., *Citizenship and Nationhood in France and Germany*, Harvard University Press, London, 1992, pp. 21–50.

17 Jacobson, D., *Rights Across Borders: Immigration and the Decline of Membership*, The Johns Hopkins University Press, Baltimore and London, 1996, pp. 8–10.

embryonic to allow political participation.[18] Consequently, they are located outside the national political community[19] and denied political rights such as the rights to vote and stand for elections[20] whereas their political participation remains contingent on their accessing citizenship through naturalisation.[21]

In contrast to political membership, social membership has become inclusive in respect of permanent regular migrants as they became eligible for non-political citizenship rights. Residence in the host State, however, must both be lawful and sufficiently stable to generate rights.[22] Hammar has coined the word *denizens* to describe the status of regular migrants who are long-term residents in host countries. *Denizens* have gained a secure residence status in the host State and as such are entitled to a wide array of rights save in the political domain.[23] Brubaker observes that in the social as well as the economic spheres citizenship no longer acts as a closure

---

18 Schuck, P.H., 'The re-evaluation of American citizenship', in: Joppke, C. (ed.), *Challenge to the Nation-State: Immigration in Western Europe and the United States*, Oxford University Press, Oxford, 1998, pp. 191–230, at p. 203.

19 For a critique of migrants' exclusion from political membership, see, for instance, Rubio-Marín, *op.cit.* (note 13), p. 58; and Legomsky, S.H., 'Immigration, federalism, and the welfare state', *UCLA Law Review*, Vol. 42, 1994–1995, pp. 1453–1474, at p. 1467.

20 Brubaker notes that the exclusion of non-citizens from modern systems of 'universal suffrage' is exemplary of modern States' self-understanding as bounded nation-States; Brubaker, *op.cit.* (note 16), p. 28. See also Soysal, Y.N., *Limits of Citizenship, Migrants and Postnational Membership in Europe*, Chicago University Press, Chicago, 1994, p. 131. The 1990 International Convention on the Protection of the Rights of All Migrant Workers and Members of their Families provides that regular migrant workers and members of their families have the right to vote and to be elected at elections of the State of employment (Article 41(1)). These rights, however, remain hypothetical as their recognition is subject to compliance with the legislation of the State of employment (Article 41(1)).

21 Naturalisation laws, however, suggest that there is an expectation that settled regular migrants will become citizens. For instance, Canadian law provides that regular resident migrants who have lived in Canada for at least three years may apply for citizenship (Citizenship (R.S., 1985, c. C-29), s. 5(1)(c)). In France, the applicant must normally have been a regular resident for at least five years (Article 21-17 of the Civil Code). In the UK, the qualifying period for citizenship is six years provided that the applicant meets the activity condition (Borders, Citizenship and Immigration Act 2009 (C 11), section 41(1)). The Act is due to come into effect in July 2011 (Hansard, 14 July 2009, Column 232). The activity condition requires of applicants that they engage in formal volunteering and civic activism (UK Government, *Document Made Available to the House to Illustrate the Government's Emerging Thinking on Active Citizenship*, 4 June 2009, para. 5, www.refugeecouncil.org.uk, under the heading 'Resources'). The activity condition is based on the concept of earned citizenship that was introduced by the UK Government's Green Paper entitled *The path to citizenship: next steps in reforming the immigration system* (Home Office, February 2008). The new path to citizenship has been strongly criticised for making access to citizenship more difficult. See, for instance, Ryan, B., 'Integration Requirements: A New Model in Migration Law', *Journal of Immigration Asylum and Nationality Law*, Vol. 22, No. 4, 2008, pp. 303–316.

22 For a critique of this legal approach to the concept of residence, see, for example, Rubio-Marín, *op.cit.* (note 13), p. 22; and Hammar, T., *Democracy and the Nation State*, Avebury, Aldershot, 1990, pp. 194–195.

23 Hammar, *op.cit.* (note 22), pp. 12–13.

mechanism in respect of permanent regular migrants.[24] Immigration status, however, remains the primary determinant of migrants' eligibility for social membership with the consequence that irregular migrants are excluded. This leaves irregular migrants confronted to a double divide: the traditional citizen/migrant divide and the regular/irregular migrant divide.

3. IRREGULAR MIGRANTS AND THE HOST STATE: 'OUTSIDERS WITHIN'

In contrast to regular migrants, irregular migrants' immigration status locates them outside the national community. As 'outsiders within', irregular migrants are assumed not to contribute to the national community[25] and not to share any of the duties borne by citizens and regular migrants. Moreover, their breach of the host State's immigration laws is deemed symptomatic of a general contempt for the law.[26] As a result, they are perceived as a continuous threat to society and are criminalised irrespective of their actual behaviour.[27] The language of illegality used by States contributes to their criminalisation and the creation of a 'culture of distrust' around this group.[28] It also emphasises their otherness. Groenendijk points out that '[h]uman beings are disqualified by being called illegal.'[29]

Irregular migrants' exclusion from all spheres of national life on account of their immigration status is rooted in the nation-State's perception of irregular migration as a threat to both the internal and external dimensions of national sovereignty, namely the nation-State's power to control its borders and the national community's right to self-determination.[30] Host States have made the 'fight' against irregular migration a priority. State controls have been enhanced and have become

---

24 Brubaker, *op.cit.* (note 16), p. 182.

25 Rubio-Marín, *op.cit.* (note 13), p. 86.

26 Legomsky, *loc.cit.* (note 19), p. 1468; Rubio-Marín, *op.cit.* (note 13), p. 86; and Bigo, D., 'The criminalisation of "migrants": the side effect of the will to control frontiers and the sovereign illusion', in: Bogusz, Cholewinski, Cygan and Szyszczak (eds), *op.cit.* (note 4), pp. 61–91.

27 Demleitner, N.V., 'The fallacy of social "citizenship", or the threat of exclusion', *Georgetown Immigration Law Journal*, Vol. 12, 1997-1998, pp. 35–64, at p. 43.

28 Cholewinski, *loc.cit.* (note 5).

29 Groenendijk, K., 'Introduction: four questions about human beings without the right papers', in: Bogusz, Cholewinski, Cygan and Szyszczak (eds), *op.cit.* (note 4), pp. xvii-xxii, at p. xix. On terminology issues, see also Cholewinski, R., *Migrants Irréguliers: L'Accès aux Droits Sociaux Minimaux* [Irregular migrants: access to minimum social rights], Council of Europe Publishing, Collection Migration, Strasbourg, 2005, pp. 9–10.

30 Dauvergne, D., 'Sovereignty, migration and the rule of law in global times', *Modern Law Review*, Vol. 67, No. 4, 2004, pp. 588–615, at p. 601. Freeman, however, argues that 'worries about the disappearance of state sovereignty over population movements are premature'; Freeman, G.P., 'The decline of sovereignty? Politics and immigration restriction in liberal states', in: Joppke, *op.cit.* (note 18), pp. 86–108, at p. 95.

increasingly sophisticated.[31] Yet a settled population of irregular migrants continues to be present in States such as France, the UK and Canada. There are several reasons for the failure of immigration enforcement. It is partly attributable to the difficulties inherent in detecting individuals who deliberately seek to evade immigration admission mechanisms, difficulties which are exacerbated by the development of people smuggling and trafficking networks.[32] Some of the primary causes for the magnitude of the phenomenon of irregular migration, however, lie with host States themselves. Migration control discourse and policies within host States fail to take in the complexities and realities of migration.[33] In particular, host States' immigration laws and policies do not appear to recognise and respond to the combined effect of the continuous demand for a cheap and flexible workforce and the persistence of significant wealth inequalities worldwide on migratory patterns. Consequently, tighter immigration controls have failed to reduce the numbers of irregular workers.[34]

Reliance on irregular migrant workforce has become a *de facto* component of States' employment policies.[35] In developed countries, the demand for a cheap, low-skilled workforce remains strong in a number of sectors of the economy.[36] Significantly, unemployment levels in host States do not affect particularly irregular migrant

---

31 Freeman, *loc.cit.* (note 30), p. 96.

32 See, for instance, Taran, P.A. and Moreno-Fontes Chammartin, G., *Getting at the Roots: Stopping Exploitation of Migrant Workers by Organized Crime, Perspectives on Labour Migration 1E, International Migration Programme*, International Labour Office, Geneva, 2003; Ventrella McCreight, M., 'Smuggling of migrants, trafficking in human beings and irregular migration on a comparative perspective', *European Law Journal*, Vol. 12, No. 1, 2006, pp. 106–129; Lee, M., 'Human trade and the criminalization of irregular migration', *International Journal of the Sociology of Law*, Vol. 33, No. 1, 2005, pp. 1–15; Piotrowicz, R., 'Irregular migration networks: the challenge posed by people traffickers to states and human rights', in: Bogusz, Cholewinski, Cygan and Szyszczak (eds), *op.cit.* (note 4), pp. 137–155; and Gallagher, A.M., 'Triply exploited: female victims of trafficking networks – strategies for pursuing protection and legal status in countries of destination', *Georgetown Immigration Law Journal*, Vol. 19, 2004–2005, pp. 99–124.

33 Kostakopoulou, D., 'Irregular migration and migration theory: making state authorisation less relevant', in: Bogusz, Cholewinski, Cygan and Szyszczak (eds), *op.cit.* (note 4), pp. 41–57.

34 Taran, P.A. and Geromini, E., *Globalization, Labour and Migration: Protection is Paramount, Perspectives on Labour Migration 3E, International Migration Programme*, International Labour Office, Geneva, 2003, p. 7.

35 Legomsky, *loc.cit.* (note 19), p. 1469.

36 These include agriculture, food-processing, construction, textile and service industries (for instance, domestic work as well as the sex sector). See, for example, Taran and Geromini, *op.cit.* (note 34), pp. 3–4; Stalker, P., *Workers Without Frontiers – The Impact of Globalisation on International Migration*, ILO, Geneva 2000; and Schierup, C-U., Hansen, P. and Castles, S., *Migration, Citizenship and the European Welfare State*, Oxford University Press, Oxford, 2006, p. 3. In 2002, it was estimated that 76,000 irregular migrants worked in Ontario's construction industry; see Jimenez, M., '200,000 illegal immigrants toiling in Canada's underground industry', Globe and Mail, 15 November 2003, available at: http://are.berkeley.edu/APMP/pubs/agworkvisa/canada111503.html. See also *supra* note 9.

workers' ability to find employment easily.[37] This is because their employability is closely linked to their exploitability. Neuman notes that 'illegal migrant workers appear to be, in many respects, an ideally exploitable source of labor.'[38] 'It is often reported that migrant labour fills the "three-D" jobs; dirty, degrading and dangerous.'[39] 'The exploitability of migrant labour, particularly when it is legally unprotected, makes it an attractive instrument for maintaining competitiveness.'[40] The UN Special Rapporteur on the Human Rights of Migrants observed that

> [t]he exploitation of migrants by unscrupulous employers and contractors who pay lower wages than they would pay a foreigner in a regular situation or a national only adds to the advantages they gain if they also do not pay their social security and taxes on earnings from the labour of these persons. Such situations force these workers to put up with excessively long working hours and unacceptable security and hygiene conditions that gravely endanger their health. They enable unscrupulous employers and contractors to threaten migrants with the possibility they will report their irregular status in the host country...[41]

Yet, because of their immigration status, irregular migrants' contributions are counted as evidence of their transgression of immigration law requirements rather than being regarded as actual contributions.[42] The author argues that the institutionalisation of irregular migration that stems from national economies' continuing reliance on irregular migrants as an expandable source of cheap labour cannot be reconciled with their location outside the national community and their ensuing exclusion from any form of membership.

4. IRREGULAR MIGRANTS AND THE WELFARE STATE

Irregular migrants' exclusion from membership on account of their immigration status causes their exclusion from the welfare State. This is because the welfare State's primary goal is to address members' claim to welfare. Banting and Kymlicka highlight that 'there are important variations in the attitude towards the claims of different

---

37 Lean Lin, L., 'Growing economic interdependence and its implications for international migration economic interdependence and its implications for international migration', in: *United Nations: Population Distribution and Migration*, United Nations, New York, 1998, p. 277.

38 Neuman, G.L., *Strangers to the Constitution*, Princeton University Press, Princeton, 1996, p. 185.

39 Taran and Geromini, *op.cit.* (note 34), p. 4. See also Abella, M.I., 'Mondialisation, marchés du travail et mobilité' [Globalisation, job markets and mobility], *Migrations et Avenir*, Vol. 14, No. 79, January-February 2002.

40 Taran and Geromini, *op.cit.* (note 34), p. 5.

41 UN Economic and Social Council, *Specific Groups and Individuals, Migrant Workers*, Report of the Special Rapporteur, Ms Gabriela Rodríguez Pizarro, submitted pursuant to Commission on Human Rights Resolution 2000/48, UN Doc. E/CN.4/2001/83, 9 January 2001, para. 54.

42 Dauvergne, *loc.cit.* (note 30), p. 601.

immigrant groups. Public debates in many countries distinguish "good" immigrant groups, who are seen as hard-working and law-abiding (…), from "bad" immigrant groups, who may be seen as illegal or lazy, or as prone to crime….'[43] Resident regular migrants' immigration status makes them 'good' migrants. Their recognition as duty bearers and contributors to the national community means that they are regarded as bound together with citizens in the social cooperation scheme that is the welfare State. The welfare State supposes that '[members] must trust each other to both take part as contributors and not take advantage as beneficiaries.'[44] Thus, the redistribution of welfare requires trust and solidarity amongst members.[45] As members, resident regular migrants are deemed 'deserving' of welfare provision in the host State.

In contrast to regular migrants, irregular migrants' immigration status portrays them as 'bad' migrants. Their lack of membership in the national community makes them 'undeserving' of welfare provision. The distinction that the welfare State operates between the 'deserving' and the 'undeserving' predates the debate on migrants' inclusion. From its inception, the welfare State distinguished between the 'deserving' and the 'undeserving' poor[46]:

> The 'deserving' poor have become needy as a consequence of a tragedy or after decades of hard work (…) The 'undeserving' poor, in contrast, have caused their poverty through moral or cultural decay (…) When the poor are characterized as morally undeserving because they are criminally or otherwise deviant or because they have failed to fulfil their duties toward society, society believes it no longer has any obligation to support them.[47]

Like the 'undeserving' poor, irregular migrants are held responsible for their hardship that arises from their 'self-inflicted illegality'. Members question their willingness to work.[48] Yet we have seen in the previous section that host States do rely on their labour.

---

43 Banting, K. and Kymlicka, W., 'Introduction, multiculturalism: setting the context', in: Banting, K. and Kymlicka, W. (eds), *Multiculturalism and the Welfare State: Recognition and Redistribution in Contemporary Democracies*, Oxford University Press, Oxford, 2006, pp. 1–45, at p. 8.

44 Crepaz, M., 'If you are my brother, I may give you a dime!', Public opinion on multiculturalism, trust, and the welfare state', in: Banting and Kymlicka (eds), *op.cit.* (note 43), pp. 92–117, at p. 109.

45 See Banting and Kymlicka, *loc.cit.* (note 43), p. 11; Braithwaite, V. and Levi, M. (eds), *Trust and Governance*, Russel Sage Foundation, New York, 1998; Miller, D., 'Multiculturalism and the welfare state: theoretical reflections', in: Banting and Kymlicka (eds), *op.cit.* (note 43), pp. 323–338, at p. 323; and Banting, K., Soroka, S. and Johnston, R., 'Ethnicity, trust and the welfare state', in: Kay, F. and Johnston, R. (eds), *Social Capital, Diversity and the Welfare State*, University of British Columbia Press, Vancouver, 2006, pp. 279–303.

46 Sainsbury, D., *Gender, Equality and Welfare States*, Cambridge University Press, Cambridge, 1996. For an analysis of the concept of the 'deserving poor', see Sher, G., 'Health care and the "deserving poor"', *The Hastings Centre Report*, Vol. 13, No. 1, 1983, pp. 9–12. See also Sales, R., 'The deserving and the undeserving? Refugees, asylum seekers and welfare in Britain', *Critical Social Policy*, Vol. 22, No. 3, 2002, pp. 456–478.

47 Demleitner, *loc.cit.* (note 27), p. 45.

48 *Idem.*

Irregular migrants are also suspected of 'milking the system for free state benefits'.[49] Such an accusation, however, is inconsistent with their exclusion from the welfare State. Moreover, it assumes a degree of membership in the national community that irregular migrants' immigration status and ensuing clandestine existence do not allow.

Irregular migrants' exclusion from the welfare State is compounded by two factors: the growing problematisation of irregular migration and the crisis of the welfare State.[50] These two factors have become intertwined as host State governments developed the view that the level of welfare provision for migrants is a significant determinant of migratory patterns. They contend that the availability of minimum social rights for irregular migrants acts as a primary pull factor and therefore sustains and encourages illegal population movements.[51] As a result, curtailments – if not denials – of welfare provision have become instrumental in attempting to control immigration and tackling irregular migration.[52] The crisis of the welfare State, and in particular the crisis of national health care systems,[53] has further bolstered the objections to irregular migrants' inclusion in the redistribution of welfare. This crisis has entrenched the distinction between 'deserving' and 'undeserving' welfare applicants. This has polarised members and non-members' respective interests[54] with the consequence that welfare provision for irregular migrants is set against competing national priorities for limited resources.

---

49 Lopez, M.J., 'Access to healthcare for legal and undocumented immigrants', *Immigration and Nationality Law Review*, Vol. 21, 2000, pp. 641–662, at p. 651.

50 Schierup, Hansen and Castles, *op.cit.* (note 36), p. 1. See also Castles, F.G., *The Future of the Welfare State: Crisis Myths and Crisis Realities*, Oxford University Press, Oxford, 2004; Huber, E. and Stephens, J.D., *Development and Crisis of the Welfare State: Parties and Policies in Global Markets*, Chicago University Press, Chicago, 2001; and Cox, R.H., 'The consequences of welfare reform: how conceptions of social rights are changing', *Journal of Social Policy*, Vol. 27, No. 1, 1998, pp. 1–16.

51 Host State governments have also used the pull factor argument in respect of forced migration. However, research suggests that welfare provision does not play a major role in shaping the decision to seek asylum in a particular State. See, for example, Robinson, V. and Segrott, J., *Understanding the Decision-Making of Asylum Seekers*, Home Office Research Study 243, Home Office Research, Development and Statistics Directorate, The Home Office, London, 2002, pp. 49–52. See also Crawley, H., Chance *or Choice? Understanding Why Asylum Seekers Come to the UK*, Refugee Council, London, January 2010, pp. 40–41, www.refugeecouncil.org.uk/Resources/Refugee%20 Council/downloads/rcchance.pdf.

52 Da Lomba, S., 'Fundamental social rights for irregular migrants: the right to health care in France and England', in: Bogusz, Cholewinski, Cygan and Szyszczak (eds), *op.cit.* (note 4), pp. 363–386, at p. 363.

53 See, for instance, Le Faou, A-L., *Le Système de Santé en Questions, Allemagne, France, Royaume-Uni, Etats-Unis et Canada* [Questions about the health system, Germany, France, the United Kingdom, the United States and Canada], Ellipses Marketing, Paris, 2003; Appleby, J. and Harrison, A., *Spending on Health Care*, King's Fund, London, 2006; Field, M.G. (ed.), *Success and Crisis in National Health Systems: A Comparative Approach*, Routledge, London, 1989; and Priest, L., *Operating in the Dark: The Accountability Crisis in Canada's Health Care System*, Doubleday Canada, Toronto, 1998.

54 Schuck, P.H. and Smith, R.M., *Citizenship Without Consent*, Yale University Press, New Haven/ London, 1985, p. 3 and pp. 103–115.

Irregular migrants' lack of membership in the national community precludes their partaking in the welfare State, which constrains their access to health care. Yet irregular migrants do have rights as persons,[55] which include the right to health care.

5. IRREGULAR MIGRANTS' RIGHT TO HEALTH CARE IN INTERNATIONAL HUMAN RIGHTS LAW

Irregular migrants are not totally lacking in rights. As persons, they are entitled to the basic human rights recognised in international human right law.[56] The right to health care has been characterised as a basic human right and is therefore bestowed on irregular migrants. The right to health care forms part of the right to health[57] which is among the social rights[58] affirmed in a range of international human rights instruments.[59] 'Article 12 of the International Covenant on Economic, Social and Cultural Rights [ICESCR] provides the most authoritative articulation of the right to health in international human rights law.'[60] '[It] is concerned with the level of health to which human rights law is committed',[61] namely 'the right of everyone to the enjoyment of the highest attainable standard of physical and mental health.'[62] Article 12 recognises the right to health care as a constituent of the right to health.[63] The core obligations arising from the right to health care have grown over the years. They were initially based on the Alma-Ata Declaration of the World Health Organization (WHO), which emphasised the provision of primary health care and

55 Parliamentary Assembly, Council of Europe, *Creation of a charter of intent on clandestine migration*, Doc. 9522, 15 July 2002, para. 31.

56 Carens, J.H., 'The rights of irregular migrants', *Ethics & International Affairs*, Vol. 22, No. 2, 2008, pp. 163–186, at p. 165.

57 General Comment No. 14, *supra* note 7, paras 4 and 11.

58 Alston, P., 'Economic and social rights', *Studies in Transnational Legal Policy*, Vol. 26, 1994, pp. 137–166, at p. 138.

59 For example, the right to health is recognised in the 1979 Convention on the Elimination of all Forms of Discrimination against Women (Article 12) and in the 1989 Convention on the Rights of the Child (Article 24). Several conventions setting out international standards for occupational health and safety have also been adopted under the auspices of the International Labor Organization (for example, the 1981 ILO Convention No. 155 concerning Occupational Safety and Health and the 1988 ILO Convention No. 167 concerning Safety and Health in Construction).

60 World Health Organization, *International Migration, Health & Human Rights*, Health & Human Rights Publication Series, Issue No. 4, December 2003, p. 32.

61 McHale, J. and Fox, M., *Health Care Law: Texts and Materials*, Thomson, Sweet & Maxwell, London, 2007, 2nd ed., p. 8.

62 Article 12(1) of the ICESCR.

63 General Comment No. 14, *supra* note 7, paras 4 and 11.

non-discrimination as key aspects of access to health care.[64] General Comment No. 3 of the Committee on Economic Social and Cultural Rights confirmed that States parties have a minimum core obligation to provide essential primary health care for all.[65] General Comment No. 14 of the Committee on Economic, Social and Cultural Rights (General Comment No. 14) offers the most authoritative statement of the core obligations arising out of Article 12 of the ICESCR.[66] States parties are under the obligation to 'ensure the right of access to health facilities, goods and services on a non-discriminatory basis', especially for vulnerable or marginalized groups'[67] as well as their equitable distribution.[68] This core obligation encompasses access to health care since the right to health includes the right to health care. Further core obligations that pertain to the right to health care require that States

> (a) (...) ensure reproductive, maternal (pre-natal as well as post-natal) and child health care;
> (b) (...) provide immunization against the major infectious diseases occurring in the community; [and]
> (c) (...) take measures to prevent, treat and control epidemic and endemic diseases...[69]

Like 'traditional' civil and political rights, economic, social and cultural rights generate three types of obligations, namely obligations to respect, protect and fulfil.[70] It follows that the States parties to the ICESCR are under the obligation to respect, protect and fulfil the right to health care, and more broadly the right to health.[71] Crucially, General Comment No. 14 stresses that '[s]tates are under the obligation to *respect* the right to health by, *inter alia*, refraining from denying or limiting equal access for all persons, including (...) *illegal migrants*,[72] to preventive, curative and palliative health

64 Declaration of Alma Ata, in WHO, *Primary Health Care: Report of the International Conference on Primary Health Care*, 1978, pp. 3–4. The Maastricht Guidelines on Violations of Economic, Social and Cultural Rights state that 'the failure of States to provide essential primary health care to those in need may amount to a violation'; International Commission of Jurists (ICJ), *Maastricht Guidelines on Violations of Economic, Social and Cultural Rights*, 26 January 1997, Part II, para. 6, available at: www.unhcr.org/refworld/docid/48abd5730.html. See also Den Exter, A. and Hermans, B., 'Constitutional rights to health care: the consequences of placing limits on the right to health care in several Western and Eastern European states', *European Journal of Health Law*, Vol. 5, No. 3, 1998, pp. 261–289, p. 265.

65 Committee on Economic Social and Cultural Rights, *The nature of States parties obligations*, UN Doc. E/1991/23/23, annex III, at 86 (1991), 14 December 1990, Article 2(1). CESCR, General Comment No. 3, General Comments, para. 10.

66 General Comment No. 14, *supra* note 7, paras 43–44.

67 *Ibidem*, para. 43(a).

68 *Ibidem*, para. 43(e).

69 *Ibidem*, para. 44(a), (b) and (c).

70 *Maastricht Guidelines on Violations of Economic, Social and cultural Rights*, *supra* note 64, Part II, para. 6.

71 General Comment No. 14, *supra* note 7, para. 33.

72 Emphasis added.

services…'[73] Non-discrimination is indeed characterised as an essential element of the right to health[74] and Article 12 does not permit discrimination on the basis of legal status.[75] Affordability is also considered central to the right to health.[76] 'Payment for health-care services (…) [must] be based on the principle of equity, ensuring that these services, whether privately or publicly provided, are affordable for all, including socially disadvantaged groups.'[77] The author shares the view that irregular migrants' socio-economic circumstances make rules requiring them to contribute towards the cost of their health care a likely obstacle to the realisation of their right to health care.[78] The obligation to respect also means that States must refrain from interfering, directly or indirectly, with the enjoyment of the right to health.[79] Moreover, the obligation to protect implies that States must prevent third parties' interferences.[80] 'Finally, the obligation to fulfil requires States to take appropriate legislative, administrative, budgetary, judicial, promotional and other measures towards the full realization of the right to health.'[81] Interferences with the enjoyment of the right to health care are therefore not permissible and States must take all the steps necessary to its realisation.

The constraints that limited national resources place on the effective realisation of social rights were acknowledged in the ICESCR.[82] Article 2(1) provides for the progressive realisation of rights to the maximum of States parties' resources.[83] Progressive realisation distinguishes economic, social and cultural rights from civil and political rights. This distinction, however, must not be exaggerated and progressive realisation does not preclude the imposition of immediate obligations on States.[84] Such obligations have been identified in relation to the right to health, 'such

73 General Comment No. 14, *supra* note 7, para. 34.

74 *Ibidem*, para. 12(b).

75 *Idem*.

76 *Idem*.

77 *Idem*.

78 Lopez, *loc.cit.* (note 49), p. 654. Médecins du Monde UK stressed that 'undocumented migrants ha[d] no income, [did] not have access to public funds and [were] unable to pay charges'; House of Lords and House of Commons, Joint Committee on Human Rights – *Written Evidence*, 'Memorandum from Médecins du Monde', para. 46, point 5, September 2006, available at: www.publications.parliament.uk/pa/jt200607/jtselect/jtrights/81/81we01.htm.

79 General Comment No. 14, *supra* note 7, para. 33.

80 *Idem*.

81 *Idem*.

82 General Comment No. 3, *supra* note 65, para. 1.

83 Article 2(1) of the ICESCR reads that '[e]ach State Party to the present Covenant undertakes to take steps, individually and through international assistance and co-operation, especially economic and technical, to the maximum of its available resources, with a view to achieving progressively the full realization of the rights recognized in the present Covenant by all appropriate means, including particularly the adoption of legislative measures.'

84 General Comment No. 3, *supra* note 65, para. 1. The 1993 Vienna Declaration declares that the two types of rights recognised in the ICESCR and the International Covenant on Civil and Political

as the guarantee that the right will be exercised without discrimination of any kind (...) and the obligation to take steps (...) towards the full realization of article 12...'[85] Significantly 'resource scarcity does not relieve States of certain minimum obligations in respect of the implementation of economic, social and cultural rights.'[86] General Comment No. 14 specifies that unwillingness to use the maximum of State resources for the realisation of the right to health always constitutes a violation of Article 12.[87] States parties which are unable to fully meet their obligations must show that every effort was made to use all their available resources.[88] Importantly, resource constraints cannot 'under any circumstances whatsoever, justify [States'] non-compliance with the core obligations set out in paragraph 43 (...), which are non-derogable.'[89]

International human rights law confers rights on irregular migrants, including the right to health care. The government's immigration power, however, does have a bearing on the normative content of international human rights law. Notwithstanding its universal premise, international human rights law forms part of international law and is therefore State-centred in nature. Thus, international human rights law is profoundly shaped by two recurrent principles of international law, namely the 'state consent supernorm',[90] which relates to the State's primary role in the creation, implementation and enforcement of international law, and national sovereignty.[91] These principles, however, are not rooted in human rights ideals. This explains the gap between human rights ideals as expressed by theorists, on the one hand, and international human rights provisions, on the other hand.[92] This also explicates why international human rights law does not compel States to confer the

Rights (ICCPR) are 'universal, indivisible and interdependent and interrelated'; Vienna Declaration and Programme of Action, World Conference on Human Rights, Vienna, 14-25 June 1993, UN Doc. A/CONF.157/23, para. 5.

85 General Comment No. 14, *supra* note 7, para. 30. Paragraph 31 further specifies that '[t]he progressive realization of the right to health over a period of time should not be interpreted as depriving States parties' obligations of all meaningful content. Rather, progressive realization means that States parties have a specific and continuing obligation to move as expeditiously and effectively as possible towards the full realization of article 12'.

86 *Maastricht Guidelines on Violations of Economic, Social and cultural Rights, supra* note 64, para. 10. This was clearly established in the *Limburg Principles on the Implementation of the International Covenant on Economic, Social and Cultural Rights,* Principles 25 to 28, UN Doc. E/CN.4/1987/17, Annex, reproduced in: *Human Rights Quarterly*, Vol. 9, No. 2, 1987, pp. 122–135.

87 General Comment No. 14, *supra* note 7, para. 47.

88 *Idem.*

89 *Idem.*

90 Buchanan, A., 'From Nuremburg to Kosovo: the morality of illegal international legal reform', *Ethics*, Vol. 111, No. 4, 2001, pp. 673–705, at p. 688.

91 Meckled-García, S. and Çali, B., 'Human rights *legalized* – defining, interpreting and implementing an ideal', in: Meckled-García, S. and Çali, B. (eds), *The Legalization of Human Rights, Multi-disciplinary Perspectives on Human Rights and Human Rights Law*, Routledge, London/New York, 2005, pp. 1–31, at pp. 17–18.

92 This remark, however, does not apply to positivists as the latter take the view that human rights do not exist outside human rights law; *ibidem*, p. 13.

full set of human rights on all persons.[93] The State-centred nature of international human rights law accounts for its inability to render legal status in the nation-State irrelevant. Consequently, the universalist ideal that underpins international human rights law and makes migrants' protection a compelling cause is set against nation-States' concerns over national sovereignty, thereby creating a serious tension between migration control and human rights protection. This tension is apparent in the text of the 1990 International Convention on the Protection of the Rights of All Migrant Workers and Members of their Families (the Migrant Workers Convention).[94] The latter was presented as the 'culmination of [an] evolutionary process which ha[d] seen the development of universal standards protecting the rights of non-nationals.'[95] Yet the extent to which protection should be afforded to irregular migrants proved particularly contentious. States fell into two camps: those which retreated behind the pull factor argument and advocated very limited rights for irregular migrants, mostly host States, and those which viewed the protection of migrant workers' rights primarily as a 'question of universal values'.[96] A compromise was reached in an attempt to accommodate both human rights and immigration control concerns. Part III of the Convention grants basic rights to *all* migrants and members of their families irrespective of their immigration status.[97] Conversely, Part IV, which enhances the rights recognised in Part III, is only applicable to regular migrants.[98] This status-based distinction sought to affirm the States' immigration power, and in particular their condemnation of irregular migration. Limited obligations, however, were not sufficient to appease host States' disquiet as to the impact of the Convention on their immigration policies and so far none of the Northern American and Western European States has ratified nor signed the Migrant Workers Convention.[99]

---

93 *Ibidem*, p. 18.

94 See Cholewinski, R., *Migrant Workers in International Human Rights Law: Their Protection in Countries of Employment*, Clarendon Press, Oxford, 1997, p. 137.

95 *Idem.*

96 *Ibidem*, p. 187. A further argument in favour of the recognition of rights for irregular migrants rested on the idea that inclusion would deter employers from turning to irregular workforce whilst improving the working conditions of national workers; *idem*.

97 These include the right to life (Article 9), the right not to be subjected to torture or to cruel, inhuman or degrading treatment or punishment (Article 10), the right to freedom of thought, conscience and religion (Article 12(1)) and the right to recognition everywhere as a person before the law (Article 24).

98 These rights include the right to equality of treatment with nationals of the State of employment in respect of access to vocational guidance and placement services (Article 43(b)), access to vocational training and retraining facilities and institutions (Article 43(c)), access to housing, including social housing schemes, and protection against exploitation in respect of rents (Article 43(d)), protection against dismissal (Article 54(a)) and unemployment benefits (Article 45(b)).

99 The Migrant Workers Convention, which entered into force on 1 July 2003, has so far been ratified by 42 States and signed by 31. On the ratification process, see MacDonald, E. and Cholewinski, R., *The Migrant Workers Convention in Europe, Obstacles to the Ratification of the International Convention on the Protection of the Rights of All Migrant Workers and Members of their Families*, UNESCO Migration Studies, United Nations Educational, Scientific and Cultural Organization, Paris, 2007;

The right to health care is enshrined in Part III and is therefore bestowed on irregular migrants. Article 28 reads

> Migrant workers and members of their families shall have the right to receive any medical care that is urgently required for the preservation of their life or the avoidance of irreparable harm to their health on the basis of equality of treatment with nationals of the State concerned...

Article 28 emphasises that 'emergency medical care shall not be refused to [migrants] by reason of any irregularity with regard to stay or employment.' This inclusiveness, however, must be measured against the limited material scope of Article 28 that fails to include all the core obligations arising out of Article 12 of the ICESCR. In contrast to Article 12, Article 28 of the Migrant Workers Convention is only concerned with emergency health care.[100] Article 28 requires States parties to provide 'any medical care that is urgently required for the preservation of life or the avoidance of irreparable harm to their health'. Article 28 further specifies that this must be delivered 'on the basis of equal treatment with nationals'. Equality of treatment with nationals in respect of general access to health care services, however, is reserved to regular migrants.[101] The material scope of Article 28 was originally broader, but the phrase 'or the restoration of their health' was repealed at the request of the US delegation.[102] Article 28 compares very disfavourably with Article 12 of the ICESCR. The original draft ensured irregular migrants' access to curative health care and therefore brought Article 28 closer to the standard set out in Article 12. Yet it still failed to match irregular migrants' entitlements under Article 12 as it did not provide for access to preventive health care.

The tension that arises from the persisting relevance of immigration status to the realisation of the human right to health care was brought to the fore in *International Federation of Human Rights Leagues (FIDH)* vs *France*, a case brought under the European Social Charter.[103] The collective complaint was lodged following the 2002

and Hune, S. and Niessen, J., 'Ratifying the UN Migrant Workers Convention: current difficulties and prospects', *Netherlands Quarterly of Human Rights*, Vol. 9, No. 4, 1994, pp. 393–404.

100 Limiting irregular migrants' right to health care to the provision of urgent medical care is not specific to the Migrant Workers Convention. See, for example, Parliamentary Assembly, Council of Europe, Resolution 1509 (2006), Human Rights for Irregular Migrants, para. 13.2, http://assembly.coe.int/main.asp?Link=/documents/adoptedtext/ta06/eres1509.htm.

101 Migrant Workers Convention Part IV, Article 43(1)(e). This right is contingent on migrants meeting 'the requirements for participation in the respective schemes' (Article 43(1)(e)). Article 45(1)(c) extends the right to access health services on the same basis as nationals to regular migrant workers' family members.

102 Cholewinski, *op.cit.* (note 94), p. 168.

103 European Committee of Social Rights, *International Federation of Human Rights Leagues (FIDH)* vs *France*, 7 October 2004, Collective complaint No. 14/2003, HUDOC database (www.echr.coe.int).

reform of the *Aide médicale d'État* (State medical assistance) (AME).[104] The latter required of irregular migrants that they contribute towards the cost of their health care as AME users. It also denied children immediate access to the AME and therefore to health care in some cases. The FIDH contended that France had breached Articles 13 (right to social and medical assistance) and 17 (right of children and young persons to social, legal and economic protection) of the Revised European Social Charter (the Charter).[105] The French Government argued that France could not possibly be in breach of its obligations under the Charter as irregular migrants fell outside its personal scope.[106] The French Government founded its position on the Appendix to the Charter which provides that

> [t]he persons covered by Articles 1 to 17 and 20 to 31 include foreigners only in so far as they are nationals of other Parties lawfully resident or working regularly within the territory of the Party concerned.[107]

The FIDH, on the other hand, took the view that the condition relating to lawful residence was only relevant in relation to equal treatment with nationals and did not therefore justify a total exclusion of irregular migrants from the benefit of the Charter's provisions on medical assistance.[108] The complaint raised the fundamental question whether immigration status and nationality could trump personhood as the basis for basic social rights. The European Committee of Social Rights (the Committee) emphasised that the Charter was a human rights instrument and as such embraced universal values such as dignity and solidarity.[109] Referring to the Vienna Declaration of 1993, the Committee recalled that 'all human rights are universal, indivisible, interdependent and interrelated'[110] and concluded that 'the Charter must be interpreted so as to give life and meaning to fundamental social rights' and that restrictions on rights must consequently 'be read restrictively'.[111] Turning to the issue of restrictions on access to health care, the Committee stressed that

> [i]t treads on a right of fundamental importance to the individual since it is connected to the right to life itself and goes to the very dignity of the human being. Furthermore, the restriction in this instance impacts adversely on children who are exposed to the risk of no medical treatment.[112]

104 This reform is discussed in section 6.1.

105 *Supra* note 103, paras 16–25.

106 *Ibidem*, para. 18.

107 Point 1 of the Appendix to the Revised European Social Charter.

108 *Supra* note 103, para. 17.

109 *Ibidem*, para. 27.

110 *Ibidem*, para. 28, referring to para. 5 of the 1993 Vienna Declaration, United Nations, General Assembly, Vienna Declaration, *supra* note 84.

111 *Supra* note 103, para. 29.

112 *Ibidem*, para. 30.

The Committee concluded that '[l]egislation or practice which denies entitlement to medical assistance to foreign nationals, within the territory of a State Party, even if they are there illegally, is contrary to the Charter.'[113]

The Committee, however, did not go as far as demanding equal treatment between nationals and irregular migrants, which is consistent with international human rights standards.

The Committee found that France had not breached Article 13 because irregular migrants were not deprived of all entitlement to medical assistance.[114] The Committee, however, held that France had fallen short of its obligations under Article 17 by depriving irregular migrants' children from immediate access to health care save in respect of emergency cases.[115] The Committee reached its conclusion by an extremely narrow majority, namely a majority of one. The contentious point related to the delineation of the personal scope of the Charter and whether it should include irregular migrants. Six out of the 13 Committee members, whilst they deplored the exclusion of irregular migrants from the scope of the Charter, took the view that their inclusion would go against the letter of the Appendix and would amount to an implicit revision of the Charter.[116] They contended that the majority's interpretation of the Appendix engaged the basic principles on the interpretation of treaties in that it totally disregarded the wording of the Charter.[117] The reasoning of the majority, however, is rooted in the universality and fundamental character of respect for human dignity. The Committee emphasised that

> [h]uman dignity is the fundamental value and indeed the core of positive European human rights law - whether under the European Social Charter or under the European Convention of Human Rights and health care is a prerequisite for the preservation of human dignity.[118]

Thus, if the decision of the Committee may be seen to deviate from the principles on the interpretation of treaties despite its assertion to the contrary,[119] it does so in order to uphold the universal principle of respect for human dignity, ensure compliance with international human rights law and give substance to the right to health care.

---

113 *Ibidem*, para. 32.

114 *Ibidem*, para. 33.

115 *Ibidem*, para. 37.

116 See, in particular, the dissenting opinion of Mr Rolf Birk; *idem*.

117 *Idem*.

118 *Ibidem*, para. 31.

119 The Committee underscored that its interpretation of the personal scope of the Charter was consistent with Article 31(1) of the Vienna Convention on the Law of Treaties; *ibidem*, para. 26. Article 31(1) reads that '[a] treaty shall be interpreted in good faith in accordance with the ordinary meaning to be given to the terms of the treaty in their context and in the light of its object and purpose.'

6. IRREGULAR MIGRANTS' ACCESS TO HEALTH CARE IN FRANCE, THE UK AND CANADA

The objective of this section is to further examine the respective relevance of immigration status and personhood as sources of rights through a comparative study of irregular migrants' access to health care in France, the UK and Canada.

In all three jurisdictions, irregular migrants' immigration status causes their exclusion from national health care systems. These jurisdictions' legal responses to irregular migrants' health care needs, however, do vary. France expressly provides for irregular migrants' access to health care, though through a separate scheme. In the UK, irregular migrants' access to the national health care system remains an exception to the rule that makes eligibility contingent on lawful residence. Finally, legal provisions on access to health care in Canada totally ignore irregular migrants.

6.1. IRREGULAR MIGRANTS' ACCESS TO HEALTH CARE IN FRANCE

The French health care system aims to address the needs of French residents. The latter are covered by compulsory public health insurance.[120] Eligibility essentially rests on two criteria: lawful residence and occupational status.[121] Because they do not meet the first criterion, irregular migrants are not insured. Access to free health care for this group, however, was rendered possible through the AME.[122] Moreover, French law provides for the regularisation of those migrants who suffer from an exceptionally serious medical condition and cannot obtain adequate treatment in their country of origin.[123]

Originally, AME applicants could establish their identity, residence in France and resources[124] by means of statements (*déclarations sur l'honneur*). In 2002, however,

---

120 Public health insurance forms part of the French social security system. The most important public health care insurance fund is the *Régime général de la sécurité sociale*. Other schemes cover self-employed people and agricultural workers (*Caisse nationale d'assurance maladie des professions indépendantes* and *Mutualité sociale agricole*).

121 *Code de la sécurité sociale (Partie Législative)*, chapter 3.

122 Article L251-1 of the *Code de l'action sociale et des familles*.

123 Article L-313-11 of the *Code de l'entrée des étrangers et du droit d'asile*. The French Government, however, has been criticised for its restrictive reading of this provision. See Report of the Observatoire du droit à la santé [Right to health observatory], *La Régularisation pour Raison Médicale en France, Un Bilan de Santé Alarmant, 1998–2008: Dix Ans d'Application du Droit au Séjour des Étrangers Malades* [Regularisation for health reasons in France, An alarming health assessment, 1998–2008: Ten years of implementation of the right of foreign nationals to remain owing to ill-health], ODSE, May 2008, p. 35, available at: www.odse.eu.org/IMG/pdf/ODSE-rapport2008_.pdf.

124 The AME is meanstested. For the period 1 October 2008 to 30 September 2009, resources were not to exceed € 8774 per tax household; *Arrêté* of 27 May 2008 *pris en application de l'article D. 380-4 du code de la sécurité sociale, Journal Officiel*, 31 May 2008.

an increase in the number of AME beneficiaries[125] prompted a more stringent approach to the processing of applications, and applicants are now required to submit comprehensive evidence in support of their claims.[126] This reform was strongly criticised for being impracticable owing to irregular migrants' circumstances[127] and for deliberately erecting yet another hurdle on their effective access to health care.[128] The rise in the number of AME users triggered two further changes to the AME. First, the *Loi de finances rectificative pour 2002* introduced the idea of a *ticket modérateur*[129] for AME users, thereby requiring them to contribute towards the cost of their health care.[130] The end of free health care for AME beneficiaries was denounced as an attempt to use the threat of ill-health as a repressive measure against irregular migrants in spite of governmental reassurances to the contrary.[131] The government attempted to present the reform as a means to control and reduce health expenditure and make AME users more responsible.[132] Yet French hospital personnel stressed that the vast majority of irregular migrants would not be able to contribute and that hospitals would be left with unpaid bills as a result.[133] This reform also marked the end of the principle of free access to health care for the poorest groups of society irrespective of nationality and legal status. This principle had been enshrined in French law since the end of the 19th century.[134] To date, however, the government has not adopted the necessary implementing measures and irregular migrants continue to have access to health care

125 The number of AME users was close to 120,000 in September 2001 and close to 180,000 in September 2002; Gissler, É. *et al.*, *Mission d'audit de modernisation, Rapport sur la Gestion de l'Aide Médicale d'État* [Modernisation audit mission, Report on state medical assistance management], Inspection générale des Finances et Inspection des affaires sociales [Finances general inspectorate and social affairs inspectorate], Paris, May 2007, p. 5.

126 *Décret* No. 2005-859 *relatif à l'aide médicale d'Etat* and *décret* No. 2005-860 *relatif aux modalités d'admission des demandes d'AME* of 28 July 2005, *Journal Officiel* No. 175 of 29 July 2005, pp. 12353–12354.

127 A report on the AME acknowledges that AME applicants are often unable to submit all the required documentary evidence; Gissler *et al.*, *op.cit.* (note 125), p. 33.

128 GISTI, Groupe Protection Sociale, 'L'accès aux soins des étrangers: les débats et les évolutions du droit' [Foreigners' access to health care : law debates and developments], *Hommes et Migration*, No. 1225, May-June 2000, pp. 13–22.

129 The *ticket modérateur* is a key feature of France's public health insurance. It corresponds to the fraction of the cost of health care that is not reimbursed by the public health insurance and is therefore borne by the insured patient. The amount of the *ticket modérateur* varies with patients' resources.

130 *Loi de finances rectificative pour 2002*, No. 2002-1576 of 30 December 2002, Article 30-1, *Journal Officiel* of 31 December 2002, p. 22070. Pregnant women, children and people suffering of serious illnesses are not required to pay the *ticket modérateur*; *idem*.

131 Condemnation of the reform emanated from many corners, including members of the medical profession, migrants support organisations, trade unions and academics. See Bissuel, B., 'Le gouvernement met fin à la gratuité des soins pour les sans-papiers' [The government puts an end to free health care for undocumented migrants], *Le Monde*, 4 March 2003, p. 11.

132 *Idem*.

133 Da Lomba, *loc.cit.* (note 52), p. 371.

134 *Loi* of 15 July 1893, *Journal Officiel de la République Française*, 18 July 1893, p. 3681.

free of charge.[135] Secondly, the *Loi de finances pour 2003* tightened the conditions for eligibility and applicants are now required to supply evidence of their continuous residence in France for a minimum period of three months, save in emergency cases.[136] The three-month residence requirement, however, had to be lifted in respect of minors following decisions of the *Conseil d'État*[137] and the European Committee of Social Rights.[138] In its follow up resolution,[139] the Committee of Ministers of the Council of Europe took note of the adoption of the Circular on the defrayal of costs of urgent care delivered to foreigners illegally resident in France and non-beneficiaries of the AME.[140] The Circular expressly acknowledges the particular vulnerability of children and adolescents and specifies that the term urgent care extends to any health care provided to minors who are not eligible for the AME.[141] Admission to the AME is for one year in the first instance and may be renewed.[142]

135 The introduction of the *ticket modérateur* provided for in the *Loi de finances rectificative pour 2002* necessitates the adoption of a *décret* by the government; *supra* note 130.

136 *Loi de finances pour 2003*, No. 2002-1575 of 30 December 2002, *Journal Officiel* of 31 December 2002, p. 22025, Article 97(1). The new residence requirement was incorporated in Article 251-1 of the *Code de l'action sociale et des familles*. The number of AME beneficiaries for 2004 fell from 170,000 in December 2003 to 145,000 in December 2004; Gissler *et al., op.cit.* (note 125), p. 5. The number of users rose again in 2005 (180,000) and 2006 (190,000); *ibidem*, p. 6. This increase was attributed to the introduction of speedier asylum procedures which gave rise to an increase in the numbers of failed asylum seekers who remained in France, many of whom became eligible for the AME; *idem*. The authors of the report on the AME, however, acknowledged that it was not possible to precisely measure the impact of the AME reforms on the number of AME beneficiaries; *idem*.

137 *Conseil d'État*, 1ère et 6ème sous-sections réunies, 7 June 2006, www.comede.org/UserFiles/File/Textes_reglementaires/Arret_CE_AME_Mineurs_7_juin_2006.pdf.

138 The decision of the *Conseil d'État* is congruent with the decision of the European Committee of Social Rights in *International Federation of Human Rights Leagues (FIDH)* vs *France, supra* note 103. This decision is analysed in section 5.

139 ResChS(2005)6 on Collective complaint No. 14/2003 by the International Federation of Human Rights Leagues (FIDH) against France.

140 Circular DHOS/DSS/DGAS, No. 2005-141 of 16 March 2005 *relative à la prise en charge des soins urgents délivrés à des étrangers résidant en France de manière irrégulière et non bénéficiaires de l'aide médicale de l'Etat (art. L. 254-1 du code de l'action sociale et des familles, issu de l'art. 97 de la loi de finances rectificative pour 2003 du 30 décembre 2003)* [Circular DHOS/DSS/DGAS, No. 2005-141 of 16 March 2005 on the implementation of urgent care delivered to foreigners resident in France in an illegal manner and non beneficiaries of State Medical Assistance (Art. L. 254-1 of the Social Action and Families Code, implementing Art. 97 of the Amending Finances Statute for 2003 of 30 December 2003)]. The health care costs incurred by these migrants are borne by the State; *ibidem*, para. 1.

141 *Ibidem*, para. II-1. The concept of urgent care also covers pre- and post-natal care provided under Article L. 2122-1 to L.2122-5 of the *Code de la santé publique* as well as abortions carried out under Article L.2212-1 of the *Code de la santé publique*. Access to natal care is in line with France's obligations under Article 12 of the ICESCR (General Comment No. 14, *supra* note 7, para. 44(a)).

142 Article 252-3 *Code de l'action sociale et des familles*.

6.2. IRREGULAR MIGRANTS' ACCESS TO HEALTH CARE IN THE UK

Eligibility for free health care on the National Health System (NHS) is conditional on whether a person is 'ordinarily resident' in the UK.[143] The test for ordinary residence was set out in *R.* vs *Barnet LBC Ex p. Shah (Nilish)*.[144] Here, Lord Scarman observed that 'ordinarily residence' was not a term of art in English law and that it should therefore be construed in its ordinary English meaning.[145] He took the view 'that "ordinarily resident" refer[red] to a man's abode in a particular place or country which he ha[d] adopted voluntarily and for settled purposes as part of the regular order of his life for the time being, whether of short or long duration.'[146] However, whilst Lord Scarman did not have irregular migrants in mind,[147] he did identify the lawfulness of residence as an important exception to the 'ordinarily resident' test. He emphasised that

> [i]f a man's presence in a particular place or country is unlawful, e.g. in breach of the immigration laws, he cannot rely on his unlawful residence as constituting ordinary residence (...) There is, indeed, express provision in the Act of 1971, section 33(2)[[148]]. But even without this guidance I would conclude that it is wrong in principle that *a man could rely on his own unlawful act to secure an advantage which could not have been obtained if he had acted lawfully.*[149]

It follows from Lord Scarman's analysis that irregular migrants may not be considered ordinarily resident in the UK because of their immigration status. The relevance of the government's immigration power to the treatment of migrants in the social sphere is therefore upheld. Subsequently, a 1999 Health Service Circular specified that, to be considered ordinarily resident, '[a] person must have an identifiable purpose for his or her residence and that purpose must have a sufficient degree of continuity to be properly described as settled. It is unlikely that anyone coming to live in the UK, intending to stay for less than six months, will fulfil these criteria.'[150] Those falling

---

143 Section 175 of the NHS Act empowers the Secretary of State for Health to charge any patient who is not ordinarily resident in the UK; NHS Act 2006, c. 41, previously Section 121 of the 1977 National Health Service, c. 49.

144 House of Lords, *R.* vs *Barnet LBC Ex p. Shah (Nilish)*, 16 December 1982, [1983] 2 A.C. 309.

145 *Ibidem*, 343 G-H.

146 *Idem*.

147 In *R.* vs *Barnet LBC Ex p. Shah (Nilish)*, *idem*, the House of Lords had to consider whether overseas students were to be considered 'ordinarily resident' for the purpose of the 1962 and 1980 Education Acts.

148 Section 33(2) of the Immigration Act 1977 (c. 77) reads that 'except as otherwise provided in this Act, a person is not to be treated for the purposes of any provision of this Act as ordinarily resident in the UK (...) when he is there in breach of the immigration laws.'

149 *Supra* note 144, 343G to 344B (emphasis added).

150 HSC 1999/018, 1 February 1999, Overseas Visitors' Eligibility to Receive Free Primary Care, para. 3. This circular is now obsolete, but it still provides guidance. The Department of Health planned

outside the scope of this definition are described as 'overseas visitors'.[151] The latter have limited access to free health care on the NHS. This begs the question whether irregular migrants can have access to health care which is free at the point of delivery as overseas visitors. The answer to this question, however, depends on whether irregular migrants seek to access NHS hospital services or NHS primary medical services.

In principle, overseas visitors are liable to pay for NHS hospital treatment. NHS hospitals are under the obligation to establish whether patients are overseas visitors; if this is the case, they are required to make and recover charges for any treatment they may provide.[152] Some services, however, are always exempted from charges irrespective of the patient's health care status. These are treatment for serious communicable diseases,[153] treatment in Accident and Emergency departments[154] and compulsory psychiatric treatment.[155] As far as HIV is concerned, only the initial diagnostic test and associated counselling are free.[156] The Department of Health recommends a strict interpretation of the concept of 'emergency' and 'immediately required treatment', confining the provision of free treatment to 'essential treatment which cannot be reasonably delayed until the patient returns to [his or her] home

---

to issue new guidance after consultation in the course of 2008, but none had been given at the time this article was written.

151 Regulation 1(2) of the National Health Service (Charges to Overseas Visitors) Regulations 1989, SI 1989, No. 306.

152 *Ibidem*, Regulation 2. The Regulations apply in England and Wales. See also Article 42 of the Health and Personal Social Services (Northern Ireland) Order 1972, No. 1265 (N.I. 14); and Regulation 2 of the National Health Service (Charges to Overseas Visitors) (Scotland) Regulations 1989, SI 1989, No. 364 (S.40).

153 Regulation 3(c) and (d) of the National Health Service (Charges to Overseas Visitors) Regulations 1989, *supra* note 151. Serious communicable diseases are exempted from charges on public health grounds and include sexually transmitted infections; Regulation 4(5)(d) of the Provision of Health Services to Persons Ordinarily Resident Regulations (Northern Ireland) 2005, Statutory Rule 2005 No. 551; and Regulation 3(c) and (d) of the National Health Service (Charges to Overseas Visitors) (Scotland) Regulations 1989, *supra* note 152.

154 Regulation 3(a) of the National Health Service (Charges to Overseas Visitors) Regulations 1989, *supra* note 151; Regulation 4(5)(a) of the Provision of Health Services to Persons Ordinarily Resident Regulations (Northern Ireland) 2005, *supra* note 153; and Regulation 3(a) of the National Health Service (Charges to Overseas Visitors) (Scotland) Regulations 1989, *supra* note 152.

155 Regulation 3(e) and (f) of the National Health Service (Charges to Overseas Visitors) Regulations 1989, *supra* note 151; Regulation 4(5)(f) and (g) of the Provision of Health Services to Persons Ordinarily Resident Regulations (Northern Ireland) 2005, *supra* note 153; and Regulation 3(e) and (f) of the National Health Service (Charges to Overseas Visitors) (Scotland) Regulations 1989, *supra* note 152.

156 Regulation 3(d) of the National Health Service (Charges to Overseas Visitors) Regulations 1989, *supra* note 151; Regulation 4(5)(e) of the Provision of Health Services to Persons Ordinarily Resident Regulations (Northern Ireland) 2005, *supra* note 153; and Regulation 3(d) of the National Health Service (Charges to Overseas Visitors) (Scotland) Regulations 1989, *supra* note 152. On the issue relating to charges for overseas visitors for HIV/AIDS treatment, see Select Committee on Health, Third Report, Session- 2004–05, www.publications.parliament.uk/pa/cm200405/cmselect/cmhealth/252/25202.htm.

country'.[157] Moreover, treatment ceases to be free if the overseas visitor is admitted to an inpatient ward or referred to an outpatient service.[158] Certain categories of overseas visitors are exempt from charges.[159] Until 2004, any person who had spent the previous 12 months in the UK, whether *legally or illegally*, had access to free NHS hospital treatment.[160] Thus, provided that they had resided in the UK for no less than one year, irregular migrants could have access to free NHS hospital treatment. The 12-month residency rule, however, was qualified by the 2004 Amendment Regulations that made the exemption from charges conditional on lawful residence in the UK.[161] This in effect introduced charges for irregular migrants save in respect of exempted NHS hospital services.

General practitioners have a duty to provide treatment which they consider to be immediately required owing to an accident or any other emergency free of charge, irrespective of the person's nationality or residency status.[162] Hence, overseas visitors, who can include irregular migrants, can receive urgent treatment which is free at the point of delivery on the same terms as ordinary residents. The current legislation stresses that '[i]t is, of course, a matter for the GP's professional judgement to determine whether treatment is immediately required in each individual case.'[163] According to the British Medical Association, immediately necessary treatment is likely to include 'treatment that is required to treat not only new conditions but also pre-existing conditions that have become exacerbated during the period of a person's stay in the UK, as well as prescriptions for medication without which the patient's

---

157 HSC 1999/018, *supra* note 150, para. 6.

158 Regulation 3(a) of the National Health Service (Charges to Overseas Visitors) Regulations 1989, *supra* note 151; Regulation 4(5)(a) of the Provision of Health Services to Persons Ordinarily Resident Regulations (Northern Ireland) 2005, *supra* note 153; and Regulation 3(a) of the National Health Service (Charges to Overseas Visitors) (Scotland) Regulations 1989, *supra* note 152.

159 These include refugees and asylum seekers whose applications have not yet been determined. See Regulations 4, 5 and 6 of the National Health Service (Charges to Overseas Visitors) Regulations 1989, *supra* note 151; Regulations 3, 5, 6 and 7 of the Provision of Health Services to Persons Ordinarily Resident Regulations (Northern Ireland) 2005, *supra* note 153; and Regulations 4, 5 and 6 of the National Health Service (Charges to Overseas Visitors) (Scotland) Regulations 1989, *supra* note 152.

160 Regulation 4(b) of the National Health Service (Charges to Overseas Visitors) Regulations 1989, *supra* note 151; and Regulation 4(b) of the National Health Service (Charges to Overseas Visitors) (Scotland) Regulations 1989, *supra* note 152.

161 Regulation 4(1)(d) of the National Health Service (Charges to Overseas Visitors) (Amendment) Regulations 2004, SI 2004, No. 614. See also Regulation 3(b)(i) of the National Health Service (Charges to Overseas Visitors) (Scotland) Amendment Regulations 2004, No. 369; Regulation 3(1)(d) of the National Health Service (Charges to Overseas Visitors) (Amendment) (Wales) Regulations 2004, No. 1433 (W. 146); and Regulation 3(c) of the Provision of Health Services to Persons Ordinarily Resident Regulations (Northern Ireland) 2005, *supra* note 153.

162 HSC 1999/018, *supra* note 150, para. 6.

163 *Ibidem*, para. 8.

symptoms may become exacerbated.'[164] The Department of Health, however, is rather prescriptive with respect to what amounts to 'emergency' and 'immediately required treatment'. It recommends that these terms be interpreted 'to mean essential treatment which cannot be reasonably delayed until the patient returns to their home country'[165] and refers to 'immediately necessary treatment for a period of up to 14 days.'[166] In respect of non-emergency treatment, general practitioners have discretion to offer overseas visitors either free treatment on the NHS or on a paying basis as private patients.[167] Private treatment is particularly encouraged when it appears that patients have come to the UK specifically to seek treatment there.[168] Irregular migrants' access to primary health care on the NHS may be hampered by their inability to meet registration requirements. Indeed, GP practices are increasingly asking for proof of identity as a condition for registration with a general practitioner.[169] Moreover, as with proof of address, surgeries are not always flexible with the type of proof that may be submitted.[170]

As the law currently stands, irregular migrants have access to free primary medical services, although in practice access may be confined to emergencies. In May 2004, however, the Department of Health launched a consultation on the exclusion of overseas visitors from free NHS primary medical services,[171] though action has yet to be taken. The Minister of State for Health stressed that the proposals aimed to 'ensure that the NHS [was] first and foremost for the benefit of residents of this country [the UK].'[172] He went on to state that, whilst overseas visitors would continue to receive emergency or immediately necessary treatment, they would no longer be eligible for free NHS primary medical services.[173] The proposals stipulate that '[w]e [the Government] wish to see closer links established between free use of the NHS and UK citizenship or residency.'[174] They further emphasise that 'the NHS is a national institution and not an *international* one'.[175] Because they strengthen the relevance of legal status to access to health care, these proposals risk exacerbating the tension that exists between a status-based approach to access to health care, which

164 General Practitioners Committee (GPC), *Overseas Visitors – Who Is Eligible for NHS Treatment? Guidance for GPS*, BMA, London, April 2006.

165 HSC 1999/018, *supra* note 150, para. 6.

166 *Idem*.

167 *Ibidem*, paras 13–15.

168 *Ibidem*, para. 15.

169 House of Lords and House of Commons, Joint Committee on Human Rights, *supra* note 78, para. 46, point 14.

170 *Idem*.

171 Department of Health, *Proposals to Exclude Overseas Visitors from Eligibility to Free NHS Primary Medical Services*, May 2004, www.dh.gov.uk/en/Consultations/Closedconsultations/DH_4087618.

172 *Ibidem*, Foreword.

173 *Idem*.

174 *Idem*.

175 *Idem* (emphasis added).

is a manifestation of the government's immigration power, and the right to health care attached to the person. The Joint Council for the Welfare of Immigrants (JCWI) expressed concern that the proposals would affect particularly vulnerable groups, namely irregular migrants and failed asylum seekers.[176]

6.3. IRREGULAR MIGRANTS' ACCESS TO HEALTH CARE IN CANADA

Canada's health care system is publicly funded and is best described as an interlocking set of ten provincial and three territorial health care systems.[177] Each provincial and territorial health insurance plan covers medically necessary hospital and doctor services, which are provided free of charge.[178]

Canada's health care system is primarily concerned with the health of Canadian residents.[179] Resident status is therefore central to admission to provincial and territorial health care systems and the definition of the term resident is critical to eligibility. The residence criterion is laid down in the Canada Health Act and is reiterated in provincial and territorial health care legislation. The Canada Health Act defines an insured person for the purpose of eligibility for registration with provincial health care systems as a resident of the province concerned.[180] The Act proceeds to define a resident as 'a person *lawfully* entitled to be or remain in Canada who makes his home and is ordinarily present in the province, but does not include a tourist, a transient or a visitor to the province.'[181]

The term resident must be further defined by reference to the Immigration and Refugee Protection Act that distinguishes between permanent residents[182] and Canadian citizens, on the one hand, and foreign nationals, on the other hand. The Act defines a foreign national as 'a person who is not a Canadian citizen or a permanent resident...'[183] Persons who have acquired permanent resident status in one

---

176 JCWI, *Response to the Consultation Paper on Proposals to Exclude Overseas Visitors from Eligibility to Free NHS Primary Medical Services (Issued by the Department of Health May 2004)*, August 2004, www.medsin.org/downloads/page_attachments/0000/1916/JCWI.pdf.

177 These provincial and territorial health care systems are: Alberta Health, British Columbia (BC) Health, Manitoba Health, New Brunswick Health, Newfoundland Health Care, Northwest Territories (NWT) Health Care, Nova Scotia Health, Nunavut Health, Ontario Health, Prince Edward island (PEI) Health Care, Quebec Health Care, Saskatchewan Health, and Yukon Health Care.

178 Three provinces - British Columbia, Ontario and Alberta - do charge health care premiums, but non-payment of a premium does not limit access to medically necessary services.

179 Canada Health Act (R.S., 1985, c. C-6), section 3.

180 *Ibidem*, section 2.

181 *Idem* (emphasis added).

182 The Immigration and Refugee Protection Act defines a permanent resident as 'a person who has acquired permanent resident status...'; Immigration and Refugee Protection Act 2001, c. 27, section 2(1).

183 *Idem*. The definition includes stateless persons.

of the provinces or territories qualify for medical coverage under its health insurance plan.[184] Foreign nationals whose ordinary place of residence is outside Canada may also be eligible for registration with provincial and territorial health insurance plans provided that they reside there lawfully,[185] thereby automatically excluding irregular migrants. Legislation in Quebec emphatically states that 'persons who may engage or continue in employment without an employment authorization' shall not be considered temporary residents.[186]

Irregular migrants, because they do not lawfully reside in Canada, cannot register with provincial or territorial medical insurance plans and are therefore liable to pay for *all* medical services. Canadian law takes a particularly harsh stance in that it does not provide for irregular migrants' access to emergency treatment free of charge.[187] In practice, however, it is unlikely that they will be refused emergency care.[188] It remains the case that irregular migrants' access to health care is at best haphazard. At worst, access may be denied unless they can pay for medical services. Irregular migrants' access to health care essentially depends on health care providers' willingness and scope to 'bend' the rules and provide treatment free of charge to non-insured persons. In recent years, a number of factors such as greater scrutiny over

184 Section 3(1) of the Alberta Health Care Insurance Act, [R.S.B.C. 1996] chapter 286; Section 2(a) of the New Brunswick Regulation 84–20 under the Medical Services Payment Act (O.C. 84–64); Section 1 of the Medicare protection Act, [RSBC 1996] 1996 chapter 286 (British Columbia); Section 3(a) of the Medical Care Insurance Beneficiaries and Inquiries Regulations under the Medical Insurance Act (O.C. 96–132) (Newfoundland); Section 1 and 3(1) of the Medical Care Act R.S.N.W.T. 1988, C.M-8 (Northwest Territories); Section 2(1) of the Health Services and Insurance Act, Chapter 197 of the Revised Statutes, 1989 amended 1992, c.20, ss. 1–17, 2002, c.5/ ss. 22–26, 2004, c.4, s. 115 and Section 2(1) of the M.S.I., Regulations made under Section 17 of the Health Services and Insurance Act R.S.N.S. 1989, c. 197 O.I.C. 69–276, N.S. Reg. 41/69 as amended up to O.I.C. 2001–327 (5 July 2001), N.S. Reg. 87/2001 (Nova Scotia); Sections 1 and 3(1) of the Consolidation of Medical Care Act, R.S.N.W.T. 1988, c. M-8 as duplicated by Section 29 of the Nunavut Act, s.c. 1993, c. 28; Section 1.1(1) and (2) of the R.R.O. 1990, Regulations 552 of Ontario's Health Insurance Act; Section 8(1) of the Health Services payment Act Regulations Chapter H-2 (Prince Edward Island); Sections 1(1) and 2 of the Regulation respecting eligibility and registration of persons in respect of *the Régie de l'assurance maladie du Québec*, c. A-29, r.0.01; Section 12(1) of the Saskatchewan Medical Care Insurance Act Chapter S-29; Section 4(1) of the Yukon Health Care Insurance Plan Regulations, Y.C.O. 1971/275; and Sections 2(1) and 33 of the Health Services Insurance Act, C.C.S.M. c. H35 (Manitoba).

185 These include foreign nationals who are students or are in lawful employment for more than six months. In respect of the former category of foreign nationals, see, for example, section 3(2) of the Regulation respecting eligibility and registration of persons in respect of the *Régie de l'assurance maladie du Québec*, c. A-29, r.0.01. In respect of the latter category, see, for instance, *ibidem*, section 3(1).

186 *Ibidem*, section 3(1).

187 This is the case in all Canadian provinces and territories.

188 Munoz, M., 'Les soins de santé pour les réfugiés et les sans-papiers: des enjeux médicaux et légaux aux questions morales' [Health care for refugees and undocumented migrants: from medical and legal challenges to moral issues], CDIM Chaire de Recherche du Canada en Droit International des Migrations, *table ronde* [Round table], 2 March 2006, http://cdim.cerium.ca/Les-soins-de-sante-pour-les.

health care expenditure, the growing problematisation of irregular migration and the criminalisation of irregular migrants have made circumventing the rules more difficult.[189] Both federal and provincial governments consider that the provision of free treatment to non-insured patients undermines attempts to efficiently allocate limited resources, at the expense of insured persons' health care.[190] Furthermore, like other host State governments, Canada regards free health care for irregular migrants as a major pull factor that frustrates the 'fight' against irregular migration.

6.4. ANALYSIS

This comparative study shows that France, the UK and Canada frame the issue of access to health care in terms of membership rights. It is argued that this approach has detrimental consequences for both members and non-members. Moreover, it is contended that the characterisation of health care as a membership right as opposed to a basic human right engages these States' international obligations.

Restrictions placed on irregular migrants' access to health care in the jurisdictions under consideration seek to protect members' interests, namely citizens and regular resident migrants. Irregular migrants' exclusion from national health care systems rests on the premise that unlawful residence necessarily implies a lack of contributions to and duties toward the national community.[191] The fact that health care resources are limited further antagonises members and non-members' interests.

> In a world of scarce resources, budgetary constraints and ever increasing demand, the value of asserting a right to health care has become apparent to those who seek to shield existing services from cutbacks and to extend access to medical care to disadvantaged groups in society.[192]

The depiction of irregular migrants as an 'undeserving' group who has a propensity to abuse health care services and place a heavy burden on health care systems makes this task even more challenging.[193] Yet the rather scant data on irregular migrants' use of health care services suggest that usage is low amongst this population and that they tend essentially to resort to these services in cases of emergency.[194] The

189 Crépeau, F., comments made during the round table, *idem*. See also Rousseau, C., *idem*.

190 Crépeau, *supra* note 189.

191 See, for example, Gissler *et al.*, *op.cit.* (note 125), pp. 32–33.

192 Giesen, D., 'A right to health care? A comparative perspective', *Health Matrix*, Vol. 4, No. 2, 1994, pp. 277–295, at p. 277.

193 Rousseau, *supra* note 189; and Lopez, *loc.cit.* (note 49), p. 654.

194 Observatoire Européen de l'Accès aux Soins de Médecins du Monde [Médicins du Monde's European observatory for access to health care], *Enquête Européenne sur l'Accès aux Soins des Personnes en Situation Irrégulière* [European Survey on Undocumented Migrants' Access to Health Care], September 2007, www.mdm-international.org/spip.php?article112. Lamara underscores the lack of statistical data on irregular migrants' health status, access to health care and living conditions;

reasons for this are many. Most irregular migrants have little or no knowledge of the rights – if any – they may have with regard to access to free health care[195] and health care personnel may not be better informed.[196] Access to health care is further hampered by convoluted procedures[197] and language barriers.[198] Another impediment lies in irregular migrants' anxiety that contact with official authorities and structures, including health care services, might bring their presence to the attention of the immigration authorities.[199] The 'fear of being caught' that comes with clandestine living is a Damoclean sword that weighs heavily on every aspect of irregular migrants' life. This concern may have severe and far-reaching consequences for irregular migrants and their families' health and well-being. Studies in France show that irregular migrants are reluctant to divulge their address as required under the AME scheme for fear that their presence might be detected.[200] In Canada, there have been reports of teenagers' refusals to consult a doctor for fear that their parents' presence may be reported to the authorities.[201] Significantly, there have been attempts to establish administrative linkages between immigration enforcement authorities and health care personnel with a view to turning the latter into immigration control auxiliaries.[202] Such linkages, it is argued, go against the States' obligations under Article 12 of the ICESCR. They interfere with the realisation and the enjoyment of the right to health care. We have already seen that irregular migrants are often reluctant to seek medical care by fear that their presence will come to the attention of the

Lamara, F., 'Migration et santé publique dans l'Union Européenne: une mise en chantier qui se fait attendre' [Migration and public health in the European Union: a project still to be developed], in: Chauvin, P. and Parizot, I. (eds), *Santé et Recours aux Soins des Populations Vulnérables* [Vulnerable populations' health and access to health care], Editions Inserm, Paris, 2005, pp. 305–321. See also Munoz, *op.cit.* (note 188).

195 Munoz, *op.cit.* (note 188).

196 Observatoire Européen de l'Accès aux Soins de Médecins du Monde, *op.cit.* (note 194), p. 6 and pp. 31–34; JCWI, *op.cit.* (note 176); Da Lomba, *loc.cit.* (note 52), p. 376; and Lopez, *loc.cit.* (note 49), p. 642.

197 See, for instance, Observatoire Européen de l'Accès aux Soins de Médecins du Monde, *op.cit.* (note 194), p. 34.

198 *Ibidem*, p. 6; and House of Lords and House of Commons, Joint Committee on Human Rights, *supra* note 78, para. 46, point 16. Munoz underscores the lack of resources of interpretation services in Quebec; Munoz, *loc.cit.* (note 188).

199 MacPherson, D.W. and Gushulak, B.D., 'Irregular Migration and Health', *Global Commission on International Migration (GCIM), Global Migration Perspectives*, No. 7, October 2004, p. 8, www.gcim.org/gmp/Global%20Migration%20Perspectives%20No%207.pdf.

200 Gissler *et al., op.cit.* (note 125), p. 24. Irregular migrants' reluctance to divulge their address is compounded by the fact that French law makes it an offence to assist irregular sojourn (Article L. 622.1 *Code de l'entrée et du séjour des étrangers et du droit d'asile*).

201 Rousseau, *supra* note 189. For the same reason, migrants are often reluctant to report cases of domestic violence and other forms of abuse; *idem*.

202 See, for instance, Prieur, C., 'Les médecins dénoncent des pressions sur l'accueil des étrangers malades' [Doctors denounce pressures relating to the reception conditions of foreigners who are ill], *Le Monde*, 24 November 2007; and Crépeau, *supra* note 189. See also Carens, *loc.cit.* (note 56), p. 168.

authorities. For the same reason, they may be unwilling 'to pursue legal protections and remedies to which they are entitled'.[203] Carens advocates the establishment of a 'firewall' with a view to ensuring that immigration law enforcement does not hinder human rights protection.[204] He posits that the proposed firewall should rest on the legal principle that 'no information gathered by those responsible for protecting and realizing basic human rights can be used for immigration enforcement purposes'.[205]

Irregular migrants' poor access to health care contributes to making them a particularly vulnerable group. Limited and haphazard access to health care has adverse health outcomes and may cause a deterioration of living conditions.[206] Studies indicate that it is not unusual for irregular migrants' health status to decline subsequent to their arrival in host States.[207] The absence of effective access to health care means that illnesses are left undiagnosed and thus untreated, that health care is sought at a late stage, and that treatment is likely to be less efficient.[208] Inadequate access to health care is also highly detrimental to irregular migrants who suffer from chronic illnesses or diseases that require long term treatment and follow up.[209] Poor access to health care may also detrimentally impact on irregular migrants' capacity to work and therefore support themselves and their families. Because irregular migrants live outside the protection of the welfare State, employment is vital to their meeting their most basic needs as well as those of their families.

The damaging consequences of poor access to health care are primarily felt by irregular migrants and their families. However, members in the national community may also be affected. Constraints on irregular migrants' access to health care may restrict their ability to contribute. In its response to the UK Government's proposals to exclude overseas visitors from free NHS primary medical services, the JCWI observed that

> whether migrant workers are documented or not, the functioning of the UK's dynamic and flexible economy depends on their participation across a range of sectors (...). Proposals which seek to limit undocumented migrants' access to primary health care services could limit their fitness to participate in the workforce and will strike at UK businesses and the flexible economy.[210]

203 Carens, *loc.cit.* (note 56), p. 167.

204 *Ibidem*, pp. 167–168.

205 *Ibidem*, p. 167.

206 On the linkage between health and socio-economic circumstances, see, for instance, Lebas, J. and Chauvin, P., *Précarité et Santé* [Deprivation and health], Flammarion, Paris, 1998; and Wilkinson, R.G., *Unhealthy Societies: The Afflictions of Inequalities*, Routledge, London, 1996.

207 See Brixi, O., 'Santé et migration' [Health and migration], in: Lebas and Chauvin, *op.cit.* (note 206), p. 99; and MacPherson and Gushulak, *loc.cit.* (note 199), pp. 12–13.

208 *Idem*; and JCWI, *op.cit.* (note 176), para. 3.5.

209 Da Lomba, *loc.cit.* (note 52), p. 366 and p. 375; and JCWI, *op.cit.* (note 176), Introduction, p. 4 and para. 3.5.

210 JCWI, *op.cit.* (note 176), p. 3.

Moreover, exclusionary policies such as the ones developed in France, the UK and Canada pose a threat to public health and risk placing an additional, yet avoidable, burden on health care resources. Restrictions on irregular migrants' access to health care are likely to leave people with contagious diseases untreated, thereby jeopardising public health.[211] This argument was at the heart of the condemnation of the AME reform. Its opponents contended, *inter alia*, that the tightening of admission requirements would in many cases be tantamount to exclusion and would consequently engage the principle of public health protection.[212] Irregular migrants' exclusion from health care systems rests on the premise that barriers on access to health care provide a means to alleviate the burden that this population is deemed to place on already overstretched health care systems. Yet, as Lopez points out, '[a] weighing and balancing of the harm of contagion and protection of public health and safety with the cost to the state (...) for medical therapy would appear to favor the government paying for the cost of treatment.'[213] The relevance of Lopez's argument is not confined to communicable diseases. Medical practice shows that early treatment and preventive health care for *all* residents is critical to maximising treatment efficiency and avoiding unnecessary costs to health care systems.[214]

Irregular migrants' exclusion from national health care systems purports to protect the national interest by restricting the distribution of welfare resources to members and preserve these systems as national institutions central to the welfare State. Yet we have established that, paradoxically, restrictions on irregular migrants' access to health care carry damaging consequences for members as well as non-members.

211 *Ibidem*, Introduction, p. 3; Lopez, *loc.cit.* (note 49), p. 642. Legomsky stresses the need to include migrants irrespective of their legal status in immunising programmes, especially against life-threatening contagious diseases; *loc.cit.* (note 19), p. 1465. Studies show that the incidence of communicable diseases such as tuberculosis tends to be significantly higher in countries of origin than in host countries in the west. See, for instance, Decludt, B. and Campese, C., 'Les cas de tuberculose déclarés en France en 1998 et 1999' [Tuberculosis cases notified in France in 1998 and 1999], *Bulletin épidémiologique hebdomadaire*, No. 10/2001, 6 March 2001.

212 See FIDH, *Réclamation collective contre la France, Réformes de l'Aide médicale d'Etat (AME) et de la Couverture maladie universelle (CMU) contraires aux articles 13,17, E et G de la Charte Européenne Révisée, Saisine du Comité européen des droits sociaux du Conseil de l'Europe, Annexe 3, Argumentaire du Gisti sur l'inconstitutionnalité de la réforme AME et CMU* [*Collective complaint against France, State medical assistance (AME) and Universal sickness cover (CMU) Reforms contrary to Articles 13, 17, E and G of the Revised European Charter, Referral to the European Committee of Social Rights, Annex 3, GISTI's Submissions relating to the unconstitutionality of the AME and CMU reform*], March 2003, hwww.fidh.org/communiq/2003/fr0503f.pdf. The principle of public health protection was upheld by the *Conseil Constitutionnel*. See, for instance, Decision 90-283 DC of 8 January 1981, para. 15 and Decision 90-287 DC of 16 January 1991, para. 24.

213 Lopez, *loc.cit.* (note 49), p. 659. In lieu of example, Lopez notes that '[t]he cost of testing for Tuberculosis would be minor in comparison with the cost of treatment for one or more individuals regardless of the status of the person tested'; *idem*. Lopez's comments relate to the situation in the United States, but they are relevant to the French, UK and Canadian contexts.

214 Gittler, J., 'Controlling resurgent tuberculosis: public health agencies, public policy and the law', *Journal of Health Politics, Policy and Law*, Vol. 19, No. 1, 1994, pp. 107–147, at pp. 117–121.

Furthermore, it is contended that the constraints placed on irregular migrants' access to health care hamper the realisation of their human right to health care and engage France, the UK and Canada's international human rights obligations, and in particular their obligations under Article 12 of the ICESCR.

As parties to the ICESCR, France, the UK and Canada are legally bound to ensure that irregular migrants present on their territory have access to preventive, curative and palliative health care.[215] This requires full compliance with the core obligations that Article 12 imposes in respect of access to health care,[216] some of which are non-derogable.[217] Accordingly, the realisation of irregular migrants' right to health care must be ensured on a non-discriminatory basis and their access to health care services may not be hindered by resource constraints.[218] Yet this comparative study of irregular migrants' access to health care shows that France, the UK and Canada are failing to fully discharge their obligations under Article 12 of the ICESCR. In all three jurisdictions, the law either constrains or does not make provision for irregular migrants' access to health care on account of their immigration status. Yet Article 12 compels these States to take all the measures necessary to the realisation of the right to health care, including legislative measures.[219] In particular, it is argued that they do not meet their obligations regarding non-discrimination on the basis of legal status and affordability.[220]

France makes provision for irregular migrants' access to health care, albeit through a separate scheme. This in itself does not violate France's obligations under Article12. However, the restrictions on access to health care stemming from the three-month residence requirement and potentially from the contribution requirement may engage its international obligations. Moreover, further breaches of Article 12 may result from the administrative barriers that irregular migrants experience when trying to apply for the AME. We have seen that this procedure is ill-adapted to their circumstances.[221] In the UK, the cases in which irregular migrants may be exempt from NHS hospital treatment charges do not match Article 12 core obligations. For instance, exempted hospital services do not explicitly refer to pre- and post-natal health care. It is contended that the introduction of charges for NHS primary medical care would aggravate the risk of non-compliance with Article 12 of the ICESCR. However, it is in Canada that irregular migrants face the greatest obstacles to the realisation of their

215 General Comment No. 14, *supra* note 7, para. 34.

216 *Ibidem*, para. 43(a) and (e) and para. 44(a), (b) and (c).

217 *Ibidem*, para. 47.

218 *Ibidem*, paras 43(a) and 47.

219 *Ibidem*, para. 33. Article 2(1) of the ICESCR places particular emphasis on the adoption of the legislative measures necessary to the realisation of the rights recognised in the Covenant.

220 *Ibidem*, paras 12(b) and 18.

221 In *International Federation of Human Rights Leagues (FIDH) vs France*, the European Committee of Social Rights observed that the exercise of AME rights by irregular migrants was not without difficulties; *supra* note 103, para. 34.

right to health care. In the absence of legal provisions, their access to health care is largely contingent on health care personnel disregarding the rules. This contravenes Canada's obligations under Article 12. General Comment No. 14 clearly states that violations of Article 12 may occur through acts of omission and that these include 'the failure to take appropriate steps towards the full realization of *everyone's* right to the enjoyment of he highest attainable standard of physical and mental health'.[222]

We have seen that the ICESCR accepts that resource constraints may impede the realisation of social rights. Resource shortages, however, do not absolve States parties from their obligations under Article 12. General Comment No. 14 clearly distinguishes between a State's unwillingness to meet its obligations and a State's inability to do so.[223] Unwillingness always gives rise to violations of Article 12, while 'non-deliberate' shortcomings may only be justified on the basis of resource constraints where State have used all their available resources.[224] Furthermore, some core obligations are non-derogable.[225] This comparative study, however, shows that France, the UK and Canada are unwilling as opposed to unable to fully discharge their obligations under Article 12. The restrictions that these States place on irregular migrants' access to health care primarily seek to affirm their immigration power. Moreover, some of these restrictions are inconsistent with non-derogable core obligations. For these reasons, it is argued that these States' shortcomings amount to violations of Article 12 of the ICESCR.

7. CONCLUSION

The question of irregular migrants' access to health care brings to the fore the tension that exists between the exercise of the government's immigration power and compliance with international human rights law. Barriers on irregular migrants' access to health care in France, the UK and Canada aim to affirm the government's immigration power. These States construe the right to health care as a membership right. This is of little consequence for regular permanent migrants as their immigration status makes them eligible for membership rights. Irregular migrants, however, are located outside the national community on account of their immigration status and are consequently denied membership rights. The characterisation of the right to health care as a human right is therefore critical to this group.

Human rights must be distinguished from membership rights in that they 'belong to human beings as such, and must be respected universally'.[226] Unlike

222 General Comment No. 14, *supra* note 7, para. 49 (emphasis added).

223 *Ibidem*, para. 47.

224 *Idem*.

225 *Idem*.

226 Miller, D., 'Irregular migrants: an alternative perspective', *Ethics & International Relations*, Vol. 22, No. 2, 2008, pp. 193–197, at p. 194.

membership rights, they do not 'come encumbered with corresponding obligations and responsibilities'.[227] Consequently, States' assumption that irregular migrants do not contribute and do not share duties with members cannot justify their being denied basic social human rights. Miller points out that

> [w]hatever burdens we think that irregular migrants can properly suffer as a result of having [breached immigration laws] forfeiting one or more of their human rights is not among them.[228]

International human rights law does not dispute the State's power to control its borders and the national community's right to self-determination. We have seen that, whilst international human rights law predicates rights on the person, it does not require of States that they extend all rights to all persons on an equal basis. States may differentiate on the basis of legal status in the nation-State. Significantly migrant-specific human rights instruments such as the Migrant Workers Convention make immigration status a determinant of the rights migrants may have in host States.[229] Thus, international human rights law does not make immigration status irrelevant to one's treatment in the social sphere. What international human rights law does, however, is to carve out a zone of protected personhood. This zone consists of the basic human rights, including social rights, that must be granted to *all* persons only by virtue of their being human beings. These rights include the right to health care as formulated in Article 12 of the ICESCR.

Yet we have shown that irregular migrants' access to health care in France, the UK and Canada falls short of the standards established by Article 12. It is contended that full compliance with this provision demands that these States instil a human rights element in their status-based approach to access to health care. This, in turn, necessitates a reassessment of the relevance of immigration status to irregular migrants' treatment in the national community and a reinstatement of personhood as a source of rights. Irregular migration is a highly complex phenomenon that 'should be addressed in a comprehensive and balanced manner, considering its causes, manifestations and effects in the countries of origin, transit and destination'.[230] Dehumanising irregular migrants, however, cannot be part of the answer and host states are urged to develop a human rights-based approach to the exercise of their immigration power.

227 *Idem.*

228 *Ibidem*, p. 195.

229 This is also the case of the instruments adopted by the International Labour Organization; these include the Migration for Employment Convention (Revised) 1949 (No. 97), the Migration for Employment Recommendation (Revised) 1949 (No. 86), the Migrant Workers (Supplementary Provisions) Convention 1975 (No. 143) and the Migrant Workers Recommendation 1975 (No. 151).

230 Parliamentary Assembly, Council of Europe, *op.cit.* (note 55), para. 11(iii).

[16]

Migrating to Australia with Disabilities: Non-discrimination and the Convention on the Rights of Persons with Disabilities*

Ben Saul**

This article interrogates how the 'health test' under Australian immigration law adversely impacts upon the human rights of persons with disabilities who seek to migrate to Australia. The article argues that Australia's longstanding health test for migrants may impose unjustifiable indirect discrimination on some migrants or refugees with disabilities, and thus infringe the equal protection obligation under the Convention of the Rights of Persons with Disabilities and the International Covenant on Civil and Political Rights. Health requirements under national migration law, as long as they are carefully crafted, are permissible in principle under international human rights law, to legitimately safeguard scarce medical resources in the community. The current Australian health test, however, is not sufficiently restricted in scope so as to comply with international human rights law. This article demonstrates that the health test is problematic because: (1) its threshold of application is set too low; (2) the quantification of disability costs is flawed; (3) the capacity of a person with disabilities to pay for treatment is not taken into account; (4) the social and economic contributions of a migrant with disabilities (and often his or her family) are not considered; (5) the evidentiary requirements are inadequate; (6) the operation of the test adversely affects the right of family unit; and (7) the test is not consistent with Australia's International refugee law obligations. The operation of the health test results in the routine, arbitrary exclusion of migrants with disabilities from Australia, in a manner not justified by any legitimate public policy concerns. The health test also embodies an outmoded 'medicalised' policy approach to disabilities, in which persons with disabilities are perceived as an economic burden and object of charity, rather than having their inherent worth and human dignity valued and their contributions to social diversity recognised.

Introduction

The adoption of the Convention on the Rights of Persons with Disabilities (CRPD) in 2006 has stimulated governments worldwide to review, with renewed vigour, whether domestic laws on the treatment of persons with disabilities conform to international standards. The purpose of the Convention is stipulated in Art 1 as 'to promote, protect and ensure the full and equal

* This article was originally published in (2010), *Australian Journal of Human Rights*, **16**, pp. 63–104.

** Associate Professor of International Law, Faculty of Law, University of Sydney, and Co-Director of the Sydney Centre for International Law Email: <ben.saul@sydney.edu.au>. Many thanks to the two anonymous referees for their helpful comments and to Ms Naomi Hart for research assistance.

enjoyment of all human rights and fundamental freedoms by all persons with disabilities, and to promote respect for their inherent dignity'.

To some extent, the CRPD particularises general human rights standards which already apply to persons with disabilities and other people alike, including principles of non-discrimination and equal treatment in the International Covenant on Civil and Political Rights (ICCPR) and the International Covenant on Economic, Social and Cultural Rights (ICESCR). The rights in those framework conventions apply to 'all individuals', which necessarily includes persons with disabilities, although the twin covenants (like some of the more specialised treaties, such as the Convention on the Elimination of All Forms of Discrimination Against Women and the International Convention on the Elimination of Racial Discrimination) do not mention 'disability' or contain disability-specific provisions. Over time, the international jurisprudence on the twin covenants has recognised disability as an 'other status' protected against discrimination (UN Committee on Economic, Social and Cultural Rights 1994, para 5), and a few of the more recent specialised and regional conventions specifically address disability (such as the Convention on the Rights of the Child, Art 23; African Charter on Human and Peoples' Rights, Art 18(4); Additional Protocol to the American Convention on Human Rights in the Area of Economic, Social and Cultural Rights, Art 18). Much normative work remained to be completed, however, in relation to strengthening international protection of persons with disabilities.

In this context, The CRPD rearticulates and sharpens the focus of general principles and provides an opportunity for national authorities to more closely review the application of general human rights to persons with disabilities. Yet, the CRPD also incrementally and, in some cases, extensively develops the law beyond the existing general principles. Some areas of the CRPD involve progressive development of the law (Kayess and French 2008, 32-33),[1] particularly as regards collective or social group rights;[2] environmental rights; rights to leisure, tourism and recreation; the transformation of certain negative rights[3] into positive obligations on the state; and the potential justiciability of even certain socio-economic rights in the CRPD.

As for implementation, the CRPD requites countries '[t]o take all appropriate measures, including legislation, to modify or abolish existing laws, regulations, customs and practices that constitute discrimination against persons with disabilities'.[4] In Australia, while federal and state anti-discrimination law has provided substantial protection to persons with disabilities, the process of entering into the CRPD has brought renewed scrutiny. Indicating its formal commitment to disability rights, Australia signed the treaty on the day that it opened for signature (30 March 2007) and soon after ratified it on 17 July 2008. A Joint Standing Committee of Treaties (JSCOT) report of June 2008 had recommended ratification (JSCOT

[1] 'Despite what might be characterised as the "official fiction" that the CRPD does not set down any new human rights, it would seem clear that it has, in fact, modified, transformed and added to traditional human rights concepts in key respects' (Kayess and French 2008, 32-33).

[2] Concerning research and development, awareness raising, social protection and poverty reduction, and international cooperation (Kayess and French 2008, 32-33).

[3] Such as non-interference in opinion and expression, or equality before the law (Kayess and French 2008, 32-33).

[4] While reservations to the Convention are expressly permitted (art 46), those which are contrary to the object and purpose of the Convention are precluded.

2008, ch 2), after considering the government's National Interest Analysis and undertaking a public consultation.

One major area of concern identified during the public consultation was Australia's treatment of migrants with disabilities (JSCOT 2008, 14-17), particularly their exclusion from Australia because of a 'health test'. JSCOT accordingly recommended a review of the *Migration Act 1958* 'to ensure that there is no direct or indirect discrimination against persons with disabilities in contravention of the Convention' (JSCOT 2008, ch 2, Recommendation 2).[5] In response, in 2009 the Minister for Immigration and Citizenship requested that the parliamentary Joint Standing Committee on Migration inquire into the health requirements (Joint Standing Committee on Migration 2009). The inquiry reported in June 2010 and made numerous criticisms of, and recommendations for improving, the health test (Joint Standing Committee on Migration 2010). Submissions to that inquiry by numerous organisations working with persons with disabilities and migrants reflected widespread, long-held and unaddressed concerns about the impact of the 'health test' on migrants and their families.[6] It remains to be seen whether the Australian government will respond favourably to the inquiry's recommendations, when successive Australian governments have habitually ignored the recommendations of parliamentary committees – particularly in election years, when political compassion for migrants typically descends to low ebb.

In 2007-08, of the 600,000 temporary and permanent visa applicants who were subject to the health test, 1,532 were refused visas on health grounds, of which 71 cases involved disabilities, 244 involved a 'health condition', and 442 were refused because a family member failed the health test (Australian Senate 2009). The Australian government maintains that the health requirements are non-discriminatory and comply with its obligations under the CRPD, since thy 'apply equally to all applicants' and 'are also based on legitimate objective and reasonable criteria' (JSCOT 2008, para 2.40; Department of Immigration and Citizenship (DIAC) 2009b, 23-24). (As this article will demonstrate, equal application of law does not necessarily meet concerns about *indirect* discrimination.) In contrast, as recently as 2009, the UN Committee on Economic, Social and Cultural Rights criticised the exemption of migration laws from Australia's anti-discrimination legislation and the resulting 'negative immigration decision based on disability or health conditions', with particularly adverse effects on refugee families (UN Committee on Economic, Social and Cultural Rights 2009, para 16).

---

5 The author discloses that he provided a legal opinion to the National Ethnic Disability Alliance which was provided to the JSCOT inquiry (JSCOT 2008, para 2.39) and to the Joint Standing Committee on Migrations (2010, paras 7.44-7, 48, 7.77).

6 Including the National Ethnic Disability Alliance, Australian Federation of Disability Organisations, Physical Disability Australia, Deafness Forum of Australia, Disability Services Commission (WA), Queensland Nurses' Union, Federation of Ethnic Communities' Councils of Australia, Action on Disability within Ethnic Communities, Immigration Advice and Rights Centre, Vision Australia, Ethnic Disability Advocacy Centre, Multicultural Mental Health Australia, National Association of People Living with HIV/AIDS, Australian Federation of AIDS Organisations, HIV/AIDS Legal Centre, Royal Society for the Blind, Disability Discrimination Legal Service, National Welfare Rights Network, Cabramatta Community Centre, NSW Young Lawyers Human Rights Committee, Migration Institute of Australia, Cerebral Palsy League, Blind Citizens Australia, National Council on Intellectual Disability, NSW Disability Discrimination Law Centre, and Royal Australasian College of Physicians.

This article interrogates how Australian migration law adversely impacts upon the human rights of persons with disabilities who seek to migrate to Australia. The article argues that the current Australian 'health test' for migrants may impose unjustifiable indirect discrimination on some migrants or refugees with disabilities, and thus infringe the equal protection obligation under Art 5 of the CRPD.[7] The Australian 'health test' (under Sch 4 of the *Migration Regulations 1994*) enables the exclusion from Australia of a non-citizen who has a 'disease or condition' which would impose certain burdens or costs on the Australian health system. The health test is then exempted from anti-discrimination protections under the *Disability Discrimination Act 1992* (DDA) by s 52 of that Act.

Health requirements under national migration law, *as long as they are carefully crafted*, are permissible in principle under international human rights law, to legitimately safeguard scarce medical resources in the community. The current Australian health test, however, is not sufficiently narrow (or restricted in scope) so as to comply with the CRPD and general human rights law, and the test may give rise to unjustifiable *indirect* discrimination (a concept explained further below) against some migrants with disabilities. As this article demonstrates, the health test is problematic because: (1) its threshold is set too low; (2) the quantification of disability costs is flawed; (3) the capacity of a person with disabilities to pay for treatment is not taken into account; (4) the social and economic contributions of a migrant with disabilities (and often his or her family) are not considered; (5) the evidentiary requirements are inadequate; (6) the operation of the test adversely affects the right of family unity; and (7) the test is not consistent with Australia's international refugee law obligations.

Consequently, under international human rights law, the health test, does not lawfully balance the interests of preserving scarce health resources against non-discrimination towards the disabled. The restrictive nature of the health test also sits uncomfortably with the movement in the CRPD away from a 'medicalised' model of disability, in which persons with disability have been conventionally perceived as an economic burden and object of charity (UN Enable nd). The more contemporary 'social model' of disability values persons with disabilities in their own right and as vital contributors to social diversity (Kayess and French 2008, 6-8). That movement is scarcely reflected in migration laws, which exclude many persons with disabilities because their care is often presumed to cost too much, in circumstances where the law prevents an accurate and humane assessment of the social and economic costs and benefits of admitting migrants with disabilities.

Migrants with disabilities face a potent risk of double discrimination because of their status as both persons with disabilities and non-nationals. They are particularly vulnerable to adverse treatment by the legal system and may experience special difficulties in accessing remedies and justice, particularly if they are situated overseas or are refugees. As others have noted, 'compassion towards non-citizens ranks very low in the domestic hierarchy of political values, and is trumped by … "national sovereignty"' and notions of social cohesion (Carney and Boucher 2009, 36-57). In such circumstances, strong rights-based protections can provide an essential counter-balance to politically expedient migration policy choices.

---

[7] The focus of enquiry here is the compatibility of Australian migration law with international human rights obligations, rather than under domestic anti-discrimination law concepts of discrimination (in the event that the DDA exemption were to be lifted).

The Migration Act exemption

The health test exemption from domestic anti-discrimination law

Section 52 of the DDA exempts from the anti-discrimination provisions of that Act: (a) the *Migration Act* and all regulations made under it; and (b) anything done by a person in relation to the administration of the *Migration Act*. The scope of the exemption encompasses a wide range of matters arising under the *Migration Act*. Pertinently, the exemption applies to the criteria for visas available (under the Act and Regulations) to non-citizens seeking to enter and remain in Australia, as well as to the administration of those visas by DIAC.[8] But for the exemption, the DDA protects against direct and indirect discrimination on the grounds of a person's disability, as those concepts are defined in the DDA.[9] The term 'disability itself is given a wide meaning under Australian law,[10] although a more contemporary approach would regard the conditions listed as 'impairments', in contrast to the socially constructed 'disability' which often flows from the perception and treatment of those conditions (Kayess and French 2008, 6-7, 21). (This article will use the term 'disability' because that is the term which continues to be used by both the CRPD and the DDA).

According to a Productivity Commission review in 2004, a primary purpose of the DDA exemption is to ensure that the criteria for assessing visa applicants cannot be challenged as

---

[8] The Howard government rejected Recommendation 12.3 of the Productivity Commission Review to limit the migration exemption to provisions dealing with entry and migration visas, and not to exempt administrative processes. Such processes include, for instance, the provision of information and other services (not exempted under other legislation), which might potentially hinder the right of disabled persons 'to utilize relevant processes such as immigration proceedings' under Art 18(1)(b) of the CRPD. Recommendation 12.3 of the Productivity Commission was accepted by the Rudd Labor government and is reflected in amendments to the DDA made in 2009; see *Disability Discrimination and Other Human Rights Amendment Act 2009*.

[9] Section 5 of the DDA defines 'direct disability discrimination' as occurring where 'a person (the *discriminator*) *discriminates* against another person (*the aggrieved person*) on the ground of a disability of the aggrieved person if, because of the disability, the discriminator treats, or proposes to treat, the aggrieved person less favourably than the discriminator would treat a person without the disability in circumstances that are not materially different', including where the discriminator fails to make reasonable adjustments for the aggrieved person, resulting in their less favourable treatment. Indirect disability discrimination is defined by s 6 of the DDA as arising where a person is required to comply with a requirement or condition which the aggrieved person is not able to comply with because of their disability, or where reasonable adjustments are not made, resulting in the person being disadvantaged. The scope of 'direct discrimination' under Australian federal law was considered by the High Court of Australia in *Purvis v New South Wales*, 2003; for a critique of the decision, see Rattigan 2004, 532.

[10] The DDA defines 'disability', in relation to a person, as total or partial loss of the person's bodily or mental functions; total or partial loss of a part of the body; the presence in the body of organisms causing disease or illness; the presence in the body of organisms capable of causing disease or illness; the malfunction, malformation or disfigurement of a part of the person's body; a disorder or malfunction that results in the person learning differently from a person without the disorder or malfunction; or a disorder, illness or disease that affects a person's thought processes, perception of reality, emotions or judgment, or that results in disturbed behaviour.

discriminatory under the DDA (Productivity Commission 2004, 343). Relevantly, the DDA exemption applies to the health requirements for visa applicants under criterion 4005-4007 of Sch 4 of the *Migration Regulations*. Those Regulations exclude an applicant who has a 'disease or condition' which would, during the applicant's proposed stay in Australia, be likely to (at 4005 (c)(i)):

> (A) require health care or community services; or
> (B) meet the medical criteria for the provision or a community service;

and the provision of such health care or community services would be likely to (at 4005(c)(ii)):

> (A) result in a significant cost to the Australian community in the areas of health care and community services; or
> (B) prejudice the access of an Australian citizen or permanent resident to health care or community services:

regardless of whether the health care or community services will actually be used in connection with the applicant. Specified diseases or conditions trigger further health investigation.[11] Certain conditions are specially designated as likely to 'prejudice the access' of Australians to health care.[12]

There is provision for the Minister to waive health requirements where an employer undertakes to meet all costs related to the disease or condition (*Migration Regulations*, Sch 4, 4006A(2)), or where the Minister is satisfied that granting the visa would be unlikely to result in (i) 'undue cost to the Australian community'; or (ii) 'undue prejudice to the access to health care or community services of an Australian citizen or permanent resident' (*Migration Regulations*, Sch 4, 4007(2)).

The health test and its exemption from the DDA are purportedly justified by the Australian authorities by reference to the public policy interests in minimising public health and safety risks to Australia, containing public health expenditure, and maintaining access to health and community services for Australian residents (Productivity Commission 2004, 343-44). As the Federal Court of Australia stated in *Minister for Immigration and Multicultural Affairs v Sligman*, 1999: 'The policy behind the test is clear. It is to limit the entry into Australia for long term residence of people who are likely to be a financial burden on the Australian community' (at [74]).

---

11 Including tuberculosis (current or past); mental illness, including bipolar disorder and depression; blindness; cerebral palsy; Crohn's disease; diabetes (if the applicant is aged 40 years or over); epilepsy; haemophilia; heart disease; hepatitis B and C; intellectual impairment; multiple sclerosis; renal failure; rheumatism; ulcerative colitis; cancer in the last five years; cystic fibrosis; HIV; and organ transplant recipient (Department of Immigration and Citizenship 2009).

12 Including services such as dialysis; organ transplants; blood/plasma products, including coagulation factors and immunoglobulin; fresh blood or blood components, for people with rare blood groups; or knee and hip joint replacements.

Non-discrimination under the CRPD

The CRPD does not confer any right upon a non-citizen with disabilities to enter a foreign country, nor is such a right available to non-citizens generally under international law. There is no human right to enter the country of which a person is not a national (UN Human Rights Committee 1986, para 5). Countries are only required to admit their own nationals, while international refugee and human rights law impose a further limited obligation not to return a person to a place where they face a risk of persecution or torture (1951 Refugee Convention, Art 33(1); 1984 Convention against Torture, Art 3(1); ICCPR, Art 7). During the drafting of the CRPD, even a limited draft proposal to extend Art 18 (on liberty of movement and nationality) to include a right to 'enjoy on an equal basis with others the right to enter and immigrate to a country other than their State or origin' was not accepted, reflecting continuing sensitivities about sovereign power to regulate immigration. Australia's 'Declaration' to the CRPD correctly observes that 'the Convention does not create a right for a person to enter or remain in a country of which he or she is not a national' (Australian Government, Declaration upon Ratifying the CRPD 2008).

Where a country does, however, exercise its discretionary authority to admit non-nationals under its domestic immigration law, such procedures must still comply with human rights law, including provisions relating to health screening and assessment. The CRPD contains no express or implied territorial limitation on its scope of application, such as might operate to withhold protection from migrants located outside Australian territory but seeking to enter it. Rather, relevant human rights protections will necessarily apply to any person subject to the application of an Australian law – that is, within Australia's functional jurisdiction – regardless of their geographic location.

Relevantly, and in the absence of an immigration-specific non-discrimination provision, Art 4(1) of the Convention imposes a general obligation on states parties 'to ensure and promote the full realization of all human rights and fundamental freedoms for all persons with disabilities without discrimination of any kind on the basis of disability'. The Convention defines 'discrimination on the basis of disability' in Art 2 as:

> … any distinction, exclusion or restriction on the basis of disability which has the purpose or effect of impairing or nullifying the recognition, enjoyment or exercise, on an equal basis with others, of all human rights and fundamental freedoms in the political, economic, social, cultural civil or any other field. It includes all forms of discrimination, including denial of reasonable accommodation.[13]

A literal reading of these provisions might suggest that discrimination on the basis of disability only occurs where such discrimination is connected with impairing some other existing human right or freedom. The similarly worded provision in Art 14 of the European Convention on Human Rights has been interpreted as providing protection against discrimination only in relation to the exercise or enjoyment of other human rights enumerated in that treaty (*Belgian Linguistic* case, 1968 at [9]). Since there is no human right to enter a foreign country in the CRPD, such interpretation would imply that Australia's migration exemption is not relevantly

---

[13] Under the DDA, the equivalent Australian law concept is 'reasonable adjustment', defined in s 4(1) following amendment by the *Disability Discrimination and Other Human Rights Legislation Amendment Act*.

connected with the impairment of a human right and thus that the protection of Art 4 is not engaged.

Article 5 of the CRPD, however, relevantly provides further non-discrimination guarantees with are *not* limited by the requirement of a connection to another human right.

> States Parties recognise that all persons are equal before and under the law and are entitled without any discrimination to the equal protection and equal benefit of the law.
>
> States Parties shall prohibit all discrimination on the basis of disability and guarantee to persons with disabilities equal and effective legal protection against discrimination on all grounds.

By analogy with the accepted understanding of Arts 26 and 2 respectively of the ICCPR, the 'equal protection' provision in Art 5 of the CRPD does not merely duplicate the general non-discrimination provision in Art 4 of the same Convention. Rather, Art 5 discretely 'prohibits discrimination in law or practice in any field regulated and protected by public authorities'.[14] For the reasons explained in the next section, that freestanding protection applies to onshore and offshore domestic migration law procedures, including the administration of the health test, notwithstanding the absence of any positive right of non-citizens to enter Australia under international law generally.

The application of the CRPD to non-citizens

Domestic migration law procedures are not quarantined from the CPRD or the general principles of non-discrimination and equal protection under the ICCPR. The CRPD applies to 'all persons with disabilities' pursuant to Art 1 (articulating the purposes of the CRPD) and Art 4 (setting out 'general obligations' under the CRPD). Applying the accepted principles of treaty interpretation (Vienna Convention on the Law of Treaties, Art 31(1)), the ordinary meaning of the phrase 'all persons with disabilities' encompasses the whole category of persons who experience disabilities and is not conditioned by any limiting or qualifying terms (such as reference to nationality, migration or refugee status). In the same manner, rights under the ICCPR generally apply to 'all individuals' (ICCPR, Art 2(1)), meaning that they 'apply to everyone, irrespective of reciprocity, and irrespective of his or her nationality or statelessness' (UN Human Rights Committee 1986, para 1).[15]

Further, the CRPD does not contain any provision equivalent to Art 1(2) of the International Convention on the Elimination of All Forms of Racial Discrimination (CERD), which provides that the CERD 'shall not apply to distinctions, exclusions, restrictions or preferences made by a State Party to this Conventions between citizens and non-citizens.[16] While there was some

---

[14] As in the application of the comparable 'equal protection' clause in the ICCPR (*Brooks v The Netherlands*, 1984, at [12.3]; UN Human Rights Committee 1989, para 12).

[15] Only in exceptional cases are some ICCPR rights reserved for citizens (such as rights of political participation under Art 25, or of admission to one's own country under Art 12) or non-citizens (such as rights concerning expulsion under Art 13). Where rights are so limited, such limitation arises by express words which clearly indicate an intention to depart from the general rule that rights apply to all persons.

[16] In any event the UN CERD Committee has stated that the provision 'must be constructed so as to avoid undermining the basic prohibition of discrimination' and so as not to detract in any way from

debate during the drafting of the CRPD concerning the scope of application of CRPD rights to non-citizens, nothing in the drafting record indicates any general agreement by states to exclude non-citizens with disabilities from CRPD rights. While the CRPD does not expressly exclude the application of CRPD rights to non-citizens with disabilities, many CRPD rights are subject to the general text under international human rights law for the limitation of rights in pursuit of legitimate policy objectives. As shown further below, rights of non-discrimination and equal protection may thus be restricted on grounds of citizenship or immigration status if the criteria for differentiation pursue a legitimate public policy aim and are proportional to achieving the aim (UN Committee on the Elimination of Racial Discrimination 2004, para 4).

Indirect discrimination under the CRPD

Under international human rights law, equal protection and non-discrimination safeguard not only against direct discrimination, but also against indirect discrimination, as is now well established in the jurisprudence of the UN Human Rights Committee in *Althammer v Austria*, 2001, at [10.2]:

> … a violation of article 26 [of the ICCPR] can also result from the discriminatory effect of a rule or measure that is neutral at face value or without intent to discriminate. However, such indirect discrimination can only be said to be based on the grounds enumerated in Article 26 of the Covenant if the detrimental effects of a rule or decision exclusively or disproportionally affect persons having a particular race, colour, sex, language, religion, political or other opinion, national or social origin, property, birth or other status. Furthermore, rules or decisions with such an impact do not amount to discrimination if they are based on objective and reasonable grounds.[17]

By extension of the accepted interpretation of equal protection and non-discrimination under international human rights law, Art 5 of the CRPD must be seen to protect – and was intended to protect – against both direct and indirect discrimination on the ground of disability enumerated in that Convention.

There are a few comparative cases directly on the specific point of discrimination on the basis of disability in migration decisions.[18] The Canadian decision of *Deol v Minister of Citizenship and Immigration*, 2000, provides some guidance. In that case, a visa applicant

obligations in the ICCPR or ICESCR (UN Committee on the Elimination of Racial Discrimination 2004, para.2; 1993, para 3).

17 Likewise under the European Convention on Human Rights, it is recognised that 'where a general policy or measure has disproportionately prejudicial effects on a particular group, it is not excluded that this may be regarded as discriminatory notwithstanding that it is not specifically aimed or directed at that group', and where there is no 'reasonable and objective justification' for it (*Hoogendijk v The Netherlands*, 2005).

18 An argument alleging disability discrimination under British immigration law in a recent case was not successful due to the failure of counsel to fully articulate the relevant arguments and because the facts were not necessarily favourable, but the UK Asylum and Immigration Tribunal indicated that the issues might otherwise have been of general importance (NM (*Disability Discrimination*) *Iraq*, 2008 at [19]). The essential claim was that by precluding third-party support to a visa applicant whose British spouse was disabled and therefore could not support her, the British legislation discriminated in the basis of disability. That case was decided prior to the UK's ratification of the CRPD on 8 June 2009.

was refused admission to Canada due to severe osteoarthritis in both knees, which would have required specialist care and knee replacement surgery. Relevantly, s 19(1) of the former *Canadian Immigration Act 1976* required the refusal of admission to persons 'suffering from any disease, disorder, disability or other health impairment' which, as a result of its 'nature, severity or probable duration', 'would cause or might reasonably be expected to cause excessive demands on health or social services'. It thus resembles Australia's health requirements, although there are differences, as explained further below.

On appeal, the applicant alleged that the statutory health requirements discriminated against him on the basis of disability and were accordingly unconstitutional under s 15 of the Canadian Charter of Rights and Freedoms. Section 15(1) of the Canadian Charter is an equal protection and non-discrimination clause which, for present purposes, is equivalent to the protection in Art 5 of the CRPD.[19] While the Canadian Immigration and Refugee Board (Appeal Division) determined that the applicant's condition did not fall within the definition of 'disability', it also proceeded to find that even if it did constitute a disability, the existence of the disability was not the basis of inadmissibility. Rather, inadmissibility was based on 'the probable excessive demand caused by the condition' (*Deol*, at 8). Such an approach underpins Australia's similar justification of its health test.

Yet, the decision of the Appeal Board – an administrative tribunal rather than a constitutional or human rights court – is far from satisfactory. Its analysis appears to be limited to whether the health requirements *directly* discriminated by overtly excluding applicants on the basis of disability per se. That surface approach did not ask the relevant deeper questions about *indirect* discrimination, in particular whether the health requirements are harder for persons with disabilities to meet and disproportionately affect them – questions which are critical in the Australian context.

Prima facie discrimination by the Australian health requirements

The Australian health requirements are framed in a facially neutral manner, since all visa applicants are subject to them and there is no explicit focus on disability as a basis for excluding persons (in contrast to the direct exclusion of, for instance, people with the disease tuberculosis) (*Migration Regulations*, Sch 4). However, as noted by the Productivity Commission, the health requirements may still potentially operate to differentiate on the basis of disabilities, by giving rise to both direct and indirect discrimination (Productivity Commission 2004, 343).

Direct discrimination may arise where additional medical tests or evidentiary requirements are specifically imposed on persons with disabilities once they have been identified as experiencing disabilities through the health screening process. There may thus be differential treatment (in policy and/or practice) compared with other visa applicants (that is, the relevant similarly situated or analogous class of person subject to regulation). Yet, some other visa applicants without disabilities are also subject to further medical tests, such as those with

[19] Section 15 of the Canadian Charter provides that: 'Every individual is equal before and under the law and has the right to the equal protection and equal benefit of the law without discrimination and, in particular, without discrimination based on race, national or ethnic origin, colour, religion, sex, age or mental or physical disability.

infectious diseases or temporary impairments. On that analysis, there is no differential treatment by the law of persons with disabilities *on account of* their disability, since there is equal treatment of the relevant similarly situated group – visa applicants with significant (and potentially costly) health issues of any kind. Differential treatment is thus seen to be based on the anticipated costs of admitting the person, rather than specifically 'because of' their disability.

Direct discrimination may also arise, however, as a result of the practical operation or administration of a facially neutral law, in circumstances where the law itself does not evidence direct discrimination. Thus, in practice, it is possible that the identification of a disability in an applicant, unlike other health conditions, might automatically trigger further investigation by DIAC, leading to routine exclusion, indicating that disability per se operates as a trigger for direct differential treatment. Empirical analysis of the operation of the health requirements may, for example, reveal a pattern of differential treatment of persons with disabilities by DIAC. Numerous organisations with expertise in the disability sector have suggested that exclusion on account of disability routinely occurs 'as a matter of course' in immigration health screening (Productivity Commission 2004, 345).

More information would, however, be required on departmental practices and the facts of individual cases before firm conclusions could be drawn on this point, since it is difficult to determine in the abstract, without clearer empirical data, whether discrimination results from the operation of the facially neutral health requirements. It could further be argued that discrimination does not arise because there is an individualised focus on the health impacts and circumstances of each individual, rather than any exclusion of a class based on the shared characteristic of disability.

Indirect discrimination may potentially arise where the Act sets standards of health requirements which persons with disabilities do not or cannot meet. Since many disabilities (defined as long-term impairments under Act 1 of the Convention) may require costly health care or community support, it is likely that a significant number of migrants with disabilities would be found to impose a 'significant cost' on the Australian community, and/or 'prejudice the access' of Australians to such services.

The analysis of whether there is prima facie indirect discrimination depends on a number of considerations. Evidently, different types of impairment require different levels of health care, as do different levels within the same category of impairment. It is plainly not impossible for a person with disabilities to satisfy the health test, particularly where the disability does not require expensive medical treatment. Statistically, it is unknown what proportion of all migrants with disabilities are refused on health grounds, and what proportion are admitted. Nor is it known what proportion of migrants without a disability are nonetheless refused on other health grounds, relative to the proportion of persons with disabilities admitted and refused. But it is clear that the health test does not always result in indirect discrimination, given that some persons with disabilities can comply with its requirements. Moreover, a discretionary power to waive the health requirements exists, which DIAC claims is regularly exercised in favour of applicants with disabilities.[20]

[20] The Department of Immigration and Multicultural and Indigenous Affairs (renamed the Department of Immigration and Citizenship in 2007) has previously indicated that the waiver is regularly exercised, including on compassionate grounds for the disabled (Productivity Commission 2004, 346).

That does not rule out the possibility, however, that people with certain types or severity of disability, requiring expensive care, are subject to prima facie indirect discrimination as a result of the requirements of the health test. As noted earlier, numerous Australian organisations working with persons with disabilities report that applicants with certain disabilities are routinely excluded under the health test, as a result of the test stipulating conditions which cannot be met *on account of the nature or severity of their particular disability.* As set out below, the issue then becomes whether differentiation is based on objective and reasonable grounds and is proportionate to the aims pursued.

That the health test may also exclude migrants without disabilities who have other health conditions is not to the point. A rule is discriminatory not only if its operation *exclusively* targets a particular group, but also if it impacts *disproportionately* upon a group, as appears to be the case in relation to applicants with certain kinds or severities of disability. Further, the test for discrimination encompasses not only whether a rule targets all persons with disabilities – a broach church indeed – but also whether people sharing a particular kind of disability are disproportionately targeted. As discussed further below, the power to waive the health requirements is not sufficient to meet the concern that applicants with disabilities may experience indirect discrimination.

Permissible limitations on equal protection under the Convention

Differential treatment alone, as explored above, is not sufficient to constitute unlawful discrimination. The next, critical question is whether there exists any objective and reasonable justification for any (direct or indirect) differential treatment under the health test. The CRPD contains no general 'limitation clause' setting out the scope of, or criteria for, permissible limitations on disability rights as a whole, nor is there any specific limitation clause in relation to the non-discrimination or equal protection provisions. The similarly worded equal protection provision in Art 26 of the ICCPR likewise contains no express limitation clause.

Under international law, however, the UN Human Rights Committee accepts that '[n]ot all differentiation of treatment will constitute discrimination, if the criteria for such differentiation are reasonable and objective and if the aim is to achieve a purpose which is legitimate under the Covenant' (UN Human Rights Committee 1989, para 13; *Broeks,* at [13]). Australia's 'Declaration' to the CRPD correctly identifies and endorses this test when it declares that the migration health test must be 'based on legitimate, objective and reasonable criteria'.[21] The test for limitations necessarily involves a degree of subjectivity and judgment, but they are still *legal* criteria which operate to constrain *political* judgments about the necessity of a particular migration or health policy.

In an early Canadian case, *Anvari v Canada Employment and Immigration Commission,* 1988, the Canadian Human Rights Tribunal considered the exclusion from Canada of a non-

[21] The Declaration does not declare that the current health test is *actually* legitimate, objective and reasonable, contrary to the view of JSCOT ('the Australian Government has made a Declaration asserting that Australia's migration processes are in full compliance with the Convention') (JSCOT 2008, para 2.35). As the Australian Human Rights Commission rightly puts it, the declaration is simply indicating that the health test is lawful *'if and to the extent that* these requirements are based on legitimate, objective and reasonable criteria' (Australian Human Rights Commission 2009, 3 (emphasis added).

citizen, who suffered from the physical disability of scoliosis due to childhood polio, under Canadian immigration legislation which excluded those with (inter alia) a 'disability', and whose 'admission would cause or might reasonably be expected to cause excessive demands on health or social services (*Anvari*). The Tribunal accepted that there was prima facie discrimination against the applicant which was directly caused by his disability, but found that the health and social services needs of Canadian society as a whole provided a bona fide justification for differentiation on the basis of disability under s 14(g) of the *Canadian Human Rights Act 1976*.[22]

Although it is an older case and an administrative tribunal, that decision provides some authority for the proposition that a country may lawfully prioritise its own health needs over those of non-citizens with disabilities seeking to enter or remain.

Such a view accords with the parliament's policy preferences underlying health test legislation – that is, to 'trade off' competing social interests (non-discrimination and public health) in favour of the 'local' community and at the expense of persons with disabilities or other non-citizens facing adverse health issues. Human rights law does not regard non-discrimination as an absolute value which takes precedence over all other social interests, although it does presuppose a careful and rational balancing of interests – which cannot be taken for granted in particular health test legislation.

Reasonable and objective justification for the Australian exemption?

On one hand, it is clearly arguable that the state has a legitimate public policy interest in minimising burdens imposed on public health services and expenditure by non-citizens, not only to protect general revenue but also to preserve access to health services by Australian citizens and permanent residents.[23] There is no global cosmopolitan order of 'open borders'. International law endorses the premise that states are generally free to determine their immigration intakes in accordance with political and economic policy priorities, to conserve resources as far as possible for the benefit of nationals and other residents.

Under the Australian health test, the individualised assessment of applicants, the availability of a (discretionary) waiver, and the taking into account of the applicant's potential means of support (at least from an employer) indicate that the health provisions are also (to some extent) *proportionate* restrictions on equal protection. The test is not applied in an indiscriminate, blanket or inflexible fashion, and less invasive means for achieving the policy objective are (sometimes) taken into account through the waiver process. The Australian government also reports that there is already considerable pressure on disability services in Australia, with

[22] Note that Canadian immigration law no longer explicitly mentions 'disability', but instead provides more general health requirements under s 38(1) of the *Immigration and Refugee Protection Act 2001*: 'A foreign national is inadmissible on health grounds if their health condition: (a) is likely to be a danger to public health; (b) is likely to be a danger to public safety; or (c) might reasonably be expected to cause excessive demand on health or social services.'

[23] Immigration programs generally are already highly selective and differentiate between non-citizens on a variety of bases, including skills, financial assets and language. Requirements concerning health, labour market, social welfare, financial and government policy considerations are 'by nature and design, discriminatory' (though not necessarily on prohibited grounds as such) (Productivity Commission 2004, 348).

29,200 people estimated to have unmet demands for assistance under the Commonwealth/State/Territory Disability Agreement (as of 2005) (DIAC 2009b, 19).

As noted earlier, although human rights law allows a 'trade off' between non-discrimination and other social interests such as public health, in the migration area the balancing of interests is frequently tilted presumptively in favour of the local community and against the foreigner. Preserving scarce public health resources is not an ultimate value which must take pre-eminence in all situations. There is a countervailing public policy interest in ensuring that persons with disabilities are not treated adversely on account of personal characteristics – permanent or debilitating impairments – which are beyond their control. The immutable nature of permanent disabilities, and the debilitating nature of other disabilities, can be what sets disability apart from other grounds of selection in immigration programs (such as skills, finances or language abilities) and over which individuals can ordinarily exercise a greater degree of human agency.

In light of the social model of disability, there is a further countervailing public interest in recognising and valuing the social diversity which comes with disability, including as it manifests in migrant communities. The policy justification for the immigration health test too readily dismisses such interest in its attempt to socially engineer a 'healthy' or 'flawless' migrant intake – one which bears little relation to the diverse health picture of the existing Australian population as a whole.

Further, Australia's migration program already 'cherry picks' the most skilled labour and business people from other countries – including, for instance, from countries where professionals such as doctors and nurses are in short supply – yet refuses to admit the natural diversity of foreign populations, including persons with disabilities. In so doing, Australia drains the capacity of developing countries to meet their own health needs and to prosper economically, while at the same time refusing to mitigate the costs it imposes on other countries by admitting a more representative intake of migrants.

The purpose of the CRPD (in Art 1) is 'to promote, protect and ensure the full and equal enjoyment of all human rights and fundamental freedoms by all persons with disabilities, and to promote respect for their inherent dignity'. It is arguable that the health requirements of the *Migration Act,* while not *expressly* targeting disabilities, will frequently present insuperable obstacles to a large number of potential migrants whose disabilities require costly treatment.

Such requirements – unless very carefully crafted – could therefore impede respect for the dignity and the right to equal treatment at law of persons with disabilities, including under immigration law. Persons with disabilities already face other obstacles in the immigration system, where, for instance, they cannot meet skills, assets or language tests on account of their disabilities – tests which of themselves may raise additional issues of indirect discrimination – and which problems are compounded further by the health requirements.

As set out below, a close examination of the nature of the Australian health test reveals substantial flaws in its construction, which makes it difficult to rationalise the test as a justifiable limitation on the right to equal protection of migrants with disabilities. Those flaws include that (1) the threshold of the health test is set too low; (2) the current quantification of disability costs is flawed; (3) the capacity of a person with disabilities to pay for treatment is not taken into account in weighing the costs; (4) the social and economic contributions of a migrant with disabilities are not considered; (5) the evidentiary requirements are inadequate;

(6) the test adversely affects the right of family unity; and (7) the test is not consistent with international refugee law obligations.

The threshold of the health test is set too low

While the Canadian decisions mentioned earlier concern health requirements with similar purposes to the Australian ones, on their face they also involve important differences in construction. Exclusion on health grounds in Canada occurs if a condition would cause 'excessive demands' on health or social services. In contrast, Australia imposes a substantially lower threshold of 'significant cost' to Australia, or 'prejudice' to the access of an Australian to health care or community services.[24]

There is seemingly a stronger justification in Canada for any prima facie differential treatment, since exclusion is permitted only where the needs of a person with disabilities impose 'excessive' demands rather than merely 'significant' costs (which may, indeed, not amount to an excessive demand). The Canadian health test is accordingly more likely to satisfy the CRPD's requirement of an objective and reasonable justification for interference with equal protection, and better balances the competing interests of non-discrimination against persons with disabilities and the preservation of local health resources.

In practice, however, the Australian and Canadian tests are not so far apart. In Australia, a 'significant cost' is set at $21,000 over five years, a figure arrived at by reference to the average per capita health and welfare expenditure in Australia, plus a 20 per cent loading to cover anticipated increases in medical costs (DIAC 2009b, 9). In Canada, the cost threshold for 'excessive demand' is the similar amount of C$25,715 over five years, an amount set by a comparable formula.[25]

At first glance, pegging the anticipated health burden of migrants to the annual per capita health expenditure on Australians may seem reasonable. The 'significant cost' threshold of $21,000 is an average of the health costs of *all* Australians, able and disabled, sick and healthy, and it is applied equally to all migrants seeking to enter or remain in Australia. The assumption underpinning the test is that the Australian community should not be expected to bear the health costs of treating migrants where those costs exceed what an average Australian resident would enjoy. Otherwise, the migration program could become a proxy global social welfare program, whereby Australians would subsidise the health costs of foreigners with disabilities or illnesses, at a level greater than that received by the average Australian. Nothing in international law or the CRPD requires countries to redistribute wealth away from one's own nationals in favour of foreigners with disabilities or illnesses, even if a country is wealthy and developed.

Yet, that policy objection is hard to sustain. The number of people who fail the health test on account of a disability is very small – 71 in 2007-08 (plus 500 family members), relative to the 600,000 people who entered Australia in that year – yet the personal costs to those excluded

24 Which include hospital services; residential, nursing home and palliative care; community health care and consultations; rehabilitation services; disability services; supported education and accommodation; home and community care; special education; and social security benefits.

25 That is, the average annual per capita health and social service costs for Canadians, or otherwise a demand on health or social services that would add to existing waiting lists and increase the mortality or morbidity rates of Canadians by denying or delaying the provision of services to them.

on a discriminatory basis are very high. There is little evidence of a 'slippery slope' problem, whereby foreigners with disabilities everywhere might seek to enter Australia because of a relaxation of its health requirements. Foreigners seeking to come to Australia must still either have a family connection or independently meet other immigration entry criteria (such as skills, language or assets). Rates of disability among non-citizens do not vary significantly from those experienced by Australians as a whole. Further, the government has not presented statistics on the average per capita health expenditure on migrants compared with Australian citizens. It is therefore unknown whether those migrants who are admitted are more or less likely to draw upon public health resources than Australian citizens – and therefore whether the per capita health costs of all Australians is a reasonable threshold in respect of migrants.

The 'significant costs' threshold is a rather indiscriminate means of dealing with migrants with disabilities. It is difficult to generalise about the health costs of persons with disabilities as a whole without more detailed analysis of particular disabilities – and it is important to avoid stereotyping persons with disabilities as an economic burden on health care systems. Yet, the reality that persons with disabilities are routinely excluded by the current threshold suggests that many persons with disabilities require treatment costing in excess of the average health costs of all Australians. That result is inevitable: the average cost of health care for all Australians includes the many people who are both healthy and without disabilities – and therefore likely to incur fewer health expenses and certainly to cost less than the average for all Australians.

By requiring migrants with disabilities not to exceed the average health costs of all Australians, the health test is setting them up to fail. A more reasonable comparison would calculate 'significant cost' for the sub-category of migrants with disabilities as the average per capita health costs of *Australians with disabilities*, so that like categories are treated alike and migrants with disabilities stood a chance of being admitted. The problem with such a test is that it too is blunt in its own way, since it would disadvantage migrants with the most acute disabilities who require the most expensive care. A medicalised hierarchy of disability would then ensue, in which some migrants with disabilities could stay in Australia as long as they are not as disabled as others.

A more calibrated test would measure migrants with disabilities against the average health costs of Australians with the *particular* disability, and at the same level of severity, of the applicant, since such a test is properly comparing similarly situated people. As an immigration screening tool, however, such a test has little value, since the medical costs of a migrant with paraplegia are presumably identical to the medical costs of an Australian with the same level of paraplegia, and likewise for people with a combination of conditions.

Some advocates of reform have argued that *any* assessment of costs is inappropriate, since it 'medicalises' disability and 'attempts to place a value on the worth of any individual in society which is a degrading and negative process' (National Welfare Rights Network 2009, 2). The CRPD is intended to reflect a '"paradigm shift" in attitudes and approaches to persons with disabilities':

> … [a] movement from viewing persons with disabilities as 'objects' of charity, medical treatment and social protection towards viewing persons with disabilities as 'subjects' with rights, who are capable of claiming those rights and making decisions for their lives based on their free and informed consent as well as being active members of society, [UN Enable nd.]

A health test the sole focus of which is the cost burden of migrants treats an applicant with disabilities as an 'object of disorder' and of assessment, rather than as a person with inherent value (Vision Australia 2009, 4).

Persons with the most serious disabilities – or those with disabilities who are most in need of expensive care – are most vulnerable to exclusion under *any* health test. Any quantification of costs will inevitably generate a hierarchy of disabilities, with persons with the most serious disabilities at greatest risk of exclusion. Perfecting the quantification of costs and improving the administration of the test only entrenches that hierarchy, since affected persons are less able to challenge the economic bases or rationality of a refusal. A migrant's worth then becomes reduced to the value of their economic life, in an economy which is often not well adapted to make use of workers with disabilities, or to placing a monetary value on the social contribution of persons with disabilities who do not work.

Such is the unavoidable effect of a public policy choice which prioritises the health care of nationals over foreigners, and 'well' foreigners over less well foreigners. Short of abolishing the health test – which does not look likely in view of current public policy – the best that can be achieved at present is improvements in the substance and procedure of the health test. The guidelines for medical officers, for instance, lack transparency and need to be exposed to publication and external security (National Ethnic Disabilities Alliance 2009, 19), so that affected persons can understand the basis on which decisions are made; accurate assessments of true health costs can be gained; and the public can be confident that persons with disabilities are not arbitrarily excluded. As detailed below, there is much room to improve the method of quantifying medical costs and in taking into account the capacity to pay for medical treatment and to offset medical costs against the economic and social contributions typically made by migrants with disabilities.

Such improvements may be cold comfort to non-nationals with the most serious disabilities who seek to move to Australia, who may always find themselves excluded under even the most refined health test, and who will hardly feel better about their exclusion because those with lesser disabilities than themselves may gain entry to Australia. Even so, Australia cannot absolve itself from all responsibility for the most vulnerable persons with disabilities overseas. By Art 32 of the CRPD, Australia has committed itself to international cooperation in promoting the rights of the disabled, including through international development programs and capacity building, technology sharing and economic assistance. Such measures are means by which Australia might seek to assist those persons with disabilities whom it excludes from entry to Australia, and who may lack adequate health care at home – even if the Convention falls short of specifying the degree of commitment required.

The current quantification of disability costs is flawed

The method of assessing whether a person's condition will result in 'significant cost' or 'prejudice to the access' of Australians must be a rational one to satisfy the human rights law requirement that the means of achieving the legitimate objective is proportionate to its attainment. If, for instance, the manner of quantifying the costs of particular conditions is arbitrary or not supported by demonstrable evidence (as to the likely costs of procedures, the likely need for treatment, the resource limitations in the health system and so on), then it is questionable whether exclusion on health grounds is a necessary or proportionate response to the policy objective of preserving scarce health resources.

Under the Australian health test, there are a number of basic flaws in the method of assessing the costs of disability. First, when determining if an applicant's condition is likely to result in significant costs or prejudice access of Australians to health care, the medical officer is explicitly directed *not* to take into account 'whether the applicant will actually use the identified health care or community services' (DIAC 2009a, para 56.4). Further, the medical officer must *not* have 'regard to the applicant's personal circumstances or any claims by the applicant that they do not intend to use the identified care or services' (DIAC 2009a, para 56.4), reflecting a 'worst case scenario' approach to financial risk assessment by the law, rather than a more reasonable, sensitive and contextual approach. The medical officer must accordingly provide a 'costing assessment based on a hypothetical person with the same severity of condition' (DIAC 2009a, para 56.4).

The courts have clarified that the health test requires more than the identification of a condition followed by a consideration of the cost of treating a hypothetical person with that generic condition. Rather, the specific nature of the particular condition experienced by the applicant must be identified, followed by an assessment of the cost of treating a hypothetical person with that level of condition (*Robinson v Minister for Immigration and Multicultural Affairs*, 2005, at [43], a case involving a child with Down syndrome). The *actual* circumstances of the applicant are not, however, the focus of the test, including whether the person's circumstances may change.

By excluding consideration of the *actual* circumstances of the applicant – that is, the extent to which they *personally* are likely or not to make use of certain medical services – the health test cannot demonstrate that excluding a person is a genuinely necessary or proportionate restriction on a person's human rights. A range of factors affect whether a person is likely to burden public disability services, including a person's capacity to pay for those services, awareness of the availability of services, the suitability of services for particular migrant groups, and cultural factors such as a preference for family care-giving (Multicultural Disability Advocacy Association 2009, 16).

By potentially excluding people who are likely *not* to use health services, the health test exceeds what is necessary to conserve scarce health resources, and in such cases the 'significant cost' threshold bears no relationship to the actual medical costs borne by the Australian health system. In such cases, direct disability may even arise, because the law is excluding migrants with disabilities from Australia, on account of their disabilities, in circumstances where they are equally as likely not to use health services as migrants without disabilities. A test more compatible with human rights law would be an 'actual person' test which considered the personal, medical employment history of the applicant or their family members (Disability Discrimination Legal Service (Vic) 2009, 3). In addition, in suitable cases, enforceable undertakings could be given by a person as to their funding or use of services.

A second objection to the method of assessing health costs concerns the computation of anticipated costs. The Guidance Notes used by medical officers to quantify the costs of particular conditions are not publicly available, and so their accuracy and suitability cannot be readily scrutinised. The Migration Institute of Australia has expressed the concern that they may be outdated and rely on inaccurate data (Migration Institute of Australia 2009, 6). Medical opinion can reasonably differ on the classification of the seriousness of particular disabilities or conditions; opinion can differ further on the appropriate nature and degree of treatment required; and opinion may also vary on the likely costs of such treatment as is likely to be required.

Cost assessment is inevitably subjective, rather than strictly mathematical (Immigration Advice and Rights Centre 2009, 6). It is not clear whether the Guidance Notes reflect this varied range of possibilities, while their application by medical officers in practice is also likely to vary. Future developments in medicine and assistive technology cannot be predicted or quantified (NSW Disability Discrimination Legal Centre 2009, 12; Human Rights Law Resource Centre 2009, 5), lending further uncertainty to cost assessments. While the 'significant cost' threshold of $21,000 includes a 20 per cent loading to account for rapid increases in the cost of medical services, no such allowance is made for new technologies which may *decrease* the costs of treating particular conditions (for instance, by replacing surgery with medication, or hospital care with home treatment).

Migration and disability law practitioners routinely report arbitrariness and over-estimation in cost assessments under the health test. The Multicultural Disability Advocacy Association suggests that cost assessments are often 'based on unwarranted assumptions about the nature of disability and the likelihood of our use of health and community services' (Multicultural Disability Advocacy Association 2009, 1). Appeals have sometimes exposed exaggerated cost estimates (Multicultural Disability Advocacy Association 2009, 8). The National Ethnic Disability Alliance also queries the capacity of medical officers to accurately assess health costs over a person's lifetime (National Ethnic Disabilities Alliance 209, 19), when so many factors may intervene.

Even within particular conditions, such as HIV / AIDS or haemophilia (Haemophilia Foundation Australia 2009, 4), the experience of a condition and the treatment required can vary greatly, and medical officers without expertise in those conditions may not be sensitive to such variability. In practice, certain conditions, such as HIV /AIDS, appear to result in routine exclusion (Australian Federation of AIDS Organisations 2009, 7), notwithstanding the development of more sophisticated guidelines for decision makers (*Notes for Guidance for Medical Officers* 2008). Canadian cases have illustrated the risks of medical officers making generic assessments of particular conditions or disabilities without paying close attention to the specific manifestation in a particular individual (*Hilewitz v Canada; De Jong v Canada*). The Australian test may not always, therefore, be utilising the relevant comparators, since its assessment of the cost of the specific manifestation of a person's disability is based on the estimated cost of a different form or grade of the disability.

Assessment by medical officers typically further do not provide clear and comprehensive details about cost calculations (Migration Institute of Australia 2009, 5), or the reasoning and information relied upon to reach the conclusion (Freehills 2009, 3). While a medical officer may take into account other medical opinions or cost calculations provided by the applicant (Migration Institute of Australian 2009, 5), 'this practice is observed to a limited extent' and insufficient weight may be given to specialist opinions (Migration Institute of Australia 2009, 6). The Australian National Audit Office has also previously criticised deficiencies in processes for approving medical officers to administer the health test (Australian National Audit Office 2007).

The capacity of a person with disabilities to pay for treatment is not taken into account in weighing the costs

The applicant's own means of support (including private health insurance coverage or support by family members or others) is not considered in the medical cost assessment made by the medical officer. In some cases, the courts have acknowledged, for instance, that the cost of purchasing prescription medication (such as anti-retroviral drugs) would ordinarily be borne by a hypothetical HIV-sufferer, so as not to burden the public 'health care' system (*X v Minister for Immigration, Multicultural and Indigenous Affairs*, 2005). Yet, even then, the over-the-counter cost does not take into account public subsidies under the Pharmaceutical Benefits Scheme (Australian Federation of AIDS Organisations 2009, 7), such that HIV sufferers are still typically excluded. The capacity to self-fund or self-insure other medical treatment or services, particularly those which are in scarce supply, is not generally taken into account.

Again, if the legitimate policy aim of the health test is the protection of scarce health resources, it is arguable that it cannot be a necessary and proportionate means of attaining that objective to screen out those who can fund their own treatment and who therefore would not burden resources or prejudice access to them by others. The health test is built on a (highly prejudicial) assumption that persons with disabilities are an inevitable cost burden, regardless of their own capacity to pay, earn income, exercise autonomy in looking after themselves, or draw on private support networks or family members to assist them. Further, in such cases, direct disability may arise, because the law excludes migrants with disabilities, on account of their disabilities, in circumstances where they are capable of demonstrating the same level of financial self-sufficiency as migrants without disabilities.

By contrast, in Canada, the capacity of family members to support the medical costs of a person with disabilities is a relevant factor in assessing whether the person would cause 'excessive demand' (*Hilewitz,* 5). An applicant may provide the authorities with a formal plan detailing how they will privately fund their own medical care, without impacting on public funds (Canadian High Commission in Australia 2009, 4). Likewise in the United States, the family of a person with disabilities may submit a contractual affidavit of support.[26]

Some reform advocates have argued that, nevertheless, it would be inappropriate to offer applicants 'a chance to "buy" their way out of the health requirement for a family member with a disability, because it tends to reduce the problem into simply creating an equally oppressive distinction between those who have and those who have not' (Disability Discrimination Legal Service (Vic) 2009, 8). It has been proposed that the potential for 'reasonable accommodations' of an applicant's health care needs should instead be considered (Disability Discrimination Legal Service (Vic) 2009, 8). Under Art 2 of the CRPD, reasonable accommodations are defined as:

> ... necessary and appropriate modifications and adjustments not imposing a disproportionate or undue burden where needed in a particular case, to ensure to persons with disabilities the enjoyment or exercise on an equal basis with others of all human rights and fundamental freedoms.

[26] Demonstrating income and assets equivalent to at least 125 per cent of the federal poverty guidelines (Action on Disability in Ethnic Communities 2009, para 15.7).

That suggestion really just shifts the focus of the balancing of economic costs from point of entry to residence in the community. To that extent, it is not really an alternative to allowing applicants to demonstrate capacity to pay in the migration process, as a condition of entry. Rather, it is an argument for a more open policy on admitting migrants and then determining what degree of support is reasonable after they have arrived. The determination of 'reasonable accommodation' would likely still allow scope for decision makers to refuse medical treatment to migrants with disabilities, on the basis that recently arrived migrants with expensive health needs would impose a 'disproportionate or undue burden' on the rest of the community. One difference, however, is that the assessment of 'undue burden' might also take into account the economic fruits (such as employment) which reasonable accommodations could enable among persons with disabilities – and which the current test ignores.

If the point of the present health test is to limit the immediate burden on public finances, then an alternative approach built around reasonable accommodations is unlikely to gain traction in policy circles. This is so particularly because after admitting migrants, politically it would be very difficult to refuse medical treatment to people then lawfully resident in Australia. Instead, permitting consideration of an applicant's capacity to pay – while generating equity concerns between different persons with disabilities – is a small way of modifying the health test which would likely result in admitting more persons with disabilities while simultaneously safeguarding resource concerns.

The social and economic contributions of a migrant with disabilities are not considered

Not only does the Australian health test exclude from consideration the applicant's capacity to pay for their own medical care, but it also regards as irrelevant the broader economic, social and cultural contributions which a person with disabilities may make to Australia if admitted (Productivity Commission 2004, 345; Disability Services Commission (WA) 2009, 1; Deafness Forum of Australia 2009, 4; ACT Human Rights Commission 2009, 1; Royal Australasian College of Physicians (RACP) 2009, 10). Economically, the health test appears to be based on an assumption that persons with disabilities are an economic burden and are unable to contribute financially to society – a 'deficit' approach. The health test thus treats as irrelevant all of the ways in which migrants with disabilities might contribute to the economy. Where a secondary applicant (such as a child with disabilities) is excluded under the health test, the economic contribution of their family members is not considered (RACP 2009, 8).

Disability advocates have frequently emphasised that many persons with disabilities contribute to economic life through employment, taxation and investment, and by generating demand for goods and services and growing the economy. They may also make unrecognised contributions through unpaid but financially valuable voluntary and community work, domestic labour, carer responsibilities, child minding and rearing, supporting family members, and so on (Cabramatta Community Care 2009, 7). Appropriate education and training, social security support, disability adjustments in workplaces, and family support can, by lessening barriers to participation, all increase the capacity of persons with disabilities to contribute further to economic life. Persons with disabilities and their families also make an intergenerational contribution to the economy (National Ethnic Disabilities Alliance 2009, 22).

The health test can also operate to generate unaccounted economic burdens of its own, such as when it results in family separation and anxiety which can adversely affect productivity and incur additional costs for counselling services in Australia. The costly administrative machinery required to assess hundreds of thousands of applicants annually – in order to exclude less than one hundred persons with disabilities – brings substantial costs of its own.

The exclusion of persons with disabilities cannot be justified under human rights law where the decision to exclude does not take into account the full range of factors relevant to determining the costs and benefits of admitting or excluding a person, including economic contributions (Australian Human Rights Commission 2009, 4). Quite apart from quantifiable economic activities, the social contributions of persons with disabilities are also overlooked by the health test. Persons with disabilities are often involved in community associations, sporting clubs, school or parent groups, and cultural organisations (Vision Australia 2009, 5). They contribute to building communities, pluralism and diversity (RACP 2009, 12), and 'social cohesion' (Human Rights Law Resource Centre 2009, 5; NSW Disability Discrimination Legal Centre 2009, 7). Such contributions are made over a lifetime, yet are not readily quantifiable (Carrington, McIntosh and Walmsley 2007). The formal irrelevance of the social contributions of migrants with disabilities in the health test process also disempowers them, by eliminating any opportunity to 'voice' their social value (Immigration Advice and Rights Centre 2009, 2).

Many advocates of reform have suggested that the health test should accordingly seek to balance the anticipated health care costs against the economic and social contributions expected from admitting a migrant with disabilities and their family (Crock 2009, 3; Public Interest Advocacy Centre/Service for the Treatment and Rehabilitation of Torture and Trauma Survivors (PIAC/STARTIS) 2009, 22; Castan Centre for Human Rights 2009, 3). Factors which might be taken into account could include age, occupation, career trajectories and family relationships (Crock 2009, 3), as well as community ties (PIAC/STARTTS 2009, 22) and other potential social contributions. In the United States, for example, the screening of migrants to determine whether they might constitute a 'public charge' takes into account not only their health status, but also their age, family status, assets, resources, financial status, education and skills, in the totality of the circumstances (*Immigration and Nationality Act,* s 1182 4(A)).

Yet, others who oppose the current health test also oppose a shift towards balancing costs and benefit, instead arguing that the health test should be narrowed only to exclude people with a narrow range of contagious conditions (such as active tuberculosis) that post a risk to public health (Australian Federation of AIDS Organisations 2009, 18). The Australian Federation of AIDS Organisations argues against substituting a cost/benefit test because of the complexities of quantifying the many (economic and non-economic) cost/ benefit variables of a condition such as AIDS, as well as the potential for privileging people from developed countries (who would typically be diagnosed and treated early, reducing future costs) over developing countries (without similar advantages). Still others, such as Australian Lawyers for Human Rights, have called to abolish the health test altogether, since it cannot be readily reconciled with anti-discrimination principles (Australian Lawyers for Human Rights 2009, 4).

At a minimum, the highly restrictive nature of the current test has provoked adverse, if impotent, reaction from some decision makers. In the case of Dr Bernhard Moeller, involving the refusal of a permanent residency to the applicant because his child was intellectually disabled, the Migration Review Tribunal observed that the case raised 'compelling and compassionate circumstances' (*Moeller* case, 2008, at [24]). The Tribunal indicated that it would have waived the health requirements had such a discretion been available to it, on account of the applicant's own significant contribution to the community as a health professional, as well as his capacity to provide for his son's treatment, and because his son was a valued member of the Australian community, with potential to develop skills and make future contributions.

The Moellers were ultimately granted permanent residency by the exercise of the Minister for Immigration's personal discretion under s 417 of the *Migration Act* (Evans 2008). Yet, that such discretion had to be exercised at all is an indication of systemic failure in the health test, which arbitrarily excludes migrants on account of disabilities which would be likely not to impose significant costs on the Australian community. Further, resource to ministerial discretion is itself problematic, for the reasons canvassed in a recent government review: it is a non-compellable, non-reviewable power, which can only be exercised after the exhaustion of a legal process which itself is substantively inadequate, and which inevitably imposes protracted hardship on applicants pending a final determination.

The evidentiary requirements are inadequate

Flaws in the method of quantifying costs are closely related to the wider procedures of assessment. In the Canadian case of *Anvari*, while the health requirements were objectively justified in principle, the applicant succeeded on the facts of that case because the government had failed to meet the high evidentiary threshold for exclusion on health grounds, which required the concurring opinions of at least two medical officers. The 'need for the best possible evidence to differentiate adversely against a person because of a disability' was an important factor supporting the Canadian statutory scheme in that case (*Anvari*).

The Canadian scheme is procedurally distinguishable from the Australian health test by requiring two concurring medical opinions, whereas one is sufficient in Australia. It is arguable that the opinion of a single medical officer about the disability condition of a visa applicant should not be regarded as sufficient to support adverse differentiation against the person on the basis of disability. Requiring two or more concurring medical opinions would be an important safeguard against arbitrary or unjustifiable differentiation against the disabled, in circumstances where medical opinions can reasonably differ on questions such as the severity of the disability and the care and treatment (and thus the expense) required (RACP 2009, 10).

As the RACP argues, the health test is medically flawed because it relies upon the discretionary judgment of only one medical officer who may not have adequate training on the relevant condition or disease (RACP 2009, 10). The health test is also not sensitive to certain important medical distinctions, as between acute illness and disability (RACP 2009, 10). RACP has also expressed a medical ethics concern that doctors are being asked to participate in a potentially discriminatory assessment process which may not be in the best interests of their patients (RACP 2009, 7-8).

In the experience of the Immigration Advice and Rights Centre, while an opportunity is provided to respond to an adverse medical opinion, additional information provided by the applicant seldom results in a reconsidered opinion (Immigration Advice and Rights Centre 2009, 12-13). Many migrants (particularly offshore and refugee applicants) are not, in any case, able to provide their own expert medical evidence to contest the view of the medical officer, due to the expense and complexity of obtaining advice from medical specialists and migration agents (National Ethnic Disabilities Alliance 2009, 11).

While there is often (but not always[27]) an avenue of merits review through the Migration Review Tribunal, the medical officer's opinion is binding on the Tribunal and, as a non-expert body, the Tribunal is not in a position to provide expert reconsideration of medical opinions. Other factors may also limit the availability of an appeal, such as delay, expense, language difficulties and cultural barriers (Immigration Advice and Rights Centre 2009, 12-13). Since primary decision makers are not required to provide reasons for decisions to refuse visa applications on health grounds, it can be very difficult to seek review and challenge the basis of the decision (PIAC/STARTTS 2009, 15). The availability of discretionary ministerial intervention is no substitute for enforceable rights of review.

The test adversely affects the right of family unity

As the *Moeller* case discussed above indicates, the health test can have particularly adverse impacts on families. For some visa categories, the 'one fail all fail' rule – in which all family members are refused visas if one family member does not meet the health test – is particularly indiscriminate in its operation, since the assessment of the potential medical costs of a family member with disabilities does not take into account the potential contributions to Australia of other family members, or the capacity of family members to support a person with disabilities (Multicultural Disability Advocacy Association 2009, 16-17).

The rule can also generate unnecessary and destructive family conflict. As the Australian Federation of AIDS Organisations observe: 'Knowledge that their own HIV positive status means that all their family will be refused protection by Australia can place an enormous burden on the person diagnosed with HIV, in terms of guilt and shame, and in terms of the reaction of the rest of their family' (Australian Federation of AIDS Organisations 2009, 11).

In other situations, such as where family members are already resident in Australia and seek to sponsor remaining relatives from overseas, the application of the health test can result in family separation, such as where a visa is refused to a child or parent with disabilities (Human Rights Council of Australia 2009, 2). Family disintegration can result from the trauma of separation (Disability Discrimination Legal Service (Vic) 2009, 3). Family separation is all too common as a result of the health test. To give just one example, a man who suffered multiple limb amputations in the armed conflict in Sierra Leone was not permitted to be reunited with his family in Australia, even though his brother and sister-in-law were trained medical professionals capable of supporting him financially (Cerebral Palsy Australia 2009, 7).

The principles of family unity and the 'best interests' of a child are well embedded in international human rights law (ICCPR, Act 23; Convention on the Rights of the Child 1989, Arts 8 and 9). Article 23(4) of the CRPD itself requires that '[i]n no case shall a child be separated from parents on the basis of a disability of either the child or one or both of the parents', and such protection applies equally to a migration process. As others have observed, health criteria that prevent persons with disabilities from exercising rights of family unity

[27] No appeal right exists for humanitarian visa applicants.

cannot be justified under human rights law (ANU College of Law (Migration Law Program) 2009, 4-5).

The test is not consistent with international refugee law obligations

Other international obligations are also relevant to Australia's treatment of refugees seeking to come to Australia. While onshore asylum seekers are exempted from the health requirements (PIAC/STARTTS 2009, 22), no such concession is extended to offshore applicants for resettlement. More than other migrants, refugees and asylum seekers may suffer from a range of interesting and complicated health conditions or disabilities, including those related to conflict and post-conflict trauma, lack of adequate medical treatment while in refugee camps or during displacement, poor nutrition, and developmental delay in children (RACP 2009, 8). A common disability in children, such as paediatric hydrocephalus, can lead to exclusion under the health test, even though it can be effectively treated by surgery that is not available in refugee camps (UN High Commissioner for Refugees (UNHCR) 2009, 7). Likewise, the early diagnosis and treatment of HIV / AIDS can be rare in refugee situations (Australian Federation of AIDS Organisations 2009, 11), increasing the likelihood of a person being excluded by the health test at a later stage once the disease has progressed.

Despite the assessed need for protection from persecution and family reunification, refugee families are routinely separated as a result of the health test. The Cabramatta Community Centre, for instance, describes the many Iraqi refugee families it assisted in 2007-09 where family members were rejected through the health test (Cabramatta Community Centre 2009, 2), while other refugees have faced difficulty in integrating in Australia because of the absence of family members with disabilities, such as mothers (Cabramatta Community Centre 2009, 2).

While a waiver is available in offshore refugee cases, UNHCR argues that 'practice suggests that it is very rarely granted and, effectively, automatic rejection of refugee cases which fail the health requirement is the norm' (UNHCR 2009, 10). In contrast, in Canada, refugees and asylum seekers are exempt from the 'excessive demand' assessment (*Immigration and Refugee Protection Act*, s 38(2)). Given Australia's international refugee law protection obligations towards refugees and their families – which admit no public health exception – such applicants should be exempt from the health test, or at least a presumption in favour of a waiver should be exercised (UNHCR 2009, 5).

Waiver of health requirements

The potential waiver of the health requirements under Sch 4 of the *Migration Regulations* is an important means of preventing blanket differentiation against persons with disabilities. Decisions whether to waive the health requirements may consider evidence of the capacity to support a person with disabilities, qualifications and employment prospects, whether there are Australian minor children, whether there are existing links to Australia, and whether there are 'any substantial compelling and compassionate circumstances' (*Migration Regulations*, Sch 4, 4005-4007). Although the waiver power may assist some applicants, it is not sufficient to ensure that Australia consistently conforms to its anti-discrimination obligations in relation to migrants with disabilities, for the reasons above.

First, the waiver is only available in respect of certain visa classes[28] and not others,[29] producing unjustifiable differentiation between different categories of migrants and leaving some persons with disabilities vulnerable to exclusion without consideration of their individual circumstances. The basis of the differentiation is that the waiver was originally intended as a concession only applicable to applicants with family ties to Australia, rather than also applying to independent migrants (Immigration Advice and Rights Centre 2009, 4). However, if the purpose of the health test is to conserve public health resources, it would be more sensible to restrict the waiver to economic migrants, who as a whole are more likely to be able to support their own health care costs than family stream migrants (Immigration Advice and Rights Centre 2009, 4).

If the waiver applies to family applicants, it also ought to extend to other visa categories and there are no other apparent justifications for not making the waiver available to all classes. In practice, there is no longer any logic to the availability of the waiver among visa subclasses; even within the family stream, the waiver applies to some subclasses but not others, while the waiver is equally available for some economic migrants but not others.

Second, the waiver is discretionary, so that even if an applicant with disabilities in the right visa class would *not* impose undue costs or cause undue prejudice, entry is not available *as of right*. If the legitimate public policy aim is the protection of scarce health resources, it is arguable that the possible exclusion of persons with disabilities who would *not* unduly burden those resources (by a failure to utilise the waiver power) cannot be objectively justified. Waiver is also available where any employer undertakes to cover the medical expenses, but *not* where the actual applicant gives such an undertaking (although this is a factor taken into account in the exercise of the minister's own waiver). Such a distinction is not justifiable.

There are also social costs to a discretionary approach. As one migrant group notes, 'it is demoralising and demeaning for us … to have to beg to have our rights recognised in this way' (Multicultural Disability Advocacy Association 2009, 19). A review of the Minister for Immigration's general discretionary powers in immigration law indicated that, across government, most decision-making had moved away from broad personal discretions towards more codified or rights-based powers (Proust 2008; Senate Committee on Ministerial Discretion in Migration Matters 2004). Personal discretions render applicants more vulnerable to arbitrariness in DIAC's administration of, and record keeping in relation to, the visa waiver power (Australian National Audit Office 2007). In place of the waiver, it would be preferable to provide clear, predictable and prospective legal criteria for use by decision makers in health decisions, enabling such matters to be considered as of right in all visa cases, and reducing the potential for the politicisation of immigration decisions which comes with discretionary ministerial powers.

---

[28] Spouse/de facto spouse, Interdependent partner, Fiancé, Dependent child, Adopted child, Refugee and humanitarian visas granted overseas, Temporary humanitarian stay, Business skills (permanent), New Zealand Citizen Family Relationship, Business (long stay) and Educational: Family visa subclasses 100, 309, 801 and 820 (Partner); 101 and 802 (Child); 102 (Adoption); 110, 310, 814 and 826 (Interdependency); 300 (Prospective Marriage); 445 (Dependent Child); and 461 (NZ Citizen Family Relationship Temporary).

[29] Subclasses 115 and 835 (Remaining Relative); 116 and 836 (Carer); 117 and 837 (Orphan Relative); 103 (Parent); 804 (Aged Parent); 143 and 173 (Contributory Parent); 864 and 884 (Contributory Aged Parent); or 114 and 838 (Aged Dependent Relative).

Third, the waiver is available if a person's condition would not result in 'undue cost' to the Australian community or 'undue prejudice' to access to health care by Australians. By implication, exclusion on health grounds is permitted where a person's condition imposes 'significant' but not 'undue' cost on Australia, or where it would 'prejudice' access to health services by Australians but not 'unduly' so.

This aspect of the test highlights the concern raised above that the Australian threshold for exclusion on health grounds is not sufficiently high to justify any direct or indirect discrimination on the basis of disability. The low bar for exclusion interferes too readily in the purpose of the CRPD in protecting the dignity of persons with disabilities, and is overly protective of access to health services for Australians without adequately balancing the competing interests.

In this regard, if persons with disabilities otherwise qualify for admission into the Australian community (for example, for family reunion), they should not be subject to discriminatory treatment on account of their disability in circumstances where there is not a sufficiently strong ground for such interference. Some cost to the Australian community must be expected and accepted; and the Canadian threshold of 'excessive' (or, synonymously, 'undue') cost better balances the interests at stake than standards of mere 'significant' cost or 'prejudice'.

Conclusion

Ironically, Australia's health test would likely exclude from Australia a glittering array of talented foreigners with disabilities or serious illnesses, from Stephen Hawking to John F Kennedy to Franklin D Roosevelt. Even the current chair of the UN CRPD Committee, the blind Australian law professor Ron McCallum, might find himself excluded if he were of another nationality and seeking to migrate to Australia. It also excludes many less well-known persons with disabilities who are capable of making considerable social and economic contributions to enriching Australian life. The current health test is constructed and operates in a blunt and arbitrary fashion which is not well tailored to the requirements of international human rights law, nor respectful of basic human dignity.

Australia has assumed an international legal obligation to ensure that its domestic law and policy comply with the requirements of the CRPD, including in its treatment of migrants. There is also a pragmatic reason to reform Australian immigration law. On 21 August 2009, Australia acceded to the Optional Protocol to the CRPD, following a JSCOT recommendation (JSCOT 2008, ch 2). The Optional Protocol came into force for Australia on 20 September 2009. Article 1 enables individuals to complain of violations to the new UN Committee on the Rights of Persons with Disabilities. In addition, Art 6 of the Optional Protocol empowers the Committee with a wider function to investigate 'grave or systematic violations' of Convention rights by a state party.

The report of the Joint Standing Committee on Migration in June 2010 reflects a belated recognition by parliamentarians that the health test has inflicted unjustifiable harm on migrants with disabilities. Its recommendations are largely responsive to the concerns raised in that inquiry and the earlier JSCOT process, both stimulated by Australia's participation in the CRPD. In broad terms, the Joint Standing Committee on Migration recommended improving the assessment of costs;[30] increasing the transparency of the process, [31] and reconsidering the DDA exemption as part of a wider review of federal anti-discrimination law (Joint Standing Committee on Migration 2010, xxii-xxv). If Australia is to avoid complaints being made pursuant to the UN procedures, with the attendant adverse publicity and embarrassment which this may entail, it is essential to reform existing discriminatory immigration practices to comply with disability rights standards. Australia has an opportunity to reconfigure its migration laws to treat migrants with disabilities in a more rational and humane manner – and to signal to the world a new era or disability rights in Australia.

References

Cases

Althammer v Austria, UN Human Rights Committee Communication, No 998/2001
Anvari v Canada Employment and Immigration Commission, D 18 / 88, 14 December 1988
Belgian Linguistic case, 23 July 1968, Series A, No 6 (1979-80) 1 EHRR 252
Broeks v The Netherlands, UN Human Rights Committee, 172/84 (1984)
Deol v Minister of Citizenship and Immigration (2000) CanLII 21099 (IRB), Canadian Immigration and Refugee Board (Appeal Division), W97-00037, 22 February 2000
Hilewitz v Canada (Minister of Citizenship and Immigation); De Jong v Canada (Minister of Citizenship and Immigration) [2003] 2 SCR 706; 2005 SCC 57
Hoogendijk v The Netherlands, European Court of Human Rights, 6 January 2005
Minister for Immigration and Multicultural Affairs v Seligman [1999] FCA 117 (1 March 1999)
Moeller case, 0807398 [2008] MRTA 1051 (25 November 2008)
NM (Disability Discrimination) Iraq [2008] UKAIT 00026
Purvis v New South Wales (Department of Education and Training) (2003) 202 ALR 133
Robinson v Minister for Immigration and Multicultural Affairs [2005] FCA 1626
X v Minister for Immigration, Multicultural and Indigenous Affairs [2005] FCA 429

Legislation

Canadian Charter of Rights and Freedoms 1982
Canadian Human Rights Act 1976
Disability Discrimination Act 1992 (Cth)
Disability Discrimination and Other Human Rights Amendment Act 2009 (Cth)

[30] By raising the 'significant cost' threshold; considering the social and economic contributions to Australia of a prospective migrant, or his or her family; recognising the contribution made by carers in the family to offset health care or community services costs; revising the 'hypothetical person test'; removing the regulatory requirement that costs will be assessed 'regardless of whether the health care or community services will actually be used in connection with the applicant'; allowing a discretion to consider mitigating factors once a person has failed the test; and considering a voluntary bond or other scheme to indemnify against, or manage health care or community service costs.

[31] By making publicly available the *Notes for Guidance*; publishing online the cost calculation methodology used by Medical Officers; and providing each applicant with a detailed breakdown of their assessed costs.

Immigration Act 1976 (Canada)
Immigration and Nationality Act, 8 United States Code
Immigration and Refugee Protection Act 2001 (Canada)
Migration Regulations 1994 (Cth)

International legal materials

Additional Protocol to the American Convention on Human Rights in the Area of Economic, Social and Cultural Rights (adopted 14 November 1988, entered into force 16 November 1999, OAS Treaty Series No 69 (1988))

African Charter of Human and Peoples' Rights (adopted 17 June 1981, entered into force 21 October 1986, 1520 UNTS 245)

Australian Government, Declaration upon Ratifying the CRPD, 17 July 2008 [Online]
Available: www.un.org/disabilities/default.asp?id=475 [2010, May 7]

Convention Against Torture and Other Cruel, Inhuman or Degrading Treatment or Punishment (adopted 10 December 1984, entered into force 26 June 1987, 1465 UNTS 85)

Convention on the Elimination of All Forms of Discrimination Against Women (adopted 18 December 1979, entered into force 3 September 1981, 1249 UNTS 13)

Convention on the Rights of Persons with Disabilities (adopted on 13 December 2006, opened for signature 30 March 2007, entered into force 3 May 2008, 993 UNTS 3)

Convention on the Rights of the Child (adopted 20 November 1989, entered into force 2 September 1990, 1577 UNTS 3)

Convention Relating to the Status of Refugees (adopted 28 July 1951, entered into force 22 April 1954, 189 UNTS 137)

International Convention on the Elimination of All Forms of Racial Discrimination (adopted 7 March 1966, entered into force 4 January 1969, 660 UNTS 195)

International Covenant on Civil and Political Rights (adopted 16 December 1966, entered into force 23 March 1976, 999 UNTS 171)

Optional Protocol to the Convention on the Rights of Persons with Disabilities (adopted 13 December 2006, entered into force 3 May 2008)

UN Committee on Economic, Social and Cultural Rights (1994), General Comment No 5, 'Persons with Disabilities (11th session) UN Doc E/1995/22

UN Committee on Economic, Social and Cultural Rights (2009), Concluding Observations on Australia (42nd session) UN Doc E/C.12/AUS/CO/4

UN Committee on the Elimination of Racial Discrimination (1993), General Recommendation 11, 'Non-citizens (Art 1)' (42nd session) UN Doc A / 46 / 18

UN Committee on the Elimination of Racial Discrimination (2004), General Recommendation 30, 'Discrimination against Non-citizens' (2004) (64th session) UN Doc CERD/C/64/Misc.11/rev.3

UN Enable (nd), Convention on the Rights of Persons with Disabilities [Online] Available: www.un.org/disabilities/default.asp?navid=12&pid=150 (2010, May 7]

UN Human Rights Committee (1986), General Comment No 15, 'The position of aliens under the Covenant' (27th session) UN Doc CCPR/C.74/CRP.4/Rev.6

UN Human Rights Committee (1989), General Comment No 18, 'Non-discrimination' (37th session) UN Doc HRI/GEN/1/Rev.5

Vienna Convention on the Law of Treaties (adopted 23 May 1969, entered into force 27 January 1980, 1135 UNTS 331)

Other references

ACT Human Rights Commission (2009) Submission to the Joint Standing Committee on Migration Inquiry into Immigration Treatment of Disability, October

Action on Disability in Ethnic Communities (2009) Submission to the Joint Standing Committee on Migration Inquiry into Immigration Treatment of Disability, October

ANU College of Law (Migration Law Program) (2009) Submission to the Joint Standing Committee on Migration Inquiry into Immigration Treatment of Disability, October

Australian Federation of AIDS Organisations (2009) Submission to the Joint Standing Committee on Migration Inquiry into Immigration Treatment of Disability, October

Australian Human Rights Commission (2009) Submission to the Joint Standing Committee on Migration Inquiry into Immigration Treatment of Disability, October

Australian Lawyers for Human Rights (2009) Submission to the Joint Standing Committee on Migration Inquiry into Immigration Treatment of Disability, October

Australian National Audit Office (2007) *Administration of the Health Requirement of the Migration Act 1958*

Australian Senate (2009) *Budget Estimates,* 27 May

Cabramatta Community Centre (2009) Submission to the Joint Standing Committee on Migration Inquiry into Immigration Treatment of Disability, October

Canadian High Commission in Australia (2009) Submission to the Joint Standing Committee on Migration Inquiry into Immigration Treatment of Disability, October

Carney T and Boucher A K (2009) 'Social security and immigration: an agenda for future research?' 23 *Zeitschrift für Ausländisches und Internationales Arbeits-und Sozialrecht* [Journal for Foreign and International Work and Social Rights] p 36

Carrington K, McIntosh A and Walmsley J (2007) *Social Costs and Benefits of Migration in Australia*

Castan Centre for Human Rights (2009) Submission to the Joint Standing Committee on Migration Inquiry into Immigration Treatment of Disability, October

Cerebral Palsy Australia (2009) Submission to the Joint Standing Committee on Migration Inquiry into Immigration Treatment of Disability, October

Crock M (2009) Submission to the Joint Standing Committee on Migration Inquiry into Immigration Treatment of Disability, October

Deafness Forum of Australia (2009) Submission to the Joint Standing Committee on Migration Inquiry into Immigration Treatment of Disability; October

Department of Immigration and Citizenship (DIAC) (2009a) *Procedures Advice manual 3*

Department of Immigration and Citizenship (DIAC) (2009b) Submission to the Joint Standing Committee on Migration Inquiry into Immigration Treatment of Disability, October

Disability Discrimination Legal Service (Vic) (2009) Submission to the Joint Standing Committee on Migration Inquiry into Immigration Treatment of Disability, October

Disability Services Commission (WA) 2009 Submission to the Joint Standing Committee on Migration Inquiry into Immigration Treatment of Disability, October

Evans C (2008) 'Statement by Senator Evans on Dr Bernhard Moeller', 26 November [Online] Available: www.chrisevans.alp.org.au/news/1108/immediarelease26-01.php> [2010, May 7]

Freehills (2009) Submission to the Joint Standing Committee on Migration Inquiry into Immigration Treatment of Disability, October

Haemophilia Foundation Australia (2009) Submission to the Joint Standing Committee on Migration Inquiry into Immigration Treatment of Disability, October

Human Rights Council of Australia (2009) Submission to the Joint Standing Committee on Migration Inquiry into Immigration Treatment of Disability, October

Human Rights Law Resource Centre (2000) Submission to the Joint Standing Committee on Migration Inquiry into Immigration Treatment of Disability, October

Immigration Advice and Rights Centre (2009) Submission to the Joint Standing Committee on Migration Inquiry into Immigration Treatment of Disability, October

Joint Standing Committee on Migration (2009) *Inquiry into the Migration Treatment of Disability,* 13 August [Online] Available: www.aph.gov.au/House/committee/mig/disability/index.htm [2010, May 7]

Joint Standing Committee on Migration (2010) *Enabling Australia Inquiry into the Migration Treatment of Disability*, report, 21 June [Online]

Available: www.aph.gov.au/house/committee/mig/disability/report.htm [2010, July 6]

Joint Standing Committee on Treaties (JSCOT) (4 June 2008) *Report 95: Treaties Tabled on 4 June, 17 June, 25 June and 26 August 2008*

Kayess R and French P (2008) 'Out of darkness into light? Introducing the Convention on the Rights of Persons with Disabilities' 8 *Human Rights Law Review* p 1

Migration Institute of Australia (2009) Submission to the Joint Standing Committee on Migration Inquiry into Immigration Treatment of Disability, October

Multicultural Disability Advocacy Association (2009) Submission to the Joint Standing Committee on Migration Inquiry into Immigration Treatment of Disability, October

National Ethnic Disabilities Alliance (2009) Submission to the Joint Standing Committee on Migration Inquiry into Immigration Treatment of Disability, October

National Welfare Rights Network (2009) Submission to the Joint Standing Committee on Migration Inquiry into Immigration Treatment of Disability, October

Notes for Guidance for Medical Officers, of the Commonwealth of Australia: Financial implications and consideration of prejudice to access for services associated with infection with human immunodeficiency virus and acquired immune deficiency syndrome (HIV/AIDS) (2008), 7 July

NSW Disability Discrimination Legal Centre (2009) Submission to the Joint Standing Committee on Migration Inquiry into Immigration Treatment of Disability, October

Productivity Commission (2004) *Review of the Disability Discrimination Act 1992*

Proust E (2008) *Report to the Minister for Immigration and Citizenship on the Appropriate Use of Ministerial Powers under the Migration and Citizenship Acts and Migration Regulations*, 31 January

Public Interest Advocacy Centre/Service for the Treatment and Rehabilitation of Torture and Trauma Survivors (PIAC/STARTTS) (2009) Submission to the Joint Standing Committee on Migration Inquiry into Immigration Treatment of Disability, October

Rattigan K (2004) 'Purvis v NSW (Department of Education and Training): a case for amending the Disability Discrimination Act 1992 (Cth)' 28 *Melbourne University Law Review* p 532

Royal Australasian College of Physicians (RACP) (2009) Submission to the Joint Standing Committee on Migration Inquiry into Immigration Treatment of Disability, October

Senate Committee on Ministerial Discretion in Migration Matters (2004) *Report,* 31 March

UN High Commissioner for Refugees (UNHCR) (2009) Submission to the Joint Standing Committee on Migration Inquiry into Immigration Treatment of Disability, October

Vision Australia (2009) Submission to the Joint Standing Committee on Migration Inquiry into Immigration Treatment of Disability, October

Part VI
The International Migrants Bill of Rights Project

[17]

INTERNATIONAL MIGRANTS BILL OF RIGHTS, WITH COMMENTARY

Table of Contents

IMBR CONTRIBUTORS*

IMBR Steering Committee Authors and Editors

Avinoam Cohen
Justin Gest
Ian Kysel
Randy Nahle
Sarah Plastino
Bianca Santos

IMBR Text and Commentary Student Authors

Georgetown University Law Center

Zach Bench
Maher Bitar
Emily Bruemmer
Sasha Filippova
Sarah Fink
Julia Follick
Justin Fraterman
Ashley Gaillard
Hadia Hakim
Thayer Hardwick
Ian Kysel
Sarah Lavin
Randy Nahle
Sarah Plastino
Bianca Santos
Justin Schwegel
Carly Stadum
Melissa Stewart
Jacob Zenn

* The International Migrants Bill of Rights (IMBR) and accompanying commentary, handbook, and indicators are the products of an ongoing collaboration of an international network of students and scholars. The materials draw significantly from the draft IMBR published by the Georgetown Immigration Law Journal in the spring of 2010, and reflect the work of a partnership between Georgetown University Law Center, the Minerva Center for Human Rights at Hebrew University of Jerusalem, and the Migration Studies Unit at the London School of Economics. The IMBR Initiative would like to thank Bianca Santos for her service as the Initiative's Program Director (2012-2013) and member of the Steering Committee (2011-present); Bianca's leadership and vision has been instrumental in our work. We would also like to express our deep gratitude to Andrew I. Schoenholtz (Georgetown University Law Center) and the Georgetown Law Human Rights Institute for contributing invaluable guidance and support to this initiative. We would like to convey our appreciation for the advice and support of Susan F. Martin (Georgetown University) and the Institute for the Study of International Migration (ISIM) throughout the drafting and revision process. We are further indebted to all of the experts who contributed their perspective in consultations with the Initiative, whose important insight into the IMBR is reflected throughout this publication, and particularly those whose engagement with the IMBR is ongoing. We received invaluable research assistance from Carolyn Armstrong (London School of Economics), Noa Bornstein-Ziv (Hebrew University) and Shannon Kisch (Hebrew University). For their assistance in organizing the publication of the IMBR, we would like to thank Michael Warley and Zach Meyers of the Georgetown Immigration Law Journal. Finally, neither this publication nor the Initiative would be possible without the generous support of the Open Society Foundations; we sincerely thank Aryeh Neier, Maria Teresa Rojas, Naomi Spitz, and Alyssa Ross for all of their support.

Hebrew University of Jerusalem

Mia Biran
Noa Bornstein-Ziv
Gallia Daor
Jacob Flex
Sharon Gefen
Nimrod Kovner
Yael Mazuz
Tomer Naor
Tamar Segev
Shlomo Shuvy
Miryam Zalkinder
Yotam Zeira

IMBR Handbook Student Authors

Adina Appelbaum
Andrew Craycroft
Lauren Esterle
Elizabeth Gibson
Nikhil Pillai
Justin Simeone
Meher Talib
Dave Wilkins

IMBR Indicators Student Authors

Adina Appelbaum
Andrew Craycroft
Lauren Esterle
Elizabeth Gibson
Nikhil Pillai
Justin Simeone
Meher Talib
Dave Wilkins

IMBR Principles

Every migrant has the right to **dignity**, including physical, mental, and moral integrity.

Every migrant has the right, without any discrimination, to the **equal protection** of the law of any State in which the migrant is present.

Vulnerable migrants, including children, women, and migrants with disabilities, have the right to the protection and assistance required by their condition and status and to treatment which takes into account their special needs.

Every migrant has the inherent right to **life**.

Every migrant has the right to **liberty and security of person**.

Every migrant has the right to recognition everywhere as a **person before the law**.

Every migrant has the right to an effective **remedy**.

Every migrant has the right to **due process** of law.

Every migrant **victim of crime** has the right to assistance and protection, including access to compensation and restitution.

Every migrant has the right to protection against discriminatory or arbitrary **expulsion** or deportation, including collective expulsion.

Every migrant has the right to seek and to enjoy in other countries **asylum**.

Every migrant has the right **against refoulement**.

Every migrant has the right to a **nationality**.

Every migrant **family** has the right to protection by society and the State.

Every migrant has the right to **freedom of thought, conscience, and religion or belief**.

Every migrant has the right to **freedom of opinion and expression**.

Every migrant has the right to **freedom of peaceful assembly and association**.

Every migrant has the right to participate in the **civil and political life** of the migrant's community and in the conduct of public affairs.

Every migrant has the right to be **free from slavery**, servitude, or forced or compulsory labor.

Every migrant has the right to **work** and to just and favorable conditions of work.

Every migrant has the right to the highest attainable standard of physical and mental **health**.

Every migrant has the right to an **adequate standard of living**.

Every migrant has the right to **education**.

Every migrant has the right to enjoy the migrant's own **cultures** and to use the migrant's own languages, either individually or in community with others, and in public or private.

PREAMBLE

RECALLING the principles proclaimed in the Charter of the United Nations which recognize the inherent dignity and worth, and the equal and inalienable rights of all members of the human family as the foundation of freedom, justice and peace in the world;

CONSIDERING the obligation of States under the Charter of the United Nations and the International Conventions on Human Rights to respect, protect and promote the human rights and fundamental freedoms of migrants;

RECOGNIZING that the ideal of free human beings enjoying freedom from fear and want can only be achieved if conditions are created whereby everyone, including migrants, may enjoy economic, social, cultural, civil, and political rights;

EMPHASIZING the universality, indivisibility, interdependence and interrelatedness of all human rights and fundamental freedoms and the need for migrants to be guaranteed their full enjoyment without discrimination of any kind;

RECALLING the Universal Declaration of Human Rights, the International Covenant on Civil and Political Rights, the International Covenant on Economic, Social and Cultural Rights, the International Convention on the Elimination of All Forms of Racial Discrimination, the Convention on the Elimination of All Forms of Discrimination Against Women, the Convention against Torture and Other Cruel, Inhuman or Degrading Treatment or Punishment, the Convention on the Rights of the Child, the International Convention on the Rights of All Migrant Workers and Members of Their Families, the Convention on the Rights of Persons with Disabilities, the International Convention for the Protection of All Persons from Enforced Disappearance, the 1951 Convention Relating to the Status of Refugees, and the Protocol thereto, International Labour Organization Conventions concerning Decent Work for Domestic Workers, concerning Migration for Employment, and concerning Migrations in Abusive Conditions and the Promotion of Equality of Opportunity and Treatment of Migrant Workers, the Convention Against Transnational Organized Crime, and the Protocols thereto, including the Palermo Protocol to Prevent Suppress and Punish Trafficking in Persons, and other relevant international and regional instruments;

RECOGNIZING the legitimate interest of States in controlling their borders and that the exercise of sovereignty entails responsibility, including in the adoption of appropriate and comprehensive migration policies;

REALIZING the importance and extent of the migration phenomenon, which involves millions of individuals and affects all States in the international community;

RECOGNIZING that migrants have special needs that may require special accommodation in certain regards;

AFFIRMING that a balance should be struck between the interest of States in preserving the cultural heritage of their peoples and the interest of migrants in preserving their cultural identity;

REALIZING that the migrant, having duties to other individuals and to the community to which the migrant belongs, is under a responsibility to strive for the promotion and observance of the rights contained herein;

CONSIDERING that migrants bring special contributions to their communities, that the ability to participate in and influence one's community is a significant part of human dignity;

RECOGNIZING the importance of governmental cooperation with civil society for upholding the rights of migrants and for promoting their participation in the civil, political, economic, social, and cultural spheres with equal opportunities, in every country;

URGING governmental, administrative, civil society, and other bodies, and actors and individuals dealing with migrants to implement this Bill in the recognition and development of principles, standards, and remedies affecting migrants;

RECOGNIZING that the rights in the present Bill shall be subject only to lawful restrictions permitted by other relevant international instruments;

AFFIRMING that nothing in this Bill shall be interpreted as restricting, modifying, or impairing the provisions of any international human rights or international humanitarian law instrument or rights granted to persons under domestic law;

AFFIRMING that nothing in this Bill shall be interpreted as implying for any State, group, or person any right to engage in any activity or to perform any act aimed at the destruction of any of the rights and freedoms recognized herein or at their limitation to a greater extent than is provided for in the present Bill; and

CONVINCED that a comprehensive and integral framework protecting and promoting the rights and dignity of all migrants will make a significant contribution to the international protection of their rights:

Commentary

(1) *Paragraph 1—RECALLING*: The first paragraph encompasses introductory preambular language from a number of complementary international and regional human rights agreements to establish that the principles of the U.N. Charter are at the center of the IMBR endeavor. These include the Universal Declaration of Human Rights (UDHR);[1] the International Cov-

1. Universal Declaration of Human Rights, G.A. Res. 217 (III) A, pmbl. ¶ 1, U.N. Doc. A/RES/217(III) (Dec. 10, 1948) [hereinafter UDHR] ("Whereas recognition of the inherent dignity and of the equal and inalienable rights of all members of the human family is the foundation of freedom, justice and peace in the world . . .").

enant on Civil and Political Rights (ICCPR);[2] the International Covenant on Economic, Social and Cultural Rights (ICESCR);[3] the International Convention on the Elimination of All Forms of Racial Discrimination (ICERD);[4] the Convention against Torture and Other Cruel, Inhuman or Degrading Treatment or Punishment (CAT);[5] the Convention on the Rights of the Child (CRC);[6] the Convention on the Rights of Persons with Disabilities (CRPD);[7] and the European Convention on Human Rights (ECHR).[8]

(2) *Paragraph 2—CONSIDERING*: The second paragraph recalls language of complementary agreements to stress the obligation of States to promote universal respect for, and observance of, human rights and freedoms,[9] and incorporates the contemporary "respect/protect/promote" language, adding a reference to the Conventions.[10] Further, it makes explicit

2. International Covenant on Civil and Political Rights pmbl. ¶ 2, Mar. 23, 1976, S. Treaty Doc. No. 95-20, 999 U.N.T.S. 171 [hereinafter ICCPR] ("Considering that, in accordance with the principles proclaimed in the Charter of the United Nations, recognition of the inherent dignity and of the equal and inalienable rights of all members of the human family is the foundation of freedom, justice and peace in the world . . .").

3. International Covenant on Economic, Social and Cultural Rights pmbl. ¶ 2, Dec. 16, 1966, 1966 U.S.T. 521, 993 U.N.T.S. 3 [hereinafter ICESCR] ("Considering that, in accordance with the principles proclaimed in the Charter of the United Nations, recognition of the inherent dignity and of the equal and inalienable rights of all members of the human family is the foundation of freedom, justice and peace in the world . . .").

4. International Convention on the Elimination of All Forms of Racial Discrimination pmbl. ¶ 2, Dec. 21, 1965, 660 U.N.T.S. 195 [hereinafter ICERD] ("Considering that the Charter of the United Nations is based on the principles of the dignity and equality inherent in all human beings . . .").

5. Convention Against Torture and Other Cruel, Inhuman or Degrading Treatment or Punishment pmbl. ¶ 2, Dec. 10, 1984, 1465 U.N.T.S. 85 [hereinafter CAT] ("Considering that, in accordance with the principles proclaimed in the Charter of the United Nations, recognition of the equal and inalienable rights of all members of the human family is the foundation of freedom, justice and peace in the world . . .").

6. Convention on the Rights of the Child pmbl. ¶ 1, Nov. 20, 1989, 1577 U.N.T.S. 3 [hereinafter CRC] ("Considering that, in accordance with the principles proclaimed in the Charter of the United Nations, recognition of the inherent dignity and of the equal and inalienable rights of all members of the human family is the foundation of freedom, justice and peace in the world . . .").

7. International Convention on the Protection and Promotion of the Rights and Dignity of Persons with Disabilities, G.A. Res. 61/106, Annex I, pmbl. (a), U.N. Doc. A/61/49 (Dec. 13, 2006) [hereinafter CRPD] ("*Recalling* the principles proclaimed in the Charter of the United Nations which recognize the inherent dignity and worth and the equal and inalienable rights of all members of the human family as the foundation of freedom, justice and peace in the world . . .").

8. Convention for the Protection of Human Rights and Fundamental Freedoms pmbl. ¶ 4, Nov. 4, 1950, Europ.T.S. No. 5; 213 U.N.T.S. 221 [hereinafter ECHR] ("Reaffirming their profound belief in those Fundamental Freedoms which are the foundation of justice and peace in the world . . .").

9. UDHR, *supra* note 1, at pmbl. ¶ 6 ("Whereas Member States have pledged themselves to achieve, in co-operation with the United Nations, the promotion of universal respect for and observance of human rights and fundamental freedoms . . ."); ICCPR, *supra* note 2, at pmbl. ¶ 5 ("Considering the obligation of States under the Charter of the United Nations to promote universal respect for, and observance of, human rights and freedoms . . ."); ICESCR, *supra* note 3, at pmbl. ¶ 5 ("Considering the obligation of States under the Charter of the United Nations to promote universal respect for, and observance of, human rights and freedoms . . ."); African Charter on Human and Peoples' Rights pmbl. ¶ 11, June 27, 1981, 1520 U.N.T.S. 217 [hereinafter Banjul Charter] ("*Firmly convinced* of their *duty* to promote and protect human and peoples' rights and freedoms . . .").

10. International Convention for the Protection of All Persons from Enforced Disappearance, G.A. Res. 61/177, pmbl. ¶ 4, U.N. Doc. A/RES/61/177 (2006), *reprinted in* 14 INT'L HUM. RTS. REP. 582 (2007) [hereinafter CPED]; CRPD, *supra* note 7, at pmbl. (b).

what is only implicit in existing international law: that migrants are entitled to enjoy the same rights and freedoms enjoyed by other persons.[11]

(3) *Paragraph 3—RECOGNIZING*: The third paragraph recognizes that the conditions necessary to achieve enjoyment of rights enunciated in complementary agreements[12] are also necessary for migrants to achieve the enjoyment of those rights.[13]

(4) *Paragraph 4—EMPHASIZING*: The fourth paragraph embodies the principle of equality and non-discrimination. It borrows paragraph (c) of the preamble of the Convention on the Rights of Persons with Disabilities,[14] affirming the nature of human rights as universal, indivisible, interdependent and interrelated and tying rights to the duty of non-discrimination, applying the language specifically to migrants.[15]

(5) *Paragraph 5—RECALLING*: The fifth paragraph recognizes, through an upward reference, that the IMBR is fundamentally rooted in, builds upon, and incorporates the core international human rights, refugee, and labor agreements.[16]

(6) *Paragraph 6—RECOGNIZING*: The sixth paragraph recognizes that States have a responsibility to manage migration in a manner that is consistent with international human rights law. It also acknowledges that the IMBR can assist governments in providing for the security and well-being of persons within their territory.

---

11. Other Agreements similarly affirm the application of rights to specific groups of persons. *See, e.g.*, CRPD, *supra* note 7, pmbl. (c) ("*Reaffirming* the universality, indivisibility, interdependence and interrelatedness of all human rights and fundamental freedoms and the need for persons with disabilities to be guaranteed their full enjoyment without discrimination . . ."); *see also*, Walter Kalin, Guiding Principles on Internal Displacement: Annotations 6, (American Society of International Law, Studies in Transnational Legal Policy, No. 38) (2000), at vii, 11, *available at* http://www.asil.org/pdfs/stlp.pdf.

12. ICCPR, *supra* note 2, pmbl. ¶ 4; ICESCR, *supra* note 3, at pmbl. ¶¶ 4-5; American Convention on Human Rights pmbl. ¶ 4, Nov. 21, 1969, O.A.S. T.S. No. 36; 1144 U.N.T.S. 143 [hereinafter ACHR].

13. *See supra* note 11.

14. *See supra* note 11.

15. *See supra* note 11.

16. UDHR, *supra* note 1; ICCPR, *supra* note 2; ICESCR, *supra* note 3, ICERD, *supra* note 4; Convention on the Elimination of All Forms of Discrimination against Women, Dec. 18, 1979, 1249 U.N.T.S. 13 [hereinafter CEDAW]; CAT, *supra* note 5; CRC, *supra* note 6; International Convention on the Protection of the Rights of All Migrant Workers and Members of their Families arts. 2, 3, 6, Dec. 18, 1990, 2220 U.N.T.S. 93 [hereinafter ICRMW]; CRPD, *supra* note 7; CPED, *supra* note 10; Convention Relating to the Status of Refugees art. 1A, July 28, 1951, 189 U.N.T.S. 150 [hereinafter 1951 Refugee Convention]; Protocol Relating to the Status of Refugees, Jan. 31, 1967, 606 U.N.T.S. 267; Convention Concerning Decent Work for Domestic Workers, June 16, 2011, I.L.O. No. 189, *available at* http://www.ilo.org/dyn/normlex/en/f?p=NORMLEXPUB:12100:0::NO:12100:P12100_INSTRUMENT_ID:2551460:NO [hereinafter ILO Convention 189]; Convention Concerning Migration for Employment, July 1, 1949, I.L.O. No. 97, 1616 U.N.T.S. 120 [hereinafter ILO Convention 97]; Convention Concerning Migrations in Abusive Conditions and the Promotion of Equality of Opportunity and Treatment of Migrant Workers, Dec. 9, 1978, I.L.O. No. 143, 1120 U.N.T.S 323 [hereinafter ILO Convention 143]; Protocol to Prevent, Suppress and Punish Trafficking in Persons, Especially Women and Children, Supplementing the United Nations Convention Against Transnational Organized Crime, GA Res. 55/25, U.N. GAOR, 55th Sess., U.N. Doc. A/45/49 (Vol. I) (Nov. 15, 2000) [hereinafter Palermo Protocol].

(7) *Paragraph 7—REALIZING*: The seventh paragraph is an adaptation of the seventh preambular paragraph of the ICRMW.[17] It acknowledges the importance and extent of global migration and stresses that it affects all States.

(8) *Paragraph 8—RECOGNIZING*: The eighth paragraph mirrors the fourth preambular paragraph of the CRC.[18] It justifies a document dedicated to the rights of migrants by acknowledging that migrants typically move in an unfamiliar, and less secure world.

(9) *Paragraph 9—AFFIRMING*: The ninth paragraph, rooted in the sixth preambular paragraph of the World Cultural Heritage Convention (UNESCO), conveys that migrants bring value to their receiving States through their cultural identity and diversity.[19]

(10) *Paragraph 10—REALIZING*: The tenth paragraph is an adaptation of the sixth preambular paragraph of the ICCPR.[20] It recognizes that, while the rights contained herein are rights to which all persons, without exception, are entitled, the rights of migrants may remain illusory if their implementation is not claimed.

(11) *Paragraph 11—CONSIDERING*: This paragraph refers to the civic rights of migrants. This is a general provision, which acknowledges that comprehensive protection of migrants' human rights depends in part on the connection between the individual and the State. The paragraph also highlights that participation in one's community is an element of the realization of human dignity.

(12) *Paragraph 12—RECOGNIZING*: The twelfth paragraph is an adaptation of the language in CRPD preambular paragraphs (l) and (y).[21] It acknowledges the critical role of the civil society sector in upholding the rights of migrants and urges governments to collaborate with civil society in the development of policies and principles affecting migrants.

(13) *Paragraph 13—URGING*: This Bill is both a compilation of existing human rights norms and a statement of the continually evolving standards and state practice regarding human rights. In this respect, the thirteenth preambular paragraph encourages all institutions and individuals dealing with migrants or charged with the implementation and protection of human rights to apply the rights, standards and remedies enumerated in this document as appropriate. If more favorable remedies exist on the national level or in other human rights documents, those more favorable remedies should be applied.

---

17. ICRMW, *supra* note 16, at pmbl. ¶ 7.
18. CRC, *supra* note 6, at pmbl. ¶ 4.
19. Convention Concerning the Protection of the World Cultural and Natural Heritage, pmbl. ¶ 6, Nov. 16, 1972, 27 U.S.T. 37, 1037 U.N.T.S. 151.
20. ICCPR, *supra* note 2, at pmbl. ¶ 6; ICESCR, *supra* note 3, at pmbl. ¶ 6.
21. CRPD, *supra* note 7, at pmbl. ¶¶ (l), (y).

(14) *Paragraph 14—RECOGNIZING*: The fourteenth paragraph emphasizes that only lawful derogations of the rights in this Bill are permitted. Some rights are subject to narrow limitations in situations that amount to public emergencies that threaten the life of the nation, such as certain situations of armed conflict.[22] Other rights in the Bill are non-derogable, such as the right to life and the right to be free from slavery.

(15) *Paragraph 15—AFFIRMING*: The fifteenth paragraph is a savings clause adapted from Principle 2 of the Guiding Principles on Internal Displacement.[23] The purpose of this paragraph is to preserve the existing legal obligations of States and to ensure that the IMBR sets a minimum standard. More favorable provisions in international, regional, or domestic law shall not be impaired by the application of the rights in this Bill.

(16) *Paragraph 16—AFFIRMING*: The sixteenth paragraph explicitly applies the prohibition of the abuse of rights principle to the human rights enumerated in the IMBR. This clause forbids the State and any entity or person from using provisions of this Bill to deprive another person of access to and enjoyment of the human rights herein. The prohibition of abuse of rights is a well-established principle of international law and included in many foundational human rights instruments, including the ICCPR and ICESCR.[24] It was initially formulated as Article 30 of the UDHR, in part in response to groups with "nascent nazi, fascist or other totalitarian ideaologies" using enumerated freedoms like speech to oppress and destroy the rights of other groups.[25] The principle is commonly invoked to prevent groups from using the freedoms of speech, assembly, and association to negate or destroy others' human rights.[26]

(17) *Paragraph 17—CONVINCED*: The seventeenth paragraph, mirroring the fifteenth paragraph of the ICRMW,[27] acknowledges that a unified document enunciating the rights of all migrants is a novel contribution to the field of international human rights law that will further efforts to respect, protect, and promote the rights of migrants.

---

22. Human Rights Comm., *General Comment No. 29 on States of Emergency*, U.N. Doc. CCPR/C/21/Rev.1/Add.11 (Aug. 31, 2001), at http://www.unhchr.ch/tbs/doc.nsf/0/71eba4be3974b4f7c1256ae200517361/$FILE/G0144470.pdf.

23. *See* Commission on Human Rights, Guiding Principles on Internal Displacement, U.N. Doc. E/CN.4/1996/52/Add.2 (Dec. 5, 1995), at http://daccess-dds-ny.un.org/doc/UNDOC/GEN/G95/146/89/PDF/G9514689.pdf?OpenElement [hereinafter Guiding Principles on Internal Displacement].

24. ICCPR, *supra* note 2, at art. 5; ICESCR, *supra* note 3, at art. 5; UDHR, *supra* note 1, at art. 30. *See also* ECHR, *supra* note 8, at art. 17; Charter of Fundamental Rights of the European Union art. 54, Dec. 7, 2000, 2000 O.J. (C. 364) 1; ICRMW, *supra* note 16, at art. 81(2).

25. *See* U.N Secretary-General, Annotation on the Text of the Draft International Covenants on Human Rights, ¶ 55, U.N. Doc. A/2929 (July 1, 1955), at http://www2.ohchr.org/english/issues/opinion/articles1920_iccpr/docs/A-2929.pdf.

26. Annotation on the Text of the Draft International Covenants on Human Rights, *supra* note 25.

27. ICRMW, *supra* note 16, at pmbl. ¶ 15.

ARTICLE 1
DEFINITION OF MIGRANT

(1) The term "migrant" in this Bill refers to a person who is outside of a State of which the migrant is a citizen or national, or, in the case of a stateless migrant, the migrant's State of birth or habitual residence.

(2) The present Bill shall apply during the entire migration process of migrants.

Commentary

(1) This Article provides a purposefully broad and inclusive definition of "migrant." Paragraph 1 establishes that "migrant" refers to individuals who are outside of the territory of the State of which they are a citizen or national, or in the case of stateless migrants, the State of birth or habitual residence. This definition captures stateless persons who have left a country to which they are indigenous or in which they are habitual residents. Thus, individuals are migrants regardless of whether their presence is temporary, lawful, for protection, or for economic or other reasons.

(2) This definition does not include individuals who are present in the territory of a State where they hold secondary citizenship or nationality. Further, it does not apply to individuals who migrate—forcibly or voluntarily—within the borders of a State in which they are citizens, nationals or habitual residents.[28] This broad definition applies to all Articles within the IMBR, except when particular enumerated rights are qualified to apply to one or more specific categories of migrants.

(3) Under current international law, there is no definitive, legal definition of who is considered a migrant for the purposes of human rights protection. Current international legal instruments related to the rights of migrants remain largely unconnected, while specific protections are limited to categories of migrants, such as refugees and asylum seekers or migrant workers.[29] The current categorizations do not articulate the protections that should apply to persons who are outside of their countries of origin or habitual residence or for stateless migrants, their country of birth or habitual residence. The term "migrant" advances the notion that all categories of migrants are entitled to a unified set of basic protections regardless of their individual circumstances. The IMBR bridges this gap in international human rights law.

(4) This Article also describes the scope of the IMBR by clarifying that the IMBR applies to the entire process of migration. Thus, the IMBR applies during all stages of the migration process, including preparation for migration, departure, transit, admission, stay in a host State, repatriation, and return to the State of nationality.

---

28. *See* Guiding Principles on Internal Displacement, *supra* note 23.
29. ICRMW, *supra* note 16, at arts. 2, 3, 6; 1951 Refugee Convention, *supra* note 16, at art 1A.

(5) *Paragraph 1*: The broad definition of migrant in Article 1 seeks to encompass definitions from a number of complementary international and regional instruments. These include the International Convention on the Protection of the Rights of All Migrant Workers and Members of Their Families (ICRMW);[30] the 1954 Convention Relating to the Status of Stateless Persons (1954 Statelessness Convention);[31] the 1951 Convention Relating to the Status of Refugees (1951 Refugee Convention);[32] the Charter of Fundamental Rights of the European Union (EU Charter);[33] the Organization of American States (OAS) Cartagena Declaration on Refugees (OAS Declaration);[34] the Organization of African Unity (OAU) 1969 Convention Governing the Specific Aspects of Refugee Problems in Africa (1969 OAU Convention);[35] and additional international instruments relating to non-citizens.[36]

(6) *Persons with Special Protection under International Law*: In line with the wide definition of "migrants," persons who are entitled to special protection under international law will receive the "most favorable standard." Nevertheless, if for any reason, *de jure* or *de facto*, the special protection ceases, these persons shall *ipso facto* be entitled to the benefits of the IMBR if they remain present within the territory of a State of which they are not citizens or nationals.

(7) *Persons with Special Status under International Law—Forced Migrants*: The term "migrant" in Paragraph 1 includes forced migrants for whom international or municipal law accords special status, including refugees, asylum seekers and the temporarily displaced, as described both in international and regional treaties, agreements and conventions.[37] Therefore, "migrants" include refugees and asylum seekers[38] who qualify for refugee status under the criteria set forth in the 1951 Refugee Convention,[39] regional

30. ICRMW, *supra* note 16, at arts. 2, 3, 6.

31. Convention Relating to the Status of Stateless Persons art. 1, Sept. 28, 1954, 360 U.N.T.S. 117.

32. 1951 Refugee Convention, *supra* note 16.

33. Charter of Fundamental Rights of the European Union, *supra* note 24, at art. 18.

34. Cartagena Declaration on Refugees (Cartagena de Indias, 22 November 1984) OAS/Ser.L/V/II.66, doc. 10, rev. 1 rev.1, ¶ 5 [hereinafter Cartagena Declaration].

35. Convention Governing the Specific Aspects of Refugee Problems in Africa art. 1, Sept. 10, 1969, 1001 U.N.T.S. 45.

36. *See* U.N. High Comm'r for Refugees, The Rights of Non-Citizens, U.N. Doc. HR/Pub/06/11, U.N. Sales No. E.07.XIV.2 (2006); Declaration on the Human Rights of Individuals Who Are Not Nationals of the Country in Which They Live, G.A. Res. 40/144, annex, Supp. (No. 53) at 252, U.N. Doc. A/40/53 (Dec. 13, 1985).

37. *See supra* notes 25-31.

38. *See infra* Commentary to Art. 11.

39. Pursuant to Article 1D of the 1951 Refugee Convention, *supra* note 16, refugees include persons who are "at present receiving from organs or agencies of the United Nations other than the United Nations High Commissioner for Refugees protection or assistance," as well as refugees "*ipso facto* . . . entitled to the benefits" of the 1951 Refugee Convention because the "protection or assistance" they receive "from organs or agencies of the United Nations other than the United Nations High Commissioner for Refugees has ceased for any reason," without their position "being definitely settled in accordance with the relevant resolutions adopted by the General Assembly of the United Nations." *See, e.g.*, U.N. High Comm'r for Refugees, Revised UNHCR Note on the Applicability of

instruments and agreements, and municipal legislation, as well as under any extended mandate[40] of the United Nations High Commissioner for Refugees (UNHCR). Additionally, "migrant" includes refugees or asylum seekers granted refuge under temporary international, regional or municipal protection schemes, or whose claims remain under review.

(8) The designation of "migrant" also applies to forced migrants who do not qualify for special status under international law, but nevertheless are forcibly[41] displaced or are compelled to find refuge in the territory of another country.[42] The term "migrant" equally refers to stateless persons who are outside of a State of birth or habitual residence.[43] Due attention should be given to the special relevance of the IMBR to the protection of migrants who do not enjoy the privilege of having the support of their country of origin, regardless of whether it ceased to exist or refuses to offer support.

(9) *Lawfully Settled Migrants*: The term migrant also encompasses persons who qualify for a durable legal status that entitles them to long-term residence, in conformity with host State immigration laws, as well as individuals who are *de facto* permitted to settle in spite of a specific residency status to the contrary.[44] Paragraph 1 also applies to spouses who migrate for marriage. Migration for marriage primarily, but not exclusively, affects women. This phenomenon is noted in particular, because such migration

---

the 1951 Convention relating to the Status of Refugees to Palestinian Refugees (2009), at http://www.refworld.org/pdfid/4add77d42.pdf (clarifying a long-standing inconsistency on the part of UNHCR with regard to the second clause of Article 1D).

40. UNHCR's current extended mandate applies to individuals "outside their country of origin or habitual residence and unable or unwilling to return there owing to serious and indiscriminate threats to life, physical integrity or freedom resulting from generalized violence or events seriously disturbing public order," including for example "foreign domination, intervention, occupation or colonialism." U.N. High Comm'r for Refugees, Self-Study Module 2: Refugee Status Determination. Identifying Who is a Refugee (Sept. 1, 2005), at http://www.refworld.org/docid/43141f5d4.html.

41. The term "forced'" "is not to be limited to physical force but includes the threat of force or coercion, such as that caused by fear of violence, duress, detention, psychological oppression or abuse of power against such person or persons or another person, or by taking advantage of a coercive environment." Prosecutor v. Krajisnik, Case No. IT-00-39-T, Judgment, ¶ 729 (Int'l Crim. Trib. for the Former Yugoslavia Sept. 27, 2006).

42. Such migrants include forcibly displaced individuals who have sought refuge because of violations of human, "economic, social and/or cultural rights, where victims perceive that survival in minimally acceptable conditions is at risk or impossible," or whose claims have not yet been filed, have been rejected or are considered inadequate, yet are still present in a country in which they are neither citizens, nationals nor habitual residents. P.A. Taran, *Human Rights of Migrants: Challenges of the New Decade*, *in* THE HUMAN RIGHTS OF MIGRANTS 29 (International Migration Vol. 38 (6), 2000).

43. Article 1 incorporates the 1954 Statelessness Convention definition, which holds that a "'stateless person' means a person who is not considered as a national by any State under the operation of its law." Convention Relating to the Status of Stateless Persons, *supra* note 31 at, art. 1. It should be noted that stateless individuals who do not fall under the IMBR are nonetheless entitled to the full spectrum of human rights enshrined in the UDHR and outlined in international and national instruments, including the Convention Relating to the Status of Stateless Persons and the 1961 Convention on the Reduction of Statelessness. *See* 1961 Convention on the Reduction of Statelessness art. 1, para. 1, Aug. 30, 1961, 989 U.N.T.S. 175.

44. Such persons include, for example, lawful permanent residents, recognized and intending immigrants, lawful long-term non-immigrant residents, and other individuals with recognized permanent status.

arrangements have the potential to make persons "vulnerable, since their legal status is linked to that of" another person.[45]

(10) *Lawful Temporary Migrants*: Paragraph 1 does not distinguish between migrants based on length of stay. Therefore, "migrant" includes persons intending to lawfully remain in the territory of another state temporarily, because such persons are equally entitled to the rights enumerated in the IMBR, including equal protection, due process and protection against discrimination. Such persons include, for example, tourists; people conducting business for a temporary period of time, including investors;[46] students and trainees;[47] and artists present within the territory of a State of which they are not a citizen or national. Nevertheless, length and original purpose of stay may serve as a relevant criterion for distinction in various contexts, as mentioned, for instance, in the commentary to Article 3(4). The IMBR also applies to irregular migrants that were, for a certain period, under regular status that excludes protection by other international instruments (such as students or tourists).

(11) *Migrant Workers*: Paragraph 1 applies fully to "migrant workers" and incorporates the definition of migrant worker from the ICRMW.[48] The IMBR adopts a broad definition of migrant to ensure a uniform standard of treatment.

(12) *Irregular Migrants*: Paragraph 1 encompasses migrants who are not lawfully present in a State of which they are not nationals or citizens. Such persons include undocumented migrants, individuals with expired status; individuals "who enter without following required immigration procedures;"[49] individuals "who enter as non-immigrants and then remain beyond the limits of their permission to remain;"[50] or persons who otherwise lack the requisite documentation to remain. "Migrant" also refers to irregular migrants who may be smuggled,[51] trafficked,[52] or otherwise irregularly entered

---

45. Nicola Piper & Margaret Satterthwaite, *Migrant Women*, *in* INTERNATIONAL MIGRATION LAW: DEVELOPING PARADIGMS AND KEY CHALLENGES 240, 49-51 (Ryszard Cholewinski, et al. eds., T.M.C. Asser Press 2007).

46. *But cf.* ICRMW, *supra* note 16, at art. 3(c) (excluding "persons taking up residence in a State different from their State of origin as investors" from the benefits of the Convention).

47. *But cf.* ICRMW, *supra* note 16, at art. 3(c) (the IMBR recognizes "students and trainees" as migrants, unlike ICRMW art. 3(e), which excludes these two categories of migrants).

48. ICRMW, *supra* note 16, at art. 2 ("The term 'migrant worker' refers to a person who is to be engaged, is engaged or has been engaged in a remunerated activity in a State of which he or she is not a national."). Under the ICRMW, the migrant worker category explicitly includes frontier workers; seasonal workers; seafarers; workers on offshore installations "under the jurisdiction of a State of which [they] are not . . . national[s];" itinerant workers; project-tied workers; specified-employment workers; and self-employed workers. *Supra* note 16, at art. 2.

49. David Weissbrodt, *Protection of Non-Citizens in International Human Rights Law*, *in* INTERNATIONAL MIGRATION LAW: DEVELOPING PARADIGMS AND KEY CHALLENGES 221, 229 (Ryszard Cholewinski et al. eds., T.M.C. Asser Press 2007).

50. Weissbrodt, *Protection of Non-Citizens in International Human Rights Law*, *supra* note 49.

51. The U.N. Protocol Against the Smuggling of Migrants by Land, Sea and Air seeks to distinguish between victims of trafficking and smuggling. Protocol against the Smuggling of Migrants by Land, Sea and Air, Supplementing the United Nations Convention against Transnational

into a State where they are not nationals or citizens. A migrant's unlawful entry into and presence within a State do not automatically abrogate or otherwise limit rights provided to all migrants in the IMBR, unless specifically noted otherwise.

(13) Defining who qualifies as a migrant brings to the fore important issues regarding the origins, destinations, patterns, volume, and intensity of global migration. Cognizant of the complexity of international migration, the IMBR has purposefully provided a broad and encompassing definition. In this context, the IMBR and the commentary suggest a dynamic blueprint for identifying various types of migration in a changing, global world. The underlying premise of Paragraph 1 is that migrants are entitled to human rights protections, regardless of their nationality, the cause of their migration, lawfulness or irregularity of their presence, or the temporary versus longstanding nature of their stay.

(14) Article 1 highlights important questions as to when an individual ceases to be a "migrant." The designation of "migrant" ceases to apply when a migrant either returns to settle in their country of nationality, citizenship or habitual residence, or when the migrant naturalizes in the State in which the migrant is a resident and thus no longer meets the definition of migrant.[53]

(15) *Paragraph 2*: The language clarifying the scope of the IMBR in Paragraph 2 is rooted in the ICRMW.[54]

(16) The broad language of Paragraph 2 affirms that the rights of migrants endure throughout the entire migration process. The migration process includes various stages of migration during which migrants may be particularly vulnerable to certain abuses. During the entirety of migration, a migrant may pass through or remain in the territory or custody of multiple States, or may interact with States in locations outside of their sovereign territory, such as the high seas. Paragraph 2 clarifies that the migrant is the possessor of the rights contained in the IMBR regardless of geographic location or relationship to the sovereign in question.

Organized Crime, GA Res. 55/25, annex III, U.N. GAOR, 55th Sess., Supp. No. 49, at 65, UN Doc. A/45/49 (Vol. I) (Nov. 15, 2000). Article 3 of the Protocol "states that smuggled migrants have consented to being transported—usually for a fee—and the relationship with the smugglers ends upon arrival. Trafficked persons, although they may consent to transportation, do so under coercive and deceptive conditions, making the consent meaningless. Most importantly, victims of trafficking are not free upon their arrival. Instead, they continue to be exploited for profit." DAVID WEISSBRODT, THE HUMAN RIGHTS OF NON-CITIZENS 207 (2008). *See also* Convention for the Suppression of the Traffic in Persons and of the Exploitation of the Prostitution of Others, July 25, 1951, 96 U.N.T.S 271.

52. Trafficking "involves the transportation of human beings for illicit purposes, such as sexual exploitation, child labor, forced labor, sweatshop labor, and other illegal activities." Weissbrodt, *Protection of Non-Citizens in International Human Rights Law*, *supra* note 49, at 207. *See also*, Palermo Protocol, *supra* note 16, at art. 3(a).

53. The acquisition of foreign citizenship does not automatically or implicitly forfeit an individual's right to citizenship in the individual's home country. *See infra* Commentary to Art. 13(7).

54. ICRMW, *supra* note 16, at art. 1(2).

(17) Paragraph 2 applies the rights' construct to the entire migration life-cycle. While destination countries have the primary obligation to safeguard the rights of all persons on their territories, abuses often begin in countries of origin, particularly in the process of migrant worker recruitment. Protecting migrants' rights as human and labor rights is also a shared responsibility of countries of origin, transit and destination, and the international community as a whole.[55]

(18) *Preparation for Migration and Departure*: Paragraph 2 applies fully to the period during which a migrant makes preparations to migrate while in the country of origin. In particular, Paragraph 2 seeks to protect migrants during migrant worker recruitment.

(19) *Transit*: Paragraph 2 encompasses migrants in transit from their country of origin to a destination country, without regard to the duration of stay in the country where a migrant is currently present. In this regard, the IMBR seeks to protect, in particular, against abuse of migrants during smuggling, trafficking in persons, and while in transit through particularly inhospitable or perilous routes.

(20) *Admission*: Paragraph 2 clarifies that the rights contained in the IMBR remain attached when a migrant seeks admission to a State. In this context, in particular, the IMBR seeks to protect against unlawful detention or expulsion of migrants seeking admission to a State.

(21) *Stay in a Host State*: Paragraph 2 applies fully to the entire duration of a migrant's stay in a destination State.

(22) *Repatriation*: Paragraph 2 also applies during the process of voluntary or involuntary repatriation of migrants. The IMBR seeks to protect the rights of migrants during expulsion or removal, and in particular, during the involuntary repatriation of vulnerable migrants, custody transfer of a migrant between States, and repatriation that takes place in dangerous, remote, or otherwise life-threatening locations.

(23) *Return to State of Nationality*: Paragraph 2 also applies when a migrant has returned to a State of nationality or origin. Notably, temporary return to a country of nationality, citizenship or habitual residence does not extinguish all rights in the host country of imminent return. A migrant's acquired rights are not forfeited upon return to the country of nationality, citizenship or habitual residence. This provision is particularly relevant in the context of cyclical migration.

---

55. Ryszard Cholewinski, *Human Rights of Migrants: The Dawn of a New Era?*, 24 GEO. IMMIGR. L.J. 615 (2010).

ARTICLE 2
HUMAN DIGNITY

Every migrant has the right to dignity, including physical, mental, and moral integrity.

Commentary

(1) Human dignity is a foundational concept in the UDHR.[56] Article 1 of the UDHR states: "All human beings are born free and equal in dignity and rights."[57] The U.N. Charter also affirms the "dignity and worth of the human person" as a basic concept.[58] Numerous international human rights instruments confirm the status of human dignity as the cornerstone of international human rights law. In identical statements in their preambles, the ICCPR, ICESCR, and CEDAW proclaim that the rights they seek to protect "derive from the inherent dignity of the human person."[59] Article 70 of the ICRMW explicitly recognizes a migrant's right to human dignity.[60] Numerous regional human rights instruments also explicitly give an affirmative right to human dignity.[61]

(2) The purpose of Article 2 is to ensure that migrants are treated with dignity. The U.N. Special Rapporteur on the Human Rights of Migrants emphasized that respecting the dignity of migrants is required by States' human rights obligations.[62] Physically, dignity means that migrants, by virtue of their humanity, must be "afforded the basic requirements to live as a human being who is valued."[63] Psychologically, dignity means that migrants must not be demeaned or treated as if they have no value.[64] Thus, the concept of human dignity requires that the value and integrity of each individual migrant be respected based on our common humanity. Violations of certain fundamental rights such as the rights to life, liberty, due process, and freedom from torture and discrimination may concurrently violate the right to dignity by their very nature.[65]

---

56. UDHR, *supra* note 1 (references to human dignity appear in the Preamble twice and in Articles 1, 22, and 23).

57. UDHR, *supra* note 1.

58. U.N. Charter, pmbl.

59. Evadne Grant, *Dignity and Equality*, 7 HUM. RTS. L. REV. 299, 303 (2007).

60. ICRMW, *supra* note 16, at art. 70.

61. *See, e.g.*, Banjul Charter, *supra* note 9, at art. 5 ("Every individual shall have the right to the respect of the dignity inherent in a human being . . ."); ACHR, *supra* note 12, at art. 11 ("Everyone has the right to have his honor respected and his dignity recognized . . . Every person has the right to have his physical, mental, and moral integrity respected . . .").

62. U.N. GAOR, 57th Sess., U.N. Doc. A/57/292 (Aug. 8, 2002) ("Migration should thus take place in conditions that respect the dignity of migrants, in line with States' human rights obligations.").

63. Grant, *supra* note 59, at 312.

64. *Id.*

65. *See, e.g.*, Pedro Miguel Vera Vera et al. v. Ecuador, Case 11.535, Inter-Am. Comm'n H.R., OEA/Ser.L/V/II, doc. 5 rev. ¶ 37 (2010), *available at* http://www.cidh.oas.org/demandas/11.535%20Pedro%20Miguel%20Vera%20y%20otros%20Ecuador%2024%20febrero10%20Eng.pdf. ("Among

ARTICLE 3
EQUAL PROTECTION

(1) All persons, including migrants, are equal before the law. Every migrant has the right, without any discrimination, to the equal protection of the law on the same basis as nationals of any State in which the migrant is present.

(2) The present Bill of Rights applies to all migrants without distinction of any kind, such as sex, race, color, language, religion or conviction, political or other opinion, national, ethnic or social origin, nationality, age, economic position, property, marital status, disability, birth, gender, sexual orientation or gender identity or other status.

(3) In this respect, the law shall prohibit any discrimination and guarantee to migrants equal and effective protection against discrimination on any ground such as sex, race, color, language, religion or conviction, political or other opinion, national, ethnic or social origin, nationality, property, marital status, disability, birth, gender, sexual orientation or gender identity or other status.

(4) Distinctions in the treatment of migrants are permissible, including in the regulation of admission and exclusion, only where the distinction is made pursuant to a legitimate aim, the distinction has an objective justification, and reasonable proportionality exists between the means employed and the aims sought to be realized.

Commentary

(1) Article 3 emphasizes two core and interrelated principles underlying the protection of the rights of migrants in the IMBR: non-discrimination and equality before the law. The phrasing of Clause 1 of Paragraph 1 emphasizesthat individual migrants are rights-bearers while the rest of Article 3 makes clear that the prohibition on non-discrimination (both under the *per se* grounds of non-discrimination in Paragraph 3 and the test established in Paragraph 4) includes and protects migrants. Importantly, the standard for distinctions permitted amongst and between migrants in Paragraph 2 creates a presumption favoring the equal protection of migrants without unduly burdening states.

the fundamental principles upon which the American Convention is grounded is the recognition that the rights and freedoms protected thereunder are derived from the attributes of the human person. From this principle flows the basic requirement underlying the Convention as a whole, and Article 5 in particular, that individuals must be treated with dignity and respect. Therefore, Article 5(1) guarantees to all persons the right to have his or her physical, mental, and moral integrity respected, and Article 5(2) requires all persons deprived of their liberty to be treated with respect for the inherent dignity of the human person. These guarantees presuppose that persons protected under the Convention will be regarded and treated as individual human beings, particularly in circumstances in which a State Party proposes to limit or restrict the most basic rights and freedoms of an individual, such as the right to liberty.")

(2) The IMBR follows the convention of human right instruments in positing a general standard of non-discrimination as broadly applicable, while explicitly allowing for variation in other articles.[66] Thus, Article 3 shall be read as the rule of general application unless specifically displaced in the circumstances prescribed by a subsequent article.

(3) *Paragraph 1*: That all persons are entitled to equality before and protection of the law is a fundamental tenet of human rights law. Both the UDHR and the ICCPR recognize the principles of equality and equal protection.[67] The principle of equal protection has been widely affirmed in other human rights instruments and by human rights treaty bodies;[68] however, the IMBR adopts a slightly different phrasing for the right in order to emphasize that equal protection must at a minimum afford protection to migrants on the same basis as nationals of a State.[69]

(4) *Equality*: The right to equality, and specifically equality before the law, is a right to be treated equally and in a non-arbitrary manner, even when the specific legal consequence of a law or action does not implicate an independent human right.[70] It also follows that, as a general rule, factual situations involving migrants must be treated consistently with those involving citizens, as well as other migrants.[71] This applies broadly—for example,

66. *See, e.g.*, Human Rights Comm., *General Comment No. 15: The Position of Aliens under the Covenant*, ¶ 2, U.N. Doc. HRI/GEN/1/Rev.1 (Apr. 11, 1986) (A more specific standard displaces the general standard).

67. UDHR, *supra* note 1, at art. 7. ("All are equal before the law and are entitled without any discrimination to equal protection of the law."); ICCPR, *supra* note 2, at art. 26. ("All persons are equal before the law and are entitled without any discrimination to the equal protection of the law.").

68. ICRMW, *supra* note 16, at art. 18 ("Migrant workers and members of their families shall have the right to equality with nationals of the State concerned before the courts and tribunals."); ACHR, *supra* note 12, at art. 24; Banjul Charter, *supra* note 9, at art. 3.

69. ICRMW, *supra* note 16, at art. 18 ("Migrant workers and members of their families shall have the right to equality with nationals of the State concerned before the courts and tribunals."); U.N. Econ. & Soc. Council, Sub-Comm'n on the Promotion and Prot. of Human Rights, *Progress Report of the Special Rapporteur on the Rights of Non-Citizens*, ¶ 50, U.N. Doc. E/CN.4/Sub.2/2002/ (June 5, 2002) ("In general, international human rights law requires the equal treatment of citizens and noncitizens.") [hereinafter ECOSOC]; U.N. Comm. on Econ., Soc. and Cultural Rights, *Consideration of Reports Submitted by States Parties under Articles 16 and 17 of the Covenant: Concluding Observations of the Comm. on Econ., Soc. and Cultural Rights, Dom. Rep.*, ¶ 34, U.N. Doc. E/C.12/1/Add.16 (Dec. 12, 1997) ("State[s] party . . . take all necessary measures to ensure that Haitian immigrants in the Dominican Republic enjoy their economic social and cultural rights fully and without discrimination.").

70. MANFRED NOWAK, U.N. COVENANT ON CIVIL AND POLITICAL RIGHTS: CCPR COMMENTARY 465 (2d rev. ed., N.P. Engel 1993).

71. NOWAK, *supra* note 70, at 467; *General Comment No. 15*, *supra* note 66, ¶¶ 1-3, 7, 9; Ibrahima Gueye et al. v. France, Comm. No. 196/1983 (3 April 1989), ¶ 9.4, U.N. Doc. Supp. No. 40 (A/44/40) at 189 (1989); Comm. on the Elimination of Racial Discrimination, *Compilation of General Comments and General Recommendations Adopted by Human Rights Treaty Bodies, Recommendation 30 on Discrimination Against Non-Citizens*, 189-90 ¶¶ 1, 3, 4, 6, U.N. Doc. CERD/C/64/Misc.11/rev.3 (2004); U.N. Econ. & Soc. Council, Sub-Comm'n on Human Rights, Sub-Comm'n on the Prot. of Human Rights, *Prevention of Discrimination: The Rights of Non-Citizens*, ¶¶ 21-23, U.N. Doc. E/CN.4/Sub.2/2003/23 (May 26, 2003); Comm. on the Elimination of Discrimination, *General Recommendation XIV, Definition of Discrimination*, (Forty-second session, 1993), U.N. Doc. HRI/GEN/1/Rev.9 (May 27, 2008); *General Comment No. 15*, *supra* note 66, ¶ 4.

in requiring equal access to criminal and civil complaint mechanisms; equal access to courts of law and administrative processes, including birth registration; and equal access to remedies and equality in the performance of civil and criminal judgments.[72]

(5) *Equal Protection*: The right to "equal protection" is a right to enjoy actual and effective protection of the law. This is a right directed at those promulgating laws and regulations. It mandates that States both refrain from enacting discriminatory laws and affirmatively promulgate measures that afford effective protection against discrimination for migrants (i.e. afford migrants substantive equality).[73] Thus, there should be equal application of national legislation to migrants as well as citizens, and legislation itself should not be discriminatory.[74]

(6) *On the Same Basis as Nationals*: Qualifying the guarantee of equal protection with the language "on the same basis as nationals" reaffirms the importance of ensuring legal protection without regard to alienage. Rather than stating that migrants bear all the same rights as nationals, this clause stresses that migrants enjoy the same protection as nationals for all coextensive rights. Notably, the IMBR does not limit these obligations to rights provided by the IMBR.[75]

(7) *Paragraph 2*: The restriction on the distinctions States may make when applying the IMBR to migrants is an essential tool to ensure States do not apply the Bill in a discriminatory manner. The restrictions in Paragraph 2 reflect similar restrictions on the application of the ICCPR in its Article 2(1).[76] This principle has been included widely in other human rights instruments as well, including in ICESCR Article 2, the American Conven-

72. The contours of equal protection, while aided by the development of international human rights norms that provide various minimum standards of treatment, continues the long international legal tradition of recognizing the juridical capacity of aliens. *See, e.g.*, ANDREAS HANS ROTH, THE MINIMUM STANDARD OF INTERNATIONAL LAW APPLIED TO ALIENS, 131, n.1 (Leiden, A.W. Sijthoff 1949) (citing The Institute of International Law Declaration of 1874 affirming that the juridical capacity of aliens "existe indépendamment, de toute stipulation des traites et de toute condition de reciprocite" (exists independent of any treaty stipulation and of any obligation of reciprocity [comity]; i.e. juridical capacity is absolute)); Comm. on the Elimination of Racial Discrimination, *Compilation of General Comments and General Recommendations Adopted by Human Rights Treaty Bodies, Recommendation 30 on Discrimination Against Non-Citizens, supra* note 71; Econ. & Soc. Council, Sub-Comm'n on Human Rights, Sub-Comm'n on the Prot. of Human Rights, *Prevention of Discrimination: The Rights of Non-Citizens, supra* note 71; U.N. High Comm'r for Human Rights, Comm. on the Elimination of Racial Discrimination, *Report of the Committee on the Elimination of Racial Discrimination*, ¶ 469, U.N. Doc. A/59/18-24 (2004); *General Comment No. 15, supra* note 66, ¶ 4.

73. NOWAK, *supra* note 71, at 468-69.

74. Human Rights Comm., *General Comment No. 18: Non-Discrimination*, U.N. Doc. HRI/GEN/1/Rev.9 (Nov. 10, 1989); RICHARD B. LILLICH, THE HUMAN RIGHTS OF ALIENS IN CONTEMPORARY INTERNATIONAL LAW 46 (Manchester Univ. Press 1984).

75. This follows general human rights principles. *See, e.g.*, UDHR, *supra* note 1, at pmbl. ¶ 1 ("Whereas recognition of the inherent dignity and of the equal and inalienable rights of all members of the human family is the foundation of freedom, justice and peace in the world").

76. ICCPR, *supra* note 2, at art. 2(1) ("Each State Party to the present Covenant undertakes to respect and to ensure to all individuals within its territory and subject to its jurisdiction the rights recognized in the present Covenant, without distinction of any kind, such as race, colour, sex,

tion on Human Rights (ACHR) Article 1(1), and the ECHR Article 14.[77] The IMBR follows the phrasing of the enumerated grounds of non-distinction in the ICRMW,[78] while adding the grounds of disability and gender, sexual orientation or gender identity to reflect progression of the law in recent years.[79]

(8) *Paragraph 3*: The restriction on discriminatory treatment is a fundamental and complementary principle of the international human rights regime. Both the UDHR and the ICCPR prohibit discrimination.[80] Paragraph 3 mandates that States refrain from discriminating against or between migrants on a number of enumerated bases;[81] however, this list should not be seen as exhaustive. It explicitly allows for breadth to encompass developments in customary international and human rights law. This wording echoes the affirmative obligation on States, to both enact non-discriminatory laws and to work to eliminate the discriminatory effect of all laws and policies.[82] As should be clear from the non-exhaustive nature of the enumerated grounds, this affirmative obligation is not limited to distinctions between migrants and nationals. It includes affirmative obligations with regard to all grounds recognized as constituting discrimination *per se*, for example, with regard to sex-based discrimination.[83]

(9) *Enumerated Grounds*: The IMBR follows the phrasing of the enumerated grounds of non-discrimination used in the ICRMW.[84] In addition to the

language, religion, political or other opinion, national or social origin, property, birth or other status.").

77. ICESCR, *supra* note 3, at art. 2; ACHR, *supra* note 12, at art. 1(1); ECHR, *supra* note 8, at art. 53.

78. ICRMW, *supra* note 16, at art. 1(1) ("The present Convention is applicable, except as otherwise provided hereafter, to all migrant workers and members of their families without distinction of any kind such as sex, race, colour, language, religion or conviction, political or other opinion, national, ethnic or social origin, nationality, age, economic position, property, marital status, birth or other status.").

79. *See* CRPD, *supra* note 7. *See generally*, THE YOGYAKARTA PRINCIPLES: PRINCIPLES ON THE APPLICATION OF INTERNATIONAL HUMAN RIGHTS LAW IN RELATION TO SEXUAL ORIENTATION AND GENDER IDENTITY, http://www.yogyakartaprinciples.org/principles_en.pdf (last visited Mar. 18, 2014) [hereinafter YOGYAKARTA PRINCIPLES]; Joslin v. N.Z., Comm. No. 902/1999, U.N. Doc. A/57/40 at 214 (2002); Jarvinen v. Finland, Comm. No. 295/1988, ¶ 6.2, U.N. Doc. CCPR/C/39/D/295/1988 (1990); *General Comment No. 15*, *supra* note 66, ¶ 3.

80. UDHR, *supra* note 1, at art 7; ICCPR, *supra* note 2, at art. 26.

81. *See* NOWAK, *supra* note 70, at 459 ("The prohibition on discrimination for reasons of certain personal characteristics has come to be the most essential element in a substantive structuring of the principle of equality . . .").

82. JAMES C. HATHAWAY, THE RIGHTS OF REFUGEES UNDER INTERNATIONAL LAW 238-39 (Cambridge Univ. Press 2005); *see also* NOWAK, *supra* note 70, at 476-79 (discussing ICCPR Committee commentaries discussing positive measures (affirmative action) to mitigate horizontally discriminatory effect, such as in the workplace).

83. *See, e.g.*, Comm. on Elimination. of Discrim. Against Women, *General Recommendation No. 21: Equality in Marriage and Family Relations*, U.N. Doc. A/49/38 (1994), at http://www.un.org/womenwatch/daw/cedaw/recommendations/recomm.htm#recom21.

84. ICRMW, *supra* note 16, at art. 7 ("States Parties undertake, in accordance with the international instruments concerning human rights, to respect and to ensure to all migrant workers and members of their families within their territory or subject to their jurisdiction the rights provided for in the present Convention without distinction of any kind such as to sex, race, colour, language,

prohibited grounds of discrimination under the ICCPR, the ICRMW and the IMBR add "conviction," "ethnic origin,"[85] "nationality,"[86] "marital status,"[87] and "disability."[88] Paragraph 3 also adds grounds considered "other status" under the ICRMW and the ICCPR, such as gender identity and sexual orientation, reflecting the progression of the law in recent years.[89]

(10) *Paragraph 4*: The IMBR adds a specific legal test for making distinctions among and between migrants. The legal standard adopted in Paragraph 4 mandates legitimate action, objective justification, and reasonable proportionality, thus distinguishing between prohibited discrimination and lawful distinctions. In selecting this standard, the IMBR creates a presumption in favor of migrants drawn from commentators and ECHR jurisprudence,[90] and explicitly rejects the more deferential standard articulated by the U.N. Human Rights Committee in General Comment 18.[91] The standard flows directly from the principles of equality and non-discrimination, as was suggested by the Human Rights Committee in General Comment 15.

(11) The IMBR explicitly selects a standard for distinctions at the most protective end of current State practice and *opinio juris*. The test represents the optimal compromise between protecting sovereign functions and safeguarding the welfare of migrants. In selecting a test that hinges on legitimacy and proportionality, the IMBR affirms that the rights of migrants derive from their fundamental human dignity and status as persons before the law, as well as their ties to the community of the host State.

(12) *Regulation of Admission and Exclusion*: The IMBR does not limit the sovereign power of States to control admission of non-citizens at their

---

religion or conviction, political or other opinion, national, ethnic or social origin, nationality, age, economic position, property, marital status, birth or other status.").

85. ICERD, *supra* note 4, at art. 1 (defining racial discrimination to include discrimination on the basis of ethnic origin); Banjul Charter, *supra* note 9, at art. 2 (prohibiting distinctions based on individuals' ethnic group).

86. *General Comment No. 15*, *supra* note 66, ¶¶ 1-2 ("In general, the rights set forth in the [ICCPR] apply to everyone, irrespective of reciprocity, and irrespective of his or her nationality or statelessness. Thus the general rule is that aliens receive the benefit of the general requirement of non-discrimination in respect of the rights guaranteed in the Covenant.").

87. CEDAW, *supra* note 16, at art. 1 (defining prohibited discrimination to include distinctions made on the basis of marital status).

88. CRPD, *supra* note 7, at art. 5(2) (prohibiting discrimination on the basis of disability); CRC, *supra* note 6, at art. 2(1) (prohibiting discrimination on the basis of disability).

89. *See generally* YOGYAKARTA PRINCIPLES, *supra* note 79; Joslin v. N.Z., *supra* note 79; Jarvinen v. Finland, *supra* note 79, ¶ 6.2; *General Comment No. 15*, *supra* note 66, ¶ 3.

90. GUY S. GOODWIN GILL, INTERNATIONAL LAW AND THE MOVEMENT OF PERSONS BETWEEN STATES 78 (Oxford Univ. Press 1978) (citing Judge Tanaka's dissent in The South West African Cases and the ECHR decision in the Belgian Linguistics cases). *See also* Joan Fitzpatrick, *The Human Rights of Migrants*, *in* MIGRATION AND INTERNATIONAL LEGAL NORMS 172, 176 (T. Alexander Aleinikoff & Vincent Chetail eds., T.M.C. Asser Press 2003); SARAH JOSEPH, JENNY SCHULTZ & MELISSA CASTAN, THE INTERNATIONAL COVENANT ON CIVIL AND POLITICAL RIGHTS: CASES, MATERIAL AND COMMENTARY 700-28 (2d ed., Oxford Univ. Press 2004).

91. General Comment 18 does not mention proportionality. *General Comment No. 18*, *supra* note 74, ¶ 13. *See also*, David A. Martin, *The Authority and Responsibility of States*, *in* MIGRATION AND INTERNATIONAL LEGAL NORMS 31, 35 (T. Alexander Aleinikoff & Vincent Chetail eds., T.M.C. Asser Press 2003).

borders or formulate immigration policy,[92] as long as the exercise of those powers is reasonable.[93] Thus, the standard acknowledges that States are allowed to, and may make such distinctions, and rejects any notion that States require an explicit "margin of appreciation."[94] Indeed, the IMBR allows States to make reasonable distinctions among and between migrants in light of foreign policy goals or on the basis of national security.[95] This standard strikes a balance between the needs and rights of States and the need to protect the rights of migrants.

(13) *Legitimate Aim*: The IMBR language permitting only those distinctions based on a legitimate aim should be read in reference to international and regional norms as well as national norms and protections (i.e. not just rights within the IMBR or the core international human rights treaties).[96] The standard does not require that distinctions only be made pursuant to law, though the broader requirements of equal protection generally do. Thus, the IMBR constrains both discretionary and non-discretionary State action.

(14) *Objectivity and Reasonable Proportionality*: The IMBR further requires States to act in a way that is objectively related to and reflects a reasonable proportionality between the means employed and the legitimate goal pursued. This test is intentionally context-specific.[97] Fundamentally, the IMBR should be interpreted as creating a continuum of reasonable and proportional distinctions.[98] Most importantly, as a migrant's contact and connection with the host State increase, any distinctions made should tend toward more favorable treatment. Consequently, migrants with less contact or connection with the host State may receive less favorable treatment, as long as the treatment they receive complies with the provisions of this Bill and other human rights protections. Thus, a State may, for example, take into account the longstanding connection of particular classes of migrants (or of

92. *See, e.g.*, Martin, *supra* note 91 (discussing James A.R. Nafziger, *The General Admission of Aliens Under International Law*, 77 AM. J. INT'L L. 803 (1983) (suggesting that states can maintain immigration regimes that give preference on the basis of, for example, economic status)).

93. U.N. Econ. & Soc. Council, Sub-Comm'n on Human Rights, Sub-Comm'n on the Prot. of Human Rights, *Prevention of Discrimination: The Rights of Non-Citizens*, *supra* note 72, ¶ 21; Human Rights Comm., Shirin Aumeeruddy-Cziffra and 19 Other Mauritian Women v. Mauritius, No. R.9/35, U.N. Doc. Supp. No. 40 (A/36/40) at 134, ¶¶ 9.2(b)2(ii)2-9.2(b)2(ii)3 (1981); Abdulaziz v. U.K., App. No. 9214/80, 9473/81, 9474/81, 7 Eur. H.R. Rep. 471, 499 (1985).

94. Gaygusuz v. Austria, App. No. 17371/90, 23 Eur. H.R. Rep. 364, 381-82 (1996) (noting the margin of appreciation doctrine, but also indicating that states must provide "very weighty reasons" to benefit from it; holding that distinctions in emergency housing assistance between Austrian and non-European community national are discriminatory in spite of State's claim of special responsibility for citizens). *See also General Comment No. 15*, *supra* note 66, ¶ 5; Poirrez v. France, App. No. 40892/98, 40 Eur. H.R. Rep. 2, 38, 46, 47 (2003) (claim to disability benefits by a Cote d'Ivoire national resident in France); Abdulaziz, 7 Eur. H.R. Rep. at 499; Proposed Amendments to the Naturalization Provisions of the Constitution of Costa Rica, Advisory Opinion OC-4/84, Inter-Am. Ct. H.R. (Ser. A) No. 4, ¶ 62 (Jan. 19, 1984).

95. *See* Martin, *supra* note 91, at 33 (discussing the traditional and historically fundamental sovereign function of regulating admission of aliens).

96. Including, for example, obligations under the 1951 Refugee Convention and 1967 Protocol.

97. Joseph et. al., *supra* note 90, at 700.

98. *See* Martin, *supra* note 91, at 35.

individual migrants) to the State when conferring benefits.[99] The standard also does not prohibit more favorable treatment *per se*, such as measures taken by a State to protect a particular national group in a time of natural disaster in the State of origin.[100]

ARTICLE 4
VULNERABLE MIGRANTS

(1) Every vulnerable migrant has the right to protection and assistance required by the migrant's condition and status and to treatment which takes into account the migrant's special needs.

(2) In all actions concerning child migrants, the best interests of the child shall be a primary consideration. States shall undertake to ensure the child migrant such protection and care as is necessary for the child's well-being, and assure to the child migrant who is capable of forming the child's own views the right to express those views freely in all matters affecting the child, the views of the child being given due weight in accordance with the age and maturity of the child.

(3) States shall take in all fields all appropriate measures to ensure the full development and advancement of women migrants for the purposes of guaranteeing them the exercise and enjoyment of human rights and fundamental freedoms on the basis of equality with men, including the provision of special protection during pregnancy.

(4) States shall undertake to ensure and promote the full realization of all human rights and fundamental freedoms for all migrants with disabilities without discrimination of any kind on the basis of disability, including through taking appropriate measures to enable migrants with disabilities to live independently and participate fully in all aspects of life.

Commentary

(1) Article 4 provides that particularly vulnerable migrants are entitled to protection and assistance required by their condition and to treatment that takes into account their special needs and legal status. According special protection to some groups of migrants does not violate the principle of equality, as objectively disparate situations should not be treated equally and specific vulnerabilities should be taken into account.[101] Human rights law deals with the special needs of certain categories of persons in specific

99. *See, e.g.*, INT'L MIGRANTS BILL OF RIGHTS, art. 10, 28 GEO. IMMIGR. L.J. 17 (envisioning that States will take substantial connection into account when creating opportunities for relief from removal).

100. For example, the practice of according temporary protection to migrants independent of *non-refoulement* obligations. Such a measure would fall within the bounds of the legal test and therefore not be discriminatory.

101. Kalin, *supra* note 11, at 22.

instruments, including protections for children,[102] women,[103] and persons with disabilities.[104] Article 4 reinforces these existing protections. When read in conjunction with the rest of the IMBR, Article 4 extends a right to special protection and treatment to all vulnerable migrants, including migrants who are vulnerable in multiple and intersecting ways, when realizing the rights contained herein.[105]

(2) *Paragraph 1*: Paragraph 1 is adapted from Principle 4(2) of the Guiding Principles on Internal Displacement. While Paragraphs 2 through 4 enumerate obligations of States toward particular vulnerable migrants—child migrants, women migrants, and migrants with disabilities—the rights in Paragraph 1 apply to all vulnerable migrants.

(3) *Origins of Paragraph 2*: The CRC Articles 3(1), 3(2) and 12(1) state that the rights contained in Paragraph 2 apply to all children, including child migrants.[106] Article 7 of the CRPD affirms that children with disabilities, including migrant children with disabilities, possess the rights in Paragraph 2.[107]

(4) *Origins of Paragraph 3*: Paragraph 3 is an adaptation of CEDAW Articles 3 and 11(2)(d).[108] The CRPD Article 6 affirms these rights for women with disabilities, including women migrants with disabilities.[109]

(5) *Origins of Paragraph 4*: Paragraph 4 applies CRPD Articles 4 and 9 specifically to migrants with disabilities.[110] Through Paragraph 4, the IMBR also stresses all principles of the CRPD, listed in CRPD Article 3.[111]

ARTICLE 5
LIFE

Every migrant has the inherent right to life. This right shall be protected by law. No migrant shall be arbitrarily deprived of life.

Commentary

(1) The right to life is a fundamental right of all persons, as codified in numerous international human rights instruments. Article 5 of the IMBR creates an affirmative responsibility on the part of States to not deprive migrants of the right to life.

102. CRC, *supra* note 6.
103. CEDAW, *supra* note 16.
104. CRPD, *supra* note 7.
105. *See* Report of the Special Rapporteur on Violence Against Women, Its Causes and Consequences, ¶¶ 12-108, A/HRC/17/26/Add.1-5 (May 2, 2011).
106. CRC, *supra* note 6, at arts. 3(1), 3(2), 12(1).
107. CRPD, *supra* note 7, at art. 7.
108. CEDAW, *supra* note 16, at arts. 3, 11(2)(d). *See also* Comm. on the Elimination of Discrimination Against Women, *General Recommendation No. 26 on Women Migrant Workers*, UN Doc. CEDAW/C/2009/WP.1/R (Dec. 5, 2008).
109. CRPD, *supra* note 7, at art. 6.
110. CRPD, *supra* note 7, at arts. 4(1), 9(1).
111. CRPD, *supra* note 7, at art. 3.

(2) In the migration context, the right to life is threatened by numerous factors and in a variety of contexts. Migrants in transit between countries face harsh conditions and dangerous routes, as a result of extremes of climate and weather as well as unsafe or overcrowded vehicles, boats, and other means of transportation.[112] Detained migrants suffer from threats to their health and safety, due to isolation, unsafe conditions, and lack of access to health care.[113] Additional rationales for enunciating the right to life in the migration context include: hate crimes against migrants; deaths during smuggling, flight, border-crossing, or otherwise when seeking entry; and violations of the right to life by border authorities or other government forces. Article 5 of the IMBR creates an affirmative responsibility of States to protect the lives of migrants, just as States have a responsibility to protect the lives of all persons subject to their jurisdiction.

(3) The language of Paragraph 1 is drawn directly from the ICCPR, Article 6.[114] The right to life is also enumerated in other international instruments, including the UDHR,[115] the ICRMW,[116] and the Guiding Principles on Internal Displacement.[117]

ARTICLE 6
LIBERTY AND SECURITY OF PERSON

(1) Every migrant has the right to liberty and security of person. No migrant shall be arbitrarily arrested, detained, or otherwise deprived of liberty.

(2) States shall ensure that deprivations of liberty occur only in accordance with and as authorized by law and only when determined to be necessary, reasonable in all the circumstances, and proportionate to a legitimate objective. States should cease the detention of children on the basis of their immigration status.

(3) Detention shall occur only as measure of last resort and shall last no longer than required by the circumstances. Detention shall occur only pursuant to an individualized determination of the need to detain, and the

---

112. Maria Jimenez, *Humanitarian Crisis: Migrant Deaths at the U.S.-Mexico Border*, ACLU of San Diego & Imperial Counties and Mexico's National Commission of Human Rights (October 2009) (estimating that migrant deaths at the southern U.S. border from approximately 1994 to 2009 ranged from 3,861 to 5,607 deaths. Although the U.S. border patrol does perform search and rescue of migrants, there have been concerns that there have been both a decrease in the number of rescues and a rise in the number of deaths in recent years). *See, e.g.*, *Europe Migrant Deaths: Record Number of Migrants Died While Trying to Reach Continent, UN Says*, HUFFINGTONPOST.COM, http://www.huffingtonpost.com/2012/01/31/europe-migrant-deaths_n_1244132.html (last visited Jul. 21, 2012) (migrants worldwide have perished trying to reach final destinations).

113. Will Matthews, *Immigration Detention: A Death Sentence for Too Many*, ACLU BLOG OF RIGHTS (Oct. 24, 2011, 2:35 PM), http://www.aclu.org/blog/immigrants-rights/immigration-detention-death-sentence-far-too-many.

114. ICCPR, *supra* note 2, at art. 6.

115. UDHR, *supra* note 1, at art. 3.

116. ICRMW, *supra* note 16, at art. 9.

117. Guiding Principles on Internal Displacement, *supra* note 23, at Principle 10.

migrant shall have the right to appeal the conditions, legality, and length of detention.

(4) Every migrant deprived of liberty shall be treated with humanity and with respect for the inherent dignity of the human person.

(5) Every migrant who has been the victim of unlawful arrest or detention shall have an enforceable right to compensation.

Commentary

(1) Article 6 affirms a number of fundamental elements of the right to liberty and security of the person as it relates to detention or other deprivations of the liberty of migrants. Paragraph 1 asserts a basic principle of the right to liberty and security of person. Implicit in this paragraph is the presumption of non-detention. Paragraph 2 reproduces core procedural protections against arbitrary detention. Paragraph 3 further protects against arbitrary detention and explicitly conditions the State's ability to detain migrants. Paragraph 4 incorporates a respect for dignity in detention conditions. Paragraph 5 asserts compensation for violations of these rights.

(2) The right of migrants to liberty and security of the person is violated with alarming frequency. States increasingly use detention at the border, criminal enforcement, and other forms of detention or deprivations of liberty to punish irregular migrants.[118] In some cases, including many involving stateless migrants, or where there are no diplomatic relations between the host State and the country of origin, a State's inability to remove migrants may render detention indefinite.[119] Additionally, the use of criminal penalties in lieu of, or to reinforce, administrative enforcement against violations of immigration law is of increasing concern.[120] Article 6 thus attempts to codify those fundamental protections necessary to ensure adequate protection of the rights of migrants when detained or otherwise deprived of liberty.

(3) *Paragraph 1*: Paragraph 1 is rooted in the rights of liberty and security of the person,[121] as well as the prohibition on arbitrary detention. It applies regardless of legal status.[122] The wording of the IMBR is adapted directly from the ICCPR Article 9(1).[123] This choice of language affirms a presumption of liberty and sets non-detention as the norm.

(4) The purpose of Paragraph 1 is to affirm that migration alone is an insufficient basis for depriving migrants of liberty and that wrongful deten-

118. *See, e.g.*, G.A. Res. 63/184, U.N. Doc. A/RES/63/184 (Mar. 17, 2009).

119. *See, e.g.*, Katherine Perks & Jarlath Clifford, *The Legal Limbo of Detention*, 32 FORCED MIGRATION REV. 42 (2009).

120. *See, e.g.*, Navanethem Pillay, Opening Remarks at the Panel Discussion on "Human Rights of Migrants in Detention Centres" (Sept. 17, 2009), *available at* http://www2.ohchr.org/english/issues/migration/taskforce/docs/HCStatementPanelMigrants.pdf.

121. Shyla Vohra, *Detention of Irregular Migrants and Asylum Seekers*, in INTERNATIONAL MIGRATION LAW 49, 49-51 (Ryszard Cholewinski et al. eds., 2007).

122. ICCPR, *supra* note 2, at art. 9; UDHR, *supra* note 1, at art. 9.

123. ICCPR, *supra* note 2, at art. 9(1).

tion is incompatible with the human right of liberty and security of person. These principles are codified in both the U.N. Charter and the UDHR.[124] In order to safeguard the rights and autonomy of migrants, the IMBR affirms a presumption of non-detention, promotes the liberty and security of person of migrants, and includes limits carefully constrained to protect the interests of sovereign States.

(5) *Paragraph 2*: Paragraph 2 is derived from Article 9(1) of the ICCPR and includes the requirements of non-arbitrariness and procedural fairness. The prohibition against arbitrary detention is a process right mandating that States precisely define the cases in which deprivation of liberty is permissible.[125] It places a legal obligation on both legislators and those enforcing the laws.[126] The general standard for determining arbitrariness is that action must be reasonable and necessary in all circumstances, and must not contravene national or international law, including the IMBR.[127]

(6) Paragraph 2 emphasizes that States should not detain children for migration-related reasons. Detention based on migration status or parental migration status is not in the child's best interest and is a violation of the CRC.[128] States should implement alternatives to deprivation of liberty, such as the Child-Sensitive Community Assessment and Placement Model.[129] States should also not detain other vulnerable groups or individuals.

(6) *Paragraph 3*: The rights in Paragraph 3 are derived from the right to be free from arbitrary detention stated in Paragraphs 1 and 4 of ICCPR

---

124. Vohra, *supra* note 121, at 53.

125. NOWAK, *supra* note 70, at 160 (noting that although a process right, liberty of the person is tied to the freedom of movement, and thus only implicated when that freedom has been abridged).

126. NOWAK, *supra* note 47, at 172.

127. NOWAK, *supra* note 47, at 173 (citing Van Alphen v. the Netherlands, Comm. No. 305/1988, U.N. Doc. CCPR/C/39/D/305/1988 (1990), at http://www.refworld.org/docid/525414304.html (finding that although a particular detention was lawful it was not reasonable or necessary in all the circumstances, and was therefore arbitrary; weighing flight risk, interference with evidence, risk of further criminal conduct, etc.); notably, detention cannot be justified by a domestic law that violates binding international minimum standards). *See* Joseph et al., *supra* note 90, at 342 (citing A. v. Australia, Comm. No. 560/1993, U.N. Doc. CCPR/C/59/D/560/1993 (1997), at http://www1.umn.edu/humanrts/undocs/html/vws560.html).

128. Comm. on the Rights of the Child, *General Comment No. 6 on Treatment of Unaccompanied and Separated Children Outside Their Country of Origin*, ¶ 61, U.N. Doc. CRC/GC/2005/6 (Sept. 1, 2005), at http://www2.ohchr.org/english/bodies/crc/docs/GC6.pdf; Comm. on the Rights of the Child, *Report of the 2012 Day of General Discussion: The Rights of All Children in the Context of International Migration*, ¶¶ 32, 78 (Sept. 28, 2012), at http://www.ohchr.org/Documents/HRBodies/CRC/Discussions/2012/DGD2012ReportAndRecommendations.pdf [hereinafter 2012 Day of General Discussion]. *See also* Special Rapporteur on the Human Rights of Migrants, *Promotion and Protection of All Human Rights, Civil, Political, Economic, Social and Cultural Rights, Including the Right to Development*, Human Rights Council, U.N. Doc. A/HRC/11/7 (May 14, 2009), at http://www.refworld.org/pdfid/4a3b51702.pdf; U.N. Secretary-General, Note to the General Assembly, transmitting Human Rights of Migrants Report of the Special Rapporteur, U.N. Doc. A/64/213 (Aug. 3, 2009).

129. INT'L DETENTION COAL. [IDC], CAPTURED CHILDHOOD ch. 6 (2012) *available at* http://idcoalition.org/ccap. *See also* 2012 Day of General Discussion, *supra* note 128, ¶ 35.

Article 9.[130] Paragraph 3 states the presumption in favor of liberty[131] by mandating that detention only occur as a measure of last resort.[132] Paragraph 3 also requires that detention shall not be continued beyond the period for which the State can provide appropriate justification.[133] Indefinite detention for immigration purposes is not lawful under international law.[134] It should be noted that excessive length of detention, or uncertainty as to its duration, also raise issues of cruel, inhuman or degrading treatment.[135]

(7) When choosing to deprive a migrant of liberty, States must first consider whether less intrusive measures, such as alternatives to institutional detention, would suffice to achieve legitimate aims.[136] Critically, however, deprivations of liberty in the context of alternatives to institutional detention must also comport with the requirements of the right to liberty and security of person. Lesser restrictions on liberty must comport with the requirement of the right to freedom of movement, protected under ICCPR Article 12.[137]

---

130. ICCPR, *supra* note 2, at arts. 9(1), 9(4).

131. Human Rights Council, Rep. of the Working Grp. on Arbitrary Detention, ¶¶ 67, 82, U.N. Doc. A/HRC10/21 (Feb. 16, 2009), at http://daccess-dds-ny.un.org/doc/UNDOC/GEN/G09/110/43/PDF/G0911043.pdf?OpenElement [hereinafter 2009 WGAD Report]; Council of Europe: Comm. of Ministers, *Guidelines on Human Rights Protection in the Context of Accelerated Asylum Procedures* (July 1, 2009), *available at* http://www.refworld.org/docid/4a857e692.html. *See also* The U.N. Refugee Agency, Executive Committee, Detention of Refugees and Asylum-Seekers, EXCOM Conclusion No. 44 (XXXVII) ¶ (b) (Oct. 13, 1986), http://www.unhcr.org/print/3ae68c43c0.html; The U.N. Refugee Agency Executive Committee, Expulsion, EXCOM Conclusion No. 7 (XXVIII) ¶ (e) (Oct. 12, 1977), http://www.unhcr.org/print/3ae68c4320.html; Comm. on the Elimination of Racial Discrimination, Concluding Observations of the Committee on the Elimination of Racial Discrimination: Bahamas, ¶ 17, U.N. Doc. CERD/C/64/CO/1 (Apr. 28, 2004); Neptune v. Haiti, Merits, Reparations and Costs, Judgment, Inter-Am. Ct. H.R. (ser. C) No. 180, ¶ 90 (May 6, 2008); Álvarez and Iñiguez v. Ecuador, Preliminary Objections, Merits, Reparations and Costs, Judgment, Inter-Am. Ct. H.R. (ser. C) No. 170, ¶ 53 (Nov. 21, 2007); Vélez Loor v. Panama, Preliminary Objections, Merits, Reparations and Costs, Judgment, Inter-Am. Ct. H.R. (ser. C) No. 218, ¶ 116, 166-71 (Nov. 23, 2010).

132. Human Rights Council, Rep. of the Working Grp. on Arbitrary Detention, ¶¶ 58-59, U.N. Doc. A/HRC13/30 (Jan. 18, 2010) [hereinafter 2010 WGAD Report] (acknowledging "the sovereign right of States to regulate migration," yet cautioning that "immigration detention should gradually be abolished . . . If there has to be administrative detention, the principle of proportionality requires it to be the last resort.").

133. A v. Australia, Comm. No. 560/1993, ¶ 9.4, U.N. Doc CCPR/C/59/D/560/1993 (Apr. 30, 1997), at http://www1.umn.edu/humanrts/undocs/html/vws560.html.

134. *Id.*

135. The Committee Against Torture has repeatedly warned against the use of prolonged or indefinite detention in the immigration context. Comm. Against Torture, Concluding Observations of the Committee Against Torture: Sweden, ¶ 12, U.N. Doc. CAT/C/SWE/CO/5 (June 4, 2008) (detention should be for the shortest possible time); Comm. Against Torture, Concluding Observations of the Committee Against Torture: Costa Rica, ¶ 10, U.N. Doc. CAT/C/CRI/CO/2 (July 7, 2008) (expressing concern at failure to limit the length of administrative detentions of non-nationals and recommending "[t]he State Party should . . . set a maximum legal period for detention pending deportation, which should in no circumstance be indefinite.").

136. C. v. Australia, Comm. No. 900/1999, U.N. Doc. CCPR/C/76/D/900/1999 (Nov. 23, 2002); *See* INT'L DETENTION COAL., THERE ARE ALTERNATIVES: A HANDBOOK FOR PREVENTING UNNECESSARY IMMIGRATION DETENTION (2011) *available at* http://www.ohchr.org/Documents/Issues/Migration/Events/IDC.pdf.

137. ICCPR, *supra* note 2, at art. 12; ECHR, *supra* note 8, at art. 2; ACHR, *supra* note 12, at art. 22; Banjul Charter, *supra* note 9, at art. 12; League of Arab States, Arab Charter on Human Rights, at art. 24, May 22, 2004, reprinted in 12 Int'l Hum. Rts. Rep. 893 (2005) (entered into force Mar. 15, 2008) [hereinafter Arab Charter].

(8) Paragraph 3 also provides migrants the right to challenge detention.[138] Clause 2 of Paragraph 3 is a synthesis of Paragraphs 1 and 4 of ICCPR Article 9.[139] Thus, it both places an obligation on States and provides a specific right to migrants. It also impliedly incorporates other commentary that has stressed the link between legal personhood (as a fundamental expression of liberty) and prohibitions on arbitrary detention and the common-law-derived right of habeas corpus.[140] This restriction applies to all forms of detention, including detention at the border, and not just detention in connection with removal.

(9) *Paragraph 4*: Most fundamentally, Paragraph 4 is rooted in the right to be free from torture and cruel, inhumane and degrading treatment.[141] The ICCPR makes a specific application of the prohibition on torture, cruel, inhumane and degrading treatment for the right of detained persons to be treated with humanity and respect for their human dignity.[142] Standards on conditions of detention are contained in various international authorities.[143] The UNHCR Revised Guidelines on Detention of Asylum Seekers similarly demand that conditions of detention for any asylum seeker deprived of liberty be humane and with respect for the inherent dignity of the person.[144]

(10) Even where deprivations of the liberty of migrants can be justified under international human rights law, additional constraints are imposed on States regarding the conditions of detention and the treatment of detainees. Accordingly, facilities holding migrants must be sufficiently clean, safe and healthy to comport with obligations of humane treatment as well as the

---

138. GUY S. GOODWIN-GILL, THE REFUGEE IN INTERNATIONAL LAW 97 (1983) ("The rule of international law requires that there be available some procedure whereby the underlying legality of executive action can be questioned, such as the writ of habeas corpus in common law jurisdictions;" citing the North Sea Continental Shelf Cases for proposition that the ICCPR "embodies and crystallizes" pre-existing rules of customary international law).

139. ICCPR, *supra* note 2, at arts. 9(1), 9(4).

140. Hamdi v. Rumsfeld, 542 U.S. 507, 555 (2004) (Scalia, J., dissenting) ("To make imprisonment lawful, it must either be, by process from the courts of judicature, or by warrant from some legal officer, having authority to commit to prison; which warrant must be in writing, under the hand and seal of the magistrate, and express the causes of the commitment, in order to be examined into (if necessary) upon a *habeas corpus*.") (quoting 1 W. BLACKSTONE, COMMENTARIES ON THE LAWS OF ENGLAND 131-133 (1765)).

141. CAT, *supra* note 5, at art. 16; ICCPR, *supra* note 2, at art. 7; ECHR, *supra* note 8, at art. 3; ACHR, *supra* note 12, at art. 5; Banjul Charter, *supra* note 9, at art. 5.

142. ICCPR, *supra* note 2, at art. 10(1). *See also* ACHR, *supra* note 12, at art. 5(2); Banjul Charter, *supra* note 9, at art. 5; Arab Charter, *supra* note 137, at art. 20.

143. First U.N. Congress on the Prevention of Crime and the Treatment of Offenders, Standard Minimum Rules for the Treatment of Prisoners (1955) *available at* http://www.globaldetention project.org/fileadmin/docs/Standard-Minimum-Rules-for-the-Treatment-of-Prisoners.pdf; Body of Principles for the Protection of All Persons Under Any Form of Detention Imprisonment, G.A. Res. 43/173, U.N. Doc. A/RES/43/173 (Dec. 9, 1988); U.N. Rules for the Protection of Juveniles Deprived of Their Liberty, G.A. Res. 45/113, U.N. Doc. A/RES/45/113 (Dec. 14, 1990); U.N. Rules for the Treatment of Women Prisoners and Non-custodial Measures for Women Offenders (The Bangkok Rules), G.A. Res. 65/229, U.N. Doc. A/RES/65/229 (Mar. 16, 2011).

144. THE U.N. REFUGEE AGENCY, DETENTION GUIDELINES: GUIDELINES ON THE APPLICABLE CRITERIA AND STANDARDS RELATING TO THE DETENTION OF ASYLUM-SEEKERS AND ALTERNATIVES TO DETENTION (2012), http://www.unhcr.org/refworld/docid/503489533b8.html.

freedom from torture and cruel, inhumane or degrading treatment.[145] Deprivations of liberty should not be punitive in nature, and migrants subject to administrative detention should not be held in criminal detention facilities.[146] To be compatible with human dignity, conditions of detention should not subject detainees to a level of suffering beyond that inherent in detention.[147] Moreover, the cumulative effect of a number of poor conditions may lead to a violation of the prohibition against cruel, inhumane and degrading treatment.[148]

(11) *Overcrowding:* One of the most frequent obstacles to the respect of human dignity and to the prohibition of cruel, inhumane and degrading treatment and other forms of ill-treatment in places of detention is overcrowding.[149] Paragraph 4 prohibits severe overcrowding and less severe overcrowding when in conjunction with other poor conditions of detention.[150]

(12) *Access to Health Care*: The right to health for all migrants, provided in Article 21 also applies to migrants deprived of liberty. Inadequate healthcare or access to essential medicines for migrants deprived of liberty may also violate the prohibition on cruel, inhumane and degrading treatment and Paragraph 4. Lastly, security measures applied during medical treatment must also comport with the requirements of Paragraph 4.[151]

(13) *Protection from Violence*: With respect to migrants deprived of liberty, the State has a heightened obligation to protect and a special duty of care.[152] Accordingly, excessive or inappropriate use of physical restraint and any physical or sexual assaults of migrants deprived of liberty may also violate Paragraph 4.

(14) *Paragraph 5*: States have an obligation to provide available, adequate, effective, prompt and appropriate remedies to victims of violations of international human rights law and international humanitarian law, including reparation.[153] In accordance with this general principle, Paragraph 5 restates the right to reparation, including compensation, for persons, includ-

---

145. CAT, *supra* note 5, at art. 16; ICCPR, *supra* note 2, at art. 7; ECHR, *supra* note 8, at art. 3; ACHR, *supra* note 12, at art. 5; Banjul Charter, *supra* note 9, at art. 8.

146. Human Rights of Migrants, International Standards and the Return Directive of the E.U., Inter-Am. Comm'n H.R., Resolution 03/08 (July 25, 2008).

147. S.D. v. Greece, App. No. 53541/07, Eur. Ct. H.R., ¶ 45 (2011); M.S.S. v. Belgium, App. No. 30696/09, 53 Eur. H.R. Rep. 2, 72 (2011); "Juvenile Reeducation Institute" v. Paraguay, Preliminary Objections, Merits, Reparations, and Costs, Judgment, Inter-Am. Ct. H.R. (ser. C) No. 112, ¶¶ 151-55 (Sept. 2, 2004).

148. Dougoz v. Greece, App. No. 40907/98, 29 Eur. H.R. Rep. CD147 (2011); Z.N.S. v. Turkey, App. No. 21896/08 Eur. Cr. H.R. (2010); Charahili v. Turkey, App. No. 46605/07, 55 Eur. H.R. Rep. 11 (2010); M.S.S. v. Belgium, 53 Eur. H.R. Rep. at 73-74.

149. Special Rapporteur on Torture, Civil and Political Rights, Including the Questions of Torture and Detention: Torture and Other Cruel, Inhuman, or Degrading Treatment or Punishment, Human Rights Council, ¶ 49, U.N. Doc. E/CN.4/2004/56 (Dec. 23, 2003).

150. Orchowski v. Poland, App. No. 17885/04 Eur. Ct. H.R., ¶¶ 122-23 (2009), at http://hudoc.echr.coe.int/sites/eng/pages/search.aspx?i=001-95314#{"itemid":["001-95314"]}.

151. Henaf v. France, App. No. 65436/01, 40 Eur. H.R. Rep. 44, 999-1001 (2005).

152. Salman v. Turkey, App. No. 21986/93, 34 Eur. H.R. Rep. 17 (2002).

153. G.A. Res. 60/147, U.N. Doc. A/RES/60/147 (Dec. 16, 2005).

ing migrants, found by domestic or international courts or other competent authorities to have been wrongfully detained.[154]

ARTICLE 7
LEGAL PERSONHOOD

(1) Every migrant has the right to recognition everywhere as a person before the law.

(2) To give effect to this right to migrants and migrant families, every child shall be registered immediately in the country of the child's birth. A child shall be provided with a birth certificate that provides permanent, official and visible evidence of a State's legal recognition of the child's existence as a member of society.

(3) Every migrant has the right to all documents necessary for the enjoyment and exercise of their legal rights, such as passports, personal identification documents, birth certificates and marriage certificates. It shall be unlawful for anyone, other than a duly authorized public official, to confiscate, destroy, or attempt to destroy identity documents, documents authorizing entry to or stay, residence or establishment in the national territory, or work permits.

Commentary

(1) *Paragraph 1*: The purpose of Paragraph 1 is to reaffirm that every person, including a migrant, has the right to be recognized as a person before the law. This right includes all of the responsibilities required of and protections offered by a legal system. The Paragraph seeks to address that while citizens may possess rights not afforded to non-citizens, the right to recognition as a person before the law is a right that must be afforded equally and is non-derogable.[155] The right is enshrined in the UDHR, Article 16 of the ICCPR, and other relevant international instruments.[156]

(2) *Paragraph 2*: The purpose of Paragraph 2 is to recognize the importance of birth registration as a means for preserving the right to recognition as a person before the law by providing an official record of the existence of a person and to allow an individual to retain documentation of this official record through the issuance of a birth certificate.[157] Regardless of

---

154. ICCPR, *supra* note 2, at art. 9(5); ECHR, *supra* note 8, at art. 5(5); Arab Charter, *supra* note 137, at art. 14.7.

155. ICCPR, *supra* note 2, at art. 4.

156. ICCPR, *supra* note 2, at art. 16; Guiding Principles on Internal Displacement, *supra* note 23, at Principle 20; Banjul Charter, *supra* note 9, at art. 5; CPRD, *supra* note 7, at art. 12.

157. Human Rights Council, Birth Registration and the Right of Everyone to Recognition Everywhere as a Person before the Law, U.N. Doc. A/HRC/19/L.24 (March 16, 2012); Human Rights Comm., *General Comment No. 17: Rights of the Child, Article. 24*, U.N. Doc. HRI/GEN/1/Rev.1 at 23, ¶ 7 (Apr. 7, 1989), at http://ccprcentre.org/doc/ICCPR/General%20Comments/HRI.GEN.1.Rev.9%28Vol.I%29_%28GC17%29_en.pdf ("Under article 24, paragraph 2, every child has the right

nationality laws of individual countries, all children should be registered immediately after birth on the territory of the country of the child's birth.[158] Birth registration should be free of charge and should be performed without delay.[159] This Paragraph seeks to address that children born to migrants do not always have equal access to birth registration and denial of registration leaves children vulnerable to statelessness, as addressed in the Inter-American Court of Human Rights case, *Yean and Bosico v. Dominican Republic*.[160] The right to registration immediately after birth is enshrined in the ICCPR, the CRC, and other relevant international instruments.[161]

(3) *Paragraph 3*: The purpose of Paragraph 3 is to recognize the importance of identity documents that provide a record of an individual's existence as a means of preserving the right to recognition as a person before the law. In the case of migrants who fall under the protection of the 1951 Refugee Convention and its 1967 Protocol or the Guiding Principles on Internal Displacement, the authorities shall issue identity documents or facilitate the issuance of new documents.[162] The protection for migrants against the destruction of such documents originates in the ICRMW.[163]

---

to be registered immediately after birth and to have a name. In the Committee's opinion, this provision should be interpreted as being closely linked to the provision concerning the right to special measures of protection and it is designed to promote recognition of the child's legal personality").

158. *See* G.A. Res. 65/197 ¶ 43(j), U.N. Doc. A/RES/65/197 (Mar. 30, 2011); H.R.C. Res. 16/12, U.N. Doc. A/HRC/16/L.13/Rev.1 (Mar. 22, 2011), at http://daccess-dds-ny.un.org/doc/UNDOC/LTD/G11/122/34/PDF/G1112234.pdf?OpenElement; Recommendation on the Nationality of Children CM/Rec(2009)13, ¶ 57 (Dec. 9, 2009), at https://wcd.coe.int/ViewDoc.jsp?id=1563529 ("States should register the birth of every child born on their territory, even in cases of the illegal presence of foreign or stateless parents, or when the parents of the child are unknown. States should not refuse the registration because of the foreign nationality of the child."); Ineta Ziemele, *Article 7: The Right to Birth Registration, Name and Nationality, and the Right to Know and Be Cared for by Parents*, A COMMENTARY ON THE UNITED NATIONS CONVENTION ON THE RIGHTS OF THE CHILD, Vol. 7, p. 25 (2007) ("A State, at least, should register a child 'immediately after birth.' This does not guarantee nationality to a child but it ensures some recognition by the legal system.").

159. Recommendation on the Nationality of Children, *supra* note 158, ¶ 57.

160. Yean and Bosico v. Dominican Republic, Judgment, Inter-Am. Ct. H.R. (ser. C) No. 130 (Sept. 8, 2005).

161. ICCPR, *supra* note 2, at art. 24; CRC, *supra* note 6, at art. 7; ICRMW, *supra* note 16, at art. 29; African Charter on the Rights and Welfare of the Child, art. 6, July, 1990 OAU Doc. CAB/LEG/24.9/49 (1990) (entered into force Nov. 29, 1999) [hereinafter African Children's Charter]; Recommendation on the Nationality of Children, *supra* note 158.

162. 1951 Refugee Convention, *supra* note 16, at art. 27 ("The Contracting States shall issue identity papers to any refugee in their territory who does not possess a valid travel document."). *See* Guiding Principles on Internal Displacement, *supra* note 23, at Principle 20(2) ("[T]he authorities concerned shall issue to them all documents necessary for the enjoyment and exercise of their legal rights, such as passports, personal identification documents, birth certificates and marriage certificates. In particular, the authorities shall facilitate the issuance of new documents or the replacement of documents lost in the course of displacement, without imposing unreasonable conditions . . .").

163. ICRMW, *supra* note 16, at art. 21 ("It shall be unlawful for anyone, other than a public official duly authorized by law, to confiscate, destroy or attempt to destroy identity documents, documents authorizing entry to or stay, residence or establishment in the national territory or work permits."). *See also* ILO Convention 189, *supra* note 16, at art. 9(c) ("Each Member shall take measures to ensure that domestic workers . . . (c) are entitled to keep in their possession their travel and identity documents.")

ARTICLE 8
REMEDY

Every migrant has the right to an effective remedy for acts violating the rights guaranteed to the migrant by the relevant domestic law as well as international law, including those rights or freedoms herein recognized.

Commentary

(1) The remedy clause of the IMBR finds its roots in Article 8 of the UDHR and Article 2(3) of the ICCPR.[164] Article 8 of the UDHR is one of a series of articles that are seen as the first articulation of a right to a fair trial in a modern, multilateral document.[165] Article 8 specifically ensures that every person is given some form of judicial or administrative recourse in the event of a violation of national or international law, and IMBR Article 8 reiterates that right for migrants. ICCPR Article 2(3) provides a remedy to persons whose rights and freedoms in the ICCPR itself have been violated. In that vein, IMBR Article 8 explicitly provides migrants with a remedy for any violations of the rights and freedoms mentioned in the IMBR.

(2) Coupled with the equality provisions found in Article 3 of the IMBR, this remedy clause provides migrants with the same ability to avail themselves of national and international law as any national of the receiving State, empowering them to seek recourse against violations of their rights by the government or private parties, in accordance with governing national and international laws. International and regional bodies have affirmed that a right to a remedy applies to all migrants, regardless of status.[166] Remedies for human rights violations must be "prompt, effective, accessible, impartial and independent, must be enforceable, and lead to cessation of or reparation for the human rights violation concerned."[167]

---

164. UDHR, *supra* note 1, at art. 8; ICCPR, *supra* note 2, at art. 2(3). *See also* ICRMW, *supra* note 16, at art. 83; ICERD, *supra* note 4, at art. 6; CAT, *supra* note 5, at art. 14; CPED, *supra* note 10, at art. 8(2); ECHR, *supra* note 8, at art. 13; ACHR, *supra* note 12, at art. 25; G.A. Res. 60/147 *supra* note 153.

165. These articles are UDHR, *supra* note 1, at arts. 8-11. *See* Beth Simmons, *Civil Rights in International Law: Compliance with Aspects of the "International Bill of Rights,"* 16 IND. J. GLOBAL LEGAL STUD. 437, 481 (2009).

166. *See* Comm. on the Elimination of Discrim. Against Women, *General Recommendation No. 26*, *supra* note 108, ¶¶ 21-22; Juridical Condition and Rights of the Undocumented Migrants, Advisory Opinion OC-18/03, Inter-Am. Ct. H.R. (ser. A) No. 18, ¶ 170 (Sept. 17, 2003); Comm. on the Elimination of Racial Discrim., *Concluding Observations on Republic of Korea*, ¶ 18, U.N. Doc. CERD/C/KOR/CO/14 (Aug.17, 2007), at http://www2.ohchr.org/english/bodies/cerd/docs/CERD.C.KOR.CO.1.pdf; Comm. on Migrant Workers, *Concluding Observations on Mexico*, ¶¶ 30-31, U.N. Doc. CMW/C/MEX/CO/1.Add.1 (June 19, 2008), at http://www2.ohchr.org/english/bodies/cmw/docs/CMW.C.MEX.CO.1.Add.1.pdf.

167. INT'L COMM'N OF JURISTS, MIGRATION AND INTERNATIONAL HUMAN RIGHTS LAW: PRACTITIONERS GUIDE NO. 6, at 123.

ARTICLE 9
DUE PROCESS

(1) Every migrant has the right to due process of law before the courts, tribunals, and all other organs and authorities administering justice, as well as those specifically charged with making status determinations regarding migrants.

(2) States shall provide legal aid and representation in criminal proceedings. States should provide legal representation to migrants in all proceedings related to their legal status as a migrant.

(3) Every migrant shall be entitled to interpretation in a language the migrant can understand in criminal proceedings. Migrants should be entitled to interpretation in a language the migrant can understand in all proceedings.

(4) The migrant shall be informed of the availability of such interpretation, aid and representation upon receiving a civil complaint, administrative summons, or upon arrest.

(5) Migrants should be free from disproportionate penalties on account of entry, presence or status, or on account of any other offense which can only be committed by migrants.

Commentary

(1) The right to due process of law is a fundamental check on arbitrary treatment and the violation of other rights. Article 9 affirms a strong principle of customary international law grounded in comity and historical notions of equality and echoed in human rights law and jurisprudence. In affirming a general right to due process for migrants, the IMBR goes further than other international instruments to give specific content to the implications of personhood for migrants before the law.

(2) The international community has long realized the importance of due process of law as a check on rights abuses. Although implicitly applicable to migrants by virtue of their personhood, a migrant's right to due process is subject to particularly pronounced abuses by governments.[168] Of particular concern is administrative detention of migrants, the increasing use of criminal sanctions as a policy response to increases in migration, and State responses to terrorism.

(3) *Paragraph 1*: Paragraph 1 affirms the general right of due process before all adjudicatory institutions to all migrants.[169] Human rights law

168. *See, e.g.*, *Orantes-Hernandez v. Gonzales*, 504 F.Supp.2d 825 (C.D.Cal. 2007); Karen Tumlin, *Immigration Detention Centers under the Microscope: Recent Reports Reveal Widespread Violations of the National Detention Standards*, 216 IMMIGRANTS' RIGHTS UPDATE 6 (2007) (reviewing U.S. government violations of its own standards regarding migrant detention).

169. UDHR, *supra* note 1, at arts. 6, 10, 11; ICCPR, *supra* note 2, at arts. 14, 16; ICERD, *supra* note 4, at art. 5(a); ICRMW, *supra* note 16, at arts. 17(1), 18(1); G.A. Res. 40/144, art. 5(1)(c), U.N. Doc. A/RES/40/144 (Dec. 13, 1985); CRC, *supra* note 6, at arts. 12(2), 40(1); ECHR, *supra* note 8, at art. 6(1).

establishes due process as an essential consequence of personhood in a fair legal regime. Due process is recognized in more than one international legal instrument as a fundamental human right, and migrants' due process rights fall under general human rights protections. Despite these general protections, heightened abuses affecting migrants require specific provisions aimed at enshrining migrants' rights to the same treatment as nationals of a State. Both classes are entitled to the respect of due process under international human rights law. Article 9(1) achieves this by reiterating the human right to due process and applying it explicitly to migrants, thereby eliminating any misconception that migrants can be treated in a manner inferior to nationals with regard to due process.

(5) The right to due process is intended to include all of the procedural guarantees of Article 13 of the ICCPR, essentially the opportunity to be represented and heard before a competent decision maker. The IMBR, like the ICCPR, prohibits collective expulsion.[170] Importantly, the IMBR does not limit the right to due process to those with lawful status, but provides this right explicitly to all migrants.[171]

(6) *Paragraph 2*: Paragraph 2 recognizes the right of migrants to be provided free legal assistance and representation in criminal proceedings when they cannot afford it. The State must provide free legal assistance and representation to low-income migrants in criminal cases where they are defendants. As far as possible, taking into account the circumstances of the individual case, the financial needs of the migrant, and the fundamental rights at stake, the State shall provide free legal assistance and representation to migrants in all proceedings related to their status as a migrant.[172] Due to the special and critical nature of administrative proceedings related to the legal status of migrants and their families, especially expulsion or deportation proceedings, the State has a duty to provide low-income migrants free legal assistance and representation in those cases wherever possible.[173]

(7) Access to counsel is an essential element of due process, and the provision of legal aid and representation to the poor is grounded in notions of state responsibility in the context of international human rights obligations.[174] ICCPR Article 14 only expressly recognizes a right to free counsel

---

170. Joseph, et al., *supra* note 90, at 378.

171. *See* Joseph, et al., *supra* note 90, at 379.

172. Article 13 of the ICCPR and Article 1.1(c) of the ECHR Protocol 7 guarantee the right to representation before the authority competent to decide on an expulsion decision. ICCPR, *supra* note 2, at art. 13; ECHR, *supra* note 8, at 1.1(c).

173. Nolan v. Russia, App. No. 2512/04, 53 Eur. H.R. Rep. 29, 1006 (Feb. 12, 2009) (finding a violation of ECHR Protocol 7 when "the Government did not furnish any explanation as to why the decision on the applicant's exclusion had not been communicated to him for more than three months and why he had not been allowed to submit reasons against his expulsion and *to have his case reviewed with the participation of his counsel*." (emphasis added)).

174. Eileen Skinnider, *The Responsibility of States to Provide Legal Aid* (The Int'l Ctr. for Crim. Law Reform and Crim. Just. Pol'y, 1999), *available at* http://www.icclr.law.ubc.ca/Publications/Reports/beijing.pdf.

in criminal cases.[175] However, the Human Rights Committee has emphasized that Article 14 applies to both criminal and civil cases.[176] The United Nations Body of Principles for the Protection of All Persons under Any Form of Detention or Imprisonment provides that a detained person is entitled to have legal counsel assigned by a judicial or other authority in all cases where the interests of justice so require and without payment if the migrant does not have sufficient funds to pay.[177] The *United Nations Basic Principles on the Role of Lawyers* states that governments shall ensure the provision of sufficient funding and other resources for legal services to the poor and, as necessary, to other disadvantaged persons, and that professional associations of lawyers should cooperate in the organization and provision of services, facilities, and other resources.[178] The principle of providing legal representation at public expense to litigants who are unable to afford it is widely accepted and observed: Canada, Australia, New Zealand, Brazil, Madagascar and South Africa have statutes or constitutional provisions providing for free civil counsel for those in need.[179] In 1979 the European Court of Human Rights ruled in *Airey v. Ireland* that free civil counsel to facilitate access to the courts was a basic right.[180] Thereafter, the Council of Europe requires its members to provide free counsel. Each country has met this requirement, but with limits in the form of merit-based and need-based eligibility standards.[181] This principle is also grounded in treaty law: the OAS Charter explicitly recognizes a right to counsel,[182] and the Inter-American Court of Human Rights and the Inter-American Commission on Human Rights have recognized that the right applies in both civil and criminal cases.[183]

(8) As a recognized human right, the right to state-funded legal assistance is essential in criminal proceedings due to the fundamental rights at stake.[184] This right is not limited to criminal proceedings and should be expanded to include all proceedings related to a migrant's status to ensure that the IMBR's

---

175. ICCPR, *supra* note 2, at art. 14(3)(d).

176. Human Rights Comm., *General Comment No. 13, Article 14 (Equality before the Courts and the Right to a Fair and Public Hearing by an Independent Court Established by Law)* ¶ 2, UN Doc. HRI\GEN\1\Rev.1 (Apr. 13, 1984), at http://ccprcentre.org/doc/ICCPR/General%20Comments/HRI.GEN.1.Rev.9%28Vol.I%29_%28GC13%29_en.pdf.

177. G.A. Res 43/173, U.N. Doc. A/RES/43/173 (Dec. 9, 1988).

178. Eighth United Nations Congress on the Prevention of Crime and the Treatment of Offenders, Havana, Cuba, Aug. 27-Sept. 7, 1990, *Basic Principles on the Role of Lawyers*, U.N. Doc. A/CONF. 144/28/Rev.1, at http://www.unhcr.org/refworld/docid/3ddb9f034.html.

179. Raven Lidman, *Civil Gideon: A Human Right Elsewhere in the World*, 40 CLEARINGHOUSE REVIEW 288 (2006).

180. *Airey v. Ireland*, App. No. 6289/73, 2 Eur. H.R. Rep. 305 (Oct. 9, 1979).

181. Lidman, *supra* note 179, at 292.

182. Charter of the Organization of the American States, art. 45, Dec. 13, 1951, 119 U.N.T.S. 3 [hereinafter OAS Charter].

183. Access to Justice as a Guarantee of Economic, Social and Cultural Rights: A Review of the Standards Adopted by the Inter-American System of Human Rights, Advisory Opinion, Inter-Am. Comm'n H.R., OEA/Ser.L./V/II.129 doc. 4 ¶ 182 (Sept. 7, 2007).

184. For a discussion of the historical development of free legal aid and the priority of criminal cases see Skinnider, *supra* note 174.

right to due process is meaningfully secured. This right has special relevance in the context of immigration proceedings due to the fundamental rights at stake, and States should make every effort to provide migrants with free legal aid and representation in proceedings related to their status or the status of their family members.[185]

(9) *Paragraph 3*: The right of a migrant to an interpreter draws from international human rights norms. In the criminal context, the ICCPR explicitly guarantees defendants the right to be informed of their charges in detail in a language they understand.[186] The ICCPR also provides for defendants to enjoy the free assistance of an interpreter.[187] In the civil context, there is no explicit international right to interpretation, but it can be inferred from the provisions of the ICCPR, the CAT and the UDHR.[188] These documents all contain language on due process and fairness that underscore the importance of a defendant's awareness of charges and proceedings.[189] Although the grounds for this requirement are much stronger in criminal cases, the civil and administrative contexts (particularly those proceedings related to a migrant's status) should also be considered important, due to the human rights interests at stake and the importance of integrity and fairness in the legal process.

(10) A defendant needs to be fully aware of the charges or details of the proceedings brought against the defendant, whether in the criminal, civil, or administrative contexts, in order to properly prepare a defense. This is especially relevant where the defendant is a migrant who may not sufficiently understand the language or legal culture of the host country. As noted in Paragraph 6 of this Commentary, while the defendant's right to an interpreter is explicit in the ICCPR for criminal matters, it is only an inferred right in the civil context. Article 9(3) explicitly provides for interpretation to be offered to migrant defendants so that they may understand in detail the charges and proceedings brought against them. It also extends the right to an interpreter, making it applicable in civil, criminal and administrative proceedings.

(11) Although the IMBR did not adopt the language of the ICCPR, which promises the "free assistance of an interpreter," the host government should

185. *See* Juridical Condition and Rights of the Undocumented Migrants, *supra* note 166, ¶ 126; Velez Loor v. Panama, Preliminary Objections, Merits, Reparations and Costs, Judgment, Inter-Am. Ct. H.R. (ser. C) No. 218, ¶ 146 (Nov. 23, 2010).

186. ICCPR, *supra* note 2, at art. 14(3)(a) ("In the determination of any criminal charge against him, everyone shall be entitled to the following minimum guarantees, in full equality . . . to be informed promptly and in detail in a language which he understands of the nature and cause of the charge against him").

187. ICCPR, *supra* note 2, at art. 14(3)(f) ("In the determination of any criminal charge against him, everyone shall be entitled . . . to have the free assistance of an interpreter if he cannot understand or speak the language used in court.").

188. *Compare* KATHY LASTER & VERONICA L. TAYLOR, INTERPRETERS AND THE LEGAL SYSTEM 73 (1994) *with* ECHR, *supra* note 8, at art. 6 (interpreted as not applying to immigration proceedings).

189. UDHR, *supra* note 1, at art. 10; ICCPR, *supra* note 2, at art. 9(2)-(5); CAT, *supra* note 5, at arts. 13, 14.

defray the costs of the interpretation service in order to ensure financial considerations do not interfere with migrant defendants' exercise of their rights.

(12) *Paragraph 4*: This Paragraph makes it mandatory that a migrant be informed of the migrant's right to free counsel, interpretation, and other aid promptly after receiving notice of the criminal, civil, or administrative proceedings to which the migrant is a party.

(13) In order to prevent abuses and to ensure the full enjoyment of the rights secured under it, the IMBR provides that migrant defendants be given notice of their entitlement to counsel and to an interpreter. In addition, migrants in civil and immigration cases must be notified of representation, aid, and interpretation at the outset of a proceeding. Due to migrants' potential unfamiliarity with local legal procedures and language, early notification of these services is critical.

(14) *Paragraph 5*: Paragraph 5 builds on language in Article 31 of the 1951 Refugee Convention.[190] Freedom from disproportionate penalties also builds on general due process and non-discrimination principles. States should particularly ensure that their detention and expulsion policies meet the appropriate proportionality standards.

ARTICLE 10
VICTIMS OF CRIME

(1) Every migrant victim of crime has the right to assistance and protection, including access to compensation and restitution.

(2) States shall provide assistance to ensure the physical, psychological, and social recovery of victims of crimes, especially where such individuals are victims of trafficking in persons.

Commentary

(1) This Article seeks to establish the right of migrant victims of crime to receive assistance and protection regardless of their immigration status. Ensuring this right may require the disaggregation of law enforcement from immigration control because concerns over immigration status may otherwise expose migrants to manipulation and abuse. Because migrant victims of crime, especially in cases of human trafficking, may experience particular trauma, States should provide assistance that ensures migrants' physical, psychological, and social recovery.

---

190. 1951 Refugee Convention, *supra* note 16, at art. 31 ("The Contracting States shall not impose penalties, on account of their illegal entry or presence, on refugees who, coming directly from a territory where their life or freedom was threatened in the sense of article 1, enter or are present in their territory without authorization, provided they present themselves without delay to the authorities and show good cause for their illegal entry or presence.").

(2) As non-citizens, migrants face unique challenges in accessing local law enforcement mechanisms. Migrants may fail to report crimes or to seek assistance due to ignorance about local laws or concerns about immigration enforcement, leaving them particularly vulnerable to crime, exploitation, and manipulation.[191]

(3) Of particular concern are victims of human trafficking, who are subjected to treatment amounting to arbitrary detention, slavery, rape, or cruel, inhuman and degrading treatment,[192] and often struggle to receive assistance even after they are discovered.[193]

(4) *Paragraph 1*: Paragraph 1 establishes the right of migrant victims of crime to receive assistance and protection from local law enforcement. This right is most strongly recognized in instruments addressing trafficking in persons, including the Protocol to Prevent, Suppress and Punish Trafficking in Persons, Especially Women and Children (Palermo Protocol) attached to the U.N. Convention Against Organized Crime,[194] and the Council of Europe Convention on Action Against Trafficking in Human Beings.[195] The IMBR draws on these and other instruments contemplating State obligations towards victims of crime to establish a general right of migrant victims of crime to protection and assistance.[196]

(5) Without an established right to protection and assistance irrespective of immigration status, migrant victims of crime may hesitate to come forward and may become susceptible to threats and intimidation by abusive partners, predatory employers, and other potential assailants.[197] This Article recognizes the right of migrants to access local law enforcement when they have been subjected to mistreatment. Moreover, public safety is best served by encouraging victims of crime to report abuse, thus denying perpetrators the opportunity to commit crimes against individuals silenced by the fear of possible immigration enforcement actions. This recognition is reflected in a growing State practice of providing special protections to migrant victims of

---

191. *See, e.g.*, Fiona David, *Law Enforcement Responses to Trafficking in Persons: Challenges and Emerging Good Practice*, *in* Trends and Issues in Crime and Criminal Justice No. 347 (Toni Makkai ed., 2007).

192. The Global Problem of Trafficking in Persons: Breaking the Vicious Cycle on "Trafficking of Women and Children in the International Sex Trade," Hearing before the H. Comm. on Int'l Relations, 106th Cong. 2 (1999) (statement of Harold Hongju Koh, Assistant Secretary of State).

193. *See* Ratna Kapur, *Migrant Women and the Legal Politics of Anti-Trafficking Interventions*, *in* TRAFFICKING IN HUMANS: SOCIAL, CULTURAL AND POLITICAL DIMENSIONS 111, 118-19 (Edward Newman & Sally Cameron eds., 2007).

194. Palermo Protocol, *supra* note 16.

195. Council of Europe Convention on Action against Trafficking in Human Beings, May 16, 2005, C.E.T.S. No. 197.

196. *See* Palermo Protocol, *supra* note 16, at art. 25(2); Recommendation on the Protection of Women Against Violence CM/Rec(2002)5 (Apr. 30, 2002). *See also* INT'L COMM'N OF JURISTS, *supra* note 167, at 83.

197. *See, e.g.*, David, *supra* note 191.

crime actively cooperating with criminal prosecutions.[198] The IMBR goes further than other instruments in recognizing that all migrant victims of crime are entitled to genuine assistance and protection.

(6) Taking appropriate measures to provide assistance and protection to migrant victims of crime may require separation of law enforcement from immigration control. When such considerations are linked through concurrent enforcement, migrant victims of crime become vulnerable to exploitation and manipulation by criminals threatening to retaliate by reporting migrants to immigration authorities. Disaggregation of law and immigration enforcement also requires meaningful protections for migrant victims of crime who depend on their abuser for immigration status.

(7) Special attention should be given to address racist and xenophobic practices by law enforcement officials toward migrant victims of crime.[199] A State's obligation to ensure that migrants are assisted without discrimination on account of race or national origin is derived from the ICERD, as further affirmed by the international community in the Durban Declaration, which states that "policies towards migration should not be based on racism, racial discrimination, xenophobia and related intolerance."[200]

(8) Because the provision of such services is costly, States should also consider supporting the right of migrant victims established in Paragraph 1 to compensation and restitution by providing victims with the ability to pursue legal action and recover damages from those responsible, particularly any business entities that have knowingly and unlawfully profited from the labor of migrants, and especially victims of human trafficking.

(9) *Paragraph 2*: Paragraph 2 recognizes that migrant victims of crime may require special assistance and support in order to recover from abuse. This is particularly the case for victims of human trafficking. The Palermo Protocol[201] and the Council of Europe Convention make special recognition of this fact.[202] The IMBR recognizes that all other migrant victims of crime, especially victims of domestic abuse, may require special assistance for addressing their physical and psychological needs, including basic assistance such as translation and counseling regarding their legal rights.

198. *See, e.g.*, Palermo Protocol, *supra* note 16, at art. 24(1) ("Each State Party shall take appropriate measures within its means to provide effective protection from potential retaliation or intimidation for witnesses in criminal proceedings who give testimony concerning offences."). *See also* INT'L COMM'N OF JURISTS, *supra* note 167, at 88.

199. *See, e.g.*, INT'L COMM'N OF JURISTS, *supra* note 167, at 34.

200. World Conference against Racism, Racial Discrimination, Xenophobia and Related Intolerance, Aug. 31-Sept. 8, 2001, *Declaration*, ¶¶ 12, 16, 38, 47-51, at http://www.un.org/WCAR/durban.pdf.

201. Palermo Protocol, *supra* note 16, art. 6(3) ("Each State Party shall consider implementing measures to provide for the physical, psychological and social recovery of victims of trafficking in persons . . .").

202. Council of Europe Convention on Action against Trafficking in Human Beings, *supra* note 195, at art. 12(1) ("Each Party shall adopt such legislative or other measures as may be necessary to assist victims in their physical, psychological and social recovery.").

This is especially important when, as is often the case, migrants may not have an understanding of local laws and customs, may struggle to access institutions providing assistance, and lack access to informal support networks due to their status. Article 10 should be read in conjunction with the rights of vulnerable migrants in Article 4, due process rights contained in Article 9, and the right to health in Article 21.

(10) Paragraph 2 seeks to ensure that migrant victims of crime are provided with special protections to address their unique vulnerabilities and any physical or psychological trauma. Especially in cases of human trafficking, States should consider providing, *inter alia*, appropriate housing; counseling and information, particularly with regard to legal rights, in a language understood by the victim; medical, psychological and material assistance; and employment, education and training opportunities.

(11) In general, regard should be had for the age, gender and special needs of victims. In the case of children, particular attention should be paid to the provision of housing, education, and other care.

(12) Non-governmental organizations often play a special role in providing assistance to migrant victims of crime, who may fear government authorities or require special expertise.[203] States are encouraged to cooperate with non-governmental organizations and other elements of civil society in providing assistance to migrant victims of crime. This perspective reflects best practices among practitioners,[204] as well as the language of instruments addressing the needs of victims of human trafficking.[205]

ARTICLE 11
EXPULSION

(1) Every migrant has the right to protection against discriminatory or arbitrary expulsion or deportation, including collective expulsion. States shall expel a migrant only when justified by the specific facts relevant to the individual concerned and only pursuant to a decision reached in accordance with and authorized by law.

(2) Migrants have a right to an effective remedy when expulsion would give rise to a violation of human rights.

(3) Except where compelling reasons of national security otherwise require, a migrant shall be allowed to submit the reasons against expulsion and to have the migrant's case reviewed by, and be represented for the

---

203. *See, e.g.*, Mark Lagon, *The Global Abolition of Human Trafficking: The Indispensible Role of the United States*, 12.1 GEO. J. INT'L AFFIRS 89, 96 (2011).

204. *See* David, *supra* note 191.

205. *See, e.g.*, Palermo Protocol, *supra* note 16, at art. 10(2) ("States Parties shall provide or strengthen training for law enforcement, immigration and other relevant officials . . . [which] should also take into account the need to consider human rights and child- and gender-sensitive issues and it should encourage cooperation with non- governmental organizations, other relevant organizations and other elements of civil society.").

purpose before, the competent authority or a person or persons especially designated by the competent authority. Pending such review, the migrant concerned shall have the right to seek a stay of the decision of expulsion.

(4) The decision to expel a migrant shall be communicated to the migrant in a language the migrant understands. Upon request where not otherwise mandatory, the decision shall be communicated to the migrant in writing and, save in exceptional circumstances on account of national security, the reasons for the decision likewise stated. The migrant shall be informed of these rights before, or at the latest, at the time the decision is rendered.

(5) Expulsion from a State shall not in itself prejudice any rights of a migrant acquired in accordance with the law of that State, including the right to receive wages and other entitlements due. A migrant shall have a reasonable opportunity before or after departure to settle any claims for wages and other entitlements due and any pending liabilities.

(6) In effectuating the expulsion of a migrant from its territory, a State shall ensure the respect of the rights guaranteed to the migrant by relevant domestic and international law, including those rights or freedoms herein recognized.

Commentary

(1) Article 11 imposes a limitation on the ability of States to remove a migrant arbitrarily or without due process of law. While the IMBR respects the sovereign right of States to remove aliens from their territories, it places restrictions on this right under international law and takes into consideration the particular vulnerability of migrants during expulsion. Arbitrary expulsion, deportation, and removal of migrants is a human rights issue with serious and complicated consequences for migrants and their families, as well as States of origin and receiving States.[206] States too often deport migrants without regard for their rights under international law, including on the basis of prohibited discriminatory grounds, en masse, and without consideration for their safety in transit or upon return.[207] The international law governing expulsion is evolving and States must take measures to ensure

206. *See, e.g.*, HUMAN RIGHTS WATCH, NO REFUGE: MIGRANTS IN GREECE 3 (2009), *available at* http://www.hrw.org/en/reports/2009/11/02/no-refugees; HUMAN RIGHTS WATCH, PUSHED BACK, PUSHED AROUND: ITALY'S FORCED RETURN OF BOAT MIGRANTS AND ASYLUM SEEKERS, LIBYA'S MISTREATMENT OF MIGRANTS AND ASYLUM SEEKERS (2009), *available at* http://www.hrw.org/reports/2009/09/21/pushed-back-pushed-around.

207. *See, e.g.*, HUMAN RIGHTS WATCH, DISCRIMINATION, DENIAL AND DEPORTATION: HUMAN RIGHTS ABUSES AFFECTING MIGRANTS LIVING WITH HIV (2009), *available at* http://hrw.org/en/reports/2009/06/18/discrimination-denial-and-deportation-0; HUMAN RIGHTS WATCH, PERILOUS PLIGHT: BURMA'S ROHINGYA TAKE TO THE SEAS (2009), *available at* http://www.hrw.org/en/reports/2009/05/26/perilous-plight-0; HUMAN RIGHTS WATCH, IRAN: HALT MASS DEPORTATIONS OF AFGHANS (2007), *available at* http://www.hrw.org/en/news/2007/06/17/iran-halt-mass-deportation-afghans.

that they protect both substantive and procedural rights of migrants during expulsion.[208]

(2) *Paragraph 1*: The prohibition on arbitrary expulsion derives from ICCPR Article 13 and from Article 22(2) of the ICRMW. Both treaties allow States to expel migrants only when the decision is reached in accordance with law and minimum process requirements are met.[209] If a State seeks to remove, deport, or expel a migrant, such a decision must be justified by an application of the facts of the particular migrant's circumstance and the applicable law. In restricting expulsion to decisions made on the basis of specific facts and in accordance with law, Paragraph 1 echoes the prohibitions on discrimination and against arbitrariness.[210]

(3) The prohibition on discriminatory or arbitrary expulsion includes collective expulsion, which is specifically prohibited in the ICRMW,[211] and in several regional instruments governing human rights, such as the Fourth Protocol to the ECHR,[212] the ACHR,[213] the African Charter on Human and People's Rights (the Banjul Charter),[214] and the Arab Charter on Human Rights (Arab Charter).[215] The Human Rights Committee has also affirmed that collective expulsion would be a violation of ICCPR Article 13.[216]

(4) Fundamental procedural protections are required in all circumstances in which a migrant is subject to a State's jurisdiction. A State must respect a migrant's substantive human rights during the entry process.[217] However, there are limited procedural protections for migrants at entry.[218]

(5) *Paragraph 2*: To ensure the right to an effective remedy, States are obligated to provide opportunities for relief from expulsion when expulsion would give rise to violation of that migrant's human rights.[219] For example, States are obligated to provide opportunities for remedy when expulsion

---

208. *See* Int'l Law Comm'n, May 7-June 1, July 2-Aug. 3, 2012, Expulsion of Aliens, U.N. Doc. A/CN.4/L.797 GAOR, 64th Sess. (May 24, 2012).

209. ICCPR, *supra* note 2, at art. 13; ICRMW, *supra* note 16, at art. 22(2). *See also* ECHR, *supra* note 8, at Protocol 7, art. 1.

210. *See* T. Alexander Aleinikoff, *International Legal Norms and Migration: A Report, in* MIGRATION AND INTERNATIONAL LEGAL NORMS 1, 19 (T. Alexander Aleinikoff & Vincent Chetail, eds. 2003).

211. ICRMW, *supra* note 16, at art. 22(1).

212. ECHR, *supra* note 8, at Protocol 4.

213. ACHR, *supra* note 12, at art. 22(9).

214. Banjul Charter, *supra* note 9, at art. 12.

215. Arab Charter, *supra* note 137, at art. 26(2).

216. *General Comment No. 15*, *supra* note 66.

217. States must respect these rights (e.g. right to life) whenever a migrant is subject to its jurisdiction.

218. *See* INT'L COMM'N OF JURISTS, *supra* note 167, at 45-46.

219. UDHR, *supra* note 1, at art. 8; ICCPR, *supra* note 2, at art. 2; CAT, *supra* note 5, at art. 14; ICERD, *supra* note 4, at art. 6; CRC, *supra* note 6, at art. 39. See also G.A. Res. 60/147, *supra* note 153 on the right to a remedy and reparation for victims of gross violations of international human rights law and serious violations of international humanitarian law.

would give rise to *refoulement*[220] or a violation of the right to respect for family life.[221] According to the U.N. Basic Principles and Guidelines on the right to a remedy and reparation, remedies for violations of international human rights must be available, adequate, effective, prompt and appropriate.[222]

(6) *Paragraph 3*: The IMBR extends to all migrants the procedural rights in Article 22(4) of the ICRMW, namely the rights to submit reasons against expulsion, to have the case reviewed by the competent authority, and to seek a stay of the decision of expulsion.[223] While ICCPR Article 13 and Article 1 of Protocol No. 7 of the ECHR only apply to migrants lawfully in the territory, the protections in ICRMW Article 22(4) apply regardless of status. Paragraph 3 follows the language in the ICRMW and applies to all migrants.[224] At the regional level, the Inter-American Court of Human Rights, the Inter-American Commission on Human Rights, and the African Commission on Human and Peoples' Rights have granted additional procedural protections by finding that fair trial guarantees apply in expulsion proceedings.[225] The Committee of Ministers of the Council of Europe recommended that "the removal order should be addressed in writing to the individual concerned either directly or through his/her authorised representative . . . . [and] shall indicate the legal and factual grounds on which it is based [and] the remedies available, whether or not they have a suspensive effect, and the deadlines within which such remedies can be exercised."[226]

(7) *Paragraph 4*: Paragraph 4 also provides fundamental procedural protections required in all circumstances to guarantee the realization, in practice and not just in theory, of the rights of migrants. Paragraph 4 seeks to enable migrants to understand and take advantage of their rights in the context of expulsion by invoking and extending to all migrants the protections of Article 22(3) of the ICRMW.[227]

(8) *Paragraph 5*: Paragraph 5 derives from Articles 22(6) and 22(9) of the ICRMW, and seeks to ensure that expulsion does not interfere with any wages or entitlements due to a migrant.[228]

(9) *Paragraph 6*: Paragraph 6 affirms that States have an obligation to uphold all other relevant legal obligations, including the obligations contained in the IMBR, when expelling a migrant. In the expulsion context, this

---

220. INT'L MIGRANTS BILL OF RIGHTS, art. 13, 28 GEO. IMMIGR. L.J. 18.

221. *See, e.g.*, *C.G. v. Bulgaria*, App. No. 1365/07, 47 Eur. H.R. Rep. 51 (2008); *Keles v. Germany*, App. No. 32231/02, 44 Eur. H.R. Rep. 12 (2007).

222. G.A. Res. 60/147, *supra* note 153, at arts. 2-3.

223. ICRMW, *supra* note 16, at art. 22(4).

224. *See, e.g.*, NOWAK, *supra* note 70, at 224; *General Comment No. 15*, *supra* note 66.

225. INT'L COMM'N OF JURISTS, *supra* note 167, at 134-136. *See also* Int'l Law Comm'n, *supra* note 208, at art. 26.

226. Twenty Guidelines on Forced Return, adopted by the Committee of Ministers of the Council of Europe on 4 May 2005 at the 925th meeting of the Ministers' Deputies, guideline 4.1. *See also International Law Commission*, A/CN.4/L.797, 24 May 2012, Draft Article 26.

227. ICRMW, *supra* note 16, at art. 22(3).

228. ICRMW, *supra* note 16, arts. 22(6), (9).

obligation prohibits States from practicing unsafe repatriations and expulsions that violate the right to life or dignity or the prohibition on cruel, inhumane or degrading treatment.[229]

ARTICLE 12
ASYLUM

(1) Every migrant has the right to seek and to enjoy in other countries asylum.

(2) States shall ensure access, consistent with relevant international and regional instruments, to fair and efficient status-determination procedures for migrants seeking asylum within their effective control, whether or not they are within the State's territory.

(3) No state shall expel or return in any matter a migrant who has been granted asylum or other international protection.

Commentary

(1) *Paragraph 1*: The purpose of Paragraph 1 is to reaffirm the well-established principle that every person, including every migrant, has a right to seek and to enjoy in other countries asylum. The omission of "from persecution" is in recognition of the practice in some countries and regions of the world of granting asylum to persons not considered to be refugees under the definition articulated in the 1951 Refugee Convention and its 1967 Protocol, or of defining the term refugee more broadly.[230] The "right to seek and to enjoy in other countries asylum from persecution" was originally enshrined in Article 14 of the UDHR[231] and reaffirmed in numerous General Assembly Resolutions.[232]

(2) *Paragraph 2*: The purpose of Paragraph 2 is to give effect to this right for migrants and strengthen the right to asylum through procedural safeguards that are absent from the 1951 Refugee Convention and 1967 Protocol.[233] These procedures should extend to the frontier and extrater-

---

229. *See also* Int'l Law Comm'n, *supra* note 208, at art. 21.

230. *See, e.g.*, Convention Governing the Specific Aspects of Refugee Problems in Africa art. 1(2), Sept. 10, 1969, 1001 U.N.T.S. 45 ("The term 'refugee' shall also apply to every person who, owing to external aggression, occupation, foreign domination or events seriously disturbing public order in either part or the whole of his country of origin or nationality, is compelled to leave his place of habitual residence in order to seek refuge in another place outside his country of origin or nationality.").

231. UDHR, *supra* note 1, at art. 14.

232. *See, e.g.*, G.A. Res. 2312 (XXII), U.N. Doc. A/RES/2312(XII) (Dec. 14, 1967); G.A. Res. 50/152, U.N. Doc A/RES/50/152 (Dec. 21, 1995).

233. Refugee Convention, *supra* note 16; U.N. HIGH COMM'R FOR REFUGEES, FAIR AND EFFICIENT ASYLUM PROCEDURES: A NON-EXHAUSTIVE OVERVIEW OF APPLICABLE INTERNATIONAL STANDARDS (2005), *available at* http://www.unhcr.org/cgi-bin/texis/vtx/search?page=search&docid=4aa76da49&query=refugee%20protection ("[I]t is generally recognized that fair and efficient procedures are an essential element in the full and inclusive application of the 1951 Convention."). *See also* U.N. High Comm'r for Refugees, *Asylum Processes (Fair and Efficient Asylum Procedures)* ¶ 4-5, U.N. Doc. EC/GC/01/12 (May 31, 2001), at http://www.refworld.org/docid/3b36f2fca.html.

ritorially, including to migrants seeking asylum and interdicted on the high seas,[234] in order to preserve the right of *non-refoulement*.[235] Fair and efficient procedures[236] include that a trained official of the State shall make a determination of refugee status and the granting of asylum and shall examine complementary protection needs to ensure that migrants in need of international protection are identified and granted such protection.[237] States should not bar the substantive determination of a migrant's claim for asylum for failure to seek asylum within a certain time limit or for seeking asylum during removal proceedings.[238] A migrant should have the right to legal assistance and representation.[239] A migrant should have a right to an effective remedy before a court or tribunal against a negative decision taken on their application for asylum or a decision to withdraw refugee status.[240]

(3) *Paragraph 3*: The purpose of Paragraph 3 is to reaffirm the principle of *non-refoulement*, deemed to be "intrinsically linked" to a granting of asylum and to reiterate that it is not limited to those formally recognized as

---

234. *See, e.g.*, *Conclusions Adopted by the Executive Committee on International Protection of Refugees*, U.N. GAOR, 34th Session, Supp. No. 12A, at 16, ¶ (c), U.N. Doc. A/34/12/Add.l (1980) ("[I]t is the humanitarian obligation of all coastal States to allow vessels in distress to seek haven in their waters and to grant asylum, or at least temporary refuge, to persons on board wishing to seek asylum."); U.N. HIGH COMM'R FOR REFUGEES, UNHCR ADVISORY OPINION ON THE EXTRATERRITORIAL APPLICATION OF *NON-REFOULEMENT* OBLIGATIONS UNDER THE 1951 CONVENTION RELATING TO THE STATUS OF REFUGEES AND ITS 1967 PROTOCOL [hereinafter UNHCR ADVISORY OPINION] (2007), *available at* http://www.unhcr.org/refworld/docid/45f17a1a4.html; The Haitian Centre for Human Rights et al. v. United States, Case 10.675, Inter-Am. Comm'n H.R., Report No. 51/96, OEA/Ser.L/V/II.95, doc. 7 rev. ¶ 156-57 (1997); Brief for U.N. High Comm'r for Refugees as Amicus Curiae Supporting Respondents, Sale v. Haitian Centers Council, Inc., 509 U.S. 155 (1993) (No. 92-344).

235. ELIHU LAUTERPACHT & DANIEL BETHLEHEM, THE SCOPE AND CONTENT OF THE PRINCIPLE OF *NON-REFOULEMENT*: OPINION, *available at* http://www.unhcr.org/419c75ce4.html.

236. *See e.g.* Cartagena Declaration, *supra* note 34, ¶ 4.

237. FAIR AND EFFICIENT ASYLUM PROCEDURES: A NON-EXHAUSTIVE OVERVIEW OF APPLICABLE INTERNATIONAL STANDARDS, *supra* note 233; U.N. High Comm'r for Refugess, *Agenda for Protection*, U.N. GAOR, 53d Sess., 32, U.N. Doc. A/AC.96/965/Add.1 (2002), at http://www.refworld.org/pdfid/3d4fd0266.pdf. *See also* Cartagena Declaration, *supra* note 34, ¶ 4; G.A. Res. 51/75, ¶ 4, U.N. Doc. A/RES/51/75 (Dec. 12, 1996), at http://www.un.org/documents/ga/res/51/ares51-75.htm.

238. 1951 Refugee Convention, *supra* note 16, at art. 31(1) ("The Contracting States shall not impose penalties, on account of their illegal entry or presence, on refugees who, coming directly from a territory where their life or freedom was threatened in the sense of article I, enter or are present in their territory without authorization, provided they present themselves without delay to the authorities and show good cause for their illegal entry or presence."); *Asylum Processes (Fair and Efficient Asylum Procedures)*, *supra* note 233, ¶ 20 ("A fundamental safeguard in some systems, which should, in UNHCR's view, be promoted for all, is the recognition that an asylum-seeker's failure to submit a request within a certain time limit or the non-fulfillment of other formal requirements should not in itself lead to an asylum request being excluded from consideration, although under certain circumstances a late application can affect its credibility. The automatic and mechanical application of time limits for submitting applications has been found to be at variance with international protection principles."); Jabari v. Turkey, 29 Eur. H.R. Rep. CD178 (2000) ("In the Court's opinion, the automatic and mechanical application of such a short time-limit for submitting an asylum application must be considered at variance with the protection of the fundamental value embodied in Article 3 of the Convention.").

239. FAIR AND EFFICIENT ASYLUM PROCEDURES: A NON-EXHAUSTIVE OVERVIEW OF APPLICABLE INTERNATIONAL STANDARDS, *supra* note 233; *Agenda for Protection*, *supra* note 237, at 32.

240. Council Directive 2005/85/EC, art. 39, 2005 O.J. (L 326/13) (EC).

refugees.[241] The principle of *non-refoulement* was articulated in Article 33 of the 1951 Refugee Convention and its 1967 Protocol[242] and applies to persons "where there are substantial grounds for believing that [they] would be in danger of being subjected to torture" under the CAT.[243] The principle of *non-refoulement* is non-derogable and is considered a cornerstone principle of international law protecting individuals.[244] This Paragraph serves as a complementary articulation of the IMBR Article 13 principle of *non-refoulement.*

ARTICLE 13
NON-REFOULEMENT

(1) Every migrant has the right against *refoulement.*

(2) No migrant shall be expelled or returned in any manner to another State where there are substantial grounds for believing that the migrant would be subjected to torture or cruel, inhuman or degrading treatment or punishment.

(3) No migrant shall be expelled or returned in any manner to the frontiers of territories where the migrant's life or freedom would be threatened on account of race, religion, nationality, membership of a particular social group, or political opinion.

(4) No migrant shall be expelled or returned in any manner to another State where there are substantial grounds for believing that the migrant would be subjected to a serious deprivation of fundamental human rights.

(5) No migrant should be expelled or returned in any manner to another State where there are substantial grounds for believing that the migrant would be subjected to other serious deprivations of human rights.

(6) States shall respect the *non-refoulement* rights of all migrants within their effective control, whether or not they are within the State's territory.

Commentary

(1) *Paragraph 1*: *Non-refoulement* is a non-derogable right possessed by all migrants. The principle of *non-refoulement* is a peremptory norm and is one of the strongest constraints on a State's ability to control entry and expulsion.[245]

241. *See, e.g.*, U.N. HIGH COMM'R FOR REFUGEES, UNHCR NOTE ON THE PRINCIPLE OF *NON-REFOULEMENT* (1997), *available at* http://www.unhcr.org/refworld/docid/438c6d972.html.

242. Refugee Convention, *supra* note 16, at art. 33.

243. CAT, *supra* note 5, at art. 3.

244. *See* Jean Allain, *The* Jus Cogens *Nature of* Non-Refoulement, 13 INT'L J. REFUGEE L. 533, 538 (2001); GOODWIN-GILL, *supra* note 138, at 97; Erika Feller, *Asylum, Migration and Refugee Protection: Realities, Myths and the Promise of Things to Come*, 18 INT'L J. REFUGEE L. 509, 523 (2006) (describing *non-refoulement* as "the most fundamental of all international refugee law obligations").

245. *See* Allain, *supra* note 244, at 538; GOODWIN-GILL, *supra* note 138, at 97; Feller, *supra* note 244, at 523 (describing *non-refoulement* as "the most fundamental of all international refugee law obligations").

(2) *Paragraph 2*: Paragraph 2 is derived from Article 3 of the CAT, which states, "No State Party shall expel, return (*refouler*) or extradite a person to another State where there are substantial grounds for believing that he would be in danger of being subjected to torture;"[246] however, Paragraph 2 provides that migrants shall not be "expelled or returned in any manner" to explicitly guard against scenarios such as chain *refoulement*, reflecting the position, as articulated by the Human Rights Committee, that "States parties must not expose individuals to the danger of torture or cruel, inhuman or degrading treatment or punishment upon return to another country by way of their extradition, expulsion or *refoulement*."[247] The Human Rights Committee and the European Court of Human Rights have interpreted the ban on *refoulement* as being inherent in the prohibitions against torture or cruel, inhuman or degrading treatment or punishment in Article 7 of the ICCPR[248] and Article 3 of the ECHR,[249] respectively. Article 13 of the IMBR understands the country of return to designate not only the country to which removal is to be effected directly, but also any other country to which the migrant may be removed afterwards.[250]

(3) *Paragraph 3*: The purpose of Paragraph 3 is to give effect to the *non-refoulement* rights of all migrants under Article 33 of the 1951 Refugee Convention, which states, "No Contracting State shall expel or return ("*refouler*") a refugee in any manner whatsoever to the frontiers of territories where his life or freedom would be threatened on account of his race, religion, nationality, membership of a particular social group or political opinion."[251] Like Paragraph 2, Paragraph 3 also recognizes that States have an obligation to ensure that migrants are not put at risk, directly or indirectly, by their return to any other country.[252] Although Article 33(2) of the 1951 Refugee Convention lists two exceptions for public order and for national

---

246. CAT, *supra* note 5, at art. 3.

247. Human Rights Comm., *General Comment No. 20: Article. 7 (Prohibition of Torture, or Other Cruel, Inhuman or Degrading Treatment or Punishment)* ¶ 9, U.N. Doc. HRI/GEN/1/Rev.9 (Mar. 10, 1992), at http://ccprcentre.org/doc/ICCPR/General%20Comments/HRI.GEN.1.Rev.9%28 Vol.I%29_%28GC20%29_en.pdf.

248. *See General Comment No. 20*, *supra* note 247, ¶ 9; Human Rights Comm., *General Comment No. 31: The Nature of the General Legal Obligation Imposed on States Parties to the Covenant*, ¶ 12, U.N. Doc. CCPR/C/21/Rev.1/Add.13 (May 26, 2004), at http://ccprcentre.org/doc/ ICCPR/General%20Comments/CCPR.C.21.Rev1.Add13_%28GC31%29_En.pdf.

249. *See, e.g.*, Soering v. United Kingdom, App. No. 14038/88, 11 Eur. H.R. Rep 439 (1989); Cruz Varas v. Sweden, App. No. 15576/89, 14 Eur. H.R. Rep. 1 (1991); Vilvarajah v. United Kingdom, App. No. 13163/87, 14 Eur. H.R. Rep. 248 (1992); Chahal v. United Kingdom, App. No. 22414/93, 23 Eur. H.R. Rep. 413 (1997); Ahmed v. Austria, App. No. 25964/94, 24 Eur. H.R. Rep. 278 (1997); T.I. v. United Kingdom, App. No. 43844/98 (2000), *available at* http://hudoc.echr.coe.int/ sites/fra/pages/search.aspx?i=001-5105.

250. *See* UNHCR ADVISORY OPINION, *supra* note 234.

251. 1951 Refugee Convention, *supra* note 16, at art. 33(1).

252. *See* UNHCR ADVISORY OPINION, *supra* note 234.

security,[253] these exceptions apply only in extreme and limited circumstances.[254]

(4) *Paragraph 4*: The purpose of Paragraph 4 is to affirm the principle of *non-refoulement* in human rights law, independent of the CAT and the 1951 Refugee Convention and Protocol. In cases of serious violations of fundamental human rights that do not fall under CAT or have a nexus to the five protected grounds in the 1951 Refugee Convention, human rights law provides robust protections against return.[255]

(5) The most fundamental of these rights is the right to life. Regional instruments,[256] international human rights treaty bodies,[257] and regional court systems[258] have all explicitly found that potential violations of the right to life trigger *non-refoulement* protections. The right to life may be threatened in various ways, including the death penalty,[259] extra-judicial execu-

---

253. 1951 Refugee Convention, *supra* note 16, at art. 33(2).

254. *See* UNHCR NOTE ON THE PRINCIPLE OF *NON-REFOULEMENT*, *supra* note 241.

255. *See* INT'L COMM'N OF JURISTS, *supra* note 167, at 95, 99; Vincent Chetail, *Are Refugee Rights Human Rights? An Unorthodox Questioning of the Relations between Refugee Law and Human Rights Law*, *in* HUMAN RIGHTS AND IMMIGRATION 19, 34, 37 (Ruth Rubio-Marín ed., 2014) ("[M]ost general human rights treaties have been construed by their respective treaty bodies as inferring an implicit prohibition on *refoulement* . . . the human rights principle of *non-refoulement* stands out as a practical and powerful means for ensuring effective respect for fundamental rights."); G.T. v. Australia, Comm. No. 706/1996 ¶¶ 8.1-8.2, U.N. Doc. CCPR/C/61/D/706/1996 (1997), at http://www.refworld.org/docid/4ae9acbfd.html.

256. *See, e.g.*, Cartagena Declaration, *supra* note 34, ¶ 3 ("[T]he definition or concept of a refugee . . . includes among refugees persons who have fled their country because their lives, safety or freedom have been threatened by generalized violence, foreign aggression, internal conflicts, massive violation of human rights or other circumstances which have seriously disturbed public order."); Convention Governing the Specific Aspects of Refugee Problems in Africa, *supra* note 35; Council Directive 2011/95/EU, art. 15, 2011 O.J. (L 337) 9, 18 (Subsidiary protection of non-return includes risk of serious harm, defined as: "(a) the death penalty or execution; or (b) torture or inhuman or degrading treatment or punishment of an applicant in the country of origin; or (c) serious and individual threat to a civilian's life or person by reason of indiscriminate violence in situations of international or internal armed conflict.").

257. *See, e.g.*, *General Comment No. 6*, *supra* note 128 ("States shall not return a child to a country where there are substantial grounds for believing that there is a real risk of irreparable harm to the child, such as, but by no means limited to, those contemplated under articles 6 [right to life] . . . of the Convention."); *General Comment No. 31*, *supra* note 248, ¶ 12 ("[T]he article 2 obligation requiring that States Parties respect and ensure the Covenant rights for all persons in their territory and all persons under their control entails an obligation not to extradite, deport, expel or otherwise remove a person from their territory, where there are substantial grounds for believing that there is a real risk of irreparable harm, such as that contemplated by articles 6 [right to life] and 7 of the Covenant, either in the country to which removal is to be effected or in any country to which the person may subsequently be removed."); G.T. v. Australia, *supra* note 255, ¶ 8.1.

258. *See* Bader v. Sweden, App. No. 13284/04, 46 Eur H.R. Rep. 13, 206 (2005) (finding that deportation of the applicant to face execution would violate the right to life). The European Court of Human Rights often deals with alleged violations of the right to life in the context of examining violations of the right to be free from torture, inhuman or degrading treatment or punishment. *See, e.g.*, Na v. United Kingdom, App. No. 25904/07, 48 Eur. H.R. Rep. 15, 378 (2009); Said v. the Netherlands, App. No. 2345/02, 43 Eur. H.R. Rep. 14, 256 (2005). *See also* Haitian Centre for Human Rights v. United States of America, Decision, Case 10.675, Inter-Am. Comm'n H.R., Report No. 51/96, OEA/Ser.L./V/II.95, doc. 7 rev. at 550 (1997).

259. Kaboulov v. Ukraine, App. No. 41015/04, 50 Eur. H.R. Rep. 39, 998 (2010).

tions,[260] or lack of appropriate medical care.[261]

(6) The right to be free from torture and other cruel, inhuman or degrading treatment or punishment is the most analyzed and discussed *non-refoulement* trigger in human rights law. The right is non-derogable.[262] States must not "expose individuals to the danger of torture or cruel, inhuman or degrading treatment or punishment upon return to another country by way of their extradition, expulsion or refoulement."[263] Most Human Rights Committee and European Court of Human Rights jurisprudence regarding *non-refoulement*, including cases that implicate other rights, falls under analysis of this rule.

(7) *Paragraph 5*: Paragraph 5 urges States to consider forgoing expulsion of a migrant where there are substantial grounds for believing that the migrant would be subjected to other serious deprivations of human rights.

(8) International human rights bodies and regional frameworks recognize *non-refoulement* protection for situations of generalized violence, which may implicate a broad range of rights.[264] Certain States and regions use temporary protection regimes to ensure that migrants are not returned to areas of war or other crisis.[265] Situations such as sudden natural disasters or slow-onset disasters may threaten migrants' right to life, as well as other rights such as health, housing, food, and adequate standard of living.[266] While cases that

260. *See, e.g.*, The Haitian Centre for Human Rights et al. v. United States, Case 10.675, Inter-Am. Comm'n H.R., Report No. 51/96, OEA/Ser.L/V/II.95, doc. 7 rev. ¶ 156-57 (1997); Baboeram v. Suriname, Comm. Nos. 146/1983. 148-154/1983, CCPR/C/24/D/146/1983, (Apr. 4, 1985), at http://www1.umn.edu/humanrts/undocs/session40/146-1983.htm.

261. *See* D. v. United Kingdom, App. No. 30240/96, 24 Eur. H.R. Rep. 423, 436-38 (1997) (finding article 2 claims indissociable from article 3 claims).

262. Saadi v. Italy, App. No. 37201/06, 49 Eur. H.R. Rep. 30, 758-59 (2009) para. 127; Chahal v. U.K., App. No. 22414/93, 23 Eur. H.R. Rep. 413, 437 (1997).

263. *General Comment No. 20*, *supra* note 247.

264. *See, e.g.* Cartagena Declaration, *supra* note 34, at 190-193 ("the definition or concept of a refugee . . . includes among refugees persons who have fled their country because their lives, safety or freedom have been threatened by generalized violence, foreign aggression, internal conflicts, massive violation of human rights or other circumstances which have seriously disturbed public order."); Convention Governing the Specific Aspects of Refugee Problems in Africa, *supra* note 230; Council Directive 2011/95/EU, *supra* note 256, at art. 15 (Subsidiary protection of non-return includes risk of serious harm, defined as: "(a) the death penalty or execution; or (b) torture or inhuman or degrading treatment or punishment of an applicant in the country of origin; or (c) serious and individual threat to a civilian's life or person by reason of indiscriminate violence in situations of international or internal armed conflict."); Na v. United Kingdom, App. No. 25904/07, 48 Eur. H.R. Rep. 15, 356 (2009) ("The Court has never excluded the possibility that a general situation of violence in a country of destination will be of a sufficient level of intensity as to entail that any removal to it would necessarily breach Article 3 of the Convention. Nevertheless, the Court would adopt such an approach only in the most extreme cases of general violence, where there was a real risk of ill-treatment simply by virtue of an individual being exposed to such violence on return.").

265. INT'L COMM'N OF JURISTS, *supra* note 167, at 67-73.

266. *See* Vikram Kolmannskog & Lisetta Trebbi, *Climate change, natural disasters and displacement: a multi-track approach to filling the protection* gaps, 92, no. 879 International Review of the Red Cross 713 (2010), *available at* http://www.icrc.org/eng/assets/files/review/2010/irrc-879-kolmannskog-trebbi.pdf.

implicate such rights as health[267] and adequate standard of living[268] have been evaluated by the European Court of Human Rights under humiliating and degrading treatment, both the Human Rights Committee and the European Court of Human Rights have held that potential violation of other rights could produce *non-refoulement* protections. For example, States should not return a migrant to a country where there are substantial grounds for believing that the migrant would be denied the right to a fair trial,[269] be denied the right to hold and manifest religious beliefs,[270] or be arbitrarily detained.[271] States should adjust their expulsion procedures to uphold all human rights of each individual within their jurisdictions.

(9) *Paragraph 6*: The purpose of Paragraph 6 is to establish protection against *refoulement* for all migrants who are subject to a State's jurisdiction or effective control, whether or not the migrant is within the State's territory.[272] The scope of protection should include migrants seeking asylum or migrants interdicted on the high seas,[273] and prohibits so-called "push-backs," in which States intercept vessels at sea and summarily return migrants to sending States without an individualized determination of protection needs.[274] This "extraterritorial" understanding of *non-refoulement* is bolstered by the intent of States party to the 1951 Refugee Convention not to place migrants at risk of serious harm or persecution,[275] and the nature of the IMBR as a set of norms derived from the fundamental dignity of all migrants, rather than from their ties to a particular sovereign.

267. D. v. United Kingdom, App. No. 30240/96, 24 Eur. H.R. Rep. 423, 436-38 (1997).

268. M.S.S. v. Belgium, App. No. 30696/09, 53 Eur. H.R. Rep. 2, (2011) (taking into consideration the fact that the asylum-seeker was "living in the street, with no resources or access to sanitary facilities, and without any means of providing for his essential needs" for several months).

269. *See* A.R.J. v. Australia, ¶ 6.15, U.N. Doc. CCPR/C/60/D/692/1996 (Aug. 11, 1997), at http://www.refworld.org/docid/4028adfa7.html.

270. *See* Z and T v. United Kingdom, App. No. 27034/05, Eur. H.R. Rep. (28 February 2006), at http://www.refworld.org/docid/45ccab042.html.

271. *See* Z and T, Eur. H.R. Rep.; Tomic v. the United Kingdom, App. No. 17387/03, Eur. H.R. Rep. (June 9 2003), at http://echr.ketse.com/doc/17837.03-en-20031014/view/ (stating that there is the potential for flagrant arbitrary detention to raise *non-refoulement* issues).

272. UNHCR ADVISORY OPINION, *supra* note 234.

273. *See e.g. Conclusions Adopted by the Executive Committee on International Protection of Refugees*, *supra* note 234, ¶ (c) ("[I]t is the humanitarian obligation of all coastal States to allow vessels in distress to seek haven in their waters and to grant asylum, or at least temporary refuge, to persons on board wishing to seek asylum."); UNHCR ADVISORY OPINION, *supra* note 234; The Haitian Centre for Human Rights et al. v. United States, Case 10.675, Inter-Am. Comm'n H.R., Report No. 51/96, OEA/Ser.L/V/II.95, doc. 7 rev. ¶ 156-57 (1997 Brief for U.N. High Comm'r for Refugees as Amicus Curiae Supporting Respondents, Sale v. Haitian Centers Council, Inc., 509 U.S. 155 (1993) (No. 92-344); Medvedyev v. France, App. No. 3394/03, 51 Eur. H.R. Rep. 39, 919-21 (2010) (extending applicability of the ECHR to a French warship's interception and effective control of a boat on the high seas).

274. *See* Hirsi Jamaa v. Italy, App. No. 27765/09, 55 Eur. H.R. Rep. 21 (2012).

275. *See* UNHCR ADVISORY OPINION, *supra* note 234.

ARTICLE 14
NATIONALITY

(1) Every migrant has the right to a nationality.

(2) Every person has the right to the nationality of the State in whose territory the person was born if the person does not have the right to any other nationality.

(3) States shall provide for, and should encourage, the naturalization of migrants, subject to limitations and conditions that are non-arbitrary and accord with due process of law.

(4) States shall recognize the right of expatriation and renunciation of citizenship, subject only to conditions and limits based on compelling considerations of public order or national security.

(5) Neither marriage nor the dissolution of marriage shall automatically affect the nationality of either spouse or their children. States shall not remove the nationality of a citizen who marries a non-citizen unless the citizen takes affirmative steps to renounce citizenship. States shall grant women equal rights with men with respect to the nationality of their children.

(6) No migrant shall be arbitrarily deprived of nationality nor denied the right to change nationality. States should not consider a migrant's acquisition of foreign nationality to be an automatic or implied basis of renunciation of the nationality of the State of origin.

(7) States should allow children having multiple nationalities acquired automatically at birth to retain those nationalities.

Commentary

(1) The foundation of this Article is the fundamental right of every person to a nationality. This right includes the ability to change one's nationality without arbitrary interference by a sovereign State.[276] States should also take reasonable measures to combat statelessness, and should not act so as to render persons stateless. This Article affirms that unreasonable barriers to the renunciation or acquisition of a nationality must not be erected. Furthermore, to better enable migrants to achieve full enjoyment of the social, political, cultural, labor, and other rights within this Bill, States should encourage the naturalization of resident lawful migrants. While this Article recognizes the general right of sovereign States to determine when to bestow citizenship and nationality rights,[277] this Article also recognizes necessary

---

276. *See* UDHR, *supra* note 1, at art. 15 ("(1) Everyone has the right to a nationality. (2) No one shall be arbitrarily deprived of his nationality nor denied the right to change his nationality.").

277. International law has long recognized citizenship and nationality laws as falling within the sovereign powers of States. *See* Convention on Certain Questions Relating to the Conflict of Nationality Law arts. 1, 2, Apr. 12, 1930, 179 L.N.T.S. 89. *See also* MICHAEL WALZER, SPHERES OF JUSTICE 39 (1983) (arguing that the survival of democratic communities depends upon their exercise of some control over membership status within their own national communities).

limits[278] on this power: in particular, States may not unreasonably burden the free movement of persons by way of unduly restrictive citizenship and nationality laws, nor may States exercise their sovereign powers over citizenship and nationality in a manner that conflicts with international law norms. A non-exhaustive list of such norms includes preserving gender equality, marriage rights, and rights of the child. This Article articulates the limits applicable to States' sovereign power to prescribe citizenship and nationality laws. Pursuant to Article 1, a migrant who gains citizenship in a host State ceases to be a migrant.

(2) Migrants frequently encounter problems of legal status as a result of the citizenship and nationality laws of both receiving States and States of origin. In particular, migrants may encounter resistance in naturalizing where they reside, and they may risk the unwanted forfeiture of nationality rights and privileges in a State of origin as they seek or obtain nationality in another State. In each of these cases, this Article favors inclusion under citizenship and nationality laws, and this Article strongly disfavors the involuntary renunciation of one's citizenship and nationality under a State's internal laws. In the case of an otherwise stateless person, this Article recognizes that person's right to the nationality of the State in which they were born should no other nationality be available to them.

(3) *Paragraph 2*: The goal of Paragraph 2 is to ensure that everyone has the right to a nationality. A person's right to the nationality of the state in which the person was born is explicitly provided for in the ACHR,[279] the European Convention on Nationality of 1997,[280] the Convention on the Reduction of Statelessness,[281] and the Hague Convention on Certain Ques-

---

278. There is ample modern and historical support for placing boundaries around the scope of a sovereign State's power to draft its citizenship and nationality laws. Article I of the 1930 Hague Convention on Nationality recognized that such laws must be consistent with international conventions, international custom, and general principles of international law. *See* Convention on Certain Questions Relating to the Conflict of Nationality Laws, *supra* note 277, at art. 1. The earlier advisory opinion of the PCIJ in the *Tunis-Morocco* case already suggested that, in the future, international law would develop so as to impose restrictions on sovereign States' authority to draft and administer nationality laws. *See* Nationality Decrees Issued in Tunis and Morocco (French Zone) on November 8th, 1921, Advisory Opinion, 1923 P.C.I.J. (ser. B) No. 4, at 24 (Feb. 7). The *Nottebohm* case directly incorporates considerations of international law norms in evaluating the legitimacy of a sovereign's nationality laws. Nottebohm (Liech. v. Guat.), 1955 I.C.J. 4, 23 (Apr. 6). More recently, the Strasbourg European Convention on Nationality of 1997 declared in Article III, Paragraph 2 that States shall determine their own nationality laws only insofar as such laws are consistent with international conventions, customary international law, and general international principles regarding nationality. European Convention on Nationality art. 3.2, Nov. 6, 1997, ETS No. 166.

279. ACHR, *supra* note 12, at art. 20 ("Every person has the right to the nationality of the state in whose territory he was born if he does not have the right to any other nationality.).

280. European Convention on Nationality of 1997, *supra* note 278, at art. 7 ("Each State Party shall provide in its internal law for its nationality to be acquired by children born on its territory who do not acquire at birth another nationality.").

281. Convention on the Reduction of Statelessness, *supra* note 43, at art. 1 ("A Contracting State shall grant its nationality to a person born in its territory who would otherwise be stateless.").

tions Relating to the Conflict of Nationality Laws,[282] and is implicit in the UDHR[283] and the CRC.[284] The realization of a person's right to the nationality of the State in which they were born would ultimately lead to the elimination of statelessness if this right were universally exercised. However, States need not confer nationality automatically under these treaties. States should ensure that there is an expedited process for acquiring nationality for those who would otherwise be without a nationality. A process that is so onerous as to defeat the object and purpose of this right is a violation of this right.

(4) *Paragraph 3*: Naturalization of resident lawful migrants should be encouraged, as naturalization furthers the exercise of a migrant's other rights and preserves the right to change one's nationality. The goal of naturalization is justified by the inherent inequality involved in having two distinct classes of residents within one State. This dichotomy of legal status is particularly problematic when a non-naturalized class is subject to the laws of a State without enjoying participation and voting rights within the sovereign State.[285] Temporary workers present one example of such a problem: despite formal guarantees of legal protections, these migrants frequently encounter difficulties in exercising their rights and in enforcing fair working conditions, while the availability of such vulnerable, often low-wage workers may also damage the bargaining power of local unions and worsen wage and working conditions for naturalized workers in the same industry.[286] Thus, naturalization not only improves the condition of the migrant, but it also preserves the legal rights of already naturalized residents and citizens in the receiving State.

(5) Factors that strengthen a claim to naturalization include: duration of residence; economic, social, and family ties; community and linguistic integration; legal status; the best interest of the child; and humanitarian grounds. This list of factors for evaluating the strength of a naturalization claim is non-exhaustive, and these factors must be applied in a case-by-case

---

282. Convention on Certain Questions Relating to the Conflict of Nationality Laws, *supra* note 277, at art. 15 ("Where the nationality of a State is not acquired automatically by reason of birth on its territory, a child born on the territory of that State of parents having no nationality, or of unknown nationality, may obtain the nationality of the said State.").

283. UDHR, *supra* note 1, at art. 15(1) ("Everyone has the right to a nationality."). This conference of a universal right does not specify which state has the corresponding duty of providing the nationality, however the most logical construction of this article is that each person has at a minimum the right to the nationality of the country in which the individual is born.

284. CRC, *supra* note 6, at art.7(1) ("The child shall be registered immediately after birth and shall have the right from birth to a name, the right to acquire a nationality . . .), art. 8(1) ("States Parties undertake to respect the right of the child to preserve his or her identity, including nationality . . ."). Because birth registration and right to nationality are both included in the same paragraph of article 7 of the CRC it is implicit in this article that the child shall be both registered in the state in which it is born and entitled to acquire the nationality of that state.

285. *See* PHILLIP COLE, PHILOSOPHIES OF EXCLUSION 10 (2000).

286. *See* Jennifer Gordon, *Transnational Labor Citizenship*, 80 S. CAL. L. REV. 503, 553-56 (2007) (regarding the domestic and foreign workers' rights problems posed by the existence of a temporary worker system instead of one resulting in the naturalization and subsequent unionization of foreign workers).

analysis of individual naturalization claims. Under such an analysis, the absence of any one factor or set of factors is not *per se* dispositive of a claim to naturalization; conversely, a very strong claim under any one factor—such as the right to family unification or the necessary interests of the child—may suffice on its own to sustain a claim. A necessary result of this balancing of factors favoring or disfavoring a claim to naturalization is that the unlawful status of a migrant's entry into a State shall not absolutely bar the migrant's ultimate naturalization in that State.

(6) *Paragraph 4*: The right of expatriation is itself a norm of international law.[287] To properly protect this right, exceptions allowing for States to refuse expatriation must be read narrowly: "[C]ompelling considerations" should be limited to necessary, proportional responses to *existing* exigencies, and not merely broad-based, preemptive policies directed at hypothetical, future threats to State sovereignty. Thus, while an imminent threat of grave national harm may sustain a State's refusal to allow citizens to expatriate, more abstract concerns regarding the long-term preservation of State resources will not justify refusing expatriation.

(7) *Paragraph 5*: In keeping with the trend of gender-neutral citizenship law and the concept that the renunciation or acquisition of a nationality should be a positive act, this Paragraph recognizes both the equality of men and women with regard to their own nationality in the act of marriage, and with respect to the nationality of their children as affirmed by CEDAW[288] and the Convention on the Nationality of Married Women.[289] In the event that a State retains laws that automatically confer nationality upon marriage, this Bill shall not be taken as an affirmative action for the renunciation of other nationalities. In particular, the act of marriage must not result in gender discrimination by automatically changing the nationality of one spouse to reflect that of the other—as has most often been the case with women having their nationalities changed forcibly to reflect the nationality of their husbands.[290] This Paragraph further incorporates important considerations of gender equality as, in the case of illegal forced marriages, this Paragraph prevents further harm from being visited upon forced migrants by ensuring

287. *See, e.g.*, UDHR, *supra* note 1, at art. 15(2) (noting that "no one shall be . . . denied the right to change his nationality").

288. CEDAW, *supra* note 16, at art. 9(1), (2) ("States Parties shall grant women equal rights with men to acquire, change or retain their nationality. They shall ensure in particular that neither marriage to an alien nor change of nationality by the husband during marriage shall automatically change the nationality of the wife, render her stateless or force upon her the nationality of the husband . . . States Parties shall grant women equal rights with men with respect to the nationality of their children"). *See also*, Unity Dow v. Attorney-General, Court of Appeal, July 3, 1992, 1992 BLR 119 (CA) (Bots.) (holding that the automatic bestowal of the father's nationality to the exclusion of the mother's infringed the right not to be discriminated against on the basis of sex).

289. Convention on the Nationality of Married Women, art. 1, opened for signature Feb. 20, 1957, 309 U.N.T.S. 65 (". . . neither the celebration nor the dissolution of a marriage between one of its nationals and an alien, nor the change of nationality by the husband during marriage, shall automatically affect the nationality of the wife.").

290. *See* CEDAW, *supra* note 16, at art. 9(1).

that nationality in the involuntary spouse's State of origin is not simultaneously and involuntarily surrendered upon marriage. Likewise, it ensures gender equality for children of marriages between nationals of two different States.

(8) *Paragraph 6*: Paragraph 6 incorporates two important concerns. First, the renunciation of nationality should be an affirmative process; second, States should not construct "trap doors" through which the enjoyment of one's rights in areas such as marriage results in the inadvertent loss of nationality. One has a clear right under international law to marry the person of one's choosing.[291] Exercise of this right must not nullify the enjoyment of other essential rights, such as those regarding nationality.

(9) Paragraph 6 is the clearest articulation of this Article's policy favoring the recognition of plural citizenship, and the policy strongly disfavoring any renunciation of citizenship not involving an active declaration of intent from the individual citizen directly affected by the loss of citizenship. While States retain authority to draft domestic citizenship laws that do not recognize plural citizenship rights, transparency and effective notice should always characterize citizenship laws. This Paragraph also favors trends towards the recognition of plural citizenship in at least some circumstances. Paragraphs 6 and 7 complement each other, such that plural nationality acquired automatically by any means—just as plural nationality acquired automatically and specifically through marriage—should not constitute an automatic renunciation of one's original nationality.

(10) *Paragraph 7*: This Paragraph builds upon and clarifies the existing nationality rights of children. Just as every person is entitled to a nationality, every child must have the right to acquire a nationality.[292] The right to acquire a nationality necessarily includes the right to preserve that nationality.[293] Paragraph 6 of this Article establishes that a full recognition of these rights should extend to the recognition of a child's plural nationalities acquired automatically at birth. Moreover, preserving equality between men and women with respect to the nationality of their children[294] requires the acceptance of plural nationality under this Paragraph. Traditionally, there has been some resistance in international law to allowing for dual or plural nationalities;[295] however, there is a strong movement towards the recog-

---

291. *See, e.g.*, UDHR, *supra* note 1, at art. 16(1), (2).

292. *See, e.g.*, ICCPR, *supra* note 2, at art. 24(3); CRC, *supra* note 6, at art. 7(1).

293. *See* CRC, *supra* note 6, at art. 8(1).

294. *See* CEDAW, *supra* note 16, at art. 9(2).

295. *See* Convention on Certain Questions Relating to the Conflict of Nationality Law, *supra* note 277, at pmbl. ("Being convinced that it is in the general interest of the international community to secure that all its members should recognise that every person should have a nationality and should have one nationality only."). In the second paragraph of Article 12, the Convention provides "[t]he law of each State shall permit children of consuls de carrière, or of officials of foreign States charged with official missions by their Governments, to become divested, by repudiation or otherwise, of the nationality of the State in which they were born, in any case in which on birth they acquired dual nationality, provided that they retain the nationality of their parents." The Convention seems more

nition of plural nationalities, and those States still formally rejecting the practice often acquiesce by failing to enforce internal laws requiring exclusive nationality.[296] This Bill favors the trend towards recognition and adopts the position that, in general, the interests of the children covered by this Paragraph shall best be served by permitting plural nationality.

ARTICLE 15
FAMILY

(1) Every migrant family is entitled to protection by society and the State.

(2) States shall take all appropriate measures to facilitate the reunification of migrant family members with nationals or citizens.

(3) Children with no effective nationality have the right to return to either parent's State of origin and to stay indefinitely with their parent or parents regardless of the children's citizenship.

(4) States should grant derivative immigration status and timely admission to dependent family members of migrants who are lawfully settled within the State. States should consider extending derivative immigration status to non-dependent family members of lawfully settled migrants.

Commentary

(1) This Article establishes the importance of the family and addresses family rights that are especially pertinent to migrants. It builds upon prior international legal precedent in establishing a right that should not be controversial.[297] The most crucial and basic social grouping is the family. Families may be by biological ties, but may also include individuals with mutual dependencies.[298] As migration can lead to extended periods of family separation and uncertainty, State treatment of the family can greatly impact

---

worried about children being able to renounce their dual nationality with respect to children of career diplomats. T. Alexander Aleinikoff, *Between Principles and Politics: U.S. Citizenship Policy*, *in* FROM MIGRANTS TO CITIZENS 119, 137-41 (T. Alexander Aleinikoff & Douglas Klusmeyer eds., 2000), *reprinted in* THOMAS ALEXANDER ALEINIKOFF ET AL., IMMIGRATION AND CITIZENSHIP: PROCESS AND POLICY 90-91 (2008).

296. *See* Peter J. Spiro, *Dual Nationality and the Meaning of Citizenship*, 46 EMORY L.J. 1411, 1453-58 (1997). *But see* Karin Scherner-Kim, *The Role of the Oath of Renunciation in Current U.S. Nationality Policy—To Enforce, To Omit, or Maybe To Change?*, 88 GEO L.J. 329, 370 (2000) (arguing that States *should* enforce the laws refusing to allow for recognition of plural nationalities).

297. "This standard should not be controversial as it merely reflects broad international agreement [as embodied in various human rights treaties]." *See* Ryan T. Mrazik & Andrew I. Schoenholtz, *Protecting and Promoting the Human Right to Respect for Family Life: Treaty-Based Reform and Domestic Advocacy*, 24 GEO. IMMIGR. L.J. 651, 672 (2010).

298. The definition of "family" should be construed broadly. *Id.* at 653-54 ("Because one's family can include parents, siblings, grandparents, adult children, and others, establishing the existence or non-existence of a family life involves a fact-based, flexible, and substantive evaluation of situations where the right to respect for family life might attach."). *See also* Yogyakarta Principles, *supra* note 79, at 27 ("Everyone has the right to found a family, regardless of sexual orientation or gender identity. Families exist in diverse forms. No family may be subjected to discrimination on the basis of the sexual orientation or gender identity of any of its members.").

the protection families receive in regard to other rights. Migrants are particularly vulnerable when separated from their family. The family's right to be together and the family's right to reunify once separated are of utmost importance.

(2) *Paragraph 1*: This Paragraph defines the protection given by society and the State to the family grouping. The right to protection of the family by the State is derived directly from ICCPR Article 23(1): "The family is the natural and fundamental group unit of society and is entitled to protection by society and the State."[299] ICESCR Article 10(1) also establishes that "[t]he widest possible protection should be accorded to the family, which is the natural and fundamental group unit of society, particularly for its establishment and while it is responsible for the care and education of dependent children."[300] Article 12 of the UDHR guards against "arbitrary interference" with the family, among other things, including "privacy . . . home or correspondence."[301] The CRC and CEDAW also protect the right to family relations as expressed through ensuring that the family is not separated from the child or retaining a family structure under law.[302] This extends the right of ICRMW Article 44(1), which establishes that "States Parties, recognizing that the family is the natural and fundamental group unit of society and is entitled to protection by society and the State, shall take appropriate measures to ensure the protection of the unity of the families of migrant workers."[303]

(3) A State is responsible for protecting families, with no discrimination between citizens and non-citizens. The prohibition against discrimination on the basis of national origin can be found in Article 2(2) of the ICESCR, which guarantees all rights in that Convention "without regard . . . to social origin" and in Article 2(2) of the ICCPR. Furthermore, the right to non-interference with the family is protected by the ICCPR. Article 17 of the ICCPR states that: "(1) No one shall be subjected to arbitrary or unlawful interference with his privacy, family, home or correspondence, nor to unlawful attacks on his honour and reputation. (2) Everyone has the right to the protection of the law against such interference or attacks."[304]

(4) The conception of the family as the "fundamental group unit of society" is recognized in international law[305] and is derived from social

299. ICCPR, *supra* note 2, at art. 23(1).
300. ICESCR, *supra* note 3, at art. 10(1).
301. UDHR, *supra* note 1, at art. 12.
302. CRC, *supra* note 6, at arts. 8-10, 16; CEDAW, *supra* note 16, at arts. 9, 16.
303. ICRMW, *supra* note 16, at art. 44(1).
304. ICCPR, *supra* note 2, at art. 17. *See also* Mrazik & Schoenholtz, *supra* note 297, at 683. Mrazik and Schoenholtz outline this protection, stating that the inclusion of "arbitrary" as a qualifier "suggests a need for a measure of discretion in state decisions that affect an individual's right to respect for family life."
305. ICCPR, *supra* note 2, at art. 23(1); ICESCR, *supra* note 3, at art. 10(1); UDHR, *supra* note 1, at art. 16(3); CRC, *supra* note 6, at arts. 8-10, 16; ICRMW, *supra* note 16, at art. 44(1).

needs, biological connections, and dependency relationships between the individuals in the family unit. The right to protection of the family implies the right of family members to live together.[306] The "two main principles" that underlie the "right to respect for family life" are: "(1) the family is the natural and fundamental unit of society, and (2) maintaining the family unit is in the best interests of the child."[307]

(5) *Paragraph 2*: The rights contained in this paragraph derive from the CRC's right of a child to be raised by the child's family.[308] Children should not be separated from their parents against their will, and in cases where children are separated, family reunification should be pursued unless contrary to the best interests of the child.[309] Children separated from their parents "face greater risks of, *inter alia*, sexual exploitation and abuse, military recruitment, child labor (including labor for their foster families) and detention."[310] In particular, this Paragraph intends to prevent situations in which a migrant child is born in the parents' host country and granted legal status or citizenship in that country only to be forbidden from returning with the parents to the parents' country of origin. In accordance with the CRC, separation should only occur when it is in the best interests of the child, and should not occur on the basis of citizenship. This right should be read in the context of the IMBR's broad *non-refoulement* provision.[311]

(6) Children are entitled to special protection and assistance by the State when they are temporarily or permanently deprived of their family.[312] Under the CRC, discrimination based on national or social origin is impermissible and therefore States have an obligation to provide special protection and assistance to all children regardless of national or social origin. Furthermore, Article 22 of the CRC, which refers to children who are seeking refugee status or are refugees, calls on States Parties to assist the United Nations in "trac[ing] the parents or other members of the family of any refugee child in order to obtain information necessary for reunification with his or her family."[313] If the family cannot be found, then "the child shall be accorded

306. Human Rights Comm., *General Comment No. 19: Article 23 (Protection of the Family, the Right to Marriage and Equality of the Spouses)*, U.N. Doc. HRI/GEN/1/Rev.9 (July 27, 1990), at http://ccprcentre.org/doc/ICCPR/General%20Comments/HRI.GEN.1.Rev.9%28Vol.I%29_%28GC19%29_en.pdf.

307. Mrazik & Schoenholtz, *supra* note 297, at 652.

308. CRC, *supra* note 6, at art. 9(1).

309. *General Comment No. 6, supra* note 128, ¶ 79 ("The ultimate aim in addressing the fate of unaccompanied or separated children is to identify a durable solution that addresses all their protection needs, takes into account the child's view and, wherever possible, leads to overcoming the situation of a child being unaccompanied or separated.").

310. *Id.* at ¶ 3.

311. INT'L MIGRANTS BILL OF RIGHTS, art. 13, 28 GEO. IMMIGR. L.J. 18. *See also General Comment No. 6, supra* note 128, ¶ 82 ("Family reunification in the country of origin is not in the best interests of the child and should therefore not be pursued where there is a 'reasonable risk' that such a return would lead to the violation of fundamental human rights of the child.").

312. CRC, *supra* note 6, at arts. 20(1), 22(2).

313. CRC, *supra* note 6, at art. 22(2).

the same protection as any other child permanently or temporarily deprived of his or her family environment for any reason, as set forth in the present Convention."[314] This Paragraph also relates to State obligations to children under IMBR Article 3(2).[315]

(7) The CRC also requires States to treat applications of children or parents to enter or leave for the purpose of family reunification in a "positive, humane and expeditious manner." Such applications "shall entail no adverse consequences for the applicants and for the members of their family."[316]

(8) *Paragraph 3*: A child should grow up in a family environment[317] and should be raised by the child's parents.[318] Understanding that the migration process can cause differences in citizenship and effective nationality between children and their parents, this Paragraph ensures that citizenship or *de facto* statelessness will not prevent children from joining their parents, should they return to the State of origin or to another new location.

(9) *Paragraph 4*: This Article builds on the foundation of the family as the fundamental group unit of society. The right to protection of the family implies the ability of family members to live together.[319] The first portion of this Paragraph emphasizes the right to migrate for dependent family of lawfully settled migrants. The CRC provides that "applications by a child or his or her parents to enter or leave a State Party for the purpose of family reunification shall be dealt with by States Parties in a positive, humane and expeditious manner."[320] Additionally, the ICRMW instructs States to "take measures that they deem appropriate and that fall within their competence to facilitate the reunification of migrant workers with their spouses or persons who have with the migrant worker a relationship that, according to applicable law, produces effects equivalent to marriage, as well as with their minor dependent unmarried children."[321] The European Court of Human Rights has upheld the right of a child (or of a substantial equivalent) to join the child's lawfully resident parents under the ECHR right to family.[322]

(10) Distinctions among family members that follow the standard presented in Article 3(4) of this Bill (made pursuant to a legitimate aim, with an objective justification, and with reasonable proportionality between the means employed and the aims sought to be realized) are valid; this Paragraph is not meant to supplant the Bill's equal protection article.

314. CRC, *supra* note 6, at art. 22(2).
315. INT'L MIGRANTS BILL OF RIGHTS, art. 3(2), 28 GEO. IMMIGR. L.J. 15.
316. CRC, *supra* note 6, at art. 10(1).
317. CRC, *supra* note 6, at pmbl.
318. CRC, *supra* note 6, at art. 9; *see* OPEN SOCIETY JUSTICE INITIATIVE, EXPERT OPINION ON THE RIGHT TO FAMILY LIFE AND NON-DISCRIMINATION (2008).
319. *See General Comment No. 19*, *supra* note 306; ICCPR, *supra* note 2, at pmbl. ¶ 2.
320. CRC, *supra* note 6, at art. 10(1).
321. ICRMW, *supra* note 16, at art. 44(2).
322. Sen v. Netherlands, App. No. 31465/96, 36 Eur. H.R. Rep. 7 (2001).

(11) The second portion of this Paragraph encourages States to consider extending lawful status to non-dependent family members of lawfully settled migrants. The extension of derivative immigration status to non-dependent family members of lawfully settled migrants follows from several human rights instruments that establish the family as the "fundamental group unit of society," including the ICCPR, the ICESCR, the UDHR, the CRC, and the ICRMW.[323] The animating concern throughout this Article is that, as the fundamental group unit of society, the family is deserving of State protection, and this includes both individuals who are dependent and those who are non-dependent but comprise part of a family.

ARTICLE 16
FREEDOM OF THOUGHT, CONSCIENCE AND RELIGION OR BELIEF

(1) Every migrant has the right to freedom of thought, conscience, and religion or belief.

(2) This right shall include freedom to have or to adopt a religion or belief of one's choice, and freedom, either individually or in community with others and in public or private, to manifest one's religion or belief in worship, observance, practice and teaching. Migrants shall not be subject to coercion that would impair their freedom to have or to adopt a religion or belief of their choice.

(3) States shall undertake to have respect for the liberty of parents and, when applicable, legal guardians to ensure the religious and moral education of their children in conformity with their own convictions.

Commentary

(1) *Paragraph 1*: The purpose of Paragraph 1 is to reaffirm the right to freedom of thought, conscience and religion for migrants. This is of particular importance for migrants who may practice a religion unfamiliar to their country of residence. Under Article 4(2) of the ICCPR, the right to freedom of thought, conscience and religion is non-derogable.[324] The right to freedom of thought, conscience and religion was enshrined in Article 18 of the UDHR, Article 18 of the ICCPR and other international instruments.[325] According to the Human Rights Committee General Comment 22, the rights

---

323. *See* ICCPR, *supra* note 2, at art. 23(1); ICESCR, *supra* note 3, at art. 10(1); UDHR, *supra* note 1, at arts. 12, 16(3) (protecting against "arbitrary interference with . . . privacy, family, home or correspondence); CRC, *supra* note 6, at arts. 8, 9, 10, 16; ICRMW, *supra* note 16, at art. 44.

324. ICCPR, *supra* note 2, at art. 4(2).

325. ICRMW, *supra* note 16, at art. 12; ECHR, *supra* note 8, at art. 9; Banjul Charter, *supra* note 9, at art. 8; ACHR, *supra* note 12, at art. 12; Declaration on the Elimination of All Forms of Intolerance and of Discrimination Based on Religion or Belief, G.A. Res. 36/55, art. 1(1), U.N. Doc. A/RES/36/55 (Nov. 25, 1981).

protected in this Article are "far-reaching and profound."[326] Additionally, according to General Comment 15, the rights guaranteed in the Convention "apply to everyone . . . irrespective of his or her nationality" and "must be guaranteed without discrimination between citizens and aliens."[327]

(2) *Paragraph 2*: The purpose of Paragraph 2 is to reaffirm that the freedom of thought, conscience, religion or belief includes the right to retain one's religion or belief, the right to change one's religion or belief, the right to adopt a religion or belief, and the right to adopt atheistic views.[328] These rights encompass the right to worship or assemble in connection with a religion or belief, including through ritual or ceremonial acts.[329] These rights are without limit.[330] The second clause of this Paragraph supports these rights by reaffirming the right to be free from coercion. The protection of these rights for migrants are of particular importance when they are members of a minority religion or belief and are vulnerable to State agents or others who may try to convert or prevent the conversion of persons through unethical or forcible means.[331] The text of this Paragraph derives from Article 18 of the UDHR, Article 18 of the ICCPR, and other international instruments.[332]

(3) *Paragraph 3*: The purpose of Paragraph 3 is to reaffirm the right of migrant parents or legal guardians to provide religious and moral education to their children. This includes a respect for the cultural identity and values of the country from which migrant children may originate.[333] Children should have access to religious and moral education in accordance with the wishes of their parents and should not be compelled to receive instruction against the wishes of their parents. The text of this article derives from Article 18 of the ICCPR, Article 14 of the CRC, and other international instruments.[334]

---

326. Human Rights Comm., *General Comment No.22: Article 18 (Freedom of Thought, Conscience or Religion)*, ¶ 1, U.N. Doc. CCPR/C/21/Rev.1/Add.4 (Sept. 27, 1993), at http://ccprcentre.org/doc/ICCPR/General%20Comments/CCPR.C.21.Rev1.Add4_%28GC22%29_En.pdf.

327. *General Comment No. 15*, *supra* note 66, ¶¶ 1-2.

328. *General Comment No. 15*, *supra* note 66, ¶ 7; U.N. Secretary-General, *Implementation of the Declaration on the Elimination of all Forms of Intolerance and of Discrimination Based on Religion or Belief*, ¶¶ 70-80, U.N. Doc. E/CN.4/1997/91 (Dec. 30, 1996).

329. *General Comment No. 22*, *supra* note 326, ¶ 4; G.A. Res. 36/55, *supra* note 325, at art. 6(a)-(c).

330. Special Rapporteur of the Comm'n on Human Rights on Freedom of Religion or Belief, *Elimination of all Forms of Religious Intolerance, transmitted by Note of the Secretary-General*, ¶¶ 49-53, U.N. Doc. A/60/399 (Sept. 30, 2005).

331. *Elimination of all Forms of Religious Intolerance*, *supra* note 330, ¶¶ 40-68; *see* ICCPR, *supra* note 2, at art. 27; Human Rights Comm., *General Comment No. 23: Article 27 (Rights of Minorities)*, ¶ 5.2, U.N. Doc. CCPR/C/21/Rev.1/Add.5 (Apr.26, 1994), at http://ccprcentre.org/doc/ICCPR/General%20Comments/CCPR.C.21.Rev1.Add5_%28GC23%29_En.pdf.

332. Declaration on the Elimination of All Forms of Intolerance and of Discrimination Based on Religion or Belief, *supra* note 325, at art. 1(1).

333. CRC, *supra* note 6, at art. 14(2).

334. CRC, *supra* note 6, at art. 14(2); ICCPR, *supra* note 2, at art. 18 (4); ICRMW, *supra* note 16, at art. 12 (4); Declaration on the Elimination of All Forms of Intolerance and of Discrimination Based on Religion or Belief, *supra* note 325, at art. 5.

ARTICLE 17
FREEDOM OF OPINION AND EXPRESSION

(1) Every migrant has the right to hold opinions without interference.

(2) Every migrant has the right to freedom of expression; this right shall include freedom to seek, receive and impart information and ideas of all kinds, regardless of frontiers, either orally, in writing or in print, in the form of art, or through any other media of the migrant's choice.

Commentary

(1) *Paragraph 1*: The purpose of Paragraph 1 is to reaffirm the well-established principle that every person, including every migrant, has the right to freedom of opinion. The right to freedom of opinion was originally enshrined in Article 19 of the UDHR.[335] Paragraph 1 tracks the language from Article 19 of the ICCPR and Article 13 of the ICRMW.[336] The Human Rights Committee has stated that the freedom of opinion contained in ICCPR Article 19 extends to protect the right of an individual to change their opinion and the freedom not to hold or express an opinion.[337] The Human Rights Committee has also stated that no individual may be subjected to an impairment of the individual's human rights based on actual, perceived or supposed opinions.[338] There are no exceptions or reservations to the right to freedom of opinion,[339] and therefore, the Human Rights Committee has declared that it can never become necessary to derogate from the freedom of opinion during a state of emergency.[340]

(2) *Paragraph 2*: The purpose of Paragraph 2 is to reaffirm the well-established principle that every person, including every migrant, has the fundamental right to freedom of expression. The UN General Assembly has declared that the "freedom of information is a fundamental human right and . . . the touchstone of all the freedoms to which the United Nations is consecrated."[341] It is important to note that the guarantee protects both the right to impart information and the right to seek and receive information and ideas.[342] The "right to freedom of expression" was originally enshrined in

---

335. UDHR, *supra* note 1.

336. ICCPR, *supra* note 2, at art. 19; ICRMW, *supra* note 16, at art. 13.

337. Human Rights Comm., *General Comment No. 34: Article 19 (Freedoms of Opinion and Expression)* ¶¶ 9-10, U.N. Doc. CCPR/C/GC/34 (Sept. 12, 2011), at http://ccprcentre.org/doc/ICCPR/General%20Comments/CCPR-C-GC-34.pdf.

338. *General Comment No. 34*, *supra* note 337, ¶ 9.

339. Toby Mendel, *Restricting Freedom of Expression: Standards and Principles; Background Paper for Meetings Hosted by the UN Special Rapporteur for Freedom of Opinion and Expression*, CENTRE FOR LAW AND DEMOCRACY 2010, at 3.

340. *General Comment 34*, *supra* note 337, ¶ 5.

341. Calling of an International Conference on Freedom of Information, G.A. Res. 59/1, U.N. Doc. A/RES/59 (Dec. 14, 1946).

342. Mendel, *supra* note 339, at 4-5; Mavlonov v. Uzbekistan, Comm. No. 1334/2004, ¶ 8.4, U.N. Doc. CCPR/C/95/D/1334/2004 (Apr. 27, 2009), at http://www.refworld.org/docid/4ac9aaa22.html

Article 19 of the UDHR. Paragraph 2 tracks the language from Article 19 of the ICCPR and Article 13 of the ICRMW.[343]

ARTICLE 18
FREEDOM OF PEACEFUL ASSEMBLY AND ASSOCIATION

(1) Every migrant has the right to freedom of peaceful assembly and association.

(2) These rights shall include freedom to form associations and trade unions in the State of residence for the promotion and protection of the migrant's economic, social, cultural, and other interests.

Commentary

(1) *Paragraph 1*: The purpose of Paragraph 1 is to reaffirm the right to peaceful assembly and association for migrants. The right to peacefully assemble and the right to associate are enshrined in many of the core human rights instruments, including the UDHR,[344] the ICCPR,[345] the CRC,[346] the ICERD,[347] the ECHR,[348] the Banjul Charter,[349] and the ACHR.[350] The Human Rights Committee has further interpreted the ICCPR to ensure that "aliens receive the benefit of the right of peaceful assembly and of freedom of association."[351] The UN Human Rights Council has highlighted the importance of these rights and reiterated that the rights apply to migrants.[352] The Special Rapporteur on the Rights to Freedom of Peaceful Assembly and of Association was even more explicit in stating that

---

(holding that the refusal of Uzbek authorities to register a newspaper denied the right of both the expression rights of the editor but also of the reader to receive information and ideas).

343. ECHR, *supra* note 8, at art. 10; ACHR, *supra* note 12, at art. 9; Banjul Charter, *supra* note 9, at art. 13.

344. UDHR, *supra* note 1, at art. 20(1) ("Everyone has the right to freedom of peaceful assembly and association.").

345. ICCPR, *supra* note 2, at art. 21 ("The right of peaceful assembly shall be recognized."), art. 22(1) ("Everyone shall have the right to freedom of association with others . . .").

346. CRC, *supra* note 6, at art. 15(1) ("States parties recognize the rights of the child to freedom of association and to freedom of peaceful assembly.").

347. ICERD, *supra* note 4, at art. 5(d)(ix) (". . . States Parties undertake to prohibit and to eliminate racial discrimination in all its forms and to guarantee the right of everyone, without distinction as to race, colour, or national or ethnic origin, to equality before the law, notably in the enjoyment of the following rights: The right to freedom of peaceful assembly and association . . .").

348. ECHR, *supra* note 8, at art. 11(1) ("Everyone has the right to freedom of peaceful assembly and to freedom of association with others, including the right to form and to join trade unions for the protection of his interests.").

349. Banjul Charter, at art. 10(1) ("Every individual shall have the right to free association provided that he abides by the law."), art. 11 ("Every individual shall have the right to assemble freely with others.").

350. ACHR, at art. 15 ("The right of peaceful assembly, without arms, is recognized."), art. 16(1) ("Everyone has the right to associate freely for ideological, religious, political, economic, labor, social, cultural, sports, or other purposes.").

351. *General Comment No. 15*, *supra* note 66, ¶ 7.

352. G.A. Res. 15/21, ¶ 1, U.N. Doc. A/HRC/RES/15/21 (Oct. 6, 2010).

the rights of assembly and association in the ICCPR apply to non-nationals, including stateless persons, refugees, and migrants.[353]

(2) The right to peacefully assemble and associate facilitates the exercise of many other rights and is essential to a functioning democracy. The right allows individuals to "express their political opinions, engage in literary and artistic pursuits and other cultural, economic and social activities, engage in religious observances or other beliefs, form and join trade unions and cooperatives, and elect leaders to represent their interests and hold them accountable."[354] For migrants, who often do not have the right to vote, who are often of a cultural, ethnic, or religious minority, and who are often in labor situations with few bargaining rights, the ability to assemble and associate without fear of reprisal is an important way to engage in the polity and to claim other civil, cultural, economic, political and social rights.[355]

(3) *Paragraph 2*: The freedom to form associations and trade unions is explicitly enumerated in several of the core human rights documents, including the UDHR,[356] the ICCPR,[357] the ICESCR,[358] the ICERD,[359] theICRMW,[360] and the ECHR.[361] The right to form and join trade unions is also protected by the International Labour Organization in ILO Convention No. 87.[362] Additionally, the ILO Congress declared in 1998 that all members of the ILO have the obligation to respect, promote, and realize certain

353. Report of the Special Rapporteur on the Rights to Freedom of Peaceful Assembly and of Association, ¶ 13, U.N. Doc. A/HRC/20/27 (May 21, 2012).

354. G.A. Res. 15/21, *supra* note 352, at pmbl.

355. Report of the Special Rapporteur on the Rights to Freedom of Peaceful Assembly and of Association, *supra* note 353, ¶ 12.

356. UDHR, *supra* note 1, at art. 23(4) ("Everyone has the right to form and to join trade unions for the protection of his interests.").

357. ICCPR, *supra* note 2, at art. 22(1) ("Everyone shall have the right to freedom of association with others, including the right to form and join trade unions for the protection of his interests.").

358. ICESCR, *supra* note 3, at art. 8(1) ("The States Parties to the present Covenant undertake to ensure . . . The right of everyone to form trade unions and join the trade union of his choice, subject only to the rules of the organization concerned, for the promotion and protection of his economic and social interests.").

359. ICERD, *supra* note 4, at art. 5(e)(ii) (". . . States Parties undertake to prohibit and to eliminate racial discrimination in all its forms and to guarantee the right of everyone, without distinction as to race, colour, or national or ethnic origin, to equality before the law, notably in the enjoyment of the following rights: The right to form and join trade unions.").

360. ICRMW, *supra* note 16, at art. 26(1) ("States Parties recognize the right of migrant workers and members of their families: (a) To take part in meetings and activities of trade unions and of any other associations established in accordance with law, with a view to protecting their economic, social, cultural and other interests, subject only to the rules of the organization concerned; (b) To join freely any trade union and any such association as aforesaid, subject only to the rules of the organization concerned . . .").

361. ECHR, *supra* note 8, at art. 11(1) ("Everyone has the right to freedom of peaceful assembly and to freedom of association with others, including the right to form and to join trade unions for the protection of his interests.").

362. Convention Concerning Freedom of Association and Protection of the Right to Organise (No. 87), art. 2, July 9, 1948, 68 U.N.T.S. 17 [hereinafter ILO Convention 87] ("Workers and employers, *without distinction whatsoever*, shall have the right to establish and, subject only to the rules of the organisation concerned, to join organisations of their own choosing without previous authorization." (emphasis added)).

fundamental rights, including freedom of association.[363] Freedom of association includes the right to form and join an association, to operate the association freely and to be protected from undue interference, to access funding and resources, to take part in the conduct of public affairs, and to not be subject to unlawful termination.[364] The freedom to join trade unions applies to workers, not only regardless of citizenship, but also "irrespective of their migratory status."[365] This right should be read in concert with the labor rights protected by this Bill in Article 20.

ARTICLE 19
CIVIL AND POLITICAL LIFE

(1) Every migrant has the right to participate in the civil and political life of the migrant's community and in the conduct of public affairs.

(2) This right shall include the freedom to participate in public affairs of their State of origin and to vote and to be elected at elections of that State, in accordance with its legislation.

Commentary

(1) The right to civil and political life extends from the idea that it is in the interest of all people to have a voice in the policies that affect them. As emphasized in the IMBR preamble, "migrants bring special contributions to their communities, [and] the ability to participate in and influence one's community is a significant part of human dignity." Migrants often create new familial and community roots in their location of residence while still maintaining similar connections in their State of origin. This Article encourages States to extend civic rights to migrants by providing some avenues for migrant voices to be heard.

(2) *Paragraph 1*: The language "participate in the civil and political life" allows for a range of interpretations. In practice, States should grant voting rights for migrants in local elections, but can also facilitate civic participation by soliciting comments on pertinent proposed laws or policies, soliciting migrants' opinions through a representative on deliberative or advisory

363. International Labour Conference, Geneva, Switz., June 1998, *ILO Declaration on Fundamental Principles and Rights at Work*, art. 3 (June 18, 1998), at http://www.ilo.org/declaration/thedeclaration/textdeclaration/lang—en/index.htm [hereinafter ILO 1998 Declaration].

364. Special Rapporteur on the Rights to Freedom of Peaceful Assembly and of Association, *supra* note 353, ¶¶ 53-76.

365. Advisory Opinion on Undocumented Migrants, *supra* note 166, ¶ 157 ("The safeguard of [freedom of association and to organize and join a trade union] for migrants has great importance based on the principle of the inalienable nature of such rights, which all workers possess, irrespective of their migratory status, and also the fundamental principle of human dignity embodied in Article 1 of the Universal Declaration, according to which '[a]ll human beings are born free and equal in dignity and rights.'")

bodies, and providing full information about civic rights and duties.[366] The right may also be realized in part by facilitating association and assembly, whether on community or trade-group grounds.[367] Assembly and association rights will also support migrant participation in the conduct of public affairs by allowing migrants to exert "influence through public debate and dialogue with their representatives or through their capacity to organize themselves."[368]

(3) The right to participate in the civil and political life of the community builds on ideas in the ICCPR and the ICERD.[369] Though these documents limit civic rights on the basis of citizenship, they serve as evidence of the importance of these concepts to the full enjoyment of human rights. The Human Rights Committee explicitly mentions the possibility that permanent residents might "enjoy [civic] rights on a limited basis, for example, by having the right to vote in local elections or to hold particular public service positions."[370] While international human rights law does not require direct electoral participation for migrants, European countries—and the European Union as a whole—provide successful models of non-citizen participation in civil and political life, including local elections.[371] In addition, immigrant suffrage is a growing trend and currently available on some level in more than forty countries.[372] This immigrant suffrage trend reflects strong policy arguments in favor of enfranchising migrants, especially those migrants who pay taxes, may be drafted into military service, and otherwise bear the responsibilities of citizenship to the host country.[373]

---

366. *See* European Convention on the Participation of Foreigners in Public Life at the Local Level, Explanatory Report, Feb. 5, 1992, C.E.T.S. No. 144.

367. *See, e.g.*, European Convention on the Participation of Foreigners in Public Life at the Local Level, *supra* note 366.

368. Human Rights Comm., *General Comment No. 25: Article 25 (The Right to Participate in Public Affairs, Voting Rights and the Right of Equal Access to Public Service)* ¶ 8, U.N. Doc. CCPR/C/21/Rev.1/Add.7 (Aug. 27, 1996), at http://ccprcentre.org/doc/ICCPR/General%20Comments/CCPR.C.21.Rev1.Add7_%28GC25%29_En.pdf (describing one way in which citizens may take part in the conduct of public affairs).

369. ICCPR, *supra* note 2, at art. 25 ("Every citizen shall have the right . . . to take part in the conduct of public affairs."); ICERD, *supra* note 4, at art. 5(c) ("Political rights, in particular the right to participate in elections—to vote and to stand for election—on the basis of universal and equal suffrage, to take part in the Government as well as in the conduct of public affairs at any level and to have equal access to public service.").

370. *General Comment No. 25*, *supra* note 368, ¶ 3.

371. *See, e.g.*, European Convention on the Participation of Foreigners in Public Life at the Local Level, *supra* note 366 (guaranteeing freedom of expression, assembly and association, encouraging the establishment of consultative bodies to represent foreign residents at local levels, and guaranteeing the right to vote and to stand for election in local authority elections); Maastricht Treaty, art. 8b, Feb. 7, 1992, 1992 O.J. (C 191) 1 ("Every citizen of the Union residing in a Member State of which he is not a national shall have the right to vote and to stand as a candidate at municipal elections in the Member State in which he resides, under the same conditions as nationals of that State.").

372. IMMIGRANT VOTING PROJECT, http://ronhayduk.com/immigrant-voting/around-the-world/ (last visited May 10, 2014) (updated list of all countries that provide such rights, as well as extensive discussion of the topic).

373. *See* Gabriela Evia, *Consent by All the Governed: Reenfranchising Noncitizens as Partners in America's Democracy*, 77 S. CAL. L. REV. 151 (2002); Elise Brozovich, *Prospects for Democratic Change: Non-Citizen Suffrage in America*, 23 HAMLINE J. PUB. L & POL'Y 403 (2000) (arguing in

(4) *Paragraph 2*: Paragraph 2 is derived from ICRMW Article 41 and requires States of origin to allow their citizens living abroad to vote and be elected.[374] The right to vote externally draws support from the principle of universal suffrage. The UDHR recognizes the right of every person to take part in government, directly or through freely chosen representatives, and to have equal access to public service.[375] The ICCPR and various regional instruments grant citizens the right to vote and to stand for election without unreasonable restrictions;[376] however, the Human Rights Committee and the European Commission on Human Rights have stated that residency requirements are generally considered reasonable requirements for voting.[377] While there is significant divergence in State practice regarding who is eligible for external voting, and many migrants' voting rights are effectively suspended during migration,[378] over 100 countries expressly allow their citizens to vote from abroad.[379] The trend in State practice to enable and encourage external voting is particularly prominent for elections in post-conflict States.[380]

ARTICLE 20
LABOR

(1) Every migrant has the right to be free from slavery, servitude, or forced or compulsory labor.

(2) Every migrant has the right to work, and States shall take progressive measures to safeguard this right.

---

favor of non-citizen voting rights in America); Jamin B. Raskin, *Legal Aliens, Local Citizens: The Historical, Constitutional and Theoretical Meanings of Alien Suffrage*, 141 U. PA. L. REV. 1391 (1993).

374. ICRMW, *supra* note 16, at art. 41 ("Migrant workers and members of their families shall have the right to participate in public affairs of their State of origin and to vote and to be elected at elections of that State, in accordance with its legislation").

375. UDHR, *supra* note 1, at art. 21.

376. ICCPR, *supra* note 2, at art. 25 ("Every citizen shall have the right and the opportunity, without any of the distinctions mentioned in article 2 and without unreasonable restrictions . . . to vote and to be elected at genuine periodic elections which shall be by universal and equal suffrage and shall be held by secret ballot, guaranteeing the free expression of the will of the electors."). *See also* Banjul Charter, *supra* note 9, at art. 13; ACHR, *supra* note 12, at art. 23; ECHR, *supra* note 8, at art. 3.

377. *General Comment No. 25*, *supra* note 368, ¶ 11 (e.g. residence requirements that exclude homeless from voting are not reasonable). *See* X v. United Kingdom, App. No. 7566/76 Eur. H.R. Rep. (1976), *available at* http://echr.ketse.com/doc/7566.76-en-19761211/view/ ("This right [universal suffrage] was neither absolute nor without limitations but subject to such restrictions imposed by the Contracting States as are not arbitrary and do not interfere with the free expression of the people's opinion.").

378. JEREMY GRACE, CHALLENGING THE NORMS AND STANDARDS OF ELECTION ADMINISTRATION 35-38 (IFES, 2007), *available at* http://www.ifes.org/~/media/Files/Publications/White%20Paper Report/2007/593/IFES%20Challenging%20Election%20Norms%20and%20Standards%20WP.pdf. *See* Kim Barry, *Home and Away: The Construction of Citizenship in an Emigration Context*, 81 N.Y.U. L. REV. 11, 51 (2006); NYU Law School.

379. Barry, *supra* note 378.

380. Barry, *supra* note 378; INTERNATIONAL IDEA, A PREVIEW OF THE FORTHCOMING INTERNATIONAL IDEA HANDBOOK ON EXTERNAL VOTING (International IDEA, 2006) *available at* http://www.idea.int/elections/upload/External_voting_Preview_withlayout_07june06_final.pdf. *See also* Caroline Carter, *The Right to Vote for Non-Resident Citizens: Considered through the Example of East Timor*, 46 TEX. INT'L L. J. 655, 673 (2011).

(3) Every migrant has the right to just and favorable conditions of work, including fair and equal remuneration, minimum working age, maximum hours, safety and health standards, protection against unfair dismissal, and collective bargaining.

(4) States shall ensure the effective abolition of child labor.

(5) States shall ensure the elimination of discrimination in respect of employment and occupation.

(6) Migrants shall be entitled to treatment at least as favorable as that accorded to citizens with respect to labor conditions and employment.

(7) States should require that migrant workers who are recruited in one country for work in another receive a written job offer, or contract of employment that is enforceable in the country in which the work is to be performed, addressing the terms and conditions of employment prior to crossing national borders for the purpose of taking up the work to which the offer or contract applies.

Commentary

(1) This Article reaffirms a number of existing labor rights found in key international human rights instruments. The right to work, as provided by ICESCR, is an inherent part of human dignity. The essence of the right to work is not an absolute right to obtain employment, but rather the right to freely choose employment and to not to be unfairly deprived of employment.[381] The right to freely choose work necessarily includes an absolute prohibition of slavery, servitude, and forced labor. The right to work also entails a range of rights in the workplace.

(2) In addition to the core human rights instruments, the ILO Declaration on Fundamental Principles and Rights at Work establishes that all Member States, even if they have not ratified the appropriate Convention, have obligations arising from membership in the ILO to respect, promote and realize the principles and rights in four categories: freedom of association and the effective recognition of the right to collective bargaining, the elimination of forced or compulsory labor, the abolition of child labor, and the elimination of discrimination in respect of employment and occupation. The ILO has eight fundamental conventions that cover these four principles.[382] The four principles are addressed in this IMBR labor article.

---

381. ICESCR, *supra* note 3, at art. 6(1).

382. ILO Convention No. 29 concerning Forced or Compulsory Labor, June 10, 1930, 39 U.N.T.S. 55 [hereinafter ILO Convention 29]; Abolition of Forced Labour Convention (No. 105), Jan. 17, 1959, 320 U.N.T.S. 291 [hereinafter ILO Convention 105]; Discrimination (Employment and Occupation) Convention (No. 111), June 15, 1960, 362 U.N.T.S. 31 [hereinafter ILO Convention 111]; Equal Remuneration Convention (No. 100), May 23, 1953, 165 U.N.T.S. 303 [hereinafter ILO Convention 100]; ILO Convention 87, *supra* note 362; Right to Organise and Collective Bargaining Collection (No. 98), July 18, 1951, 96 U.N.T.S. 257 [hereinafter ILO Convention 98]; Convention Concerning Minimum Age for Admission to Employment (No. 138), June 19, 1976, *available at* http://www.ilo.org/ilolex/cgi-lex/convde.pl?C138 [hereinafter ILO Convention 138]; Convention

(3) Many migrants leave their native countries in search of better economic prospects. Even those motivated by other factors such as persecution, discrimination or armed conflict must earn a livelihood upon settling in a receiving State. Migrants often must overcome significant obstacles in finding employment, including language barriers, lack of knowledge of the local job market, non-recognition of qualifications from the State of origin and poor understanding of local employment laws.

(4) Upon securing employment, migrants face additional challenges, including discrimination, harassment, poor and unsafe working conditions, persistent job insecurity and fear of expulsion upon employment termination. These challenges often persist because local labor laws may be inapplicable to migrants or governments may simply refuse to apply relevant laws to situations of migrant employment. Migrants also are often employed in the informal economy, where it is much harder for them to obtain the protection of the State, particularly when migrants are in an irregular status.

(5) Numerous migrants arrive in receiving States as the result of smuggling or human trafficking operations. Such migrants are typically subject to highly exploitative terms of employment and are sometimes compelled into commercial sex work or other forms of forced labor. Migrants are also often highly susceptible to various forms of economic exploitation and physical abuse, as their ability to remain in the receiving State may be tied to continued employment with the same sponsoring employer. This last problem is particularly acute for those migrants employed as domestic workers.[383]

(6) One of the reasons States typically restrict immigration is to protect the domestic labor market, shielding native workers from competition and attempting to ensure low levels of unemployment. However, States sometimes encourage the migration of certain classes of workers in order to fill a lacuna or restructure the domestic labor market. Special categories or conditions of employment are created to promote the inflow of these migrants and to regulate their activities upon arrival. However, such measures may facilitate exploitative or discriminatory practices on the part of employers.[384]

Concerning the Prohibition and Immediate Action for the Elimination of the Worst Forms of Child Labor (No. 182), Nov. 19, 2000, 2133 U.N.T.S. 161 [hereinafter ILO Convention 182].

383. *See* J.M. RAMIREZ-MACHADO, DOMESTIC WORK, CONDITIONS OF WORK AND EMPLOYMENT: A LEGAL PERSPECTIVE (ILO 2003), *available at* http://www.ilo.int/wcmsp5/groups/public/---ed_protect/---protrav/---travail/documents/publication/wcms_travail_pub_7.pdf; U.N. Econ. & Soc. Council, Comm'n on Human Rights, *Report of the Special Rapporteur: Ms. Gabriela Rodríguez Pizarro on Specific Groups and Individuals: Migrant Workers, Submitted Pursuant to Commission on Human Rights Resolution 2003/46*, U.N. Doc. E/CN.4/2004/76 (Jan. 12, 2004), *available at* http://daccess-dds-ny.un.org/doc/UNDOC/GEN/G04/102/37/PDF/G0410237.pdf.

384. JEAN-MICHEL SERVAIS, INTERNATIONAL LABOUR LAW, 226-27 (2005).

(7) *Paragraph 1*: The prohibition of servitude, slavery, and forced labor has long been recognized in international law as one of the first peremptory norms.[385] Slavery is outlawed by the 1926 Slavery Convention, and the prohibition of slavery and servitude can be found in the UDHR, ICCPR, ECHR, ACHR, ACHPR and ICRMW.[386] Forced labor is defined by ILO Convention No. 29 as "all work or service for which the said person has not offered himself voluntarily."[387] Forced labor is banned in the ICCPR, ICESCR, ICRMW, ECHR, ACHR, ACHPR, as well as in ILO Conventions Nos. 29 and 105.[388]

(8) *Paragraph 2*: The right to work derives from numerous human rights instruments, including the UDHR, ICESCR, ICERD, CEDAW, CRC, ICRMW, ADRDM, and the Additional Protocol to the ACHR.[389] The core elements of the right to work are the rights to freely choose employment and to not be unfairly deprived of employment.[390] The right to work also entails a range of rights in the workplace.

(9) *Paragraph 3*: The right to just and favorable conditions of work is detailed in Article 7 of the ICESCR. It is also provided by Article 5 of ICERD, and Banjul Charter Article 15, which asserts the right to work under equitable and satisfactory conditions.[391]

(10) The right to just and favorable remuneration is enshrined in UDHR Article 23. The UDHR links this right to the ability of the individual to provide an "existence worthy of human dignity" for himself and his family.[392] This right is echoed in the American Declaration of the Rights and Duties of Man Article XIV, ICESCR Article 7, ICERD Article 5 and the ILO Philadelphia Declaration.[393] Article 25 of the ICRMW provides that migrant

---

385. *See, e.g.*, M. Cherif Bassiouni, *International Crimes: "Jus Cogens" and "Obligatio Erga Omnes,"* 59 LAW & CONTEMP. PROBS. 63, 68 (1996).

386. *See* UDHR, *supra* note 1, at art. 4; ICCPR, *supra* note 2, at art. 8; ECHR, *supra* note 8, at art. 4; ACHR, *supra* note 12, at art. 6; Banjul Charter, *supra* note 9, at art. 5; ICRMW, *supra* note 16, at art. 11.

387. ILO Convention 29, *supra* note 382.

388. ICCPR, *supra* note 2, at art. 8; ICESCR, *supra* note 3, at art. 6; ICRMW, *supra* note 16, at art. 11; ECHR, *supra* note 8, at art. 8; ACHR, *supra* note 12, at art. 6; Banjul Charter, *supra* note 9, at art. 10; ILO Convention 29, *supra* note 382; ILO Convention 105, *supra* note 382.

389. *See* UDHR, *supra* note 1, at art. 23; ICERD, *supra* note 4, at art. 5(e)(i); CEDAW, *supra* note 16, at art. 11; CRC, *supra* note 6, at art. 32; ICRMW, *supra* note 16, at art. 11; American Declaration of the Rights and Duties of Man, O.A.S. Res. XXX, adopted by the Ninth International Conference of American States (1948), *reprinted in* Basic Documents Pertaining to Human Rights in the Inter-American System, art. 24, OEA/Ser.L.V/II.82 doc.6 rev.1 at 17 (1992); ACHR, *supra* note 12, Protocol in the Area of Economic, Social and Cultural Rights, art. 6.

390. ICESCR, *supra* note 3, at art. 6(1).

391. *See also* Convention concerning Termination of Employment at the Initiative of the Employer (No. 158), June 22, 1982, *available at* http://www.ilo.org/dyn/normlex/en/f?p=NORMLEXPUB:12100:0::NO:12100:P12100_ILO_CODE:C158.

392. *See* UDHR, *supra* note 1, at art. 23.

393. *See also* Convention concerning the Portection of Wages (No. 95), Sept. 24, 1952, *available at* http://www.ilo.org/dyn/normlex/en/f?p=NORMLEXPUB:12100:0::NO:12100:P12100_ILO_CODE:C095; ILO Convention 100, *supra* note 382; Equality of Treatment (Social Security) Convention, Apr. 25, 1964, *available at* http://www.ilo.org/dyn/normlex/en/f?p=NORMLEXPUB:12100:0::NO:12100:P12100_INSTRUMENT_ID:312263:NO.

workers should enjoy treatment not less favorable than that received by nationals with regard to remuneration.

(11) The right to form trade unions is a more specific application of the right to freedom of association indicated in Article 18. The explicit right to form and join trade unions is found in UDHR Article 23, ICERD Article 5, ICCPR Article 22 and ECHR Article 11. ACHR Articles 15 and 16 do not mention union organization, but do recognize the right to freedom of association, a right that has commonly been interpreted to encompass the right to join unions. Even so, none of these treaties explicitly recognizes the right to collective bargaining. In mandating this right, the IMBR draws inspiration from ILO Conventions Nos. 87 and 98, which both provide for the right to union organization as well as the right to collective bargaining. The collective bargaining right is further guaranteed by ILO Convention No. 154, is part of the ILO's Philadelphia Declaration, and is implicit in the ILO Constitution.[394]

(12) States should also follow the standards set in ILO Convention No. 189 Concerning Decent Work for Domestic Workers to ensure that domestic workers are protected by and benefit from labor laws.

(13) *Paragraph 4*: The effective abolition of child labor is one of the ILO's four fundamental principles of work and is binding on all ILO members, regardless of whether they have signed the corresponding conventions. In addition, the ICESCR protects children from economic and social exploitation, and requires a minimum age of employment.[395] The CRC also requires States to protect all children "from all forms of economic exploitation and from performing any work that is likely to be hazardous or to interfere with the child's physical, mental, spiritual, moral, or social development."[396]

(14) *Paragraph 5*: Prohibition of discrimination in the workplace is guaranteed by the ICESCR and the ICERD and is one of the ILO fundamental principles.[397] IMBR Article 3 provides protection against discrimination, including in the workplace. The Committee on the Elimination of Racial Discrimination explicitly recommends that States "take measures to eliminate discrimination against non-citizens in relation to working conditions and work requirements, including employment rules and practices with discriminatory purposes or effects." The Committee also explains that while States

394. Virginia Leary, *The Paradox of Workers' Rights as Human Rights*, *in* 29 HUMAN RIGHTS, LABOR RIGHTS, AND INTERNATIONAL TRADE 22 (Lance A. Compa and Stephen F. Diamond, eds., 1996).

395. *See* ICESCR, *supra* note 3, at art. 10.

396. *See* CRC, *supra* note 6, at art. 32(1).

397. *See* Comm. on Econ, Soc. & Cult. Rights, *General Comment No. 18: The Right to Work* ¶ 18, U.N. Doc. E/C.12/GC/18 (Feb. 6, 2006); Comm. on Econ, Soc. & Cult. Rights, *General Comment No. 20: Non-Discrimination in Economic, Social, and Cultural Rights* ¶ 30, U.N. Doc. E/C.12/GC/20 (July 2, 2009) (stating that ICESCR rights apply "to everyone including non-nationals, such as refugees, asylum-seekers, stateless persons, migrant workers and victims of international trafficking, regardless of legal status and documentation"); ILO 1998 Declaration, *supra* note 363.

may condition jobs upon a work permit, labor and employment rights attach when an employment relationship is established.[398] ILO Conventions Nos. 100 and 111 provide ILO standards on the elimination of discrimination.

(15) Additionally, the Committee on the Elimination of Discrimination Against Women has commented specifically on the human rights abuses of women migrant workers, and the need for specific measures to guarantee equality.[399]

(16) *Paragraph 6*: Paragraph 6 is derived from Article 25 of the ICRMW. Article 25 stresses that regardless of immigration status, migrants shall receive treatment at least as favorable as citizens in workplace conditions. The ICRMW specially lists remuneration, hours of work, rest, safety, health, termination of employment, and minimum working age. The Paragraph is also supported by ILO Convention No. 97 and Articles 10 and 12(g) of ILO Convention No. 143.[400]

(17) *Paragraph 7*: Paragraph 7 is based on Article 8 of ILO Convention No. 189 Concerning Decent Work for Domestic Workers, and is supported by the ILO Multilateral Framework for Labour Migration.[401] The terms and conditions of employment should include the name and address of the employer and of the worker; the address of the usual workplace or workplaces; the starting date and, where the contract is for a specified period of time, its duration; the type of work to be performed; the remuneration, method of calculation and periodicity of payments; the normal hours of work; paid annual leave, and daily and weekly rest periods; the provision of food and accommodation, if applicable; the period of probation or trial period, if applicable; the terms of repatriation, if applicable; and terms and conditions relating to the termination of employment, including any period of notice by either the domestic worker or the employer.[402]

---

398. *See* Comm. on Elimination of Racial Discrim., *General Recommendation No. 30: Discrimination Against Non-Citizens* ¶ 33, U.N. Doc. CERD/C/64/Misc.11/rev.3 (Oct. 1, 2004). *See also* Juridical Condition and Rights of the Undocumented Migrants, *supra* note 166 ("[T]he migrant acquires rights that must be recognized and ensured because he is an employee, irrespective of his regular or irregular status in the State where he is employed.")

399. *See* Comm. on the Elimination of Discrim. Against Women, *General Comment No. 26 on Migrant Women Workers*, U.N. Doc. CEDAW/C/2009/WP.1/R (Dec. 5, 2008).

400. ILO Convention 97, *supra* note 16, at art. 6 ("Each Member for which this Convention is in force undertakes to apply, without discrimination in respect of nationality, race, religion or sex, to immigrants lawfully within its territory, treatment no less favourable than that which it applies to its own nationals in respect of the following matters: [remuneration, hours of work, minimum age, collective bargaining, social security, etc.].")

401. ILO Convention 189, *supra* note 16, at art. 8; INTERNATIONAL LABOUR ORGANIZATION, ILO MULTILATERAL FRAMEWORK ON LABOUR MIGRATION: NON-BINDING PRINCIPLES AND GUIDELINES FOR A RIGHTS-BASED APPROACH TO LABOUR MIGRATION 13.3 (2006), *available at*: http://www.ilo.org/migrant/information-resources/publications/WCMS_178672/lang--en/index.htm ("[Governments should give due consideration to licensing and supervising recruitment by] ensuring that migrant workers receive understandable and enforceable employment contracts").

402. *See* ILO Convention 189, *supra* note 16, at arts. 7, 8.

ARTICLE 21
HEALTH

Every migrant has the right to the enjoyment of the highest attainable standard of physical and mental health, including equal access to preventive, curative, and palliative health services, and the right to an adequate standard of living and to the underlying determinants of health.

Commentary

(1) The right to the enjoyment of the highest attainable standard of health is a foundational human right.[403] Beyond the importance of health to individual and societal flourishing, it is strongly linked to and necessary to the provision of many other human rights, such as the right to human dignity and the right to life.[404] It was first enunciated in the Constitution of the World Health Organization,[405] and later enumerated in the UDHR,[406] the ICESCR,[407] and many other international and regional human rights treaties.[408] It is understood as the right to health care that is available, accessible, acceptable, and of appropriate and good quality.[409] Additionally, mothers are accorded special protection during a reasonable period before and after childbirth.[410] An adequate standard of living and the underlying determinants of health include, but are not limited to, access to safe and potable water and adequate sanitation, an adequate supply of safe food, nutrition and housing, healthy occupational and environmental conditions, and access to health-related education and information, including information about sexual and reproductive health.[411] States are obligated to respect the right to health, meaning they cannot limit access for any persons regardless of immigration status.[412] Legal measures securing access to health care for migrants,

---

403. Comm. on Econ., Soc. & Cult. Rights, *General Comment No. 14, The Right to the Highest Attainable Standard of Health* ¶ 1, U.N. Doc. E/C.12/2000/4 (Aug. 11, 2000).

404. *See General Comment 14*, *supra* note 403 ¶ 3; *see also* Purohit and Moore v. Gambia, African Comm'n on Human and People's Rights, Comm. No. 241/2001, ¶ 84, Sixteenth Activity Report 2002-2003, Annex VII. ("enjoyment of the human right to health . . . is crucial to the realization of all the other fundamental human rights and freedoms").

405. World Health Organization Constitution pmbl, Apr. 7, 1948, 14 U.N.T.S. 185.

406. UDHR, *supra* note 1, at art. 25.

407. ICESCR, *supra* note 3, at art. 12(1).

408. CRC, *supra* note 6, at art. 24; CEDAW, *supra* note 16, at art. 12; ICERD, *supra* note 4, at art. 5; Banjul Charter, *supra* note 9, at art. 16; African Charter on the Rights and Welfare of the Child, *supra* note 161, at art. 14; European Social Charter, art. 11, *opened for signature* March 5, 1996, C.E.T.S. 163 (entered into force Jan. 7, 1999).

409. *General Comment 14*, *supra* note 403, ¶ 12. Though the ICRMW only explicitly grants emergency medical care and access to health services contingent on participation in regulatory schemes, Article 81(1) states that more favorable rights from other instruments (like the general right to health) are retained. ICRMW, *supra* note 16, at art. 81(1).

410. CRC, *supra* note 6, at art. 24(2); CEDAW, *supra* note 16, at art. 12(2); ICCPR, *supra* note 2, at art. 10(2); UDHR, *supra* note 1, at art. 25.

411. *General Comment No. 14*, *supra* note 403, ¶ 11.

412. *General Comment No. 14*, *supra* note 403, ¶ 34; *see also* Eur. Comm. Soc. Rights, Int'l Fed. of Human Rights League v. France, Complaint No. 14/2003 ¶ 32 (Nov. 3, 2004) (stating "legislation

particularly irregular migrants, are lacking in many countries and where they exist, migrants and health providers are often unaware of them and the laws remain unimplemented.[413] Administrative, financial and linguistic barriers exacerbate this lack of access, as does a fear of being reported to police or immigration authorities.[414] Due to these widespread difficulties in accessing health care, many migrant populations are particularly at risk of violations of their rights to health.

ARTICLE 22
EDUCATION

(1) Migrants and their children have the right to education.

(2) States shall make primary education free and compulsory for all children including migrants and their children. Access to public pre-school educational institutions or schools shall not be refused or limited by reason of the irregular situation with respect to stay or employment of either parent or by reason of the irregularity of the child's stay in the State.

(3) States shall encourage the development of secondary education and shall make it accessible to all, including migrants and their children, on the basis of equal treatment with nationals.

(4) States shall make higher education equally accessible to all, including migrants and their children, on the basis of capacity.

Commentary

(1) This Article clarifies that the well-established right to education applies to migrants and their children regardless of their legal status. The Article provides paragraphs corresponding to the three stages of education that are covered by various human rights treaties. Paragraph 2 clearly expresses that migrants and their children are encompassed in the obligation to provide free and compulsory primary education as well as preschool education. Paragraph 3 reiterates the international law obligation of all States to provide secondary education to migrants and their children on the basis of equality of treatment with nationals. Paragraph 4 duly treats higher education.

---

or practice which denies entitlement to medical assistance to foreign nationals, within the territory of the State Party, even if they are there illegally, is contrary to the Charter"); Federal Constitutional Court (2012, in German), 1 BvL 10/10 vom 18.7.2012, Absatz-Nr. (1-140), *press release available at:* http://www.bundesverfassungsgericht.de/pressemitteilungen/bvg12-056en.html (finding that German Asylum Seekers Benefit Act violates human right to a minimum existence because the benefits had not been updated in 19 years).

413. U.N. High Comm'r for Human Rights, *Right to Health Fact Sheet No. 31*, at 19 (June 2008), *available at* http://www.ohchr.org/Documents/Publications/Factsheet31.pdf.

414. *Right to Health Fact Sheet No. 31*, *supra* note 413, at 18; WORLD HEALTH ORG., INTERNATIONAL MIGRATION, HEALTH AND HUMAN RIGHTS, 21-23 (2003), *available at* http://www.who.int/hhr/activities/en/intl_migration_hhr.pdf.

(2) *Paragraph 1*: The right to education is well established in international and regional human rights instruments.[415] In spite of the numerous international conventions that recognize and reiterate the right to education for all people, this right is not always practically accessible to migrants and their children. The inaccessibility of education is particularly acute for migrants and for children whose parents are not lawfully settled in the host state.

(3) *Paragraph 2*: The right to education, and specifically the right to free and compulsory primary education, is formally recognized in the UDHR,[416] the ICESCR,[417] the CEDAW,[418] and the CRC.[419] This right to education has also been incorporated into regional organizations such as the Charter of the OAS and the ECHR.[420] The Committee on Economic, Social, and Cultural Rights has explicitly interpreted the right to education to extend "to all persons of school age residing in the territory of a State party, including non-nationals, and irrespective of their legal status."[421]

(4) This Article highlights the non-discrimination principle and provides a universal floor by guaranteeing primary and secondary education for all children on a basis of equality of treatment with nationals.[422] Because

---

415. ICESCR, *supra* note 3, at art. 13; ICERD, *supra* note 4, at art. 5(e)(v); CEDAW, *supra* note 16, at art. 10; CRC, *supra* note 6, at arts. 28, 29; ICRMW, *supra* note 16, at arts 12(4), 30, 43(1)(a), 45(1)(a), 45(4); CRPD, *supra* note 7, at art. 24; Banjul Charter, *supra* note 9, at art. 17; ECHR, *supra* note 8, at art. 2; African Charter on the Rights and Welfare of the Child, *supra* note 161, at art. 11.

416. UDHR, *supra* note 1, at art. 26(1) ("Everyone has the right to education. Education shall be free, at least in the elementary and fundamental stages. Elementary education shall be compulsory."); *see* Filartiga v. Peña-Irala, 630 F.2d 876, 883 (2d Cir. 1980) (using the Universal Declaration of Human Rights as evidence of customary international law norms).

417. ICESCR, *supra* note 3, at art. 13 ("The States Parties to the present Covenant recognize the right of everyone to education . . . Primary education shall be compulsory and available free to all.").

418. CEDAW, *supra* note 16, at art. 10 ("States Parties shall take all appropriate measures to eliminate discrimination against women in order to ensure to them equal rights with men in the field of education and in particular to ensure, on a basis of equality of men and women . . .").

419. CRC, *supra* note 6, at art. 28 ("States Parties recognize the right of the child to education, and with a view to achieving this right progressively and on the basis of equal opportunity, they shall, in particular . . . [m]ake primary education compulsory and available free to all.").

420. Charter of the Organization of American States, *supra* note 182, at art. 49 ("The Member States will exert the greatest efforts, in accordance with their constitutional processes, to ensure the effective exercise of the right to education . . . Elementary education, compulsory for children of school age, shall also be offered to all others who can benefit from it. When provided by the State it shall be without charge."); ECHR, *supra* note 8, at Protocol 1, art. 2 ("[n]o person shall be denied the right to education"). Unlike the OAS Charter that creates an affirmative obligation to provide compulsory elementary education, ECHR, Protocol 1 creates a "negative" right under which States may not deprive people of educational opportunities. Publicists have interpreted this negative construction of the right as deriving from the fact that the EU Member States did not think about the necessity of establishing a public education system, since each of the Member States already had a system in place. Further, since the adoption of Article 28 of the CRC all signatories have an affirmative obligation to provide free primary education to all children.

421. Comm. on Econ., Soc, & Cult. Rights, *The Right to Education*, ¶ 34, E/C.12/1999/10 (Dec. 8, 1999).

422. While the language from the various treaties does not specify that primary education shall be granted on a basis of equality of treatment, the greater requirement is that it be not only free, but compulsory. Based on its fundamental nature, it should be argued a fortiori that primary education should be granted on the basis of equality of treatment with nationals.

linguistic barriers can further disadvantage migrants and their children, the IMBR incorporates the right to preschool education from the ICRMW.[423] States should also refrain from using school lists as a way to find and remove irregular migrants. Such a practice would force migrant parents to not send their children to school because of the threat of expulsion, rendering the right to education a nullity for migrant children lacking sufficient legal status.

(5) *Paragraph 3*: The right to secondary education is likewise provided for in international treaties and legal instruments. The UDHR,[424] the ICESCR,[425] the CEDAW,[426] and the CRC provide for the right to secondary education.[427] The human rights bodies that monitor and interpret these treaties reaffirm that the principle of non-discrimination applies to all migrants, regardless of status.[428] On the national level, Article 13 of the French Constitution says that the organization of free and secular public education at all levels is a duty of the state.[429] While France is a leading example of constitutional guarantees, in countries such as Canada, the United States, and Germany, the right to education is not explicitly recognized. Nevertheless, courts in these countries have effectuated a right to education for all classes of people within equal protection principles.[430]

(6) *Paragraph 4*: International law instruments also protect the right to access to higher education. The UDHR,[431] the ICESCR,[432] and the

---

423. ICRMW, *supra* note 16, at art. 30 ". . . Access to public pre-school educational institutions or schools shall not be refused or limited by reason of the irregular situation with respect to stay or employment of either parent or by reason of the irregularity of the child's stay . . .".

424. UDHR, *supra* note 1, at art. 26(1) (implying that the right to education is not limited to elementary education).

425. ICESCR, *supra* note 3, at art. 13 ("Secondary education in its different forms, including technical and vocational secondary education, shall be made generally available and accessible to all by every appropriate means.").

426. CEDAW, *supra* note 16, at art. 10 ("States Parties shall take all appropriate measures to eliminate discrimination against women in order to ensure to them equal rights with men in the field of education and in particular to ensure, on a basis of equality of men and women . . .").

427. CRC, *supra* note 6, at art. 28 ("States Parties recognize the right of the child to education, and with a view to achieving this right progressively and on the basis of equal opportunity, they shall, in particular . . . Encourage the development of different forms of secondary education, including general and vocational education, make them available and accessible to every child, and take appropriate measures such as the introduction of free education and offering financial assistance in case of need . . .").

428. Comm. on the Rights of the Child, *General Comment No. 1: The Aims of Education* ¶ 10, U.N. Doc. CRC/GC/2001/1 (Apr. 17, 2001); *General Comment No. 6*, *supra* note 128, ¶¶ 12, 18; Comm. on Econ., Soc. & Cult. Rights, *General Comment 13: The Right to Education*, U.N. Doc. E/C.12/1999/10 (Dec. 8, 1999); *General Comment 30*, *supra* note 398, ¶¶ 30-31.

429. 1946 Constitution Oct. 27, 1946, pmbl. (Fr.).

430. For example, although the United States Constitution does not discuss the right to education, the Supreme Court of the United States in *Plyler v. Doe* held that States could not use the legal status of migrants as grounds for denying migrant children the educational resources that are available to citizens. Plyer v. Doe, 457 U.S. 202, 205 (1982).

431. UDHR, *supra* note 1, at art. 26(1) ("Everyone has the right to education . . . higher education shall be equally accessible to all on the basis of merit.").

432. ICESCR, *supra* note 3, at art. 13(2) ("The States Parties to the present Covenant recognize the right of everyone to education . . . . Higher education shall be made equally accessible to all, on the basis of capacity, by every appropriate means, and in particular by the progressive introduction of free education.").

CRC[433] all guarantee the absolute right to access higher education on the basis of merit. This right to education has also been incorporated into the CEDAW[434] and the charters of regional organizations such as the OAS and the ECHR.[435]

ARTICLE 23
CULTURE

(1) Every migrant has the right to enjoy the migrant's own cultures and to use the migrant's own languages, either individually or in community with others, in public or private.

(2) The right to cultural enjoyment includes the freedom of migrant parents to ensure the religious, cultural, linguistic, and moral education of their children, in conformity with their convictions, by choosing for their children schools other than those established by the public authorities.

(3) States shall not impede, but should encourage and support, migrants' efforts to preserve their cultures by means of educational and cultural activities, including the preservation of minority languages and knowledge related to a migrant's culture. Nothing in this Article shall mean that States may not adopt measures to promote acquisition and knowledge of the majority, national, or official language or languages of the State.

(4) States should take appropriate steps to promote public awareness and acceptance of the cultures of migrants by means of educational and cultural activities, including minority languages and knowledge related to the migrant's own culture.

Commentary

(1) Article 23 asserts the fundamental right of migrants to enjoy their own cultures. Accordingly, the Article proposes a framework for respecting, protecting and promoting migrants' cultural rights that derives from both the civil and political rights regime as well as the economic, social and cultural rights regime. This framework, in recognition of the many ways in which culture may be manifested, is expansive in order to effectively promote respect for the cultures of migrants.

(2) The UDHR states that "[e]veryone has the right to freely participate in the cultural life of the community."[436] The UDHR also protects cultural

433. CRC, *supra* note 6, at art. 28 ("States Parties recognize the right of the child to education, and with a view to achieving this right progressively and on the basis of equal opportunity, they shall, in particular . . . [m]ake higher education accessible to all on the basis of capacity by every appropriate means.").

434. CEDAW, *supra* note 16, at art. 10 ("States Parties shall take all appropriate measures to eliminate discrimination against women in order to ensure to them equal rights with men in the field of education and in particular to ensure, on a basis of equality of men and women . . . .").

435. OAS Charter, *supra* note 182, at art. 49; ECHR, *supra* note 8, at art. 2, note 7.

436. UDHR, *supra* note 1, at art. 27.

rights that may be "indispensable for [a person's] dignity and the free development of [the person's] personality."[437] The ICCPR recognizes the right of migrants, as "ethnic, religious, or linguistic minorities . . . to enjoy their own culture . . . or to use their own language."[438] Article 27 of the ICCPR also recognizes minorities' right to "practice their own religion."[439] The IMBR promotes a framework that respects the communal nature of cultural development and practice. This document, following the ICCPR, applies to all persons, without regard to nationality or status.[440] Consequently, this Article reaffirms States' obligation to provide equal protection for the cultural rights of all people, including migrants. Drawing from both the UDHR and the ICCPR, this Article affirms that migrants may participate in and contribute to both the national culture of the State in which they reside and the minority culture of a migrant community or communities.

(3) *Paragraph 1*: A migrant's right to a cultural identity includes the right to reject—as well as accept—in whole or in part, association with a particular group identity, as emphasized by the phrase "individually or in community" in Article 23(1) of the IMBR. Thus, neither the State nor a cultural group should assume that a person's cultural background automatically demonstrates adherence to particular loyalties, beliefs, or practices. The right to a cultural identity is rooted in the individual right to self-determination and does not by itself provide a right to make decisions on behalf of others without their consent. Protecting cultural rights should be seen as opening doors and never as coercive.

(4) *Paragraph 2*: This Paragraph promotes parents' rights to educate their children in conformity with their beliefs as a universal human right with special bearing on migrants. Human rights instruments recognize a parental right to direct the moral upbringing of one's children.[441] The ICESCR recognizes that the right derives from "respect for the liberty of parents."[442] This right takes on additional practical importance when considered in the context of migration. This Paragraph should be construed to permit the education of temporary migrant workers' children in the language of the migrants' State of origin and, as far as possible, in accordance with the educational standards of that State of origin. In the case of settled migrants, migrant children's interest in preserving their culture and maintaining a

437. UDHR, *supra* note 1, at art. 22.

438. ICCPR, *supra* note 2, at art. 27.

439. *Id.*

440. ICCPR, *supra* note 2, at art. 2(1).

441. ICCPR, *supra* note 2, at art. 18(4); UDHR, *supra* note 1, at art. 2(3); ECHR, *supra* note 8, at Protocol 1, art. 2; ICESCR, *supra* note 3, at art. 13(3); Declaration on the Elimination of All Forms of Intolerance and of Discrimination Based on Religion or Belief, G.A. Res. 36/55, ART. 5(1), U.N. Doc. A/RES/36/55 (Nov. 25, 1981); ICRMW, *supra* note 16, at art. 12; UNESCO Convention against Discrimination in Education, art. 2(b), Dec. 14, 1960, 429 U.N.T.S. 93 (*entered into force* May 22, 1962).

442. ICESCR, *supra* note 3, at art. 13(3).

culturally-based support network may be in competition with their interest in successful integration in the host State. States should take measures to ensure that such balancing decisions are left to the discretion of migrant parents. States with an objective of educating all children within the State system should pursue this objective not through compulsion, but through balancing, such as providing meaningful alternatives to elements that infringe on the rights contained herein.

(5) *Paragraph 3*: Paragraph 3 clarifies the obligations established in paragraph 23(1) of this Article, and underscores the importance of State support for migrants' efforts to preserve their cultures and languages. Under Paragraph 3, States are not obligated to allocate resources to language and cultural preservation, but such a practice is encouraged and resources that are available should be distributed on a non-discriminatory basis.[443] Official support for such activities should complement the activities of stake-holders from within relevant migrant communities. Paragraph 3 also encourages efforts by signatory States to promote the social, cultural, and/or linguistic integration of migrants. This recognizes the fundamental importance of understanding and communication in fostering tolerant relationships between migrant and non-migrant communities. However, integration must be balanced against respect for migrants' rights. For example, the European Court of Human Rights has suggested that "pursu[ing] an aim of indoctrination . . . might be considered as not respecting . . . [the] religious and philosophical convictions [of migrants]."[444]

(6) *Paragraph 4*: According to the UDHR, "recognition of the inherent dignity and of the equal and inalienable rights of all members of the human family is the foundation of freedom, justice, and peace in the world."[445] States' obligations to respect, protect, and promote the human rights of migrants suggests that States should encourage understanding and tolerance of migrants' cultures through appropriate cultural activities because tolerance and respect for migrants will depend in part on knowledge of minority cultures. The ICRMW affirms, "States Parties shall ensure respect for the cultural identity of migrant workers and . . . may take appropriate measures to assist and encourage efforts in this respect."[446] These efforts may include, *inter alia*, incorporating the study of migrants' culture or history in public education, providing funding for museums, teaching minority languages in public school systems, facilitating the organization of cultural fairs, and supporting public broadcasting in minority languages.

---

443. *See* ICRMW, *supra* note 16, at art. 45(4).
444. Folgerø v. Norway, App. No. 15472/02, 46 Eur. H.R. Rep. 47, 1187 (2007).
445. UDHR, *supra* note 1, at pmbl.; *see also* ICCPR, *supra* note 2, at art. 27; ICERD, *supra* note 4, at art. 7.
446. ICRMW, *supra* note 16, at art. 31.

Name Index